CAPITALISTS AND CHRISTIANS

Alfred (later Sir Alfred) Owen (right) and the evangelist
Billy Graham, at a Birmingham Youth for Christ rally
in Birmingham Town Hall in the late 1940s (probably
on the occasion of Billy Graham and Cliff Barrows' visit
on 28 May 1949); photo from the Owen family
collection.

Capitalists and Christians

*Business Leaders and the Churches
in Britain, 1900–1960*

DAVID J. JEREMY

CLARENDON PRESS · OXFORD
1990

Oxford University Press, Walton Street, Oxford OX2 6DP
Oxford New York Toronto
Delhi Bombay Calcutta Madras Karachi
Petaling Jaya Singapore Hong Kong Tokyo
Nairobi Dar es Salaam Cape Town
Melbourne Auckland
and associated companies in
Berlin Ibadan

Oxford is a trade mark of Oxford University Press

Published in the United States
by Oxford University Press, New York

British Library Cataloguing in Publication Data
Jeremy, David J. (David John) 1939–
Capitalists and Christians.
1. Great Britain. Industries. Role of christians
I. Title   261.85

ISBN 0-19-820121-4

Library of Congress Cataloging in Publication Data
Jeremy, David J.
    Capitalists and Christians: business leaders and the churches in
  Britain, 1900–1960/by David J. Jeremy
      p.   cm.
    Includes bibliographical references.
    1. Capitalism—Religious aspects—Christianity—History of
  doctrines——20th century. 2. Great Britain—Church history—
  20th century. 3. Great Britain—Commerce. I. Title.
   BR115.C3J47   1990
305.5′54′0882—DC20   90-35341
ISBN 0-19-820121-4

Typeset by BP Integraphics Ltd.
Printed and bound in
Great Britain by Bookcraft Ltd.
Midsomer Norton, Bath

To Joanna and Michael
Rebecca and Mark

If riches increase, set not your heart upon them.

(Psalm 62: 10, AV)

'Lord, thou deliveredst unto me five talents; behold I
have gained beside them five talents more.'
His lord said unto him, 'Well done, thou good and faithful servant: thou hast been faithful over a few things,
I will make thee ruler over many things: enter thou into
the joy of thy lord.'

(Matthew 25: 20–1, AV)

Acknowledgements

The research behind this study was undertaken while I was Research Fellow in the Business History Unit at the London School of Economics. The writing was completed in between my teaching commitments at Manchester Polytechnic. Necessarily I have incurred many debts within and beyond both these institutions. First and foremost I am indebted to the Leverhulme Trust which financed me to work full-time on this project over the two years 1985–7 (Grant no. A/85/43). At the LSE Geoff Jones (when acting director of the Unit) lent his support to my grant application, a seminar on the topic and publication of the seminar papers (as *Business and Religion in Britain*). Les Hannah (when director of the Unit), to whom I owe the opportunity to work on British entrepreneurs (as editor of the *Dictionary of Business Biography*), subsequently maintained positive encouragement for my work, bringing the formation of business values into my field of interest. In searching for obituaries, Mrs Alison Sharp relieved me of some of the burden, and Michael Bywater, with his knowledge of London sources, of more. Richard Kacznyski and Adam Lubansky of the LSE's computer services department resolved the problems of an IT beginner and Gus Stewart, responsible for the administration of research grants at LSE, efficiently handled that side. At the Polytechnic my head of department George Zis has given the encouragement and opportunity without which the writing could not have been completed in a reasonable time. The Polytechnic's library, computing, and reprographic services have supplied excellent back-up support.

Next I must thank those who generously gave me interviews or admitted me to their family or private archives. The lists are lengthy (and are detailed among the sources). In particular I am grateful to Godric Bader, the late Dr Kathless Bliss, Gordon Bridge, Sir Adrian Cadbury, O. H. W. Clark, George Goyder, the Reverend Dr John Huxtable, Jack Keiser, A. David Owen, Professor Ronald Preston, Mrs Faith Raven, the Reverend Bruce Reed, Sir Basil Smallpeice, and Ronald G. Stansfield. Others, like Mr A. Forrester-Paton and Mrs E. Holderness, supplied information by correspondence. All their perspectives and/or their archives, coming from various sorts and levels of churchmanship, opened my understanding to many of the people, issues, and movements that have occupied the terrain between business and church.

Professional archivists have also been helpful in directing my attention to relevant records in their custody. Via Dean Edward Carpenter and Mr W. D. Pattinson, Secretary-General of the General Synod of the Church of England, I was introduced to Dr Brenda Hough, the General Synod's Archivist, and her colleague Dr Pat Kelvin who was then cataloguing CBF papers. Dr Hough's combined helpfulness and archival hospitality met no equal. At the Church Commissioners' Archives, London; St Deiniol's Library, Hawarden (David Anscombe); and Sion College, London, I was met by helpful staff. Dr Ray Refaussé of the Church of Ireland's Representative Body supplied copies of past yearbooks. For the Roman Catholic Church, which could not be treated adequately due to the nature of that church's organization and the design of this research, the Westminster Diocesan archivist (Miss Elizabeth Poyser) provided useful introductions. For Methodists I am indebted to the co-operation of the staff of the *Methodist Recorder*, who allowed me unlimited access to early runs, and at the John Rylands Library, Manchester, to the staff in charge of the Methodist Archives (Alison Peacock in particular). The staffs of the Dr Williams's Library and the Friends' House Library were as helpful as those of the more general institutions: the British Library, the Institute of Historical Research (Rosemary Taylor), Manchester Central Reference Library, the Mitchell Library in Glasgow, the National Library of Scotland in Edinburgh and Newcastle-upon-Tyne Reference Library (John Airey). At Cadburys I was much assisted by Basil Murray and Helen M. Davis, and at Unilever by Maureen Staniforth and Jocelyn Butler. For access to Lever materials I am grateful to Mr Peter Humphries, when he was church secretary of Christ Church, Port Sunlight, and to the staff of the Port Sunlight Heritage Centre (Ailsa Bowers in particular). Archivists of The Leys School (Geoff Houghton) and Kingswood School (John Gardner) answered my queries about alumni. At Rubery Owen members of the Owen family, especially A. David and Jim Owen and Mrs Grace Jenkins, facilitated my research.

Various private individuals in the churches have supplied information. For Congregationalists the Reverend Drs John Huxtable and Geoffrey Nuttall came to my aid. In my efforts to identify Methodist lay people I am obliged to Alan Rose, editor of the *Proceedings* of the Wesley Historical Society, for advertising my queries, and to all those who responded with information: a lack of space prohibits me from mentioning them all. In the same breath, however, I must record my thanks to Laurie Gage for supplying me with so many scarce Nonconformist works, and at reasonable prices. The Reverend George Thompson Brake provided many useful introductions to fellow Methodist ministers. Two other old church friends contributed information and inspiration to my assessment of Nonconformist businessmen. John Barfield, manager of the Baptist Union Corporation Ltd., assembled occupational data on members of the BU Council in the mid-1950s. The Reverend Donald M. MacKenzie's pulpit ministry at Westcliff-on-Sea tempered my evaluations of churchmen, clerical or lay, more than he might guess.

For knowledge of the Scottish business and church scenes I am grateful most of all to Professor R. H. Campbell. He has kindly commented on the Scottish section and given me the benefit of several conversations on the topic of this book. To the Reverend James L. Weatherhead, Principal Clerk of the Church of Scotland, and to the Reverend Stuart Borthwick of Clydebank I am also obliged. The Reverend Dr R. Tudur Jones, of Bala-Bangor College, enlarged my understanding of Welsh Nonconformity.

Numerous fellow historians (economic, business, ecclesiastical) including some of the above have, over the years, given me ideas, clues, encouragement. I wish to thank Philip S. Bagwell, Theo Barker, David Bebbington, Clyde Binfield, Emily Boyle, John Briggs, Ken Brown, Roy Coad, Tony Corley, Louis M. Cullen, Richard Davenport-Hines, Charlotte Erickson, Douglas Farnie, Ronald Ferrier, Francis Goodall, Howard Gospel, Edwin Green, Tony Howe, David S. Johnson, Edgar Jones, Bill Kennedy, Geoff Milburn, Nick M. Morgan, Michael Moss, Charles Munn, Derek Oddy, Phil Ollerenshaw, Gordon Read, Bill Reader, Lesley Richmond, Iain Russell, Christine Shaw, Tony Slaven, Brian Stanley, Alison Turton, Geoff Tweedale, Oliver Westhall, and Peter Young. Professor David Martin at LSE confirmed my early suspicion that the topic of this volume was both important and neglected. John Hacche and Susan Evans, colleagues at Manchester Polytechnic, resolved Welsh language and statistical difficulties respectively. Most recently I am grateful to Dr Bryan Wilson for the opportunity to try some of this book on his sociology of religion seminar at All Souls College, Oxford. At the Oxford University Press, Ivon Asquith encouraged me with a contract at the outset of my Leverhulme grant. Two anonymous referees and the OUP editor, Tony Morris, sensibly prevailed on me to condense what was an even longer book than this present one. For her meticulous and indefatigable copy-editing Jacqueline Pritchard has my gratitude and admiration.

All the members of my immediate family have made unique and substantial contributions. Despite infirmity my parents have maintained their loving interest, now fifty years strong. Joanna, my elder daughter, and Michael, her husband, provided relaxing diversions in the West

Country. Rebecca, my younger daughter, rendered sterling service in relieving me of several tedious chores during her vacations from Aston University. She more than shared the work of inputting 20,000 names into a personal computer; she assisted in turning literary biographical information on business leaders into machine-readable codes; and she cross-checked church lay leaders' names against the *Directory of Directors*. For me she significantly reduced the laboriousness of unavoidably labour-intensive research. Mark, her boyfriend, supplied timely accommodation in Edinburgh. Theresa, my wife, spurred with love, common sense, and impatience, as ever. My heartfelt thanks to them all.

Two thoughts remain. In making these acknowledgements I am more than likely to have missed someone: if so, I hope they will accept my apologies. Secondly, it must be emphasized that no one listed in these acknowledgements is responsible for the blemishes that survive in the following pages. As always, they lie at the author's door.

Contents

List of Tables

Abbreviations

AGBO	Sir Alfred (George Beech) Owen
BCC	British Council of Churches
B.Ce.	birth certificate
BCM	*Bible Christian Magazine*
BDP	*Birmingham Daily Post*
BFBS	British and Foreign Bible Society
Bt	Baronet
BUL	Birmingham University Library
BU of S.	Baptist Union of Scotland
BWW	Baptist Union, *Baptist Who's Who*
CAC	Chapel Affairs Committee (Wesleyan Methodist)
Catholic WW	*Catholic Who's Who*, 1931, 1938, 1951
CBF	Central Board of Finance
CCFCL	Council on the Christian Faith and the Common Life
CFC	Christian Frontier Council
CHA	Church of England, Church House, Archives (now Church of England Record Office, London SE16)
CNL	*Christian News-Letter*
C. of E.	Church of England
C. of S.	Church of Scotland
COPEC	Conference on Christian Politics, Economics and Citizenship
CSL	Church Socialist League
CSSM	Children's Special Service Mission
DBB	D. J. Jeremy and C. Shaw (eds.), *Dictionary of Business Biography* (London, 1984–6)
DBF	diocesan boards of finance
DD	*Directory of Directors*
DNB	*Dictionary of National Biography*
DQB	Dictionary of Quaker Biography
DSBB	A. Slaven and S. Checkland (eds.), *Dictionary of Scottish Business Biography* (Aberdeen, 1986)
EA	(World's) Evangelical Alliance
FBI	Federation of British Industries
HMC	Head Masters' Conference
ICF	Industrial Christian Fellowship
IME	Institution of Mechanical Engineers
IVF	Inter-Varsity Fellowship
JRL	John Rylands Library
MLPWW	Methodist Church, *Methodist Local Preachers' Who's Who*

MM	*Methodist Monthly*
MMS	Methodist Missionary Society
MNC	Methodist New Connexion
MP	Primitive Methodist
M. Rec.	*Methodist Recorder*
MUL	Manchester University Library
MW	Wesleyan Methodist
NGL	National Guilds League
PC	Privy Counsellor
PM	*Primitive Methodist*
PMM	*Primitive Methodist Magazine*
PMMS	Primitive Methodist Missionary Society
PODL	*Post Office Directory of London* (Kelly's)
PP	*Parliamentary Papers*
ROA	Rubery Owen Archives
Rt. Hon.	Right Honourable
SCM	Student Christian Movement
SOAS	School of Oriental and African Studies, London University
SRO	Scottish Record Office
TCF	Twentieth Century Fund
UCCF	Universities and Colleges Christian Fellowship
UFCS	United Free Church of Scotland
UMFC	United Methodist Free Churches
UMM	*United Methodist Magazine*
WEA	Workers' Educational Association
Wes. Mag.	*Wesleyan Magazine*
WMUSS	Wesleyan Methodist Union for Social Service
WS	Writer to the Signet (solicitor in Scotland)
WW	*Who's Who*
WW Wales	*Who's Who in Wales*, 1921, 1937
WWC	Congregational Union, *Who's Who in Congregationalism*
WWFC	*Who's Who in the Free Churches*, 1951
WWM	Methodist Church, *Who's Who in Methodism*
WWMP	M. Stenton and S. Lees (eds.), *Who's Who of Members of Parliament* (Hassocks, Sussex, 1976–81)
WWW	*Who Was Who*
YB	*Year Book*
YMCA	Young Men's Christian Association
YWCA	Young Women's Christian Association

1914	38
1920	15.2
1935	26.5
1946	14.3
1950	11.8
1955	9.6
1960	8.5
1988	1

The above table may help the reader to appreciate the magnitude of philanthropic gifts, church incomes, etc., mentioned in the text. It shows that £1 sterling in 1914 would purchase 38 times as much as £1 in 1988, and in 1960 8.5 times as much.

Source: Central Statistical Office, 'Internal Purchasing Power of the Pound' (December 1989).

INTRODUCTION

Business Leaders and Churches: Issues and Approaches

If William Lever's soap works at Port Sunlight were typical, capitalists on the eve of the First World War cast long religious shadows. To Port Sunlight on the Mersey estuary, opposite but upstream from Liverpool, came crowds of visitors year after year during the summers of Britain's industrial and imperial ascendancy. In their thousands they trooped around the model village, admiring the wide, tree-lined streets and the spaciously laid houses and gardens. Mostly semi-detached and built in English vernacular styles, of black-and-white half-timber or Ruabon brick, each block of houses had a unique design. Public buildings, sometimes in Gothic or Georgian lines, included shops (four), village hall, men's social club, girls' institute, vast dining hall, open air swimming pool, gymnasium, cottage hospital, hotel, and church. From the village visitors might pass to the giant soap factory next door. Nearly as many worked in the factory as lived in the village: 3,000 in the former, 3,600 in the latter in 1907. From elevated walkways in the works visitors might look down on room after room of employees toiling in well-ventilated and hygienic conditions on the production, packaging, and dispatch of soap to the far corners of the earth.[1]

Port Sunlight was the creation of the extraordinary William Hesketh Lever (1851–1925). The son of a Bolton grocer and Congregationalist, at 21 he became his father's partner; at 35 he struck out on his own into soap manufacturing, starting at Warrington in 1885 and then moving to a greenfield site, Port Sunlight, in 1888. First and foremost a salesman,

[1] W. L. George, *Labour and Housing at Port Sunlight* (London, 1909); W. L. Creese, *The Search for Environment* (New Haven, Conn., 1966); E. Hubbard and M. Shippobottom, *A Guide to Port Sunlight Village* (Liverpool, 1989).

he was hugely successful in marketing branded soaps. Improving soap by the use of vegetable rather than mineral oils, he sold his brands, from Sunlight to Monkey Brand, Vim, and Lux, with a mixture of aggression, ingenuity and ruthlessness unmatched in the trade. By 1907 he had set up subsidiary companies and factories in half a dozen countries, in Europe, North America, and Australia. Soap made Lever a very rich man. His personal assets were valued at £1.5 million in 1897, at almost £3 million in 1912. He entered Parliament, was created a baronet in 1911, was raised to the peerage in 1917, and died as Viscount Leverhulme of the Western Isles.[2]

Lever was an autocrat but a paradoxical one. He expected obedience from his subordinates but admired independence of spirit and wished to find it in his company village if not in his company. He was also a man of capital as well as personal wealth. The ordinary shares and hence controlling ownership in Lever Brothers belonged to him. It was hardly surprising, therefore, that when in the late 1890s the village magazine carried an article by one of his Continental managers in defence of socialism, Lever was highly disturbed. Dissatisfactions in the village threatened his hopes of engineering a community which was at once subservient to his leadership and yet vigorous and spirited within the bounds he set. To attain his goals he would have to shape village opinions.[3]

To this end he used the well-tried paternalistic ploys of hiring a minister of religion as his welfare officer and building a company church in the village. As he told the crowd who filled the Gladstone Hall (which at lunchtimes accommodated 800 works diners under the gaze of a fine collection of Victorian paintings) on a Friday evening late in August 1900: 'When I first called on Mr Walker I did so without taking the Divine Services Committee into my confidence, because I felt that if Mr Walker could not come, it would be a severe blow to them, and that I had better say nothing about it until I knew. There's an old saying which runs "Never tell what you are doing until you have done it." '[4] In style and substance this was vintage Lever. From the start he overturned the Congregational (and democratic) principle, with which his upbringing would have familiarized him, of the right and duty of the local congregation to choose their minister.

[2]   W. J. Reader, 'William Hesketh Lever', *DBB*.

[3]   The sources for this material on Lever are in D. J. Jeremy, 'The Devices of a Paternalist', unpublished conference paper (École des Hautes Études Commerciales, University of Montreal, 1–4 May 1986).

[4]   *Progress*, 1 (1900), 539.

Lever's choice of minister was masterly. The Reverend Samuel Gamble Walker was a Wesleyan minister who had worked in the poorer districts of Chester, Manchester, and Birkenhead and, more to the point, had been active on behalf of the Independent Labour Party. As Lever told Port Sunlighters, 'There are many ministers who are in sympathy with Capitalists. But I never yet knew a Capitalist who needed anyone to help him.'[5] Between 1900 and 1907 when he left, Walker assumed a leadership role in the various village institutions. He was chairman of the Men's Social and Bowling Club, the Dramatic Society, the Port Sunlight Football Association Club, and the annual flower shows of the Horticultural Society. In the intellectual life of the village he presided over the Scientific and Literary Society and the University Extension lectures held under its auspices. At celebratory occasions, like the opening of new facilities or the Christmas Eve social gatherings when Lever customarily read Dickens's *Christmas Carol* to excited Port Sunlighters (epitomizing the warm paternalistic relationship Lever cherished), Walker invariably sat on the platform. With Lever he was initiated into Freemasonry, though did not ascend its rungs as high as his employer. Yet on only one occasion in the annals of the company magazine did he vent his earlier radical views, when in 1902 he went as far as condemning Britain's wealthy landowners for industrial poverty: in contrast Lever was liberating the land for the occupation of the labouring classes. Of course Walker had in mind the comparison between the ample, healthy conditions at Port Sunlight and the squalid slums of the typical northern industrial city. All the evidence nevertheless suggests that Walker had become the captive prophet in the captive company village. And at Port Sunlight Balaam had no ass.

Similarly Christ Church, the church Lever built at Port Sunlight, commenced as a captive of capitalist and company. Lever bore the £25,000 cost of the village church, though ownership was vested in the Congregational Union of England and Wales from 1903. He chose the name. He decided that it should be designed in Perpendicular Gothic style. Mrs Lever laid the foundation stone in 1902 and opened it two years later. Lever chose the hymnbooks and insisted on a robed choir, a professional organist and bell ringing, thereby imposing his liturgical preferences on the new congregation. Senior company managers and directors sat on the ruling body of Christ Church. No doubt Lever's hand was behind the extraordinary decision of the Christ Church Committee under Walker's chairmanship in 1902 to place all those not in the employment

Ibid.

of Lever Bros. Ltd., or who had left the company, on a separate communicants' roll distinct from the church membership roll. Since a Port Sunlight tenant who lost his job with the firm had just one week in which to vacate his house, this seems like a clear attempt to keep the church locked into the policies of company and village, ultimately the policies of William Hesketh Lever.

These attempts to make religion an instrument of business failed. Between 1900 and 1907 the population of Port Sunlight grew from 2,000 to 3,600 yet the membership of Christ Church merely rose from 50 to 140 in 1911. In contrast the Sunday School grew from 230 in 1900 to 1,300 in 1911. Eventually Lever tired of trying to manipulate the village church and in the last two decades of his life directed his considerable energies into the promotion of Freemasonry. From the company's point of view that too could be a valuable tool. The international character of Freemasonry could be useful in facilitating the movement of information and managers between Lever Bros. at Port Sunlight and its multiplying overseas subsidiaries. It was also a cohesive device which could be deployed at Port Sunlight when the disruptive forces of growth needed to be held in check. Significantly Lever founded five lodges and one Royal Arch chapter at Port Sunlight. In the Lady Lever Art Gallery, opened in memory of his widow in 1922, Lever reserved one section of the building for a Masonic hall for the use of local lodges. All the evidence suggests that Lever the paternalist tirelessly sought to use religious and pseudo-religious devices to promote the forces of order over the period when his company and his company town were expanding at their fastest rate. It may be significant that deep down, perhaps to the end of his days, Lever lacked a strong Christian faith. Angus Watson of Skipper sardines (a fellow Congregationalist) recorded that Lever had no faith in immortality and that 'Material things meant much to him, because the preparation for the spiritual life was, after all, secondary.' And the Reverend J. D. Jones, a former chairman of the Congregational Union, recalled that one night after he had preached at Port Sunlight and was returning in Lever's car, Lever suddenly turned to him and said ' "Did you believe all you said tonight?" I replied: "I should not have said it if I did not believe in it." "Well!" he said, "I came nearer to being converted tonight than I have ever been in my life." '[6]

Capitalism and religion are among the most potent phenomena in

[6] Both Watson and Jones are quoted in C. Binfield, 'Business Paternalism and the Congregational Ideal', in D. J. Jeremy (ed.), *Business and Religion in Britain* (Aldershot, 1988).

modern society; blended, they present a cauldron of conflicts and perplexities. With the onset of industrialization in Britain from the late
eighteenth century, the Puritan ethic was one of the major ideological
alternatives available to aspiring and successful industrialists.[7] Though
diluted by the economics of Adam Smith, the secular self-help notions
of Samuel Smiles, and the social Darwinism of Herbert Spencer, the
Calvinist code morally and spiritually energized English capitalism
through the decades of Victorian prosperity. All this is well known and
well explored in contrast to the twentieth-century experience.[8] Since
1900, and earlier, economic decline, the rise of socialism, state intervention, and mounting unbelief, to say nothing of changes in industrial
structure and social theology, have apparently opened a wide chasm
between capitalist entrepreneurs and the practice of the Christian religion. Apparently: the word is deliberately chosen. One of the purposes
of this study is to discover the extent of linkages between business leaders
and the churches. One finding is that business leaders and businessmen
were much closer to the churches than might be suspected.

Historians have traditionally followed one of two broad alternatives
in analysing the relationship between capitalism and religion. Marxists,
seeing religion subordinate to economic circumstances, have emphasized
religion as a tool of social control. Thus E. P. Thompson regards early
Methodism as 'a ritualised form of psychic masturbation', its 'box-like,
blackening chapels standing in the industrial districts like great traps
for the human psyche'.[9] Religion served masters not men. It inculcated
obedience in workers and allowed them to vent their workplace frust-
rations in weekend revivalist fervour. At the other pole of debate, heirs
of Max Weber, the German sociologist, view religion as an engine of
economic change. For them capitalism was motivated and rationalized
by the religious varieties of Protestantism. The Puritan ethic was not
simply one of two or three alternative ideologies capable of powering
capitalism. It was the dominant one.[10] Neither of these models is
assumed at the outset of this study. Instead a stance of critical empiricism
is taken. That is, the evidence is tested for answers to a series of questions

---

[7]   S. G. Checkland, 'Cultural Factors and British Business Men, 1815–1914', in K.
Nakagawa (ed.), *Social Order and Entrepreneurship* (Tokyo, 1977).

[8]   See the essays and sources in Jeremy (ed.), *Business and Religion*.

[9]   E. P. Thompson, *The Making of the English Working Class* (London, 1965), 368.

[10]   For a summary of the debate unleashed by Weber see R. W. Green (ed.), *Protestantism
and Capitalism* (Boston, 1959); K. Samuelsson, *Religion and Economic Action* (London,
1959); M. Morishima, 'Ideology and Economic Activity' (London, 1986).

informed by an empathetic but not blinkered view of capitalists and their dilemmas and of churchmen and theirs.

What are those questions? How have answers been sought? The first cluster of questions relates to Marxist assertions that religion has been the opiate of the people. To what extent have capitalists in twentieth-century Britain tried to introduce religion into an industrial context? What use have they made of it there? The major quantitative research exercise behind this volume has been directed at discovering what proportions of the British business élite have (*a*) received strong religious (Christian) influences in their upbringing, and (*b*) actually retained church connections in adulthood. The exercise does not of course show the extent to which entrepreneurs and managers attempted to impose religious provisions as a form of social control. It does, however, suggest what might have been the minimal strength of the relationship between capitalism and religion.

A second group of questions concerns the formation of business values. These values, however defined, it is widely acknowledged, lie behind Britain's relative industrial decline and failure of entrepreneurial nerve. What have the churches taught with respect to business values? Have they always been muted towards capitalism? How has their teaching changed? Official church teaching aside, what of the ordinary experience of church or chapel? What standards, skills, and social networks useful in business have they provided?

Thirdly, there is the wide area of religion in business. What were the theoretically recognized limits to religion in business at the end of the nineteenth century? How extensive was paternalism? How did paternalists attempt to use religion to control their workforces? Was William Lever typical? When entrepreneurs gave way to professional managers did religious instrumentality fade? Did Christian perspectives among managers then move from the purely religious (building a church, holding a service of some kind, or employing a chaplain, for example, within the orbit of the firm) to the ethical level (following certain standards, values, practices which were ascribed by their upholders to their Christian faith)? Answers to these questions have been the most difficult to reach because the written evidence is so elusive, more so in the managerial corporation than in the family-owned and run firm, and because motivations are rarely expressed and scarcely single or simple.

The last set of questions deals with business people in church, especially in the national leaderships of the various denominations. The opposite side of the coin to religion in business, this area is largely unknown territory. What is generally clear is that since the nineteenth century the major denominations have become more centralized, more structured, more professionally run. The systems and modes adopted by their central organizations have often derived from the world of business. What part have businessmen and women played in these processes? Have the skills of entrepreneurs and managers in the midst of the churches been used rationally? Have business people been more than fund-raisers and benefactors? Have they advised on organizational structure, acted as investment consultants, played any part in shaping larger policies or doctrines, influencing business values (to complete the circle)? There is another facet to this topic. At a local level what parts have been played by the rich man, frequently a businessman, in the local congregation? Did he find a new role when it became clear that nineteenth-century paternalism no longer fitted prevailing social patterns? Or did rich men find more opportunities in inter-denominational organizations, 'penumbra' church activities?

At the risk of boring the reader, the techniques by which answers to these questions have been sought need some explanation. Without this the strengths and weaknesses of the study can hardly be assessed. Clearly great care has to be taken if the landscape between business and church is to be properly surveyed. It simply will not do to wheel out a few familiar heroes, claiming that they represent the population occupying this terrain. Yet that is precisely what one or two recent studies have done.[11] Two groups of people have to be identified: business leaders and church leaders. Only some sort of objective sampling could satisfactorily identify them.

Business leaders have been defined as those holding the positions (regardless of title) of chairman and managing director (or their equivalents in the case of a partnership) of the 100 largest companies in the UK economy at benchmark dates between 1900 and 1960.[12] A labour measure (number of employees) rather than a capital measure (e.g. market value, capital issued, turnover) for company size was preferred for several reasons. In contrast to other measures, data on labour can be obtained for dates across the period. They can be used in conjunction with data for the whole economy, collected for the Censuses of Production. They are particularly appropriate to a study about interpersonal relationships between captains of industry and churches. The dates chosen, 1907, 1935, and 1955, coincide with or are within a year of a Census

[11] I have in mind I. C. Bradley, *Enlightened Entrepreneurs* (London, 1987).

[12] Names of individual chairmen and managing directors were obtained from *Stock Exchange Year Books*, company histories, or the companies themselves. Sources for the information about employments will be published in a forthcoming article.

of Production. In the case of 1955 difficulties in securing data yielded a sample of 96 rather than 100 companies (see Appendix I). For companies employing over 100,000 people additional managing directors (one per 100,000 employees) were included in the samples. The result was a sample of 616 positions in three business élites corresponding to the pre-1914 period, the inter-war years, and the post-war decade. Some individuals obviously held more than one of these positions in one or more of the three benchmark years (see Appendix II).

Business people in the leadership of the major Christian church denominations were identified in a similarly objective way. For the same benchmark dates (1907, 1935, 1955), or as close to them as possible, the names of all those sitting on the national committees or holding national offices in the major denominations were copied from denominational handbooks on to a personal computer database using Lotus 123. By re-ordering these names it became apparent that some individuals occupied more than two or three committee places. With some arbitrariness it was decided that those holding five or more places should be regarded as the lay leaders of their denomination. These 'workhorses' were then pursued to ascertain whether they had business connections. One standard test was to check these people against the members of the business élites. Another, applied across the denominations, was to check the *Directory of Directors* to see how many of the 'activists' in the churches were members of the Institute of Directors and, where they were, on which companies' boards they sat. Such a task, involving the logging of over 20,000 names, would have been enormously time-consuming before the introduction of the computer. As it was I needed typing assistance to complete this part of the project which has taken four years altogether.

This tedious computer exercise has allowed some of the critical questions mentioned above to be answered quantitatively. It has moreover substantially contributed to the formulation of qualitative findings. The reason for this is simple. Out of the computer searches have come the men (few women) who inhabited the social landscape linking together the worlds of business and church. From this population more specific sources and questions developed. As noted, the technique is bound to omit some individuals. And, as Professor R. H. Campbell reminds me, people who sit on committees are not necessarily the most politically powerful. The assumption generally holds, however, that power is more likely to be vested in multiple office holders in a bureaucracy than in non-multiple office holders. Sometimes exceptional individuals or families (for example, the Coats among the Scottish Baptists) can be traced from other sources. In addition the computer exercise has been complemented by a number of case-studies which both test quantitative findings and flesh out the bare bones of names and numbers. It has therefore been possible to identify some of the most active figures on the crowded stage at the intersections of business and church and to pose to them the kinds of question challenging not only the historian but also present-day people in business, church, and related policy-making.

Finally two caveats must be entered. First this study is confined to the major Christian denominations. Little is said about members of modern religious sects or about Jews in business, though both groups appear in tables of aggregated data. Second the most regrettable omission has been any consideration of the role of business leaders in the Roman Catholic Church. Because of the objective method adopted for identifying church leaders and because committees of laity had no part in the government of the Catholic Church in this period it is not possible to apply a comparable technique for identifying Catholic laymen or charting changes in their influence.

PART I

Contexts

I

Business Structures, Religious Structures, and Business Élites, 1900–1960

Paternalism, frequently harsher if not more intrusive than that found at Port Sunlight, characterized very many late Victorian businesses. As a pattern of attitudes and behaviour on the part of employers, an employer ideology, it was vanquished in twentieth-century Britain partly by changes within the firm, partly by changes in the firm's environment. The latter would include the spread of political rights, the extension of the powers of the state, the widening of educational opportunities, the growth of the mass media, and much more than can be mentioned here. Inside the firm the salient changes related to size and structure. We must begin this study with a consideration of these for two reasons. First, they altered the business leaders' scope for action of a religious or ethical kind. Second, they help at a heuristic level to define the firms and managers who will comprise the samples of business leaders to be investigated (as explained in the Introduction).

I BUSINESS STRUCTURES

This study is primarily concerned with big business. Heads of largest employers wielded wide powers within their firms and outside them set the pace in offering new models of company organization and behaviour. Hence the primary focus. What then were the major changes in the size and structure of big businesses and how did these affect their religiously disposed heads?

Table 1.1, derived from Appendix I, summarizes changes in the size of the 100 largest firms (by employment measure) in the UK economy between 1900 and 1960. Several trends are evident. First, while the

TABLE 1.1. *Workforce of 100 largest companies as share of UK workforce, 1907, 1935, 1955*

	1907	1935	1955
UK workforce[a]	17,838,000	20,722,000	21,797,000
Workforce of 100 largest employers[b]	1,420,054	2,260,181	4,643,512
Percentage share in 100 largest companies	7.96	10.9	21.30

[a] Data for 1911, 1931, 1951, excluding public administration and the armed forces.
[b] Data for 1907, 1935, 1955; 96 companies for 1955.

Sources: B. R. Mitchell and P. Deane, *Abstract of British Historical Statistics* (Cambridge, 1962), 60–1. Author's data on largest companies' workforces.

occupied workforce grew between 1907 and 1955 by nearly four million, three million people moved into the employment of the 100 largest firms. These firms nearly trebled their share of the workforce. At the same time the average size of these 100 firms was rising. In most sectors the largest firms at least doubled the size of their workforces between 1907 and the 1930s (Table 1.3), before the various nationalizations distorted this measure of private industry. In other words work in large industrial organizations was the increasingly common experience of employees. Secondly, industrial activities were in flux. At the beginning of the period most employees in the largest firms were in manufacturing and transport (Table 1.2) but by the 1950s transport's share had halved while the shares of employees in mining, distribution, and finance had appreciably increased. Of the top 20 firms in 1907, 11 were railway companies. New industries, based on chemical, electrical, motor vehicle, and aviation technologies, produced large firms between the wars, firms such as ICI, Associated Electrical Industries, GEC, Austin, Morris, and Hawker Siddeley Aircraft. Services also emerged. Retail chains tentacled across cities and provincial towns, bringing Woolworths, Home & Colonial, W. H. Smith & Son, Marks & Spencer alongside the CWS. The names, but not the number, of high street banks became fewer: Midland, Lloyds, and Barclays in the front rank, Westminster and National Provincial behind. By the 1950s the post-war Labour Government's nationalization programme had created new giants. The General Post Office, an industrial titan throughout the period, was now joined by the British Transport Commission, the National Coal Board, the British Electricity Authority, and the Gas Council. Newcomers to the circle of largest private employers included the builders and contractors Wimpey and Laing and the film producer, distributor, and exhibitor the J. Arthur Rank Organization. The general picture, then, is of shifts among largest employers from old to new industries, from manufacturing and transport

TABLE 1.2. *Sectoral shares of workforce of 100 largest companies, 1907, 1935, 1955*

Sector	1907		1935		1955[a]	
	No.	%	No.	%	No.	%
Mining	70,997	5.00	102,987	4.56	704,000	15.16
Manufacturing	535,478	37.71	997,102	44.12	1,783,261	38.40
Building	7,500	0.53		0.00	37,000	0.80
Utilities	22,000	1.55	22,000	0.97	333,400	7.18
Transport and communications	739,428	52.07	894,488	39.58	1,281,233	27.59
Distribution	44,651	3.14	170,246	7.53	367,676	7.92
Finance			73,358	3.31	98,442	2.12
Entertainment					38,500	0.83
TOTAL	1,420,054	100.00	2,260,181	100.00	4,643,512	100.00

[a] 96 companies.

Source: Author's data on 100 largest companies' workforces.

towards distribution and financial services: a simple reflection of what was happening in the economy as a whole.

Growth in large firms hinged on profit margins and was measured by net profits and market share. Owners and managers incessantly sought higher returns on the working of their resources. Cutting unit costs of production was the most ready method. In expanding markets this could be achieved by increasing the scale of production (gaining economies of scale), in contracting markets, by lowering wage rates or sacking workers. Market share might be pushed up in one or both of two ways: internally generated growth or merger with rivals. Mergers, which occurred in waves in the 1900s, the 1920s, and the late 1950s–1960s, accounted for most growth.[1]

Growth, whether by merger or internal expansion, posed new problems. The point was soon reached when a workforce was so large or the number of plant sites so numerous that neither one man nor his brothers and sons could manage the business efficiently. At Port Sunlight in 1909 William Lever, the Napoleon of soap manufacture, ruled his 3,600 employees (and hundreds more elsewhere in the UK) through six directors, 125 managers, 104 salesmen, and 803 staff.[2] By the turn of the century hierarchies of professional managers, in the largest firms often drawn from the railways or government-owned businesses, were

[1] For over 75 per cent in the period 1919–30 according to one calculation: L. Hannah, *The Rise of the Corporate Economy* (2nd edn., London, 1983), 98.
[2] Lever Bros., *The Co-Partnership Trust in Lever Brothers Ltd.* (Port Sunlight, 1909): author's calculation from lists of co-partners.

TABLE 1.3. *Average sizes of 100 largest firms (by employment), 1907, 1935, 1955*

Sector	1907	1935	1955
Mining	8,875	10,299	704,000
Manufacturing	8,925	15,873	29,234
Building	7,500		18,500
Utilities	11,000	22,000	166,700
Transport	30,810	99,388	160,154
Distribution	8,930	15,477	26,263
Finance		12,226	16,407
Entertainment			19,250
Total employment	1,420,054	2,260,181	4,643,512
Total no. of firms	100	100	96

Source: Author's data on 100 largest employers, 1907, 1935, 1955.

beginning to emerge. Managerial power triumphed with the invention of the multi-divisional corporation. Pioneered in the USA, it was introduced into Britain in the 1920s. In essence the multi-divisional structure consisted of a head office and autonomous operating divisions which it controlled through interlocking directors and functional managers.[3] In Britain it was adopted first by Nobel Industries and then by ICI after its formation from the merger between Nobel Industries, Brunner, Mond, the British Dyestuffs Corporation, and United Alkali in 1926.[4] With huge numbers of employees—ICI had 56,000 in the UK alone in 1935—large managerial hierarchies were needed. However, the diffusion of the multi-divisional occurred slowly in Britain until the 1950s. As late as 1953 only 8 per cent of largest firms (by asset size) had adopted it. By 1970 it was found in three-quarters of large British corporations.[5] Of the 96 largest employers in 1955 29 can be casually identified as firms in which founding families or self-made entrepreneurs remained in command. Hierarchies of professional managers stretched below them. In co-ordinating economic activities managers tended to remove economic transactions from the market, sweeping them into the firm and thus provoking further enlargements of managerial bureaucracies.

The managerial revolution, as all these changes were called, introduced new motivations, new attitudes, new limits to business management.

---

[3] See A. D. Chandler, *Strategy and Structure* (Cambridge, Mass., 1962) and idem, *The Visible Hand* (Cambridge, Mass., 1977).

[4] See W. J. Reader, *Imperial Chemical Industries* (London, 1970–5), i and Hannah, *Rise*, 70–89.

[5] D. Channon, *The Strategy and Structure of British Enterprise* (London, 1973), 68–70.

The interests of professional managers, whether their background was in accountancy or engineering, were not the same as those of family-firm owners. The latter focused on profits in order to build up reserves against the unprofitable years of adverse trading conditions, and on dividends healthy enough to support the owners' accustomed standard of living. Professional managers sought profits in order to build up their firm's organizational size and with it their own status and power; unlike older paternalists, they were much less interested in 'community-based entre-preneurship' than in national or international organizational efficiency; and, responsible ultimately to their shareholders, they were inhibited in their fields of action in ways unknown to family owner-managers. Another trend in twentieth-century Britain, the expanding power of the state, also tended to curtail managements' scope for idiosyncratic or capricious action in the public corporation.

What were the implications of these developments for managers intent on conducting their business from a Christian perspective, at either a religious or an ethical level? Hypotheses, to be tested later, can be hazarded. Recurrent depressions of the trade cycle are likely to have induced a closer conformity to economic norms than to religious ideals. Managerial corporations would replace the *ad hoc* welfare of a company village like Port Sunlight with more rational and systematized schemes run by personnel managers. These possibilities are examined in Chapter 4. Professional managers in public companies would have much less scope to exercise their religiously based ideals than family-firm owners. In fact the professional managers' operational mode was likely to be confined to an ethical level inside the firm, which did not preclude oppor-tunities of associating with company-focused religious activity originating outside the firm. This possibility emerges in Chapters 5 and 6.

2 RELIGIOUS STRUCTURES

The wide array of church denominations presented in Table 1.4 indicates the range and diversity of religious choices available to lay and business people in the period under study. Scarcely a town in England and Wales by 1900 can have failed to offer either an episcopalian or a Nonconformist church of some description; in Scotland and Ireland, a presbyterian or episcopalian one. The differences they represented sprang from several directions. Some acquaintance with these will help to define the factors shaping the business leaders' religious stances either in youth or adul-thood.

TABLE 1.4. *An anatomy of sects, denominations, and churches in Britain, 1750–1960*[a]

Date established	Denomination	Theology	Liturgy	Local leaders	Organization/polity
England					
Early AD	Roman Catholic	Trinitarian	Ritualistic	Priest	Hierarchy under bishops and pope
16th c.	Church of England	Trinitarian	R. and non-R.	Priest	Hierarchy under two archbishops. State church
16th c.	Congregationalists	Trinitarian	Formal worship	Minister	Local church autonomous
16th c.	Presbyterians	Trinitarian	Formal worship	Minister	Hierarchy of courts
17th c.	Baptists	Trinitarian	Formal plus believer's baptism	Minister	Local church autonomous
17th c.	Unitarians	Unitarian	Formal worship	Minister	Local church autonomous
17th c.	Society of Friends (Quakers)	Trinitarian	Informal worship; reliance on inner voice of Holy Spirit	Lay elders and ministers	Local meeting under national Yearly Meeting
1784	Wesleyan Methodists	Trinitarian	Formal worship	Minister	Conference (annual) of ministers
1797	Methodist New Connexion	Trinitarian	Formal worship	Minister	Conference (annual) of ministers and laity
1805	Independent Methodists	Trinitarian	Formal worship	Lay ministers, i.e. unpaid, part-time	Conference of church reps.
1810	Primitive Methodists	Trinitarian	Emotional worship	Minister	Conference (annual) of ministers and laity
1815	Bible Christian Methodists	Trinitarian	Informal worship	Minister	Conference (annual) of ministers and laity
1830	Christian Brethren	Trinitarian	Sober worship; believer's baptism	Lay elders	Local church autonomous
1830	Catholic Apostolic Church (Irvingites)	Trinitarian	Charismatic worship	Priest	Hierarchy under apostles and bishops
1857	United Methodist Free Churches	Trinitarian	Formal worship	Minister	Conference (annual) of ministers and laity
1865	Salvation Army	Trinitarian	Informal worship	Officer	Centralized structure: army model

TABLE I.4. *cont.*

Date established	Denomination	Theology	Liturgy	Local leaders	Organization/polity
1907	United Methodist Church: union of Methodist New Connexion, Bible Christians, and the United Methodist Free Church	Trinitarian	Formal worship	Minister	Conference (annual) of ministers and laity
1915	Elim Foursquare Gospel Alliance	Trinitarian	Charismatic worship; believer's baptism	Pastor	Centralized under board of overseers
1932	Methodist Church: union of Wesleyans, Primitive, and the United Methodists	Trinitarian	Formal worship	Minister	Conference (annual) of ministers and laity
Scotland					
1560	Church of Scotland	Trinitarian Calvinistic	Formal worship	Minister	Presbyterian, i.e. a hierarchy of courts: kirk session or parish court; presbytery (many parishes); synod (many presbyteries); General Assembly (nation). Clergy and laity sit at all levels. State church
1690	Episcopal Church in Scotland	Trinitarian	Similar to liturgy of Church of England	Priest	Hierarchy under bishops
1733	Original Secession Church	Trinitarian Calvinistic	Formal worship	Minister	Presbyterian. Anti-Erastian (anti-state control)
1743	Reformed Presbyterians	Trinitarian Calvinistic	Formal worship	Minister	Presbyterian
1761	Relief Church	Trinitarian Calvinistic	Formal worship	Minister	Presbyterian. Anti-Erastian. More tolerant than the Secession

TABLE I.4. *cont.*

Date established	Denomination	Theology	Liturgy	Local leaders	Organization/polity
1843	Free Church of Scotland	Trinitarian Calvinistic	Formal worship	Minister	Presbyterian. Anti-patronage. Formed on the principle of spiritual independence, i.e. state should support state church but not exert legal control
1847	United Presbyterian Church: union of Secession and Relief Churches	Trinitarian Calvinistic	Formal worship	Minister	Presbyterian
1876	Reformed Presbyterians join Free Church				
1892	Free Presbyterians: strict Calvinists (most in the Highlands) who seceded from the Free Church				
1900	United Free Church of Scotland: union of Free and United Presbyterian Churches	Trinitarian Calvinistic	Formal worship	Minister	Presbyterian
1900	A minority remained in the Free Church, being known as the 'Wee Frees'				
1929	United Free Church united with the Church of Scotland, though a minority in the UFCS remain independent to the present				

The Baptists, Congregationalists, Methodists, Brethren, and Salvation Army were also represented in Scotland; the Roman Catholics have had a strong presence in Scotland.

Wales

Date established	Denomination	Theology	Liturgy	Local leaders	Organization/polity
1536–9	The Church in Wales	Trinitarian	Liturgy of Church of England	Priest	Hierarchy under English archbishops. State church until 1920
1639	Welsh Independents Union formed in 1872	Trinitarian	Formal worship	Minister	Local congregation autonomous
1730	Presbyterian Church of Wales: first General Assembly for whole of Wales, 1864	Trinitarian Calvinistic	Formal worship	Minister	Presbyterian

Baptists and Methodists, Brethren, and Salvation Army were also represented in Wales where some of the churches were organized in separate language groups.

TABLE I.4. *cont.*

Date established	Denomination	Theology	Liturgy	Local leaders	Organization/polity
Ireland					
1537–60	Church of Ireland	Trinitarian	Liturgy of Church of England	Priest	Hierarchy under English archbishops. State church until 1871
1642	Presbyterian Church in Ireland	Trinitarian	Formal worship	Minister	Presbyterian

In the 26 counties which formed the Republic after 1922 the dominant religion was Roman Catholic (perhaps 80% of the population in the 19th century). In Northern Ireland (the six counties comprising Ulster) over 60% of the population were Protestant by the 1870s. Presbyterians outnumbered episcopalians 3:2. Small groups, many of them presbyterian, have abounded in Ulster.

Alternatives to the orthodox denominations in the nineteenth century
A number of sects, new and theologically unorthodox, most originating in the USA, spread to England before 1920. By approximate date of arrival in England they included the following:

1810 Swedenborgianism (New Jerusalem Church)
1837 Church of Jesus Christ of the Latter-Day Saints (Mormons)
1848 Christadelphians
1878 Seventh-Day Adventists
1890 Theosophy
1900 First Church of Christ Scientist
1914 Jehovah's Witnesses

a These lists are not exhaustive.

Various kinds of social affinity were one source of religious diversity.[6] An ethnically specific denomination was the Catholic Church in Ireland. Regional affinity was exemplified by the Bible Christians (Methodists) of the South-West or the Church of Scotland in Lowland Scotland. Political biases distinguished other denominations, for example the identification of the Church of England as the Tory Party at prayer or the alliance between Nonconformity and Liberalism. A common socioeconomic status drew others to particular denominations. Artisans and their upwardly mobile descendants, the small and medium businessmen, usually supported one of the Nonconformist denominations who emphasized diligence, sobriety, frugality, self-help: virtues that underpinned the middle classes. The connection helps to explain the flourishing state of Nonconformity in Victorian suburbs.

Doctrine, ritual, and organization, what the sociologists call the 'utility' of a church, also contributed to the multiplicity of denominations. Doctrine, buffeted by German scholarship, pivoted on the interpretation of Scripture, for which there were three broad alternatives. The Catholic Church placed it in the hands of the church, personified in pope and priest. Unitarians subjected it to reason. Evangelicals preserved the Reformation view of *sola scriptura*: Scripture, the final authority on faith and conduct, was its own interpreter under the Spirit of God. While the polar positions of Catholics and Unitarians are readily described, a range of intermediate positions lay between them. In the Church of England, High Churchmen (Anglo-Catholics) emphasized the church collective, as the mystical body of Christ, apostolic succession and priestly authority. Low Churchmen (Evangelicals), like most Nonconformists, held the priesthood of all believers, stressing the individual and his right of direct access and accountability to God. Among Nonconformists most differences derived from questions of church government, though Baptists distinguished themselves also by insisting on believer's baptism for church membership.

With ritual, differences approximated to Catholic and Anglican on one hand, Nonconformist and presbyterian on the other. While episcopalians underlined the authority of their bishops and priests with robes, ornaments, processions, and prepared liturgies, Nonconformists originally rejected all distinctions beyond the ministerial dog collar and the

---

[6] The following analysis is based on A. D. Gilbert, *Religion and Society in Industrial England* (London, 1976); O. Chadwick, *The Victorian Church*, i and ii (London, 1971–2); D. W. Bebbington, *The Nonconformist Conscience* (London, 1982); R. Currie *et al.*, *Churches and Church-Goers* (Oxford, 1977); H. MacLeod, *Class and Religion in the Late Victorian City* (London, 1974); and other sources listed in the Bibliography.

Genevan preaching gown. By 1900 this stereotyped picture of Victorian church worship was changing. Surpliced choirs and printed service sheets were appearing in the larger middle-class, usually urban, chapels. While Roman observances were gaining ground in the Church of England, Quakers and Brethren followed the most simple of service routines in bare chapels. In Nonconformist and presbyterian circles doctrinal differences could be the subject of keen intellectual debate, engaging the allegiance of businessmen raised on such a diet. Ritual exercised an emotional influence. If 'rites satisfy "a cultural demand" not otherwise met by society',[7] those relatively deprived of ritual could be expected to seek it if and when they considered changing their denominational affiliation. William Lever, as High Church as a nominal Congregationalist might decently be, evidently found additional ritual satisfaction from his extensive Masonic involvements.[8]

Church organization will emerge in subsequent chapters. At this point it is sufficient to observe only the broadest features. Table 1.4 outlines the polities (forms of church government) by which the major denominations were administered. They ranged from the highly centralized and exclusively clerical hierarchy of the Roman Catholic Church to the decentralized and lay government of the Brethren. These two characteristics, extent of centralization and extent of lay participation, offered the laity, and businessmen in particular, additional kinds of utility.

Centralization among the Protestant churches usually implied the growth of bureaucracy and with it some loss of clerical power. In the Church of England this progressively happened after the creation of the Ecclesiastical Commission in 1836. It was set up to take over episcopal and capitular (cathedral) estates and to redistribute church income into newly populous, urban-industrial areas. By 1906 the Commission had nearly 100 staff to administer properties whose rents totalled £1.72 million, securities (mostly gilts) worth £11 million and mortgages valued at £7.7 million.[9] In the dioceses a handful of professional laymen (architect, surveyor, accountant, canon law expert), some part-time, assisted bishops and senior clergy.[10] A bishop funded his secretary out of his

   [7] Currie et al., Churches, 63.
   [8] Progress, 25 (1925), 130; D. J. Jeremy, 'The Devices of a Paternalist', unpublished conference paper (École des Hautes Études Commerciales, University of Montreal, 1–4 May 1986).
   [9] Ecclesiastical Commissioners, Reports of Committees 1907, file 8,034, Memo on the Official Establishment, p. 21, Table A; C. of E., YB 1907.
   [10] PP Commission on Cathedrals C3712; C. of E., YB 1907.

own budget.[11] The largest Nonconformist denominations had, or were in process of setting up, centralized bureaucracies. The Wesleyans' central offices were scattered across London but two more were in Manchester. The Congregationalists established their national headquarters in Memorial Hall, Farringdon Street, London, after it opened in 1875. Unitarians had Essex Hall, off the Strand, after 1885. Quakers started to develop a centralized staff of administrators in London in the 1890s. At the turn of the century the Primitive Methodists had a publishing house in Aldersgate Street, London, and two or three other departmental headquarters in the metropolis but three other departments were in northern cities. The Baptist Union opened a new headquarters in Southampton Row, central London, in 1903. The development of centralized bureaucracies was viewed with deep suspicion in some quarters and some denominations, however. As late as 1906 the denomination officers of the Methodist New Connexion were scattered around nearly a dozen northern cities.[12] In Scotland the head offices of the Church of Scotland were located in Queen Street, Edinburgh, while the United Free Church of Scotland, excluded from their headquarters by the House of Lords judgement of 1904 (see Chapter 9), occupied various properties in Edinburgh and Glasgow until 1911 when the George Street, Edinburgh, premises were built.[13]

Several trends lay behind the moves towards centralization and bureaucratization. One was the relative decline of most denominations. Table 1.5, showing religious densities (church members, however defined, as a percentage of the population aged 15 and over), suggests a decay in all denominations apart from the Catholics and the Church of Scotland between 1900 and 1960. In absolute figures the denominations' membership rolls started to drop at dates spread across the period. Baptists peaked in 1906, Congregationalists in 1911, English Presbyterians in 1916, Anglicans in 1926, Methodists in 1932, Quakers and the

[11] J. Barnes, *Ahead of His Time* (London, 1979), 156.

[12] The topic of church administration in Nonconformity deserves a separate study. These examples come from (Methodist) Wesleyan, *Minutes of Conference* (London, 1907); R. T. Jones, *Congregationalism in England 1662–1962* (London, 1962), 312–13; Unitarians, *Essex Hall YB* (London, 1907); S. H. Mellone, *Liberty and Religion* (London, 1925); E. Isichei, *Victorian Quakers* (Oxford, 1970), 107; A. S. Peake, *The Life of Sir William Hartley* (London, 1926), 126; E. A. Payne, *The Baptist Union* (London, 1959), 158; Methodist New Connexion, *Minutes of Annual Conference* (London, 1906).

[13] C. of S., *YB* 1902; G. M. Reith, *Reminiscences of the United Free Church General Assembly (1900–1929)* (Edinburgh, 1933), 120.

TABLE 1.5. *Religious densities for major denominations, 1906, 1936, 1956*

Denomination	1906	1936	1956
Church of England[a]	8.9930	7.579	6.672
Congregationalists[b]	1.9510	0.936	0.634
Presbyterians[a]	0.3810	0.269	0.217
Baptists[b]	1.7420	1.161	0.876
Methodists[c]		2.308	1.936
Wesleyan	1.8690		
Primitive	0.7700		
United	0.5430		
Quakers[c]	0.0479	0.042	0.043
Church of Scotland[d]	22.4980	34.350	34.369
United Free Church of Scotland[d]	15.7090	0.617	0.647
Episcopal Church in Scotland[d]	4.2870	3.436	2.762
Church of Wales[e]	—[f]	10.333	—[f]
Presbyterian Church of Wales[e]	12.923	9.567	7.335
Roman Catholics[c]	5.900[g]	6.430	9.200
Roman Catholic Church in Ireland	74.2000[h]		74.700[i]
Church of Ireland	13.0000[h]		10.600[i]
Presbyterian Church in Ireland	9.9000[h]		10.200[i]

Note: Religious density = church membership (however defined) as a percentage of the population aged 15 and over.

[a] England.
[b] England and Wales.
[c] Great Britain (England, Wales & Scotland).
[d] Scotland.
[e] Wales.
[f] Not applicable.
[g] Figure for 1911.
[h] Figure for 1901.
[i] Figure for 1961.

Sources: Robert Currie and Alan Gilbert, 'Religion' in A. H. Halsey (ed.), *Trends in British Society since 1900* (London, 1972), 444–50. Figures for Quakers calculated from R. Currie *et al.*, *Churches and Church-Goers* (Oxford, 1977), 157–8, and B. R. Mitchell and P. Deane, *Abstract of British Historical Statistics* (Cambridge, 1962), 10. The 1936 figure for Roman Catholics is derived from Currie *et al.*, *Churches and Church-Goers*, 153.

Church of Scotland in 1956, Roman Catholics in the late 1960s.[14] One response to decline was merger, as Table 1.4 summarizes. After 1900 the major church mergers were those which produced the United Free Church of Scotland in 1900, the augmented Church of Scotland in 1929, the Methodist Church in 1932. The formation of the British Council of Churches in 1942 was part of the same trend. With merger came the chance to reshape church bureaucracies, to occupy new headquarters, in short to strengthen the centralizing tendency. The creation of permanent central church executives implied the need for additional resources,

[14] R. Currie and A. Gilbert, in A. H. Halsey (ed.), *Trends in British Society since 1900* (London, 1972); Currie *et al.*, *Churches*; P. Brierley (ed.), *UK Christian Handbook 1983* (London, 1982).

particularly financial. An idea of the amounts of money to be stewarded in the major denominations is given in Table 1.6. By the 1930s the Church of England at national and local levels had an income in the order of £16 million, the Church of Scotland around £2.7 million, and the Methodist Church of £3.95 million. Specialized executives also required some kind of semi-independent supervision. For both these functions devout businessmen were most suited.

In the two established churches, the Church of England and the Church of Scotland, dependence on the wealth of the laity was nothing like as great as among the non-established denominations. In the latter, therefore, persons of organizational ability, civic weight, or personal wealth had a special welcome. Such attributes were theoretically not sufficient unless accompanied by evidences of personal faith and piety. Just how reliant the churches were on their laity is indicated by Table 1.7. In 1907 the major denominations' central assemblies, conferences, councils, and committees had over 7,200 lay positions to be filled, a figure which had slipped to around 6,200 by 1955.

How attractive were these positions to the laity? As Table 1.7 shows, the more centralized denominations had more national places to offer laymen and women. Thus the Church of England, the Methodists, the Quakers, the Church of Scotland, and the United Free Church of Scotland (pre-1929) all had a higher number of central positions than denominations with a congregational polity—the Baptists or the Congregationalists, for example. Conceivably any businessman interested in attaining a national presence would be attracted to a denomination with greater rather than lesser opportunities for this. The extent of those opportunities can be calculated as the ratio between national offices and national members, as in Table 1.7. From this it is clear that the most democratic of the centrally governed denominations was the Society of Friends (the Quakers) with one national office for every 24 members in 1907 and for every 17 members in 1955. They were followed by the Methodist Wesleyans, the Methodist New Connexion, and the English Presbyterians in 1907; by the Methodists and the Church in Wales in 1955.

Yet the picture is not that simple even for the centrally governed denominations. The environment of the churches has to be considered. Since the late nineteenth century British society has grown increasingly apathetic towards Christianity and churchgoing. Tensions between sacred and secular have become harder to resolve. Hence the supposition that there was always an adequate supply of able laity and people in business to fill all the churches' national positions cannot be taken for granted.

TABLE 1.6. *Annual church incomes, 1900–1960 (in £s, uncorrected for inflation or deflation)*

	1907	1925/1932	1935/1939	1955
Church of England				
Sees	98,908		?	?
Cathedral churches	192,460		?	?
Ecclesiastical benefices	4,213,662		1,000,000	?
Ecclesiastical/Church Commissioners	1,247,827		3,250,000	11,227,390
Queen Anne's Bounty	700		2,340,000	
Central Board of Finance			145,000	208,000
Diocesan Boards of Finance			650,355	?
Voluntary parish contributions	6,000,000		?	9,230,910
Total	11,753,557		16,000,000	20,666,300
Methodists pre-Union of 1932				
Wesleyans				
By collections and subs		447,929		
By assessment		61,473		
By dividends on investments		42,289		
Other sources		73,516		
Total		625,207		
United Methodists				
By collections and subs		49,781		
By assessment		18,246		
By dividends on investments		14,223		
Other sources		9,714		
Total		91,964		
Primitive Methodists				
By collections and subs		57,684		
By assessment		37,355		
By dividends on investments		2,560		
Other sources		10,244		
Total		107,843		
Pre-Union total		825,014		
Methodists post-Union				
Trust incomes			1,550,000	
Connectional funds			900,000	
Church and circuit incomes			1,500,000	
Total			3,950,000	
Church of Scotland		1,200,000		
Endowments	360,000			
Central church income			979,057	1,477,210
Voluntary parish contributions	520,997		1,720,791	3,620,726
Total	880,997		2,699,848	5,097,936
United Free Church of Scotland				
Estimates for 1925		1,500,000		

Notes: Church of England 1907: 1890 property return; Church of England parish contributions 1907: Estimate of Archbishops' Committee for 1910; Church of England, total revenue from all sources late 1930s: estimate made by Sir Richard Hopkins in the early 1950s.

Sources: *Official Year-Book of the Church of England*, 1907, 1937, 1957; *The Economist*, 16 Sept. 1944; CHA, CBF, Box 596, 'Proposed Statement of Sir Richard Hopkins on the Finances of the Church', 1951–2; *Minutes of the Uniting Conference of the Methodist Church, 1932*; *Minutes of the Methodist Conference, 1937*; *Church of Scotland Year Book*, 1909, 1937, 1957; Gavin White, '"Whose Are the Teinds?" The Scottish Union of 1929', in W. J. Shiels and D. Wood (eds.), *The Church and Wealth* (Oxford, 1987), 386.

TABLE 1.7. *Numbers of national lay offices compared to church memberships/adherents, 1907, 1935, 1955*

Denomination	1907			1935			1955		
	Offices	Members	Ratio	Offices	Members	Ratio	Offices	Members	Ratio
England									
Church of England	555	2,023,000	3,645	407	2,299,573	5,650	343	2,167,503	6,319
Congregationalists	178	288,292	1,620	325	275,247	847	401	200,583	500
Presbyterians	259	85,774	331	409	81,715	200	74	69,651	941
Baptists	47	267,737	5,697	66	251,025	3,803	58	202,239	3,487
Methodists	2,428	802,470	331	1,430	759,835	531	1,079	684,992	635
Wesleyan Methodists	1,671	446,368	267						
Primitive Methodists	407	206,445	507						
United Methodist constituents									
Bible Christians	48	32,317	673						
Methodist New Connexion	184	37,017	201						
United Methodist Free Churches	118	80,323	681						
Quakers	775	18,860	24	1,012	19,301	19	1,220	21,343	17
Scotland									
Church of Scotland	684	512,248	749	1,229	919,313	748	979	917,848	938
United Free Church of Scotland	824	506,088	614	132	21,826	165	69	24,856	360
Episcopal Church in Scotland	137	51,289	374	n/a	61,151		n/a	56,528	
Congregationalists		36,714		n/a	39,530		n/a	35,467	
Baptists	179	21,142	118	311	23,311	75	283	19,235	68
Wales									
Church in Wales		138,782		457	195,744	428	486	176,723	364
Independents (Congregationalists)	36	173,289	4,814	50	159,693	3,194	39	140,949	3,591
Calvinistic Methodists (Presbyterians)	112	185,935	1,660	137	182,221	1,330	137	150,077	1,095
Baptists	11	137,507	12,501	n/a	122,375		18	99,750	5,542

TABLE 1.7. *cont.*

Denomination	1907			1935			1955		
	Offices	Members	Ratio	Offices	Members	Ratio	Offices	Members	Ratio
Ireland									
Church of Ireland[a]	603	581,089	964	644	490,504	762	596	457,261	767
Presbyterian Church in Ireland[b]	431	443,276	1,028	438	418,998	957	416	429,168	1,032
TOTAL	7,259	6,273,492	864	7,047	6,321,362	897	6,198	5,853,273	944

Notes: English Presbyterians, 1955: source omits most committee members.
Most 'Revd Drs' have been eliminated from the Church of Scotland and United Free Church of Scotland lists by reference to the various *Fasti*.
Episcopal Church of Scotland, 1935, 1955: sources omit committee members.
Congregational Union in Scotland: sources do not distinguish between clergy and laity and omit committee members.
Baptist Union of Wales: 1907, 1955 council members only; 1935 church records missing.
Episcopalian memberships are for communicants.
The Roman Catholic Church, being run by a wholly clerical hierarchy, had no representative lay bodies at a national or regional level in this period.
[a] Membership figures under 1935, 1955 refer to 1936–7, 1951–61.
[b] All Presbyterians included.

Sources: Currie *et al.*, *Churches and Church-Goers*, for church memberships. Denominational yearbooks, data abstracted by author. Baptist Union of Wales: data from Mr P. D. Richards, assistant secretary.

TABLE 1.8. *Age structures of business élites, 1907, 1935, 1955*

	Chairmen			Managing directors		
	1907	1935	1955	1907	1935	1955
Average age	61	62	62	55	57	57
Standard deviation	11	9	8	11	9	8
Cases	86	94	90	72	82	85
Total in cohort	100	100	96	101	103	116

On the demand side, those churches with a London headquarters presumably stood a better chance of recruiting from the national figures brought to the capital by business or politics than denominations based outside London. Yet this has to be qualified since many distinguished Scotsmen on the London scene regularly commuted northwards and could have happily accommodated General Assembly meetings in Edinburgh in their schedules. Again, much depended on creating national structures that would best utilize the abilities of men in business. If church councils simply became talking shops, devoid of decision and action, or if they were confined to theological issues and speculations, businessmen would find them tiresome and exhausting. They might then be expected to confine their church interests to their local church or to a denomination where a decision/action rather than an intellectual/ theological debate mode might be made to prevail, much as Lever operated at Port Sunlight. Or perhaps they would move on to an interdenominational scene. Chapters 7–10 explore how businessmen seized the utility of lay leadership in the churches and in interdenominational organizations.

3 BUSINESS ÉLITES

The 100 largest firms in 1907, 1935, and 1955 identified in the first section of this chapter provide the framework for objectively chosen business élites. Biographies of the chairmen and managing directors (or their equivalents) of these firms, listed in Appendix II, supply clues to individuals' religious links. Equally importantly, when treated collectively the biographical data reveal the broad characteristics of the whole business leadership and how these changed over time. Three characteristics are the concern of this section: the age structures, origins, and education of the three business élites.

As might be expected, chairmen tended to be an older group than managing directors. Table 1.8 shows the difference in their average ages as five or six years. Between the 1900s and the 1950s the average age of both edged upwards, from 61 to 62 for chairmen, from 55 to 57 for managing directors. Extremes of age were greatest in 1907 when three chairmen were octogenarians and 17 were septuagenarians, three were in their thirties and 11 in their forties. By the 1950s there was only one octogenarian chairmen (Sir John Craig of Colvilles), ten were in their seventies. Consonant with the vigour required of managing directors, there were seven septuagenarians in 1907, four in 1935 (when there was also an 80-year-old, Sir Thomas Callendar), and three in 1955. The youngest managing directors, most in family firms, appeared in 1907 when one, Benjamin Palin Dobson, was in his late twenties and four were in their thirties. By 1955 only two were in their thirties.

These age structures suggest that the dominant formative influences for nearly all those in the 1907 élite, all in the 1935 élite and all but a score in the 1955 élite were Victorian and Edwardian. Besides recollections of imperial grandeur, class-based social relations, luxury for the few and acute poverty for the many, and much else, their images of Britain related to the virtues of business success and the respectability of churchgoing. Those notions would change. Almost as much as churchgoing, business activities became publicly less esteemed after the cataclysm of the First World War.

Formative influences shaping the three business élites can be defined more closely, however. Table 1.9 summarizes what has been discovered about social origins. The social classification follows that of Charlotte Erickson,[15] a very broad classification based on occupation which has been preferred because of deficiencies in the historical data. Two difficulties have to be kept in mind in interpreting the data. First, information is absent for about a quarter of the chairmen and a third to a half of managing directors. It is likely that the missing individuals, lacking a *Who's Who* entry or an obituary in *The Times*, were not socially prominent and therefore came from lower rather than higher social classes. Second, the definition of class, based on father's occupation, cannot be consistently derived because it comes from a mixture of sources. Some (like birth certificates) give the father's occupation at the birth of the business leader, some (like obituaries) offer no indication of the date at which the father attained a particular occupation. In addition, occupations are very occasionally combined, e.g. the father of the 8th Earl of Bessborough, chairman of the London, Brighton & South Coast Railway, was

---

[15] C. Erickson, *British Industrialists* (Cambridge, 1959), 230–2.

TABLE 1.9. *Social origins of chairmen and managing directors*

	Class	1907		1935		1955	
		n	% of N	n	% of N	n	% of N
Chairmen							
Class I							
Nobility	11	8	10.4	1	1.4	2	2.5
Partner, owner, director	12	31	40.3	26	35.1	28	35.0
Merchant, banker	13	8	10.4	8	10.8	8	10.0
Landowner, farmer	14	4	5.2	3	4.1	2	2.5
Professional (excl. clerics)	15	11	14.3	15	20.3	14	17.5
Clergyman	16	1	1.3	4	5.4	3	3.8
Senior manager	17	8	10.4	7	9.5	6	7.5
Gentleman	18	2	2.6	0	0.0	0	0.0
Total		73	94.8	64	86.5	63	78.8
Class II							
Retail tradesman or craftsman	21	1	1.3	3	4.1	3	3.8
Clerk, foreman	22	1	1.3	1	1.4	3	3.8
Craftsman, self-employed	23	2	2.6	2	2.7	3	3.8
Total		4	5.2	6	8.1	9	11.3
Class III							
Skilled manual employee	31	0	0.0	3	4.1	5	6.3
Class IV							
Unskilled, semi-skilled employee	41	0	0.0	1	1.4	3	3.8
			100.0		100.0		100.0
N		77		74		80	
Cohort			100		100		96
N as % of cohort			77.0		74.0		83.3

TABLE 1.9. *cont.*

Class		1907		1935		1955	
		n	% of N	n	% of N	n	% of N
Managing directors							
Class I							
Nobility	11	0	0.0	0	0.0	0	0.0
Partner, owner, director	12	20	41.7	20	33.3	24	37.5
Merchant, banker	13	1	2.1	3	5.0	1	1.6
Landowner, farmer	14	1	2.1	1	1.7	2	3.1
Professional (excl. clerics)	15	11	22.9	9	15.0	11	17.2
Clergyman	16	5	10.4	6	10.0	4	6.3
Senior manager	17	5	10.4	5	8.3	8	12.5
Gentleman	18	0	0.0	0	0.0	0	0.0
Total		43	89.6	44	73.3	50	78.1
Class II							
Retail tradesman or craftsman	21	1	2.1	4	6.7	2	3.1
Clerk, foreman	22	1	2.1	4	6.7	4	6.3
Craftsman, self-employed	23	2	4.2	4	6.7	2	3.1
Total		4	8.3	12	20.0	8	12.5
Class III							
Skilled manual employee	31	1	2.1	4	6.7	4	6.3
Class IV							
Unskilled, semi-skilled employee	41	0	0.0	0	0.0	2	3.1
			100.0		100.0		100.0
N		48		60		64	
Cohort			101		103		116
N as % of cohort			47.5		58.25		55.2

Notes: N = total number of cases; n = subset of N.

both a peer and a Church of England clergyman.[16] In these cases the higher social classification has been chosen for coding, except for peers. Peers in business have been classified as partners, company directors, managers, etc. (sub-classes 12, 13, 17) rather than as nobility (sub-class 11). Both these defects in the data mean that the results in Table 1.9 are biased upwards to an unknown extent and towards business classes to a known extent.

There are sufficient data, however, to reveal broad trends. The strongest features confirm the salient findings of Charlotte Erickson for the steel industry. The British business system failed 'to make the best use of the abilities latent in society'.[17] Less than 10 per cent of chairmen and managing directors in these samples, as in hers, came from the two lower classes, who comprised over 70 per cent of the population by the 1920s. Second, men in business fathered businessmen. This was more true of these business leaders than of the steelmen alone. Whereas the proportion of steel manufacturers who were sons of businessmen dropped from 48 to 28 per cent between 1905 and 1953,[18] the proportions of chairmen in subclasses 12, 13, and 17 in Table 1.9 fell from 60 to 51 per cent and those of managing directors from 54 to 52 per cent between 1907 and 1955. The group who seem to have gained were the sons of senior managers who were more likely to succeed as managing directors than sons of directors were to become chairmen.

The data disclose other changes in the social origins of business leaders. Sons of peers and baronets, a source concentrated among chairmen, markedly abandoned business between the 1900s and the 1950s. Removing the primary classification of business occupation (explained above) shows among chairmen 13 sons of peers in 1907, 11 in 1935, but only 5 in 1955; among managing directors there were just three in 1935. Business peerages and baronetcies figured most heavily in the business élite of the inter-war years when they accounted for 10 chairmen and three managing directors. Boot, Reckitt, Smith, Wills, Ritchie, Samuel, Lindsay, Fairfax, McLaren, and Burbidge (the family names of these chairmen) and Joicey, Cozens-Hardy, and Burbidge (of the managing directors) are notable because, as will be seen in later chapters, nearly all had church or religious connections.

From the lowest classes came two dozen among the 230 chairmen and 172 managing directors whose fathers' occupations are known. In 1935

---

[16] *Complete Peerage.*
[17] Erickson, *British Industrialists*, p. xv.
[18] Ibid. 231.

chairmen in this group included Sir Harry McGowan, of the mighty ICI, son of a Glasgow brass finisher; and William Richard Morris, Lord Nuffield, of Morris Motors, son of a Walthamstow draper's assistant. By 1955 nine of the chairmen of the UK's biggest employers could claim lower-class origins. Sir John Craig, of Colvilles steel, the son of a Lanark iron puddler, Harley Drayton, of BET, elder son of a Streatham gardener, and Lionel Fraser, of Babcock & Wilcox engineers, oldest son of the butler to Gordon Selfridge, will be encountered later.

Eleven managing directors are known to have had lower-class fathers. They included McGowan of ICI in 1935 and John Bedford, of Debenhams, son of a Birmingham brass caster, in 1955. From society's point of view this represented a feeble utilization of its potential human resources; from the individual's angle it intimated that rags to riches was rarely achieved in Britain, across two generations anyway.

Despite this, the lower middle and working classes (II, III, and IV) made some gains between 1900 and 1960. They started from a very low baseline, with tiny or nil shares of the business élite in 1907. Typical of sons of class II fathers among the chairmen of 1907 were men like William Lever and George Livesey, son of an Islington clerk, who became head of the country's second largest utility, the South Metropolitan Gas Co. By 1935 sons of clerks and retailers included Sir Josiah Stamp, chairman of the London, Midland & Scottish Railway, the son of a London cheesemonger; or Simon Marks, chairman of Marks & Spencer, son of a Leeds bazaar operator. Lord Hives, chairman of Rolls-Royce and the son of a Reading factory clerk, exemplified these social origins in 1955. Among managing directors from class II were (in 1907) Arthur Dorman, steelmaker and son of a Kent saddler; (in 1935) Frank Pick of London Passenger Transport Board, son of a Lincolnshire draper; and (in 1955) Paul Chambers of ICI, son of a Southgate commercial clerk.

The other social stratum to demonstrate pronounced success was the professional classes (including clergymen), whose shares of offspring among the ranks of chairmen rose from 17 to 27 per cent between 1907 and 1935 and remained above 20 per cent in 1955. These in fact were the most successful of outsider groups to invade the highest business circles. Some were the sons of military and naval officers, like Sir Benjamin Browne, of shipbuilders Hawthorne, Leslie & Co., or Sir Andrew Noble of Armstrong, Whitworth the armaments and engineering firm. Others were the offspring of legal men, like Dudley Docker of the Metropolitan Amalgamated Railway Carriage & Wagon Co., and Sir John Beale of GKN and the British Iron & Steel Co., both sons of solicitors;

or Lord (Hamar) Greenwood of Dorman, Long & Co. and Frank Gill of Standard Telephones & Cables, whose fathers were barristers. A number were engineers, like the father of Lord Joicey, the coal-mine proprietor, or William Lorimer of the North British Locomotive Co. and the Steel Co. of Scotland. The most successful profession in getting their sons into big business chairmanships was the engineers, followed by army and navy officers and the clergy (of whom more in Chapter 3). Among managing directors the sons of professional fathers fell from 23 to 9 per cent of the cohort 1907–1955 (Table 1.9).

What this analysis of social origins demonstrates is that the majority of business leaders hailed from the upper middle classes. This is hardly surprising but confirmation of the point is important for the present study. It is now possible to proceed safely on the assumption that the individuals in the business élites studied here were shaped by the religious habits and values of the middling classes. However, while parental class constituted the first moulding influence for promising business leaders it was by no means the last. Fresh boundaries defined other formative influences.

It has been argued that an individual's success in reaching the highest levels in business has hinged upon place. If this is so it will help us come somewhat closer to the nature of formative religious influences. W. D. Rubinstein, studying millionaires, concluded that a Whittington syndrome has been at work. London has held the greatest concentration of wealth in the British economy and as the industrial regions have declined relative to the South-East so the attraction of London has increased during the twentieth century.[19] There is some evidence for this in the careers of the business leaders analysed here (see Table 1.10). In the careers of chairmen for whom place of birth is known, the proportion born in London rose appreciably between 1907 and 1955, as did the proportion born in London and the rest of the South-East. Among managing directors the London-born share rose though the rest of the South-East lost proportionately.

London of course was a city with many faces. Since few born in London were the sons of lower-class parents, scarcely any of these business leaders knew the steaming tenements north of the Strand or in the East End so familiar to mission workers, Salvation Army officers, and social investigators at the turn of the century. Working-class Londoners did not appear among the chairmen until 1955 and then the fathers concerned had plied skilled or semi-skilled trades—gardener, butler, carpenter—in healthy

[19] W. D. Rubinstein, *Men of Property* (London, 1981), 102–10.

southern and western suburbs like Streatham, Kensington, and Camberwell (the fathers of Drayton, Lionel Fraser, and Godber). Theirs, as Lionel Fraser recalled of Kensington, was 'a thoroughly genteel neighbourhood' and for him (denied the chance of playing in the street) meant a cramped flat, a high-walled passage, and play in Kensington Palace Gardens.[20]

More typical of the London-born chairmen in the business élites were the sons of middle-class fathers who occupied suburban houses and villas. For example, Arthur Chamberlain of Kynochs was born in Camberwell in 1842 when that suburb was still young;[21] Sir Hallewell Rogers of BSA was born in Hampstead in 1864 when its architectural irregularities and its picturesque heath were defying charges of suburban monotony;[22] and Alexander Henderson of the Great Central Railway, born at 25 Upper Winchester Street, Islington, in 1850, was raised in the tree-lined suburb of Ealing.[23] The managing directors born in London experienced not dissimilar circumstances in their growing years. Geographical origins strengthen the impression that the Victorian and Edwardian religious life of London potentially played an important part in the early years of a significant section of these business élites.

The other major geographical source of business leadership was Scotland. Its contribution is clear from Table 1.10. Scottish origins outnumbered London ones in 1907 and still ranked second to London in the 1950s when Scotland produced a sixth of the chairmen and a sixth of the managing directors of the biggest companies. Partly this is explained by the presence of Scottish-located companies among the largest 100 employers—in 1907 there were 19 Scottish companies in the top 100. By 1955 there were just six (of 96) compared to nearly 17 per cent of Scottish chairmen and managing directors among the top 100 firms. A very considerable southwards migration of Scots into the upper echelons of British business had clearly occurred as big business in Scotland had relatively declined. In some cases individuals went south early in their careers and worked their way up through an English firm, as did Sir David Milne-Watson in the Gas Light & Coke Co., Sir Robert Sinclair in Imperial Tobacco, or William Hunter McFadzean in British Insulated Callender's Cables. Alternatively, individuals moved south when their Scottish companies were absorbed into English, mostly London-headquartered, ones. In this second category were William Whitelaw

[20] W. L. Fraser, *All to the Good* (London, 1965), 15.
[21] H. J. Dyos, *Victorian Suburb* (Leicester, 1961).
[22] D. J. Olsen, *The Growth of Victorian London* (London, 1976), 232.
[23] D. Wainwright, *Henderson* (London, 1985), 14.

TABLE 1.10. *Geographical origins of chairmen and managing directors*

	1907		1935		1955	
	n	% of N	n	% of N	n	% of N
Chairmen						
London	11	14.7	15	20.5	14	20.9
Other South-East	5	6.7	6	8.2	5	7.5
East Anglia	0	0.0	0	0.0	0	0.0
South-West	6	8.0	4	5.5	3	4.5
West Midlands	2	2.7	6	8.2	9	13.4
East Midlands	3	4.0	1	1.4	0	0.0
North-West	10	13.3	6	8.2	7	10.4
Yorkshire	10	13.3	8	11.0	6	9.0
North	3	4.0	2	2.7	4	6.0
Wales	0	0.0	2	2.7	3	4.5
Scotland	16	21.3	13	17.8	11	16.4
Northern Ireland	2	2.7	0	0.0	0	0.0
Ireland (predecessor cos. of Rep.)	2	2.7	0	0.0	0	0.0
Canada	1	1.3	0	0.0	1	1.5
USA	3	4.0	4	5.5	1	1.5
UK offshore islands	0	0.0	2	2.7	0	0.0
Holland	0	0.0	0	0.0	1	1.5
Germany/German states	1	1.3	1	1.4	1	1.5
Austria–Hungary	0	0.0	1	1.4	0	0.0
India	0	0.0	1	1.4	0	0.0
Australia	0	0.0	0	0.0	1	1.5
Baltic States	0	0.0	1	1.4	0	0.0
Totals	75	100.0	73	100.0	67	100.0
N	75		73		67	
Cohort	100		100		96	
N as % of cohort	75.0		73.0		69.8	

TABLE I.IO. *cont.*

	1907		1935		1955	
	n	% of N	n	% of N	n	% of N
Managing directors						
London	8	14.0	8	13.0	14	22.0
Other South-East	6	11.0	5	8.0	4	6.0
East Anglia	0	0.0	0	0.0	1	2.0
South-West	5	9.0	4	7.0	4	6.0
West Midlands	2	4.0	8	13.0	12	18.0
East Midlands	0	0.0	1	2.0	1	2.0
North-West	7	12.0	9	15.0	4	6.0
Yorkshire	3	5.0	4	7.0	5	8.0
North	4	7.0	2	3.0	3	5.0
Wales	0	0.0	1	2.0	0	0.0
Scotland	12	21.0	9	15.0	11	17.0
Northern Ireland	2	4.0	0	0.0	0	0.0
Ireland (predecessor cos. of Rep.)	1	2.0	2	3.0	2	3.0
Canada	1	2.0	0	0.0	1	2.0
USA	1	2.0	3	5.0	1	2.0
South America	0	0.0	0	0.0	1	2.0
UK offshore islands	1	2.0	1	2.0	0	0.0
Holland	0	0.0	0	0.0	1	2.0
Germany/German states	3	5.0	0	0.0	0	0.0
Italy	1	2.0	0	0.0	0	0.0
Austria-Hungary	0	0.0	1	2.0	0	0.0
India	0	0.0	0	0.0	0	0.0
Far East	0	0.0	1	2.0	0	0.0
Australia	0	0.0	0	0.0	0	0.0
Baltic States	0	0.0	1	2.0	0	0.0
Totals	57	100.0	60	100.0	65	100.0
N	57		60		65	
Cohort	101		103		116	
N as % of cohort	56.4		58.25		56.0	

Notes: N = total number of cases; n = subset of N.

of the London & North Eastern Railway (formerly with the North British Railway), Sir Harry McGowan of ICI (formerly with Nobels), and Sir William Fraser of Anglo-Iranian Oil, later BP (formerly with Scottish Oils). The migration was important in preserving a sizeable representation of Scottish religious experience, and the values derived from it, amidst the British business élite.

Surprisingly, immigrants (excluding all Irish-born) accounted for a very small proportion of chairmen, though rather more of the managing directors. About 5 per cent of chairmen in 1907, 12 per cent in 1935, and 7 per cent in 1955 were born abroad, less than 3 per cent in any year coming from Europe. Among managing directors the proportions for the same years moved from 11 to 12 to 6 per cent. This group includes not only one or two Jewish immigrants like Sir Montague Burton, who remarkably migrated alone at the age of 15 from Lithuania,[24] and Hugo Hirst, the creator of GEC; but also the sons of expatriate Scots, like Lord Pirrie, of Harland & Wolff, born in Quebec, and Sir Eric Geddes, of Dunlop Rubber, born in India. Eight chairmen and five managing directors were born in the USA. The religious backgrounds these immigrants brought were very mixed but largely reinforced the Christian and Jewish traditions already established in Britain at the opening of the twentieth century.

Besides paternity and place, education ranked high as an aggregate formative influence. Parents and locality might shape the individual's early years but schooling, particularly that received during impressionable teenage years, could be even more important. When school replaced family, as it did for Victorian teenage boys sent to boarding schools—public schools primarily—teachers, peers, and the school ethos dominated most other environmental character-forming experiences. Public schools, in the English Victorian sense of fee-paying boarding schools designed to sieve middle- and upper-class sons through a predominantly classical curriculum and transform them into Christian gentlemen, was, in the words of W. J. Reader, 'a purely English invention'.[25] Exactly which schools qualified for the title of 'public school' was never clearly determined though membership of the Head Masters' Conference, organized in 1869 to set standards, is one criterion. Starting with the heads of thirteen 'new', i.e. of Victorian foundation, public schools the HMC grew until in 1937 it had 200 members.[26] After the Clarendon Com-

---

[24] Eric M. Sigsworth, 'Sir Montague Maurice Burton', *DBB*.
[25] W. J. Reader, *At Duty's Call* (Manchester, 1988), 84.
[26] S. J. Curtis, *History of Education in Great Britain* (4th edn., London, 1957), 183.

mission of 1861 charged that insufficient attention was given to 'modern' subjects such as modern languages, history, English, mathematics, and science, public schools developed a 'modern' side, invariably regarded as more suited for less able pupils than the classical stream. Public schools nevertheless remained the experience of a very small proportion of teenage boys. Dr Reader estimates that only 20,000 boys, or 1 per cent, of 15 to 19 year-old boys attended leading public schools (then 64 in all by J. R. de S. Honey's definition) in 1901.[27]

An elementary education system, providing basic literacy and numeracy for children up to their teens, had been established by the Church of England and the Nonconformists from the 1830s. By 1871 the male literacy rate was 80 per cent, suggesting that this proportion of boys was by then attending some kind of elementary school. At a secondary level the old grammar schools, originally endowed charitable foundations, were pressured by late eighteenth-century inflation and rising middle-class aspirations to charge fees, reform their curricula, and send pupils into the Oxford and Cambridge Local examinations organized after the 1850s. Under the impetus of the Taunton Commission of the 1860s, which investigated 800 endowed schools, 3,000 'middle-class fee-paying academic grammar schools' were organized. Some joined the HMC and were transmuted into public schools. Children of the tradesmen-artisan class had to wait for secondary education until after 1870 when the first state-run schools, the Board Schools, were established.[28]

One main point emerges from Table 1.11 (which should be used with caution: data are not available for all individuals and attendance is no guide to performance). The teenage education of chairmen in big business was most commonly that of the public school. The position is explored in Table 1.12. Among chairmen 40 per cent in 1907 attended a UK public school; by 1955 this was the school background of over half the chairmen—still well below the 65 per cent found for chairmen of largest firms (by asset size), 1905–71, by Stanworth and Giddens, who included unknowns (not included here).[29] Among managing directors the proportion was smaller, at 31 per cent, in 1907, but by 1955 was slightly larger than that of the chairmen. When kinds of public school are differentiated an interesting shift appears. At the beginning of the

---

[27] Reader, *At Duty's Call*, 84.

[28] M. Sanderson, *Education, Economic Change and Society in England, 1780–1870* (London, 1983), 17, 35, 59.

[29] P. Stanworth and A. Giddens, 'An Economic Élite', in Stanworth and Giddens (eds.), *Élites and Power in British Society* (Cambridge, 1974), 84.

TABLE I.II. *Secondary school education of chairmen and managing directors*

	1907		1935		1955	
	n	% of N	n	% of N	n	% of N
Chairmen						
Overseas schools	0	0.0	5	7.5	3	4.2
Scottish schools						
Non-HMC	5	8.5	5	7.5	4	5.6
HMC	2	3.4	6	9.0	4	5.6
English and Welsh schools						
State—elementary	0	0.0	0	0.0	4	5.6
State—grammar	1	1.7	2	3.0	4	5.6
Denominational, non-C. of E., Non-HMC	4	6.8	5	7.5	3	4.2
Other charitable fdns. incl. C. of E.	10	16.9	1	1.5	6	8.3
Private school/tutor	2	3.4	2	3.0	0	0.0
Public—Clarendon nine	22	37.3	21	31.3	21	29.2
Public—other HMC (1935)	11	18.6	17	25.4	20	27.8
Other fee-paying (prep, commercial, etc.)	0	0.0	0	0.0	1	1.4
Military	2	3.4	1	1.5	1	1.4
Scientific	0	0.0	2	3.0	1	1.4
Known but unclassified	0	0.0	0	0.0	0	0.0
Totals	59	100.0	67	100.0	72	100.0
N	59		67		72	
Cohort	100		100		96	
N as % of cohort	59.0		67.0		75.0	

TABLE I.II. cont.

	1907		1935		1955	
	n	% of N	n	% of N	n	% of N
Managing directors						
Overseas schools	2	4.7	2	4.2	3	3.7
Scottish schools						
Non-HMC	8	18.6	5	10.4	5	6.2
HMC	2	4.7	2	4.2	3	3.7
English and Welsh schools						
State—elementary	1	2.3	1	2.1	0	0.0
State—grammar	1	2.3	1	2.1	9	11.1
Denominational, non-C. of E., non-HMC	3	7.0	4	8.3	2	2.5
Other charitable fdns. incl. C. of E.	0	0.0	3	6.3	2	2.5
Private school/tutor	1	2.3	0	0.0	1	1.2
Public—Clarendon nine	8	18.6	5	10.4	17	21.0
Public—other HMC (1935)	14	32.6	18	37.5	25	30.9
Other fee-paying (prep, commercial, etc.)	2	4.7	2	4.2	5	6.2
Military	0	0.0	1	2.1	4	4.9
Scientific	0	0.0	2	4.2	1	1.2
Known but unclassified	1	2.3	2	4.2	4	4.9
Totals	43	100.0	48	100.0	81	100.0
N	43		48		81	
Cohort	101		103		116	
N as % of cohort	42.6		46.6		69.8	

Notes: Clarendon Commission (1861–4) schools: Eton, Charterhouse, Harrow, Merchant Taylors', Rugby, St Paul's, Shrewsbury, Westminster, Winchester. Head Masters' Conference members in 1935 listed in Truman and Knightley Ltd., *Schools* (London, 1935), 164–71.
N = total number of cases; n = subset of N.

twentieth century chairmen came from the ancient public schools and managing directors from the rest. By 1955, however, the less prestigious HMC schools were catching up among chairmen and the Clarendon Nine had considerably increased their share of the managing directors. It could be that when the business leader attended a particular school it had not joined the HMC. It may be safely assumed, however, that in most cases the earlier character of the school was not very dissimilar from its late Victorian and Edwardian manifestations.

Public schools depended on middle-class fathers, sizeable proportions of whom were in the professions and in business;[30] big business conversely depended on the public schools to feed its upper echelons. The content of public school education changed surprisingly little during the half-century before the First World War. Following Thomas Arnold, it was generally agreed that the overarching purpose of education was religious and moral, not vocational, training. The function of public schools was to produce Christian gentlemen, men of character fit to lead nation and empire, and their subordinate institutions—including companies, some of the largest private organizations in society. Character-building came from several distinctive elements in public schools—the monitorial system and fagging, long hours on the playing fields (which later degenerated into games-worship), and the influence of masters who were usually Church of England clergymen on their way up the preferment ladder. Classical studies were acceptable as a complement to Christian teaching and as a means of sharpening intellectual skills through massive rote learning and minute accuracy in linguistic exercises.[31]

From public or grammar school business leaders frequently readied themselves for business leadership via either an apprenticeship or a university education. Apprenticeship, the time-honoured training for many professions with the gaping exception of the church, entailed learning by doing. But was this the most efficient way for engineers to learn

[30] The proportion of school income provided by fees varied greatly; older foundations tended to have a larger proportion from endowments: see T. J. H. Bishop and R. Wilkinson, *Winchester and the Public School Élite* (London, 1967), 234–7. That fathers were middle class is clear from E. A. Allen, 'Public School Élites in Early-Victorian England', *Journal of British Studies*, 21 (1982), 87–117. Allen found that in the first half of the nineteenth century 45 per cent of known fathers of boys at Merchant Taylors' and 57 per cent at Harrow were in the professions while 24 per cent at Merchant Taylors' were in business; Harrow, the province of Whig aristocrats and politicians, had only 6 per cent of known fathers in business.

[31] This depiction of the public schools is derived from W. J. Reader, *Professional Men* (London, 1966), 104–6 especially. For the ethos of nineteenth-century public schools see D. Newsome, *Godliness and Good Learning* (London, 1961).

TABLE I.12. *Public school backgrounds of business leaders, 1907, 1935, 1955*

Kind of public school (but all in HMC, 1935)	Chairmen						Managing directors					
	1907		1935		1955		1907		1935		1955	
	No.	%	No.	%	No.	%	No.	%	No.	%	No.	%
Scottish	2	2.33	6	6.45	4	4.40	2	2.74	2	2.41	2	2.00
Denominational	1	1.16	1	1.08	3	3.30	2	2.74	3	3.61	1	1.00
Clarendon Nine	22	25.58	21	22.58	21	23.08	8	10.96	5	6.02	17	17.00
Other HMC of 1935	13	15.12	17	18.28	18	19.78	11	15.07	15	18.07	24	24.00
Total	38	44.19	45	48.39	46	50.55	23	31.51	25	30.12	44	44.00
Total business leaders with 13+ education (% from public schools)	63 (60.3)	73.26	67 (67.2)	72.04	70 (65.7)	76.92	43 (53.5)	58.90	44 (56.8)	53.01	81 (54.3)	81.00
Total for whom biog. data	86	100.0	93	100.0	91	100.0	73	100.0	83	100.0	100	100.0
Total in cohort	100		100		96		101		103		116	

TABLE 1.13. *Higher education of chairmen and managing directors*

	1907		1935		1955	
	n	% of N	n	% of N	n	% of N
Chairmen						
University						
Oxford	8	22.9	11	27.5	13	33.3
Cambridge	12	34.3	12	30.0	12	30.8
London	3	8.6	3	7.5	0	0.0
Scottish	4	11.4	2	5.0	4	10.3
Other UK universities	0	0.0	4	10.0	2	5.1
Other UK institutions						
Technical	3	8.6	0	0.0	3	7.7
Night/part-time	0	0.0	0	0.0	0	0.0
Teacher training	0	0.0	0	0.0	1	2.6
Military/naval	1	2.9	3	7.5	3	7.7
Overseas university/college	4	11.4	5	12.5	1	2.6
Total	35	100.0	40	100.0	39	100.0
N	35		40		39	
Cohort		100		100		96
N as % of cohort		35.0		40.0		40.6

TABLE I.13. *cont.*

	1907		1935		1955	
	n	% of N	n	% of N	n	% of N
Managing directors						
University						
Oxford	4	19.0	2	10.0	7	17.5
Cambridge	2	9.5	4	20.0	12	30.0
London	2	9.5	0	0.0	5	12.5
Scottish	5	23.8	2	10.0	3	7.5
Other UK universities	2	9.5	6	30.0	8	20.0
Other UK institutions						
Technical	0	0.0	3	15.0	3	7.5
Night/part-time	1	4.8	0	0.0	0	0.0
Teacher training	0	0.0	0	0.0	0	0.0
Military/naval	2	9.5	1	5.0	2	5.0
Overseas university/college	3	14.3	2	10.0	0	0.0
Totals	21	100.0	20	100.0	40	100.0
N	21		20		40	
Cohort	101		103		116	
N as % of cohort	20.8		19.4		34.5	

Notes: N = total number of cases; n = subset of N.

science or physicians their medicine? By the 1870s the rise of a very different 'modern' and technical educational system extending to university level in Germany, productive in many observers' opinion of that state's military might, sparked a controversy about the kind of education most appropriate to the needs of an industrial society. The debate continues to the present. In the nineteenth century the older universities, Oxford and Cambridge, were wedded to the classics and for the first half of the century largely turned out parsons. By the 1870s reforms had begun, but only slowly at Oxbridge. By 1900 at Cambridge, for example, only 11 per cent of fellowships were in the natural sciences; at Oxford in 1906 only 7 per cent of graduates went into business.[32] In response to the needs of industry, in the face of foreign competition and the deficiencies of the older universities, industrialists lent their weight and resources to founding colleges, soon expanded into universities, where science and engineering subjects were taught. By the 1890s and 1900s some, like Manchester, Birmingham, Newcastle, and Bristol, were sending a third or a half of their students into industry. The Universities of Scotland Act of 1858, which inaugurated the four-year degree course with honours in Maths and sciences, 'made possible the education of an industrial technocratic class' north of the border.[33] Despite the efforts of Sir William Ashley at Birmingham and initiatives at Cambridge and the London School of Economics, a great gap remained in so far as management education was concerned. Degrees in which accountancy and administration were major components did not become available until after the First World War, partly due to the ascendancy of mathematical economics in the universities, partly to the deep and widespread suspicions industrialists (often rightly) harboured towards university training.[34]

Whether a public school, Oxbridge-trained classicist was better suited to the needs of business and industry than an engineering graduate[35] depended on where one focused. The country's business and industrial

[32] M. Sanderson, *The Universities and British Industry, 1850–1970* (London, 1972), 35, 53.

[33] Ibid. 152.

[34] Ibid. *passim*.

[35] From the Royal College of Science (originally Chemistry) (1845), the Royal School of Mines (1851), or the City and Guilds Central Technical College (1884)—which merged in 1907 to form Imperial College—or from University College, London, the top science and engineering institutions in the country at the beginning of the twentieth century: G. W. Roderick and M. D. Stephens, *Education and Industry in the Nineteenth Century* (London, 1978), 104.

structures needed men both on the bridge and in the engine-room: strategists as well as tacticians and technical experts. For business leaders, particularly company chairmen concerned with identifying long-term objectives and the allocation of resources for reaching those goals, a purely vocational education was being viewed with disquiet by the 1950s.[36] To be preferred was a broader undergraduate education in the humanities, such as Oxbridge classics or American liberal arts courses provided. Products of management schools and engineering courses were better suited to middle management positions.

These are some of the considerations which lurk behind the data presented in Table 1.13. The proportions going to university or college were roughly similar to those attending public school in the case of chairmen in 1907 and 1935: around 40–45 per cent. By 1955 an appreciably larger proportion had been to public school than had gone on to university. The data confirm the findings of Stanworth and Giddens, 46 per cent of whose chairmen had been to university.[37] Among managing directors there was a marked rise in the number of university-trained men, moving from 27 to 40 per cent, 1907–55, suggestive of the rise of technocrats.

This collective biography of the British business élites between 1907 and 1955 reveals a number of group characteristics which have implications for the interactions between these élites and the churches. Because of their age, members of the élites were raised in Victorian or Edwardian society, or else were brought up by parents, nannies, and teachers whose world view was certainly Victorian. A sense of religion was built into their early years. Since a high proportion, of chairmen at least, were the sons of businessmen and professionals, many were educated at public schools—over 40 per cent of chairmen, over 30 per cent of managing directors, on conservative estimates. Many of these went on to university. All these influences, translated into a religious mode, spelt only one thing: the Church of England. This conclusion is hardly sensational. It will, however, be more closely probed in Chapter 3.

[36] M. Newcomer, *The Big Business Executive and the Factors that Made Him* (New York, 1955), 67.
[37] Stanworth and Giddens, 'Economic Élite', 85.

PART II

Formations

2

Church Views of Business, 1900–1960

A consensus view of what the churches taught about business is difficult to discover. Not least because the churches themselves found it hard to think clearly and delicate or dangerous to pronounce definitely on the questions it posed. They could have had no compunction in condemning the likes of Jabez Spencer Balfour, the Congregationalist and dishonest chairman of the Liberator Building Society which crashed in 1892 leaving 1,400 bankrupted aged spinsters and widows in its wake.[1] In Scotland the *United Presbyterian Magazine* did not hesitate to denounce the City of Glasgow Bank directors, headed by a Free Churchman, whose dishonesty led to the bank's collapse in 1878 and losses of £6 million, much borne by 1,800 stockholders, a quarter of them spinsters, widows, and married women.[2] In some denominations indeed business failure among members had been regarded as likely evidence of moral failure which therefore required investigation by church deacons or elders.[3]

Violations of civil or criminal law were clear-cut cases. What of the other aspects of business behaviour on which the Old and New Testaments explicitly or implicitly counselled, sometimes with apparent ambiguity? For example, what about the ownership of private property, the foundation of capitalism? The lure of Canaan, the Promised Land, centred heavily on its abundant fruitfulness, flowing with milk and honey; but Mosaic Law from the Ten Commandments onwards condemned

[1] Esmond J. Cleary, 'Jabez Spencer Balfour', *DBB*.

[2] A. C. Cheyne, *The Transforming of the Kirk* (Edinburgh, 1983), 138; R. E. Tyson, 'The Failure of the City of Glasgow Bank', *Accountant's Magazine* (Apr. 1974).

[3] This happened to Sir Samuel Morton Peto, the great Victorian railway contractor, after he became bankrupt in 1866. See F. and B. Bowers, 'Bloomsbury Chapel and Mercantile Morality', *Baptist Quarterly* (1984).

the coveting of property. In the New Testament, the gospel is directed at the poor and Christ warned that rich men would as soon enter the kingdom of heaven as a camel would pass through the eye of a needle; yet he spoke approvingly of profitable stewardship. Prophetic voices from the early Church Fathers onwards continued to warn against wealth but yet to lend it qualified approval.[4] So did Luther and Calvin, the Reformers whose theology shaped Protestant Britain for over four centuries.[5]

Truth to tell, the post-Constantine church and its Roman, Orthodox, and Protestant successors found it impossible to avoid secular and material entanglements.[6] Like almost every other religious institution before or since, the church in England (in the sense of a clerical organization), whether in its Roman, Anglican, or Nonconformist manifestations, has depended on the laity to endow it with property, subscribe a portion of its income, advise on its investments, assist in its administration, and much else. Even association with the rogues of business was seemingly unavoidable. Before his first bankruptcy (in 1898), the ex-Baptist deacon and company promoter E. T. Hooley claimed, 'Eminent divines of the Church of England would come praying me for money to restore their cathedrals, while the politicians simply fell over each other in their endeavours to gain my ear.'[7] Hooley also asserted in later years that, to celebrate Queen Victoria's Jubilee, he had presented a communion set of gold plate to the Dean and Chapter of St Paul's. A few weeks later his financial empire collapsed. Despite the tainted gift and despite the donor's distress the cathedral authorities kept their plate and Hooley heard nothing more from them.[8] The most flawed laymen have served and funded the church: how could the clergy bite the hand that fed?

There was another reason, besides the difficulties of theological interpretation and the churches' reliance on wealthy laymen, that made it hard for the churches to formulate a clear statement of their teaching about business. Industrial society had alienated many more poor than rich as it spread out across the face of nineteenth-century Britain. Belatedly the 'Condition of England' debate in the 1880s and 1890s wakened the churches to their failure to reach the industrial working classes. Con-

---

[4] See M. Wilks, 'Thesaurus Ecclesiae' and other essays in W. J. Sheils and D. Wood (eds.), The Church and Wealth (Oxford, 1987).

[5] R. H. Tawney, Religion and the Rise of Capitalism (London, 1936).

[6] See the string of examples in Sheils and Woods (eds.), Church and Wealth.

[7] E. T. Hooley, Hooley's Confessions (London, 1924), 24; Kenneth and Margaret Richardson, 'Ernest Terah Hooley', DBB.

[8] Hooley, Confessions, 154–5.

cern for the inner cities, evidenced among the churches by William Booth's Salvation Army, the Wesleyans' central halls, and the Anglo-Catholics' missions, relatively both obscured and diverted church teaching on business ethics. Obscurity came from the preoccupation with the private relief of the poor, diversion from the rise of socialism. The churches' ten thousand compassions, for the poor, orphans, prisoners, prostitutes, the blind and deaf, the insane, sick, and aged, sailors, and soldiers, swelled across the decades of the nineteenth century but fell short in the end of meeting the vast army of human needs: ultimately state action had to be mobilized.[9] But in the welter of charitable activities the businessman was seen primarily as benefactor, almost by definition on the side of the angels.[10]

The most radical nineteenth-century intellectual response to the injustices and agonies of industrial society came from socialist thinkers, notably Marx and Engels. Their *Manifesto of the Communist Party*, translated into English in 1888, exhorted the working classes to unite in a class struggle the goal of which was the abolition of private property. Communism, as expounded by Marx and Engels, could hardly be embraced by the propertied middle classes. Nor could it command the wholehearted allegiance of the followers of Christ. The *Manifesto* assumed that Christianity had succumbed to eighteenth-century rationalism. The vestiges of 'religious liberty and freedom of conscience merely gave expression to the sway of free competition within the domain of knowledge'.[11] Religion Marx dismissed in his German study of Hegelian philosophy (1844) as 'the opiate of the people. . . . The criticism of Religion is . . . a criticism of the vale of misery. . . . The removal of Religion as the illusory happiness of the people means the demand of the people for their real happiness.'[12] Yet the experience of the early church suggested a primitive form of communism. The Acts of the Apostles chapter 2 (AV) recorded, 'And all that believed were together, and had all things common, And sold their possessions and goods, and parted them to all men, as every man had need.'

[9] F. K. Brown, *Fathers of the Victorians* (Cambridge, 1961); K. Heaseman, *Evangelicals in Action* (London, 1962); D. W. Bebbington, *The Nonconformist Conscience* (London, 1982); O. Checkland, *Philanthropy in Victorian Scotland* (Edinburgh, 1980) provide a comprehensive picture of the churches' outpouring of charitable endeavour.

[10] This point is well made by R. H. Campbell, 'A Critique of the Christian Businessman and His Paternalism', in D. J. Jeremy (ed.), *Business and Religion in Britain* (Aldershot, 1988).

[11] K. Marx and F. Engels, *Manifesto of the Communist Party* (repr. Moscow, 1955), 91.

[12] Quoted in E. Rogers, *A Christian Commentary on Communism* (London, 1959), 92.

This text was one starting-point for the Christian Socialists, who adopted their name in 1850. But their ideals lay in the direction of communitarian or co-operative production on Owenite lines, rather than Marxist class struggle.[13] One of them, Charles Kingsley the cleric and novelist, (probably unknowingly) echoed Marx when in 1848 he declared that the Bible had been misused as 'an opium dose for keeping beasts of burden patient while they were being overloaded' and as a 'book to keep the poor in order'.[14] Although the theological leader of the Christian Socialists, F. D. Maurice, has been reinterpreted as a Tory paternalist,[15] he made a fundamental contribution. Maurice emphasized that the kingdom of Christ was here and now, rather than in the future (so immanent that he equated it with the English state of his own day). If the early Christian Socialist leaders were upper- and middle-class Anglicans, rank and file were frequently Nonconformist laymen with Chartist and trade union backgrounds; few were Nonconformist ministers, for their livelihood depended on middle-class congregations.

By the 1880s many younger clergy, especially those ministering in city slums, were touched in varying degrees by ideas of radical social reform.[16] The Christian Socialist movement remained largely upper class but now diversified. Stewart Headlam's Guild of St Matthew (reformed 1877) merged Maurician and Tractarian with aesthetic and even Fabian streams.[17] The Christian Social Union (formed 1889) tended to be more academic. Its founder was Henry Scott Holland, Canon of St Paul's; its first president B. F. Westcott, Bishop of Durham; and its other luminary the High Churchman Charles Gore, successively, 1902–19, Bishop of Worcester, Birmingham, and Oxford. Their thinking inspired many later, many lesser, writers and movements, not all sympathetic to their ideas.[18] One way to assess whether this theological ferment produced any Christian views of business is to see what the most perspicacious among Anglican and Nonconformists after 1900 had to say on two of the pertinent issues: the relationship between the church and the world; and prescriptions for economic systems.

[13] E. R. Norman, *The Victorian Christian Socialists* (Cambridge, 1987).

[14] C. Kingsley, *Politics for the People*, quoted in O. Chadwick, *The Victorian Church*, i (London, 1971), 353.

[15] E. R. Norman, *Church and Society in England, 1779-1970* (Oxford, 1976), 170–5. Cf. Chadwick, *Victorian Church*, i, 346–63.

[16] O. Chadwick, *The Victorian Church*, ii (London, 1972), 273.

[17] J. Oliver, *Church and Social Order* (London, 1968), 2–3.

[18] The best available surveys are Oliver, *Church and Social Order* and relevant chapters in Norman, *Church and Society*.

I THE RELATIONSHIP BETWEEN THE CHURCH AND THE WORLD

Axiomatically none of the advanced church thinkers took the view that religion should be divorced from economics or business. Such a separation was commonly held. Why, was demonstrated by the brilliant Oxford historian, churchman, and socialist Richard H. Tawney, who had come under Gore's influence while an undergraduate at Balliol. In the first Scott Holland Memorial Lectures, delivered at King's College, London (appropriately where F. D. Maurice once taught), in 1922, Tawney took up and modified Max Weber's theory that Calvinism was the parent of capitalism. He argued *inter alia* that since the late seventeenth century the individualistic rather than the collectivist element in Calvinism had triumphed and with it the separation of religion and social ethics. In the words of an eighteenth-century writer, 'trade is one thing and religion is another'.[19] The essence of that transformation Tawney saw in his own day as 'a dualism which regards the secular and the religious aspects of life, not as successive stages within a larger unity, but as parallel and independent provinces, governed by different laws, judged by different standards, and amenable to different authorities'.[20] Adam Smith, the father of modern economics, reinforced the dualism. 'In Smith's writings, religion and morality, together with paternalism, were all effectively banished from business and government; religion was relegated to the private sphere where it could have no contact with either.'[21] Apart from the Quakers and a few lone voices in the Nonconformist denominations, until the 1880s church leaders and preachers tacitly accepted this notion of two kingdoms and stayed resolutely within their own.

But there were other reasons why churchmen kept religion and business in different compartments. By the turn of the century proponents of the 'social gospel', the attempts to bring religious principles to bear on economic behaviour, were often identified with liberal Christianity. Liberals followed the theories and methods of the German theologians, who called on science and historical scholarship to question the tradi-

---

[19] Tawney, *Religion and the Rise of Capitalism*, 192. Tawney was not the first to blame the Reformation for divorcing Christian morality from the economic realm: Archdeacon Cunningham had briefly done so in a lecture at the London School of Economics in 1913. Norman, *Church and Society*, 224.

[20] Tawney, *Religion and the Rise of Capitalism*, 279.

[21] S. G. Checkland, 'Cultural Factors and British Business Men, 1815–1914', in K. Nakagawa (ed.), *Social Order and Entrepreneurship* (Tokyo, 1977), 60.

tional teachings of the church—about the miracles, the reliability and authority of the biblical texts, even the divinity of Christ.[22] Conservative theologians and evangelicals, who dominated the Nonconformist and Scottish churches and represented a large group in the Church of England, fearing the association, eschewed the call to radical social reform. Instead they emphasized private charity and other church teachings, particularly on evangelism. Missionary endeavour demanded priority because, it was emphasized in the late nineteenth century, it would hasten the second coming of Christ and thus end the world's present suffering. The disillusioned suffragette leader Christabel Pankhurst, for example, held the premillennial belief that the imminent visible coming of Christ made the struggle for social reform pointless.[23] Rather differently, other church leaders distrusted their competence to pronounce on matters relating to technical subjects like economics and business.

No such constraints held back emerging proponents of the 'social gospel'. To them, the individualistic, palliative acts of charity, with which nineteenth century Christians had remorselessly attacked social problems could never succeed by themselves. In addition social, economic, and political systems and structures had to be captured and reshaped in accordance with a Christian ethic and order. The Christian Social Union's aims of 1889 included 'To claim for the Christian Law the ultimate authority to rule social practice' and 'To study how to apply the moral truths and principles of Christianity to the social and economic difficulties of the present time.'[24]

Nonconformist ministers sat closer, but often less comfortably, to men of business and the business world than prelates of the Church of England. Disestablished, Dissenting pastors looked down on pews of commercial men and faced them across vestry tables when the ruling bodies of local congregations met to decide a gamut of delicate issues including the pastor's salary. The real or putative intimidation did not silence all prophets, however. Shocked by the exploitation of women under the Contagious Diseases Act, the Reverend Hugh Price Hughes, a Wesleyan 'Day of Judgement in breeches',[25] became the shrill mouthpiece

---

[22] This is necessarily a simplified summary of liberal theology. See Chadwick, *Victorian Church*, ii, 40–111.

[23] T. P. Weber, *Living in the Shadow of the Second Coming* (Oxford, 1979), 103–4. On the other hand, many premillennialists were spokesmen for civic reform and like the English Wesleyan evangelist Gypsy Smith denounced alcohol, prostitution, and other forms of vice.

[24] Oliver, *Church and Social Order*, 5.

[25] Arthur Porritt, quoted by Bebbington, *Nonconformist Conscience*, 41.

of the Nonconformist conscience in the 1880s. Until his death in 1902 he led the Forward Movement, committed to social improvement via legislative reform and social action aimed at the urban masses. Central halls were one product of the Forward Movement and stirred by Hughes many younger Wesleyan businessmen like Joseph Rank the miller subscribed to central hall projects. Whether they saw them as vehicles of the gospel of individual salvation or as agencies for collective relief and reform (Hughes's emphasis) was not always clear.[26]

A strip of Hughes's mantle fell on Samuel E. Keeble, a Wesleyan minister and regular contributor in the 1890s to the *Methodist Times* edited by Hughes. In the preface to the first (1896) edition of his *Industrial Day Dreams: Studies in Industrial Ethics and Economics*, Keeble, then at Sheffield with eighteen years' standing in the ministry, rebuked religious individualism. A solution to 'the social problem . . . depends not merely upon the possession of the Christian temper—though that is of vital importance—but upon the direct application of the ethical standards of Christianity as tests, and of Christian principles as guides, to these problems as such'.[27] He also roundly rejected the two kingdoms approach: 'To this hour it is maintained in the schools and the public press that political economy and Christianity have nothing to do with each other, that the one is "science," and the other "morals". . . . Political economy is largely a science of human relations. No such science can help being moral; it is *immoral* when it is otherwise.'[28] Such a message proved unpopular with the wealthy trustees at Sheffield Brunswick Chapel and Keeble, rebuked by his superintendent minister, was moved to lesser church charges. He went on in 1905 to found the Wesleyan Methodist Union for Social Service, as close as Wesleyans then came to Christian Socialism, whose members included the Reverends W. F. Lofthouse and Henry Carter.[29]

Ministers in other Nonconformist churches were also trying to reclaim economic activity as an area for the application of Christian morality. Again, until the 1890s they were voices crying in the wilderness. Among Congregationalists the Reverend R. W. Dale at Carr's Lane, Birmingham, from 1867 and into the 1880s 'set out to show "the sacredness

---

[26] Bebbington, *Nonconformist Conscience, passim*; K. S. Inglis, *Churches and the Working Classes in Victorian England* (London, 1963), 85–100; P. S. Bagwell, *Outcast London* (London, 1987).

[27] S. E. Keeble, *Industrial Day Dreams* (London, 1907), pp. vii–viii.

[28] Keeble, *Industrial Day Dreams*, 189.

[29] M. L. Edwards, *S. E. Keeble* (London, 1949), 1–30. Material relating to the WMUSS and the ministerial Sigma Fellowship are in the John Rylands Library, Keeble papers.

of what is called secular business" and to present "a new and Christian conception of the industrial and commercial pursuits of mankind."'[30] Among Quakers Edward Grubb denied any notion of separating faith and business but inclined towards the redemption of individuals rather than systems: 'selfishness, after all, is not a quality of systems, but of human beings'.[31] In Scotland before 1900 the smallest of the large presbyterian denominations, the United Presbyterians, led the way in their periodical literature and among some of their ministers in emphasizing the ethical aspects of the gospel. A few ministers in the Church of Scotland welcomed socialism. Others in the Free Church expressed sympathy for trade unions and opposition to Highland land laws. In the Church of Scotland in 1901 a Scottish Christian Social Union was formed; the General Assembly set up its first permanent committee on social problems in 1912. In the United Free Church a similar committee was instituted in 1909. By 1914 the two largest denominations in Scotland were turning from an individualized version of the faith to a 'new Christian social concern based on a suspicion or rejection of the existing order, and which expressed itself in social criticism and in more dynamic and radical forms of social action'.[32] Finally, Roman Catholic social theology also moved to the left in the last decade of the nineteenth century.[33] Pope Leo XIII's encyclical *Rerum Novarum* (1891) on the rights and duties of capital and labour marked the shift. Expounding the encyclical in the *Tablet* in 1903 the Bishop of Newport observed that while the Pope started by 'laying down the lawfulness of private property', he moved on to 'laying down that every man who is willing to labour has a right to such a wage as will secure to himself and his family a frugal and sufficient maintenance'.[34]

The First World War, in which 3,000 Anglican chaplains served, exposed an appalling ignorance of the Christian faith; it also eroded class divisions and strengthened the determination to achieve social

[30] E. P. Hennock, *Fit and Proper Persons* (London, 1973), 161.

[31] E. Grubb, *Christianity and Business* (London, 1912), 118. Interestingly he changed his view of an individualistic approach. In *Social Aspects of the Quaker Faith* (London, 1899), 193, he commended the American Charles M. Sheldon's *In His Steps*; in *Christianity and Business*, 127, he regarded modern society as too complex to admit a 'mechanical imitation of what Jesus did or would do'.

[32] Cheyne, *Transforming of the Kirk*, 153, quoting D. C. Smith, 'The Failure and Recovery of Social Criticism in the Scottish Church, 1830–1950' (Edinburgh Ph.D., 1963), 436.

[33] R. H. Preston, *Church and Society in the Late Twentieth Century* (London, 1983), 87–8 briefly analyses this shift.

[34] *Tablet* 7 Mar. 1903.

reform and the more equitable distribution of wealth.[35] Awakened by the horrors of the First World War, those in the Christian Socialist tradition seized the opportunity to move the established church towards clearer statements on economic and industrial behaviour. The 'outstanding expression of Christian thought about post-war society'[36] was the Report of the Archbishops' Fifth Committee of Inquiry, *Christianity and Industrial Problems* (1918)—the five enquiries issued from the National Mission of Repentance and Hope of 1916, the church's reponse to war. The members of the committee which produced the Fifth Report included four bishops in the Christian Social Union (one of them Gore), R. H. Tawney, Albert Mansbridge (founder of the Workers' Educational Association), and George Lansbury (editor of the *Daily Herald* and then between two terms as Labour MP). Signatories also included two or three prominent industrialists such as F. W. Gilbertson, the South Wales tinplate manufacturer,[37] and W. L. Hichens, the chairman of Cammell Laird, the Birkenhead shipbuilding firm.[38]

The authors of the Fifth Report defied Adam Smith: 'we think it our duty to point out that Christianity claims to offer mankind a body of moral teaching which not only is binding upon individuals in their personal and domestic conduct but also supplies a criterion by which to judge their economic activity, their industrial organisation and their social institutions.'[39] The significance of the Fifth Report emerged two years later when it was affirmed by the Lambeth Conference Committee on Industrial and Social Problems (the personnel of the two committees heavily overlapped). The resolutions of the 1920 Lambeth Conference (which condemned the 'internecine conflict between capital and labour' and urged 'accepting as the basis of industrial relations the principle of co-operation in service for the common good in place of unrestricted competition for private or sectional advantage', as well as asserting again that 'God cannot be excluded from politics, or industry, or from any of our social relationships'[40]), were 'popularised in the Church by the work of the Industrial Christian Fellowship, founded in 1919 by amalgamating the CSU with the Navvy Mission (founded in 1877)'.[41] Further confirmation of the sea change came when the new National Assembly

---

[35] Norman, *Church and Society*, 239–40.
[36] Oliver, *Church and Social Order*, 49 ff.
[37] Graeme M. Holmes, 'Francis William Gilbertson', *DBB*.
[38] R. P. T. Davenport-Hines, 'William Lionel Hichens', *DBB*.
[39] *Christianity and Industrial Problems*, 9.
[40] Norman, *Church and Society*, 245.
[41] Ibid.

of the Church of England in 1923 appointed a Standing Committee on Social and Industrial Questions. The official teaching of the Anglican church which had prevailed for nearly two centuries was reversed. No matter their mixed record on involvement in industrial arbitration,[42] the Church of England episcopacy was committed to the new principles of social criticism.

As E. R. Norman has observed, one of William Temple's roles was 'to push the orthodoxy of social radicalism further down the ecclesiastical hierarchy, until it reached the parish pulpit with the frequency with which, previously, it had reached the episcopal palace'.[43] Under Temple's rising leadership and the Life and Liberty Movement, a more interdenominational approach to social problems was forged out of the war. From the Interdenominational Conference of Social Service Unions (presided over by Gore) in 1919 came the idea, born in the London-based 'Collegium' (a seminar for senior Student Christian Movement workers) run by Temple, for a general Christian conference on social questions. It materialized in 1924 when under Temple's chairmanship 1,500 delegates, mostly from Britain, assembled in Birmingham for the Conference on Christian Politics, Economics and Citizenship, known as COPEC. Delegates discussed twelve reports prepared by commissions which had gathered data from study groups around the country. The first report, *The Nature of God and His Purpose for the World*, 'laid a sound theological foundation for the practical suggestions of later reports, and warded off the criticism that the social gospel lacked a theological basis'[44] The merging of religion and economics was now a respectable but by no means universal position in the mainline denominations. When in 1941 Temple came to write his immensely influential *Christianity and Social Order* his first chapter, 'What Right Has the Church to Interfere?', dealt with this issue. Now, however, he was writing to convince the ordinary thinking person with Christian sympathies (the book sold 150,000 copies within twelve months of appearing in 1942), not church theologians.

Among Nonconformists the teaching that churches had a social as well as an individual gospel to proclaim, and a duty to apply it to secular systems and institutions, was achieved by a growing number of clerical voices, sometimes in the wilderness, sometimes in denominational conferences. A powerful theological defence of the social gospel was advanced at the annual meetings of the Congregational Union in 1905 when the Reverend Dr P. T. Forsyth gave his chairman's address on

[42] Norman, *Church and Society*, 257–9.
[43] Ibid. 281.
[44] Oliver, *Church and Social Order*, 68.

'A Holy Church the Moral Guide of Society'. Christ, he asserted, came 'so to save souls and found churches as to make Christian nations and thus change Society to the Kingdom of God'.[45] To Congregational businessmen like William Lever, Albert Spicer, Halley Stewart, or George Alfred Wills, owners of large-scale businesses if they were not all in the top hundred employers,[46] P. T. Forsyth's address was as discomforting as it was challenging. Along the way he remarked, 'The Bible, both in the Old and New Testaments, shows an anti-capitalist tendency.' Admittedly capitalism had brought many benefits as well as many scourges. But, thinking no doubt of the world of his own co-religionists Balfour and Hooley, he went on, capitalism 'has begun in its own interests seriously to limit freedom. . . . A monopolist Trust can force the workman to choose between its terms and starvation. And so with the shopkeeper. The shops become tied houses.'[47] Forsyth's real concern was not capitalism as such but the spirit of greed and exploitation which it so usually engendered. It simply was not good enough to point to the benefactions of Christian philanthropists:

A billionaire at the head of a vast monopoly may be a sincere Christian, nay, a generous and lavish Christian. But his simple personal faith will not of itself give him the power and insight to apply the Christian moral principle to the accepted standard of the age. And as a matter of fact such faith has had more effect on the disposal of wealth than on the moral making of it. The current ethic of giving may be far more Christian than that of getting.[48]

Forsyth's sympathies lay with the small businessman and against the monopoly capitalist. His vision of social transformation rested on the application of a Christian morality that would usher in the kingdom of God.

The most influential Nonconformist study after those of Keeble, Grubb, and Forsyth was *The Christian Ideal for Human Society* (1930) by Alfred Garvie, Forsyth's successor as principal at New College, London. Former chairman of the Congregational Unions of Scotland and of England and Wales, former moderator of the Federal Council of Free Churches, dean of the faculty of theology in London University, Garvie was deeply involved in COPEC and in developing inter-church

---

[45] P. T. Forsyth, *A Holy Church the Moral Guide of Society* (London, c. 1905), 12.

[46] For lists of business leaders arranged by denomination see D. J. Jeremy, 'Religious Links of Individuals Listed in the *DBB*', in Jeremy (ed.), *Business and Religion*, 188–205.

[47] Forsyth, *Holy Church*, 43, 45.

[48] Ibid. 46.

relations.[49] In *The Christian Ideal* he observed, 'Adam Smith's *Wealth of Nations* (1776), admirable as it may be as an analysis of industry and commerce in his own land and in his own day, is not applicable to all countries for all time.' (Again the attack was directed at the core of the opposing ideology.) The Christian church had been insufficiently critical of capitalism. Business and economic behaviour ought to be subjected to three Christian standards: stewardship towards God should be fulfilled in the service of man; the power over others implied in the possession of wealth should be exercised with due regard for the dignity of the human personality; and, thinking of employees no doubt, moral obligations are mutual.[50] Influential though Garvie's work was, its very length and dense prose made it a forbidding treatise which few businessmen can have read.

In the face of national economic depression and following the Methodist Union of 1932, the largest and most business-orientated Nonconformist denomination agreed a radical statement of its position. The 'Declaration of the Methodist Church on a Christian View of Industry in Relation to the Social Order' of 1934 showed that a majority of denominational leaders had rejected the two kingdoms theology: 'industry ought therefore to be an instrument for establishing the Kingdom of God on earth'.[51] The implications of this were by no means clear to Methodist captains of industry, however. It certainly did not mean that all Methodist businessmen assented, for example, to nationalization (which was then on the Labour Party's agenda). Nor did it even mean that Methodists agreed that the pulpit should make pronouncements about economic behaviour. This ambivalence among Methodists emerges in Chapter 8 where the writings of Sir Josiah Stamp, leading industrialist and Methodist layman, are examined.

The view that religion had authority to reform the economic order did not go unchallenged. Among its more distinguished critics were Archdeacon Cunningham (d. 1919), who argued that faith should set economic goals not specify economic methods, and W. R. Inge, Dean of St Paul's, who was wary of mixing politics and religion.[52] Temple's fellow bishop, Hensley Henson of Durham, assailed the assumption of COPEC that 'the Christian Revelation includes adequate direction on political and economic matters'. In the primary episcopal charge to his

---

[49] His influence on the Baptist leader Ernest A. Payne is indicated in W. M. S. West, *To Be a Pilgrim* (Guildford, 1983), 22.

[50] A. Garvie, *The Christian Ideal for Human Society* (London, 1930), 349, 359–360.

[51] Methodist Church, *Declarations of Conference on Social Questions* (London, 1959), 25.

[52] Oliver, *Church and Social Order*, 48, 53.

clergy, *Quo Tendimus?* (1924), he restated the idea of separate spheres, with the New Testament supreme in one but not all. *Inter alia*, he also reasserted that it 'is fundamental in Christ's religion that the redemption of the world must be effected through the redemption of individuals'.[53] This was also the position of the majority of evangelicals both within and outside the Church of England until the late 1950s.[54]

Men of Christian conscience in business therefore faced various alternative Christian stances on the basic issue of whether the industrial structures of a fallen world could be claimed for the kingdom of God. The more radical argued that salvation was collective as well as individual, and that it applied to systems as well as people; this flowed from their rejection of the old assumption of separate spheres for religion and economics. The more conservative took the opposite position on these aspects of the issue. The gospel was for the individual, Smithian economics for society. In between were those who either doubted the two kingdoms philosophy or else were dissatisfied with religious individualism.

2 CHURCH PRESCRIPTIONS FOR BUSINESS AND ECONOMIC SYSTEMS

If by the 1920s the churches were urging their members to apply the faith to economic and industrial questions, what sort of possibilities were they holding out? Not surprisingly, biblical injunctions about social justice, expounded within the new tradition of social criticism against the background of war and then of high inter-war unemployment, led to the discussion of a variety of questions. Among them were wealth, competition, labour relations, property, and profit. Broadly, three kinds of solution emerged among church leaders and activists trying to advance theological insights into the realms of either theoretical economics or practical industrial matters.

First there was a range of piecemeal recommendations, usually couched in general terms, sometimes requiring voluntary action, sometimes state intervention. All envisaged gradualist change. In *Property: Its Duties and Rights* (1913), a symposium edited by Gore and the 'definitive expression of the Christian attitude on the subject',[55] property was

---

[53] Norman, *Church and Society*, 309–11; Oliver, *Church and Social Order*, 74–5.
[54] See the section on Bruce Reed and Christian Teamwork in ch. 6 and Randle Manwaring, *From Controversy to Co-existence: Evangelicals in the Church of England, 1914–1980* (Cambridge, 1985), 202.
[55] Oliver, *Church and Social Order*, 9.

recognized as necessary for the expression of personality; an important distinction was made between property for use and property for power; and the right of the state to regulate it in the interests of citizens was acknowledged. Adumbrating Tawney, Scott Holland challenged that individualism could ever be isolated: 'personality is always collective in basis'. Ultimately, it should be remembered by those on whom property had endowed power, 'Back to God all rights run.'[56] Another collection of essays, which came out of Temple's Collegium, *Competition: A Study in Human Motive* (1917), saw competition as the basis of modern industry but a basis corrupted by vested interest and economic privilege. Short of demolishing the competitive system, the vices of competition could only be eliminated by state intervention—and it recommended a more progressive tax system to fund the social reforms necessary to combat the evil results of competition.[57] The authors acknowledged that changed organizations and systems (the overall form of which they would not guess at) would only be effective if accompanied by changed hearts and motivations.[58] *Industry and Property* (1924), ninth of the COPEC reports, launched a series of proposals, many heard before (especially in the Fifth Report) like those on reform of the laws of inheritance in order to effect the more equitable redistribution of personal wealth.[59] The Methodist Church's Declaration of 1934 was another general call for change, requiring voluntary, progressive action on the part of industrialists. Among essentials prescribed for a 'New Christian Social Order' were the abolition of economic poverty, the just distribution of the fruits of industry, and adaptations to the means of control of industry. The last recalled the Whitley Councils of the First World War.[60]

The second kind of solution was of a very different order. During the decade before the First World War, when the Labour Party secured 30 seats in the Commons (1906) and industrial unrest reached new heights, more radical theories attracted the founders of the Church Socialist League (formed under P. E. T. Widdrington, Vicar of St Peter's, Coventry, and others in 1906). CSL members were mostly priests, mostly Anglo-Catholic, mostly in the North of England, and all anti-capitalist. Under Gore's influence men such as Paul Bull and J. N. Figgis were

---

[56] H. S. Holland, 'Property and Personality', in C. Gore (ed.), *Property* (London, 1913), 187, 192.

[57] Oliver, *Church and Social Order*, 11–14.

[58] J. Harvey *et al.*, *Competition* (London, 1917), 157–58.

[59] Oliver, *Church and Social Order*, 70–1; Norman, *Church and Society*, 298–301.

[60] Methodist Church, *Declarations of Conference*, 31–4.

attracted to the Community of the Resurrection at Mirfield (of which Gore was founder and later superior). Thaxted in Essex, where the turbulent Conrad Noel was priest for three decades, was another centre of what might be described as left-wing Christian Socialism.[61] One of the most prominent laymen in the CSL was Maurice Reckitt, a fugitive from the family starch business (income from which presumably gave him the leisure to think and write) and a maverick in his adopted subjects of economics and sociology (he had read history at Oxford).[62] On the eve of the war its members included Tawney, Lansbury, and A. J. Penty, a young architect.

From the group came some of the more eccentric aberrations of Christian Socialism—for that is how they must have seemed to the majority of clerics and to a responsible Christian in business like George Cadbury. Conrad Noel, who welcomed the first phases of the Russian revolution in 1917, countenanced revolution and 'the use of centralised state power for social regeneration'.[63] Penty saw social renewal coming through the restoration of craftsmanship and the revival of rural life. His was one of the variants of a neo-medieval social vision lent credence by Tawney's *Acquisitive Society* (1920), which damned the competitive spirit of capitalism and by implication elevated the economic system of medieval Christendom. When the CSL was reorganized as the League of the Kingdom of God in 1923 it retained its hostility to capitalism. Its basis included the statement, 'The Catholic faith demands a challenge to the world by the repudiation of capitalist plutocracy and the wage system, and stands for the social order in which the means of life subserve the common weal.'[64]

One seductive ideal which attracted the CSL after 1914 was Guild Socialism. National Guilds, Reckitt's particular panacea, rejected collectivism and state socialism, just as much as they distrusted profit-sharing and co-partnership. Instead Reckitt preached a scheme with strong trade unions, a single closed shop union for each industry, ownership of capital by the state but management in the hands of 'the democratic self-governing guilds'.[65] Reckitt found in Fabian ranks many sympathisers and in 1915 they formed the National Guilds League. Prototype guilds were set up in the furniture, clothing, and building trades, among others. They foundered on the rocks of trade depression and conflict within

[61] Norman, *Church and Society*, 246–51; Oliver, *Church and Social Order*, 17–21.
[62] J. S. Peart-Binns, *Maurice B. Reckitt* (Basingstoke, 1988).
[63] Norman, *Church and Society*, 248.
[64] Peart-Binns, *Reckitt*, 71.
[65] Oliver, *Church and Social Order*, 63.

the NGL between various factions which shaded into Marxists and Communists. Few survived the early 1920s.[66]

From the NGL Reckitt turned to Christendom, a group of CSL Anglo-Catholics who started meeting in 1920 at Paycocks, the medieval house owned by the Buxton family at Coggeshall, Essex. They took their name from *The Return of Christendom* (1922), a volume of their papers edited by Gore. Searching for 'Christian sociology', by which was meant distinctly Christian principles derived from Christian theology, many of the Christendom members hoped to identify a true and specific Christian order of arrangements for any given aspect of society.[67] *The Return of Christendom* has been judged 'a muddled and ill-balanced book'.[68] One of its contentions was that the financial system, not private property or industrial competition, was the root of society's economic ills. For a specific solution the Christendom group adopted Major C. H. Douglas's theory of Social Credit, an underconsumption theory analysed in Britain and condemned as unsound and unworkable by the Labour Party in 1922, the Macmillan Committee on Finance and Industry in 1931, and sundry economists of various political persuasions. Hugh Dalton described it as 'an intellectual nightmare ... an administrative monstrosity'.[69] Two erroneous assumptions underlay Douglas's economics. First, that the full costs of production were not redistributed as purchasing power: a supposition which led Douglas to suggest that producers should sell their goods below cost price and accept social credits as compensation. Second, that bank loans not fully covered by cash are imaginary creations causing economic disequilibrium: a situation which he thought would be rectified by the public control of banks.[70] Reckitt's friend Philip Mairet perpetuated Douglas's heresies by publishing a collection of Douglas's works in 1934.[71] The Christian Socialists thus aligned themselves against the prevailing financial system, some of whose more illustrious members were simultaneously instrumental in safeguarding Anglican investments, including clerical salaries and pensions.[72]

---

[66] Peart-Binns, *Reckitt*, 56–63.

[67] Norman, *Church and Society*, 318–22

[68] Oliver, *Church and Social Order*, 123.

[69] J. C. Stamp, *Motive and Method in a Christian Order* (London, 1936), 240–41. See also Elizabeth Durbin, *New Jerusalems: The Labour Party and the Emergence of Democratic Socialism* (London, 1985), 137.

[70] Oliver, *Church and Social Order*, 123–8.

[71] C. H. Douglas, *The Douglas Manual* (London, 1934).

[72] See Ch. 7.

The Christendom group remained active through the 1920s and 1930s as the leading socialists in the Church of England. In nose-diving into a heap of specific economic prescriptions, sometimes more socialist than Christian, on occasion utterly unsound, they alienated all but the most glassy-eyed businessmen, to say nothing of academically trained economists. Strong criticisms were launched at the group, some by its own members. If you could identify a Christian order for society (which proved increasingly elusive), would the state necessarily accept it?, asked V. A. Demant.[73] A non-philosophical criticism came from Hensley Henson as he privately mused over the COPEC conference: 'Will not this passionate insistence on a definitely "Christian" version of every human concern carry those who make it into the difficult business of life with minds closed to truth, and obsessed with politics which are not in any genuine sense Christian at all?'[74]

Out of this kind of impasse came a third sort of solution to the genuine concern of churchmen to bring the Christian ethic to bear on the social and economic structures and systems of their day. Its advocates were Dr Joseph H. Oldham (1874–1969) and Archbishop William Temple. Oldham, son of an army officer, was converted while a student at Trinity College, Oxford, through the ministry of the American evangelist Dwight L. Moody.[75] He signed the pledge of the Student Volunteer Missionary Union, came under the spell of John R. Mott, and went out to India, the land of his birth, as a missionary with the Scottish YMCA. After four years ill health forced him in 1901 to return to Scotland where he trained for the United Free Church of Scotland at New College, Edinburgh. Though only briefly a missionary and never ordained, Oldham became a foremost missionary statesman and ecumenical leader. His main achievements in these fields were the organization of the Edinburgh World Missionary Conference (1910) and successive international missionary councils in the 1920s; a prophetic analysis and condemnation of racism in South Africa, *Christianity and the Race Problem* (1924); and, in the 1930s, his chairmanship of the research department of the Life and Work Movement out of which, as out of the Edinburgh Conference and other initiatives, sprang the British and World Councils of

[73] Norman, *Church and Society*, 321–2.
[74] Quoted ibid., 310.
[75] The information on Oldham's background comes from two articles by his biographer, Kathleen Bliss: 'Joseph Houldsworth Oldham', *DNB 1961–1970*; and 'The Legacy of J. H. Oldham', *International Bulletin of Missionary Research* (Jan. 1984).

Churches.[76] Oldham moved in the same circles as Temple and both men were involved in the Life and Work conferences of the 1930s. As the dictators dug their grip into Euro-Asia, the deepening confrontation between church and state shifted Oldham's attention away from the traditional missionary concern about rival religions to the challenge of totalitarianism and 'scientific' humanism. He 'set himself to make contacts with Christian leaders in all parts of the world who realised the growing menace of this secularism, and to further a vast programme of international study and research, with groups in the countries of two hemispheres'.[77] Among them was Temple, then Archbishop of York. After three years' preparation a conference was held at Oxford in summer 1937 under the title of 'Church, Community and State'. These concerns led Oldham to explore the relation of the church to contemporary society, the field in which Temple was specially interested. While Temple's contributions, primarily his *Christianity and Social Order*, have been amply appraised, Oldham's role in offering a new theological approach and a vehicle to implement it has been much overlooked.[78]

While Temple, as head of a state church, sowed the seed with a wider audience through speaking, preaching, writing, convening conferences, and dealing with the great and the good in the land, Oldham, handicapped by deafness (which forced him to carry a 'vast hearing aid'[79]), watered the plants with the *Christian News-Letter* and the Christian Frontier Council. The *CNL* was a fortnightly magazine founded in 1939 under the auspices of the interdenominational Council on the Christian Faith and the Common Life. The Christian Frontier Council was a lay movement formed in February 1942.[80] Both derived from Oldham's view of the relationship between religion and society. He did not accept the old notion of separate spheres, neither did he share the Christendom group's belief in Christian blueprints for every kind of social relationship and arrangement. Instead, his ideas derived from two Roman Catholic philosophers, Baron Friedrich von Hugel and Jacques Maritain. Von Hugel argued that the relationship between church and state was a dual

---

[76] For the relations between these various bodies see the diagram in F. A. Iremonger, *William Temple* (London, 1948), 388.

[77] Ibid. 409.

[78] Norman, *Church and Society*, mentions Oldham but neglects his Christian Frontier idea. Iremonger, *Temple*, barely notices the Christian Frontier. C. Barnett, *The Audit of War* (London, 1986), wholly missed Oldham. The late Dr Kathleen Bliss's promised biography of Oldham would have filled the gap.

[79] Bliss, 'Oldham', *DNB*.

[80] See ch. 6.

one: 'in its confession of faith [the church] makes universal claims. But in its institutional embodiment it exists within society as one human interest or activity alongside of other interests and activities, such as government administration, law, industry, education, medicine, science and art.'[81] These other departments of life have an autonomy of their own, independent of ecclesiastical direction or control. As an institution the church 'must in the vast majority of instances either content itself with proclaiming generalities or expose itself to the charge of intruding into spheres beyond its competence'.[82] The church was confined to enunciating universal Christian truths. How, then were those truths to be directed into the secular departments of life? From Maritain's view that the Christian in his secular calling must act as a Christian without committing the church to a particular policy binding on all Christians, Oldham took a new line. Christians must be encouraged to work out their Christian principles within their secular spheres. This fresh emphasis on the vocation of the laity, underscored by Temple and promoted by the Christian Frontier Council, created new opportunities for lay leaders with Christian commitment. The challenge was to discover what Temple was calling ' "middle axioms"—maxims for conduct which mediate between the fundamental principles and the tangle of particular problems'.[83] As will be seen, in the 1940s a number of leading businessmen were drawn into 'Frontier' work.

These then were the main currents of thought which the churches offered their laity in the secular world: the complete separation of faith and business; a variety of generalized pronouncements suggesting a gradualist approach to the problem of reconciling Christian ethics with secular systems; the pro-socialist, anti-capitalist schemes of Christendom; or the possibility of reaching principles informed by Christian ethics but applicable only to specific areas of secular activity. For the sensitive Christian conscience confronted by ethical and social choices in business, it amounted to a choice between abdication, lassitude, hostility, or exploration. Given the confused and competing voices it is doubtful whether

[81] J. H. Oldham, 'The Frontier Idea', *Frontier* (1960), 247.

[82] Ibid. 250. The problem of competence was noticed at the Lambeth Conference of 1920. In their encyclical letter the bishops observed, 'In the technical side of economics, which is a science for experts, the Church has no authority. But whenever in the working out of economic or of political theory moral issues are directly involved, the Church has a duty to see that the requirements of righteousness are faced and fairly met.' C. of E., Anglican bishops, *Conference, 1920: Encyclical Letter* (London, 1920), 18–19.

[83] W. Temple, 'Introduction', *Malvern, 1941* (London, 1941), p. vii; Preston, *Church and Society*, 141–56.

the alternatives were always heard or fully understood. If they were, businessmen would surely find the first and second easiest, the third almost unthinkable, and the last most demanding. However industrialists and businessmen understood these confusing signals, churchmen, mostly those of middle or High Churchmanship, heard a clear call to recapture ground lost to Adam Smith. Victorian church initiatives like the Anglicans' Navvy Mission Society or the Church of Scotland's Mission to Tinkers took on a new complexion and substance as they were transformed into movements with new strategies like the Industrial Christian Fellowship and industrial chaplaincies. Under the catalytic pressures of the Second World War these initiatives either burst into life or else gained new footings, as explored in Chapter 6.

3

Christian Influences in the Formation of Business Values, Skills, and Networks in British Business Élites, 1900–1960

Growing up before the First World War, as did most members of these business élites, inevitably brought Englishmen in contact with the Christian religion. Victorian culture was an intensely religious culture. Religious encounters came by various means and in differing degrees of intensity. The tenets and vigour of Christianity impinged upon the individual from infancy. Parents and relatives; Sunday School; local church; school; national church and political figures; newspapers; friends; and later wife and her family: the list might grow longer but more tenuous. Here it is assumed that the most forceful agencies of religious influence would be family, school, and church.

I FAMILY

Father's occupation is the first indicator of Christian influence through the family. All clergymen, it might be assumed, would exercise a powerful Christian example to sons, especially in a Victorian household. Clergymen among the fathers of the three business élites at first sight seem few in number (see Table 3.2).

Nine company chairmen (including a peer in holy orders) and 15 managing directors, 3.5 per cent and 8.7 per cent of known cases (over two-thirds of the whole sample) respectively, were sons of clergymen. In fact these are relatively high proportions. Clergymen represented under 0.5 per cent of the occupied population of England and Wales in 1871 and 1911.[1] Taken by élite, there was a noticeable but temporary

---

[1] *PP* (1873) LXXI Population Census, 1871, p. xxxv; ibid. (1913) LXXIX Population Census, 1911, 2.

rise in clerical social origins between the three cohorts of business leader: 5.6 per cent (of known cases) of the 1907 business élite were sons of clergymen, 7.5 per cent of the 1935 group, and 4.9 per cent of the 1955 group. Possibly this reflects the high-water mark of religious observance in late Victorian England.

Examined individually the 24 cases of clerical origins reveal some interesting differences over time. Of the seven whose offspring ascended to the 1907 business élite, all but one were Church of England clerics; of the ten clerical fathers of the 1935 élite, however, only three were Anglicans; in the 1955 élite only two of seven cases were Anglican clerics. Gains were clearly registered by Nonconformists and Celts. The one non-Anglican clerical father of the 1907 group was the Irish Presbyterian father of Sir William Crawford. The seven non-Anglican clerical fathers of the 1935 élite were a Congregational minister who was simultaneously an oilcake and brick manufacturer (Sir Halley Stewart whose son Malcolm was chairman and managing director of London Brick & Forders Ltd. and of the Associated Portland Cement Manufacturers, and is therefore counted four times); a Church of Scotland minister (father of Robert Horne, later Viscount Horne); and a Welsh Dissenting minister (father of Sir David Owen). The denominational affiliation of the Reverend John Hyde (father of Frederick Hyde) is unknown. Methodists, Congregationalists, and Scots predominated among the clerical paters of the 1955 business élite. The father of Sir Ivan Stedeford (chairman and managing director of Tube Investments, so counted twice) served, due to the various Methodist church unions, as Bible Christian minister, minister of the United Methodist Church (and president of its Conference in 1928–9) and Methodist minister. The father of Sir Oliver (later Lord) Franks became Principal of the Congregationalists' Western College in Bristol. The fathers of Sir Robert Harvey and Sir James Reid Young were Scottish clergymen.

Anglican clergyman possessed certain advantages for sons proceeding into the business world. They were themselves educated, 70 per cent of them having been at Oxford or Cambridge in the 1880s.[2] They frequently owned property and were used to estate management on a small scale. Of the 23,000 clergymen listed in *Crockford's* in the 1880s 13,000 were beneficed, possessing freehold land and house.[3] However, entry to parson's freehold helped to tie Anglican clerics to an aristocratic and agricultural social order. Some 64 per cent of the 11,342 livings

[2] O. Chadwick, *The Victorian Church*, ii (London, 1972), 247.
[3] Ibid. 167, 247.

in the Church of England (in England and Wales) were 'in the gift of private patrons, that is in the hands of the aristocracy and gentry' in the early 1830s.[4] The situation had not much changed by the end of the century.[5] Rare, however, was the father of Edward Ponsonby who was clergyman, peer (the 7th Earl of Bessborough), and landed proprietor (with an income of £22,000 a year from 35,000 acres of Irish estates).[6] Other fathers were much lower down the clerical and social ladders. When Alexander Butterworth was born his father was still a curate; at Alfred Hewlett's birth his father was a schoolmaster in training for the priesthood. A keen awareness of the value of property and its management nevertheless was part of the average Anglican clergyman's world view.

If the general run of Anglican clerical fathers were not wealthy they certainly lived in comfort compared to their Nonconformist counterparts. Above all else, they knew the value of education and managed to afford it for their sons. Nearly every clergyman's son in the three business élites went to public school: Frederick Wrench to Haileybury, Aretas Akers-Douglas to Eton, C. H. Hornby to Harrow, Alexander Butterworth and Nigel Gresley to Marlborough, William D. Phillipps to Hereford College School. Some of these sons followed the normal path for bright public school boys and went on to university: Wrench, Akers-Douglas, and Hornby went up to Oxford, Butterworth to London University. University established friendships which opened doors, sometimes into high-level management, as in the case of Hornby whose friendship with William Frederick Danvers Smith took him into the partnership of W. H. Smith & Sons.[7] Other clerical fathers, however, overcame the prejudices of a landed mentality and allowed their sons to go into industry straight from school. Alfred Hewlett's father, in charge of a chapelry in industrial Lancashire, articled his son to the agent and colliery manager of the Earl of Bradford. Phillipps's father apprenticed his son to Scott Russell, the builder of Brunel's *Great Eastern*. Gresley was apprenticed in the Crewe Works of the London & North Western Railway.

Sons of Nonconformist ministers were also well educated, though in general Nonconformist ministers (outside Scotland) were less likely than Anglican clergymen to be university-educated. In 1901 22 per cent of

---

[4] F. M. L. Thompson, *English Landed Society in the Nineteenth Century* (London, 1963), 71.

[5] Chadwick, *Victorian Church*, ii. 207.

[6] *Complete Peerage*.

[7] C. Wilson, *First with the News* (London, 1985), 190–1.

Congregational ministers had no training at all.[8] All non-Anglicans were barred by religious tests from full academic opportunity at Oxford or Cambridge until 1871. In the 1935 group Percy Malcolm Stewart, fifth son of Sir Halley Stewart, attended one of the better schools in the towns where his father located: University School, Hastings; King's School, Rochester; and the Royal High School, Edinburgh. Robert Stevenson Horne attended George Watson's College, Edinburgh. In the 1955 business élite sons of Nonconformist and Scottish ministers went to grammar or lesser public schools: Sir Oliver Franks to Bristol Grammar (a public school); Sir Ivan Stedeford to Shebbear College and then King Edward VI's Grammar, Birmingham (also a member of the HMC); Sir Robert Harvey to Daniel Stewart's College, Edinburgh; Sir James Young to Paisley Grammar School. Less than half the non-Anglican clergymen's sons proceeded to university, most of them Scots. Horne and Young went to Glasgow University, Harvey to Edinburgh, Franks to Oxford. Three graduated with first-class degrees and Franks launched into a most distinguished career, winning distinction as don, Civil Servant, diplomat, university administrator, and businessman.

What of the specifically Christian influences of Anglican or Nonconformist clergymen on their sons? Until they went away to boarding school, and maybe afterwards, there would be attendance at domestic devotions, Sunday and even weeknight services and meetings, traces of theological debate at mealtimes. Low Churchmen and evangelical Nonconformists would hope, even expect, their children to enter into the experience of faith in Christ. More liberal theologians might be less demanding of their sons. Few glimpses of clerical paternal influence remain for these élites. Sir Oliver Franks, when questioned about the heroes in his own career, told his interviewer, 'I have no hero in fiction or in real life. . . . The person whose intellectual quality I admire most is my father.'[9] The parsonage or manse, as other professions also proved, could provide the sort of climate which suited the production of enterprising minds and nerves.

Other parents—and these are impossible to quantify—exercised a strong Christian influence over the small boys who would one day become Britain's business leaders. George Cadbury's father John Cadbury started the day with a 7 a.m. ramble across the Edgbaston fields with his dogs, often taking his children as well. When 8 a.m. breakfast (served punctually) was over, the family Bible reading followed, allowing John to

---

[8] Chadwick, *Victorian Church*, ii. 183.
[9] *Dark Horse* (Dec. 1954), 14.

open his cocoa and chocolate business at 9 a.m.[10] A. G. B. Owen recalled his father, head of a medium but expanding engineering business in the Black Country, as the head of a godly home ('I won't call it Christian but godly'). He took his sons to church (Anglican) where he was church-warden; and on Sunday nights put them on his knees to tell them Bible stories and teach them to read them.[11]

Some fathers loomed large in childhood and adulthood. A particularly awesome father was Joseph Rank. Among his fellow Wesleyans he had the reputation of 'thorough God-fearing uprightness'[12] and that was vigorously relayed to his eight children, especially his three sons. Every Sunday morning, afternoon, and evening, rain or shine, there were services at the Wesleyan chapel, when the family lived at Hull and Joseph Arthur Rank was too young to be sent away to school. At home Joseph banished alcohol, forbade smoking, and frowned on public dances and theatre-going. He nevertheless enjoyed domestic, and very energetic, polkas, lancers, and waltzes. His other rare relaxation was cricket, which he taught his sons and which regularly drew him and his family to Scar-borough for an annual holiday in cricket week. Heavily built, hard (physically and morally), loud, and blunt, Joseph Rank left an indelible impression on his sons. Conversion three years after his marriage and five years before Joseph Arthur, his youngest son, was born radically altered his life, though not the shape of his personality. His passion to serve Christ occupied nearly every moment outside his business hours. Even within those hours he fearlessly told his employees what his religion meant: 'the business has been very successful. I don't put all the success down to myself. I put a lot of it down to God. I also put a lot of it down to you—that is, office staff, millers—all of you.'[13] In accordance with his Christian principles he closed his mills after midnight on Saturday until Monday morning.[14] He gave generously of his income and his time to his church. Such a formidable example of piety his sons must have found it difficult to follow. His eldest son, who divorced to marry a divorcee, incurred his father's displeasure for massively indulging his passion for horse-racing. His youngest boy, however, never allowed fame and fortune as J. Arthur Rank, film magnate, to disturb his faith as a Methodist.

[10] A. G. Gardiner, *The Life of George Cadbury* (London, 1925), 15.
[11] A. G. B. Owen, 'Lessons from the Experience of a Business Man' (June 1946).
[12] *M. Rec.* 23 July 1896.
[13] R. G. Burnett, *Through the Mill* (London, 1945), 18–20, 25, 30, 37, 46, 70–1, 112; A. Wood, *Mr Rank* (London, 1952), 27–8.
[14] Burnett, *Through the Mill*, 75.

The influence of mothers was also important in the early lives of a number of the business leaders. George Cadbury's mother was 'a woman of retiring nature, but of great firmness of mind and character'.[15] J. Arthur Rank's mother, a gentle farmer's daughter, counterbalanced his father's impact.[16] Some mothers are known to have had a particular Christian influence. Geoffrey Heyworth's mother impressed Sir William Lever by her piety when she secured a job interview for her son.[17] Of his mother, W. Lionel Fraser recalled, 'I did not attempt to plumb the profounder things of life for myself, but was willingly and obediently guided by my dominant, though never dominating, mother. She taught us to say our prayers, which we did every night, somewhat unmeaningly I'm afraid—unless we had some personal request to make. . . .'[18]

2 SCHOOL

The majority in the three business élites received a grounding in denominational religious instruction at primary or secondary school levels. Since the Reformation the religion of the Church of England had been embodied in the statutes of the vast majority of school foundations, many the forerunners of the nineteenth-century public schools. In the pursuit of mass literacy during the early nineteenth century Anglicans outstripped Nonconformists in setting up low-cost elementary schools (spanning primary and early secondary education). By the late 1850s about 75 per cent of children attending state-inspected schools (by no means all schools admitted state inspectors) were taught the tenets of the Church of England.[19] By 1900 the state church still dominated primary education, administering 52 per cent of primary schools, compared to 34 per cent run by the state.[20]

The situation in the public schools can be quantified to some extent. Denominational biases of public schools were advertised. In the list of the 176 public schools belonging to the Head Masters' Conference in 1935 (fifty years past the zenith of religious influence in education), 67 per cent recorded their religious teaching as Church of England, 21

[15] Gardiner, *George Cadbury*, 17.
[16] Burnett, *Through the Mill*, 30, 35.
[17] Maurice Zinkin, 'Geoffrey Heyworth', *DBB*.
[18] W. L. Fraser, *All to the Good* (London, 1965), 32–3.
[19] S. J. Curtis, *History of Education in Great Britain* (4th edn., London, 1957), 250.
[20] A. H. Halsey *et al.*, 'Schools', in Halsey (ed.), *Trends in British Society since 1900* (London, 1972), 166.

per cent as undenominational.[21] Examining 89 independent public schools in England and Wales in 1942 the Fleming Committee found that 71 per cent were affiliated with the Church of England, nearly 7 per cent with the Roman Catholic Church, and a similar proportion equally shared by Methodists and Quakers. Nearly half the 89 schools were required by their statutes to appoint members of the Church of England as their headmaster.[22] Thus, for the majority of boys passing through a secondary education the teaching and worship of the Church of England would have been hard to avoid.

At least three major problems confront the attempt to define the role of the school as an agency of religious influence. First, for men born in the nineteenth century the names of primary schools have often been forgotten or have changed since. Then, when the name of the school is known, there are often difficulties in discovering its religious orientation. Last, even when information on these matters is available, it is usually unclear what the individual derived from received religious influences. While the first difficulty is often insuperable, the other two are less intractable. Religious orientation may be reached by merging primary and secondary educational experience. At secondary stage convinced (but affluent) Nonconformist or Roman Catholic parents publicized their denominational preferences in choice of public or church school for their offspring. However, less affluent Nonconformist parents had a decreasing chance, and less affluent Catholic parents possibly an increasing chance, of sending their sons to denominational secondary schools as the nineteenth century passed. The impact of religious teaching in school may be assessed for its minimal contribution to the training of the generality of pupils.

Analysis of the business leaders' merged primary and secondary education experience yielded the results in Tables 3.1 and 3.2. The evidence of these tables largely overturns that emerging from an analysis of the *Dictionary of Business Biography* which lumped together all kinds of religious influence, not just schools.[23] Table 3.2, derived in part from Table 3.1, based on stratified and chronologically separated samples of business élites, demonstrates, as was earlier suspected, that the Church of England had a disproportionately large influence in shaping the values of the business élites. It shows too that schools have been the prime

[21] Truman & Knightley Ltd., *Schools* (12 edn., London, 1935), 164–71.

[22] Fleming Report, 1944 quoted in J. C. Dancy, *The Public Schools and the Future* (London, 1963), 67.

[23] D. J. Jeremy, 'Important Questions about Business and Religion in Modern Britain', in Jeremy (ed.), *Business and Religion in Britain* (Aldershot, 1988), 16.

TABLE 3.1. *Religious links of schools attended by chairmen and managing directors*

	1907			1935			1955		
	n	% of N	% of cohort	n	% of N	% of cohort	n	% of N	% of cohort
Chairmen									
Episcopalian									
Church of England	32	72.73	32.00	35	70.00	35.00	38	79.17	39.58
Episcopal Church in Scotland		0.00	0.00		0.00			0.00	
Church in Wales		0.00	0.00		0.00			0.00	
Church of Ireland		0.00	0.00		0.00			0.00	
Total	32	72.73	32.00	35	70.00	35.00	38	79.17	39.58
Presbyterian									
Church of Scotland	1	2.27	1.00	3	6.00	3.00		0.00	
Free Church of Scotland, United Presbyterian, UFCS		0.00			0.00			0.00	
English/Welsh Presbyterian		0.00			0.00			0.00	
Irish Presbyterian		0.00			0.00			0.00	
Total	1	2.27	1.00	3	6.00	3.00		0.00	
Nonconformist									
Baptist		0.00		1	2.00	1.00		0.00	
Brethren		0.00			0.00			0.00	
Congregational	2	4.55	2.00		0.00			0.00	
Methodist: Wesleyan	1	2.27	1.00	1	2.00	1.00	2	4.17	2.08
Methodist: undifferentiated		0.00			0.00			0.00	
Methodist: pre-1932 sect		0.00			0.00		1	2.08	1.04
Quaker	1	2.27	1.00	2	4.00	2.00	1	2.08	1.04
Salvation Army		0.00			0.00			0.00	
Unitarian		0.00			0.00			0.00	
Others e.g. Moravian	2	4.55	2.00		0.00			0.00	
Total	6	13.64	6.00	4	8.00	4.00	4	8.33	4.17

TABLE 3.1. cont.

	1907			1935			1955		
	n	% of N	% of cohort	n	% of N	% of cohort	n	% of N	% of cohort
Protestant		0.00		1	2.00	1.00		0.00	
Roman Catholic		0.00		1	2.00	1.00	1	2.08	1.04
Neo-Christian (20th c. sects)		0.00			0.00			0.00	
Unspecified Christian		0.00			0.00			0.00	
Jewish		0.00		1	2.00	1.00		0.00	
Non-denominational	5	11.36	5.00	5	10.00	5.00	5	10.42	5.21
TOTALS									
N (number of schoolings with religious links)	44	100	100.00	50	100	100.00	48	100	96.00
Cohort									
N as % of cohort			44.00			50.00			50.00
Managing directors									
Episcopalian									
Church of England	17	62.96	16.83	15	51.72	14.56	34	79.07	29.31
Episcopal Church in Scotland		0.00			0.00			0.00	
Church in Wales		0.00			0.00			0.00	
Church of Ireland		0.00			0.00			0.00	
Total	17	62.96	16.83	15	51.72	14.56	34	79.07	29.31
Presbyterian									
Church of Scotland	2	7.41	1.98	1	3.45	0.97		0.00	
Free Church of Scotland, United Presbyterian, UFCS		0.00			0.00			0.00	
English/Welsh Presbyterian		0.00			0.00			0.00	
Irish Presbyterian		0.00			0.00			0.00	
Total	2	7.41	1.98	1	3.45	0.97		0.00	

TABLE 3.1. cont.

	1907			1935			1955		
	n	% of N	% of cohort	n	% of N	% of cohort	n	% of N	% of cohort
Nonconformist									
Baptist		0.00			0.00			0.00	
Brethren		0.00			0.00			0.00	
Congregational	2	7.41	1.98		0.00			0.00	
Methodist: Wesleyan	1	3.70	0.99	3	10.34	2.91		0.00	
Methodist: undifferentiated		0.00			0.00			0.00	
Methodist: pre-1932 sect		0.00			0.00		1	2.33	0.86
Quaker	2	7.41	1.98	1	3.45	0.97	1	2.33	0.86
Salvation Army		0.00			0.00			0.00	
Unitarian		0.00			0.00			0.00	
Others e.g. Moravian		0.00			0.00			0.00	
Total	5	18.52	4.95	4	13.79	3.88	2	4.65	1.72
Protestant		0.00			0.00			0.00	
Roman Catholic	1	3.70	0.99	2	6.90	1.94		0.00	
Neo-Christian (20th c. sects)		0.00			0.00			0.00	
Unspecified Christian		0.00			0.00			0.00	
Jewish		0.00		1	3.45	0.97		0.00	
Non-denominational	2	7.41	1.98	6	20.69	5.83	7	16.28	6.03
TOTALS	27	100.00		29	100.00		43	100.00	
N (number of schoolings with religious links)									
Cohort	101			103			116		
N as % of cohort	26.7			28.2			37.1		

Notes: N = total number of cases; n = subset of N.

Sources: Author's biographical files on chairmen and managing directors in the three élites.

TABLE 3.2. *Religious schooling of business élites compared to religious densities in the population (chairmen and managing directors combined)*

	1907 share of élite schools		RD	S/RD	1935 share of élite schools		RD	S/RD	1955 share of élite schools		RD	S/RD
	n	%			n	%			n	%		
Church of England	49	34.51	8.990	3.84	50	43.48	7.580	5.74	72	47.06	6.670	7.06
Church of Scotland	3	2.11	22.498	0.09	4	3.48	34.350	0.10			34.370	
Congregational	4	2.82	1.950	1.44			0.940	0.00			0.630	
Methodist	2	1.41	3.180	0.44	4	3.48	2.310	1.51	4	2.61	1.936	1.35
Quaker	3	2.11	0.048	44.01	3	2.61	0.042	62.11	2	1.31	0.043	30.40
Roman Catholic	1	0.70	5.900	0.12	3	2.61	6.430	0.41	1	0.65	9.200	0.07
N	142	100.00			115	100.00			153	100.00		
Cohort	201				203				212			

Notes: N = number of chairmen and managing directors whose obituaries have been traced; n = subset of N; RD = religious density; S = % receiving religious schooling.

Sources: Tables 1.5, 3.1.

instrument in mediating that influence. Particularly spectacular is the indication that differentials between Anglican religious densities (which were eroding) and their shares of school inputs into national business élites more than doubled between 1907 and 1955. Clearly, over the first half of the twentieth century, the Church of England relatively increased its share of school-level opportunities to mould future national business élites, contrary to assumptions about the extent of decline of religious values in an increasingly secular society.

More spectacular is the suggestion of the Quakers' enormous relative success in preparing or placing their members in the three business élites. In 1907 their share of the business élite was about 44 times as great as their religious density.[24] By 1935 the differential was over 62 times greater. This fell to a differential of 30 times by 1955, due to a falling away in the business élite rather than to decline in Quaker religious density. No other denomination throughout the period, including the Anglicans, achieved such a disproportionately successful representation of their school alumni in the national business élites.

Measured against religious density in the population no other Christian denomination besides the Anglicans and Quakers consistently surpassed parity between religious density and share of religious schooling in the national business leaderships throughout the period. Congregationalists slumped below parity by 1935. Methodists did not achieve parity until the 1930s. Roman Catholics never attained it. The Church of Scotland, which appears to have done badly also, would be more fairly tested by a sample of business leaders drawn from Scotland only.

Behind the preponderant influence of the Church of England indicated in Tables 3.1 and 3.2 is the role of the public school. Predominant in chairmen's backgrounds were schools belonging to the Head Masters' Conference (a rough definition of a public school): they educated 112 out of the 296 chairmen. Among managing directors attendance at public schools was more widely distributed: they educated 87 of the 320 managing directors. To the religious influences of the public schools, then, we must turn for an understanding of the Christian influences that shaped the values and attitudes of the business élites.

The nature of established church influence in the public schools is hardly surprising. The view that education and religion were partners in shaping the moral perfection of both individual and society, though centuries old, experienced a rebirth under the impact of the Evangelical

---

[24] In my *DBB* analysis in *Business and Religion*, 16–17, the figure for the Quakers' religious density in 1901 errs by a factor of 10: it should read 0.054, not 0.54.

and High Church revivals. Spearheaded by reforming headmasters, pre-eminently Thomas Arnold at Rugby, 'godliness and good learning' were injected into the public schools by Church of England clergymen.[25] In mid-Victorian England, when the 1907 business leaders were growing up, the orthodox public schoolmaster was 'a classically-educated clergy-man with a good academic record, perhaps on his way to a bishopric. His idea of the purpose of public-school education would be to produce Christian gentlemen.'[26] The role of an Anglican clergyman in the life of the majority of public schools changed but nevertheless persisted. By the 1950s clerics, still becoming public school headmasters and RE teachers, were more often chaplains whose work was mostly pastoral.[27] However, before the 1920s, if not later, they were very much part of the authority structure of the school. In their province were matters of discipline and behaviour as well as Scripture teaching, New Testament Greek, and sherry for visiting preachers.

The religious impact of the public schools on business leaders can be traced clearly for Eton and Harrow, the most heavily represented schools. Together they were attended by 45 chairmen and 13 managing directors. Each provided similar numbers to the 1907 and 1935 business élites (11 and 9 from Eton, 10 and 8 from Harrow, respectively). How-ever, a quantitative difference appeared in the 1955 élite: here Eton (with 13) secured nearly twice as many places as Harrow (with 7). Taking the average age of all three élites as 60 it can be assumed that the old Harrovians and Etonians were at school in the periods 1847–57, 1885–95, and 1905–14. What was the religious temper of the schools in these years?

Politically Harrow was regarded as the counterpoise of Tory Eton. Though it devoted itself to educating sons of the gentry and titled nobi-lity, two-thirds of its pupils in the period 1825–50 were sons of the pro-fessional classes. Most pupils, recent research has shown, went into the professions.[28] A violent institution before 1829, Harrow in the mid-1840s was emerging from the reforming but harsh zeal of Christopher Words-worth, a High Church cleric and later Bishop of Lincoln. Evangelicals deserted the school and sent their sons to Eton or to new foundations. Wordsworth's successor, Charles Vaughan, much younger and more conciliatory in his methods of discipline, also ruled by the Arnoldian

[25] D. Newsome, *Godliness and Good Learning* (London, 1961), 'Introduction'.

[26] W. J. Reader, *Professional Men* (London, 1966), 104.

[27] Dancy, *Public Schools*, 67–73.

[28] E. A. Allen, 'Public Schools Élites in Early-Victorian England', *Journal of British Studies*, 21 (1982).

vision. The 'deep religious feeling that shone through his sermons seems to have been so contagious that it almost made Harrow into a religious community'.[29] However, as the historian of the public schools adds, 'The aristocratic character of the school balked any attempts to create either much general industry or much religious idealism.'[30] By the end of the century Harrow was dedicated to preparing its boys for 'the big things: diplomacy, politics, the Services'.[31] Individualism was sacrificed to conformism, Christianity to gentlemanliness.

Eton held all the terrors of the pre-Arnoldian public school—its unhealthiness, bullying, and violence—until well into the 1840s. Moral reforms and religious concern came slowly and through assistant masters and tutors like the Reverend Edward Coleridge, rather than through a reforming head.[32] By 1860 the spirit of athleticism at Eton had brought with it a secularizing and military influence: 'many masters were laymen, and the rifle corps had been founded. The religious revival had degenerated into Philistine efficiency.'[33] Athleticism reached its zenith at Eton in the 1880s and 1890s under Edmund Warre, neither much of a scholar nor spiritual guide but 'the very essence of a two-fisted healthy country gentleman'.[34] Both chapel and classroom suffered as games crowded out all other activities— in any case Eton chapel was very long and the boys could not always hear the sermons.[35] Though modern science and commercial expansion challenged the Arnoldian vision, it was the Boer War which, in stirring Eton to the defence of empire, strengthened notions of moral health based on patriotism, loyalty, obedience, and courage, rather than religion. Despite the presence of Arnoldian progressives, military virtues edged Christian ones out of the gentlemanly ideal in the years before 1914.[36]

What did the Anglican business leaders recall of their public school religion? Generalizations are impossible. Most people forget the details of their school-days and businessmen have a notoriously short recollection of the past, as well as a reluctance to record memories of it. Little

---

[29] E. C. Mack, *Public Schools and British Opinion, 1780–1860* (New York, 1938), 344.

[30] Ibid. 345.

[31] H. A. Vachell, *The Hill: A Romance of Friendship* (London, 1905), quoted in Mack, *Public Schools and British Opinion since 1860* (New York, 1941), 250.

[32] Mack, *Public Schools, 1780–1860*, 362–71.

[33] Ibid. 369.

[34] Mack, *Public Schools since 1860*, 128.

[35] Recollection of Lord Hailsham of his days at Eton in the 1920s, recalled when interviewed by Roger Royle, on Radio 2, 8.30 a.m., Sunday 4 Sept. 1988.

[36] Mack, *Public Schools since 1860*, 127–33, 216–20, 238–41. For the rise of British patriotism see W. J. Reader, *At Duty's Call* (Manchester, 1988), esp. 94.

evidence is therefore available from their side. At least one, Sir Henry Babington Smith, Secretary of the Post Office in 1907, thought so much of his public school (Eton) that he had his funeral service conducted in the school chapel prior to burial in Eton cemetery.[37] A. G. B. Owen, whose grounding in Bible knowledge helped him carry off the School Certificate and Higher School Certificate prizes in Scripture at Oundle, recalled of his RE teaching, 'it wasn't the Bible as you and I know it; it was full of holes, teaching of the modernistic kind; it was split up into different authors, all co-ordinated together to make a book'.[38] Neither of these pieces of evidence suggests anything more than that public school religion could have a positive or a negative impact on its products. For most public school boys, subjected to the ceaseless observance of the *Book of Common Prayer* and the services of the Church of England, religion suggested where ultimate values in life were to be found.[39]

What of the Nonconformist schools? The Congregationalists' Mill Hill School was attended by the tobacco manufacturers William Henry Wills (later Lord Winterstoke) in the early 1840s and his second cousin George Alfred Wills in the late 1860s–early 1870s; and also by the ship-builder Herbert Babington Rowell (of R. & W. Hawthorn-Leslie & Co.) in the 1870s.[40] Under Thomas Priestley in the 1830s the school spent one hour out of 42 in the school's week on Bible study but 'the Chaplain was not a good disciplinarian, and each class regarded his advent as a signal for disorder, such as the tying of all the ten candlesticks together, and so being able to pull them all over with one twitch'.[41] In 1869 the school appointed Dr R. F. Weymouth as headmaster and a new era began. However, it was one of Weymouth's appointees to the staff who made the greatest impression on most Mill Hillians of the 1870s: James A. H. Murray, the great lexicographer and editor of the *Oxford English Dictionary*, with his 'naturally friendly, unconventional approach to his pupils' made the school a much pleasanter and intellectually stimu-lating place in which to grow up'.[42] In addition Murray must have com-

[37] *The Times*, 3 Oct. 1923.

[38] Owen, 'Lessons'.

[39] Lord Hailsham, *The Door Wherein I Went* (London, 1975), 7–27 attests to the twin influences of the Christian religion and the classics which shaped his thinking during his years at Eton in the 1920s.

[40] B. W. E. Alford, 'George Alfred Wills' and 'William Henry Wills', *DBB*; J. F. Clarke, 'Herbert Babington Rowell', ibid.

[41] N. G. Brett-James, *Mill Hill* (London, 1938), 31–41.

[42] K. M. E. Murray, *Caught in the Web of Words* (New Haven, Conn., 1977), 108–16.

municated some of the deep Scottish Congregationalist faith in God which, he attested at the end of his days, directed every step of his life.[43] While at Mill Hill, Murray secured preachers for the school chapel and often preached there himself.

More influential in shaping the business élite were the schools of the Quakers and Methodists. In relative terms these were very influential; in absolute terms they were not. Only 22 members of the three business élites are known to have attended Nonconformist schools in England and Wales. Of the 22, eight attended Quaker schools, eight Methodist schools, three the Congregationalists' Mill Hill School, two the Moravian school at Leeds (in fact one individual, William Lawies Jackson, later 1st Lord Allerton, counted twice because he was chairman of both the Great Northern Railway and the Cheshire Lines Committee), and one (Lord Stamp) a Baptist school. In absolute terms Quaker schools predominated among the Nonconformist institutions attended by the 1907 business élite. The Methodists overtook the Quakers in the 1935 élite and stayed ahead in the 1955 élite. Which schools predominated and what were the distinctive features of their religious ethos?

Of the three with a Quaker education in the 1907 élite, George Cadbury (counted twice, being chairman and equivalent of managing director) attended a day school in Edgbaston where the staple diet was the classics; supplementing school, there were lessons at home in French from a refugee. Most of his religious training came at home.[44] The other, John Wigham Richardson, attended four schools or tutors before boarding for two years (1850–2) at the Friends School, York. In the 1935 élite William F. Tuke and Edward Cadbury attended Oliver's Mount School, Scarborough; William Adlington Cadbury went to Friends' schools, first at Southport and then Hitchin. And in the 1955 élite both Paul Strangman Cadbury and Laurence Cadbury boarded at Leighton Park, Reading.

All these schools felt something of the theological currents which swept through the Quaker movement in the nineteenth century, notably the departure from an eighteenth-century evangelical and personal religion to the mystical and social religion of the Friends' founder.[45] So George Cadbury and Wigham Richardson memorized biblical texts. 'As a boy [George Cadbury] used to carry a Bible in his pocket and learn Scripture by heart as he walked along the road. His intimacy with the Bible was

[43] G. F. Timpson (ed.), *Sir James A. H. Murray* (1957).

[44] Gardiner, *George Cadbury*, 14–17.

[45] W. A. C. Stewart, *Quakers and Education as Seen in Their Schools in England* (London, 1953), 131–4.

extraordinary. It was the one literature that appealed to him.'[46] In the late 1880s and early 1890s, when Edward Cadbury and William Tuke were at Scarborough, there was still a a good deal of Scripture memorization.[47] A change came in the late 1890s when Quakers, led by Edward Grubb the Quaker thinker and apologist, started to adopt the findings of German Higher Criticism and explored the ethical and social implications of the Inner Light.[48] In response to the rising affluence of Friends, and a disturbing leakage from the Society,[49] a Quaker public school was established in 1890. Leighton Park, at Reading, offered humanities and science teaching as well as classics to wealthier Friends who wanted a university education at Oxford or Cambridge for their sons. Nevertheless Quaker influence was firmly retained through the obligatory Sunday service, Scripture lessons, school committees and denominational visitors and staff recruitment networks. In short it was a Quaker replica of a progressive public school. For Laurence Cadbury, Leighton Park kindled a strong interest in maths, science, and music, antipathy towards the classics (or at least the classics master), and a pleasure in reading the Bible which he first learned from his parents George and Elizabeth Cadbury.[50]

Among the eight business leaders educated in Methodist institutions, six attended the same school, The Leys School, Cambridge. They were John Campbell Boot (son of Jesse Boot), 2nd Lord Trent; Sir William Clare Lees; Sir Robert Abraham Burrows; and Alexander Forrester-Paton, all in the 1935 élite; J. Arthur Rank, Lord Rank, and Sir Henry J. Ross (who transferred to The Leys from George Watson's College, Edinburgh), in the 1955 élite. The others with a Methodist schooling were Richard Thomas (in the 1907 élite) who went to Wesley (now Queen's) College, Taunton, and Sir Ivan Stedeford (counted twice, being chairman and managing director of Tube Investments in 1955) who attended the Methodist Bible Christians' School, Shebbear College in North Devon, before his father moved to a Birmingham circuit and he was transferred to King Edward VI's School. The business leaders who went to The Leys were all there within the space of two decades.

---

[46] A. G. Gardiner quoted in J. F. Crosfield, *A History of the Cadbury Family* (1985), ii. 495.

[47] Stewart, *Quakers and Education*, 133–4.

[48] J. Dudley, *The Life of Edward Grubb* (London, 1946); *The Times*, 23 Jan. 1939; Stewart, *Quakers and Education*, 134.

[49] T. A. B. Corley, 'How Quakers Coped with Business Success', in Jeremy (ed.), *Business and Religion*, 164–87.

[50] Sir A. Cadbury, *Laurence John Cadbury* (1982), 5–6, 21.

Clare Lees, one of three brothers sent to the school (one of whom became Archbishop of Melbourne), was there in 1888–90. The others passed through within the fifteen years 1895–1909. Boot and Rank were contemporaries. Forrester-Paton left shortly before they arrived. Burrows finished during their first year. Ross arrived in Boot's last year.[51] Clearly in training future business leaders, The Leys vastly outstripped the 18 Methodist secondary schools founded before 1900.[52] What is the explanation for this success? What sort of Christian influence did Leysians receive at this time?

One explanation for the success must be that the school was founded for the purpose of educating the sons of Methodist businessmen. Certainly it sent twice as many of its pupils into industry as did one of the ancient public schools.[53] All six Leysians in the business élites were the sons of considerable businessmen on their way to further commercial success. The eponymous businesses of Jesse Boot and Joseph Rank are well known. Clare Lees's father had a calico printworks in Manchester.[54] Burrows's family had interests in Lancashire collieries.[55] Forrester-Paton's forebears had manufactured woollen yarns in Alloa since the eighteenth century and had several mills in the town by the 1890s; his father was partner in the firm though did not live to see the formation of Patons & Baldwins Ltd. in 1919.[56] Ross's father, William Henry Ross, was an accountant and key figure in Distillers Co. Ltd.[57] Most of the six were not high fliers at school, though Forrester-Paton gained five passes in his Higher School Certificate. Five were in the modern stream— this may have been a conscious choice, to fit them for business. Boot ended his time at The Leys in the remove form. Boot, Burrows, and Forrester-Paton got into either or both the 1st or 2nd football and lacrosse teams; all three were made prefects. Boot also captained the school Bisley

---

[51] The Leys School, *Handbook and Directory* (12th edn., Cambridge, 1934).

[52] These schools are listed in F. C. Pritchard, *Methodist Secondary Education* (London, 1949), 334–5.

[53] An occupational analysis of 1,567 living alumni in 1934 show that 34 per cent of Old Leysians were in industry of all kinds (excluding agriculture and business-related professions like accountancy and engineering). This compares very well against Winchester where under 17 per cent of Wykehamists born between 1860 and 1922 went into business. See The Leys School, *Handbook* (1934), 273–86; T. J. H. Bishop and R. Wilkinson, *Winchester and the Public School Élite* (London, 1967), 69.

[54] Roger Lloyd-Jones, 'Sir William Clare Lees', *DBB*; G. Turnbull, *A History of the Calico Printing Industry of Great Britain* (Altrincham, 1951), 438.

[55] *The Times*, 21 Aug. 1964.

[56] A. Forrester-Paton, 'The Romance of Patons Yarn' (typescript).

[57] R. B. Weir, 'William Henry Ross', *DSBB*.

team. Rank played in the 2nd lacrosse team. Ross and Clare Lees were utterly undistinguished at school. Three of the six went on to higher education. Clare Lees went to Owens College (later Manchester University) for one year. Boot attended Jesus College, Cambridge, but left after two years without a degree. Ross proceeded to Heriot Watt College where he was a medallist.[58]

Such performances contrasted sharply with the general record of the school where godliness and good learning complemented each other to a high degree. The Leys had been set up under the auspices of the Wesleyan Methodist Conference in 1875, in response to the needs of the expanding Wesleyan middle classes, facilitated by the removal of theological entrance tests at Oxford and Cambridge. The first headmaster, the Reverend Dr William Fiddian Moulton, son of a line of Wesleyan ministers, distinguished himself as scholar, ministerial tutor, and in 1890 president of the Wesleyan Methodist Conference. Under Moulton a Wesleyan version of the Arnoldian vision unfolded at The Leys. The school, never larger than 200 boys at any time in its first three decades, by 1907 had sent 250 to Cambridge alone where 50 first-class degrees and six fellowships resulted. Two pupils gained B.Sc. degrees from London University while still at school.[59]

The religious achievements of the school were similarly superlative, as might be expected from a reading of the announced objectives of the school: 'The Leys has failed of its sovran purpose if it has failed to foster a high moral tone, or even a definitely religious one, to wield an influence in the broadest and deepest sense evangelical.'[60] Moulton, head until his death in 1898, centred the school's religious life on evening prayers and, on Sundays, worship in the local Hills Road Wesleyan Chapel.[61] He refrained from building a school chapel (on which public schools normally focused their religious activities), viewing the local chapel as an important link with the wider Wesleyan world—though after his death a chapel was added to the school. There were other dimensions to the religious scene at The Leys, as was noted in 1908:

Private prayer and Scripture reading have never been out of vogue in dormitory, nor has attendance at various voluntary devotional meetings, some conducted by masters, some by strangers, and some confined to the boys themselves, been a matter of exception and remark. Not a few have been led to a deep and

[58] The Leys School, *Old Leysian Directory* (7th edn., Cambridge,1908); *Handbook*, 1934.
[59] The Leys School, *Old Leysian Directory* (1908), 4. D. Baker, *Partnership in Excellence* (Cambridge, 1975), 178.
[60] The Leys School, *Old Leysian Directory* (1908), 5.
[61] Baker, *Partnership*, 105, 195.

definite religious sense, while many have carried hence the inspiration for a whole-hearted service of God and the world.[62]

Among devotional activities mentioned were The Leys Christian Union (formed 1882) and the Leysian Mission (formed 1886). The former promoted Christian fellowship and private devotion among the boys. The latter, based on London premises to accommodate boys or Old Leysians, represented the school's concern for the outcast of the metropolis. New buildings in the City Road were opened by the Prince and Princess of Wales in 1904. Again the results of these influences were impressive:

a multitude of Old Leysians undoubtedly are proving their Alma Mater a mother in God, and her children sons of the Highest and brethren of the lowliest. Achievements, and even distinctions, on such lines are just those which the men concerned are little likely to return for purposes of our record, and which less readily come to knowledge from other sources than do academic and athletic and professional successes. But by way of sheer facts we may cite the part taken by Old Boys in the evangelistic, educational, and medical branches alike of the Central China Wesleyan Mission, in the African Presbyterian and China Inland Missions, the Sunderland, Bolton, Sale, West London, and East London Missions, at Toynbee, Mansfield and Bermondsey Settlements, in addition to the toil and wealth expended all the years upon the mission directly sustained by the School, and bearing its name.[63]

This was the essence of the religious influence surrounding the boys at The Leys before 1907: as serious and earnest in moral purpose as the Quaker schools, more intense on the issue of personal religious faith: vastly different in religious tone from Harrow and Eton. Thus equipped before the First World War, a third of the boys emerging from The Leys regularly went into business and industry (see Table 3.3).

3 LOCAL CHURCH

Given the respectability of religion among the Victorian middle classes, it may be assumed that those from middle-class homes were brought up in churchgoing families. Thus at least 75 per cent of the business élites studied here would have gone to church in their youth. What did it mean to them? Generalized and, in a few cases, particularized answers are possible.

Services in the Church of England or (for those not away at boarding

[62] The Leys School, *Old Leysian Directory* (1908), 5–6.
[62] Ibid. 6.

TABLE 3.3. *Occupations of Old Leysians alive in 1934 and 1956*

	1934		1956	
	No.	%	No.	%
Business occupations				
Minerals/mining (1956)	14	0.9	14	0.7
Trade and manufacture	433	26.4	540	26.1
Builders and contractors	18	1.1	32	1.5
Transport	51	3.1	29	1.4
Insurance	20	1.2	29	1.4
Banking	34	2.1	37	1.8
Stockbroking	26	1.6	24	1.2
Land agents, surveyors, auctioneers	31	1.9	54	2.6
Hotel management			7	0.3
Total	627	38.2	766	37.1
Professions related to business				
Accountants	70	4.3	127	6.1
Engineers	127	7.7	149	7.2
Architects	27	1.6	41	2.0
Chemists	17	1.0		
Scientists	19	1.2	28	1.4
Total	260	15.8	345	16.7
Non-business occupations				
Army/armed forces (1956)	26	1.6	51	2.5
Art	9	0.5	5	0.2
Civil Service/local government (1956)	38	2.3	49	2.4
Church (various kinds)	63	3.8	51	2.5
Dentistry	22	1.3	27	1.3
Drama	8	0.5	9	0.4
Education	79	4.8	95	4.6
Farming	122	7.4	176	8.5
History	8	0.5		
Law	189	11.5	219	10.6
Literature and journalism	27	1.6	32	1.5
Medicine	149	9.1	227	11.0
Music	15	0.9	11	0.5
Optics			4	0.2
Total	755	46.0	956	46.3
GRAND TOTAL	1,642	100.0	2,067	100.0

Source: Handbook and Directory of The Leys School (Cambridge, 1934; 1956).

school) Sunday School provided some idea of the basic beliefs of Christianity and a knowledge of the Bible. The Ten Commandments were prominently displayed on wall boards in nearly every parish church and were recited in the Communion service. The Apostles' Creed, containing a summary of Christian doctrine, had to be memorized by confirmation candidates.[64] In these ways a clear idea of the rudiments of

[64] Chadwick, *Victorian Church*, ii. 148–150; *Book of Common Prayer*, 234–6, 281–7.

Christian morality was instilled into churchgoing children. High Church or Roman Catholic priests encrusted and possibly mystified their core teaching with elaborate ritual. Among Nonconformists it was possible for children to escape the creeds, but not a knowledge of the Bible. In the presbyterian churches of Scotland and Ireland the labours of memorization were much extended by the Westminster Confession of Faith. Common to almost all churches was Bible teaching, first in the elementary stories told by Sunday School teachers, later, as understanding dawned, in the meatier presentations of pulpit masters and princes.

Another generalization about the impact of the local church on the early experience of these business leaders can be hazarded. It stems from the various denominations' definitions of membership (in turn deriving from their distinctive theologies). For the Church of England, the state church, membership was part of the birthright of all citizens. Membership was bestowed on the baby when its parents made a confession of faith on their child's behalf in the service of infant baptism. When the child grew into adulthood a personal realization of the parents' faith was expressed in the service of confirmation. This was preceded by classes held by the local clergy. Of uncertain length and quality, they were intended to clarify the candidate's understanding and assurance of faith. Taken by the bishop, the confirmation service required the candidate publicly to renounce the devil, the world, and the flesh, to confess his belief in the articles (doctrines) of the church, and to swear to obey 'God's holy will and commandments'.[65] At the other end of the denominational spectrum, the Religious Society of Friends (Quakers) also practised birthright membership for infants born to Quaker parents.[66] Most of the other major denominations also practised birthright membership. The chief exception was the Baptists, who adhered to believer's baptism as the necessary evidence of inward faith, the prerequisite of full membership.

While the Church of England, apart from its Evangelical clergy, viewed baptism and confirmation as sufficient membership qualifications, most of the other Protestant bodies looked for an inward conversion experience as well. The established church (consonant with its relationship with the state and, among some clergy, an optimistic theological estimate of human nature) viewed the world as, to quote Henry James's mixed metaphors, 'a sort of rectilinear or one-storied affair, whose accounts are kept in one denomination ... of which a simple algebraic sum of

---

[65] Book of Common Prayer, 281–2.
[66] Society of Friends, *Church Government* (London, 1931), 16–18.

pluses and minuses will give the total worth'.[67] Most Nonconformists
and Evangelical Anglicans saw human nature as a divided self: 'In the
religion of the twice-born, on the other hand, the world is a double-storied
mystery. Peace cannot be reached by the simple addition of pluses and
the elimination of minuses from life. . . . There are two lives, the natural
and the spiritual, and we must lose the one before we can participate
in the other.'[68] In these churches the younger generation were frequently
challenged by the need to pass through this conversion experience. Like
Bunyan's 'Christian' each was to struggle to the Cross and find 'his
burden loosed from off his shoulders'.[69] Born-again souls embarked
on a pilgrimage in which battle could be expected as Christian standards
met those of the world head on. What is more, no area of the individual
Christian's life was outside the battleground. Men cherishing this experience, unprepared though they might be to pronounce on broader this-
worldly relationships between religion and business, carried a clear idea
of personal moral standards into the levels of business activity in which
they engaged—even if they temporized in their application.

Since the peak age for conversion was between 14 and 17,[70] the local
church rather than the more dispassionate public school was likely to
be the agency of a conversion experience. 'Local church' conjured up
different images and recollections to different individuals. What follows
is illustrative of some of the possibilities in the backgrounds of the business leaders. For those raised at home rather than boarding school, local
church could be synonymous with all that was meant by local community. This would have been especially true of those raised in the
more defensive and tightly knit congregations outside the established
church. Sir Harold Bellman (1886–1963) (who is not in these élites),
virtual creator of the Abbey National Building Society, a close friend
of fellow Methodist Lord Stamp (who is), recalled in classic terms what
this meant to him at a Wesleyan chapel in Paddington:

Sunday was the day for best clothes, button-holes, music, happy fellowship
and good cheer. It was sometimes our duty to offer hospitality to special preachers
visiting the church for the day. I recall several men of distinction who passed
through our home on these occasions. These included Presidents and Past Presidents of the Wesleyan Conference and Principals of the Ministerial training
colleges. . . . I owe a special debt to the old chapel. It was there in the Bible

[67] W. James, *The Varieties of Religious Experience* (repr. London, 1947), 172.
[68] Ibid.
[69] J. Bunyan, *The Pilgrim's Progress* (repr. London, 1947), 46.
[70] K. D. Brown, *A Social History of the Nonconformist Ministry in England and Wales 1800–1930* (Oxford, 1988), 54–5.

class and Guild I was encouraged to speak. I started by reciting at an early
age, and later read the lesson in church on anniversary day. I think that early
experience gave me some degree of immunity from nervousness on a public
platform. ... The old chapel attracted in those years a great company of youth,
some of whom possessed a mental equipment much above the average. Some
of them won distinction in the Civil Service, the professions, and in business.
... In those days the church at Fernhead Road had a succession of fine preachers.
I recall many of them with gratitude for the inspiration they gave, and their
friendship. ... Letting my mind's eye rove over that congregation in the days
of the old chapel's great influence there are several lay personalities which focus
my attention. ... As I look back on these and other stalwarts I am conscious
of the great contribution they made—the encouragement they gave, the good
advice so sincerely proffered, and in most cases the example even better than
precept they afforded. Even those who fell from grace furnished an object lesson
and a warning.[71]

Here were the better community elements of chapel life: the enchant-
ments of music, the acquisition of public speaking and debating skills,
the sharpening of mental faculties, domestic encounters with great men,
above all the webs of friendship and the preacher's powers to support
and inspire daily living.

In the business élites glimpses of these themes may be found. William
Wallace between the ages of 6 and 21 (when he left Sunderland, his
birthplace) sat under the ministry of the Reverend Ebenezer Rees at
Grange Congregational Church. He recalled the Welsh minister as 'intel-
ligent, eloquent and bubbling over with true Christian kindness. He
also had a saving sense of humour; I remember his announcing a hymn
and saying "Let us all sing; and those of us who can't, let us at least
make a joyful noise."'[72] Frank Pick, at Salem Chapel, York (also Congregationalist) came under the influence of one of the more liberal ministers, the Reverend John Hunter. However, since Hunter moved to Hull
(and later to Glasgow) when Pick was 3 years old, the influence must
have been exerted through Hunter's occasional visits to York or through
his writings. Five years before Pick was born Hunter gave 'a course
on Christianity and Present-Day Questions, touching on the relation
of Christianity to Culture, Science, Politics, Trade, the Organisation
of Society and the Theatre'. In this Hunter attacked the two spheres
idea (see Chapter 4):

Christianity has quite as much to do with day books and ledgers as it has to
do with prayer books and hymn books, with counting houses and workshops

---

[71] H. Bellman, *Cornish Cockney* (London, 1947), 40–3.
[72] W. Wallace, *I Was Concerned* (1985), 22.

as much as with churches and pews. . . . Everything which has to do with moral principle, with righteousness, truth, justice, goodwill among men, has to do with the kingdom of Christ. The affairs of the city have as much to do with His kingdom as church and chapel matters—there will never be a true public spirit till we remember that. A man cannot neglect his duties as a citizen without incurring guilt in the sight of Christ.[73]

This was part of Hunter's legacy to Salem Chapel and among those who absorbed it was the future manager and moulder of the London Underground.[74]

For some the local church was the means of entering the experience of personal conversion. This was the case with Gordon Radley, the first engineer to become Director-General of the General Post Office. Originally his father was a member with the Brethren but switched to St George's parish church, Leeds (an Evangelical living belonging to the Simeon Trustees) in order that the children might have a broader upbringing. Raised in an austere though loving household and surrounded by younger sisters, Gordon Radley grew into an intensely shy and private person, certainly not one to wear his religion on his sleeve. Simultaneously, as two of his sisters recall, he developed an independent as well as an enquiring mind. In his teens he left St George's and went to a local Baptist church. Here he underwent a conversion experience and then took the step of believer's baptism.[75]

John Laing, born into a Brethren family, was early and frequently faced with the need for conversion, of personal faith in and commitment to Christ. No wonder that he made a profession of faith at the early age of 7 in response to an evangelistic meeting in the Carlisle Brethren Assembly. For Laing belief in God was never an intellectual problem: his childhood conviction remained unshaken throughout his life. It was, however, most seriously tested when in his late twenties he took the family building firm into an ambitious civil engineering contract which backfired and could have seriously damaged the firm's and his own prospects.[76] Church for Laing, too, was an opportunity to develop leadership qualities. At the age of 21 he was appointed clerk (secretary) of the Carlisle Brethren meeting. Three years later the last of the Carr brothers (the biscuit manufacturers who exchanged the Society of Friends for the Brethren in the late 1860s when the Quakers seemed to be losing

[73] L. S. Hunter, *John Hunter, DD* (London, 1921), 44–5.
[74] Michael Robbins, 'Frank Pick', *DBB*.
[75] Information kindly supplied by Lady Dorothy Radley.
[76] R. Coad, *Laing: The Biography of Sir John W. Laing CBE* (London, 1979), 33, 46–54.

their evangelical emphases)[77] died and Laing took over effective leadership of the assembly. Within months he and the younger members of the meeting brought in an American-style evangelist to conduct public revival meetings, with a beneficial effect on all the evangelical churches in Carlisle.[78]

Radley's conversion was swift and Laing's early in life. In contrast, J. Arthur Rank moved slowly from indifference to faith. This reflected his own cautious personality. Evidently he was not converted at The Leys School, despite all the opportunities for the experience created there. Indeed he and his two brothers rejected their father's faith. Unlike them, J. Arthur came back to that faith. After the First World War, during which he served in an ambulance unit and so escaped his father's powerful shadow, he started Sunday School teaching in Reigate Wesleyan Methodist Church. This marked the beginning of his Christian commitment.[79]

Certainly not all early church experiences were so positively received. Lionel Fraser, who eventually became a Christian Scientist, probably typified the majority in the business élites:

We went regularly to Sunday School at St Mary Abbots Church. I was also confirmed at this church, and to this day I blanch at the awful swear-word which came as a cry from my heart when, during the Confirmation Service, an almost new bowler which my father had somehow procured for me was moved by one of my friends so that I flattened it completely when I sat down!

It is a little difficult, in retrospect, to analyse exactly what my attitude was then to religion. . . . I think my attitude was not untypical of many other young people of those days. . . . I believed in heaven and hell, and I went to church because I felt it proper to do so. God had no particular significance for me except as a sort of glorified person up in the sky somewhere, to give me things at times and to help me, to whom I was ready to render thanks and praise for benefits received. As I have said, I attended Sunday School, and later took a Bible Class of my own; eventually I became a Churchwarden and served on the local Church Council of St Peter's, Bayswater. Although there was no depth in my approach to religion, the Church of England gave me a standard for which I shall always remain extremely grateful. . . . I was accepting the teachings of Christianity in an unquestioning fashion as they were taught to me, not reasoning things out for myself. But I recognise I had a sheet-anchor of a valuable kind.[80]

[77] Susan I. Dench, 'Jonathan Dodgson Carr', *DBB*.
[78] Coad, *Laing*, 55–6.
[79] Wood, *Mr Rank*, 37.
[80] Fraser, *All to the Good*, 32–3.

If nominal faith was the experience of the majority in the middle, on the other extreme from conversion was the rejection of faith and church. William Richard Morris, Viscount Nuffield, one of the most generous of modern philanthropists, whose benefactions totalled £30 million, was 'not much interested in religion'.[81] No doubt there were many others of whom this could be said. None in the business élites is known to have been a militant atheist, however.

The local church, or networks of local churches, was important in shaping members of the business élites in one other very important respect. All family businesses sooner or later faced the problem of the succession. Marriage partners for heirs or heiresses needed to be selected carefully and no better mechanism was available than in the local church or denominational connection. Here families and individuals came to know one another well and to find agreement on the deepest questions and attitudes in life. Not surprisingly, those business leaders who in adulthood were the most vigorous of Christians in their respective churches were those who selected wives with a shared religious background. John Laing married Beatrice Harland the daughter of a Stockton-on-Tees chartered accountant and head of a staunch Brethren family.[82] Four of the six Leysians are known to have married co-religionists. John Campbell Boot married Margaret Joyce Pyman, sister of two Leysians who had shipowning and shipbuilding interests in West Hartlepool.[83] Robert Burrows married Eleanor Doris Bainbridge, daughter of Arthur Emerson Bainbridge, son of Emerson Muschamp Bainbridge, prominent Wesleyan and the founder of a large department store at Newcastle-upon-Tyne. Arthur's brother Thomas was a leading layman among the Wesleyans.[84] J. Arthur Rank married Laura Ellen, eldest daughter of Sir Horace Brooks Marshall (later 1st Baron Marshall of Chipstead), a wholesale newspaper distributor and Wesleyan friend of Joseph Rank, J. Arthur's father.[85] Forrester-Paton, whose family belonged to the United Presbyterian Church of Scotland, married Mary Emma Louise Shaw, daughter of Thomas Shaw MP, Lord Advocate of Scotland (later 1st Baron Craigmyle) who held four national positions on the committees of the United Free Church of Scotland (formed in

---

[81] R. J. Overy, 'William Richard Morris', *DBB*.

[82] Coad, *Laing*, 57–9.

[83] The Leys School, *Handbook* (1934), 180, 227.

[84] A. and J. Airey, *The Bainbridges of Newcastle* (Newcastle-upon-Tyne, 1979), 76–8, 102–30.

[85] Roger Manville and Joseph Rank, 'Joseph Arthur Rank', *DBB*.

1900 by the union of the United Presbyterians and the Free Church) in 1907.[86]

Nearly all the five Cadburys married wives in the Society of Friends. In the 1907 élite George Cadbury, who married twice, chose each time a wife from a Quaker family (Mary Tylor, daughter of Charles Tylor, a London writer and lecturer; after her death, Elizabeth Mary Taylor, daughter of John Taylor, a member of the London Stock Exchange).[87] In the 1935 élite Edward Cadbury (one of George's sons) married Dorothy, the daughter of Dr Francis Howitt of Nottingham; William Adlington Cadbury (one of George's nephews) married Emmeline Hannah, daughter of Dr William Wilson who served as a medical missionary in Madagascar with the Friends' Foreign Missionary Association. In the 1955 élite Paul Strangman Cadbury (grandson of George's brother Richard) met his wife, Rachel Wilson, in France during the First World War while both were serving in the Friends' Ambulance Unit.[88] The other Cadbury in that élite, Laurence John Cadbury (son of George Cadbury by his second wife), stepped outside the Society of Friends in finding his wife. He married Joyce Mathews, the daughter of a Unitarian estate agent in Edgbaston, Birmingham. Although their children went to Quaker public schools Laurence was one of those Quakers who moved to the established church, if he had any allegiance to a denomination.[89] Laurence Cadbury was certainly not the only one to find that marriage led to (or strengthened) the resolve to switch denominations. Josiah Stamp (1st Baron Stamp), raised as a Baptist, moved across to the Wesleyans under the influence of his wife, Olive Jessie Marsh, the daughter of a Twickenham builder.[90] Other marriages that spanned denominational divides included Sir Oliver Franks's marriage to the daughter of a prominent Quaker, Herbert Tanner.

None of these marriages (so far as is known) was arranged in the sense that partners were chosen by parents. Nevertheless there is the suspicion that parents, particularly devout Victorian parents, ensured that their offspring moved in vetted circles and met only those potential

[86] Information kindly supplied by Alastair Forrester-Paton, son of Alexander Forrester-Paton; *WWW*; UFCS, *The Principal Acts of the General Assembly* (Edinburgh, 1907), 413–30.

[87] *DNB*.

[88] Rachel Wilson was the daughter of Kenneth and Isabel Wilson. Isabel was the daughter of George Cadbury by his first wife; Kenneth ran Albright & Wilson the chemical manufacturers. Information from Sir Adrian Cadbury.

[89] Crosfield, *Cadbury Family*, ii. 375, 385–6, 525, 570–2. Information from Sir Adrian Cadbury.

[90] *DNB*.

partners of whom they approved. That is not a criticism of the mechanism: it may be a virtue of it. Possibly the Quakers and the Brethren were more tightly bonded than other churches: the point deserves greater investigation than is possible here.

4 CONCLUSIONS

The foregoing two chapters both answer and raise questions. However tentative, some answers have to be accepted in order to move forward to the next stage of the investigation. How extensive were Christian influences in the early experiences of the British business élites? Which denominations were most effective in shaping the formative years of business leaders? Which agencies of Christian teaching predominated? What kinds of teaching, moral and religious, were absorbed?

Christian influences, when merged as in Table 3.4 (which must be used cautiously), apparently affected between 50 and 60 per cent of chairmen across the period and around 35 per cent of managing directors. These percentages (excluding the Jewish proportions) could well be much higher because pertinent data were untraced for 30 to 40 per cent of the samples. Quantitatively the most influential denomination, expectedly, was the Church of England, largely because of the predominance of the public school as an agency of Christian teaching—in turn due to the British businessman's preference for a public school education for his sons and to the church presence in the foundation of the major public schools.

When set against non-school influences it does seems that school religion accounted for anywhere between a quarter and a third of all possible kinds of religious influence. However the agencies were neither alternative nor mutually exclusive. Pious parents in early childhood, public school in term time, local church in holidays, all could play a part.

The anecdotal nature of the evidence about kinds of Christian teaching and influence makes it difficult to reach any hard and fast conclusions. A radical Christian social ethic was largely explored and espoused by the Anglo-Catholic wing of the Church of England. By 1901 Anglo-Catholics accounted for 30 per cent of parochial clergy in the Anglican Church.[91] On this basis no more than 30 per cent of business élites

[91] J. E. B. Munson, 'The Oxford Movement by the End of the Nineteenth Century: The Anglo-Catholic Clergy', *Church History*, 44 (1975), 388. An estimate in 1877 put the proportion of Anglo-Catholic clergy close to 50 per cent (12,000 out of 23,000 clergy were High; 5,000 were Low, 1,000 Broad and 5,000 doubtful): D. W. R. Bahlman, 'Politics and Church Patronage in the Victorian Age', *Victorian Studies*, 22 (1979), 266–7.

TABLE 3.4. *Received religious influences (all kinds) of chairmen and managing directors*

	1907		1935		1955	
	n	% of N	n	% of N	n	% of N
Chairmen						
Episcopalian						
Church of England	39	65.0	31	51.0	37	64.0
Episcopal Church of Scotland	0	0.0	0	0.0	0	0.0
Church in Wales	0	0.0	0	0.0	0	0.0
Church of Ireland	1	2.0	0	0.0	0	0.0
Total	40	67.0	31	51.0	37	64.0
Presbyterian						
Church of Scotland	2	3.0	3	5.0	1	2.0
Free Church of Scotland, United Presbyterian, and UFC	2	3.0	1	2.0	0	0.0
English/Welsh Presbyterian	0	0.0	1	2.0	1	2.0
Irish Presbyterian	2	3.0	0	0.0	0	0.0
Total	6	10.0	5	9.0	2	4.0
Nonconformist						
Baptist	0	0.0	3	5.0	0	0.0
Brethren	0	0.0	0	0.0	2	3.0
Congregational	6	10.0	2	3.0	3	5.0
Methodist: Wesleyan	1	2.0	2	3.0	4	7.0
Methodist: undifferentiated	0	0.0	0	0.0	0	0.0
Methodist: pre-1932 sect	0	0.0	0	0.0	1	2.0
Quaker	3	5.0	5	8.0	1	2.0
Salvation Army	0	0.0	0	0.0	0	0.0
Unitarian	1	2.0	1	2.0	0	0.0
Others Nonconformist e.g. Moravian	0	0.0	0	0.0	0	0.0
Total	11	18.0	13	21.0	11	19.0

TABLE 3.4. *cont.*

	1907		1935		1955	
	n	% of N	n	% of N	n	% of N
Protestant	0	0.0	2	3.0	0	0.0
Roman Catholic	0	0.0	2	3.0	1	2.0
Neo-Christian (20th c. sects)	0	0.0	0	0.0	0	0.0
Unspecified Christian	2	3.0	1	2.0	0	0.0
Jewish	0	0.0	4	7.0	6	10.0
Non-denominational	1	2.0	3	5.0	1	2.0
TOTALS						
N	60	100.0	61	100.0	58	100.0
Cohort	100		100		96	
N as % of cohort		60.0		61.0		60.0
Managing directors						
Episcopalian						
Church of England	20	52.6	16	39.0	32	59.3
Episcopal Church of Scotland	0	0.0	0	0.0	0	0.0
Church in Wales	0	0.0	0	0.0	0	0.0
Church of Ireland	0	0.0	0	0.0	0	0.0
Total	20	52.6	16	39.0	32	59.3
Presbyterian						
Church of Scotland	3	7.9	1	2.4	3	5.6
Free Church of Scotland, United Presbyterian, and UFC	1	2.6	2	4.9	0	0.0
English/Welsh Presbyterian	0	0.0	0	0.0	0	0.0
Irish Presbyterian	2	5.3	0	0.0	0	0.0
Total	6	15.8	3	7.3	3	5.6

TABLE 3.4. *cont.*

	1907		1935		1955	
	n	% of N	n	% of N	n	% of N
Nonconformist						
Baptist	0	0.0	0	0.0	0	0.0
Brethren	0	0.0	0	0.0	1	1.9
Congregational	5	13.2	4	9.8	0	0.0
Methodist: Wesleyan	1	2.6	1	2.4	1	1.9
Methodist: undifferentiated	0	0.0	1	2.4	2	3.7
Methodist: pre-1932 sect	0	0.0	1	2.4	1	1.9
Quaker	2	5.3	1	2.4	1	1.9
Salvation Army	0	0.0	0	0.0	0	0.0
Unitarian	0	0.0	0	0.0	0	0.0
Other Nonconformist e.g. Moravian	0	0.0	0	0.0	0	0.0
Total	8	21.1	8	19.5	6	11.1
Protestant	0	0.0	0	0.0	0	0.0
Roman Catholic	1	2.6	3	7.3	2	3.7
Neo-Christian (20th c. sects)	0	0.0	0	0.0	1	1.9
Unspecified Christian	1	2.6	2	4.9	0	0.0
Jewish	1	2.6	5	12.2	5	9.3
Non-denominational	1	2.6	4	9.8	5	9.3
TOTALS						
N	38	100.0	41	100.0	54	100.0
Cohort	101		103		116	
N as % of cohort	37.6		39.8		46.6	

Notes: N = total number of cases; n = subset of N.

who attended the Church of England or related schools were exposed to radical Christian social theology before the First World War, which meant the vast majority of those in the three élites studied here. On the other hand at least 25 per cent of parish clergy were Evangelical at the turn of the century, so that proportion of those in the élites attending church-linked schools may have adhered to a traditional social ethic, sitting comfortably with the separation of business and religion.[92]

The business leaders in these élites were almost entirely products of the nineteenth century. In the words of George Kitson-Clark, the nineteenth century was 'a most religious century'.[93] The doyen of ecclesiastical historians pinpoints the implications of this:

The most marked character in Victorian religion is the sense of vocation, and this sense carried with it a powerful sense of the sacredness of time and the sin of wasting it. They were servants of God, under his eye, and their hands found plenty to do in his cause, in mission, social reform, commerce, administration, empire, evangelism, ministry to the sick. Life therefore was earnest enough to prevent them from writing lightly of morality or its religious aspect.[94]

With or without a conversion experience, this was the essence of the values with which their religious upbringing equipped these business leaders for life.

[92] R. Manwaring, *From Controversy to Co-existence: Evangelicals in the Church of England, 1914–1980* (Cambridge, 1985), 2.
[93] G. Kitson-Clark, *The English Inheritance* (London, 1950), 143.
[94] Chadwick, *Victorian Church*, ii. 466.

PART III

Advance or Retreat?
Christians in Big Business

PROLOGUE

Church and Industry Links Quantified

If Marx was right about religion being the opiate of the people, capitalists could be expected to administer it. In doing so they would, like Lever at Port Sunlight, in varying degrees engage in the religious activities they wished to utilize. These might range from building a church, a religious activity with social and economic dimensions, to providing various welfare benefits, social and economic actions which could have a religious character if the entrepreneur responsible was prepared to attribute them to his beliefs. What evidence is there of religious connections in the adult careers of the business leaders in the three samples drawn for this study? In what proportions of the samples did religion figure in the business leaders' careers?

A survey of the biographical notices, obituaries, or biographies of individuals in the three business élites provides a starting-point for quantitative answers. Excluding *Who's Who* notices (which are invariably silent on such matters as religious attachment) these kinds of profile have been assembled for approximately four-fifths of individuals in the business élites. Table 4.01 summarizes the evidence on church links in these sources. It has to be used with care because 'adult religious affiliation' is a formula that has been used for a very wide range of church linkages, ranging from national or local office-holding to benefactions, membership, simple attendance, or burial rites. It has to be construed, therefore, as indicating the religious preference that an individual business leader would have acknowledged when pressed by a recruiting sergeant or a hospital admissions staff. Because there is no way by which a historian can infallibly distinguish between active and nominal Christians, this minimalist definition seems to be the most useful for present purposes.

Three features of this kind of Christian presence in the British business

TABLE 4.01. *Adult religious preferences of members of the UK's business élites, 1907, 1935, 1955*

Denomination	Chairmen						Managing directors					
	1907		1935		1955		1907		1935		1955	
	No.	%	No.	%	No.	%	No.	%	No.	%	No.	%
Episcopalian												
Church of England	33	41.3	31	34.1	17	21.0	21	32.3	19	23.8	16	20.3
Episcopal Church in Scotland	3	3.8										
Church in Wales	1	1.3					2	3.1				
Church of Ireland												
Total	37		31		17		23		19		16	
Presbyterian												
Church of Scotland	4	5.0	5	5.5	3	3.7	1	1.5	3	3.8	1	1.3
United Free Church of Scotland	4	5.0					2	3.1	2	2.5		
English/Welsh Presbyterian			1	1.1	1	1.2					1	1.3
Irish Presbyterian	2	2.5					2	3.1				
Total	10		6		4		5		5		2	

TABLE 4.01. cont.

Denomination	Chairmen						Managing directors					
	1907		1935		1955		1907		1935		1955	
	No.	%	No.	%	No.	%	No.	%	No.	%	No.	%
Nonconformist												
Baptist												
Brethren			2	2.2	1	1.2			1	1.3	1	1.3
Congregationalist	4	5.0	1	1.1	1	1.2	3	4.6	3	3.8		
Methodist: Wesleyan			1	1.1	2	2.5					2	2.5
Methodist: other												
Quaker	3	3.8	2	2.2	1	1.2	1	1.5	1	1.3	1	1.3
Unitarian	2	2.5					1	1.5	1	1.3		
Other												
Protestant (undefined)					2	2.5			1	1.3	1	1.3
Total	9		6		7		5		7		5	
Roman Catholic			2	2.2	1	1.2	2	3.1	2	2.5	1	1.3
20th. c. sects					1	1.2					1	1.3
Jewish			4	4.4	5	6.2			6	7.5	4	5.1
TOTAL	56	70.0	49	53.8	35	43.2	35	53.8	39	48.8	29	36.7
Total obituaries traced	80	100.0	91	100.0	81	100.0	65	100.0	80	100.0	79	100.0
Total in cohort	100	100	100	100	96	101	101	100	103	100	116	100

Note: Adult religious preferences ranged widely from simple regular attendance at Sunday worship to active church leadership to a minimal rite of passage (wedding or burial).

élites emerge from the table. First, a Christian presence was always stronger among chairmen than among managing directors. This probably reflected the differing social and educational backgrounds of the two groups, as outlined in Chapter 1. Second, among both chairmen and managing directors the numbers of nominal and active Christians declined from over half the business élite before 1914 to well under a half (if numbers of Jews are deducted from numbers of Christians) by the 1930s. This doubtless echoed the spreading doubts about religion and the secularization of society which marked the war and post-war years. Third, among both chairmen and directors and in every élite year the largest group of Christians were members of the Church of England. They accounted for nearly two-fifths in 1907, a share which fell to one-fifth in the 1950s. This overturns the findings emerging from the *Dictionary of Business Biography*[1] and suggests again that an objectively selected sample, such as this one, will yield a very different picture from one grounded in a collection of prominent business figures. This present one more accurately captures the business élite as defined by company position. The other suggests that religious allegiance and philanthropy were integral to the prominence sought or attained by *nouveaux riches* Nonconformists; with that came honours, official biographies, and long obituary notices, grist for subsequent historians.

If the Church of England claimed the largest shares of the business élites, it was eclipsed in relative terms by the Quakers. That much is apparent from Table 4.02. Whereas the Anglican Church's proportion of the business élite of 1907 was just over four times its religious density (the percentage of its adherents in the population aged 15 and above), the Society of Friends had a share over forty times their religious density. Both Anglicans and Quakers suffered heavy falls in this ratio by the 1950s, and Quakers more heavily than Anglicans. Even so, the Quaker representation in the business élite of 1955 was nearly thirty times the Quaker religious density, a ratio nearly ten times greater than that of the Anglicans. The predominance of Anglicans by absolute measures and of Quakers by relative measures confirms frequently expressed impressions. What is remarkable is the size of the Quaker representation.

One further quantitative exercise provides another frame of reference for the anecdotal evidence. That is a rough comparison between the major denominations' relative inputs into educating the business élites and their relative returns in terms of adult affiliations among the business

---

[1] D. J. Jeremy, 'Important Questions about Business and Religion in Modern Britain', in Jeremy (ed.), *Business and Religion in Britain* (Aldershot, 1988), 17.

TABLE 4.02. *Adult religious preferences of UK's business elites compared to religious densities, 1907, 1935, 1955*

Denomination	1907				1935				1955			
	N	%	RD	RP/RD	N	%	RD	RP/RD	N	%	RD	RP/RD
Church of England	54	37.24	8.990	4.142	50	29.24	7.580	3.858	33	20.63	6.670	3.093
Church of Scotland	5	3.45	22.490	0.153	8	4.68	34.350	0.136	4	2.50	34.300	0.073
Congregationalist	7	4.83	1.950	2.477	2	1.17	0.940	1.245	1	0.63	0.630	1.000
Methodist	1	0.69	3.180	0.217	4	2.34	2.310	1.013	4	2.50	1.936	1.291
Quaker	3	2.07	0.048	43.125	3	1.75	0.042	41.667	2	1.25	0.043	29.070
Roman Catholic	2	1.38	5.900	0.234	4	2.34	6.430	0.364	2	1.25	9.200	0.136
Sect (20th-c.)						0.00			2	1.25		
Jew			0.720		10	5.85	0.650	9.000	9	5.63	0.490	11.490
Total (no. of obituaries from Table 4.01)	145	100.0			171	100.0			160	100.0		
Total in cohort	201				203				212			

Notes: RD = religious density; RP = religious preference; N = total number of cases.
The religious density for Jews is expressed as a percentage of Jewish marriages among all marriages.
No figures are available for a calculation of the RD of 20th-century sects as a whole.

Sources: Author's data summarized in Table 4.01; religious densities from sources for Table 1.5.

leaders. Table 4.03 presents the ratios. Again the table must be interpreted with some caution. The religious schooling–religious density ratio applies only to secondary schooling; it is taken from Table 3.2 in which the number of traceable obituaries mentioning early background has been applied as the denominator in the percentage calculation. The adult affiliation ratio is based on those cases in the three cohorts for whom there was biographical information relating to adulthood. Consequently the schooling–religious density ratios probably understate the true situation. If the distortion can be neglected, then the salient feature of the comparison is that after 1907 in most denominations religious schooling inputs were higher than adult religious affiliation outputs in the careers of the business élites. Anglicans, Methodists, and Quakers in the 1930s and 1950s seem to have invested more in the careers of business leaders than they received back from the business leaders as adult religious commitment. In the 1950s only Catholics experienced the reverse. However, the data seem too qualitative and incomplete to support any large theoretical edifice. Weight and meaning are lent to these statistics by examining individual cases.

One other question remains. Is there any relationship between denominational allegiances and industrial sectors in the business élites? It is sometimes asserted, for example, that Anglicans commanded the services sector while Nonconformists stuck to manufacturing. Or that Nonconformists, especially Quakers and Methodists, went into 'clean' trades like confectionery manufacture partly because of low barriers to entry but also for reasons related to religion and morality—chocolate and toffee being less socially hazardous than alcohol and tobacco. Table 4.04 presents a summary of the business élites data on the relationship. Business activities by industrial sectors have been plotted for all those in the three élites whose adult religious preferences are known. Religious links have been aggregated under major forms of church polity. (A much larger sample would be needed to correlate individual denominations with separate industries.)

Among chairmen the table shows among other things that Anglicans did indeed have a strong presence in the service sector and a growing presence in the financial sector, responding to some extent to the shifts away from manufacturing experienced by the British economy in the twentieth century. At the beginning of the century Anglicans among chairmen included Sir George Livesey (South Metropolitan Gas Co.); railwaymen like Richard Grosvenor, 1st Lord Stalbridge (London & North Western Railway), Sir George Armytage (Lancashire & Yorkshire Railway), W. L. Jackson, 1st Lord Allerton (Great Northern Railway and

TABLE 4.03. *Religious schooling compared to adult religious preferences in business elites expressed as ratios of religious density, 1907, 1935, 1955*

	1907			1935			1955		
	School Share/RD (1)	Adult P/RD (2)	Col. 2/col. 1 (3)	School Share/RD (4)	Adult P/RD (5)	Col. 5/col. 4 (6)	School Share/RD (7)	Adult P/RD (8)	Col. 8/col. 7 (9)
Church of England	3.84	4.14	1.08	5.74	3.86	0.67	7.06	3.09	0.44
Church of Scotland	0.09	0.15	1.64	0.10	0.14	1.34		0.07	
Congregationalist	1.45	2.48	1.71		1.24			1.00	
Methodist	0.44	0.22	0.49	1.51	1.01	0.67	1.35	1.29	0.96
Quaker	43.96	43.13	0.98	62.14	41.67	0.67	30.47	29.07	0.95
Roman Catholic	0.12	0.23	1.97	0.41	0.36	0.90	0.07	0.14	1.92
Total cases	142	145		115	171		153	160	
Total in cohort	201	201		203	203		212	212	

Notes: RD = religious density; P = preference.

Sources: Tables 1.5, 3.2, 4.02, and their sources.

TABLE 4.04. *Industrial distribution of members in business élites with known religious preferences, 1907, 1935, 1955*

Industrial sector	Episcopalian		Presbyterian		Nonconformist		Roman Catholic		Sect		Jewish	
	No.	%	No.	%	No.	%	No.	%	No.	%	No.	%
Chairmen												
Élite of 1907												
Mining	2	2.50	1	1.25	1	1.25						
Manufacturing	19	23.75	7	8.75	7	8.75						
Services	16	20.00	2	2.50	2	2.50						
Finance												
Professions												
Miscellaneous												
Total	37	46.25	10	12.50	10	12.50						
Élite of 1935												
Mining	3	3.30	1	1.10	1	1.10						
Manufacturing	19	20.88	3	3.30	3	3.30	2	2.20			2	2.20
Services	7	7.69	2	2.20	1	1.10					2	2.20
Finance					1	1.10						
Professions												
Miscellaneous	2	2.20										
Total	31	34.07	6	6.59	6	6.59	2	2.20			4	4.40
Élite of 1955												
Mining												
Manufacturing	9	11.11	4	4.94	4	4.94	1	1.23	1	1.23	3	3.70
Services	4	4.94			1	1.23					2	2.47
Finance	4	4.94			1	1.23						
Professions												
Miscellaneous					1	1.23						
Total	17	20.99	4	4.94	7	8.64	1	1.23	1	1.23	5	6.17

TABLE 4.04. cont.

Industrial sector	Episcopalian		Presbyterian		Nonconformist		Roman Catholic		Sect		Jewish	
	No.	%	No.	%	No.	%	No.	%	No.	%	No.	%
Managing directors												
Élite of 1907												
Mining	2	3.08	1	1.54								
Manufacturing	15	23.08	3	4.62	5	7.69						
Services	6	9.23	1	1.54			2	3.08				
Finance												
Professions												
Miscellaneous												
Total	23	35.38	5	7.69	5	7.69	2	3.08				
Élite of 1935												
Mining	1	1.25			2	2.50						
Manufacturing	10	12.50	3	3.75	4	5.00	2	2.50			4	5.00
Services	4	5.00	2	2.50	1	1.25					2	2.50
Finance	4	5.00										
Professions												
Miscellaneous												
Total	19	23.75	5	6.25	7	8.75	2	2.50			6	7.50
Élite of 1955												
Mining	6	7.59			4	5.06	1	1.27	1	1.27	1	1.27
Manufacturing	7	8.86	2	2.53	1	1.27					3	3.80
Services	1	1.27										
Finance												
Professions												
Miscellaneous	2	2.53										
Total	16	20.25	2	2.53	5	6.32	1	1.27	1	1.27	4	5.06

Notes: Mining: Standard Industrial Classification (1968) Order 2; manufacturing: SIC (1968) Orders 3–20; services: SIC (1968) Orders 21–3; finance: SIC (1968) Order 24; professions: SIC (1968) Order 25; miscellaneous: SIC (1968) Order 26.
Total obituaries (chairmen): 1907: 80; 1935: 91; 1955: 81; total obituaries (managing directors): 1907: 65; 1935: 80; 1955: 79.

the Cheshire Lines Committee), and Tonman Mosley, later 1st Lord Anslow (North Staffordshire Railway); and several in distribution, like Robert Grosvenor, 2nd Lord Ebury (Army & Navy Co-operative Society) and W. F. D. (Freddy) Smith, 2nd Viscount Hambleden, and William Whiteley (of their eponymous retailing firms). Churchmen among the managing directors of service industry companies included David Milne-Watson (Gas Light & Coke Co.), Ammon Beasley (manager of the Taff Vale Railway, made famous or infamous, depending on one's viewpoint, by a trade union conflict that culminated in the Taff Vale judgement), William Forbes (London, Brighton & South Coast Railway), and Charles Awdry (W. H. Smith & Son).

The diminution of the Anglican presence in service industries by the mid-1930s presumably resulted partly from the post-war merger of railway companies, partly from spreading unbelief. The twelve Anglican chairmen and managing directors of service companies in 1935 headed firms like the Gas Light & Coke (Milne-Watson), the Post Office (Albert Lee), the Port of London Authority (Lord Ritchie), Cunard (Sir Percy Bates), the Southern Railway (Robert Holland-Martin), John Barker (Sir Sydney Skinner), Debenhams (Sir Frederick Richmond), and W. H. Smith (William Henry Smith, 3rd Viscount Hambleden). Almost the same number of Anglicans, but a smaller proportion as chairmen and a larger proportion as managing directors, appeared in the service sector in 1955. Clearly inheritors and successors were falling into existing religious patterns for some of the same firms crop up again: W. H. Smith (the Honourable David John Smith) and the Port of London Authority (Leslie E. Ford) being obvious cases. In addition Anglicans headed the British Electricity Authority (Sir Henry Self), the Post Office (Sir Gordon Radley), British Electric Traction (Harley Drayton), BOAC (Basil Smallpeice), and the London Transport Executive (Sir John Elliot).

Anglicans accounted for most of the church-affiliated heads of largest firms in the financial sector. No firms in the sector were large enough for inclusion in the sample of 1907. By 1935 the five big banks and the Prudential Assurance Co. had enough employees to enter the sample. Of the twelve positions of leadership they offered half were occupied by Anglicans: Colonel Colin Campbell and William F. Tuke, chairmen of the National Provincial and Barclays Banks respectively; Frederick Hyde, general manager of the Midland; Anthony W. Tuke, general manager of Barclays, under his father; George F. Abell, chief general manager of Lloyds; and Sir Joseph Burn, general manager of the Prudential. The same six firms maintained places in the 1955 cohort. This time five of the twelve leadership slots were held by Anglicans. However, four were bank chairmen: Walter Gibbs, 4th Lord Aldenham (Westminster Bank); William G. A. Ormsby-Gore, 4th Lord Harlech (Midland); David John Robarts (National Provincial), a Church Commissioner 1957–65; and Anthony W. Tuke (Barclays). William Gerald Edington was chief general manager of the Midland.

As for the Nonconformists, it is not at all clear from this data that in big business they concentrated in manufacturing. Part IV (Chapter 8 in particular) presents much more data on this point. It does seem that Quakers concentrated in confectionery. However two with suspected Quaker leanings, J. W. Beaumont Pease and Sir Oliver Franks, were bank chairmen, of Lloyds in 1935 and 1955 respectively. Nor is it clear that Nonconformists avoided firms menacing the health and morals of the community: the persistence of the Wills family in tobacco manufacture and of Methodists in the asbestos firm of Turner & Newall underline that.

Part III of this study is concerned with the business leaders' projection of their religious commitment, however they perceived that, into their firms. If the proportion of the largest firms' chairmen who had adult church connections was as high as 70 per cent in 1907 and 42 per cent in 1955, how did that emerge in their firms? Did they hold business and religion apart as Tawney claimed? Did they use religion as an instrument of control as Pollard, Joyce, and other historians found in nineteenth-century factory communities? Were they affected by the varieties of Christian Socialism? Did they adopt the ideas of Oldham and Temple? How far each élite pursued these possibilities is explored in the next four chapters.

4

Christians in Big Business Leadership before 1914

I PERSPECTIVES ON FIRMS

If churchmen among business leaders were most numerous in the twentieth century in the decade before the First World War, what was the nature of their influence within the firm? Quantitative analyses reveal that Anglicans and Quakers had the strongest presence absolutely and relatively, respectively. They will be studied in the second part of this chapter. Before looking at them, this chapter takes a random sample of the 100 largest firms and, through their chairmen's and managing directors' careers and through company histories, aims to reach conclusions about the opportunities to wield religious influence within the firm at this time.

A random 1 in 10 sample, taking firms ranked 2, 12, 22 etc. in the list of the 100 largest firms ranked by size in 1907 and presented in Appendix I, produces the following firms in descending order of employment size:

London & North Western Railway Co.
Sir W. G. Armstrong, Whitworth & Co. Ltd.
United Collieries Ltd.
Bleachers' Association Ltd.
Kynoch Ltd.
Singer Manufacturing Co. Ltd.
Fairfield Shipbuilding & Engineering Co. Ltd.
Scott's Shipbuilding & Engineering Co. Ltd.

Cheshire Lines Committee
Doulton & Co. Ltd.

The ten firms, one in mining, seven in manufacturing, and two railway companies, epitomized the activities in which the largest companies in Britain engaged at the turn of the century. Four employed more than 10,000, the others more than 4,000. The LNWR with over 70,000 was the largest. Within the parameter of size, two other firm characteristics governed the possibilities for chairmen and managing directors to exercise religiously inspired preferences: numbers of plants and company organization.

Three of the ten firms had single (or virtually single) plants, the others had multiple plants and sites. Two of the single-plant firms, Fairfield Shipbuilding & Engineering and Scott's Shipbuilding & Engineering, were shipbuilders on the Clyde, Fairfield at Govan close to Glasgow and Scott's much further down at Greenock. Scott's actually had two yards separated by one they did not own until the mid-1930s.[1] The third single plant was also on the Clyde, but on the northern bank some seven miles from Glasgow, this was the Singer factory at Clydebank which made sewing machines.

In contrast the typical firm in the sample had multiple plants, usually spread widely. Most diffused were the two railway companies, the LNWR with 1,700 miles of line and over 700 stations, and the Cheshire Lines Committee with 141 miles of line and 70 stations. United Collieries had recently absorbed the numerous coal-mines of 31 constituent firms, located in the counties of Lanark and Linlithgow. The Bleachers' Association had at least 50 dyeworks and bleacheries, nearly all within easy reach of Manchester. Kynoch's the ammunition manufacturer of Birmingham had 11 plants; Doulton the pottery manufacturer of Lambeth and Stoke-on-Trent, 6 straddled between London and Scotland; and Armstrong, Whitworth, the shipbuilding, armaments, and engineering combine of Newcastle-upon-Tyne and Manchester, 4 plants.[2]

All were limited companies except the two railways, which were differently regulated. The LNWR was governed by its parliamentary act of incorporation. The Cheshire Lines Committee was jointly and equally

[1] *Two Centuries of Shipbuilding by the Scotts at Greenock* (3rd edn., Manchester, 1950), 233.
[2] See C. Shaw, 'The Large Manufacturing Employers of 1907', *Business History*, 25 (1983), 52–3, for plants of firms solely in the manufacturing sector. For the mining and railway firms see W. B. Skinner, *The Mining Manual* (London, 1907), 1097; G. A. Sekon, *The Railway Year Book for 1908* (London, 1908), *passim*.

owned by the Great Northern, the Great Central, and the Midland railway companies. Important though the legal basis was, the companies differed more significantly with respect to organization. The railways had developed the most advanced managerial structures of their day, run by professional managers accountable to boards of politically powerful and wealthy figures representing shareholders' interests. On the railways geographical and functional responsibilities were exercised through the line-and-staff system. Thus railway managers stood in two hierarchies, one defined by activity, one by territory. In these developments the LNWR had been a pioneer.[3]

If ownership and control were most completely divorced on the railways, the other firms in the sample exhibited variations in their relationships between owners and managers. Singer was a subsidiary of the famous American parent company (founded in 1851) which opened its Scottish plant at first in Glasgow in 1867. In 1886 American managers brought their Scottish operation, which had been moved to Kilbowie (Clydebank) in 1884, more in line with their Elizabethport, NJ, works where they had recently adopted complete interchangeability and ended the system of inside contracting.[4] In short, scientific management and its accompaniment of professional managers characterized Singer.

Three firms in the sample were large-scale mergers executed in the merger wave at the turn of the century. United Collieries was formed by eight firms in 1898 to which another 23 colliery concerns, again mostly family businesses, were added in 1902. This second expansion was engineered by London financiers including J. R. Ellerman.[5] The acquisition of the 23 collieries overextended the firm's capital resources and a struggle ensued between the preference shareholders and the debenture holders, leading to a change of directors.[6] The Bleachers' Association, a merger of 53 family firms carried out in 1900, likewise soon encountered difficulties, this time because members of the constituent family firms insisted on an unwieldy structure to preserve their interests. Until a five-strong board of management was formed in 1904 and a small finance committee

---

[3] T. R. Gourvish, *Mark Huish and the London & North Western Railway* (Leicester, 1972).

[4] D. A. Hounshell, *From the American System to Mass Production, 1800–1932* (Baltimore, 1984), 120 and *passim*.

[5] SRO, Quarter Sessions records, CS 241/456/1–8; W. D. Rubinstein, 'John Reeves Ellerman', *DBB*.

[6] H. W. Macrosty, *The Trust Movement in British Industry* (London, 1907), 96–8; Skinner, *Mining Manual*, 1097.

in 1906, the chairman, Herbert Shepherd Cross, found it almost imposs-ible to wheel his 49 directors into line.[7]

The third large-scale merger was Armstrong, Whitworth, formed in 1897 when Armstrongs completed their purchase of Whitworths. Arm-strongs employed about 20,000 at a series of works mostly at Elswick on the Tyne where they produced warships, guns, and ammunition. Whitworths employed 2,000 at Openshaw, Manchester, engaged on the manufacture of machine tools, armour plate, and gun mountings. Even before Lord Armstrong's death in 1900 the whole firm came under the control of Sir Andrew Noble, who succeeded Armstrong as chairman. Noble ousted the Rendels and, aided by two of his four sons, ran the firm with a style distinguished by 'capricious autocracy, sterilising debate, and stifled innovation and management development'.[8] He overruled the London manager, 'transacting all the London business himself from lodgings or his club in London'.[9] Thus big businesses formed by merger, because they were so recently converted from family firms, still offered scope for the exercise of family preferences.

Organizationally the other four firms in the sample were marginally different again. Kynoch's had been reconstructed in 1888 when active shareholders turned out the founder and installed their own chairman, Arthur Chamberlain.[10] Chamberlain ran the firm until his death in 1913 when his son, also Arthur, succeeded him. Though assisted by a most energetic managing director, A. T. Cocking, it was Arthur Chamberlain, sen., who ran the firm with undisputed, despotic control. A strict paterna-list, he was opposed to both employers' associations and trade unions and 'wanted free bargaining on both sides with no conflicts of loyalty with peer groups'.[11]

Whereas Chamberlain was obliged to follow a founder whose business concerns had been displaced by political ambition, and to that extent had to reassert a strong paternal style, Henry Lewis Doulton inherited a well-established paternalist firm with a high public profile. After the death of his father Sir Henry Doulton, he converted the firm into a limited company, taking all the ordinary shares, a third of the preference shares, and a third of the debentures himself. A sharp contrast to his father, Lewis Doulton was quiet, unassuming, and loathed personal pub-

[7] Macrosty, *Trust Movement*, 141–4; J. J. Mason, 'Herbert Shepherd Cross', *DBB*.
[8] R. J. Irving, 'Andrew Noble', *DBB*.
[9] Quoted in D. Dougan, *The Great Gun-Maker* (Newcastle-upon-Tyne, 1970), 154.
[10] Jennifer Tann, 'George Kynoch', *DBB*.
[11] Barbara M. D. Smith, 'Arthur Chamberlain', *DBB*; Kynoch Ltd., *Under Five Flags* (Birmingham, 1962), 29–51.

licity. His forte was production; his concerns those of a self-effacing paternalist. In 1910, when the company reported bad results for a third year running (due to depression in the building trade), he accepted a silver wedding gift from his employees with the sincerely felt remark that 'there are few things dearer to my heart than the knowledge of the goodwill that has existed between the various members of our family and the staff for so many years—I might say generations. ... I am sure there was never greater need for this kindly feeling to be maintained than at the present time.'[12]

Fairfield Shipbuilding & Engineering was similar to Kynoch and Doulton in that it was a family firm, originally John Elder & Co. Like Kynoch's, new blood had been injected into it, in the form of William Pearce, a young naval architect in the 1860s. Pearce built it up and in 1886 converted it into a limited company with the Fairfield name. Shortly after, he died in his mid-fifties. His achievement was remarkable. Within twenty years he had become a millionaire, big businessman, and MP with a baronetcy to his name.[13] His only son Sir William George Pearce eventually succeeded as chairman of Fairfields but his inheritance and his training (at Rugby, Cambridge, and the Bar) diverted him from a technical background and his tastes kept him far south on his Wiltshire estate in the Kennet valley. In mitigation of the image of the absentee industrialist, a contemporary profile reported, 'Sir William is unfailing in the attention he bestows on the Fairfield Shipbuilding and Engineering Company, Limited. Although principally residing in England, he is in almost daily communication either with the works at Govan or with the London office. He is also largely interested in shipowning ...'[14]

Scott's Shipbuilding & Engineering, founded in 1711, was distinguished by the success with which the family had defied the syndrome of rags to riches to rags in three or four generations. This was the family firm *par excellence*.[15] Its chairman in 1907, Charles Cuningham Scott, was head of the sixth generation of the shipbuilding family. Educated briefly at a private school in England and then at Fettes and Edinburgh University, he started his apprenticeship in university vacations, working his way through the various departments in the firm's two shipyards—an early example of what in 1910 was reported as 'the now popular "sand-

[12] D. Eyles, *Royal Doulton, 1815–1965* (London,1965), 133–4, *passim*.
[13] Anthony Slaven, 'William Pearce', *DSBB*.
[14] *Bailie*, No. 1594 (6 May 1903), 1.
[15] See *Two Centuries of Shipbuilding*, which is mostly about the products of the shipyards with a short section on the family and nothing about management or the workforce.

wich" system'.[16] He became a managing director when his father died in 1903 and when his uncle died two years later he took over as chairman.[17]

Thus, of the ten firms in this sample from the 100 largest in 1907, six were managed by heads of the families who owned the controlling shareholdings. The two railway companies were run by hierarchies of professional managers. Singer was being reshaped by scientific management principles. United Collieries' position is obscure. The Bleachers' Association was still trying to subordinate the old family interests to the objectives of the new combination; in local plants traditional family figures ruled as the new managers. In Kynoch's, Armstrong, Whitworth, Fairfields, Scott's, and Doulton's family members and paternalist styles, not necessarily of uniform intensity, also dominated.

Despite, therefore, the increases in scale achieved in the nineteenth century, and especially in the merger wave which began in the late 1890s, inheritor business families managed six in ten of the largest businesses. Family management implied possibilities for paternalism. Patrick Joyce, one of the few to 'get inside' the culture of the late nineteenth-century factory, argues that 'the paternalism of the family firm was vastly more important than is generally recognised. In the changed technological and cultural environment after mid-century this piecemeal, unsung paternalism cut more deeply into operative life than had the paternalism of the early founders of industry.' Paternalism revived in the late nineteenth century because, he argues, 'it was the paternalist employer who most successfully translated dependence into deference'.[18] The essential elements of this new paternalism were personal relations between master and men; patriarchal provision of moral codes and welfare benefits, outside and inside the factory; dutiful respect and diligence matched by self-help as the appropriate responses of the employee; and all rooted in religion. 'The sense of mission and duty, complementing the new stress on community around mid-century, is to be located in the imperatives of a severe northern religion. It is also to be understood in terms of an almost messianic faith in the civilising power of industry, itself an aspect of the nineteenth century God of Progress.'[19] Of course the big business offered different kinds of possibilities for paternalism from the small factory. Joyce found evidence of 'familiar' and 'feudal' forms. The feudal, with its notion of duties and rights binding the big employer

[16] *Bailie, No.* 1956 (13 Apr. 1910), 1.
[17] *The Times*, 13 Feb. 1915.
[18] P. Joyce, *Work, Society and Politics* (Brighton, 1980), p. xx.
[19] Ibid. 141.

to his workers, caused less resentment than the familiar, the common life-style of the small master and his men.[20]

If paternalism old and new was essentially a set of relationships, it was most visibly expressed in the welfare provisions a company offered its employees—part of management's employment relations, in contrast to its work (workplace) relations or industrial (trade union) relations, as defined by Howard Gospel.[21] A whole range of options was available: profit-sharing, employee housing, pensions, self-improvement facilities for the employee, schooling for his children, medical and recreational provisions, and religious facilities. Few large and expanding companies did not offer some combination of these. They were bestowed at the behest of the company directors, who welcomed the chance of combining benevolence with instrumentality. Joseph Melling emphasizes the latter: 'each welfare service is designed, or functions, to meet the basic labour requirements of the employer: namely, supply, efficiency and discipline'.[22] Starting from Chandler's insights on managerial corporations, Robert Fitzgerald discovered a more complex interaction at work. He found a difference between industrial welfare in natural monopolies like railways and industrial welfare in competitive trades like most of the manufacturing industries. Natural monopolies, and especially those that were highly capitalized, needed to invest more in the stability and reliability of their workforces. Market control enabled them to plan long term. Managerial hierarchies induced more structured and rational welfare schemes, to reward managers as much as shop-floor employees.[23] These findings lead to the expectation that most large companies, at the turn of the century, would be continuing their *ex gratia* welfare policies while a minority would be developing regulated schemes managed by a welfare department.

Several questions arise. To what extent were the big businesses of 1907 paternalistic? Did they evince feudal paternalism? Or was their paternalism moving into another stage, that of the rational welfare scheme? Was such a scheme more likely to arise in a managerial hierarchy than in a family firm? Most germane to this study, were religious structures utilized as instruments of paternalism? Any adequate answer to

[20] Ibid. 161.

[21] H. Gospel, 'Managerial Structure and Strategies', in H. Gospel and C. Littler (eds.), *Managerial Strategies and Industrial Relations* (London, 1983).

[22] J. L. Melling, 'British Employers and the Development of Industrial Welfare' (Glasgow Ph.D., 1980), 16.

[23] R. Fitzgerald, *British Labour Management and Industrial Welfare, 1846–1939* (Beckenham, 1988).

these questions would require a separate study. The last question must occupy attention here. On this, evidence about the companies in the 1 in 10 sample is unfortunately slight. What is available can be quickly presented, starting with the firms run by managerial hierarchies, the railways and Singer.

The London & North Western Railway had a long history of paternalism and of welfare schemes, primarily in the town where it located its locomotive works, Crewe.[24] And religious weapons certainly had been in their armoury of welfare provisions. In the intensely sectarian battleground of nineteenth-century education, the LNWR directors consistently favoured the established church rather than the Nonconformists, from 1842 when construction of the town's first church and school commenced until 1887 when the last denominational school was opened. After the 1870 Education Act, however, the company subordinated its religious preferences to economic ones. The rational basis of this new policy was bluntly announced by Lord Stalbridge the LNWR chairman in 1894: 'What is done at Crewe ... in subscribing to schools, is only done after most careful consideration as to whether it is cheaper for the shareholders to pay a subscription or to pay the rate necessary to support a school board, the only consideration moving the directors being the economy which can be effected to the shareholders.'[25]

Stalbridge, fourth son of the 2nd Marquess of Westminster and one of the few peers in big business in 1907, had made his reputation in politics as Gladstone's Chief Whip in the 1880s. He had been a director of the LNWR since 1870 and became chairman in 1891. Inheriting a rigid attitude towards trade unions and collective bargaining from his predecessor, Sir Richard Moon, he readily adopted the paternalist tradition established on the LNWR.[26] His obituary recalled him as 'more than a shareholders' chairman. He felt keenly the responsibilities of the company towards the great army of men—over 80,000—in its employment, and as chairman furthered a number of beneficent schemes which advanced the welfare of the employees.'[27] Three were recorded: the LNWR Savings Bank (set up in 1895) which guaranteed 3.5 per cent interest; the supplementation (in 1900) of the superannuation fund of

[24] W. H. Chaloner, *The Social and Economic Development of Crewe, 1780–1923* (Manchester, 1950), ch. 2.

[25] Ibid. 61–2, 222–8.

[26] For Richard de Aquila Grosvenor, 1st Baron Stalbridge, see *Complete Peerage*; *The Times*, 20 May 1912; G. Alderman, *The Railway Interest* (Leicester, 1973), 116–19, 209.

[27] *The Times*, 20 May 1912.

the salaried staff (10,000 employees) with a widows' and employees' fund; and in 1897 'the conversion of the entire system of the LNWR into an ambulance centre of the St John Ambulance Association'.[28] Stalbridge acted as president of the last-named and personally distributed awards at annual meetings. This was as far as he allowed any of his Church of England convictions to express themselves in business—in contrast to his predecessor Moon whose strong Anglicanism led him to oppose the extension of Sunday train services.[29] Sir Frederick Harrison, the general manager of the LNWR in 1907, was probably an Anglican also—his second wife was the daughter of a clergyman.[30] Whether this helped his promotion to the position by the LNWR board under Stalbridge in 1893 is doubtful because Harrison had been moving much earlier in his career up the rungs that led to the top.[31]

It is most unlikely that the experience of the Cheshire Lines Committee was any different from that of the LNWR at the turn of the century. From the mid-1880s, when Liberalism became more radical, railway boards swung to the Right, as Geoffrey Alderman has shown. Stalbridge was exceptional in being both a leader of the railway interest and a Liberal, but he was a Unionist and a prominent one. More typical was the chairman of the Cheshire Lines Committee, William Lawies Jackson, 1st Baron Allerton, 'a man with a thoroughly Conservative and commercial background'.[32] Jackson, the eldest son of a Leeds leather merchant, was an immensely capable administrator who went into local and national government and bestrode the worlds of politics and industry. He served in Salisbury's first and second governments. In 1895 he was elected chairman of the Great Northern Railway and this took him on to the board of the Cheshire Lines Committee. He was elected deputy chairman of the Railway Companies' Association, the railway directors' parliamentary pressure group (formed in 1867), and succeeded Stalbridge as chairman in 1900. He opposed union recognition.[33] To Jackson, a devout Anglican and high-ranking Freemason,[34] the stance of managerial paternalism would have come easily. His manager, James Pinion, was an Ulsterman whose career was previously spent on railways in Ireland.

[28] Ibid. 18 May 1912.
[29] M. C. Reed, 'Richard Moon', *DBB*.
[30] *WWW*.
[31] *The Times*, 2 Jan. 1915.
[32] Alderman, *Railway Interest*, 119.
[33] Ibid. 119, 186–7, 210, 301.
[34] W. G. Rimmer, 'William Lawies Jackson', *DBB*.

Ill health forced him to resign in 1910 and he died the following year.[35] Not without flair (he put railway-owned steamers on Belfast Lough to improve services), it is unlikely that he would deviate in an area like the paternalistic application of religion (or strict neutrality towards religious issues) from the wishes of a board headed by Jackson but counterbalanced by Sir Alexander Henderson, chairman of the Great Central Railway and son of a devout Presbyterian.[36]

At Clydebank the Singer factory was run by an American manager, Franklin Atwood Park, an austere, aloof, and precise man who seldom went into the factory without his works superintendent through whom he communicated to subordinates. 'Park was small in stature, neatly built and well-dressed. He wore pince-nez spectacles with tinted lenses and used the technique of the piercing glance and "dead pan" face to good effect. He did not speak a dozen words if half a dozen would do.'[37] Above all he was an able administrator. No evidence has been found of his church links, if he had any.

Not surprisingly, in view of its American parentage, Singer under Park deployed *ex gratia* welfare rather than rational schemes. Not until 1947 did the company adopt a contributory pension scheme.[38] A glimpse of the regime governing Singer employees and its implications for welfare provisions is apparent in an episode in the company's industrial relations' record. Until 1911, a time when nationwide syndicalist hopes were stirring workers to a new militancy, industrial relations at Singer had been peaceful. That March a management attempt to cut piecework rates for the unskilled by speeding-up triggered a strike. It spread from department to department, lasted for three weeks, and involved 11,000 workers (the workforce doubled between 1900 and 1914). Ultimately it failed because the engineers capitulated to Park's tactic of holding a plebiscite, of appealing directly to the workers rather than negotiating with their strike committee.[39]

In the context of Singer the episode illustrates the unyielding, hardline approach of American managers: their Taylorite scientific management of work relations was associated with *ad hoc*, *ex gratia* policies in employment relations and opposition to collective bargaining in industrial rela-

---

[35] *Transport* 29 Apr. 1904; Sekon, *Railway Year Book,* 372; *Railway Gazette,* 29 Dec. 1911.

[36] D. Wainwright, *Henderson* (London, 1985), 14.

[37] A. Dorman, 'A History of the Singer Company (UK) Ltd. (Clydebank Factory)' (typescript, 1972), 40.

[38] Ibid. 102.

[39] Ibid. 11–15; I. McLean, *The Legend of Red Clydeside* (Edinburgh, 1983), 100–2.

tions.[40] Park summed up the Singer position to the strike and to its industrial relations when he told the *Glasgow Herald*, 'It is all a matter of public interest. We are fighting a public battle when we oppose the socialistic teaching which is at the bottom of the whole business.'[41] The firm was not opposed to ameliorating the working conditions of its employees but it was adamantly opposed to any disturbance of its relationships with labour, which it placed in a public social context. In this context welfare provisions were distributed as privileges accorded when management deemed fit, not as rights employees might claim when objectively assessed needs qualified them. Run by a professional manager who could be recalled to the USA at any time (Park was recalled in 1912, and promoted to vice-president of Singer, after eight years at Clydebank), there was little or no room for religious instrumentality at the top of the firm. This does not, of course, exclude the possibility of such instrumentality being exercised much lower down the firm, for example, in hiring policies.

What of the six firms where family owners still exerted some sort of paternalist influence in management functions? Here there was the greatest opportunity to exercise religious motives and means for religious or secular ends. In none of the six firms, however, is there evidence that the religious convictions of their chairmen and managing directors spilled over into policies which had religious means or religious ends. This judgement might be altered with more complete information. Even if true, it would not alter the fact that nearly all the chairmen and some of the managing directors had some form of religious affiliation in their private lives—which is hardly surprising given the age in which they lived, and the findings of Table 4.01. It might be speculated that 'religious inputs' were related to their own personal success in business. It might also be guessed that 'religious inputs' played some part in shaping, consciously or subconsciously, their motivations in business decision-making. Neither speculation is susceptible of demonstration, however. All that can be done here is to indicate the nature of the church links and place it alongside what little is known about the individuals' management records with particular attention to welfare policies.

At Kynoch's Arthur Chamberlain was a Unitarian. Like his famous brother Joseph he attended the Church of the Messiah in Broad Street, Birmingham, and like him married into the Kenricks, another prominent Unitarian business family in Birmingham.[42] While Arthur Chamberlain

[40] I use these terms as defined in Gospel, 'Managerial Structure and Strategies'.

[41] Quoted in Dorman, 'History of the Singer Co.', 13.

[42] E. P. Hennock, *Fit and Proper Persons* (London, 1973), 83, 94.

personally was a fearsome figure—characterized by 'an almost pathologi-
cal probity', a detachment that bordered on ruthlessness and a relentless
abhorrence of intemperance—his improvements to working conditions
and welfare were remarkably progressive. With respect to the former,
he was one of the first to cut hours to 48 a week (1894) and he improved
safety standards in areas where explosives were handled. After reading
B. Seebohm Rowntree's classic study *Poverty* (1901), and discovering
that a man, wife, and three children needed a 'minimum necessary expenditure per week' of 21s. 8d.,[43] he increased the minimum wage for adult
male workers to 22s. a week. As for welfare provisions, Chamberlain's
policies at Kynoch's were exemplary for their day. To a sick club (1891)
he added vaccination against smallpox and a convalescent home in the
1900s. Besides sick pay, he awarded staff (but possibly not workers)
14 days' paid holiday after one year's service and a pension after ten
years' service. The sick and needy within his firm, his biographer notes,
especially attracted his attention.[44]

Of the three firms engaged in shipbuilding, Armstrong, Whitworth
seems to have been the most progressive in the area of welfare. A profit-
sharing scheme had been extended from Armstrongs to the new merged
company in 1897.[45] Until their limitations were criticized, mostly by
Fabians, some thought that profit-sharing schemes (paying a fixed share
of company profits in addition to wages and salaries) brought a more
equal distribution between labour and capital of the returns of industry,
a goal of the Christian Socialists.[46] From the employer's point of view
profit-sharing had the powerful attraction of increasing employee loyalty
to the firm while weakening employee allegiance to a union. There were,
however, mixed motives for profit-sharing schemes and their reputation
has been reasserted by recent research (see next chapter). Precisely how
widespread was the scheme at Armstrong, Whitworth is unknown.
Almost certainly, workforce control rather than Christian Socialist ideals
inspired the Armstrong, Whitworth scheme, however. Typifying the
company's industrial relations, and suggestive of its employment relations, was Colonel Henry Dyer, the man appointed by the board to
manage the Whitworth end of the merged firm. In 1897–8 he led the
newly formed Engineering Employers' Federation in its bitter dispute

[43] B. S. Rowntree, *Poverty* (London, 1902; 4th edn., 1902), 110.
[44] Barbara Smith, 'Arthur Chamberlain', *DBB*; Kynoch Ltd., *Under Five Flags, passim.*
[45] Fitzgerald, *British Labour Management*, 166.
[46] R. A. Church, 'Profit-Sharing and Labour Relations in England in the Nineteenth
Century', *International Review of Social History*, 16 (1972), 12.

with the Amalgamated Society of Engineers which severely curbed union strength in the engineering industry.[47]

Although the Armstrong, Whitworth chairman, Sir Andrew Noble, outside business was noted in his later years for pheasant shooting and addiction to Sir Walter Scott's novels rather than religious involvements, his vice-chairman and financial adviser[48] amply compensated for his lack of interest. William Donaldson Cruddas, son of one of Sir William Armstrong's partners, was a very active Anglican. He was a member of the Bishop's Commission on Church Extension following the establishment of the see of Newcastle in 1882. At Elswick, where most of the company's works were located, he built and endowed St Stephen's parish church. At Byker, lower down the Tyne than the Newcastle bridges that Elswick-built ships had to negotiate, and close to the site of new warship yards after 1911, he built and endowed St Mark's parish church. In the city of Newcastle itself he was benefactor and chairman of the Newcastle City Mission. All of which suggests that while Cruddas may have been unwilling or unable to bring religion into the firm, he was determined that church institutions would visibly function in close proximity to the shipyards he helped to direct.[49]

Firms in shipbuilding, an industry in the 1900s characterized by giant single products, assembly production, a skilled workforce, intense competition, and vulnerability to economic cycles, directed their welfare efforts into industrial housing. Until the First World War this was seen as the best instrument for solving labour supply problems.[50] The war pressured the shipbuilders into making stronger efforts to train and retain their skilled men. Hence not until the war did Fairfields have a shipyard canteen or Scott's introduce such facilities for apprentices as a club, indoor and outdoor sports areas, and a lecture hall.[51] The heads of Fairfields and Scott's all had private religious convictions and allegiances but the evidence is lacking to link these to policies within the firm.

Sir William G. Pearce, the largely absentee chairman of Fairfields, died suddenly at the age of 46 from appendicitis at his London home in November 1907.[52] The funeral service, held near his Wiltshire estate,

---

[47] Jonathan H. Zeitlin, 'Henry Clement Swinnerton Dyer', *DBB*.

[48] Whom I have taken as the equivalent of a managing director.

[49] D. J. Rowe, 'William Donaldson Cruddas', *DBB*; for the impending move of warship-building below the Newcastle bridges: *Shipbuilder*, 5 (1910–11), 72.

[50] Fitzgerald, *British Labour Management*, 164–9.

[51] Ibid. 167–8.

[52] *The Times*, 4 Nov. 1907.

left intriguing clues to his religious sympathies.[53] It brought together four clergymen representing rather different forms of polity and church-manship. The Reverend Roger Kirkpatrick, the Church of Scotland parish minister of Govan, presumably represented the Govan community. Of the three Church of England priests who officiated, the local rector was ex officio. However, the other two, brought down from London, were like chalk and cheese. One was Canon Joseph McCormick, Rector of St James's, Piccadilly, 'among the most noted evangelical preachers and pastors of his day'.[54] Presumably Pearce, when in London, attended St James's, one of the most capacious West End churches. The other, the Reverend Stewart Headlam, was a High Churchman without a parish, a prominent Christian Socialist (he founded the Guild of St Matthew in 1877), and a wealthy eccentric. Though he indulged his upper-class tastes for ballet and the theatre, he had a genuine compassion for the working classes, joined the Fabians, and preached (usually in secular Labour Churches) around the *mot*, 'If you want to be a good Christian, you must be something very like a good Socialist.'[55] Headlam had gone up to Trinity College, Cambridge,[56] where Pearce was educated two decades later. Perhaps this was the connection between Sir George and the socialist priest. If the chairman of Fairfields had as intense an interest in socialism as Headlam it was not manifest in Fairfields' management.

The engineering side at Fairfields was in the hands of Alexander (later Sir Alexander) Gracie.[57] All that is known of his church links is that in 1930 he collapsed and died in Westminster Chapel in London's West End (a Congregational pulpit)[58] and that his funeral was held in Westbourne Church, Glasgow, which was in the United Free Church of Scotland before the union of 1929.[59] In life Gracie had few interests outside his industrial ones. One Glasgow weekly commented, 'It is matter for regret that able men like Mr Gracie are too busy in the interests of the industrial army to apply part of their experience and judgment towards the guidance of legislation and the discharge of civic duties.'[60]

[53] Ibid. 8 Nov. 1907.

[54] F. A. Iremonger, *William Temple* (London, 1948), 167.

[55] E. R. Norman, *Church and Society in England, 1779-1970* (Oxford, 1976), 175-9 and *passim*.

[56] *WWW*.

[57] *Bailie*, No. 2077 (7 Aug. 1912), 1-2.

[58] *The Times*, 3 Mar. 1930.

[59] Ibid. 7 Mar. 1930; J. A. Lamb, *The Fasti of the UFCS, 1900-1929* (Edinburgh, 1956), 259.

[60] *Bailie*, No. 2077 (7 Aug. 1912), 2.

Industrial relations under Gracie left much to be desired. Fairfields was one of the shipyards affected by labour disputes during the First World War and an Admiralty observer pronounced, 'The Fairfield Company on the Shipbuilding side, are by a long way the worst timekeepers in the District. I believe it is due largely to methods of management.'[61] For the pre-war decade a recent examination of the Fairfield records shows the firm to have been keenly competitive in most of its naval work (there was evidence of some collusion with other firms), suggesting either that bad management was widespread in shipbuilding or that it was induced at Govan by wartime conditions.[62]

Little is yet known about the management and their welfare strategies at Scott's of Greenock.[63] The chairman, Charles Cuningham Scott, after his marriage switched from his family's Presbyterian allegiance to the Episcopal Church of Scotland.[64] James Brown, the engineering manager at Scott's, a thoroughly trained engineer (a Whitworth Scholar who subsequently worked in yards in England and Spain as well as on the Clyde before joining Scott's[65]), was 'an active and faithful member' of the Finnart Church of Scotland at Greenock but was not an office-bearer.[66]

From his father Sir Henry Doulton, Lewis Doulton inherited an Anglican allegiance and a number of welfare commitments. At Lambeth, where his own father had set up as a potter, Sir Henry, like other employers in the vicinity, had drawn his workforce from the 'formless enormity of South London'.[67] The formation of a company village, and all the opportunities for employee control that offered, was out of the question. Like his neighbouring urban employers he had therefore spread his welfare into the community. Like Barclays the Quaker brewers, he contributed to the London City Mission whose workers 'served as primitive industrial psychologists in their riverside walks'.[68] One of the London City Missionaries ran a Potters' Temperance Society 'along with the benevolent society, maternity society and cricket club at his

[61] Quoted in McLean, *Legend*, 41.

[62] C. More, 'Armaments and Profits', *Business History*, 24 (1982), 175–85.

[63] Mr Johnston Robb of Greenock is planning to write a company history of the firm.

[64] Information from Mrs Helen C. Sutherland, daughter of C. C. Scott, in letter to author, 31 Mar. 1987.

[65] IME, *Proceedings* (1941), 141.

[66] Information from Robin Brown, son of James Brown, in letter from Johnston Robb to author, 19 Apr. 1987.

[67] J. Cox, *The English Churches in a Secular Society* (London, 1982), 112.

[68] Ibid. 113.

Lambeth Walk Mission Hall, and directed his attention in particular to the kilnburners, "a very rough sort".[69] Lewis Doulton evidently maintained something of the personal paternalism by which his father cemented the loyalty of his best craftsmen: 'to the end, Mr Doulton displayed the keenest interest in the welfare of the firm's employees, and it can definitely be said that there are many old servants of the firm, at Lambeth, Stourbridge, and Burslem, as well as in Lancashire and Scotland, who will retain very happy memories of the kindly personal interest which he took in them as individuals—an interest which he never relaxed.' However, the obituary note suggests that he might have been more denominational than his father in some of his welfare activities: 'for many years [he] was a staunch supporter of efforts associated with the Parish Church of Lambeth and a trustee of the Archbishop Temple's Lambeth Boys' School.'[70] Like his father, the focus of his paternal interest was Lambeth, a bias that possibly strained employment relations in a company with plants so widely spread.

The last of the six firms in the sample and known to have family owners among its managers was the Bleachers' Association. A third of its branch managers eligible for commission payments in 1905–6 had surnames identical to the branch they managed; the proportion of family managers was probably rather higher than this.[71] In 1907 its 53 constituent companies were still being welded together by its four-man board of management, which was checked by a finance committee of the board of directors. The company chairman, Herbert Shepherd Cross, was heavily guided by both of these.

Cross, Anglican and Tory and educated at Harrow and Oxford, had run the family bleachworks at Mortfield, Bolton, with his elder brother. After he was elected MP for Bolton in 1881 he bought a London house and left the firm's management largely in his elder brother's hands. At Mortfield the two brothers developed 'the bleachworks estate as extensive, alcohol-free model working-class buildings'.[72] After selling out to the Bleachers' Association and after his brother's death, Shepherd Cross

[69] Ibid.

[70] *Pottery Gazette*, 1 Jan. 1931.

[71] Quarry Bank Mill, Bleachers' Association Papers, item 293, Minutes of the Board of Management, 31 Mar. 1906.

[72] J. J. Mason, 'Herbert Shepherd Cross', *DBB*. In 1910 the Mortfields Bleachworks' dwelling houses numbered only 13 (including one inhabited by Shepherd Cross) plus a farm and two cottages. Quarry Bank Mill, Bleachers' Association Papers, item 376, Inventory of Mortfield Bleachworks, 21.

transferred administration of the Mortfield branch to a professional manager.[73]

What happened to welfare provisions when the Bleachers' Association took over the Mortfield company village and presumably a number of similar sets of welfare arrangements in the other constituent firms? The picture is unclear and changed slowly until after the First World War. One works applied to the board of management for permission to obtain a lease for land for a bowling club. In 1906 the board of management decided that with respect to agreements with employees 'In future all such agreements to be under the seal of the Subsidiary Company', suggesting the decentralization of labour relations. On the other hand, when these threatened the commercial interests of the whole group, a centralized policy was imposed. Thus when the question of works holidays arose, 'The Board feel that the Manchester holidays and arrangements are more important to the Association as Bleachers than the local holidays, and arrangements for the operatives should (if possible) be made in accordance therewith.'[74] After the First World War the various local welfare arrangements were rationalized into company-wide schemes. These covered superannuation, pensions, two showpiece company villages, and at many works canteens, social clubs, bowling greens, and tennis courts. All this was the work of the Association's third chairman, Sir Alan Sykes, a tepid Anglican. His biographer concludes, 'Behind all these initiatives lay perhaps less a philosophy of business than an attempt to recreate in the Bleachers' Association the paternalism of the family firm and the comradeship and co-operation which Sykes had valued in the freemasons and Volunteers.'[75]

The firm-level evidence for religious interventions, either as means or ends, in big businesses before the First World War therefore suggests several conclusions. First, that most chairmen and managing directors had in their private lives some kind of church adherence, most often Anglican. Second, that they did not extend their religious convictions into their firms in an overt way, either using them as an instrument to control employees or by making the firm an arena for religious proselytizing. Third, if, as Joyce contends, paternalism was an expression of religious concern, then nearly all firms were associated with this. Any

[73] The formula adopted was 'Mr Vickers should have full control of both sides of the Works subject to Mr H. Shepherd Cross': so the interference of the original family owner was not excluded. Quarry Bank Mill, Bleachers' Association Papers, item 293, Minutes of the Board of Management, 8 Feb. 1907.

[74] Ibid. 28 Mar. 1905, 26 Oct. 1906, 8 Feb. 1907.

[75] A. C. Howe, 'Alan John Sykes', *DBB*.

test or evidence of religious commitment is almost impossible to demonstrate, however. Welfare was in the self-interest of employers regardless of their religious or non-religious sensibilities. Clearly there were differences between the paternalism projected by family owners and that administered by a managerial corporation like a railway company. The major difference with respect to firm-based religious means and ends is that the family owner-managers had much more scope than professional managers. Large-scale firms with strong managerial hierarchies, especially those with near-monopoly control of their markets, rationalized their welfare schemes as Fitzgerald found, and in these schemes religious and political elements had no overt place. In the other sort of firm it seems that even the most pious of family owner-managers, like Cruddas at Newcastle, was either unwilling or unable to do more than make provision for religious worship close to shipyard or factory gates. Actually, it was still possible in a family-owned firm to bring religious means and ends to bear as will be shown in the next chapter. Detailed work might unearth more cases. The sampling method deployed in this chapter, however, suggests that the intensity and length of William Lever's religious shadow was rarely found in big business in the 1900s.

2 PERSPECTIVES ON ISSUES

The question of religion in big firms can be examined from the angle of issues as well as of firms. Perhaps the issues which most divided businessmen from church leaders by the 1890s lay in the area of labour relations. What position should, and did, church-connected big businessmen adopt when pressed by their church leaders to bring labour questions into the arena of theological debate? Did Christian convictions and principles prevail over commercial interests? Reaching a generalized answer would require the construction of test samples of committed churchmen and non-religious businessmen, all faced with roughly similar sets of business circumstances and decisions. Even if this were done satisfactorily the results could be interpreted differently. Laying off workers could be condemned as a ruthless capitalist technique or justified as beneficial for long-term employment prospects, as R. H. Campbell has argued.[76]

Some comparisons may be made. By juxtaposing contrasting groups of churchmen in the business élite of 1907 and gauging their willingness to bring Christian principles (however they may have perceived them)

[76] R. H. Campbell, 'A Critique of the Christian Businessman and His Paternalism', in D. J. Jeremy (ed.), *Business and Religion in Britain* (Aldershot, 1988).

into their labour policies, the role of religion in business may be better assessed. The evidence is limited and often incomplete. Consequently more detailed work may produce modified conclusions. The two groups chosen for comparison are the Anglicans and Quakers, quantitatively the largest in the élite—the Anglicans absolutely and the Quakers relatively. Attaining valid comparisons is rendered difficult by differing levels of churchmanship as well as differing industrial circumstances. Anglicans shaded down to those with a nominal allegiance scarcely distinguishable from the habits of a non-churchgoer. Even Quakers became 'worldly'.[77]

Two sets of Anglican and Quaker industrialists have been identified for comparative purposes:

(a) Quakers and Anglicans in the old industries of coal-mining, iron and steel, and related industries in the North-East of England. By the last quarter of the nineteenth century these industries faced stiffening foreign competition intensified by cyclical depressions. The favoured entrepreneurial response was to cut back on labour costs, the most easily reducible costs, in an attempt to support profit margins. Since the region had a strong tradition of religious adherence many industrialists inherited and held distinctive religious beliefs.

(b) Quakers and Anglicans in new and expanding industries with little or no foreign competition and growing domestic markets associated with Britain's rising standard of living. Such industries, like food processing and electrical goods manufacturing, utilities and retail distribution, most rapidly developed in the Midlands and South of England where London was a major market. While the religious features of these regions defy simple characterization, some of the industries, like food processing and retailing, were favoured by Quakers if not Nonconformists (see Prologue to Part III).

(a) Quakers and Anglicans in the old industries of the North-East

Five company chairmen and five managing directors (or their equivalents) had Anglican associations and centred their activities in the North-East in 1907. Of the former, Sir Benjamin Chapman Browne[78] of Hawthorn, Leslie & Co.; George Burton Hunter[79] of Swan, Hunter & Wigham Richardson; and Sir Andrew Noble of Armstrong, Whitworth

---

[77] T. A. B. Corley, 'How Quakers Coped with Business Success', in Jeremy (ed.), *Business and Religion*.

[78] J. F. Clarke, 'Benjamin Chapman Browne', *DBB*.

[79] J. F. Clarke, 'George Burton Hunter', *DBB*.

were shipbuilders; Arthur Dorman[80] of Dorman, Long was a steelmaster; and James Joicey,[81] Baron Joicey of Chester-le-Street, of Sir James Joicey & Co., a coalmaster. The managing directors were William Cruddas of Armstrong, Whitworth; Malcolm Dillon[82] of Palmers Shipbuilding & Iron Co.; John Wigham Richardson,[83] Hunter's ageing associate, all shipbuilders; and Arthur Dorman (his own managing director) and Walter William Storr[84] of Bolckow Vaughan, both iron and steel men. All the shipbuilders ran yards on the Tyne; Joicey's colliery empire was also headquartered at Newcastle; the two steelmen operated further south on the Tees at Middlesbrough. On their churchmanship, Browne was High Church, Hunter was Evangelical, Cruddas associated with Evangelical causes, Richardson was an ex-Quaker, Noble inclined to be tepid. Of the five positions held by Quakers in the 1907 business élite two were in the North-East. Arthur Francis Pease, chairman and managing director of the much-troubled Pease & Partners at Darlington on Teesside,[85] was probably still loyal to his clan's Quakerism.[86]

The challenge for industrialists of Christian principle to develop distinctive policies towards labour occurred as the coal industry experienced a secular price fall beginning in 1873. Cyclical collapses affected all staple trades and in coal especially led to confrontations with organized labour. The example of Sir Joseph Pease, head of the Pease empire of banking, coalmining, iron, railway, and woollen interests, suggested an enlightened, benevolent stance. He was among the first employers in the North-East coal industry to accept the principle of trade union recognition (providing the unions promoted 'the orderly functioning of the labour market').[87] Impelled as much by a deep Quaker-inspired concern to keep his employees at work as by an outlook shaped by mid-Victorian liberalism and prosperity, he propped up a number of loss-making subsi-

[80] Jonathan S. Boswell, 'Arthur John Dorman', *DBB*.

[81] A. A. Hall, 'James Joicey', *DBB*; in 1918 Joicey was invited to join the Organization Committee of the Church Board of Finance but declined; he nevertheless allowed his name to be used by the CBF and subscribed £5,000 to the CBF's Central Church Fund. (CHA, CBF/ORG/MEN/Jo, Joicey to Revd J. H. Ellison, 13 Apr. 1918, Joicey to Revd Frank Partridge, 12 Oct. 1918; CBF/ORG/SAC/2, undated 'List of Subscriptions of £100 and over').

[82] Erickson Workcards.

[83] J. F. Clarke, 'John Wigham Richardson', *DBB*.

[84] Erickson Workcards.

[85] M. C. Kirby, *Men of Business and Politics* (London, 1984), 91–116.

[86] M. W. Kirby, 'The Failure of a Quaker Business Dynasty', in Jeremy (ed.), *Business and Religion*, 159.

[87] Ibid. 152.

diaries for three decades, far longer than long-term commercial interests dictated. He might have succeeded had not early deaths carried off his ablest successors and a fortune-hunting peer made off with one of the family heiresses, taking her cash out of the partnership's reserves.[88] The crunch came in 1902 when Barclay & Co., the recently formed merger of Quaker banking partnerships, offered to take over the Peases' Darlington bank of J. & J. W. Pease. Negotiations necessarily involved the examination of accounts. To the horror of the Peases, William B. Peat the distinguished accountant pronounced the bank insolvent. The firm was only spared from bankruptcy by a guarantee fund launched by Sir Christopher Furness, the Teesside industrialist and a member of the United Methodist Free Churches,[89] to which numerous North-East industrialists, including Arthur Dorman, subscribed large sums. Their actions were 'a result of sentiment and considerations of commercial stability in the region'.[90]

Insolvency forced the resignation of septuagenarian Sir Joseph Pease and his two sons from the board of Pease & Partners. They gave up many of their public offices and sold their estates. One son even borrowed money from servants. In humiliation Sir Joseph went to live with an unmarried daughter in Cornwall and died within six months of the firm's collapse. His only consolation was to hear that the Guisborough Monthly Meeting, as was customary, had investigated his business failure, deeply regretted the calamity, and concluded 'that the Pease family had not forfeited the respect of the meeting'.[91]

The Pease débâcle served as an object lesson. A Quakerly concern for the interests of labour might be put above the interests of capital in a situation of industrial growth: it was inappropriate when a business or industry faced long-term erosion of profitability. The lesson was quickly learned by the remaining Peases themselves. When Sir Joseph's nephew Arthur Francis Pease took over as chairman and managing director on the death of Sir David Dale in 1906, a new order began. He became a leading figure in the Durham Coal Owners' Association and made public pronouncements fully in keeping with the policy of the employers' association (the Mining Association of Great Britain) to the effect that 'the objective economic conditions of the industry dictated that wage reductions in response to depressed selling prices were no

[88] Kirby, *Men of Business*, 73–116, esp. 87 on motivation.
[89] Gordon Boyce, 'Christopher Furness', *DBB*; Methodist UMFC, *Minutes of the Assembly* (London, 1907), 269.
[90] Kirby, *Men of Business*, 107.
[91] Kirby, 'Failure', 158.

longer a matter for negotiation, and that in the event of trade union opposition colliery owners should resort to the tactics of the lock-out'.[92] To the Sankey Commission in 1919 he gave evidence, which did not always stand up to logical probing, against the possibility of the coal industry either being nationalized or merged in a large combine.[93] The proprietors' propensity towards intransigent sectionalism, which Sir Joseph long resisted, had won the day.

The example of the Peases was not lost on Anglican industrialists in the North-East. While they were happy to support church extension funds they declined to accept the ideas of the Christian Socialists as principles by which to run their firms. For example, Arthur Dorman, at Middlesbrough, donated a peal of bells to Saltburn parish church in 1902 in memory of his brother, personally gave at least £1,000 to Archbishop Lang's church extension fund in 1911, and committed his firm to giving £1,000 to that scheme. He did what he could in a marginal way when a national coal strike forced the Middlesbrough steelmasters in 1912 to lay off many of their regular men: Dorman, Long paid them 10s. a week—but it was to be paid back in easy instalments when work resumed.

Despite these expressions of benevolence towards the church and labour, Arthur Dorman evidently believed in the separation of business and religion when it came to tackling industrial unrest. At the 1912 Church Congress held at Middlesbrough, in a session on 'The Industrial Unrest: Causes and Remedies' chaired by Lang, the Archbishop of York was forced publicly to regret that the town had

not produced either a working man or an employer who, when the Church Congress asked them to consider these questions, had something to say about them. That reveals, I think, our very great weakness, that we want a much larger number both of our employers and working men to try to think out these questions on their moral as well as economic grounds, and to give us, bishops and clergy, the guidance which we so often need.[94]

As a recent investigator, Peter Stubley, comments, 'Where we may ask, was the ironmaster, Arthur Dorman, later described as "a committed churchman"? Where, for that matter, were any of the other ironmasters who had served on the Archbishop's Church Extension Committee from

---

[92] Ibid. 159.

[93] *PP* (1919) XI, Cmd. 359, pp. 303–12.

[94] C. Dunkley (ed.), *The Official Report of the Church Congress 1912* (London, 1912), 75.

1909 to 1911?'[95] At that same Church Congress, to which both Lang and Gore (the Christian Socialist) contributed papers, Sir Benjamin Browne sent in an address in which he defined the duty of the church: 'Let her more and more teach employers and workmen to sympathise with each other's difficulties and to smooth each other's path.'[96] Neither the clerics nor Browne clarified how this would be done. None of the other Anglican business leaders, large employers of labour, took the opportunity to discuss with church leaders where Christian principles might be applicable to their situation as captains of industry. Explaining this in the case of Anglican businessmen in the North-East requires some reference to secular business difficulties in the older industries of coal, iron and steel, and shipbuilding which dominated the region. It may also be related to popular anti-clericalism. As much as trade unionists, businessmen resented interfering parsons. Albert Vickers, head of the Sheffield competitor of Armstrong, Whitworth, expressed the sentiment : 'I have never given anything to a Church since the Engineers' Strike of 1898, when the parsons most wickedly took the side of the men without knowing anything about it.'[97]

(b)   Quakers and Anglicans in the new industrial sectors of the Midlands and the South

The most prominent of the Quakers holding five positions in the 1907 élite was George Cadbury, effectively the senior managing director as well as chairman of the family cocoa manufacturing firm in Birmingham.[98] In the same business but near Bristol, Joseph Storrs Fry[99] chaired the family firm (the religious affiliation of his associate Francis James Fry has defied identification). With an 80 per cent rise in average real wages in the UK between 1850 and 1900, cocoa manufacturers, like sugar refiners, clearly benefited from the rise in disposable incomes.[100] What men of Christian principle might do in an industry enjoying

---

[95] P. Stubley, 'The Churches and the Iron and Steel Industry in Middlesbrough, 1890–1914' (Durham MA, 1979), 66–8, 110, 116.

[96] C. Dunkley (ed.), The Official Report of the Church Congress, 1912, 63.

[97] Cambridge University Library, Vickers Archives 1006, Albert Vickers to Mrs E. Dunn, 20 Sept. 1910: a reference I owe to Dr R. P. T. Davenport-Hines.

[98] Basil G. Murray, 'George Cadbury', DBB. See also C. Dellheim, 'The Creation of a Company Culture: Cadburys, 1861–1931', American Historical Review, 92 (1987).

[99] Gillian Wagner, 'Joseph Storrs Fry', DBB.

[100] B. R. Mitchell and P. Deane, Abstract of British Historical Statistics (Cambridge, 1962), 343–4, 356–7.

steadily rising demand and comfortable profits was illustrated by their firms.

From the start of his experimental industrial community at Bournville, Birmingham, in 1893–4, George Cadbury rejected the traditional concept of the company village as an instrument of employee discipline and control. He sold his first 140 houses at Bournville at cost price on 999-year leases. Only when the leaseholders sold their houses at a profit—of between 10 and 20 per cent—did George modify the contractual arrangement. Even so, he imposed a legal separation between village and factory. In 1900 he conveyed the whole estate of 330 acres and 313 houses, property valued at £172,724, to trustees responsible to the Charity Commissioners. Although members of the Cadbury family formed the first Bournville Village Trust, and George himself was chairman, the Trust Deed guaranteed the execution of the founder's wishes: 'of alleviating the evils which arise from the insanitary and insufficient accommodation supplied to large numbers of the working classes, and of securing to the workers in factories some of the advantages of outdoor village life, with opportunities for the natural and healthful occupation of cultivating the soil'.[101] Under the Bournville Village Trust a series of co-partnership and housing societies developed the estates built after 1900, the Trust ensuring that they were mostly affordable by working-class tenants, that they were well designed and landscaped, and that they were let or leased at break-even rates. In sharp contrast to William Lever's Port Sunlight, the other company-associated large-scale housing experiment of the day, Bournville was emphatically not a company town, a tool of the employer, but a garden village, the inviolate environ of families from a mixture of classes. Working conditions at Bournville, described in detail by George's son Edward in 1912 and recently reinterpreted as a form of scientific management, were among the most enlightened of their day. For example, the firm abolished fines in 1898, replacing them with record keeping and piece rates. Employees, carefully screened on recruitment, were treated humanely and not simply as adjuncts to machines.[102]

Religious convictions undeniably informed George Cadbury's vision and his Bournville experiment. His theology of Man and society derived largely from his reading of the Bible and his years as an Adult School teacher. In 1906 he told a committee of Church of England bishops,

---

[101] Bournville Village Trust, *The Bournville Village Trust, 1900–1955* (Bournville, 1955), 10.

[102] E. Cadbury, *Experiments in Industrial Organization* (London, 1912); M. Rowlinson, 'The Early Application of Scientific Management by Cadbury' *Business History*, 30 (1988),' 377–95.

'Largely through my experience among the back streets of Birmingham I have been brought to the conclusion that it is impossible to raise a nation, morally, physically and spiritually in such surroundings, and that the only effective way is to bring men out of the cities into the country and to give every man his garden where he can come into touch with nature and thus know more of nature's God.'[103] Edenic encounters were made more likely at Bournville because George Cadbury from the start insisted on the professional landscaping of the estates and on ample gardens for each house. Himself a vegetarian, he believed that the garden was almost as important as the house itself. During his lifetime Bournville gardens averaged 600 square yards and, it was discovered from a survey in the early 1900s, residents were cultivating garden produce valued at 2s. 6d. a week throughout the year, the equivalent of a third of an average rent.

At the heart of Cadbury's ideal for an industrial village was the family. When the bishops asked George Cadbury, 'What is the supreme joy you get out of life?' he replied, 'God placed man in families and man's truest joy ought to be in his own home.' He nevertheless added that exclusive devotion to family brought a man 'nothing like the same amount of joy as if he gave up some time and labour for the good of others'.[104] At Bournville therefore he deliberately fostered mixed housing, siting more expensive homes (appropriate to managers) between clusters of smaller, basic houses (intended for working-class families). He set up a Village Council to run social activities (though this rather overlapped at times with the societies at the works) and he provided a number of social amenities. Not as numerous as those at Port Sunlight, they included shops, schools (built in 1905 and administered by the Local Education Authority), recreation grounds, and a meeting house for religious worship. Of course Bournville benefited only a few thousand people—at George's death the village comprised nearly 1,500 houses. For this reason he was anxious to see that his experiment was widely emulated. To incite replication he had to demonstrate that the village was not a charitable concern but an affordable proposition, both for the householder and the operating Trust. This he did but, despite much publicity, no other non-Quaker heads of big business in the UK copied Cadbury's trust-controlled, large-scale industrial community. Instead the potential of the garden village was promoted by Ebenezer Howard (a Congregationalist) and those associated with him in the Garden City

---

[103] A. G. Gardiner, *The Life of George Cadbury* (London, 1925), 107.
[104] Ibid. 108.

movement, eventually in such communities as Letchworth, Welwyn Garden City, and Hampstead Garden Suburb.[105]

George Cadbury's most overt religious act in his business life was the holding of morning prayers at the beginning of each working day. The practice started in 1866, when George adopted it from Joseph Storrs Fry in Bristol. Essentially it was an extension of the middle-class Victorian practice of family prayers.[106] In many a small business, where employees lived with their master, it was not uncommon. Cadbury simply carried it over into the factory when he still employed a small (between 70 and 80 in number) workforce. The service began with a Scripture reading, followed by silence for prayer. Later a hymn accompanied by an organ was added. The daily service continued for thirty years. In accordance with George Cadbury's principles, particularly his commitment to religious liberty, the services were strictly undenominational. They were a moment of worship, not an opportunity for evangelism. When, eventually, accommodation became a problem the workforce was divided into three and each section attended worship on a weekly basis. The services remained popular throughout much of George Cadbury's lifetime, with the men's committee requesting the management committee in 1911 that 'in the absence of the directors, one of the local clergy or ministers should be invited to conduct the service'. Dean Kitchin in 1910 recorded his memory of one visit: 'It was a women's day . . . the short reading, kind words and simple prayer, preceded by a hymn sung by three thousand women's voices, was a revelation of religious purity and simplicity at full force.'[107] Around the time of the First World War morning service in the factory lapsed.[108] An example has also been found of George offering encouragement to one of his young salesmen (and presumably fellow Quaker) by sharing a scriptural text with him on the occasion of his first sales trip.[109]

These examples illustrated George Cadbury's treatment of labour at home. His moral intervention with one section of the firm's cocoa suppliers showed how far he was prepared to go in subordinating business to religious principles abroad. In 1901 the board of Cadbury Brothers Ltd. received reports that their supplies of cocoa from the Portuguese

[105] E. Gauldie, *Cruel Habitations* (London, 1974), ch. 16.
[106] G. M. Young (ed.), *Early Victorian England, 1830–1865* (Oxford, 1934), ii. 49.
[107] Gardiner, *George Cadbury*, 29.
[108] *George Cadbury, 1839–1922: Memorial Number of the Bournville Works Magazine* (1922), 47.
[109] Dellheim, 'Creation', 34.

West African islands of São Tomé and Príncipe, off the coast of equatorial Africa, were cultivated by slave labour.[110] São Tomé (whose name denominated both islands) produced a sixth of the world's supply of cocoa, the crop being 'not the finest in the world, but useful to the manufacturer because of the excellence and great regularity of its preparation' and in price ranked with South American cocoa. No more than a third of the São Tomé crop was exported to Britain.[111] Yet it was a major source for British manufacturers. Cadburys imported 45 per cent of their cocoa supplies from the Portuguese islands in 1901, a proportion which peaked at 60 per cent in 1903.[112] See Table 4.1.

TABLE 4.1. *Cadburys' imports of cocoa from São Tomé, 1900–1908*

	Coca from São Tomé (tons)	% of firm's UK consumption	Total output of São Tomé (tons of 1,000 kilos)	% of world output
1900	2,547	45.2		
1901	3,248	54.7		
1902	3,414	52.2	17,619	14.27
1903	3,941	60.2		
1904	3,498	56.8		
1905	2,937	48.2		
1906	2,803	47.2		
1907	3,122	49.5		
1908	1,979	32.1		
1912			36,012	15.52

Sources: Cadbury Ltd. Archives, Committee of Management minutes, minute 204, 15 Mar. 1910; Arthur W. Knapp, *The Cocoa and Chocolate Industry* (London, 1930), 169.

As James Duffy has shown,[113] in England the question of West African slavery after 1900 drew together three distinct groups whose interests at times conflicted. The Anti-Slavery Society, heavily supported by Quakers, resumed harsh attacks on the Portuguese Government and planters. The British Foreign Office, concerned to preserve the supply of African labourers from Portuguese Mozambique to South Africa, responded cautiously, even equivocally. The English cocoa manufacturers—Cadburys, Frys, and Rowntrees, all Quakers—shared a passionate and historic hostility towards slavery. However, until they had irrefutable proof that contract labour had degenerated into slavery they could not justify boycotting São Tomé cocoa. After all, contract

[110] W. A. Cadbury, *Labour in Portuguese West Africa* (London, 1910).

[111] W. A. Cadbury, *Labour*, 2.

[112] Cadbury Ltd., Archives, Committee of Management minutes, minute 204, 15 Mar. 1910. I am grateful to Sir Adrian Cadbury and Mr Basil Murray for this data.

[113] J. Duffy, *A Question of Slavery* (Oxford, 1967), chs. 7 and 8.

labour was employed under British rule in the Transvaal. The urgent task for the English cocoa manufacturers, therefore, was to find irrefutable evidence to decide the question and meantime handle the matter as discreetly as possible.

The Cadbury board took the lead in attempting to square conscience with commerce. They voted £1,000 towards investigation costs. William Adlington Cadbury, George's nephew and fellow director, was assigned the task of resolving the issue. He went to Lisbon in 1903 to meet planters and the British Ambassador. When these meetings failed to settle the question he sent an independent (but Quaker) agent, Joseph Burtt, to São Tomé. Burtt spent ten months in Lisbon learning Portuguese before setting out for São Tomé in June 1905. Accompanied by Dr W. Claude Horton of Birmingham he travelled on to Angola in 1906 and returned home in April 1907 with a report that had cost over £3,000 to assemble.[114] Its verdict: contract labour was tantamount to slave labour.[115] Burtt signalled his findings ahead of his report. The Anti-Slavery Society wanted action. At their instigation they and the manufacturers met the Foreign Secretary in October 1906. George Cadbury wanted a gunboat to collect conclusive evidence. Sir Edward Grey would have none of that. Diplomatic moves were the best way forward and the cocoa manufacturers ought to postpone their planned boycott.[116] The catalyst of crisis appears to have been H. W. Nevinson, a former reporter with the *Daily News*, the Liberal newspaper partly owned by George Cadbury. He might have taken the commission given to Burtt but was unprepared to spend time learning Portuguese.[117] Instead he speedily went out to the islands, suffered from fever most of the time,[118] and on returning published *A Modern Slavery* (1906) which brought the issue to the public's attention. It failed, however to catch headlines though interest was mounting.[119] Indeed George Cadbury and the other directors of the *Daily News* instructed its editor to withold any mention of the São Tomé affair because they 'were afraid it might wreck the

[114] *BDP*, 1 Dec. 1909. George Cadbury estimated the cost of the Burtt Commission as £2,819 including a fee of £700 to Burtt. This sum was borne by the four cocoa manufacturers, Cadbury, Fry, Rowntree, and Stollwerck. Later Messrs Cadbury paid Burtt another £500.

[115] Ibid. 4 Dec. 1909. I am grateful for the help of Sir Adrian Cadbury and the Cadbury Ltd. Librarian Mrs Helen Davies for locating and supplying the reports of the Cadbury libel action which appeared in the *BDP*, 29 Nov.–7 Dec. 1909.

[116] Ibid. 1 Dec. 1909.

[117] G. Wagner, *The Chocolate Conscience* (London, 1987), 91.

[118] *BDP*, 3 Dec. 1909.

[119] Wagner, *Chocolate Conscience*, 91–3.

work we were trying to do'.[120] Still the matter was unresolved. William A. Cadbury had visited Lisbon again in 1905 and still the Portuguese Government and planters procrastinated. Ultimately in autumn 1908 he decided to go to São Tomé and the accessible parts of Angola guided by Burtt, dispatching a secret agent into the difficult interior. On 26 September 1908, just as Cadbury and Burtt were about to sail for West Africa, the storm the manufacturers dreaded burst upon them. The Conservative *Evening Standard* accused the firm of profiting from and being indifferent to the 'monstrous trade in human flesh and blood against which the Quaker and Radical ancestors of Mr Cadbury thundered in the better days of England'.[121] George Cadbury was forced to defend the name of his family and firm and brought a libel action against the *Standard*. It was now more imperative than ever to settle the São Tomé question.

Fortunately, William had already arranged for someone familiar with the language and geography of Angola to travel around the interior and investigate charges of slavery without attracting notice or arousing antagonism. This was the Brethren missionary Charles Albert Swan (1861–1934), with whom William Cadbury had been in touch for several years. Swan, converted as a muscular young clerk in Sunderland, had been captivated by Livingstone's missionary vision for Africa and had gone out to Angola in 1886 in search of Frederick Stanley Arnot, the pioneer Brethren missionary. He had found Arnot and remained to work among the tribes of the interior until 1903 when he and his wife had moved to Lisbon. Here, probably, they first met William Cadbury.[122]

Echoes of Service, the Brethren missionary newsletter for prayer partners edited from Bath, carried in its issue of September 1908 a rather mysterious announcement: 'Some friends in England have requested Mr Swan to pay a short visit to Central Africa to obtain information on certain special matters, the character of which is not advisable to state *till his return*.' It explained that Swan 'our brother' would have 'valuable opportunities for service amongst both Portuguese and natives' and be enabled to visit 'those with whom he was associated in service for many years': for these reasons Swan viewed the opportunity 'as of the Lord'. Swan, it informed, would be leaving Lisbon for Lobito on 1 October.[123]

According to plan, Swan reached Angola and toured the mission

[120] *BDP*, 4 Dec. 1909.

[121] Gardiner, *George Cadbury*, 226.

[122] A. G. Ingleby, *Pioneer Days in Darkest Africa* (London, 1946); C. A. Swan, *The Slavery of To-Day* (Glasgow, 1909).

[123] BUL, Cadbury Papers, 180/93.

stations of five societies working in the interior. William Cadbury secretly paid all his expenses, communicated with him only through the *Echoes of Service* editorial office, and ordered him to destroy all their correspondence when he returned from Angola.[124] By April 1909 Swan was on his way back to Lisbon aboard the SS *Portugal* having gathered testimonies from missionaries and natives 'embodying the points suggested by you [William Cadbury] & T. B. [Travers Buxton] ... backing the same up with scores of actual cases which have come under their [the missionaries'] observation, giving names of persons & places &c', even photographs—the very information Travers Buxton and Mackie the British Consul at Loanda had never secured (possibly because the missionaries preferred to protest directly to the Portuguese).[125]

All the incontestable evidence assembled by William Cadbury and Joseph Burtt on one hand and Charles Swan and western missionaries on the other came before the public in spring and summer 1909. In May Cadbury published his *Labour in Portuguese West Africa*. On 2 June Swan presented a copy of his report to the Foreign Office. On 22 June a letter condemning Portuguese contract labour as slavery and signed by 19 missionaries in Angola was published in *The Times*. In August Swan's report was published as *The Slavery of To-Day*.

The receipt of Swan's evidence made the cocoa manufacturers' boycott of the São Tomé producers, announced in March 1909, permanent. Yet even before conclusive proof of slavery arrived from Charles Swan the board of Cadbury Brothers had started to look for ways of replacing their Portuguese suppliers. In 1907 they dispatched one of their expert contacts from Trinidad to the British West African colony of the Gold Coast to explore the potential of the indigenous cocoa crop. In December 1908 the first shipment of Gold Coast cocoa, a mere eight tons, arrived at Bournville. William Cadbury visited the Gold Coast on his way back from Angola early in 1909.[126] By 1912 the Gold Coast was producing more cocoa beans than São Tomé, indeed it had become the world's largest supplier and in the 1920s accounted for 40 per cent of the world's cocoa.[127] A short-term commercial reversal in the interests of moral principle had produced a lasting business advantage.

[124] BUL, Cadbury Papers, 180/916, 918, 926, William Cadbury to Swan, 20 Apr. 4 May, and 5 July 1909. For this Brethren network see R. Coad, *A History of the Brethren Movement* (2nd edn., London, 1976), 220.

[125] BUL, Cadbury Papers, 180/914, Swan to William Cadbury, 3 Apr. 1909.

[126] *BDP*, 2 Dec. 1909.

[127] A. W. Knapp, *The Cocoa and Chocolate Industry* (London, 1930), 169. My thanks to Basil Murray for this reference.

In the short term, however, none of these outcomes was so clear-cut. Sir Edward Carson KC MP, counsel for the defendant in the libel case brought by Cadbury Bros. Ltd. against the *Standard* Newspapers Ltd. and heard in Birmingham Crown Court over seven days in December 1909, read the evidence quite differently—he would of course, given his clients and the political animosity which infused the trial. Carson, whom 'no one could excel in the art of scoffing and sneering at evidence given by witnesses who were against him' (the words of Rufus Isaacs KC MP, counsel for the plaintiff), time and again hammered at the Cadbury defences, especially those of William A. Cadbury.[128] Why did they continue trading with São Tomé eight years after they suspected or knew of slavery?[129] Why did they suppress reports of São Tomé slavery submitted to the *Daily News*?[130] Was not São Tomé contract labour just the same as Chinese indentured labour in the Transvaal?[131] Was it not true that the prices of São Tomé cocoa had been falling during the years of alleged inaction?[132] The case hinged, as Isaacs was quick to see, on two issues: whether the Cadburys and their associates had done nothing about the São Tomé situation; and whether what they had done was really a sham.[133] Mr Justice Pickford agreed. 'Was this a dishonest plot to delay the matter being brought before the British public in order to enable the plaintiffs to go on buying slave-grown cocoa which they knew they ought to give up': this issue and this alone he instructed the jury to decide.[134]

In their defence William A. Cadbury and his uncle George stood solid against the innuendo and accusation Carson threw at them. To begin with they opened all their related company minute and account books for inspection to prove beyond doubt that from the start they had been determined to find out the truth of the São Tomé matter and then to act according to their Quaker consciences.[135] Did the delay amount to sham? The Cadburys pointed time and again to William's efforts in 1903, 1905, and again in 1909 (on his way back from Angola) to persuade the Government and planters' representatives in Lisbon to take action. Delay had come from Portuguese procrastination and from uncertainty about the facts. Enough evidence was submitted to show not only that

---

[128] *BDP*, 6 Dec. 1909.   [129] Ibid. 6 Dec. 1909.
[130] Ibid. 4 Dec. 1909.   [131] Ibid. 4 Dec. 1909.
[132] Ibid. 4 Dec. 1909.   [133] Ibid. 30 Nov. 1909.
[134] Ibid. 7 Dec. 1909.   [135] Ibid. 6 Dec. 1909.

the Cadburys had put up substantial sums of money to get at the truth but also that William Cadbury had placed his own safety at considerable risk in venturing into Angola. A battery of additional arguments defended the Cadbury position. First, the manufacturers had nothing to gain or lose in abandoning São Tomé cocoa. Cadburys at this time had only one small plantation (and that was in the West Indies) and could easily switch to other suppliers (as events proved). Indeed, as their records show (Table 4.1) Cadburys had been reducing their dependence on São Tomé since 1903. Equally their reliance on São Tomé could be maintained if slavery were unproven.[136] One of George Cadbury's concerns was that the native labour should not suffer as a result of his firm moving to other suppliers.[137] Second, the manufacturers delayed imposing a boycott because they were urged by the Foreign Secretary, Sir Edward Grey, to leave the matter in the hands of the diplomats. The Cadbury board in fact took the view that the issue was too big for a firm or group of firms to handle. It belonged, historically, to state policy. Having taken this position they were bound to adhere to it until damning evidence of slavery should determine a commercial rather than a political response.[138] Third, it was doubtful whether a boycott would succeed in pressuring the Portuguese into making reforms because American and most German cocoa manufacturers declined to join.[139] Fourth, the moral aspects of this commercial relationship defied easy implementation. When Sir Edward Carson in an electric moment in the trial asked George Cadbury the catch question, 'You are incapable of making a profit out of anything produced by slave labour?', he sagely replied 'One has to use common sense and sentiment. Sentiment told me I should give up buying at once, but common sense told me I would do no good if I did.'[140] So imperfect was knowledge of the West African labour market that for a long while the undisputed moral standard simply could not be applied by the manufacturers unilaterally. Finally, the profits made by Cadburys from São Tomé cocoa 1902–8, on sales of £1,336,632, were given to 'benevolent purposes'.[141] The jury were out for less than an hour and returned a verdict for the plaintiffs with damages of one farthing—a derisory sum hinting that a high moral stance was expected of Quakers with their long record of struggle against slavery. Still, Cad-

---

[136] Ibid. 2, 3 Dec. 1909. [137] Ibid. 4 Dec. 1909.
[138] Ibid. 1 Dec. 1909. [139] Ibid. 3 Dec. 1909.
[140] Ibid. 4 Dec. 1909. [141] Ibid. 2, 4 Dec. 1909.

bury Brothers Ltd. were awarded costs which, with five KCs and nine counsel altogether, must have been substantial.[142]

The Cadburys' major tactical error was in trying to censor the *Daily News*. Regarded as an unfair use of patronage,[143] it might have been managed in a less heavy-handed way. However, that side of the story awaits full treatment. As for the deceit of industrial espionage, itself contrary to high moral or commercial principle, William Cadbury would probably have argued that the end justified the means. In any case he announced his association with Swan soon after Swan got back to England, in the Preface to the second edition of his *Labour in Portuguese West Africa* which appeared in 1910. Swan in his role as William Cadbury's agent insisted that he was doing nothing illegal since Portugal had already outlawed slavery. Indeed he was careful to emphasize in *The Slavery of To-Day* that he was not quarrelling with the Portuguese but with the institution of slavery.[144]

Were men of religion the tools of businessmen? Swan and the Angolan missionaries did not see it this way. In fact, quite the opposite as Swan made clear to a Portuguese visitor when he got back to Lisbon:

Mr Cadbury was one of the first to tell us, as missionaries, that we had failed in our duty for not speaking out more publicly of what we knew in connection with the awful Slave Trade. Because of this & of what had been said and written by others about the Missionaries, I decided to go out again to Angola & consult with my fellow-missionaries & this visit has resulted in the step we had taken at home.[145]

The Cadburys were exceptional in keeping a balance when subordinating business to religious considerations. Joseph Storrs Fry, also in the expanding confectionery industry, also a Quaker who stayed 'plain', spent far more time, energy, and money on his religious commitments both within and outside the Society of Friends than was good for the family firm.[146] 'Clinging to the chairmanship despite blindness and increasing age, he never understood the harmful effects of backward–looking business practices and indiscriminate private benefactions.'[147]

[142] Ibid. 7 Dec. 1909; Wagner, *Chocolate Conscience*, 101–2.

[143] Wagner, *Chocolate Conscience*, 89, 98.

[144] Swan, *Slavery*, 20.

[145] BUL, Cadbury Papers, 180/926, Swan to William Cadbury, 5 July 1909.

[146] S. Diaper, 'J. S. Fry & Sons', in C. Harvey and J. Press (eds.), *Studies in the Business History of Bristol* (Bristol, 1988).

[147] Corley, 'How Quakers Coped with Business Success', 173. See also Gillian Wagner, 'Joseph Storrs Fry', *DBB*.

So much for Quakers in an expanding industry in the Midlands and South of England. What about Anglicans in growth industries, to whom the Cadburys and Frys might be properly compared? The 1907 business élite included a number in this category. With some, however, the strength or quality of their churchmanship was open to doubt. The intensity of David Milne-Watson's allegiance to the Church of England is unclear. General manager of the Gas Light & Coke Co., he received a Church of Scotland education at Merchiston Castle but was memorialized according to Anglican rites.[148]

For different reasons the quality of the churchmanship of Hugo Hirst and William Whiteley may be questioned. Hirst, managing director and prime architect of the General Electric Co. (GEC), was an immigrant Bavarian Jew who, after his naturalization in 1889, 'dropped Judaism for the Anglican Church' in doing 'his utmost to pass as a British gentleman'.[149] Whiteley, founder and owner of the huge West London department stores that bore his name, was an excessively harsh paternalist towards the thousands of shop assistants who lived above the premises, summarily fining and firing them. A nominal Evangelical Anglican, he peppered his staff with endless moral maxims which exhorted frugality and self-help. His methods aroused deep hostility in Bayswater and his private life was scandalous. After he was murdered early in 1907 by a man claiming to be his illegitimate son a widespread satisfaction aroused 4,000 petitions and 180,000 signatures in defence of his assassin.[150]

Of some there could be no doubt of their Anglicanism but little evidence that they were bringing Christian morality into their businesses, let alone the vexed area of labour relations. The economic and social effect of Huntley & Palmers on the town of Reading was one which neither the Quaker nor the Anglican members of the founding families ought to have been proud. A prolonged depression in trade starting in 1903 led the company to hold down wages when retail prices were rising, and to use short time and redundancies as further cost-cutting ways of maintaining profits.[151] Under a board chaired by W. Howard Palmer (baptized and buried in the Church of England[152]) whose manag-

[148] *The Times*, 4, 10 Oct. 1945.

[149] R. P. T. Davenport-Hines, 'Hugo Hirst', *DBB*.

[150] W. Philpott, 'William Whiteley', *DBB*.

[151] T. A. B. Corley, *Quaker Enterprise in Biscuits* (London, 1922), 174–7, 192–5; S. Yeo, *Religion and Voluntary Organisations in Crisis* (London, 1976).

[152] *Reading Standard*, 24 Mar. 1923; *The Times*, 21 Mar. 1923; information from T. A. B. Corley.

ing director was William Bullivant Williams (a devout and generous member of St Peter's Church, Caversham[153]) this policy culminated in 1911–12 in violent agitation, union protests (few in the company were yet in a union) and a vigorous public debate. The directors and a fifth of the workforce denied that alleged grievances had substance. Another section of employees, local trade unionists, the socialist Countess of Warwick, and the editor of the *Berkshire Chronicle* were equally adamant that they did. When the Archdeacon of Oxford, among other prominent outsiders, wrote to the company about the workers' complaints the company 'retorted that the *Chronicle*'s partisanship sprang from the editor's pose as a Tory Democrat, since he was a disappointed parliamentary candidate for the Borough'.[154] The criticisms of local church leaders were disregarded and, if possible, penalized. Thus the Vicar of St John's and St Stephen's lost Palmer support when he publicly complained of his parishioners' low wages. The minister of Carey Street Baptist Chapel, perhaps with less to lose, obliquely attacked Huntley & Palmers in 1912 by welcoming the proposal to set up a CWS jam factory in the town.[155]

Change in Huntley & Palmers' wages policy tarried until 1914. It was helped in part by a social survey conducted by A. L. Bowley, the distinguished statistician, then professor of mathematics and economics at Reading University College. He found in 1912 that 19 per cent of the town's population, and 47 per cent of children not earning, were living in primary poverty: a finding which even the restrained academic investigators found shocking. To this situation Huntley & Palmers heavily contributed because they were the town's major employer and were guilty of exploiting their monopoly position in paying relatively low wages. The threat of government intervention under the Trade Boards Act of 1909, designed to abolish 'sweated trades' where wages were abnormally low, may also have spurred the Huntley & Palmers board in July 1914 to decide to reduce the working week to 48 hours and thereby raise wages: a step delayed until the war was over.

Huntley & Palmers had some welfare facilities but these hardly compensated for the aggregate effects of the firm's wages policy. The most positive labour relations measure taken by Howard Palmer was the setting up of works committees. First came a consultative committee of workers to advise on welfare matters following the 1911 National Insurance Act which ended the company Sick Fund of sixty years' standing. In 1915 this was superseded by a General Committee of 52 employees, initially

[153] *Reading Standard*, 24 Mar. 1917; information from T. A. B. Corley.
[154] Corley, *Quaker Enterprise*, 176.
[155] Yeo, *Religion*, 117.

formed to persuade operatives to subscribe to the Government's National War Loan. 'The unprecedented feature of the new factory committee was its power to discuss freely wide areas of the company's business.'[156] Plainly, economic considerations, the findings of social scientists, state pressures, the contingencies of wartime, all had a far more persuasive effect on the Anglican–Quaker directors of Huntley & Palmers than the opinions of church leaders. However devout, these business leaders were minded to keep business and religion separate.

More conscious efforts to relate business practices to religious beliefs and their perceived moral implications for labour relations were made by the Anglican heads of two other firms in growth industries in the South of England. One was W. H. Smith & Son, the other the South Metropolitan Gas Co. At the top of the W. H. Smith & Son empire of newsagents, bookstalls, and circulating library in 1907 were William Frederick Danvers Smith and Charles Awdry, the senior members of the proprietorial partnership. Freddie was the son of the William Henry Smith 'Old Morality', whose Christian faith informed a sense of duty that took him into politics and Cabinet posts under Disraeli and Salisbury. In philanthropic, and modestly in political, public service his son followed him. Freddie, who succeeded to his mother's title in 1913 when he became 2nd Viscount Hambleden, was recalled by an obituarist with understandable exaggeration as 'a true Christian gentleman, with never a mean or unkind thought, content simply to do his duty without seeking honours or reward. A loyal son of the Church himself, he was kindly tolerant of those who did not share his beliefs, and I think was inclined to place works before faith in the reckoning of a man's final worth.'[157] Charles Awdry, scion of the Wiltshire gentry, and also a product of New College, Oxford, was surrounded by relatives in the church (he married the daughter of the Right Reverend George Moberly, Bishop of Salisbury; his brother became a bishop; and one of his daughters married a professor of pastoral theology at King's College, London). Awdry himself was recalled as 'an active supporter of the Winchester College Mission'.[158]

In the labour relations of W. H. Smith & Son the strong Christian beliefs of the partners in the two decades before the First World War were most obviously manifested in their welfare measures. Personnel matters by 1900 were Awdry's special concern. A Superannuation Fund had been set up in 1894 and a year later a Pension Fund for 'non-clerkly

[156] Corley, *Quaker Enterprise*, 192–3.
[157] *The Times*, 18 June 1928.
[158] *The Times*, 29 Mar. 1912; *Burke's Landed Gentry, 1937*.

staff' followed. Membership of this was compulsory, to avoid the potential for caprice embedded in *ad hoc* welfare arrangements. Noting these, Charles Wilson observes, 'In most respects, the partners were abreast of the best contemporary practices vis-a-vis staff, and in some respects ahead.'[159] Union recognition was granted before 1914. Not all labour policies were so advanced, however. Awdry blocked another partner's suggestion that newsboys be given uniforms—which might have relieved the household budgets of several thousand families. And for over fifty years the partners resisted every attempt to allow heating in the firms' 1,300 bookstalls, most on drafty railway platforms.[160]

Lastly there were the labour policies of Sir George Livesey, the septuagenarian chairman of the South Metropolitan Gas Co. A practical gas engineer and manager, Livesey was a devout Anglican and for a decade had been a Sunday School superintendent. His most progressive measure, to which he attached Christian motivation, was profit-sharing. It was less costly in the London gas industry where production was capital-intensive and since the 1870s had been heavily rationalized, with the Gas Light & Coke Co. supplying consumers to the north of the Thames and the South Metropolitan those to the south. However, the manner of its introduction was unfortunate. Livesey proposed profit-sharing at the end of October 1889, two months after a strike for a closed shop by the newly formed Gas Workers' Union. From his point of view it was one device for breaking the power of a union which had committed itself to lightning strikes and mass resignations. He couched his rationale for profit-sharing in philanthropic terms: 'Let the money that would be spent in a strike form the beginning of a fund for the men's benefit, to be increased in future by giving them every year a share in the profits of the Company in addition to their wages.'[161] When he confined the scheme to non-union men a two-month strike (December 1889–early February 1890) broke out, a well-known episode in what later came to be known as 'New Unionism' of unskilled and semi-skilled workers. Eventually unions were excluded from the South Metropolitan. Two aspects of the episode are relevant to the present study.

First, there was Livesey's subsequent insistence that profit-sharing was a Christian expression of a new relationship between masters and men. The South Metropolitan scheme became the flagship for the socialist- and Christian socialist-inspired co-partnership movement. Livesey, as

[159] C. Wilson, *First with the News* (London, 1985), 285.
[160] Ibid. 281–91.
[161] *PP* RC on Labour (1893), C 6894, q. 26,836. I am grateful to Francis Goodall for help here.

unifier of the two sides of industry, succeeded in influencing the Labour Co-partnership Association to such an extent that in 1898 it changed its definition of a labour co-partnership association to include 'the association of labour with capital in a partnership'.[162] In return he dropped his 'free labour clause' (i.e. limitation to non-union men) from the South Metropolitan scheme which enabled the company to join the Labour Co-partnership Association. In his more idealistic moments Livesey made pronunciations like 'Co-partnership is Christianity in Business.'[163] His own version certainly left some room for doubt in the minds of South Metropolitan employees. Bonuses could not be wholly withdrawn. After 1900 at least 50 per cent had to be invested in the company's shares. The company secretary's permission was required before an employee could sell his shares. On the other hand, the difficulties placed in the way of employees wanting to spend their money were, it was alleged, designed to induce saving and especially saving to buy a home. In addition, a case might be made that Livesey had achieved a much better balance between returns to labour and returns to capital, implying a redistribution of wealth which Christian Socialists could only applaud. The ratio of bonus to wages and salaries in the period 1896–1914 stood at 7 per cent or more, much higher than the 4 per cent paid to the company's ordinary stockholders or the 3 per cent paid to its debenture stockholders.[164] Against this it could be argued that a capital-intensive industry like gas production had relatively low labour inputs requiring modest absolute sums for distribution as bonus.

Second, in the attempts to settle the gas workers' strike in December 1889, Livesey agreed to deal with clerical arbitrators. However, neither Nonconformist nor Catholic clergymen succeeded in bringing a swift end to the dispute. Livesey first met a Nonconformist triumvirate: the Reverends Andrew Mearns (Congregationalist and author of the *Bitter Cry of Outcast London*), Dr John Clifford (Baptist), and Hugh Price Hughes (Wesleyan). Hughes too passionately took the side of the men (as Mearns confessed the following day), provoking Livesey to tell him to 'mind your own business and leave us to manage ours without interference'.[165] Cardinal Manning was no more effective.

Church and more recently Fitzgerald have seen profit-sharing as the carrot in combination with the sticks of stern paternalism and investment in labour-saving automatic stoking machinery. Perks has cast serious

---

[162] Fitzgerald, *British Labour Management*, 199.
[163] Francis Goodall, 'George Thomas Livesey', *DBB*.
[164] Church, 'Profit-Sharing', 11; *Stock Exchange Official Intelligence for 1907*.
[165] *PP* RC on Labour (1893), C 6894, q. 26,882.

doubt on the interpretation of profit-sharing as merely an anti-union tactic.[166] Matthews, looking at the gas industry generally, found inconclusive evidence for profit-sharing as a counter to unionism or a means of improving industrial relations.[167]

Livesey certainly saw it as a means of bridging the two sides of industry. Simple profit-sharing (defined as the allocation of shares to workers) was transmuted into co-partnership in 1898 with the election of two employee directors by employee shareholders—a move which raised élitist objections from the governor of the Gas Light & Coke Co., and possibly his general manager Milne-Watson.[168] By the end of 1907 5,003 out of an estimated 6,000 full-time equivalent employees were co-partners in the South Metropolitan scheme.[169]

What conclusions emerge from an issues approach? In the older staple industries Anglicans faced with declining profit margins appear to have followed a policy of separating religion from business. In similar economic circumstances the Quaker Peases apparently allowed Christian-inspired benevolence, even religious principle, to check rational entrepreneurial policies, until disaster struck. Relatively expansive economic conditions enjoyed by the cocoa manufacturers; strong management within the Cadbury firm provided by a vigorous younger generation of sons; inter-firm co-operation; and the support of British public opinion: all made the Cadburys' ethical action in the market-place easier. The unexpected outome for the Cadburys was a market substitution which guaranteed their cocoa supplies to an extent they could scarcely have imagined in 1901. Not all Quakers in expanding industries attained this felicitous balance between morality and business, as the Fry case illustrated. The Anglicans in expanding industries, even those most aware of a duty to bring business within the scope of Christian ethics, showed little interest in heeding clerical remonstration or guidance, let alone clerical mediation in labour relations, where episcopal interventions were usually unsuccessful anyway.[170] Some like the Palmers clearly resented any intrusions from clergy. Among Anglicans, in the labour relations area at least, a policy which was approved by some sections of the church (e.g. the Christian Socialists), and so might be labelled as Christian, was adopted

---

[166] Church, 'Profit-Sharing', 2–16; Fitzgerald, *British Labour Management*, 57–67; R. B. Perks, 'Real Profit Sharing', *Business History*, 24 (1982), 156–74.

[167] D. Matthews, 'Profit-Sharing in the Gas Industry, 1889–1949', *Business History*, 30 (1988), 321.

[168] Fitzgerald, *British Labour Management*, 63.

[169] Goodall, 'Livesey', *DBB*.

[170] Norman, *Church and Society*, 158.

if it served the business purposes and motives (often mixed) of the entrepreneur concerned. Anglicans seem to have been less successful in implementing high moral purposes within the firm. This may be related to the confusion in the mainline churches about social theology. Economics and ethics were still separate (see Chapter 2). It may also be related to differentials in the role of the laity. Chances for theological and ethical debate were commonplace to Quakers and many other Nonconformists. Among Anglicans the laity were still very much subordinated to the clergy, one factor behind the lament of the Archbishop of York at the Church Congress in 1912. In short, religion rarely influenced business behaviour and was much less likely to do so among Anglicans, the majority in the business élite, than among the most socially conscientious of Nonconformists, the Quakers. If the finding is not unexpected, developments after 1918 hold some surprises.

5

Christians in Big Business Leadership between the Wars

Before the First World War it had been widely accepted by both church-men and businessmen that religion and business did not mix. In the business community there were some exceptions, primarily the Quakers, who were ready to surrender business interests to religious principle. A Nonconformist paternalist like William Lever went in the other direc-tion, deploying religious institutions instrumentally for business ends. Yet in most denominations clergy and laity alike seem to have compart-mentalized ethics and economics. Between the wars, however, this pos-ition was reversed. First among Church of England bishops (who swung round towards the views of earlier Christian Socialists), later among some of the ruling bodies of the Nonconformists, the view gained ground that Christian moral teaching should rule economic and business behav-iour. However, as Chapter 2 outlined, it took nearly two decades to reach a formula for applying Christian morality to secular activity that was acceptable to capitalists as well as churchmen. By the end of the 1930s Dr Joseph Oldham and Archbishop William Temple were advanc-ing an alternative to the old 'separate spheres' doctrine that accommo-dated capitalism and hence appealed to businessmen. Their response is examined in a later chapter.

Until this new relationship had been defined and demonstrated, how-ever, businessmen had little but the older stances to follow. In essence, as the previous chapters illustrate, this meant that owner-managers with strong religious convictions expressed them within the firm through wel-fare provisions, religious provisions, or both. Purely religious provisions could range from the construction of a church near the factory or com-pany village to the assembling of the workforce for prayer at the beginning of the working day or, as at Port Sunlight, the more subtle tactic of employing a clergyman as company welfare officer. All these and similar attempts to bring religious opportunities within the firm, whether motivated by sincerely felt religious zeal or commercially driven hopes of extending worker control, were most readily accomplished in a family-owned and managed firm.

Between the wars, however, many family owners, especially in big business, were withdrawing from management and leaving that to professional managers. Regional disparities, sharply evidenced in the scarcely relieved depression afflicting the older industries of the North of England, and the boom conditions enjoyed by the new industries of the Midlands and the South, threatened the security cherished by family owner-managers. These conditions put a premium on the skills of the new breeds of accountant and professional administrator to rationalize or rescue in the North and to co-ordinate rapid company growth in the South.[1] With the withdrawal of family owners from management went the decay of religious provisions: managers were responsible to directors and directors to shareholders; paternalists only to themselves and their consciences. Unless the managerial firm was operating in a community in which religious values were politically dominant (as in Northern Ireland or Liverpool) there was little opportunity to legitimate religious practices, either instrumentally or non-instrumentally.

In these decades too, welfare provisions underwent widening modification. The need to ensure a steady labour supply, whether in natural monopolies or competitive industries, accelerated in the 1920s and 1930s as the proponents of rationalization argued for alternatives to the market mechanism to combat economic depression. Merger, horizontal integration, the closure of excess capacity, scientific management, all were part of what was variously understood as rationalization. So too was the creation of labour markets internal to the firm and with them came the reorganization of welfare schemes.[2] Instead of ad hoc arrangements, inappropriate, even intolerable, to trained managerial hierarchies or skilled labour forces, systematic welfare provisions run by personnel officers were increasingly adopted. In the field of pensions alone, for example, the number of occupational pension schemes approved under the 1921 Finance Act rose from 924 in 1928 to 2,156 in 1938.[3] The structural and cost features of rationalization meant that systematic welfare

[1] L. Hannah, *The Rise of the Corporate Economy* (2nd edn., London, 1983), 78–81, indicates the roles of professional managers in a few large and successful firms.

[2] Ibid. 27–40; R. Fitzgerald, *British Labour Management and Industrial Welfare, 1846–1939* (Beckenham, 1988), *passim*.

[3] L. Hannah, *Inventing Retirement* (Cambridge, 1986), 149.

tended to be adopted in larger rather than smaller firms. In addition the encroaching powers of the state were taking a growing number of welfare decisions out of management's hands. Except in the minority of paternalist firms which survived among the largest businesses in Britain, welfare could no longer be regarded as a sign of managerial consciences tuned by religious convictions.

How then did big business leaders with Christian beliefs and rejecting a 'separate spheres' doctrine attempt to integrate faith and work in the area of the firm? At an individual level there were clear Christian teachings, widely accepted if not consistently observed, about personal honesty, fair dealing, consideration for the weak, and so forth. Moving beyond the individual to the group, and laying down principles or codes of behaviour for all managers or all employees in the company, was much more difficult. What standards should the Christian observe when acting as chairman or managing director? That is, what might be expected of all chairmen and managers seeking to conform to Christian codes? On this kind of question some sort of collective agreement was plainly necessary. Instead, therefore, of sampling the firms in the list of largest employers of 1935 to discover on a firm-by-firm basis what was happening to management responses to the possibilities of applying Christian ethics (an exceedingly difficult if not impossible task, in view of the lack of literary evidence on this area), a different approach from that adopted in Chapter 4 is followed. Since businessmen were being asked by church leaders to admit external (church) ethics into their workplace, it seems appropriate to discover how business leaders responded at the level of collective public debate. The focus will be on those business leaders heading the firms listed as the largest employers of 1935, particularly on Quakers, Methodists, and Anglicans.

1 QUAKER INDUSTRIALISTS

Quaker employers pioneered attempts by industrialists to develop a distinctive Christian stance towards the challenges and threats of post-war business. The first conference of Quaker employers, of which three more would follow, gathered on 11–14 April 1918, a long wartime weekend. They met at Woodbrooke, the large house near Selly Oak, Birmingham, once George Cadbury's home, which in 1903 he had given to the Society of Friends for a settlement and training centre. The instigator of the conference was John Coleby Morland, director of Clark, Son & Morland Ltd., the Glastonbury sheepskin rug manufacturers. As one of the few

TABLE 5.1. *Quaker industrial conferences: individual conferees by industry*

Industry	1918	1928	1938	1948
Agriculture		3	2	
Mining	2			
Manufacturing	44	68	62	69
Construction	2	3		
Utilities				
Transport	1			1
Distribution	5	8	7	5
Finance	2	2	2	2
Professional services		1	4	4
Miscellaneous services	6	6	5	2
Civil Servants			2	
Academics			3	6
Conference organizers	3	4	1	
Unaffiliated		5	6	4
Unknown affiliation	21		21	26
Total attending	86	100	115	119
Interested but not attending		17	26	46
GRAND TOTAL	86	117	141	165

employers sitting on the Society of Friends' War and Social Order Committee (set up by the Society's Yearly Meeting in 1915), he was concerned that Quaker employers should engage in the debate about war and social order and in 1917 arrangements were set in hand for the 1918 conference.

As the conference chairman, Arnold Rowntree MP (nephew of Joseph Rowntree and a director of the York-based chocolate firm) acknowledged in his opening address, 'War has revolutionised the industrial outlook.'[4] By April 1918, despite the final desperate attempts of Ludendorff's armies to break through the Allies' trenches before American reinforcements arrived, the end of the war was in sight. Responses to peacetime rather than wartime, to prospects of reconstruction rather than military preparedness, therefore occupied the 80 Quaker employers who assembled for their first conference. Critically, and at times severely, they reviewed their own record and what they perceived as their altered position in British industry. What firms did these employers (and those who gathered again at Woodbrooke in 1928, 1938, and 1948) represent? What views and policies emerged from their decennial discussions? What were the results of these conferences?

The backgrounds of the Quaker employers meeting for the four confer-

---

[4] A. S. Rowntree, 'The Industrial Outlook', in J. E. Hodgkin (ed.), *Quakerism and Industry* (Darlington, 1918).

TABLE 5.2. *Quaker industrial conferences: conferees from firms in the manufacturing sector*

	1918	1928	1938	1948
Industry				
Food, drink, tobacco	9	17	21	30
Coal and petroleum products				
Chemicals	9	6	3	2
Metals	4	4	3	4
Mechanical engineering	7	7	5	5
Instrument engineering				
Electrical engineering		2	3	2
Shipbuilding		1		
Vehicles				
Other metal goods		3	1	2
Textiles	3	2	2	2
Leather	3	6	6	5
Clothing and footwear	2	4	4	4
Bricks, pottery, glass	1	1		1
Timber, furniture				
Paper, printing, publishing	4	13	12	12
Other manufactures	2	2	2	
Total	44	68	62	69
Number from large firms				
Cadburys	4	7	13	23
Cadbury-related firms		2	4	2
Reckitts	3	2		
Rowntrees	2	4	6	3
Rowntree-related firms		1		
Stewarts & Lloyds	2			
Family firms				
Individuals with same surname as their firm's name	43	56	49	34
TOTAL NUMBER OF ATTENDERS	86	100	115	119

ences between 1918 and 1948 are summarized in Tables 5.1 and 5.2. Predominantly they came from manufacturing, from firms smaller than the largest, and from family firms. A closer look at the manufacturing sector (Table 5.2) shows that food, chemicals, and mechanical engineering provided the larger numbers of Quaker employers in 1918; the same industries together with leather and paper in 1928; food, mechanical engineering, leather, and paper in 1938; and the same again in 1948.

Of all the firms represented in 1928 only two (Cadburys and Reckitts) appeared in the list of the UK's 100 largest employers of 1935; and in 1938 only one (Cadburys) was in the list. Rowntrees were in the largest 100 by 1955. Yet many firms were notable if not sizeable in their respective industries. This is clear from the 1928 conference report which listed all the firm and industry affiliations of members. In food, besides

Cadburys and Rowntrees there were W. & R. Jacob (biscuits), Lamb Bros. (marmalade), and the sardine business of Angus Watson (a leading Congregational layman, he was guest speaker this year). In chemicals, besides Reckitts, there was Stafford Allen & Sons, John & E. Sturge, and Albright & Wilson. In mechanical engineering: Joseph J. Armfield, Brayshaw Furnaces & Tools, Christy & Norris, R. C. Gibbins & Co., The Horsehay Co., W. Sisson & Co., and Tuke & Bell. In leather, clothing, and footwear: Clark, Son & Morland, Edward & James Richardson (leather), C. & J. Clark (shoes), and the Spirella Co. of Great Britain (corsets). In paper and publishing: the Daily News Ltd. (of which the Cadburys were proprietors), Morland & Impey, Cambrian News (Aberystwyth) Ltd., Rippin & Baker, E. S. & A. Robinson, and Hazell, Watson & Viney. Ralph D. Sweeting came from Swan, Hunter & Wigham Richardson, the Tyneside shipbuilders. Harold J. Morland came from Price, Waterhouse the chartered accountants, worried perhaps about a coming meeting with the Trade Facilities Act Advisory Committee at which, as auditor of the Royal Mail Steam Packet Co., he would have to defend the accounts of Harland & Wolff, a company in the Royal Mail group. He can scarcely have imagined that his position would lead him in 1931 to stand trial for aiding Lord Kylsant, chairman of Royal Mail, in publishing a false balance sheet.[5]

Although it is not possible to identify the exact number of family firms represented at the conferences, eponymously named firms are one indicator. Between the wars approximately half the conference members came from firms bearing their own names (see Table 5.2). Most were, by national standards, small. The largest were represented by several, or in the case of the Cadburys as many as nine, individuals drawn from family clans. However, in 1928 and 1938 the big family firms like Cadburys and Rowntrees were also being represented by individuals not bearing the family name. Presumably some were the new university-trained men whom George Cadbury jun. in 1928 had urged his fellow proprietors to hire. Though as he said then, if a son was unfitted to follow his father into the ownership of a firm, 'Our selection will therefore be in the first instance from among those most interested financially, that is from among the sons of the biggest shareholders and directors.'[6]

What did these conferences discuss? In 1918 discussions were set

[5] E. Green and M. Moss, *A Business of National Importance* (London, 1982), 78, 140–2. Morland was found not guilty but Kylsant was convicted of publishing a false prospectus and sentenced to twelve months' imprisonment.

[6] G. Cadbury jun., 'Training for Business Management', in Quaker Employers' Conference, *Quakerism and Industry* (London, 1928), 40.

against two backgrounds. First there was the contemporary view of Quaker social responsibility. That, as John Child demonstrates, had four main features: a dislike of exploiting fellow human beings; a stress on hard work, frugality, efficiency, personal renunciation, and service (a large part of the Puritan code); a tradition of egalitarianism and democratic relationships; and an abhorrence of conflict between men.[7] The other background was the social upheaval wrought by war. In 1918 a mixture of hope and apprehension prevailed as Quaker employers contemplated a future very different from their paternalist past. The war years had apparently plunged old social attitudes into the melting pot. Classes were intermixed in the armed forces; women went out to work; membership of trade unions rose by more than 50 per cent. Most directly relevant to Quaker employers contemplating post-war changes was the proposal made in mid-1917 by the parliamentary Reconstruction subcommittee, chaired by the Deputy Speaker J. H. Whitley. To reduce industrial conflict Whitley Councils would be formed, 'composed of representatives of employers and workers in each industry, ... intended to discuss everything—not just wages and conditions, but participation, job security, technical education, and improvement of management—"affecting the progress and well-being of the trade from the point of view of those engaged in it, as far as this is consonant with the general interest of the community"'.[8]

One central issue in 1918, therefore, and to a diminishing extent in 1928 and 1938, was that of worker control of industry. How far could Quaker employers go in allowing workers to participate in running industry? The question recurred because the Whitley scheme was briefly successful, with 3.25 million workers in small-scale industries covered by 1920.[9] At the 1918 conference Arnold Rowntree hailed the Whitley Report as 'a great landmark in industrial history' but it 'only provides one instrument towards the reorganisation of industry'.[10] J. Bernard Shewell of Morland & Impey, loose-leaf binder manufacturers, welcomed the Whitley Councils scheme. Such Councils might discuss 'works rules, methods of pay, bonus rates, alterations in working hours, matters affecting health, safety and conditions of work, cases of theft and misconduct, canteens, means of getting to work, dismissal of

[7] J. Child, 'Quaker Employers and Industrial Relations', *Sociological Review*, NS 12 (1964), 294.
[8] K. Middlemas, *Politics in Industrial Society* (London, 1979), 137.
[9] C. L. Mowat, *Britain between the Wars* (London, 1956), 37.
[10] Rowntree, 'Industrial Outlook', 19.

employees, thrift schemes, holidays &c &c'.[11] J. Edward Hodgkin of Motor Union Insurance Co. could not believe that all Quaker employers would be so enthusiastic because they 'really believed in autocracy in business'.[12] Francis E. Marriage, of the Colchester milling firm, strongly regretted such opposition.

But John Child is surely wrong to conclude that Quaker employers at first accepted power sharing with workers.[13] Right from the beginning the consensus opinion put clear limits on the extent of worker control in industry. In 1918 Seebohm Rowntree relayed to the conference the views of the London group of Quaker employers (who, like other groups round the country, met to prepare for the Birmingham meeting). They believed 'it was probable that ultimately there would be a demand for a much wider participation in the control of business; but a great many of them felt they could not agree to that at the present time. In industrial control they agreed that the workers should co-operate with them on equal terms; but for the present employees should not have a say in either the financial or commercial sides of the business.'[14] And that was the position written into the report issued by the 1918 conference.[15] It remained the view in 1928. In his welcome speech Edward Cadbury flatly stated, 'at present I see no way in which he [the worker] can be given any effective control in large scale industry'.[16] The final report that year noted, 'some firms discuss their business problems with them [works councils], make periodical statements on the state of trade and the prospects of employment; and explain their balance sheets'. However, 'The duty of making prompt decisions, and carrying out contracts still must remain the function of Direction, and we see no method under present circumstances by which this can be shared with employees.'[17]

The position was unaltered by the 1938 conference. One of the ablest thinkers at the 1928 and 1938 conferences was William Wallace, a solicitor and LSE commerce graduate by training, who began as assistant to B. Seebohm Rowntree in 1919 until appointed Rowntree company secretary in 1929 and director in 1931 (eventually becoming chairman in

[11] J. B. Shewell, 'The Status of the Worker', in J. E. Hodgkin (ed.), *Quakerism and Industry* (Darlington, 1918), 59.
[12] Hodgkin (ed.), *Quakerism and Industry*, 65.
[13] Child, 'Quaker Employers', 301.
[14] 'Consideration of the Report', Hodgkin (ed.), *Quakerism and Industry*, 69.
[15] Ibid. 135.
[16] E. Cadbury, 'Welcome', in Quaker Employers, *Quakerism and Industry* (1928), 1.
[17] 'Report', in Quaker Employers, *Quakerism and Industry* (1928), 89.

1952).[18] Brought up a Presbyterian and then a Congregationalist, Wallace clearly belonged to the Society of Friends when in 1938 he was assigned the delicate task of summarizing the conclusions of the meetings in lieu of a report. In a paper keenly sensitive towards Quaker theology he asserted, 'Share in management should depend upon capacity, and capacity alone. It follows that a sense of brotherhood does not involve management of businesses by mass meetings or show of hands. It is the duty of the employer to see that his business is conducted with maximum efficiency. . . . Efficiency is the first duty owed by an employer.'[19]

Besides worker control, unemployment was the other theme occupying the minds of Quaker employers between the wars. In 1918 they had no idea of the extent of unemployment which awaited the country. J. Coleby Morland believed that chronic unemployment in the towns could best be tackled by concentrating on rural unemployment. George Cadbury jun. could envisage the return of trade fluctuations and cyclical unemployment. B. Seebohm Rowntree thought they should 'try to de-casualise labour as far as possible, to overcome the difficulties of the seasonal trades, and to consider whether in their own businesses they could create Unemployment Funds'.[20] Unemployment was discussed again in 1928, too briefly in the opinion of William Weir of Swinton & District Steam Laundry.[21] As it was, the main paper by H. F. Scott Stokes of Clark, Son & Morland devoted most space to reviewing the various types of state legislation by which the worker was cushioned against accidents, sickness, unemployment, and old age. Other employers gave illustrations of the ways in which they curbed seasonal unemployment, found new openings for their own unemployed, or developed schemes for supplementing the state unemployment insurance scheme.[22]

The chronic unemployment of the 1930s slump evoked national rather than firm-level prescriptions from the Quaker employers. The conference chairman, Herbert G. Tanner of E. S. & A. Robinson the Bristol paper manufacturers, drew attention to the paradox of 'poverty in plenty' in 1930s Britain: 'no Christian can be satisfied with a state of affairs under

[18] W. Wallace, I Was Concerned (1985). I am grateful to Mr W. T. Bushell for a copy of this.

[19] W. Wallace, 'Quaker Ideals in Industry', in Quaker Employers' Conference, Quakerism and Industry (London,1938), 110, 114.

[20] Hodgkin (ed.), Quakerism and Industry, 103, 105, 107.

[21] Quaker Employers, Quakerism and Industry (1928), 64.

[22] H. F. Scott Stokes, 'Security of the Worker' and subsequent discussion in Quaker Employers, Quakerism and Industry (1928), 50–61.

which there are 1.75 millions of unemployed, and of those in more or less regular employment, a large percentage receive a wage insufficient to provide the bare necessities of physical existence for themselves and their families.'[23] Laurence Cadbury reviewed the extensions of public control of industry since 1928, from the marketing boards to the London Passenger Transport Board, worrying that they represented tendencies towards monopoly. Neither did he have confidence in Harold Macmillan's scheme to set up a state board for every industry jointly controlled by capital and labour. It would only delay the transfer of resources from declining to growing industries. The advancing power of the state, the frightening goals of which the totalitarian dictators were almost daily exhibiting (the month before the Quaker employers met in 1938 Hitler's troops invaded Austria), also disturbed Laurence Cadbury. Hence on both political and economic grounds he only cautiously accepted that unemployment might be relieved by public works.[24]

The answer according to Shipley N. Brayshaw, a mechanical engineer with Brayshaw Furnaces & Tools of Stockport, was a planned economy. Striving to avoid both capitalism and socialism he proposed a grandiose blueprint for a planned economy. In brief, his scheme pivoted on a hierarchy of central planners under whom both the currency issue and price levels would be regulated by a standard of living index. As for unemployment, he envisaged a labour reserve of 200,000 unemployed whose members would be constantly changing. 'Men and women on the reserve would be expected to get into, and/or keep themselves in, first-class condition. They would have access to gymnasia, swimming baths, and outdoor games as well as lectures and cultural enjoyment.'[25] This vision of a smoothly working planned economy smacked of Major Douglas's preposterous Social Credit scheme.[26] The prime merit of Brayshaw's blueprint was that it opened the minds of individualistic employers to the possibilities of central planning, which came with Keynesian clarity after 1945.

The Quaker employers' conferences, as John Child showed, concentrated heavily on labour relations. That concern reflected the central problems of inter-war industry. On the capital side one topic did, how-

[23] H. G. Tanner, 'Review of Industrial Changes in the Last Ten Years', in Quaker Employers, *Quakerism and Industry* (1938), 4.

[24] L. J. Cadbury, 'Public Control of Industry', in Quaker Employers, *Quakerism and Industry* (1938), 12–32.

[25] S. N. Brayshaw, 'Planning Industry for the Utilisation of all Available Abilities', in Quaker Employers, *Quakerism and Industry* (1938), 33–54.

[26] See J. C. Stamp, *Motive and Method in a Christian Order* (London, 1936), 172, 239–48.

ever, exercise sustained interest: that of surplus profits. Surplus profits
were vaguely defined in 1918 as excessive profits, which some businesses
certainly made in wartime. Alfred J. Cudworth thought these should
be distributed between shareholders and workers through profit-sharing.
Thinking in 1918 was rather divided. While some employers enthusiasti-
cally supported profit-sharing and co-partnership, voices from the trade
union side reminded employers of the unpopularity of these schemes
among unionists. The final report pronounced, 'We cannot believe that
either the proprietors or the workers are entitled to the whole of the
"surplus profits" of the business, though they might reasonably ask for
such a share as would give them an interest in its financial prosperity.
The possibilities of Profit-Sharing and Co-Partnership are therefore a
suitable field for experiment.'[27]

When William Wallace addressed the problem in 1928 the subject
came much more sharply into focus. He predicated his definition of
surplus profit on the duty of the employer, enjoined implicitly by the
Society of Friends' 'Foundations of a True Social Order' (eight statements adopted by the Yearly Meeting of 1918) and by Article 427 of
the Treaty of Versailles, to provide a living wage for all employees. In
case the definition of a living wage escaped his hearers and readers,
Wallace reminded them that B. Seebohm Rowntree had defined this
quite precisely at the 1918 conference.[28] The other prime duty of an
employer, Wallace observed, was to attain higher efficiency in order to
have more profits to distribute to both capital and labour. From these
premises he moved to specify and rank the charges on the product
of industry: a minimum wage to the rank and file and salaries to managers
just sufficient to secure the necessary managerial ability; then a charge
for the maintenance and renewal of the necessary capital, with deficiencies made good out of later surpluses; next any remaining margin should
be used to increase the minimum wage up to what Seebohm Rowntree
defined as a 'human needs' basis; finally, if there were any profits remaining these were to be regarded as surplus profits and ought to be equally
distributed between labour, direction, capital, and the community. So
persuasive were Wallace's arguments that they were adopted in the final
conference report of 1928 and repeated again in the report of 1938.[29]

[27] Hodgkin (ed.), *Quakerism and Industry*, 110–21, 141.

[28] When he gave a figure of 44s. as the minimum weekly wage for a married man
with a wife and three children to support. See Benjamin Seebohm Rowntree, 'Wages',
44–7. The principles of his calculation came from his classic study, *Poverty* (London,
1901).

[29] W. Wallace, 'The Workers' Share of the Product', in Quaker Employers, *Quakerism
and Industry* (1928), 15–25, 86–8; idem, 'Quaker Ideals', 114–15.

So much for the major topics discussed and positions reached by the inter-war Quaker employers' conferences. What impact did they have? As Child observed, Quaker employers were prone to the Utopian inclination. Their vision of what might be was far removed from current reality. That much is apparent from the almost pontifical statements of the 'Foundations of a True Social Order' (1918). 'The Fatherhood of God, as revealed by Jesus Christ, should lead us towards a Brotherhood which knows no restriction of race, sex or social class.' Again, 'Our rejection of the methods of outward domination and of the appeal to force applies not only to international affairs, but to the whole problem of industrial control.' Or, 'Mutual service should be the principle upon which life is organised. Service, not private gain, should be the motive of all work.'[30] In their inter-war conferences the Quaker employers tried desperately to reconcile these ideals to the hard practicalities of owning and running family businesses, large and small. Some, like John H. Guy, a director of John Mackintosh & Sons the Methodist toffee manufacturer, confessed defeat: 'I ... maintain that the central purpose of business conducted for private profit is fundamentally irreconcilable with the central purpose of Christianity, and one must give way to the other.'[31] Most were happy to follow the leads given by George Cadbury jun., Edward Cadbury, Seebohm Rowntree, Arnold Rowntree, and, in a younger generation, William Wallace, in edging forward reforms within the existing industrial structures. As the 1918 report emphasized, 'The duty of the individual employer, not the duty of the State or of society, is the subject we have sought to explore.' Ideals of brotherhood and service were therefore to some extent realizable in the context of labour relations. By 1938, as seen above, the limitations of this approach were clearly recognized, hence the discussions about the role of the state and economic planning.

The Quaker employers were well aware of their liability to depart from reality. Consequently in 1928 the conference chairman Arnold S. Rowntree reviewed the permanent results of the first conference. He noted four. First, a number of firms, including Cadburys, started experiments in works councils. A United States committee produced an influential report on *The Church and Industrial Reconstruction* reaching conclusions very similar to the Quaker employers' report of 1918.[32] 'It is possible, too, that some of the provisions in the Treaty of Versailles

<hr>

[30] Quaker Employers, *Quakerism and Industry* (1928), 97 where all eight 'Foundations' are printed.

[31] J. H. Guy, 'Quandary of a Financial Executive in Competitive Business', in Quaker Employers, *Quakerism and Industry* (1938), 31.

[32] I am grateful to Professor Peter D. Marshall for identifying this.

relating to labour were influenced by it in some degree.' (William Wallace agreed that Seebohm Rowntree's concept of the basic or living wage was written into the Treaty.) Fourthly, out of the 1918 conference had come Seebohm Rowntree's experiments 'with a different type of Conference at Oxford with employers, administrators and workers, which proved so successful that 25 other similar gatherings have since been held'.[33]

That was not all. Some employers adopted profit-sharing or co-partnership schemes in an attempt to inject the ideals of brotherhood and service into their firms. Harry H. Payne described how his Birmingham shoe-repair business had grown under a co-partnership scheme from four employees in 1920 to a staff on ninety sites in 1938.[34] Payne said nothing about trade union recognition. W. Dent Priestman, outlining his profit-sharing scheme in 1918, indicated that the Amalgamated Society of Engineers' representative in his works had no hesitation in recommending the arrangements he was following.[35] Profit-sharing was a mid-Victorian form of extending ownership and control (considered above in Chapter 4, s. 2). Consequently it received much less attention in the conferences than the newer idea of works councils.

As important as these tangible achievements of the Quaker conferences of employers was their impact on management philosophy. 'Quaker employers' concepts played an important role in the ready acceptance by British managerial thought of its most recent modern inspiration—the ideas of the Harvard, so-called "human relations in industry" school.[36] Quaker employers' belief that personal qualities determined industrial relationships prepared the way in Britain for the adoption of Elton Mayo's 'scientific' approach to industrial problems such as fatigue, monotony, dexterity, morale, and the like. Edward Cadbury at Bournville and Seebohm Rowntree at York had, through their welfare departments, been developing personnel management since before the First World War. Out of their firms came many of the British pioneers of management philosophy like Urwick, Sheldon, and Wallace. By 1938 the conference of Quaker employers was listening to papers which were referring to vocational guidance materials published by the National Institute of

[33] A. S. Rowntree, 'Review of Industrial Changes during the Last Ten Years', in Quaker Employers, *Quakerism and Industry* (1928), 4; Wallace, 'Workers' Share', 17.

[34] H. H. Payne, 'An Experiment in Giving the Workers a Greater Share of Control and Product', in Quaker Employers, *Quakerism and Industry* (1938), 73–8.

[35] W. D. Priestman, 'Priestman's Profit-Sharing Scheme', in Hodgkin (ed.), *Quakerism and Industry*, 92–3.

[36] Child, 'Quaker Employers', 308.

Industrial Psychology and to Mayo's *Human Relations in Industry* (1933).[37]

Finally, it might be argued that the Quaker employers' attitudes and discussions served as a model for other business leaders with Christian consciences. On rare occasions the model was pressed home sharply. At the 1918 conference Seebohm Rowntree, referring to the shift system at Port Sunlight, declared, 'Lord Leverhulme's scheme of three shifts of six hours each per day was monstrous.'[38] The published remark must have been the tip of an iceberg of informed opinion and gossip circulating about fellow employers at the Woodbrooke conferences. Doubtless some percolated back to the targets of criticism through the circles of the employers' federations to which some of the larger employers belonged.[39] Overall the Quaker employers kept their feet firmly on the ground, seeking changes beneficial to their employees as well as their profit levels and rejecting the kind of absurd panaceas with which the Anglican Christendom group became infatuated.

2 METHODIST BUSINESSMEN

In the inter-war business élite Methodists were more than twice as numerous as Quakers, but in absolute numbers they were still insignificant. Of 203 chairmen and managing directors in charge of the 100 largest companies in 1935 only four have been identified as Methodists. Among chairmen there was Sir Josiah Stamp of the London, Midland & Scottish Railway. Among managing directors there were Peter Frederick Blaker Bennett of Joseph Lucas Ltd.; Robert Abraham Burrows of Manchester Collieries; and Edward James George of Consett Iron. Only Stamp was as prominent a Methodist as he was businessman.

Of Bennett (who subsequently combined his outstanding career as an industrialist with a dozen years as Conservative MP for Edgbaston) it was recalled, 'Brought up a Methodist, he did good work for that denomination in his younger days, as a local preacher, as a Sunday School superintendent, and as an organiser of boys' clubs.'[40] In 1935

---

[37] G. E. Whiting, 'The Friends' Appointment Board', in Quaker Employers, *Quakerism and Industry* (1938), 84; H. E. Collier, 'The Needs of Everyman', in Quaker Employers, *Quakerism and Industry* (1938), 96.

[38] Hodgkin (ed.), *Quakerism and Industry*, 64.

[39] Apparently with some difficulty, especially when Quaker employers wanted to pay higher rates than the federations recommended. See Hodgkin (ed.), *Quakerism and Industry*, 68.

[40] *The Times*, 30 Sept. 1957.

he was in his mid-fifties so presumably by then had relinquished the church posts of his early career; certainly he does not appear in either of the two main denominational handbooks of the early 1930s. At his death in 1957, when he was Baron Bennett of Edgbaston, his funeral took place at Four Oaks Methodist Church, Sutton Coldfield.[41]

Burrows's upbringing as a Wesleyan (he attended The Leys School it will be recalled) carried through into his adult life but not to such an extent that he combined high business responsibility with high denominational office.[42] His highest business offices were reached after the Second World War. Sir Robert Burrows was remembered as an early member of the National Coal Board, one of the last chairmen of the LMS Railway, and as chairman of Remploy. His adult religious associations are implied in a lyrical memorial:

This [a slice of south Lancashire between Warrington and Wigan] is the land of Cobden and Bright, the land of Free Trade, and the flowering of Wesleyism [sic]. In that day the motor car and the weekend habit had not yet torn a hole in local social life—a life festooned around the religious communities. The nonconformist conscience not only made for hard work, it also impelled a spirit of service to fellow men. Of this Robert Burrows was an outstanding leader by example—president and patron of societies and institutions, a standard bearer of Liberalism to the point of feeling his reluctant duty to stand for Parliament.[43]

Unlike Burrows, who entered business through a family firm, but like Stamp and Bennett, George was a self-made manager. In 1935 he was nearly 70 and had spent thirty years in the management of Consett Iron Co. Again only a trace of his religious affiliation remains: his obituary noted, 'For over 60 years he has been a Methodist local preacher.' He is unlisted as such in the two denominational directories of 1933–4.[44]

Methodists in big business or in smaller businesses were much less co-ordinated or collective in reflecting on business issues than their Quaker counterparts. They met to discuss the classic moral burdens of Nonconformity but not business ethics per se. For example they gathered at Reading in June 1934 for the annual conference of the National Commercial Temperance League, a temperance organization for business people.[45] Few Methodist laymen in business published their opinions about the area of faith and business.

The only major article on this topic to appear in 1934, prior to the

---

[41] Ibid. 3 Oct. 1957.
[42] At least not in 1935.
[43] The Times, 15, 24 Aug. 1964.
[44] Ibid. 26 Oct. 1950; WWM 1933; MLPWW 1934.
[45] M., Rec. 21 June 1934.

important denominational statement that year about the church's view of industry, came from the Reverend Ernest Barrett, a former Primitive Methodist, who had been in the ministry since 1899 and in 1934 was one of the denomination's two General Book Stewards (publishing manager).[46] His piece defended Christian employers from charges of hypocrisy, appealing to psychology for an understanding of the saint-on-Sunday, slave-driver-on-Monday personality. Nowhere did he offer the morally based policies the Quakers were then currently forging. His perspective was that of the individual not the individual employer in the firm or the firm in its industry. This kind of emphasis, springing from the indvidualistic and experiential theology of the Methodists, was hardly surprising.

What was surprising was that Methodists failed to mobilize the large reservoir of talent among their members for tackling questions in the area of Christian ethics in industry. Among those reported in the *Methodist Recorder* in the mid-1930s were Sir Josiah Stamp, Sir Harold Bellman of the Abbey Road Building Society, Baron Rochester (transport contractor), Baron Marshall of Horace Marshall & Sons (publishers and newspaper and book wholesalers), Viscount Wakefield of C. C. Wakefield & Co. (oil manufacturers), Sir Thomas Rowbotham (head of a Stockport engineering firm), Joseph Rank (flour miller), his son J. Arthur Rank (rising film magnate), the 1st Baron Runciman, and his son the Right Honourable Walter Runciman, President of the Board of Trade (in shipping).[47] Only one of these men appeared in the objectively selected business élite of largest employers of 1935. They were nevertheless prominent men in business. In addition the Montague Burton Professor of Industrial Relations at Leeds University, Dr John Henry Richardson, who had worked in the Research Division of the International Labour Office at the League of Nations, Geneva, in the 1920s, was profiled as a prominent Methodist in 1934.[48] Here was collective ability and experience to rival that ever assembled at Woodbrooke. It remained largely latent potential.

Belonging to a strongly clerical denomination they shared the denominational decision-making process with the clergy through the formal machinery of the annual Methodist Conference. Their main opportunity for creating a Christian business ethic came at synod (district) meetings

[46] Revd Ernest Barrett, 'Can a Business-Man be a Good Christian?', *M. Rec.*, 5 July 1934.

[47] These names are drawn from reports of various annual meetings or other events in *M. Rec.*, 4 Jan., 8, 29 Mar., 26 Apr., 3 May, 28 June, 15, 22 Nov., 27 Dec. 1934. All are in *WWM 1933*.

[48] Methodist Church, *The Methodist Book-Almanack, 1934* (London, 1934), 72.

and the national Conference. During those inevitable interstices between sessions, over lunch and dinner breaks or other moments of relaxation, businessmen chancingly or deliberately met and sorted out their positions.

By the 1920s a rift was clearly developing between the ministers in the Christian Socialist tradition of Hugh Price Hughes and Samuel Keeble on one hand and some of the lay leaders with backgrounds in commerce and industry on the other. A good example of this occurred on 12 May 1926, on the last day of the General Strike. At the Second London Synod meetings in Central Hall, Westminster, the Reverend Henry Carter, General Secretary of the Wesleyan Methodist Temperance and Social Welfare Department (a close friend of Keeble), explained how Wesleyans came to be associated with the Archbishop of Canterbury's statement on the strike. He and the Reverend Dr Scott Lidgett, another Wesleyan minister of Christian Socialist convictions, had met with Carter's friend Prebendary P. T. R. Kirk of the Church of England's Industrial Christian Fellowship on 5 May to discuss the strike situation.[49] This led to meetings at Lambeth Palace and the Archbishop of Canterbury's *Appeal from the Churches* published on 7 May. That statement and a letter to *The Times* lent credence to the notion that the Nonconformist churches and the Church of England saw the coal-mine owners as the sinners and the miners as the sinned against.[50] To this many on the side of capital took exception, as Henry Carter soon discovered. After he had sat down, Sir Robert Perks, the ageing but still vigorous Wesleyan layman and businessman, got up and attacked Carter 'furiously', alleging that the denomination's Committee of Privileges (on which businessmen were well represented), the church's advisory committee on external relations, should act on behalf of Wesleyans. The issue was reopened in the Synod's afternoon session (with Carter asserting that the Committee of Privileges was too cumbersome, inadequately informed and lacking interdenominational links). Nor did it rest there. Carter learned from ministerial colleagues that 'when the Synod was assembled at tea, as the guests of Sir Robert Perks, he took the opportunity of attacking me and the administration of the Department vehemently'.[51] When one of his clerical friends wrote to Sir Robert in Carter's defence, Perks retorted acidly,

It is, however, useful to have some kindly critic who can tell me how to act

[49] JRL, Keeble papers, file 5, carbon copy of memo starting 5 May 1926.
[50] E. R. Norman, *Church and Society in England, 1779–1970* (Oxford, 1976), 338–9.
[51] JRL, Keeble papers, file 5, memo of 5 May 1926, paragraph for 12 May 1926.

at my tea-tables. . . . I hope that you will have a very pleasant and useful career in our ministry; and that you will not be subject to many critics writing you about your sermons and your general conduct. I am glad to say that this is the first instance in which I have ever received in my very long connection with Methodism a letter from any preacher similar to the one you have felt it your duty, as you say, to send to me.[52]

An anonymous notice in *The Times*, suspected to be from Perks, disclaimed any association between the Wesleyan Church and the archbishop's letter.[53]

Perks was still alive when the Methodist Conference of 1934, the second after Methodist Union, adopted 'The Declaration of the Methodist Church on a Christian View of Industry in Relation to the Social Order' (see Chapter 2), but he was in his mid-eighties and in the last months of his life. Nevertheless it is hard to believe that there were no undercurrents of opposition to this triumph for socialist ministers. Unfortunately the relevant papers have not yet been deposited in the Methodist Archives.

That Declaration was the work of Henry Carter. Supporting him were the 24 ministers and 26 lay members of the denomination's Temperance and Social Welfare Committee. They included the ageing Samuel Keeble and the youthful Donald Soper among ministers; and among the laity one or two from the Labour Party (like Charles G. Ammon, former Labour MP) and radical Liberals like Isaac Foot MP and Dingle Foot MP. Conspicuous by their absence were Lord Wakefield, Lord Marshall, either of the Ranks, Sir Harold Bellman, or Sir Josiah Stamp, the most influential among Methodist businessmen in the mid-1930s. Few of the representatives of industry and commerce on the Temperance and Social Welfare Committee were of first-rate significance. John Crowlesmith, a director of Hazell, Watson & Viney, University of London Press, and the English University Press, represented some of the more prestigious companies in his industry; he was firmly behind Carter.[54]

Carter's main backers from business were Sir Luke Thompson and

---

[52] Ibid. file 5, xerox of letter from Sir R. W. Perks to Revd G. E. H. Johnson, 14 May 1926.

[53] Ibid. file 5, cutting from *The Times*, 15 May 1926.

[54] At the end of the General Strike in 1926 he told Carter over lunch that 'rumours that many employers were disposed to use the present opportunity "to smash the Unions" were all too well-founded. He had had great difficulty in discussions that morning with employers in the printing trade to hold them to anything like a reasonable view of the settlement that ought to be achieved with their employees.' Ibid. file 5, memo of 5 May 1926, paragraph for 13 May.

Lord Rochester. Thompson, Unionist MP for Sunderland, was director of the family firm of John Thompson & Sons (Sunderland) Ltd., coal merchants.[55] In seconding the adoption of the 'Declaration Concerning a Christian View of Industry in Relation to the Social Order' he acknowledged the significance of the subject but confined himself to the generalization that nothing was more important than 'this question as to whether our civilisation was to be a Christian one or not'.[56] In presenting his Department's report, including the Declaration, Carter expressed gratitude to Lord Rochester 'for the service he had rendered since the death of Mr J. H. Beckly, as Acting Treasurer of the Department'.[57] It would be very interesting to know the views held by Rochester (Ernest Henry Lamb), who in his early years, before the First World War, had trained as an electrical engineer and formed the New System Private Telephone Co. before taking over the family firm of transport contractors, Lamb Sons & Co.[58]

One Methodist business leader, chairman of the second largest employer-company in the United Kingdom in 1935, vocally declined to follow the idealistic and sometimes unthinking line being hewed by the denomination's Christian Socialist ministers. To its credit the denomination twice provided a platform for his views, which the radical clergy could not have found altogether palatable. In contrast to the Quaker industrialists in big business, Josiah Charles Stamp (1880–1941), 1st Baron Stamp of Shortlands in the County of Kent as he became in 1938, represented the new breed of professional managers.[59]

Until the age of 31 he was an unknown Civil Servant in the Inland Revenue. His career then commenced a stellar trajectory when after three years' home study, without tuition and in the midst of a busy family life, he took an external London University B.Sc. in economics and gained high first-class honours. During the First World War he devised Excess Profits Duty for Reginald McKenna, an achievement that gained him the ear of successive Chancellors of the Exchequer. After the war, *inter alia*, he sat on the Royal Commission on Income

[55] *WWW*; *DD 1935*.
[56] *M. Rec.*, 26 July 1934.
[57] Ibid. 26 July 1934.
[58] *The Times*, 14 Jan. 1955; *WWW*.
[59] Unless otherwise stated, biographical information on Stamp comes from Michael Bywater, 'Josiah Charles Stamp', *DBB*, a concise but extremely informative entry. It draws on the other main sources on Stamp: J. H. Jones, *Josiah Stamp, Public Servant* (London, 1964); A. M. Stamp, *Josiah Stamp and the Limitations of Economics* (London, 1970).

Tax (1919), the Colwyn Committee on Taxation and the National Debt (1924), and, most importantly, the Dawes Committee on German reparations. He was knighted in 1920. Although less rapid at first his industrial career found him engaged on pioneering in Britain the enormously important divisional management structure. Harry McGowan recruited him in 1919 to what became Nobel Industries, as company secretary and director. Besides drawing up the company's first consolidated balance sheet (1922), he devised the legal and accounting instruments designed to integrate dozens of subsidiaries into the parent company, in an American-style relationship between main head office and operating company—'one of Nobel Industries' principal legacies to ICI'.[60] At ICI Stamp played a notable part in negotiations with its rivals when ICI wanted to secure an oil-from-coal process from the Germans.[61] Stamp also became highly critical of the technical subterfuges of the accounting profession and delivered several broadsides against them.

Given McGowan's autocratic and manipulating style, it did not take much to persuade Stamp to accept the post of president of the executive of the London, Midland & Scottish Railway in 1926 on the understanding that he would succeed as chairman when Sir Guy Granet retired. Between 1927 and 1941 Stamp reigned over the LMS and its 220,000 employees. He set up a powerful management team, including Harold Hartley the Oxford scientist and Ernest J. H. Lemon the Derby locomotive engineer. With that calibre of managerial support Stamp was able to continue his public engagements and positions—such as the Mond–Turner talks (between employers and labour), the Court of the Bank of England, and the Young Commission (reparations). He wrote numerous books, mostly on taxation, finance, statistics, and railway practice, received a string of honorary doctorates, distinguished vice-presidencies, and the like, all amounting to a full-column entry in *Who's Who*. The only blemish on his public record was his unperceptive espousal of all things German which continued through the early Nazi years. As late as 1938 he visited Germany as Hitler's guest. With tragic irony he died in April 1941 when German bombers made a direct hit on his home at Shortlands, killing him, his wife, and their eldest son.

Raised a Baptist, Stamp became a staunch Wesleyan Methodist after his marriage to Olive Marsh, the schoolteacher daughter of a Greenwich builder, in 1903. Their early social life revolved around the Wesleyan church at Twickenham.[62] Stamp made no attempt to conceal the fact

---

[60] W. J. Reader, *ICI* (London, 1970–5), i. 393.   [61] Ibid. ii. 42.
[62] H. Bellman, *Cornish Cockney* (London, 1947), 225.

of his Christian commitment. Quite the reverse: when the Wesleyan Methodist Church and (after 1932) the Methodist Church offered him the platform he seized the chance to write and lecture about the relationship between economics and the Christian ethic. However, as professional manager in command of a huge workforce and responsible to shareholders, Stamp could not tread all the ground covered by the inter-war Quaker employers' conferences. He could certainly pursue the duty of an employer to achieve maximum efficiency. He might also make some experiments in industrial relations. What he, unlike the Quaker paternalists, could not contemplate was the possibility of surrendering control or ownership to the workforce.

In seeking to give expression to his faith in industrial matters Stamp encountered another limitation. He was enormously busy. His close friend Harold Bellman recalled his life-style:

On one occasion we were both due to address a meeting in Liverpool. We travelled together in his chairman's coach attached to the rear of the express. His secretary joined us at Euston and he dictated throughout the journey until we reached Crewe. There she left the train and came back to London to complete her side of the work. At stops *en route* he had brief discussions with his station-masters and local officials. The meeting over he retired for the night in his sleeping-berth, the coach was attached to another train and in the morning after an early breakfast he was ready for his business appointment in Scotland.[63]

Speeches and writings therefore comprised the prime method by which Josiah Stamp sought to carry his faith into business.

On what occasions did he speak or write? What was his message? One platform he might have used was that of the very popular annual meetings of the Abbey Road Building Society which between the wars offered its members entertaining and elevating as well as informative gatherings. He had become the Society's honorary president in the early 1920s at the instigation of the secretary Harold Bellman.[64] As the *Methodist Recorder* reminded its readers when reporting the annual meeting of the Society in 1934, the Abbey Road Building Society had started in a church vestry (of the Abbey Road Baptist Church in 1875). It might have been a chance to develop high ethical themes. If Stamp's speeches of 1925–9 and 1934 were typical, he declined the opportunity.[65] Similarly, when asked to discuss national economic prospects with the deno-

[63] Bellman, *Cornish Cockney*, 223.
[64] Ibid. 225–6; Esmond J. Cleary, 'Charles Harold Bellman', *DBB*.
[65] *M. Rec.*, 8 Mar. 1934. The speeches he made to the Abbey Road Society between 1925 and 1929 are reprinted in Stamp's *Criticism* (London, 1931), 271–88.

minational newspaper at the beginning of the year Stamp adhered to economic observations.[66]

Instead he chose, until the late 1930s at least, to decant his thoughts on the relationship between the Christian ethic and economics at specific church-based, rather than business-based, occasions. The first came in 1926 when he was invited to deliver the first Beckly Social Service Lecture. This was funded with £2,000, at the instigation of the Reverend Samuel Keeble, by John Henry Beckly, a draper of Plymouth and treasurer of the Methodist Temperance and Social Welfare Department (then run by the Reverend Henry Carter). Keeble presided at the first lecture and cannot have liked the message of individualism he heard from Stamp.[67] The lecture was published the same year as *The Christian Ethic as an Economic Factor*. Ten years later he gave the fourth Fernley–Hartley lecture, funded by the old Wesleyan Fernley and Primitive Methodist Hartley lecture trusts which had been merged in 1932. This was published in 1936 as *Motive and Method in a Christian Order*. Three years later he published *Christianity and Economics*, his last major contribution to the subject, for which Rufus M. Jones, the Quaker historian and theologian, wrote an introduction. This association with the Society of Friends presumably helped to purge Stamp's reputation of former Nazi links.

The Christian Ethic is a badly organized book.[68] However, it staked out a position which Stamp defended in his later works. His message was grounded in rigorous economics. He did not envisage the church, through the conversion of the nation, being able to solve all economic problems. 'If the moral conversion of the race is likely to be a slow task, so equally is the spread of clear ideas. A soul like a walnut and a mind like a ragbag are the two enemies of all millenia.'[69] Perhaps he was, as Norman suggests, criticizing the social radicalism of the bishops.[70] Certainly, as Oliver argues, he was drawing attention 'to the need to narrow the gap between the morality of the converted individual and that of the largely amoral organisations of which he is a member'.[71] Stamp's main concern was to distance the church from economic institutions and to place a new onus on the individual Christian to work out social redemption. As he emphasized in 1926, 'The ethical does not

---

[66] *M. Rec.*, 4 Jan. 1934.
[67] *WWM 1933*; M. L. Edwards, *S. E. Keeble* (London, 1949), 72–3.
[68] Jones, *Stamp*, 260 makes this point. Readers of *Christian Ethic* will agree.
[69] J. C. Stamp, *The Christian Ethic as an Economic Factor* (London, 1926), 20.
[70] Norman, *Church and Society*, 332.
[71] J. Oliver, *The Church and Social Order* (London, 1968), 114.

determine a particular scheme [capitalism or state socialism]—it makes many schemes work.'[72] *Motive and Method*, a book aimed at Methodist local preachers, had two concerns: one for the 'plannees', the citizens, of the new society that economists and planners were projecting; the other for those churchmen who were misguidedly taking up the ideas of 'Social Credit' (see Chapter 2 above). Stamp questioned whether the morality required of individuals was identical to that demanded of individuals acting in groups: 'in what precise sense can . . . the National Union of Railwaymen love the Railway Stockholders' Union?'[73]

Christianity for Stamp 'consists in the case of a single man raised from sin to conquest, from feebleness to moral strength, from meanness to beauty, rather than in a "clear programme" of action for unemployment or exchange control'.[74] In examining motives and mechanisms in economic activity he could see no workable alternatives to the price system, differential rewards on the factors of production, in a word: 'individualistic capitalism and the competitive system have been and still are a rich soil in which wheat and tares both flourish'.[75]

His last word on the subject, *Christianity and Economics* took a more historical approach. It gave him the chance to reflect on the years since the Beckly Lecture. He preserved the essence of his former opinions but noted what he saw as the church's reversal of an earlier position. 'In 1929 the Church had to combat a worship of material ideals and possessions, and yet a few years later was putting all its emphasis on material prosperity in its social gospel, and weakening its usefulness as a spiritual force. Who will turn, when he is sore of soul, to the parson who is specialising in banking reform?'—a clear knock at the Christendom group.[76] Stamp's views were a curious mixture of old and new. Economic systems were neutral. Their morality was determined by the individuals who operated them. Christianity was about converting the individual. If the pulpit (his word for church leaders) wanted to change economic systems it should stick to its last and concentrate on the conversion and moral education of individuals. Addressing his remarks to a clerical and lay audience, Stamp spoke as Olympian economic technocrat. The economic structures of a fallen world could not be claimed for God; salvation belonged to the individual. It would be interesting to know on what sort of level he discussed his business problems with

[72] Stamp, *Christian Ethic*, 69.   [73] Stamp, *Motive and Method*, 40.
[74] Ibid. 48.   [75] Ibid. 113.
[76] J. C. Stamp, *Christianity and Economics* (London, 1939), 168.

the practical industrialists he regarded as his peers. Bellman gave one clue: 'It is a curious reflection that both Stamp and Keynes, who were considered heretical in their day, came to serve on the Court of the Bank of England. Stamp had a tremendous admiration for Keynes, and "Maynard", as he always called him, was never far from his thoughts.'[77] Stamp's preference was for the theoretical, the academic, the awareness of life's enormous complexities. Did his faith in the moral neutrality of economic and social systems change before his death? It would be astonishing if it did not. If Methodist entrepreneurs and managers followed Stamp's lead—and Bellman recalled that 'huge audiences acclaimed him in business assemblies and in the universities'[78]—it is hardly surprising that they attempted no concerted action as Christian industrialists. More positively, his demolition of Douglas's Social Credit theory, which Stamp consigned to an Appendix in *Motive and Method*, spared Methodists and his other admirers from a misbegotten economic heresy then absorbing the energies of radical Anglicans in search of social justice.

3 ANGLICAN INDUSTRIALISTS

What of Anglicans in big business between the wars? Were they any better organized or any more articulate than the Quaker employers? Who, in the first place, were they? Of the 31 chairmen and 19 managing directors heading the largest companies in 1935 and identified as belonging to the Church of England no more than nine or ten had religious affiliations above the level of the parish church. By the late 1930s one of them, William Henry Smith the 3rd Viscount Hambleden, was becoming caught up in what emerged as the most exciting initiative for lay people in business leadership. Before this development, big businessmen had grappled with the moral implications of their faith in two organizations in the Church of England. One was the Industrial Christian Fellowship, the other COPEC. For differing reasons both failed to satisfy the ethical needs of industrial leaders. They are considered in turn.

The Industrial Christian Fellowship (ICF) was formed in 1920 as a direct result of the Archbishops' Report on *Christianity and Industrial Problems* (1918) and the inadequacies of existing church initiatives in industry. The exhausted Christian Social Union and the moribund

---

[77] Bellman, *Cornish Cockney*, 226.   [78] Ibid. 228.

Navvy Mission were merged in January 1919 and renamed the ICF.[79]
Its objectives clearly encompassed individuals and industrial systems:

I. To present Christ as the living Lord and Master in every department of
human life, and to proclaim the supreme authority of the Christian law of love
II. To minister to all engaged in the industrial world, seeking to win them
to personal discipleship of Jesus Christ, and to unite all classes in a bond of
Christian fellowship and prayer. III. To study, under the guidance of the Holy
Spirit, how to apply the moral truths and principles of Christianity to the social,
economic, and industrial systems of the world.[80]

In the early years a number of industrialists sat on the 300-strong ICF
Council. However, as Gerald Studdert-Kennedy shows, several who had
supported the old Navvy Mission dropped out when the general director,
the Reverend P. T. R. Kirk, 'ran a strong line on the greed and social
irresponsibility of the coal-owners'. Among those who resigned was Sir
John Dewrance, chairman of Babcock & Wilcox and Kent Coal Con-
cessions.[81] One who stayed was (William) Lionel Hichens.

Hichens, the successful chairman of Cammell Lairds the Birkenhead
shipbuilders for thirty years from 1910, had been a member of Milner's
'Kindergarten' responsible for reconstructing the Boer colonies after the
South African War. He had powerful Anglican friends including the
2nd Earl of Selborne and Robert H. Brand of Lazards the merchant
bankers.[82] He served the ICF as one of its three (later two) trustees
during the 1920s and 1930s.[83] Hichens emerged from the First World
War, during which he had played an important part in reorganizing
Canadian munitions production, with a strongly Smithian suspicion of
the encroachments of the state in industry and a concern that at times
organized labour was too powerful. He regarded the current organizational proposals for Guild Socialism, Syndicalism, Co-Partnership, and
Whitley Councils as insufficient of themselves in treating Britain's industrial relations problems. Instead he appealed to a mutuality of rights
and duties: 'In the industrial world our duty clearly is to regard our
work as service which we render to the rest of the community, and it
is obvious that we should give, not grudgingly or of necessity, but in

[79] Oliver, *Church and Social Order*, 60–2; Norman, *Church and Society*, 245–6.
[80] 'Object' printed at the front of the ICF, *Annual Reports*.
[81] G. Studdert-Kennedy, *Dog-Collar Democracy* (London, 1982), 19–21; Christine Shaw,
'John Dewrance', *DBB*.
[82] Studdert-Kennedy, *Dog-Collar Democracy*, 23–8; R. P. T. Davenport-Hines, 'William
Lionel Hichens', *DBB*.
[83] Studdert-Kennedy, *Dog-Collar Democracy*, 23; ICF, *Annual Report* (1935–6), 1.

full measure.'[84] In his position as ICF trustee and progressive industrialist and by his numerous speeches and short papers in defence of a new realism in industry, Hichens made a widespread public impact. Within the ICF he emphasized, according to a recent examination, the spirit of the gospel operating through individuals to transform society and industry; organic bonds of goodwill and service across sectional and class lines; and respect for the first duty of the industrialist to make his business efficient. When pressed to choose between capital and labour, between the survival of industry and providing a living wage, as he was in the depression of the early 1920s, Hichens reluctantly came down on the side of capital.[85] His views were reminiscent of those of Josiah Stamp whom Hichens would have regularly met at LMS board meetings in the 1930s.

Despite the influence of a powerful industrialist like Hichens, few other business leaders joined him on the Council of the ICF. Scarcely a handful of distinguished (by title at least) lay people sat on it in 1935. Of 101 lay persons that year 43 were females and of these 32 were single ladies.[86] The laity on the ICF Council were mostly not of the first rank by any social reckoning.[87] Consequently, perhaps, the ICF, despite its third declared objective, never became an effective forum for debate or springboard for action by captains of industry belonging to the Church of England. They certainly suspected the Christian Socialist sympathies of many of the higher clergy involved in it, but (perhaps with moderating relief) would have noted that the ICF by the 1930s was preoccupied with its first and second objectives. Between the wars the ICF undertook the evangelistic mission of the church in city after city in Britain's industrial heartland. Its most famous missioner was G. A. Studdert-Kennedy, 'Woodbine Willie' of the trenches of the Western Front.[88]

In the 1920s the ICF succeeded in alienating both socialists and capitalists. At times the ICF seemed to have moved far from its Christian Socialist antecedents. Woodbine Willie's response to Ernest Bevin at a public meeting in February 1921 suggested something of this: 'If the Church went hand in hand with the Labour Party she would "make one of the greatest mistakes in her history."'[89] Alienation of capitalists,

---

[84] W. L. Hichens, *The New Spirit in Industrial Relations* (London, 1919), 28.

[85] Studdert-Kennedy, *Dog-Collar Democracy*, 137, 149, 170–6.

[86] ICF, *Annual Report* (1935–6), 1–2.

[87] Studdert-Kennedy, *Dog-Collar Democracy*, 22.

[88] W. Purcell, *Woodbine Willie* (London, 1962); Studdert-Kennedy, *Dog-Collar Democracy, passim*.

[89] Studdert-Kennedy, *Dog-Collar Democracy*, 171.

and much public opinion, accompanied its futile attempt to mediate between the miners and the coalowners after the General Strike in 1926. Ironically, if Seebohm Rowntree was right, the ICF intervention (which appeared to take the side of the miners) queered the pitch for another group of mediators and thereby may have been responsible for protracting the coal strike by six months.[90] But that may be too simple an analysis of a complex series of events. As Norman observes, 'Church social radicalism had developed in isolation from realities—in episcopal palaces, at Conferences and study-groups, in Theological Colleges and University common rooms. In 1926 the door had been opened and a very cold blast had withered the hot-house growths. The Church's passion for social criticism survived the experience, but its growth was stunted.'[91]

The other vehicle which might have acted as a catalyst for developing a Christian position for industrialists between the wars was COPEC. Of the Twelve Commissions appointed in 1921 to organize the sessions of the Conference on Christian Politics, Economics and Citizenship, that on Industry and Property presented the crucial opportunity for clear-thinking, experienced business leaders of Christian conviction to inject realism into Christian social radicalism. The opportunity was lost. Although William Temple (prime mover of COPEC) had resigned from the Labour Party on becoming Bishop of Manchester in 1921, COPEC, as Edward Norman convincingly argues, was spearheaded by churchmen and laymen with political affinities on the Left, explicitly with the League of the Kingdom of God.[92] Thus the scales were loaded against the representatives of capital from the start.

That was not the only reason why COPEC disappointed practical industrialists of Christian persuasion like Josiah Stamp.[93] No strong case was being made in defence of a redeemed capitalism. Stamp had yet to put pen to paper on the subject. Of the five industrialists sitting on the 30-strong Industry and Property Commission only one could match Stamp in intellectual brilliance and business experience. That was William Piercy who gained a first class B.Sc.(Econ.) at LSE in 1913, served with distinction in central government during the war, and afterwards joined Harrisons & Crosfield, East India merchants. Through his wife he was connected with the Earls of Chichester and the Balfours

[90] Norman, *Church and Society*, 339–40; F. A. Iremonger, *William Temple* (London, 1948), 337–44.
[91] Norman, *Church and Society*, 340.
[92] Ibid. 284–7.
[93] Stamp, *Christian Ethic*, 18–19, 83–8, for example.

of Burleigh. (He later had a successful career in finance, especially in the area of financing small and medium-sized industrial companies, for which he was raised to the peerage in 1945.[94]) But neither Piercy nor any of the industrialists produced positive insights when their minds went over the ground of Christian industrial ethics in 1921–4.

This was perhaps hardly surprising in the case of Piercy's industrial colleagues. Frank Gilbertson, head of a medium-sized West Glamorgan family firm of sheet steel and tinplate manufacturers and spokesman for his industry, despised the coalowners, the industrial malefactors of the inter-war years, not least for their grasping resistance of rationalization.[95] That much made him sympathetic to COPEC aims. A life-long churchman and prominent layman of the Church in Wales, he would loyally follow the lead given by his archbishops, and the COPEC reports simply reiterated *Christianity and Industrial Problems*, the Report of the Archbishops' Fifth Committee of Inquiry (1918), albeit to a wider audience. Sir Max Muspratt, chairman of the United Alkali Co. (and another chemist by training), headed the sick giant of his industry which only received the necessary injection of new technology and reorganization when it was swallowed up in ICI in 1926. Politically Radical (until 1926 anyway), presumably the Commission's emphases of the service motive, co-operative effort, minimum wages in industry, and reversing inequalities of wealth between individuals held some appeal for him as he battled to revive his dying corporation.[96] John Pybus, son of a prominent Wesleyan in Hull, was managing director of the English Electric Co., on the board of which sat Lionel Hichens. The limits of Pybus's assent to the high ideals of COPEC became apparent to himself and his intimates, if not all the general public, two years later when he helped to manage the *British Gazette* (the Conservative Government's partisan newspaper run by Winston Churchill) during the General Strike.[97] Angus Watson, the Congregationalist and founder of Skipper sardines (which he sold out to William Lever), would applaud COPEC's acknowledgement of the need for individual conversion prior to the transforming of social structures; however, he lacked the economic training to evaluate ethical and economic relationships.[98]

---

[94] Martin Chick, 'William Stuckey Piercy', *DBB*.
[95] Graeme M. Holmes, 'Francis William Gilbertson', *DBB*.
[96] Peter N. Reed, 'Max Muspratt', *DBB*.
[97] R. P. T. Davenport-Hines, 'Percy John Pybus', *DBB*.
[98] Richard Perren, 'James Angus Watson', *DBB*; Watson had in his sights the financiers more than the industrialists: A. Watson, *The Faith of a Business Man* (London, 1936), 90–2.

Piercy apart, the industrial men, two chemists, an electrical engineer, and a fish canner, were too practical and too specialized as men of affairs to understand fully or to counter in kind the theoretical and academic arguments put up by academics (led by Tawney), legal men (by Sir Henry Slesser), or newly mobilizing social workers (led by Henry Mess). They were more used to dealing with labour leaders or trade unionists (represented on the Commission by Ben Turner from the newly formed Council of the Trades Union Congress), men of similar specialism and narrowness of outlook. In this way the industrialists on the Industry and Property Commission were outgunned by Christian Socialists of one kind or another. A single dissenting voice was raised in defence of industry. Miss Ada Streeter, honorary secretary of the Industrial Committee of the National Council of Women of Great Britain, staff member of the Catholic Social Guild, and formerly first organizing secretary of the Catholic Women's League, included among her reasons for not, as Catholic representative on the Commission, signing the report, 'That the blame for our present difficulties does not lie wholly with Employers, Proprietors and Industrialists'.[99]

Industrialists at last in the late 1930s began to make a constructive contribution to the debate over the application of Christian ethics to society. For this the credit must go largely to two men, Archbishop William Temple and Dr Joseph Oldham. William Temple's ethical thought may not have been original, deriving from the Christian Social Union of the 1890s:[100] it certainly gathered weight and attention as he moved up the episcopal ladder. Oldham provided the idea that the institutional church in most cases could only proclaim moral generalities in the area of industrial behaviour. The onus for introducing a Christian perspective to any secular activity must lie with individual Christians (see Chapter 4 above). Temple shared this view and lent his support to the vehicles Oldham forged to mobilize the laity, including industrialists.

The first of those vehicles was the weekly *Christian News-Letter*, issued under the auspices of the interdenominational Council on the Christian Faith and the Common Life, one strand in the web of ecumenical councils organized between the wars and forerunner of the British Council of Churches. The CCFCL first met at Lambeth Palace under the chair-

---

[99] COPEC Reports, vol. ix *Industry and Property* (London, 1924), 199; *Catholic WW 1931*. Norman, *Church and Society*, 299 states that Muspratt also dissented but this is not evident from the conclusion and list of signatories to the Industry and Property report.

[100] Norman, *Church and Society*, 282.

manship of the Archbishop of Canterbury (Cosmo Lang) in November 1938. Besides Lang and Temple (by now Archbishop of York) and the Bishop of Bristol (C. Salisbury Woodward) for the Church of England, it included the Reverend Dr Scott Lidgett, now a venerable radical, for the Methodists, J. H. Oldham, and Sir Walter Moberly, former Vice-Chancellor of Manchester University and currently the first full-time chairman of the University Grants Committee.[101] Other major denominations soon joined, the Reverend M. E. Aubrey for the Baptists, the Reverend S. M. Berry for the Congregationalists. One or two younger clergymen were recruited from the full-time staff of the Student Christian Movement. A. D. Lindsay, the Master of Balliol College, Oxford, and a distinguished philosopher, and Walter Oakeshott, High Master of St Paul's School, were among the lay people co-opted. Professor Henry Clay the economist was one whose name was considered but for some reason never came on to the Council. By the outbreak of war nearly two dozen individuals from a wide spread of fields and ages, as well as the churches, assembled and were taking up a number of issues at the instigation of Oldham.

At the outset the Council (CCFCL) considered a memorandum (the basis of 'The Rebirth of the West') drafted by Oldham about its objectives.[102] Among these was the hope of developing links with thinkers and writers. Oldham reported that he had a list of upwards of 100 people who could be enlisted. His vision would need permanent staff and a budget, a Commission to serve the Council. As ever, Oldham had a plan of action. He had recently organized the merger of the Christian Social Council and the British Christian Council to form a Commission on Social and International Responsibility. Initially designed to act as a clearing house for church and interdenominational agencies of education, this would be the instrument the Council needed. Oldham saw it as 'a medium through which the Council [CCFCL] could penetrate the work of the individual Churches.'[103] The Council agreed and calculated that, with grants and donations from the Commission's parent bodies, they would have to appeal to the churches for no more than £1,340 of the £4,000 required for the initiatives Oldham was proposing.[104]

Meantime Oldham moved the Council forward by means of his favourite method of working, through small groups thrashing out discussion

---

[101] BCC, CCFCL minutes 1938–42, 10 Nov. 1938.
[102] Which apparently has not survived.
[103] BCC, CCFCL minutes, 10 Nov. 1938.   [104] Ibid.

documents and policy statements. In March 1939 he reported that one group, who had been meeting for eighteen months and were extending their Oxbridge contacts, had now produced two discussion papers, 'one by Professor H. A. Hodges outlining the tasks involved in the development of a Christian philosophy of man and society, and the other by Professor Karl Mannheim dealing with an empirical approach to the study of modern society. It was hoped that after further consideration and elaboration these two papers would provide the basis for a programme of work in which wide cooperation could be obtained.'[105] Hodges was professor of philosophy at Reading University. Mannheim, professor of sociology at London University and one of the founding giants of his discipline, was about to publish his immensely influential *Man and Society in an Age of Reconstruction* (1940). Evidently these first discussion papers came out of the 'Moot', the group of Christian intellectuals Oldham was gathering round Mannheim and T. S. Eliot.

At its second and fully representative meeting the Council on the Christian Faith and the Common Life considered Oldham's memorandum, 'The Rebirth of the West'. William Temple agreed with its diagnosis:

The acuteness of crisis was concealed in Great Britain by a residual and widespread feeling for the Christian religion which became evident in times of national emergency. It was, however, true that for many people Christian doctrine was entirely meaningless. Nineteenth century humanism had undermined the Christian biblical view and people deeply influenced by this movement lived in a different 'universe of discourse'. He felt the memorandum was right in claiming that a movement was needed which was equally conscious of both these points and he felt sure that there would be a welcome for such a move if we were able to talk a language that other people could understand.[106]

Faced with lengthening totalitarian shadows in Europe—Hitler was even then completing the Nazi occupation of Czechoslovakia and Stalin's USSR promised no better hopes for democracy and Christianity—a wide range of people in Britain were prepared to look again at the philosophical and religious foundations of their own society. Oldham was correct to see a dangerous division among those 'forces resisting the new paganism' between 'those who took their stand on Christian ethics and for whom Christian doctrine was almost meaningless' and those 'convinced that the Christian ethic must have an objective and religious foundation'. As he saw it, 'It was an urgent task to build bridges between [the] two

---

[105] Ibid. 29 Mar. 1939.   [106] Ibid.

groups.' Sir Walter Moberly put the issue clearly to the meeting: would they agree to supporting an initiative which, through mobilizing intellectual and cultural opinion, would bring humanitarians around 'a nucleus of people deeply committed to the Christian faith but adopting as their objective in public policy the creation of an England which could be in some (necessarily diluted) sense Christian'? The focal point for the movement would be Oldham's statement, its objectives, what Moberly called 'an intermediate way'. The Council agreed, leaving Oldham to forge its instruments.[107]

He evidently spent some time over summer 1939 working out the kind of precise strategy that Aubrey had urged at the March meeting. Britain's declaration of war on Nazi Germany rendered much of this redundant. It also lent a new urgency to his task. Out of this crucible Oldham presented his proposals for a *News-Letter*, first published in November 1939 with the title of *Christian News-Letter*. The impact of that weekly publication, small but highly influential, will emerge later. At this point it is important to notice that early on Oldham relied on one or two businessmen for financial acumen and some funding.

One was Harold Judd, a chartered accountant and partner in Mann, Judd & Co. During the First World War Judd was one of the number of businessmen recruited to Lloyd George's Ministry of Munitions in 1915, rising to Deputy Controller of Contracts. At the outbreak of war in September 1939 he was appointed Controller of Salvage. Born in China to missionary parents, Judd came to share their faith and in 1935 served the Presbyterian Church of England as vice-convenor of the foreign missions committee of its General Assembly.[108] He first attended the Council on the Christian Faith and the Common Life at its March 1939 meeting and was elected chairman of its finance sub-committee, intimating that it might be possible to raise funds more quickly than his ecclesiastical and academic colleagues envisaged. In September, as treasurer of the Council, he was added to its business committee.[109]

The other businessman who lent his weight to Oldham's efforts was Lord Hambleden, whose chairmanship of W. H. Smith & Son placed him in the 1930s business élite. Only 36 in 1939, he had a deep personal Anglican faith like his father, the 2nd Viscount Hambleden. After his premature death following an operation in 1948, Lord David Cecil recalled of him that

---

[107] Ibid.

[108] *WWW*; *The Times*, 7, 11 Jan. 1961; Presbyterian Church of England, *Official Handbook* (London, 1935–6), 14.

[109] BCC, CCFCL minutes, 29 Mar., 27 Sept. 1939.

Hambleden was born to great public responsibilities, and he dedicated himself to them with a selfless devotion. ... He had a very strong character. Though very humble, he always made up his mind about people and things regardless of conventional opinion and carried out his convictions in face of whatever difficulty. But with strength went sensitive sweetness. Religion, a passionate and personal religion, coloured his whole outlook.[110]

Within the firm he was beginning to collect a reputation for caring more about staff welfare than profits.[111] Hambleden was clearly one of those personalities the Council, right from the start, wanted among its members to attract the financial support of businessmen.[112] His name was suggested at the Council's March 1939 meeting and he joined the following September. His, like Judd's, was no mere ornamental involvement. With T. S. Eliot and Philip Mairet the Swiss-born designer, Fabian, former actor, journalist, and friend of Maurice Reckitt,[113] Hambleden volunteered to spend one evening a week serving as the editorial board for the *Christian News-Letter*—if Oldham, the editor, and his assistant the Reverend A. R. Vidler so wished.[114] After Hambleden's death it was recalled, 'It was chiefly his generosity which made possible the capital outlay involved in launching the *News-Letter*.'[115] Hambleden thus became the first big businessman to become involved in Oldham's new task of directing Christian ethics into a secular world. In the 1940s this would shift into the area of business.

By the 1940s then, Quaker employers were most sensitized in the matter of relating business behaviour to the ethic implicit in their religious faith. Methodist employers were likely to fall in behind Josiah Stamp and preserve the old separation between economics and religion, though this was being attacked by radical clergy. Anglicans could, through the efforts of Archbishop William Temple and Dr Joe Oldham, see a new way forward involving the mobilization of the laity. Under the stresses and strains of war and its aftermath some of these efforts to relate faith and business would gather a new momentum.

---

[110] *The Times*, 1, 5 Apr. 1948.

[111] C. Wilson, *First with the News* (London, 1985), 339.

[112] BCC, CCFCL minutes, 10 Nov. 1938, comment by Miss Eleanora Iredale who had served as secretary with the Pilgrim Trust project which produced *Men Without Work* (1938), an investigation which involved Moberly, Lindsay, and Oldham—and also Sir Edward Peacock the merchant banker and central banker. See Iremonger, *Temple*, 441–2.

[113] *The Times*, 20 Feb. 1975.

[114] BCC, CCFCL minutes, 29 Mar., 27 Sept. 1939.

[115] *CNL* 309 (14 Apr. 1948), 7.

6

Christians in Big Business Leadership during the 1940s and 1950s

If the business environment seemed to shift rapidly between the two world wars, it changed more dramatically in the 1940s and 1950s. Total war, a difficult period of peacetime readjustment which included the nationalization of some industries, more expansive conditions, but with them sharper international competition: this was the context in which big business developed in these decades. In those firms taken over by the state, professional managers quickly replaced former owner-managers, thus rolling back further the scope for paternalism in big business. In large family firms remaining in the private sector the limits of paternalism were tested by increases in scale and the influx of professional managers necessitated by diseconomies of size. In the 1950s the divisional structure started a rapid spread through the largest companies in the British economy. Christians in big business now found themselves even more clearly placed either in the category of capitalist or bureaucrat, paternalist or professional manager. Who were the churchmen in big business leadership in the 1950s? In what ways did they try to relate their faith to the advanced industrial society in which they found themselves? What sort of problems did they encounter?

As seen earlier, profiles on 160 of the 212 chairmen and managing directors heading the 96 largest company employers in 1955 have been assembled. Of these 160, 63 have left traces of some kind of religious association. For some this was as weak as a Church of England burial, for others as strong as the allocation of half his waking hours which John Laing gave to religious involvements. Of the 63, 33 were associated with the Church of England, 3 with the Church of Scotland, 2 with the English Presbyterians, 2 with the Brethren, 1 with the Congregationalists, 4 with the Methodists, 1 with the Quakers, 2 with the Roman Catholics, 2 with the Christian Scientists.

In the case of the Anglicans a large proportion appear to have been private or nominal churchgoers. For some their religious involvement was confined to the local parish church. This had varying shades of meaning and differing implications for their business life. Thus Harley Drayton, chairman of British Electric Traction Co. which employed 70,000, 'at weekends became a countryman and a serious farmer: pampering his pigs and dispensing claret after his shooting parties, reading the lesson in the parish church and enjoying the country-squire life on his 700-acre [Suffolk] estate'.[1] Another kind of established church association was possible in the life of the City, linked to the pageantry of City ceremonial on one hand and charitable activity on the other. So W. G. Edington, chief general manager of the Midland Bank, was a member of the Parochial Church Council of St Lawrence Jewry-next-Guildhall.[2] Marshal of the RAF Lord Tedder, chairman of the Standard Motor Co., had Anglican religious sympathies formed by his education at Whitgift Grammar School, Croydon.[3] These and his wartime dealings with the company led him to commend John Laing & Son Ltd., contractors for the RAF, for their 'faith and determination which have accepted risks and overcome obstacles'.[4]

Anglicans were not the only ones for whom religion could be a largely private matter. William Fraser, 1st Baron Strathalmond of Pumpherston, chairman of BP, 'was a fairly strong Presbyterian who when in London used to worship at St Columba's, Pont Street'.[5] Robert Harvey, Deputy Director General of the Post Office and another from a Scottish presbyterian background, was known among his intimates as 'a very reserved person' who 'never talked about his faith' which was assumed to be 'vigorous and strong'. He and his family were regular worshippers at Banstead Presbyterian Church, Surrey, and whenever Harvey was abroad, as in 'the early heady days of international negotiations on the first Comsat systems, I recall snatching, with him, rare opportunities

---

[1] John Hibbs, 'Harold Charles Gilbert Drayton', *DBB*.

[2] *Midland Chronicle*, Aug. 1968; for Edington's conservative influence over the Midland see A. R. Holmes and E. Green, *Midland* (London, 1986), 214–21.

[3] *The Times*, 5 June 1967. His biographer omits any reference to the religious impact of his schooling: R. Owen, *Tedder* (London, 1952).

[4] J. Laing & Son Ltd., *Teamwork* (London, 1950), Foreword.

[5] Information from Dr R. W. Ferrier, BP historian, 30 Jan. 1986. For Fraser see R. W. Ferrier, 'William Milligan Fraser', *DBB*; *The Times*, 2 Apr. 1970.

for a Sunday service in strange churches, with unfamiliar patterns of worship in places in Europe, USA, and Canada.'[6]

Other business leaders of strong Christian convictions and the propensity for religious association did not, apparently, see the world of business as a sphere for the application of Christian ethics. For them work was an area where individual colleagues might be influenced but organizational structures and modes of operation much less, if at all. Whether they understood its antecedents or not, they stood in the older Puritan tradition of 'individualism congenial to the world of business'.[7] The tradition produced some of the finest as well as some of the most hypocritical men of business. Against such a glaring example of apparent insincerity as Lord Overtoun at the turn of the century has to be set Sir John Craig chairman of Colvilles Ltd., the Scottish iron and steel manufacturers, in 1955. In early adulthood a Free Church of Scotland elder, and utterly dedicated to his firm of which he saw himself 'as simply a trustee acting for the Colville family', his career evoked carefully weighed and remarkable comments from the academic company historian: 'The history of Colvilles, under his chairmanship, cannot be fully understood without appreciating that "his religious sincerity reflected itself in his whole life and a career which might have received its initial impetus from personal ambition, quickly resolved itself into one of service for his fellow men."' Or again, 'of all the obituaries that by David Graham, of the Dalzell Works, who knew him well, was possibly the most profound: "The secret of his active and interesting career lay in the fact that he walked with God."'[8]

So far as is known most of these men, and quite a number of others whose church allegiance might be described variously as nominal, formal, private, or in some sense separate from business, did not associate with any organized Christian invasions of business. That is they made little attempt to take their faith, in either its religious or ethical expressions, into their firms in visible, organized fashion. John Craig, an ardent national office-holder in the YMCA, presumably saw that organization as a sufficient vehicle by which he might share his faith with thousands of industrial workers, including his own employees. The point begs a lot of questions, many of which cannot be answered from individual biographies of the business leaders. How did they respond to the radical social theology popularized by William Temple? Did they retain the

[6] Dr James H. H. Merriman, formerly chairman of the National Computing Centre, to the author, 7 Sept. 1986.

[7] R. H. Tawney, *Religion and the Rise of Capitalism* (London, 1936), 234.

[8] Peter L. Payne, 'John Craig', *DSBB*.

separation of business and ethics/religion? If not, how far were they pre-pared to admit Christian ethics/religion into their firms? Presumably firm owners had much more freedom than professional managers in a large corporation. How did Christians in these two positions reconcile Christian imperatives with the big business situations in which they found themselves? As noted in Chapter 2, advanced thinkers in the churches in the inter-war years were calling for the recapture of intellectual territory lost during the eighteenth-century Enlightenment. Provoked, inspired, led by a few of these church professionals, a number of industrialists embarked on experiments aimed at taking the faith once more into the workplace, whether boardroom or shop-floor. This chapter sets out to trace these endeavours. Under the clouds of war there was the Christian Frontier Council. After the war came new advances in industrial mission at Sheffield and later Luton. The industrial chaplains movement, strong in Scotland, spread in the period. Finally, evangelicals began to stir themselves.

I THE CHRISTIAN FRONTIER COUNCIL

The Christian Frontier Council (CFC) was the second of the vehicles by which J. H. Oldham, supported by Temple, hoped to mobilize the laity into applying their faith to their working lives. It grew out of the *Christian News-Letter* (*CNL*), his first vehicle (see Chapter 5). Within two months of its launch, shortly after the outbreak of war, Oldham reported that the *CNL* had 9,081 subscribers.[9] However, the Council, and with it the *CNL* which it sponsored, had multiple concerns. The Council as part of the ecumenical movement was anxious to advance the cause of Christian unity. Living in the shadow of totalitarianism, it was concerned to promote a distinctive Christian response to the threats from Right and Left. Operating in what was now recognized by the less somnolent of churchmen to be a secular society, at best indifferent at worst hostile to the Christian faith, it wanted to awaken its allies to the challenge of unbelief. And then there were the unchurched masses, particularly in the industrial cities, whose plight was deeply worrying. Oldham indeed regarded the spiritual state of England to be so unchris-tian that in the summer of 1939 he was planning 'an evangelistic mission in this country in which persons from other lands would help'. The outbreak of war forced the postponement of the Council's evangelistic

[9] BCC, CCFCL minutes 6 Feb. 1940.

task but not its commitment to ecumenical education and 'the awakening of a deeper sense of social responsibility' among Christians.[10]

While the Council on the Christian Faith and the Common Life, and its successor (after 23 September 1942) the British Council of Churches, pursued the two major causes of ecumenism and the reform of the educational system (which led with mixed bouquets for the churches to the Education Act of 1944),[11] Oldham took up what Cosmo Lang called 'pioneer work'.[12] In July 1940, before the bombing of its offices in Balcombe Street forced the removal of the *CNL* to Oxford, Oldham circulated a memo expressing his fear,

of the supreme danger of the nation getting engrossed in the immediate peril and forgetting that this was only a part of the immense dangers threatening mankind. He could see only one way of encountering these dangers. That was to create a unifying centre, some rallying point for the Christian and liberal forces in this country, which had to be mobilised and directed to cope with the swiftly moving events that might engulf us at any moment. He did not mean the creation of a new political party, but the centre had to possess a moral, spiritual and intellectual authority.[13]

He reported that he had unofficially approached Professor O. S. Franks of Glasgow University, then working at the Ministry of Supply, to act as the key person at the unifying centre. Franks declined (and went on to become British Ambassador at Washington, chairman of Lloyds Bank, and one of the most eminent of Oxford dons).

The feeling of the Council was that they should move forward somehow. The laymen, like most of the clergy, on the Council responded sympathetically though wondered where Oldham's vision would lead them. Lord Hambleden wanted more definition and a stress on doctrine. Henry Brooke, then Conservative MP for West Lewisham, urged speedy action. A. D. Lindsay, Master of Balliol, argued that if Oldham was proposing a call to the nation he should form a political party; if he wanted a call to the churches, they had to 'think out the implications

[10] Ibid. 27 Sept. 1939.

[11] This has scathingly been described as 'an enormous pudding of negotiation' which deflected politicians from the important task of shaping an educational system suited for a scientific and technological society. C. Barnett, *The Audit of War* (London, 1986), 281 and following. Barnett is surely right to condemn the futilities of denominationalism but he should beware of downplaying the need for the members of a technological society to be well equipped with moral values: scientists and engineers have no special claim to political and moral authority.

[12] BCC, CCFCL minutes, 29 July 1941.

[13] Ibid. 9 July 1940.

of Christian brotherhood in various fields and then put that to the Churches'. Harold Judd, who had resigned the Council treasurership due to pressure of work at the Ministry of Supply, being replaced by Hambleden, called for swift action rather than the perfection of a campaign plan.[14]

Oldham gave the matter a great deal of thought and prayer. He was now in his late sixties, serving the Council on the Christian Faith and the Common Life as both its secretary and the editor of the weekly *CNL*. With the latter he had the able help of a personal assistant-cum-secretary, Miss Iredale. However, it became clear to A. D. Lindsay after the *CNL* move to Manchester College, Oxford, that Oldham and his assistant should be doing less not more.[15] At the end of July 1941 Oldham resigned from the Council secretaryship. With the prospects of the Council being absorbed in the new British Council of Churches, the Council's sub-committee on staffing advised 'the creation of a semi-independent committee, largely lay, to supervise pioneer work, including the Christian News-Letter'.[16] In July 1941 Oldham suggested he should 'give his attention to the study of the Structure of Society' with 'adolescence as the point of entry'.[17] The Council minutes for February 1942 do not seem to have survived so we are unsure of the remainder of the formative thinking behind the Christian Frontier (as it was initially called) which first met on 26 February 1942.

Through the Christian Frontier J. H. Oldham hoped to realize his dream of mobilizing a core of laity who would act as the leaven of society. Those who joined him (and one clergyman assistant) at the Frontier's first meeting, at St Ermin's Hotel, Westminster, were Sir Walter Moberly (in the chair), Edwin Barker (YMCA connections), Henry Brooke MP (and after the war deputy-chairman of the Southern Railway), M. Chaning-Pearce, Harold Judd, Walter Oakeshott, and Henry U. Willink (Conservative MP for Croydon and Minister of Health 1943–5). They decided that the laymen present plus A. D. Lindsay, T. S. Eliot, Lord Hambleden, A. Wilfrid Garrett (H. M. Chief Inspector of Factories), Mrs J. L. Stocks (Principal of Westfield College, University of London), and John F. Wolfenden (headmaster of Uppingham School) would form the Council of the Christian Frontier. Others were soon added. At the Frontier's second meeting in March 1942 Harold C. Dent (editor of

[14] BCC. Judd's work at the Ministry of Supply necessitated his resignation at the meeting on 6 Feb. 1940.
[15] Ibid., minutes, 3 Feb. 1941.
[16] Ibid., committee minutes, staffing subcommittee, 11 July 1941.
[17] Ibid., minutes, 29 July 1941.

The Times Educational Supplement), Professor Oliver Franks, George A. Goyder (general manager of the Newsprint Supply Co. through which paper was channelled to the major newspapers during the war), Humphrey C. B. Mynors (Bank of England and former Cambridge economics don; a Director of the Bank in 1949[18]), Reginald Pugh, Clifton Robbins, and Barbara Ward (assistant editor of *The Economist*) joined; Lady Cripps (wife of Sir Stafford) and John Newsom (Hertfordshire County Education Officer) were on the edge of joining. Among other early recruits to the Christian Frontier Council, but who was unable to attend very much, was Allan Campbell Macdiarmid, chairman and managing director of Stewarts & Lloyds. George Woodcock, then secretary to the TUC Research and Economic Department, attended as a visitor. At the third meeting Oldham was delighted and relieved to welcome Mrs Kathleen Bliss a Girton graduate, former missionary in India, and as passionate an ecumenist as himself. With her presence he would be able to keep the *Christian News-Letter* going.[19] In short Oldham attracted a group of very able lay people who, if they were not directly involved in policy-making, were very close to policy-makers. It is surprising that some, with their wartime engagements, were able to find the time for the CFC's monthly meeting. That they did so reflected the value they attached to the work of the CFC in offering a forum for pro-Christian thinking about post-war reconstruction.

The functions of the Christian Frontier Council agreed in April 1942 were :

1. To create opportunities outside the sphere of organised religion for the discussion of Christian beliefs, standards and practice, and their application to current problems.
2. To examine the nature of the forces working in modern society, in administration, industry, education &c, and to endeavour to direct them towards a more Christian order.
3. To understand the efforts being made by various groups to influence these forces and to co-operate with those of their activities which are contributing towards Christian ends.[20]

Oldham's mode of operation in pursuit of these goals was essentially that of debate. He organized weekend conferences where papers on specific topics were discussed, study groups, and provocative articles in *CNL*.

---

[18] *The Times*, 26 May 1989.
[19] BCC, CFC minutes, 26 Feb. 18 Mar., 14 Apr., 4 May, 18 June 1942. For Dr Kathleen Bliss see *The Times*, 21 Sept. 1989, and *Independent*, 23 Sept. 1989.
[20] BCC, CFC minutes, 14 Apr. 1942.

For example, at the first conference, at Wadham College, Oxford, in July 1942, the CFC heard and discussed papers on industrial problems, the political situation, the religious basis of the Frontier's work, and the adolescent problem.[21]

The industrial situation was one of the key areas where, Oldham realized, the battle to Christianize society would be lost or won. By September 1942 he was acknowledging that the *CNL* was excessively dominated by academic contributors.[22] A much stronger representation from industry was needed. One way Oldham achieved this was through study groups. By late summer 1942 the CFC was running or forming seven of these, four relating to industry: on managers (convened by Pugh), on industrial relations (convened by Robbins), on the co-ordination of industry (no convenor yet) and on the profit motive in industry.[23] The last was run by George Goyder, G. W. Davis (an unidentified addition to the CFC in June 1942), and a newcomer Basil Smallpeice.

Smallpeice, in his mid-thirties, was Shrewsbury-educated and a chartered accountant by training (and he took an external London University B.Com. while completing his articles). In the 1930s he worked first as a cost accountant with Hoover Ltd., the UK subsidiary of a managerially progressive American parent; then as chief accountant and company secretary at Doulton & Co., a traditional English firm in which family control was giving way to professional management (see Chapter 4, s. 1). During the war he moved into management at Doulton's. Professional barriers against chartered accountants leaving public practice and entering industry stirred Smallpeice to hold discussion groups for half a dozen similarly positioned accountants. They wanted a change of status but they also wanted to relate accounting to the wider tasks of management. On their behalf Smallpeice wrote four articles that were published in the *Accountant* in 1941, on 'The Future of Auditing'. His uncle godfather sent copies to George Bell, the Bishop of Chichester, who in turn sent them to J. H. Oldham.[24]

Oldham was impressed. In no time he drew Smallpeice into the CFC. Smallpeice (who eventually became managing director of British Overseas Airways and thus appeared in the UK business élite of 1955) attended the CFC conference at Wadham College in summer 1942 and first sat

[21] BCC, CFC minutes, 18 June 1942.
[22] *CNL* 152 (23 Sept. 1942).
[23] BCC, CFC minutes 10 Sept. 1942.
[24] Sir B. Smallpeice, *Of Comets and Queens* (Shrewsbury, 1981), 1–25; Robin Higham, 'Basil Smallpeice', *DBB*.

on the CFC the following November.[25] In the intervening September
Oldham published the newcomer's 'The Profit Motive in Industry' in
the *CNL* with the comment, 'It has grown out of discussion among
a group of younger business men and has been submitted to a number
of persons with a knowledge of industry, and revised in the light of
their comments.'[26] Smallpeice's article made the interesting distinction
between the profit motive as personal incentive and as the rule of thumb
by which industrial decisions were made. Concerned with the latter he
asked two questions: in the sphere of economics whether the profit rule
'helps or hinders industry in fulfilling its function in society'; in the
sphere of ethics 'whether it is in harmony or in conflict with profession
of the Christian faith'. To both he saw the profit rule as an impediment.
With the authority of experience he observed that the exclusive pursuit
of financial profitability could restrict output, encourage short- rather
than long-term views, block innovation, and cause unemployment. The
object of the article, as he said in conclusion, was 'to show clearly that
there is evil here to be fought and overcome'.[27]

Smallpeice wrote other articles for the *CNL*. Perhaps the most useful
was that on the management revolution, a response to James Burnham's
influential American study *The Managerial Revolution* (1943). Smallpeice
called for more care in the selection and training of managers who,
he believed, should be selected primarily for their ability to plan and
to lead rather than for their technical ability. He noted the wartime
interruption of the professionalization of management in Britain: after
the war the examination schemes offered by three or four institutions
would resume. With them would come the opportunity to assert that
'Professional standards are moral standards, not standards of con-
venience.' In underlining that 'a new centre of power has come into
existence' Smallpeice clearly presented a challenge to Christians in
management.[28]

The most powerful industrialist to join Oldham's Christian Frontier
Council was Samuel Courtauld, chairman of Courtaulds the textile
manufacturers. He had spent his life in the family firm and seen it explode
in size and profitability through the adoption of new technology: from

[25] BCC, CFC minutes, 18–20 July, 5 Nov. 1942.
[26] *CNL* 152 (23 Sept. 1942).
[27] B. Smallpeice, 'The Profit Motive in Industry', *Christian News-Letter*, Supp. to No.
152 (23 Sept. 1942), repr. in *Accountant* 3 Oct. 1942.
[28] B. Smallpeice, 'The Managers of Industry', *Christian News-Letter*, Supp. to No. 180
(21 Apr. 1943).

the doomed black mourning silk manufacture of its Victorian heyday it had been rescued in the twentieth century by a switch to the manufacture of viscose rayon. Over the decade before the First World War the firm's total profits rose from £85,000 to £470,000; gross cash income reached over £6 million in 1929; in the 1930s it never fell below £1 million.[29] 'High profits made Samuel Courtauld feel guilty.'[30] They made him a millionaire but consequently increased the heavy sense of social responsibility imparted by his Unitarian upbringing: 'unto whomsoever much is given, of him shall be much required.'[31] In the 1930s he rationalized lower prices as passing on to customers the firm's cost savings. Privately he concluded that a greater degree of government control over the economy was necessary, views he publicized during the early years of the war in letters to *The Times*. Keynes encouraged him to publish and in 1942 he set out his ideas in an influential article in the *Economic Journal*.[32] Neither a Conservative (he turned down the offer of a peerage in 1937) nor a socialist, Courtauld 'was moved by a characteristically Victorian vision of perfectability, and sought its realisation in an harmonious middle-way'.[33] The appreciation of art and literature he inherited from his mother found outlets in picture collecting and friendships with prominent literary and artistic figures like the Sitwells and T. S. Eliot and the Bloomsbury set.[34] Possibly it was through Eliot that he was drawn into Oldham's acquaintance, for although Eliot rarely attended the CFC meetings, which came to be dominated by senior people in the Civil Service and in business, he was close to Oldham in the 'Moot', a group of intellectuals including Eliot, Karl Mannheim, and Michael Polanyi who met between 1938 and 1947.[35]

Courtauld first attended a CFC meeting on 5 November 1942 (a Thursday evening, at the usual wartime venue, 19 Dean's Yard, Westminster) as a visitor. Clearly some mutual appraisal occurred for the following month he was invited to join the Council and accept the treasurership made vacant by Lord Hambleden's concentration on the work of the newly formed British Council of Churches.[36] Courtauld's

[29] D. C. Coleman, *Courtaulds* (Oxford, 1969), ii. 40, 151, 315.

[30] Ibid. ii. 219.

[31] Luke 12: 48 (AV).

[32] S. Courtauld, 'An Industrialist's Reflections on the Future Relations of Government and Industry', *Economic Journal*, 52 (1942).

[33] Coleman, *Courtaulds*, ii. 219–21.

[34] D. C. Coleman, 'Samuel Courtauld IV', *DBB*.

[35] D. Kettler *et al.*, *Karl Mannheim* (London, 1984), 130–44. A. R. Vidler, *Scenes from a Clerical Life* (London, 1977), 116–19.

[36] BCC, CFC minutes, 8 Oct., 5 Nov., 3 Dec. 1942.

association with the group lasted until his death in December 1947, although serious illness prevented him attending after the March 1946 meeting. No other businessman of Samuel Courtauld's stature belonged to the CFC. On the Council he played a low-key part. He introduced only one discussion (on the minimum wage[37]) but presumably assumed a crucial role as treasurer and soon after as chairman of the CFC finance committee in place of Judd.[38]

To suggest that by the mid-1950s the CFC was running out of steam would be an exaggeration. Rather it was changing direction, as the composition of its Council indicated. The group still had the participation and ear of highly influential academics and politicians. Brooke was now Financial Secretary to the Treasury and just a few years away from becoming Home Secretary. Moberly carried great weight in the university world although he had retired from the UGC in 1949 and was in his seventies. Some of the founding members, besides Brooke and Moberly, were still there, Barker, Goyder, and Judd, for example. Other figures of consequence who soon joined the CFC included L. John Edwards, elected to the CFC in 1945 when he was Parliamentary Private Secretary to Stafford Cripps (President of the Board of Trade) and taking its chair ten years later when he was a Privy Counsellor and member of the Opposition.[39] Among donnish Civil Servants there was Sir John Maud, Permanent Secretary at the Ministry of Fuel and Power and formerly Permanent Secretary at the Ministry of Education; he joined the CFC in May 1944 when he was at Second Secretary level.[40] Another member of distinction in the 1950s and one who had joined the CFC in May 1944, was Sir Kenneth Grubb. His reputation stood high in Anglican and Foreign Office circles. Belonging to an Evangelical family clan, he had gone from Marlborough into the First World War and then, after a conversion experience, into intrepid missionary work in South America. One of his achievements was the pioneering collection of missionary statistics. Controller of Overseas Publicity in the Ministry of Information during the Second World War, he had afterwards become president of the Church Missionary Society and sat in the House of Laity of the Church Assembly, becoming its vice-chairman.[41] By the late 1950s, he was also director of Latin American Trade Ltd. and

---

[37] Ibid., minutes, 10 Mar. 1943.   [38] Ibid. 6 July 1943.
[39] Ibid. 14 Mar. 1945, 1950s *passim*; *WW 1958*.
[40] BCC, CFC minutes, 3 May 1944; *WW 1958*.
[41] Sir K. Grubb, *Crypts of Power* (London, 1971).

Editorial Services Ltd. and was publicity consultant to the J. Arthur Rank Organization.[42]

For various reasons, not always clarified in the minutes, members of Council dropped out. J. H. Oldham, the guru of the Christian Frontier, retired as the Council's chief officer at the end of 1947, to be succeeded in 1949 by the Reverend Dr A. R. Vidler, Canon of St George's Chapel, Windsor. Oldham moved on to the Council itself, attending regularly until December 1951.[43] Sometimes CFC members were not re-elected by the Council; sometimes they retired due to pressure of business. Three losses from the Christian Frontier's Trust in 1955 were Humphrey Mynors, now Deputy-Governor of the Bank of England; Walter Oakeshott, now Rector of Lincoln College, Oxford; and John Rodgers, a director of the J. Walter Thompson Co. Ltd. and the British Market Research Bureau Ltd. since 1931, now Conservative MP for Sevenoaks.[44] Henry Brooke, now Minister of Housing and Local Government, resigned in 1959, as did Basil Smallpeice, now managing director of BOAC, 'owing to his inability to attend meetings'.[45]

Perhaps as a consequence of this haemorrhage of talent the late 1950s successors of the first CFC members came from outside the UK business élite. Only Smallpeice straddled the two circles in 1955. An undated Christian Frontier Council membership list from the late 1950s or early 1960s shows that of 39 members 11 had business backgrounds, but few of these were big business heads (as defined in this study). Besides George Goyder there were John Arkell, Controller, Staff Administration, at the BBC; Stuart Dalziel, production control manager, Smith's Industrial Instruments Ltd.; Sir Arthur fforde, former solicitor (partner in Linklater & Paines) and headmaster (of Rugby) and then Chairman of the BBC; Alastair P. Forrester-Paton, a director of Patons & Baldwins; Thomas M. Heron, retired managing director of Cresta Silks Ltd.; Henry Mance, partner in Willis Faber, insurance underwriters on Lloyd's; Guthrie Moir of Associated-Rediffusion; Maurice Parsons, Director of the Bank of England; J. B. Peile, director of Turton Bros. & Matthews; and Eberhard Wedell of the Independent Television Authority.[46] Of these Sir Arthur fforde and Sir Henry Mance (as he became in 1971 part way through four consecutive years as chairman of Lloyd's) were already, or on the

---

[42] *WW 1958.*

[43] BCC, CFC minutes, 26 Nov. 1947, 26 Jan., 6 Apr. 1949, 10 Dec. 1951; *WW 1958.* Vidler, *Scenes*, 119–21, 134–5, 144–5.

[44] BCC, CFC minutes, 23 Nov. 1955; *WW 1958.*

[45] BCC, CFC minutes, 23 Apr. 1959.

[46] Ibid., papers, register of members volume.

way to becoming, the most prominent and powerful in their respective business spheres. fforde resisted pressures to commercialize the BBC.[47] Mance introduced a number of innovations into Lloyd's while he was chairman, including the admission of women and foreign nationals and the streamlining of internal procedures; he was remembered as 'a most distinguished and universally beloved personality'.[48] Parsons, who joined the Council in 1960, became Deputy-Governor of the Bank of England and then chairman of the Bank of London & South America but suffered a mental breakdown which ended his career.[49]

What then did the Christian Frontier Council achieve in advancing Oldham's objective of penetrating business and industry with the Christian ethic? (It should be underlined that this was but one of the CFC's target areas.) First, the CFC provided a forum for debate and the chance for radical ideas to be aired by policy-makers. The monthly frequency of CFC meetings allowed topics to be aired almost immediately they came into the public eye. Thus in 1945, Smallpeice introduced discussion with a topical paper on ownership. In it he proposed the radical idea of relegating the shareholder to 'the position of simple creditor; and sought to establish that limited liability, as created by the Companies Act, was an immoral device'. This move towards nationalization met a cool reaction: 'The desirability of some means whereby the various partners in industry could be represented on the higher control to form responsible social organisms was not questioned, though the need for the specific demolition work recommended by the paper was open to doubt.'[50] The CFC discussed numerous other topics, ranging in the 1940s from the Beveridge Report to the Education Bill, the atomic bomb, housing, the universities, broadcasting, propaganda, Russia, and Palestine.

All of which exposed members of the Council, and the subscribers to the CNL (numbering 10,000 in the early 1940s[51]), to a wide range of expert opinion. In the area of industry and business, however, there were relatively few published articles. Between 1939 and 1945, the first 230 issues of the CNL contained only eleven discussion papers dealing with management, business, or industrial relations. Between 1953 and 1961, when the CNL appeared in quarterly issues, ten articles on industrial questions were published, a rather higher strike rate.

Perhaps the greatest asset of the CFC was its function as a bridge

---

[47] The Times, 29 June 1985.   [48] Ibid. 17 June 1981.
[49] Ibid. 26 July 1978.   [50] BCC, CFC minutes, 14 Mar. 1945.
[51] CNL 41 (7 Aug. 1940).

between upwardly mobile, mid-career policy-makers from the various governing sectors and institutions of the economy. Oldham was particularly adept at spotting talent and equally successful in persuading people from different backgrounds to come together in pursuit of a common theme. Intellectuals, academics, politicians, senior Civil Servants, industrialists, managers, and trade unionists, all were intermingled in the multifarious discussion groups and conferences skilfully orchestrated by Oldham under the umbrella of the CFC. Two examples will suffice. In 1943 Barbara Ward (economist and journalist), Basil Smallpeice (accountant and manager), and W. G. Symons (HM Factory Inspector) produced a lengthy paper on 'Responsibility in the Economic System', the main thesis of which was that 'economic power today was irresponsible'.[52] This was accepted but the second paper the three produced under that title and dealing with the public or private company (which suggested that shares be converted into securities with a fixed and low rate of interest) claimed mixed support.[53] Secondly, in September 1951, at the CFC's conference on 'Man in Industry' at Glyn House, Kingsgate, Broadstairs, a wide spectrum of power groups was present. Smallpeice gave the introductory address on the Friday evening; at the Saturday morning symposium Gordon Bridge, personnel manager at Reckitt & Sons, Victor Feather of the TUC, Thomas Milner Heron of Cresta Silks (a socialist-minded entrepreneur and Christendom group friend of Maurice Reckitt[54]), and Jack Shelley spoke on the individual in industry; on the Saturday afternoon discussion groups were formed by the 53 conference members who included Henry Brooke, Basil Blackwell the bookseller and publisher, Sir Wilfrid Garrett, Kenneth Grubb, Sir John Maud, J. H. Oldham, A. Forrester-Paton, Crofton E. Gane (the Quaker furniture-maker), Alan Sainsbury (possibly of the grocery multiple; today Lord Sainsbury), as well as trade unionists led by Feather.[55] Ronald G. Stansfield, then a Scientific Civil Servant, recalls these conferences as times of sharp stimulus to faith and intellect.[56]

CFC meetings were not only times of intellectual cut and thrust intended to broaden the horizons of specialists. In Smallpeice's experience, and probably that of others on the Council, Joe Oldham and

[52] BCC, CFC minutes, 28 July 1943.
[53] Ibid., minutes, 22 Sept. 1943.
[54] J. S. Peart-Binns, *Maurice B. Reckitt* (Basingstoke, 1988), 56.
[55] BCC, CFC minutes, 28–30 Sept. 1951. Information from Lord Sainsbury, 16 March 1990.
[56] I am most grateful to Ronald Stansfield for putting me on the track of so many people in the CFC and for affording me a long taped interview on 4 Nov. 1986.

Kathleen Bliss proved to be wise and discreet spiritual counsellors whose encouragement strengthened the Christian faith of their lay colleagues.[57] In Smallpeice's case his strengthened faith enabled him to give a broadcast talk on the BBC and to publish it in his professional magazine on 'My Faith and My Job'. Unashamedly he told that his Christian faith braced his will to do the best he could in his work; required him to look upon his staff as human beings and not mere units of labour; and allowed him to see accountancy as a tool not a source of values or of managerial direction.[58] In its implications for new initiatives in industry the other achievement for which the Christian Frontier could take some credit was George Goyder's influential book the *Future of Private Enterprise* (1951). In his review for *The Frontier* Ronald Stansfield succinctly summarized Goyder's case. 'He is concerned to build a common purpose in industry, shared not only by the workers, management and shareholders, but also by the consumers, the local community and the community at large. He realises that a morally-acceptable purpose is essential for the continued healthy development of industry.'[59] Goyder advocated a co-operative structure, citing the example of the Carl Zeiss Works in Jena, with the board of directors functioning as trustees with the prime task of ensuring that the company's responsibilities to itself, its shareholders, workers, and consumers were carried out. Legally, and Goyder had a high regard for the power of law, all these duties would be written into the company's articles of association whose safeguarding was the special duty of the trustees.[60] Goyder's ideas, forged in the CFC, triggered other innovative approaches. Ernest Bader, one of the few entrepreneurs ever to have given away his company, transferred his plastics resin business, Scott Bader Ltd., to a company limited by guarantee (the Scott Bader Commonwealth Ltd.) under a scheme inspired by Goyder.[61] In turn Bader's pioneering work provided one of several models from which E. F. Schumacher, Economic Advisor to the National Coal Board, developed his ideas about 'intermediate technology' based on smaller working units, communal ownership, and regional workplaces.[62]

---

[57] Author's interview with Sir Basil Smallpeice at the Athenaeum, 25 Nov. 1986.

[58] B. Smallpeice, 'My Faith and My Job', *Accountant*, 15 Sept. 1945. 'My Faith and My Job' was a long-running series on the radio in the 1940s: K. M. Wolfe, *The Churches and the BBC* (London, 1984), 311, 457.

[59] R. G. Stansfield, 'Social Responsibilities of Industry', *Frontier*, 2 (1951), 239.

[60] G. Goyder, *The Future of Private Enterprise* (Oxford, 1951), 97–107.

[61] David J. Jeremy, 'Ernest Bader', *DBB*.

[62] E. F. Schumacher, *Small Is Beautiful* (London, 1973), 230–7.

Against these achievements, in advancing the Christian ethic into business and industry, must be set two major failings. First, the CFC really missed the chance to develop enduring grass-roots support. In 1939 40 discussion groups up and down the country were reported to be using the *CNL*.[63] Four years later the Council learned that in Manchester a 17-member group including 'three trade unionists, the Vice-Chancellor of the University, the chairman of the Cotton Board, Lord Stamford, the President of the Federal Free Church Council and the Dean of Manchester' had been organized. It had grown out of the Religion and Life week held in the city in summer 1942.[64] Clearly there was the possibility of going further and developing study groups for sectional interests, care being taken to keep them anchored to a multi-professional core. The chance was lost. Perhaps Oldham feared being sucked into party politics or sectional interests. Certainly he favoured the derivation of abstractions and principles for specialists to apply to their own walks of life. Some of this wartime support was transient, occasioned by the need of the hour, as in the case of Sir Raymond Streat, chairman of the Cotton Board.[65] There was none-the-less a foundation which might have been exploited further.

Two other reminders of the possibility of a national network of support groups that might have included specialist sections occurred after the war. Goyder and Oldham attended a weekend conference at Wigan in 1946 organized under the auspices of the Student Christian Movement (SCM) for those who had gone into industry and who kept in contact through the SCM's Industrial Register.[66] There was a Medical Group and a Politics Group under the aegis of the CFC[67] and since the CFC had access to mailing lists and names of potential supporters through the *CNL* mailing list, the British Council of Churches (under the loose authority of which the CFC operated), and the SCM (which it supported financially), the practicalities of establishing a system of grass-roots support were perfectly feasible.

In the 1950s the matter again arose. This time it would have been one way of extricating the *CNL* from financial difficulties. Basil Blackwell, who joined the CFC in 1950 and whose firm was publishing the *CNL*, proposed the formation of a society of readers of the *Frontier*, as the *CNL* was later named. Some thought it might be linked to the

---

[63] *CNL* 6 (6 Dec. 1939).
[64] BCC, CFC minutes, 10 May 1943.
[65] M. Dupree (ed.), *Lancashire and Whitehall* (Manchester, 1987), ii. 109–10.
[66] BCC, CFC minutes, 21 Nov. 1946.
[67] Ibid. 28–30 Sept. 1946.

Ecumenical Fellowship of the British Council of Churches. After protracted discussion the proposal was again rejected.[68]

The second opportunity lost by the CFC came in the early 1950s also. John Marsh, director of the Industrial Welfare Society (later the Industrial Society), 'asked if the Frontier Council would issue a short statement on principles which should be observed by a Christian in industry in the present difficult time, which could be reinforced by the example of Christian industrial leaders who pledged themselves to abide by such principles'. The Council judged it was not qualified to issue such a statement and advised Marsh to approach the Church of England's Social and Industrial Commission.[69] Since Grubb, Goyder, Judd, and Moberly were all present, this must represent the traditional position of the CFC. That is, it would act as a sounding board but not as fount of authority. This can only be regretted in the light of subsequent attempts by Christians in business to produce just that sort of code of practice.

Despite its prominent figures in the late 1950s and early 1960s the Christian Frontier Council had lost much of the impact it had made in wartime. Under the menace of Hitler the wide acceptance of a need for the moral bracing of the nation had made it easier to harness eminent figures to the task of opinion formation. And popular assent to the Christian ethic had been more readily given in the face of Nazism. By the mid-1950s peacetime's rising economic prosperity was dispelling the atmosphere of urgency that had bolstered the CFC's perceived mission of equipping the laity to shape the dominant values of society. Furthermore the ascendancy of sociology was presenting alternative tools and with them the ideas of moral relativity which threatened to erode the Christian ethic, however that was defined. The essence of Christian theology itself was also coming under attack from within the church and if that could not be agreed it was no wonder that the force of its ethical implications suffered.

2 INDUSTRIAL MISSIONS

While the Christian Frontier Council, as part of its remit, aimed at the head of the industrial system, the two other initiatives of the period started at the grass-roots. The first of these was the experiment in industrial mission which grew out of the industrial chaplains movement. The churches had made scattered attempts to reach the industrial population

[68] Ibid. 17 Oct., 13 Dec. 1950, 14 Jan., 25 Feb., 5 May, 14 Sept. 1952.
[69] Ibid. 31 Mar. 1952.

at places of work earlier than the 1940s. For example, the Archdeacon of Aston reported in 1942 that he had 'ten years' experience of work in factories in Birmingham'.[70] War, however, lent a new imperative to the churches' endeavours in industry. In summer 1941 Churchill moved Beaverbrook from the Ministry of Aircraft Production to the Ministry of Supply with orders to accelerate munitions production. As part of that programme more munitions factories were built, employing at their height in late 1942 nearly 290,000 people. Many Royal Ordnance Factories were in isolated areas and about 50,000 employees required hostel accommodation. Moral problems in the hostels demanded the particular attention of industrial chaplains.[71] The Commission of the Churches for International Friendship and Social Responsibility, the appropriate interdenominational body of the time, set up a committee on chaplaincies among munitions workers to deal with the whole area. Some idea of the extent of industrial chaplaincy is given by the attendance at a conference for industrial ROF chaplains in September 1942 convened by the Committee. Some 36 chaplains or deaconesses attended: 13 Anglicans, 6 Baptists, 3 Congregationalists, 5 Presbyterians, 8 Methodists, and 1 Church of Scotland minister; of the 36, 8 were females.[72] Many private firms during the war also appointed industrial chaplains, not least to act as social workers and to help boost morale. At Singer on the Clyde, for example, the industrial chaplain, the Reverend J. Kingsley Fairbairn (prompted by a request from the BBC to broadcast Sunday Evening Community Hymn Singing from the Singer works), instigated a works choir, which developed into a concert choir and continued into the 1950s.[73]

In the face of wartime pressures the Church of Scotland vigorously took up the challenge to provide industrial chaplains. The church's Home Board set apart one of its members to organize industrial chaplains in 1942. By May 1943 90 ministers were acting as industrial chaplains, a figure that topped 250 by spring 1944. The organizer visited 'Shipyards, Works and Factories in many parts of the country, ranging from Aberdeenshire to Midlothian and Ayrshire in the West ... [and] attended meetings of Directors in Board-rooms and workers' representatives in

[70] BCC, miscellaneous papers, Conference on Chaplaincies among Munitions Workers, 31 August–2 Sept. 1942.

[71] Peggy Inman, *Labour in the Munitions Industries* (London, 1957), 180, 242–57; Sir B. Butlin, *The Billy Butlin Story* (London, 1982), 134–9.

[72] BCC, miscellaneous papers, Conference on Chaplaincies among Munitions Workers, 31 Aug.–2 Sept. 1942.

[73] *Red S. Review*, 25 (Dec. 1954), 18–19.

Conferences'.[74] From ministering to camps of 'Bevin Boys' at the end of the war, chaplains turned to working among workers in the industrial schemes of peacetime, such as hydro-electric projects in the North of Scotland, railway staff hostels, and airports. As war came to an end and civilian patterns of life returned the number of industrial chaplains fell back to 230 where it stayed 1945–7 but then climbed again to 330 in 1952–3 whence it fell again to 200 in 1958–9. The vast majority of these chaplaincies were part-time. What they entailed could range from visiting the shop-floor to holding services in the works.[75] The reactions of managers were evidently sufficiently positive to admit such a large number of chaplains to their works. Union reactions were rarely recorded in the church's Home Board Reports though in 1952 the refusal of the National Union of Mineworkers to co-operate was noted.[76]

Peace saw the industrial chaplains movement contract, but much more so in England than in Scotland. The Bishop of Wakefield reported that 'for a period of years, between 1940–47 every large works in Barnsley had its Chaplain. This particular effort was initiated by the Christian Social Council of the town and it was inter-denominational.'[77] Such coverage fast diminished, as it had almost everywhere after the war. In 1953 the *Daily Mirror* reported the 330 industrial padres in Scotland and scathingly compared their activities to the neglect of England's industrial population: 'South of the border the parish tea and jolly jumble sale is too often regarded as the best approach. The time for that is dead and gone.'[78] In fact the Church of England was awakening to industrial opportunities. There were signs of a rich diversity of approach, if not widespread activity, in the early 1950s.

In response to a circular from the British Council of Churches, the Social and Industrial Council of the Church of England's General Assembly in 1952 asked all the bishops to gather information about 'work on the shop floor in industry'. Out of the 43 dioceses in the two English provinces of Canterbury and York no more than 31 appear to have replied. Of these only 22 could report definite initiatives being taken by clergymen in industry. They added up to the involvement of at least

[74] C. of S., *Reports* (1943), Report of the Home Board, 192–3.

[75] Ibid. (1943–60), Reports of the Home Board, *passim*.

[76] On the debatable grounds that its constitution, binding it to religious freedom, would require all denominations to send in industrial chaplains.

[77] CHA, Social and Industrial Council SICL/T/IND/1, response from the Bishop of Wakefield, 12 June 1952.

[78] *Daily Mirror*, 18 May 1953.

29 priests (or priests in training) and 3 laymen (including two ICF missioners).[79] Besides scanty coverage, they revealed a significant division of opinion about the merits of industrial chaplains. In fact six different views on how the church was to get into industry emerged—in addition to the older view, maintained by the Industrial Christian Fellowship and most of the Nonconformist ministers, that clergy in industry were there to undertake evangelistic missions aimed at personal conversion.

At Newcastle (perhaps harking back to the situation at the beginning of the century) the bishop tersely noted,

It is a matter of deliberate policy not to have special clergymen appointed for this work, and I need not bother you about the principles behind this decision. On the other hand, in an organised way, the laity who work in the factories and shipyards are systematically instructed in the manner that their witness should take in their industrial surroundings, and most of the clergy concerned are alive to the problem.[80]

The Bristol experience concurred: the major need was for

a trained, instructed, informed and equipped laity. The work of the Church in the field of Industrialised Society comes to a halt because our laity are so very badly informed about their faith, about how to make it live, about how to apply it to the group in which they are drawn for work. We have nothing to compare with the Communist cadre system, nor have we the same discipline. Until we get this we may as well wash our hands of trying to do anything at all—a handful of clergy will never make the required impact.[81]

The hazard in relying on the laity was the formation of cells which 'tend to attract the wrong type of "perfectionist" and alienate just the people we must reach'.[82]

A second view was that the parish priests could routinely encompass industrial areas in their ministry. This was the opinion in Lincoln and Liverpool. 'Experience has shown that the most valuable work is done by the incumbent of the parish in which the factory is situated. . . . *Factory Chaplains*. We have tried the experiment of appointing a Chaplain to the factory and once to a hostel in which factory workers were housed, but by and large the experiment did not work', was the verdict on Merseyside.[83] A third alternative meant engaging the parish priest as a full-time

---

[79] CHA, Social and Industrial Council SICL/T/IND/1, minutes, 18 June 1952, item 6 and Appendix.

[80] Ibid., Appendix, 6.

[81] Ibid., Appendix, 2.

[82] Ibid., Appendix, 8.

[83] Ibid., Appendix, 5.

industrial chaplain. This was the route followed by Southwark in London. A full-time missioner to industry and commerce had been based on Southwark Cathedral since 1945. He edited a contact magazine 'which aims at interpreting the Church to the business world and endeavours to throw a Christian searchlight on modern problems'. This he distributed through his contacts with management, personnel officers, and trade union officials. So high was his reputation that he had a standing invitation to the TUC Congress and was a member of the Southwark Chamber of Commerce. Much of his time was spent regularly visiting docks, railway centres, fire service and telecommunication headquarters. 'It is essential to keep in circulation. Wear out plenty of shoe leather and avoid Committees like the plague!'[84]

A fourth possibility was to allow a firm to hire a clergyman on a full-time basis. Stewarts & Lloyds at Corby had appointed two Free Church ministers as welfare officers and the Quaker firm of Scott Bader took at least two former Baptist ministers on to its staff with hopes of infiltrating the workforce with Christian attitudes and behaviour patterns.[85] Worker-priests, as in France, were a fifth possibility. A couple of examples were cited in the diocesan evidence that came to the Committee. At Eythorne Colliery on the Kent coalfield there were two 'priest-workmen. They work as miners, drawing miners' pay and working alternate shifts. Too early to express a judgement, but so far it seems to be working happily.' However, it was the last kind of experiment, the Industrial Mission at Sheffield, which commanded most interest, not least because one of its sponsors, the Bishop of Sheffield, sat on the Church Assembly's Social and Industrial Council.

Two men were responsible for what was widely recognized as the most innovative post-war attempt to relate the church to industrial society. One was Leslie Stannard Hunter (1890–1983), son of the Reverend Dr John Hunter, the Scottish Congregational preacher. Like his father he was neither Evangelical nor High in his churchmanship. 'Among the people and influences which shaped his life and thought, it became his habit to put his father first; von Hugel second; and third, the SCM.'[86] After New College, Oxford he became travelling secretary for the SCM 1913–21, and was ordained. His career in the church then unfolded: a year at St Martin-in-the-Fields with Dick Sheppard; Canon Residentiary of Newcastle Cathedral 1922–6; Vicar of Barking 1926–30;

[84] Ibid., Appendix, 8.

[85] Ibid., minutes, 28 June 1952, 6; S. Hoe, *The Man Who Gave His Company Away* (London, 1978), 129–39.

[86] G. Hewitt (ed.), *Strategist for the Spirit* (Oxford, 1985), 14.

Archdeacon of Northumberland 1931–9; finally, Bishop of Sheffield 1939–62. On Tyneside, at Barking and in Sheffield during the war, Hunter grew deeply dissatisfied with the Church's response to urban industrial society. A friend of William Temple from SCM days and cognizant of the initiatives J. H. Oldham was pioneering, he spent time meeting business and labour leaders, into whose company he was inevitably thrown by wartime emergencies.[87] The chance of establishing a bridgehead in industry came in 1944 when he addressed the works council of the Steel, Peech & Tozer branch (at Rotherham) of the United Steel Cos.: 'they said "send us one of your men in here if he can talk a language we can understand."' Diffidently, Hunter introduced E. R. Wickham as his industrial chaplain.[88]

Hunter and Edward Ralph Wickham had met in 1938 when Wickham was ordained in Newcastle. Wickham, 'a Londoner of sharp wit who had worked his way to ordination in the Church of England through part-time studies',[89] was curate of Shieldfield, Newcastle-upon-Tyne, before serving as industrial chaplain at Royal Ordnance Factory No. 5, at Swynnerton, Staffordshire, 1941–4.[90] With the end of the war in sight and prospects of returning to general parish work, Wickham gladly accepted Hunter's invitation to take a sinecure chaplaincy and to use it as the base for developing industrial mission work among the steel workers of South Yorkshire. Wickham's arrival in Sheffield coincided with the challenge from the Steel, Peech & Tozer works council.

For the first two years Wickham spent his time building up contacts. Entry to factories was gained in different ways and at various levels, most at shop-floor. Slowly he gained 'that web of personal relationships which is the very heart and foundation of a serious contribution that the Church might make'.[91] His method was to visit regularly and talk informally with the men 'as individuals, and as groups within departments of the works, in melting shops, mills, foundries, forges, machine shops and offices, and to become accepted by the working teams of

---

[87] Unfortunately Hunter destroyed all his papers before his death, the Hewitt biography says relatively little about the beginnings of the Sheffield Industrial Mission, and E. R. Wickham's early correspondence was inaccessible to me. The most able survey of industrial missions is E. H. Lurkings, 'The Origins, Context and Ideology of Industrial Mission, 1875–1975' (London, Ph.D., 1981).

[88] M. Atkinson, 'A Sort of Episcopal Fly on the Walls of British Industry', Hewitt (ed.), *Strategist for the Spirit*, 159.

[89] Lurkings, 'Origins', 141.

[90] *Crockford's Clerical Directory, 1969–70.*

[91] E. R. Wickham, *Church and People in an Industrial City* (London, 1957), 245.

men there'.[92] His objective was to activate the laity, not through cells or underground movements or militant meetings, but though 'lay projects', open to all and enabling the participants to find Christian perspectives.[93] As Lurkings notes, these contrasted sharply with the 'conversionist' approach of the Industrial Christian Fellowship which Wickham, with his historical perspective on industrial class conflict,[94] rejected because 'it made use of ideas and concepts which had very little meaning for an estranged working class living in a markedly secular culture and also because it emphasised "personal" conversion in such a way as to obscure the social meaning of the gospel'.[95] With Hunter's continued backing, Wickham's work grew. A second chaplain joined him in 1948, a third in 1951, and 'when he left Sheffield in 1959 to become Bishop of Middleton he was leading a team of full-time staff consisting of six Anglican priests and a woman worker'.[96]

Among the Nonconformists in England industrial chaplaincy of the Sheffield kind was slow to develop. The outstanding parallel but a much later (and more enduring) experiment began in 1954 when the Reverend Bill Gowland, Methodist minister, was stationed at Luton and set up the Luton Industrial Mission, a community centre which offered social activities and a base to support his visits to factories. Gowland also wrote a book, which grew out of his experience as a Methodist minister and factory chaplain in Reading and Manchester in the 1940s and early 1950s. His approach combined the objective of personal conversion with that of producing 'a demonstration by laymen in industry of the relevance of the Christian faith to the life of the world and the personal needs of men'.[97] In 1957 he founded Luton Industrial College which was established as a department of the Methodist Church's Home Missions Department. 'In the very inadequate rooms of the Community Centre he organised courses of all kinds, for shop-stewards, for managers, for social workers, youth, clergy and others.' In the eleven years to 1968 6,000 people went through his courses.[98] This denominational legitimization of the industrial mission stood in some contrast to the Anglican experience. The recommendation, made in 1959 by a working party

[92] Ibid. 247.
[93] Ibid. 252–3.
[94] Wickham wrote his historical analysis of Sheffield, *Church and People*, while building up the Industrial Mission.
[95] Lurkings, 'Origins', 158.
[96] Ibid. 161.
[97] W. Gowland, *Militant and Triumphant* (London, 1954), 38.
[98] Lurkings, 'Origins', 201–2.

chaired by Sir Wilfrid Garrett, that the Church of England set up an 'industrial secretariat' to co-ordinate a lay-based network of industrial missions was never implemented.[99]

Although there was a wide variety of routes by which the churches were seeking to move into industry, the Church of England at least was keenly aware of one hazard they all ran: the very real danger that industrial chaplains would become shuttlecocks in the untiring match between management and shop-floor. Any arrangement making chaplains financially dependent on management was frowned upon by the Standing Committee of the Church Assembly's Social and Industrial Council. They judged the practice of chaplains 'receiving any direct payment from the Management of a firm ... wrong in principle, as it placed the man in an impossible position and would also arouse acute suspicion on the part of the trade unions'. The Committee instructed the Bishop of Sheffield and the Archdeacon of Stow to draft and circulate a short document 'indicating the kind of dangers which were envisaged, particularly as to the question of the need for payment to be made to clergy in Industry through an approved channel, and also regarding the general method of approach to the work'.[100]

How then did managements and especially members of the business élite respond to these fresh overtures from the churches in the 1940s and 1950s? In small and medium firms managements sometimes expected the chaplain to be company welfare officer, as at Crittalls the window frame manufacturers of Silver End, Essex: 'much factory and office visiting; official work with the Crittall Athletic and Social Club; ... etc.'.[101] Other managements were apathetic and quite indifferent to the work of industrial chaplains. This was a not uncommon observation in the diocese of Wakefield. On the other hand some employers welcomed the chaplain and gave him a free hand. An Anglican priest in Colchester reported 'Visiting Messrs Davey, Paxman & Co's factory of 2,000 employees; managing director (Sir John Greaves) very interested in the Church's work and gave complete freedom to visit.'[102] The last was hardly surprising: Greaves was a churchman and on one of the financial bodies advising the Bishop of Chelmsford.[103]

At Sheffield among the large firms, E. R. Wickham's approach indicated a clear awareness of the dangers of dependence on managment.

---

[99] Ibid. 209–11.
[100] CHA, SICL/T/IND/1, minutes, 18 June 1952, minute 6.
[101] Ibid., Appendix, 10.   [102] Ibid., Appendix, 10–11.
[103] *WW 1958*.

In the early days his first priority was to establish good relations with the shop-floor. One indicator of his success in gaining grass-roots support was the extent of the men's voluntary subscriptions to the Sheffield Industrial Mission. At Samuel Fox & Co. Ltd., a subsidiary of the United Steel Cos., the number of employees contributing to the Mission rose from 1,538 in 1949 to 2,650 in 1960, their average weekly subscriptions falling from 1.31d. to 1.11d.[104]

Not until 1954 did Wickham organize special discussion meetings for managers. Such an approach was soundly based. The attitudes of managers could easily engender a role conflict in the industrial chaplain. As Lurkings notes, 'Managers, on the other hand, tend to welcome the chaplain as the representative of the "protestant ethic" and to assume that in his conversations with shop floor personnel he will uphold the virtues of honesty, hard work, thrift and deference to properly constituted authority.' As a result the industrial chaplain faced conflicting role expectations and 'in order to maintain his acceptability he has to present himself differently in different situations and commitment to a radical ideology would make it more difficult for him to do so'. The church aims to be inclusive so the chaplain is pressured to seek involvement with all social groups. Any attempt to engage in a prophetic social criticism, however, immediately loses acceptability with one or other social group.[105] Such was the dilemma of the industrial chaplain.

Since Hunter destroyed his personal papers and Wickham declines to discuss the subject, the role of big business leaders in the Sheffield Mission remains out of sight. Hunter's contacts with steel industry leaders were certainly good. At Kelvinside Academy, Glasgow, he had been taught to play tennis by Allan (later Sir Allan) Macdiarmid, chairman and managing director of Stewarts & Lloyds from 1926 until his death in 1945. Macdiarmid had Baptist influences in his background but in adulthood cut loose from denominational ties, although he 'retained a speculative interest in religious questions'.[106]

[104] MUL, Sheffield Industrial Mission papers, Box 8, S. Fox & Co., generalia file.

[105] Lurkings, 'Origins', 165.

[106] Hewitt, *Strategist for the Spirit*, 9; Jonathan S. Boswell, 'Allan Campbell Macdiarmid', *DSBB*. One of Sir Allan's daughters, Mrs Elspeth Holderness of Oxford, who was with her father during the war, remembers him meeting Bishop Hunter on various occasions during that time. Hunter gave the address at Sir Allan's memorial service recalling him as 'a Christian man with lively human sympathies ... Not many industrialists would keep a bishop out of his bed by reading aloud favourite passages from George Meredith—and he read them well.' Information kindly supplied by Mrs Elspeth Holderness in letter to author, 31 Jan. 1989.

Sir Walter Benton Jones, chairman of the United Steel Cos., 1927–62,[107] was very sympathetic to Hunter's initiatives, judging by his support for another of Hunter's experiments on the boundary between church and industry. This was the William Temple College, set up in 1947 at first as a theological college for women, but in the 1950s providing courses for people in industry in conjunction with the Sheffield Industrial Mission. Right from the start its remit was to provide 'as sound and as thorough a course of study of the Christian Faith and its bearing upon the structures of society as is possible in two or three years'.[108] Among the industrial firms subscribing to the College between 1947 and 1951 were the United Steel Cos., the Lancashire Steel Co., ICI, and Imperial Tobacco, who each gave £1,000. Stewarts & Lloyds gave £500. The Neepsend Steel & Tool Corporation, another Sheffield steel firm, 'per Mr Stuart Goodwin' gave 4,000 ordinary shares valued at £5,000.[109] (Sir Stuart Coldwell Goodwin, knighted in 1953, was chairman and managing director of Neepsend in the 1950s.[110]) When the College moved from Hawarden in Flintshire to Rugby in 1954 Sir Walter Benton Jones was on the top table at lunch, between the wife of the Archbishop of Canterbury (Fisher) and the widow of his predecessor (Temple).[111] In 1957 the United Steel Cos. provided a £10,000 interest-free loan for the William Temple College to finance extensions.[112] The presence of Sir Walter Benton Jones as honorary treasurer of the College over the years 1955–60 doubtless explains the connection.[113]

Also close to the Bishop of Sheffield was Gerald Steel, general managing director of the United Steel Cos. from 1950 until his death in 1957.[114] In diocesan affairs he helped Hunter by serving as chairman of the Sheffield Church Extension Committee.[115] In the early 1950s he sat on the Social and Industrial Council of the Church Assembly, on which Hunter also sat. At one point, Steel seems to have had hopes for the moral transformation of industry less through industrial chaplains and more through Moral Rearmament (Frank Buchman's Oxford Movement) which, on account of its universalism, was strongly suspect in most of

[107] Jonathan S. Boswell, 'Walter Benton Jones', *DBB*.
[108] J. Keiser, *College to Foundation* (Manchester, 1986), 15.
[109] *William Temple College Report, 1947–1951*, 17.
[110] *DD 1951*; *WW 1958*.
[111] MUL, William Temple College papers, Box 1, generalia file: official opening, Rugby, 11 Oct. 1954.
[112] Keiser, *College to Foundation*, 52.
[113] *William Temple College Report, 1955*; *William Temple College Report, 1955–60*.
[114] R. Peddie, 'Gerald Steel', *DBB*.
[115] Ibid.

the churches.[116] Until 1954 at least he was on the governing body of the William Temple College: his support being evidenced by his presence on the top table at the Rugby site official opening luncheon.[117]

A little more emerges about the big business role in Methodism's venture into industrial mission at Luton. Gowland, adept at mobilizing and persuading, had the support of the Methodist Home Mission Department before he moved to Luton in 1954. Once settled there he rapidly estimated the sums needed to modernize and expand the Chapel Street premises. One of his next moves was to secure the support of the denomination's most successful and generous layman, J. Arthur Rank.[118] He went to see Rank, discussed his plans and needs. Rank was impressed. He in turn wrote a note to the Reverend Albert Hearn, secretary of the Methodist Chapel Committee (largely responsible for making grants for new church-building projects) underlining his personal interest in the 'alterations to the premises at Luton'.[119] Rank was a man with weight. He was joint treasurer of the Home Mission Department (with Lord Mackintosh of Halifax) and the key member of the Benevolent Fund bearing his father's name. Outside the church his name was well known to cinema audiences. Hearn, who had already been approached by Gowland, pushed the ball back to Rank: the extent of alterations at the Luton premises that the Chapel Committee could authorize would depend on 'the measure of help that the Joseph Rank Benevolent Trust was likely to give'.[120] The upshot was that in September 1955 the Chapel Committee approved a scheme whereby an expenditure of £16,000 on alterations to the premises at Chapel Street, Luton, would be covered by £5,000 raised by the local congregation, a grant of £1,000 from the Chapel Committee and a grant of £10,000 from the Joseph Rank Benevolent Fund.[121]

All sorts of questions arise, deserving a far more thorough treatment than is possible here. How effective were industrial chaplains or industrial missions in reaching unchurched industrial workers? Did top managers resist industrial chaplains and missions? Or did they see them as a useful

[116] CHA, Social and Industrial Council papers, SICL/T/IND/6, memo by Gerald Steel on Moral Rearmament, c. 14 Jan. 1953. See G. Lean, *Frank Buchman* (London, 1985), 435–40.

[117] MUL, William Temple College papers, Box 1, generalia file: official opening, Rugby, 11 Oct. 1954; Keiser, *College to Foundation*, 53.

[118] Roger Manville and Joseph Rank, 'Joseph Arthur Rank', *DBB*.

[119] JRL, Methodist Archives, Joseph Rank Benevolent Trust, letters vol. 6, Rank to Hearn, 17 June 1955.

[120] Ibid., Hearn to Rank, 23 June 1955.

[121] Ibid., Hearn to the Revd F. Bartlett Lang, secretary of the JRBT, 5 Sept. 1955.

counter in contests with the shop-floor? How frequently did industrial missions, like the paradigm at Sheffield, succeed in bringing both sides of industry together? At Sheffield the Mission method was, by the late 1950s, to engage all sides of industry in constructive, even cathartic, discussion in which the chaplain concentrated on neutral question-raising. Is it true that this 'appears to have failed to develop theological or social bite'?[122] The whole of the industrial chaplains subject needs a much fuller historical treatment than is presently available.

3 CHRISTIAN TEAMWORK

Few in the business élite of 1955 were evangelicals. The most prominent were John W. Laing and Alfred Owen, and in the early 1950s they were more interested in bringing business resources to the aid of Christian causes than in persuading fellow businessmen to subject their practices to Christian ethics. For Laing and Owen their priority was the conversion of individuals, not the reforming of structures. J. Arthur Rank would probably also have described himself as an evangelical. What he meant by this much misunderstood term was rather less than the views of Laing, Owen, and those who in the student world by stages in 1910, 1919, and 1928 formed the theologically conservative Inter-Varsity Fellowship of Evangelical Christian Unions—in contradistinction to what they regarded as the theologically liberal Student Christian Movement.[123] The most visible manifestation of the evangelical movement, in both the churches and the student world, after the Second World War was the evangelistic (i.e. gospel preaching) crusades of Billy Graham. The role of business figures in these will be considered later. In relation to the Christian ethic in industry they had the unexpected consequence of mobilizing an evangelical initiative.

The initiative came to be called Christian Teamwork; its inspirer, the Reverend Bruce Douglas Reed. An Australian by birth, Reed had trained at Moore Theological College, Sydney, under Canon T. C. Hammond, a well-known Evangelical, before coming to read theology at Fitzwilliam House, Cambridge, in 1949 at the age of 29. Reed was a man of many interests who added layers to his thinking. In Australia he had added Karl Barth to the Calvinism of his Presbyterian youth.

[122] Lurkings, 'Origins', 165.
[123] The two sides of this division can be traced in T. Tatlow, *The Story of the SCM of Great Britain and Ireland* (London, 1933), and D. Johnson, *Contending for the Faith* (Leicester, 1979).

While visiting Finland for the Olympic Games (in which his brother was representing Australia) in 1952, group dynamics caught his attention. The emphasis on encounter, which has remained with him, led Reed to explore biblically and theologically grounded encounters with Christ in the here and now, in several directions. On the beach at Criccieth his ideas transformed the summertime CSSM (Children's Special Service Mission) mission, some of his dramatic services attracting crowds of a thousand or more, including Huw Weldon who offered him a producer's job with the BBC (which Reed declined).

After seeing the Billy Graham film *Oil Town USA*, Reed offered his services as a counsellor to the Billy Graham Crusade to Greater London in 1954. Within a few weeks Dawson Trotman, Graham's Director of Follow-up, recruited him to take over the work of following up enquirers, of whom there were over 38,000,[124] placing them in the churches, and organizing support groups. Ten days after the Crusade finished (22 May 1954) the Crusade's British Executive Committee discovered its funds had run out. Reed almost took a job in America with the Navigators (a widespread Bible memorization and evangelistic organization in which Trotman was prominent) but was deflected by a small group of converts he was counselling and teaching. Among them was Ernest Shippam the fish and meat paste manufacturer. They surprised Reed with the offer to pay him £750 a year, with £250 for expenses. Another provided a house in Westbourne Terrace W1 for Bruce Reed and his wife Mary. From this base Reed worked among the Christian Unions in the universities, particularly Cambridge and Oxford, and annually visited church groups in Finland. Most of his efforts he concentrated in building up the Christian faith of about 80 men, mainly converts from the Billy Graham Crusade. With backgrounds ranging from the City to the theatre to business and beyond, they were facing all kinds of perplexing personal choices, arising from their new-found Christian faith, which they bounced on to Reed who became the evangelical equivalent of their father confessor.[125]

In evangelical and Anglican Church circles, despite his honorary curacy at St Paul's, Portman Square, Bruce Reed was regarded as an irregular among clerical troops. His group dynamics worried some. The

[124] Three-quarters of these made first-time decisions to follow Christ: F. Colquhoun, *Harringay Story* (London, 1955), 232–5.

[125] This paragraph is based on interviews with the Revd Bruce Reed, executive chairman, the Grubb Institute, and Miss Jean Hutton, former secretary to Bruce Reed, now consultant with the Grubb Institute, 4 Aug., 3 Dec. 1986; and Bruce Reed's manuscript 'Confidential Report on the Work of the Revd B. D. Reed 8th March, 1954 to 31st July 1955'.

potential of his lay group was seen as threatening by others. In the event, the laymen attracted by his evolving emphasis on the ministry of the laity moved in directions quite new to evangelicals. In 1956 and 1957 Reed canvassed his ideas with church leaders including the Archbishop of Canterbury and Sir Kenneth Grubb.[126] Grubb and his Methodist confidant Sydney Walton approved of Reed. Some of his ideas coincided with those of the Christian Frontier Council, whose members mostly regarded Reed as too evangelical for their likes.[127] In addition Grubb saw that Reed's work might help meet the need perceived by the World Council of Churches at Evanston (1954) for a lay movement of Christians to engage in the affairs of the world.

Christian Teamwork was officially launched on 1 July 1957 when 40 members gathered under the chairmanship of Harry Mance in the newly acquired office at the back of the Liberal Club, at 1 Whitehall Place SW1, after six months' planning by working parties set up at a conference in February. Finance was an initial problem. Annual expenses were estimated at £2,900 (including £500 office rent). In the first year half of Reed's £1,000 salary came from the International Council for Christian Leadership (headed by Abraham Vereide). Another £500 was contributed by another USA source (unspecified). £200 remained from £600 raised earlier. £200 would come from various members. This left £1,500 to be found for the first year.[128] George Goyder undertook to raise £1,000 of this and did so with contributions from Alfred Owen (£200), Sir George Schuster (£200), Ernest Bader (£200 from his firm, Scott Bader Ltd.), and his own firm, British International Paper Ltd. (£400).[129] Sir Kenneth Grubb also found a small grant from church sources.[130]

The work of the group was announced in *An Introduction to Christian Teamwork*, published in September 1957. This explained that

The Christian man ... may be living a devoted Christian life and be aware of God's guidance in his personal relationships, but as he mixes with his fellow men, he recognises that he has a wider responsibility for the injustices and unchristian conduct in the life of the world around him. ... There must be the

---

[126] Revd Bruce Reed's personal papers, Reed to Ernest Shippam, 23 Mar. 1956; Grubb, *Crypts of Power*, 226.

[127] BCC, CFC minutes, 3 June 1960: evidently Reed had proposed an Institute of the Laity. The CFC wanted to develop its own ideas about this. The Revds Peter Bide and J. Martin also presented ideas to the CFC when Reed did.

[128] ROA, 1957 CH10, Bruce Reed to A. G. B. Owen (and enclosures), 9 July 1957.

[129] ROA, 1957 CH12, George Goyder to A. G. B. Owen 29 Nov. 1957.

[130] Transcript of author's interview with Bruce Reed, 3 Dec. 1986.

two-fold emphasis of faith and practice ... The divorce between formal religion and daily life must be overcome by groups of laymen who will face frankly the paradoxes and perplexities of the twentieth century in a calm spirit of faith in God through Christ, and with belief in the validity of the law of God for today's problems.[131]

Christian Teamwork proposed a fresh way of tackling the situation. Teams of fully committed Christians would be formed, each to tackle a single large problem and then to disband when it had achieved its goal. Each team was to be united spiritually and to have spiritual counselling available—initially this was Bruce Reed's role; subsequently he also pursued an approach deriving more from group dynamics and situation analysis.

Management rather than shop-floor was served by Christian Teamwork. Among the 25 people attending Moor Park College[132] for the formative conference in February 1957 were eleven in business: Gordon Bridge, a director of Reckitt & Colman; Christopher Buxton (of the evangelical clan), in the City; Arthur Chittenden, welfare officer at Shippam's, Chichester; George Goyder, managing director of International Paper; Stanley Harries, of Radio Gramophone Development Co.; Harry Mance and Neil Mills, both Members of Lloyd's; Donald W. Milne, chartered accountant and company director; John Paterson, director of Waterlow & Sons; R. H. Perry, of Chase National Bank; and Ernest Shippam, managing director of his family firm.[133] Among the seven trustees listed in September 1957 were Goyder (who was then drafting a trust deed for the group[134]) and A. G. B. Owen. Harry Mance chaired the Panel of experts offering guidance to the teams. Sir Kenneth Grubb was a trustee, as was Sir George Schuster, a very distinguished colonial and Indian administrator between the wars. Schuster had published *Christianity and Human Relations in Industry*, the Beckly Social Service Lecture for 1951, which traced the church–morality–industry boundary being explored by the Christian Frontier Council and social scientists in the 1940s.[135] By 1961 Christian Teamwork had 322 members, most

---

[131] *Introduction to Christian Teamwork* (London, 1957), 5–6.

[132] Where Canon Richard Parsons had started an adult education college on a Christian basis: *WW 1958*; H. Holland, *The Road to Farnham Castle* (Farnham, 1986), 22–3.

[133] Grubb Institute, Bruce Reed papers, 'List of Those Attending Moor Park College Conference Feb 1st–3rd, 1957'.

[134] ROA, 1957 CH10, Bruce Reed to A. G. B. Owen, 29 Oct. 1957 and enclosure.

[135] For Schuster see obituaries in *The Times*, 8 June 1982, and *SRA (Social Research Association) News*, Oct. 1982. The latter is by Ronald G. Stansfield.

(215) in London and the South-East.[136] While membership (annual subscription one guinea per annum in 1957) was open to all 'who have a sense of Christian responsibility and wish to co-operate with other Christians, irrespective of denomination, politics, social background or nationality'[137], a majority were Anglicans.

Among members in 1961 were Michael J. H. Alison, then of the Conservative Research Department (MP and member of Cabinet in the 1980s); Sir Cyril Black MP, the Baptist property dealer; Peter J. Bessell, company director and Congregational lay preacher then straining to get into Parliament (and much later to gain notoriety for his part in the trial of Jeremy Thorpe the Liberal Party Leader);[138] Roy Coad, chartered accountant and leading layman among the Brethren; John H. Cordle MP, unhappily later caught in John Poulson's web of corruption;[139] Lieutenant General Sir John Glubb, of Palestinian fame; John Lawrence, journalist, expert on the USSR and editor of *Frontier* the successor to the *CNL*; Lord Mackintosh of Halifax, the Methodist toffee manufacturer;[140] John Marsh, director of the Industrial Welfare Society; Maurice Parsons, then Executive Director of the Bank of England; Sir Gordon Radley, just retired as Director General of the General Post Office; Douglas Thornton, managing director of Ashby & Horner Ltd. the builders; and John Wren-Lewis, Assistant Research Controller of ICI. All were in London and the South-East. In the Midlands there were, besides A. G. B. Owen at Darlaston, Staffordshire, George C. Kunzle, chairman of the Birmingham bakery and restaurant chain and Alderman Eric E. Mole, of the Pioneer Works, Birmingham, both contacts of Owen in his Youth for Christ work. Dame Isobel Cripps, widow of the Labour Chancellor of the Exchequer, was also a member. These and the trustees were the most prominent members of Christian Teamwork. The vast majority were much lower down the social strata. Quite clear, however, was an overlap between Christian Frontier and Christian Teamwork. Goyder, Grubb, Mance, Lawrence, and Mark Gibbs (a Manchester schoolmaster who later developed a ministry to the laity, the Audenshaw Foundation, under the umbrella of the British Council of Churches) belonged to both. Both organizations sought to mobilize lay Christians,

---

[136] Grubb Institute, Bruce Reed papers, 'Christian Teamwork: Address List of Members, May 1961'.

[137] *Introduction to Christian Teamwork*, 13.

[138] *The Times*, 28 Nov. 1985.

[139] A. Doig, *Corruption and Misconduct in Contemporary British Politics* (Harmondsworth, 1984), 149–51.

[140] David J. Jeremy, 'Harold Vincent Mackintosh', *DBB*.

including and especially those in business and industry. Whereas the Christian Frontier met the needs of middle and High Churchmen and those of little faith at all, and operated through the medium of debate, Christian Teamwork built on the commitment of those with an evangelical experience of conversion. What then did Christian Teamwork achieve?

The *Introduction to Christian Teamwork* of September 1957 mentioned the existence of several teams: 'One is dealing with a problem in the building trade, which requires careful handling between contractors, clients, architects and eventually with the Trade Unions. Another is concerned with the personnel problem facing executives who have Christians and non-Christians on their staffs. A large industrial works has asked for a team to try to find the best way to help both labour and management face up to the claims of Christ.'[141] By 1963 other teams were organized and some were developing into significant projects. One emerged after Richard Carr-Gomme, a young Grenadier Guards officer who had been converted through the Billy Graham Crusade meetings, approached Bruce Reed for advice on managing the houses he had inherited from his family in Abbeyfield Road, Bermondsey. Carr-Gomme's concern was to keep ageing members of the family in the community. Out of that grew the Abbeyfield Society which, for a number of years, was administered from the Christian Teamwork offices. Its first chairman was Sir Gordon Radley (see next section).[142] Others were the Richmond Fellowship for the mentally ill, the Wilverley Association for residential clubs for the elderly, the Greenlow Society for temporarily housing mothers likely to be separated from their children, and the Langley House Trust.[143] This started when a member, John Dodd (himself a survivor of the notorious wartime Changi gaol[144]), took up the case of a discharged prisoner. Team K was set up, Dodd and his wife used their own home as a half-way house, and by 1963 500 discharged prisoners had passed through four such houses under the management of the Langley House Trust. These were remarkable achievements, not least because Reed rejected the temptation to hitch his star to one of the more successful social projects. By 1963 the various teams were advised by four consultative groups (industrial, community welfare, local church, and young people) all co-ordinated by the Christian Teamwork Consultative Service directed by Bruce Reed. The Christian Teamwork Institute, the fore-

[141] *Introduction to Christian Teamwork*, 8.
[142] Information from Bruce Reed and Jean Hutton.
[143] Christian Teamwork, *Christian Consultants* (London, 1963), *passim*.
[144] *The Times*, 4 Feb. 1987.

runner of the Grubb Institute, was established to run training courses and conferences.[145]

What of the industrial consultancy team? Who were its members? What did they achieve? Team S, the 'Educating Christians for Industry' team, grew out of a meeting in December 1957 between six young men with Christian convictions who had recently entered industry and encountered dilemmas posed by industrial management. Questions relating to vocation, Christian duty, loneliness, ambition, morality, suddenly tested their faith and found them quite unprepared to give answers or make decisions. The gap between church and industry had forced itself into their personal experience. Led by Alan Boddington (area representative for Parkinson Cowan), Sandy Landale (assistant secretary, industrial relations section, for the Engineering and Allied Employers' Association in Birmingham), and David Owen (who had finished at Cambridge that summer before entering the family firm, Rubery Owen & Co. Ltd., one of the largest private companies in the UK), the group contacted Christian Teamwork, of which David's father Alfred Owen was a trustee.[146] A weekend conference was organized, bringing together younger managers in industry with 'experienced industrialists, technologists and trade unionists'.[147] From this emerged the idea of Industrial Life Conferences. Their purpose was to bring together young industrialists, apprentices, technicians, and students to consider how biblical principles might be applied to industry. Fundamental to these conferences were the assumptions that God was at work in industry (and, by implication, capitalism), that industry was an honourable vocation for a Christian, and that the gap between church and industry could best be bridged by Christian lay people working in industry. Between June 1958 and January 1963 some 200 young people attended these conferences.[148] Conference themes included 'Justice in Industrial Life', 'Ambition and Incentive in Industrial Society—the Christian and the Rat Race', and 'How Can Theological Ideas Guide Us in Industrial Problems?' Not surprisingly, because of the presence of Sir Kenneth Grubb, George Goyder, Harry Mance, Gordon Bridge, and others from the Christian Frontier Council among Bruce Reed's closest advisers, the approach adopted by Christian Teamwork in industry aimed at both individuals and the structures in which they operated: 'we must tackle both the goldfish

---

[145] Christian Teamwork, *Christian Consultants*, 12, 21.

[146] Grubb Institute, Bruce Reed papers, 'Christians in Industrial Life' (leaflet n.d.) for Team S members' names; Christian Teamwork, Address List of Members, May 1961.

[147] Christian Teamwork, *Christians Entering Industry* (London, 1963), 2.

[148] Ibid. 2–4.

and the water at the same time'.[149] The preferred method was through the conference: a weekend residential event punctuated by provocative addresses explored through carefully balanced discussion and encounter groups. Essentially, Bruce Reed and Christian Teamwork believed, in some ways like Wickham and the Sheffield Industrial Mission, that the dynamics of group encounter focused on specific cases and informed by Christian morality would solve many if not most industrial problems. Reed differed from Wickham in that his theology was evangelical and his goals more pointedly evangelistic. Nowhere did Bruce Reed and Christian Teamwork apply their approach more continuously and ambitiously than at Rubery Owen & Co. at Darlaston, in the Black Country, where Industrial Life Conferences specifically for employees were held. Their value will be explored in the next section.

4 DILEMMAS FOR CHRISTIANS IN BIG BUSINESS

Relatively few individual chairmen and managing directors were involved in these Christian invasions of industry in the 1940s and 1950s and certainly very few from the business élite of 1955 identified for this study. Nevertheless there was considerable sympathy for such initiatives on the boards of the biggest UK businesses. Of the 96 largest business employers of 1955 identified for the purposes of this study, 21 made contributions to the William Temple College in the early 1950s.[150] To these can be added at least ten more whose chairmen or managing directors are known to have been committed churchmen.[151] Thus at least a sixth of the business élite of 1955 had sufficient interest in bringing Christian perspectives to bear on industrial matters that they diverted some proportion of their companies' charitable funds into an initiative related to this area. It would be very interesting to learn the justifications they gave in persuading their boards to support the Christian Frontier

[149] Christian Teamwork, *Industrial Life Report No. 6* (London, Mar. 1962), 10, 12.

[150] MUL, William Temple College papers, Box 1, *William Temple College Report, 1951–53*, 11–12. The firms were: AEI, Barclays Bank, Boots, Bristol Aeroplane Co., British Electricity Authority, Dunlop, English Electric, GKN, ICI, Imperial Tobacco, Lloyds Bank, Metal Box, Midland Bank, National Provincial Bank, Rubery Owen, Stewarts & Lloyds, John Summers & Sons, Tube Investments, United Steel Cos., Unilever, and the Westminster Bank. Four gave sums ranging between £1,000 and £1,500: British Electricity Authority, ICI, Imperial Tobacco, and United Steel Cos.

[151] Namely Allied Bakeries, BOAC, Cadburys, Colvilles, General Post Office, Laings, Pilkingtons, Ranks, J. Arthur Rank Organization, and Rowntrees.

Council, the William Temple College, the Sheffield Industrial Mission, or Christian Teamwork. Whether it was politically based—with Christianity seen as the bulwark against the tyrannies of Fascism or Communism[152]—whether it derived from a sense of 'Establishment', or whether it sprang from a concern to promote the religious objectives of individual faith and social harmony and justice, it is now impossible to tell.

The scope for churchmen to exercise specifically Christian influences in big business was related to a large extent to the legal and structural bases of the firm. Persuading fellow directors to regard a church-linked educational institution aimed at serving the cultural and morale-building needs of the company as a cause worthy of charitable support was one thing, radical activities aimed at the religious conversion of individual employees or a restructuring of the company on religious principles were an entirely different matter. The latter were quite impossible outside the family-owned firm. A professional manager in a public corporation or a public company, answerable to his superior in the managerial hierarchy and ultimately Parliament or shareholders, had little room to experiment with radical Christian initiatives. Two cases—Sir Gordon Radley, Director-General of the General Post Office, and Alfred (later Sir Alfred) Owen, chairman of Rubery Owen Co. Ltd. in 1955—illustrate the differing opportunities and dilemmas posed by these very different managerial situations.

Alfred Owen (better known in the Black Country by his initials AGB, and in the country at large between the 1940s and 1960s by his sponsorship of the BRM (British Racing Motors) project), heir to a middle-sized engineering firm, was catapulted into the chairman's seat part-way through his engineering course at Emmanuel College, Cambridge, on the sudden death of his father in 1929.[153] The firm, which then employed 1,750 and had a turnover of nearly £580,000, produced components for the motor industry, steel work for buildings, and metal parts for aircraft. AGB had spent twelve months on the shop-floor between leaving Oundle and going up to Cambridge. A formal Anglican, he was converted through the influence of a fellow student and joined the Cambridge Inter-Collegiate Christian Union, the evangelical student body. His unusual decision not to go into the ministry but to prepare for the family firm arose from an interview with La Maréchale, daughter of General William Booth, founder of the Salvation Army, during a mission at Cam-

---

[152] One powerful argument advanced by J. H. Oldham and those in the Christian Frontier at the end of the 1930s and one reason why some industrialists made contributions to the Billy Graham Crusades in the 1950s. See pp. 190, 197 above and pp. 232, 403–5 below.

[153] An outline biography is David J. Jeremy, 'Alfred George Beech Owen', DBB.

bridge. AGB stunned his family, and many more, when on his twenty-first birthday, at a huge party for 2,000 guests given in his honour by his father (an Anglican and a churchwarden) he publicly related the details of his spiritual conversion.[154] The gesture, as he intended, fore-shadowed his determination to run his life and his business on consistent Christian principles.

It also revealed a certain naïvety: he scarcely stopped to think whether it might have been better to wait until actions and policies backed his words, whether there was a more appropriate occasion. As he saw it, faith was a simple matter and any and every opportunity should be seized to convey it to others almost regardless of circumstances. He had biblical support for his style,[155] yet it was equally a matter of his personality. In the area of faith as much as business he was impatient with protracted reflection. His preference was for quick decision and prompt action, eventually most evident in his furious work pace.[156] This personal style would prove to be one source of difficulty in bringing Christian principles to bear in business.

In the firm, welfare provisions comprised an important expression of his Christian concern for his employees, as with every devout Christian paternalist employer. AGB inherited a legacy of welfare. His father as early as 1912 had provided an Institute with canteen, staff dining room, and billiards and reading rooms, a recreation ground with bowling green and tennis courts.[157] There were workers' houses and under the terms of his father's will another 200 were built. AGB and his younger brother Ernest (who became joint managing director in the early 1930s) continued this strong tradition of company welfare. Playing fields were laid out, the works canteen extended, company societies encouraged. By 1942 the firm owned 417 houses, most at nearby Bentley and most occupied by employees.[158]

Rearmament and then war saw the firm grow massively. Between 1936 and 1946 turnover rose from £951,155 to £10 million with wartime employment peaking at around 16,000.[159] By 1949 employment had

[154] A. G. B. Owen, 'Lessons from the Experience of a Business Man' (June 1946).

[155] 2 Timothy 4: 2.

[156] His family recall that he would leave the house between 7 a.m. and 8 a.m., return the next morning at around 2 a.m., sit down for an hour, and then go to bed for his usual four hours' sleep. Through the day he gave himself little time for meals, grabbing a sandwich or his favourite, cream cakes and bananas. Author's interview with Mrs Grace Jenkins née Owen, 26 Feb. 1985.

[157] *Rubery, Owen & Co. Ltd. 1884-1944*, 10.

[158] ROA, history file, 'Rubery Owen & Co.' (typescript, 1942), 8.

[159] 'Rubery Owen & Co.' 7; A. G. B. Owen, 'Lessons', 4.

settled back to 11,000, of whom half worked for the parent company at Darlaston and the rest for 16 subsidiaries of which Brooke Tool Manufacturing Co. with 1,000 employees in Birmingham and Electro-Hydraulics Ltd. with 1,200 employees at Warrington were the largest.[160] Welfare provisions were expanded accordingly, but still stayed ahead of government requirements for large firms.[161] A medical centre, day nursery, and savings bank were set up during the war; afterwards a hostel and youth club for the firm's 250 apprentices were built and a pensions scheme introduced. Near Barmouth, North Wales, a house was purchased in 1946 to serve as the Owen Group Convalescent Home, offering up to two weeks' free accommodation for employees certified by their own and the company's doctor. A new experiment for aged employees was launched in 1949: the Sons of Rest Workshop where retired workers could be paid for work carried out at a pace slower than production line speed. Until the mid-1960s these welfare provisions, on top of wage rates sufficient to attract and hold workers in an area bustling with dozens of metal-working firms, substantially contributed to a good labour relations record at Rubery Owen.

While Alfred Owen would say that this was inspired by his Christian faith, privately he was dissatisfied with welfare alone. Behavioural questions in the firm troubled him, and in the 1930s his measures gave the firm a grudgingly admired reputation. A non-drinker and non-smoker himself, in four years after taking over as chairman 'he removed the works canteen liquor licence by so heavily subsidising lemonade that it entirely displaced alcohol'.[162] He came down heavily on all forms of dishonesty, whether among men or managers. These, however, were matters of personal morality within the firm. Not until Christian Teamwork began to act as firm consultants in 1957 did AGB begin to consider structural issues. Solutions as radical for his relationship to his company as his Christian message was to individuals outside the churches, he found too threatening to entertain. One radical solution available in the 1950s, suggested by George Goyder (see above), was some form of co-operative company structure. Several experiments were made in this direction in the 1950s. At Scott Bader, in 1951 the founder Ernest Bader effectively handed over the business to a company limited by guarantee (the Scott Bader Commonwealth Ltd.), forfeiting all but 10 per cent of his shares. The Commonwealth then distributed the operating company's profits between employees and charity (up to 40 per cent

---

[160] ROA, history file, labour force figures, sheet dated 22 July 1949.
[161] S. Pollard, *The Development of the British Economy 1918–1980* (London, 1982), 228.
[162] Jeremy, 'A. G. B. Owen', *DBB*.

on these) using the rest for reserves and taxation.[163] Ernest Bader and two of his employees came from Wellingborough to Darlaston in December 1957 to explain the system of common ownership adopted in his 200-employee firm. The meeting was reported as 'a profitable discussion on industrial relationships, and the applicability of Mr Bader's system on a larger scale. We greatly appreciated the frank way questions were answered. Christian Teamwork members who attended (22) were left with a great deal of food for thought.'[164]

The other area which troubled AGB's conscience was the place of religion in the firm. Was the workplace a legitimate realm in which to present the Christian gospel? As company owner, with his younger brother (who did not share his evangelical sympathies) and his sister, there was little to prevent him from deploying his religious beliefs and prejudices as he wished. Was it right or effectual to use his position of power to impose his views on his employees? If business and industry were legitimate areas of evangelism—and he noted that his ideological rivals, the Communists and socialists, had no compunction about peddling their ideas around the shop-floor of his works—how and when should he proceed? Outside work AGB was the mainspring in the Birmingham Youth for Christ movement, organized just after the war (see below Chapter 13). Its main meetings derived their methods in part from revivalist techniques. Were these applicable in the context of the firm? How much of the firm's time, space, or other resources was he warranted, by his understanding of biblical principles on one hand and economic considerations on the other, in devoting to purely religious activities? Some idea of AGB's responses to these questions, and an appreciation of the powers he chose to wield or not, emerge in his changing policies towards industrial chaplains.

The first of these was the Reverend Alexander Bannerman Lavelle, an Irishman who had served in an industrial parish at Rotherham before becoming Rector of Darlaston in 1936.[165] As AGB recalled, 'he was looked upon as Works Chaplain and frequently visited the workpeople'. On his removal to Wednesbury in 1944 the senior clergyman remaining in the three parish churches at Darlaston was the Vicar of St George's (non-Evangelical, compared to the other two whose clergy were appointed by the Simeon Trustees). Pastoral responsibility for the Rubery Owen workforce was not transferred to him because in AGB's

[163] David J. Jeremy, 'Ernest Bader', *DBB*.

[164] ROA, 1957 CH10, Christian Teamwork Information Sheet No. 2 (21 Dec. 1957).

[165] *WWW*.

judgement 'he was incapable of carrying out this function'.[166] Instead it passed to the Right Reverend Edward Sydney Woods (1877–1953), Bishop of Lichfield 1937–53.

Woods, formerly Vice-Principal of Ridley Hall, Cambridge, and a leader in the SCM, had made a reputation as a pastoral and civic leader while Archdeacon and Bishop Suffragan of Croydon in the 1930s. He promoted a successful experiment to censor Sunday films, for example. Like his elder brother Theodore Woods (Bishop of Peterborough and then of Winchester in the 1920s), he moved in the circles of William Temple, J. H. Oldham, the missionary, Life and Liberty, and church unity movements.[167] AGB's connection with Woods derived from his memories of visits to Oundle by the Bishop of Peterborough and apparently began during the war when, in 1942, he invited Woods to Darlaston to take a Good Friday service for employees. It attracted hundreds of workers. All machinery was halted and a simple twenty-minute service (hymn, Bible reading, choral item, short address, hymn, and then wreath-laying ceremony) was held in the Canteen Concert Hall.[168] Those who could not get in heard it over the firm's loudspeaker system. It was repeated annually.

AGB's friendship with Woods was close. The bishop carried the weight and authority in matters religious which he was accustomed to accepting. Moreover Woods, with his youthful roots in the Student Volunteer Missionary Union (late nineteenth-century parent of SCM and IVF), maintained throughout his ministry a deep concern for evangelism, a concern passionately shared by AGB. He must also have breathed something of Temple's vision into Alfred Owen's thinking when, as occasionally they did, the septuagenarian bishop and the tall robust industrialist walked arm-in-arm in the precincts of Lichfield Cathedral.[169] For his part the bishop saw Darlaston as a model which in 1951 he was planning to exhibit to the world by means of a film, demonstrating 'what it means to bring Christianity into industry; which, after all, is an absolutely essential part of making Christian democracy work; that being, as you well know, the only effective answer which the West can give to the terrible menace of this awful Communism'.[170] Woods died just a few months

---

[166] ROA, 1951 GR1, AGBO to S. R. Petley, 7 Nov. 1952.

[167] WWW; Tatlow, Story of the SCM, 151, 157, 437, 651–2, 815; F. A. Iremonger, William Temple (London, 1948), 280; The Times, 12 Jan. 1953.

[168] RO News, May 1952.

[169] Goodwill (RO house magazine) (spring 1953).

[170] ROA, 1951 LI1, Bishop of Lichfield to AGBO, 8 Mar. 1951.

after Alfred Owen had decided to move a little further with the idea of industrial chaplaincy.

He did so carefully. The gratuitous suggestion that he employ an industrial chaplain came from T. W. W. Pemberton, a young Cambridge engineering graduate working for Vickers Armstrongs at Newcastle-upon-Tyne. He had heard about AGB from a Rubery Owen representative and decided to ask Alfred Owen whether he would listen to the ideas of his brother-in-law, the Reverend David A. Wood, then a curate at Bodmin, Cornwall. Pemberton and Wood planned to mobilize the laity by giving 'a hand picked few a thorough training & forming round them small "cells" scattered as widely as possible throughout the community. These cells should gradually infect the whole country after the principle of the leaven in the measure of flour.' Until they heard about Alfred Owen, the two young men envisaged that Pemberton should acquire and run a small factory and, with Wood's involvement, 'combine the roles of efficient & honest raising of funds & the training of cell leaders'.[171]

Alfred Owen was very interested. He invited Pemberton and Wood to Darlaston for an informal meeting after which Wood asked for a chance to serve as industrial chaplain with Rubery Owen for a year. AGB discovered that Wood was a High Churchman, but approvingly noted he has 'a dynamic Christian evangelical zeal and if he is guided by the Holy Spirit I would on no account stand in his way'.[172] For reassurance on this point he consulted the Bishop of Lichfield. Bishop Woods welcomed the possibility: 'I need hardly say, that with many others in the Church, I have wrestled with this particular problem of Chaplains inside industry.' The newcomer could be overseen by a local incumbent, the most appropriate person in the bishop's judgement being the Reverend Lavelle in whom AGB already had some confidence. Bishop Woods' main concern was cost. The church was aiming at an ordinary parochial stipend of £500 per annum and this would be difficult to find. Would AGB pay the chaplain's salary?[173] The appointment promised to relieve the ageing bishop of very considerable responsibilities he was not meeting adequately.[174] The bishop's reaction was an important factor in deciding AGB to proceed further.

AGB likewise consulted some of his directors and managing directors before proceeding with the appointment of an industrial chaplain. The Rubery Owen Group consisted of a large number of companies—AGB

---

[171] ROA, 1952 GR1, T. W. W. Pemberton to AGBO, 10 June 1952.
[172] Ibid., AGBO to Bishop of Lichfield, 22 July 1952.
[173] Ibid., Bishop of Lichfield to AGBO, 23 July 1952.
[174] Ibid., AGBO to S. R. Petley, 7 Nov. 1952.

was director of 42 and chairman of 24 in 1951[175]—and in theory an industrial chaplain would have admittance to all. The most thorough critique of the scheme came from Robert J. Norton, a director of Rubery Owen (Warrington) Ltd. and Electro-Hydraulics Ltd. With Christian beliefs, he wrote with some sympathy but saw drawbacks: a working parson was like to confuse his roles and start criticizing industry rather than preaching the gospel; a group industrial chaplain would find his job impossible because of geography and because his ecclesiastical authority would not run beyond the diocese of Lichfield; and the nature of his link with a local vicar meant that the chaplain himself would be subject to no local church authority. Norton advocated a chaplain for every works in the group and that he should be the local vicar in each case.[176] Another director reminded AGB that (with AGB's approval) a local vicar already acted as chaplain to one of the group's Warrington plants.[177] One director thought that Nonconformists' views should be taken into account. Two other managing directors foresaw difficulties arising when a highly educated (high status also implied) parson tried to work alongside wholly unskilled machine operatives.[178]

Despite these misgivings, AGB decided upon a trial. In September 1952 he and the young curate met the Bishop of Lichfield and within the week Wood was given a twelve-month appointment at £9 a week, starting on 9 October.[179] The following February the company magazine introduced the new group chaplain. He had left school at 18, seen service in the Royal Navy and then the Army with which he served in Egypt as an education and welfare officer. Demobilized in 1947 with the rank of captain, he read theology at Queen's College, Cambridge before ordination in Truro Cathedral. While curate of Bodmin he was part-time chaplain to the local army barracks. He was married with a 3-year old son. The article said nothing about his cell techniques but emphasized his concern to make Christian teaching relevant to industrial society and his eagerness to learn from Darlaston employees.[180] Three years later the brave experiment was over. Reasons for its failure highlight

[175] DD 1951.
[176] ROA, 1952 GR1, R. J. Norton to AGBO, 4 Aug. 1952.
[177] Ibid., A. W. Hill to AGBO, 6 Aug. 1952.
[178] Ibid., C. E. Partridge to AGBO, 26 Aug. 1952, B. E. C. to AGBO, 14 Aug. 1952, W. D. C. to AGBO, 11 Aug. 1952.
[179] Ibid., Edith Ramsden (AGBO's secretary) to Bishop of Lichfield, 28 Aug. 1952, AGBO to Revd David Wood, 18 Sept. 1952.
[180] RO News, Feb. 1953.

the dilemmas facing Alfred Owen as he tried to inject a purely religious initiative into industry.

At bottom the experiment foundered on the rock feared by the Church of England's Social and Industrial Council: the nature of the relationship between industrialist and chaplain. Financial dependence was part of it. AGB paid the chaplain's salary and decided how long he should remain in his job. Alfred Owen disliked one aspect of the arrangement: the chaplain had to admit to employees that he was in the pay of management. Consequently AGB wrote to Bishop Woods requesting that an arrangement be made whereby the chaplain received his money from the diocese.[181]

Structural problems increased the chaplain's dependence on the chairman. The wide spread of company plants between Birmingham, Staffordshire, Lancashire, and Yorkshire and the huge number of employees (estimated by Wood as 6,000 on 75 acres of sites at Darlaston and 18,000 in total) made it quite impossible for him to cover his territory evenly. Even so, he felt obliged to maintain contact with personnel in subsidiary firms, which absorbed time and travelling costs. Within three months of arriving at Darlaston he was asking Alfred Owen for a loan to supplement £100 from his war savings and the proceeds of the sale of his old car in order to buy a utility van.[182]

There was more to the problem than this, however. In the last analysis the group chaplain was not equidistant between management and shop-floor. AGB saw him as an agent of evangelical Christianity. Wood diverged from AGB's expectations. His churchmanship was not Low, his theology not evangelical. Moreover his methods entailed allying himself with the shop-floor rather than with management or board, or even Alfred Owen himself. AGB became aware of theological differences within months of Wood's arrival.

Some time earlier AGB had appointed an ex-Salvation Army couple to superintend the company's Convalescent Home near Barmouth and also to alternate that with the work of welfare officers at Darlaston.[183] However, they saw their jobs as 'an opportunity for Christian Service and witness'; they hung texts on their office walls and came to regard themselves as works padres, achieving what the Bishop of Lichfield could not. Having thus arrogated the chaplain's job, they inevitably experienced deep resentment when David Wood arrived. Resentment turned to outrage when Wood's High Churchmanship became evident. In hector-

---

[181] ROA, 1953 GR1, AGBO to Bishop of Lichfield, 1 Jan. 1953.
[182] ROA, 1952 GR1, Wood to AGBO, 29 Dec. 1952.
[183] Ibid., AGBO, to S. R. Petley, 7 Nov. 1952.

ing and sanctimonious tones the couple wrote to AGB demanding '*an uninterrupted field*'.[184] AGB would have none of it.[185]

This settled neither the relationship between the chaplain and his pre-tenders[186] nor the relationship between the chaplain and the chairman. One disturbing feature for AGB was the way in which the cell method developed. Cell members lived together in a small male commune—for this purpose the chaplain's original factory base, a gatekeeper's cottage, was too small and Wood in spring 1954 bought an old house in Bilston. He explained the principles on which he now acted: (1) 'A permanent Mission to Industrial Society must be Church centred'; (2) 'It must be free from dependence upon particular sections of the community or powerful individuals, either of whom might be thought to be using the Church for ulterior purposes'; and (3) it must 'make a universal approach through all the facets of daily life: industrial, social and spiri-tual'.[187] He and his brother-in-law set up house for young men preparing for the ministry. They attracted four ordinands, found them jobs, mostly unskilled, in local factories, concealing their religious objectives from managements. Each day they all observed a common religious rule of morning prayer, evening prayer, and compline. Each took a turn as housekeeper—Wood at this time lived separately from his wife and son.[188]

Much of this would have disturbed AGB, although he does not seem to have committed his reactions to paper. In some ways the Bilston house was reminiscent of the university settlements set up in East London at the end of the nineteenth century inspired by the Christian Socialists.[189] What surely bothered him were the echoes of monastic life: on his copy of Wood's report he amended the word 'lay-brotherhood' to 'team'. What must also have been worrisome was Wood's appearance of escaping authority, both secular and ecclesiastical. Above all, there was the point that although Wood was hired to serve the 18,000 employees in the Rubery Owen Group, he was now shrinking his effort to a localized church base which aimed at all workplaces in its vicinity. All of this coincided with AGB's involvement in the Billy Graham Crusade to

---

[184] Ibid., Sydney R. Petley to AGBO, 24 Sept. 1952.

[185] Ibid., AGBO to S. R. Petley, 7 Nov. 1952.

[186] As Wood saw the situation, the Petleys were narrow fundamentalists with vested interests in seeing him disappear: ROA, 1953 GR1, Wood's annual report, 8 Oct. 1953.

[187] ROA, 1952 GR1, Wood to AGBO, 29 Dec. 1952; ROA, 1954 GR1, Wood to AGBO, 22 Apr. 1954.

[188] ROA, 1954 GR1, Wood to AGBO, 22 Apr. 1954; ROA, 1955 GR1, Wood's 'Notes on the Parkfield Road Experiment', *c.* summer 1955.

[189] A. Briggs and A. MacCartney, *Toynbee Hall* (London, 1954).

Greater London and Wood had the temerity to tell him that 'Although I share your hopes for the Greater London Crusade, I do not feel it is the sort of approach which would have a lasting effect on the Midlands.'[190]

AGB's reactions to the full-time, internalized company chaplaincy as it developed can be concluded from the evidence presented above. He was prepared to give £500 a year and modest office accommodation for an industrial chaplaincy. He was not prepared to let employees of his own religious persuasion prejudice him against the man appointed. Neither was he prepared to let the industrial chaplain change his strategy to such an extent that it took him outside the company and therefore beyond originally agreed duties. AGB's patience with Wood probably ran out more quickly because they did not see eye-to-eye on theology, churchmanship, or evangelism. Moreover, Wood, being a much younger man than AGB, could hardly replace Bishop Woods as AGB's confidant. It was not surprising therefore that AGB abandoned the experiment of a group industrial chaplain. After causing some anguish to the new Bishop of Lichfield, Wood left on good terms with AGB in June 1955.[191] On the positive side he succeeded in bringing more parish-based chaplains into the Owen Group,[192] and he had made valuable contacts with both the Sheffield Industrial Mission and the William Temple College (to which AGB was already subscribing).[193] Perhaps more importantly he had shown AGB the difficulties that would surely arise when the classic independence of the clergy was compromised in an industrial context.

Not surprisingly Alfred Owen thereafter avoided industrial chaplains of the worker-priest type. He briefly supported Christian evangelistic work in industry through a national, evangelical, and interdenominational association aimed at the shop-floor alone. This was the Workers' Christian Fellowship, chaired by A. Lindsay Glegg, a wealthy businessman, whose most effective evangelist was Charles Potter, a Communist

[190] ROA, 1954 GR1, Wood to AGBO, 1 Feb. 1954.

[191] ROA, 1955 GR1, Bishop of Lichfield to AGBO, 3 Dec. 1954 (Lichfield was being pressed by David Wood and appealed to AGB, adding a handwritten PS 'Do please help me'), Wood to AGBO, 9 May 1955 and enclosures, AGBO to Wood, 16 May 1955.

[192] ROA, 1955 GR1, Wood, 'Notes on the Parkfield Road Experiment': four parish priests acted as chaplains to Rubery Owen (Warrington) Ltd., Electro-Hydraulics Ltd., also at Warrington, T. S. Harrison & Sons of Heckmondwike, and the parent company at Darlaston.

[193] ROA, 1954 GR1, Wood to AGBO, 1 Feb. 1954, 30 June 1954, AGBO to Wood, 6 July 1954.

official converted through the Billy Graham Crusade.[194] When next AGB personally brought a clergyman into Rubery Owen he chose the very different relationship of client and consultant.

This developed out of AGB's acquaintance with the Reverend Bruce Reed (see above) through the Billy Graham Crusade Organisation (see below) and the CSSM beach mission at Criccieth, to which AGB regularly took his growing family in the 1950s. Christian Teamwork's first Industrial Life Conference was organized for Darlaston employees in 1957.[195] When the 8th Industrial Life Conference for Rubery Owen employees was held at Ashorne Hill near Leamington in September 1961, the firm had sent over 250 men and women (out of 6,000 at Darlaston[196]) to such conferences.

Out of these came more regular discussion groups among workers in various departments. Recalled a works superintendent: 'At first they discussed anything, but gradually started to talk about the Bible, then shop-floor problems, social work. Other groups started and interchanged ideas. Next started to visit churches, doing practical work, visiting orphanages, mental homes, parcels for hard-up people.' One shop steward of fifteen years' standing reported becoming used to reading the Bible and praying; when over 200 men and their wives decided to go to church they found services complicated. Another shop steward (a Communist), determined that 'Christianity in industry [was] not going to weaken him from a Trades Union point of view', attended a Teamwork Conference and went away impressed. Soon he was discussing 'the problem of Christianity in industry' with Bruce Reed.[197] Bruce Reed's technique was to listen and talk with the men but to force them to go to their own support groups or to their local ministers and clergy: he had no intention of setting up a church within a company.[198]

AGB's relationship with Christian Teamwork and Bruce Reed was probably akin to his friendship with the Bishop of Lichfield. Reed became his spiritual mentor. Except that he was also the spiritual mentor to many of the men as well. Reed learned, among other things, that the shop stewards and the men on the shop-floor liked and respected AGB

---

[194] ROA, 1956 FE 2/8 (box 964), file on Workers' Christian Fellowship.

[195] ROA, 1957 CH10, Christian Teamwork Information Sheet No. 2 (21 Dec. 1957): few of the 50 delegates, from all ranks of the firm, were professing Christians.

[196] ROA, 1957 CH10, Christian Teamwork Information Sheet No. 2 (21 Dec. 1957).

[197] Fragment of a Christian Teamwork Newsletter, n.d. but c. 1961 in the possession of Mrs Grace Jenkins.

[198] Author's interview with Revd Bruce Reed, 4 August 1986.

while many of the managers disliked and distrusted him.[199] In this privileged position Reed gradually encouraged AGB to look more critically at his position in the firm, a process sadly interrupted in 1969 when Sir Alfred Owen suffered a serious stroke from which he never fully recovered. Something of the direction along which the Christian Teamwork consultancy was taking AGB is suggested by the programme for the 8th Industrial Life Conference for Rubery Owen employees. Delegates from the various departments agreed that they should formulate a clear statement of their aims, partly to encourage others to join. The topic of the conference, no doubt shaped with advice from Bruce Reed, was 'What Should the Industrialist Seeking to Live as a Christian Be Committed to, Believe and Practise?'[200] Whether this was to defuse shopfloor criticism of management or boardroom policies can only be ascertained by much more research in the firm's archives. Clearly the title held sharp implications with which Sir Alfred Owen, as AGB had just become, had been wrestling for thirty years.

In stark contrast to Alfred Owen, a family-firm paternalist, stood Sir Gordon Radley, Director-General of the General Post Office in 1955 when he headed the third largest business in the UK (337,000 employees). Radley was an example of the new generation of managers. His professional background was in engineering, his religious background in the Church of England. The son of a mechanical engineer, he went from Leeds Modern School at 16 to Faraday House, London, to study electrical engineering, studies interrupted by the First World War. Afterwards his dedication and hard work brought him a top first-class honours degree and a London University gold medal. From a short apprenticeship to Bruce Peebles & Co. of Edinburgh he joined the Post Office engineering staff in 1920. Over the next twenty years he worked steadily on research topics related to plasma physics, completing a Ph.D. in that area. By 1939 he was Controller of Research, in charge of the management of all the research groups in the GPO.[201]

With his parents and two younger sisters Gordon Radley attended St Michael's and All Angels, Blackheath, London, a definitely Evangelical parish church, where he led a flourishing Crusader class in the 1920s.[202] Work and faith could not be separate in his thinking. To

[199] Ibid.

[200] Grubb Institute, Bruce Reed papers, programme for 8th Industrial Life Conference 22–4 Sept. 1961.

[201] B.Ce.; *WWW*; interview with Lady Dorothy Radley and Dr James H. H. Merriman, 27 Oct. 1986, and related correspondence.

[202] Information from Lady Dorothy Radley.

integrate them, and to help others perplexed by the challenges of modern science, he wrote a small book, *Science and Faith: The Discovery of the Unknown* (1927). It was soon to be dated by advances in both archaeology and science but revealed the exhilaration he himself felt in his laboratory and in his faith. From his own field he publicized new advances to young readers of the *Crusaders' Magazine* about how television worked and about the possibilities of long distance telephony.[203]

Out of his wartime work at Dollis Hill (where he directed 1,000 research engineers) came two important results for communications: an all-electronic telephone exchange and different ways of laying a new trans-atlantic telephone cable. After the war he began working towards these goals, meantime mounting the highest rungs in the GPO hierarchy—Deputy Engineer-in-Chief 1949, Engineer-in-Chief 1951, and then in 1955 Director General. The following year, 1956, saw the opening of TAC, the first telephone cable to be laid across the Atlantic, for which his knighthood was topped with a KCB. In his profession he was elected president of the Institution of Electrical Engineers in 1956–7 and awarded the IEE's Faraday Medal in 1958.[204]

As professional success came his way where did Gordon Radley's Christian faith become evident? Lady Radley remembers that in the war years and after he had the ability to inspire 'the loyalty and affection of those whom he was driving to the limit', which she saw as 'a response to his personal qualities that were in turn a reflection of his faith'.[205] Those subordinates who survive recall several revealing glimpses of him. A rather shy and seemingly austere man, he was in his job first and foremost dedicated to doing his work well. He had a keen sense of compassion, always concerned about the welfare of his immediate subordinates. But never would he allow sentiment to cloud his professional standards. Twice in his career he recommended the appointment of an outsider as his successor in high office, hard decisions which pained him emotionally but satisfied his professional assessment of needs and personnel.

Vexed issues relating to the making and distribution of profits did not weigh as heavily on his shoulders as on those of a sensitive Christian entrepreneur like Ernest Bader. Commercial practice was laid down by

[203] W. G. Radley, 'The Romance of Communications', *Crusaders' Magazine* (Feb. 1935); idem, 'Through Electrical Eyes', *Crusaders' Magazine* (July 1935); idem, '"TIM"', *Crusaders' Magazine* (Feb. 1936).

[204] Information from Dr James H. H. Merriman and the Institution of Electrical Engineers.

[205] Lady Radley to author, 24 Apr. 1989.

Post Office tradition (not itself immutable of course), the Treasury, and the Minister (Postmaster General). Private enterprise and competition infringed upon his experience only in his dealings with contractors and since these were mostly the large manufacturers business was conducted in a gentlemanly fashion.

In contrast to A. G. B. Owen, Radley had little room to display or promote his Christian faith within the firm. Overt Christian activity within business for Sir Gordon Radley, when he was Director-General of the GPO, was confined to two modest areas. One was sometimes evident during his lunchbreaks. He regularly worked non-stop 9 a.m. to 6 p.m., taking a short time only for lunch, eating sandwiches if anything at all. At this time of day, one of his personal assistants recalled,[206] he could be caught reading his Bible. This he kept in the one drawer in his desk he was able to lock and where he placed a few personal possessions. Incidentally, he distrusted Christians who displayed a Bible as a sort of shibboleth. Secondly he readily lent his name (and presence) to the Post Office Christian Association which had been founded in the 1890s. This group offered Post Office workers who had any interest in Christianity the chance to hear speakers at lunchtime meetings, and to share in prayer and Bible study. Sir Gordon Radley served as president of POCA while he was Director-General but kept his interest to a figurehead role.

While Sir Gordon's personal correspondence does not survive to allow a documented account of the tensions he faced in reconciling his faith to his business, it is clear that he was massively circumscribed in comparison to Sir Alfred Owen. And this was proper for someone holding a position of public accountability. It might be argued, with George Goyder and Ernest Bader (who most unwillingly surrendered his power), that capitalists like A. G. B. Owen ought voluntarily to limit their power as well as their shareholding within their companies.

5 CONCLUSION

Initiatives for taking religion into firms, either as a form of association or as an ethic on which to base business behaviour, had moved in new directions by the late 1950s. The rise of the multi-plant, multinational managerial corporation with its hierarchy of mobile professional managers almost eliminated the possibility of imposing the kinds of

[206] Gordon Pocock, interviewed 27 Oct. 1986 at IEE lunch courtesy of Dr James H. H. Merriman.

religious institutions and practices favoured by pious late nineteenth-century paternalists. For the most part religion in business had retreated from the collective realm of the company to the isolated sphere of the individual, whether entrepreneur or manager. In response to this situation Christian Frontier and Christian Teamwork adopted a leavening strategy aimed at helping individual managers work their faith through into ethical principles and stances for decision and action. The major denominations, especially the Church of Scotland, the Church of England, and the Methodist Church and primarily under the impetus of the Second World War, at last began to shoulder the responsibility of reaching unchurched industrial workers, whether shop-floor or management, in their places of work. Industrial chaplains, independent of both management and shop-floor, by various routes began to invade the workplace. However, conflicts of interest arising from attempts to serve both sides of industry proved too great for some chaplains to manage and they ran the risks either of compromising their prophetic role or else of neglecting one side or other, most easily management. Rarely in big business did traditional paternalism survive. A classic example was A. G. B. Owen's firm at Darlaston. Noticeably, he moved away from the device of a tame company chaplain, such as Lever had used at Port Sunlight, and made serious efforts to accommodate the new church-side initiatives (like industrial chaplains or Christian Teamwork) within his paternalist inclinations. In general, the task of applying the Christian faith to business lay with business professionals concerting their thinking outside the workplace and with church professionals gingerly stepping into it.

PART IV

Mammon in the Temple
Commercial Men in the Churches

PROLOGUE

The Churches' Administrative and Financial Tasks Quantified

'If I had my own life to begin again I should certainly enter the Church of England. It has its limitations, but for all that it is the freest church in Christendom. The non-episcopal churches—even the Presbyterian—are too much at the mercy of the people, of small cliques, and moneyed men' (The Reverend Dr John Hunter to his son Leslie S. Hunter (eventually Bishop of Sheffield), 10 June 1912).[1]

As seen in Chapter 1, the mainline Protestant denominations in the United Kingdom offered a large number of openings at national level to lay persons, over 7,000 in 1907 and 1935, over 6,000 in 1955 (table 1.7). In addition the churches were landlords of extensive property and recipients of large incomes. In 1925, for example, the Church of England's Ecclesiastical Commissioners received an income of £2.9 million and its Central Board of Finance £145,000. By 1935 the Church of England's annual revenues from all sources were estimated at £16 million (Table 1.6), which was nearly twice the turnover of W. H. Smith the newsagent, one of the 100 largest employers in the UK in 1935 and, like the churches, in the services sector.[2] The Church of Scotland in 1924 received income totalling £1.2 million and the United Free Church of Scotland income of £1.5 million. By 1935, after the union of 1929, the Church of Scotland had a total income of £2.7 million. The three Methodist denominations which united in 1932 were reckoned to have a combined income of £3.95 million by 1935. Surely the proper stewarding of such large sums required the application of skills found in the secular world: auditing, investment consultancy, to say nothing of the manage-

[1] L. S. Hunter, *John Hunter DD* (London, 1921), 272.
[2] C. Wilson, *First with the News: The History of W. H. Smith, 1792-1972* (London, 1985), 451.

ment of clerical pension funds and the administration of property. Maybe 'moneyed men' had some use.

The next section aims to pursue two questions. Who were the 'moneyed men', the businessmen (and women where present) in the national leaderships of the main Christian denominations in Britain? What parts did they play in the running of their churches? As in the previous section answers are sought through quantitative measures. This time, however, the samples of business leaders are compared to samples of church leaders; activists among the church leaders are identified on the basis of their office holding and their business interests traced through their directorships. Qualitatively answers are sought through a number of case-studies.

7

Businessmen and Women in the Church of England, 1900–1960

INTRODUCTION

The chapter which follows identifies and examines the lay people who played a part in the national affairs of the Church of England. Attention is focused on the Houses of Laymen of the provinces of Canterbury and York and their successor, from 1920, the National Assembly of the Church of England. These were the major, but not the only, institutional channels through which the laity might have a voice in the affairs of the church. Apart from the host of ecclesiastical and charitable societies whose objects, histories, officers' names, and financial states pack page after page of *The Official Year-Book of the Church of England* year after year, there were two others that might have been chosen for analysis: the Ecclesiastical (after 1948, Church) Commissioners and the Church Congress. Neither was appropriate, but for very different reasons. The Church Congress, modelled on the meetings of the British Association, was intended to defend church interests and vent opinion. Commencing in 1862, it held a series of meetings once a year in a major town or city, usually attended by large audiences who came to hear prominent speakers on a wide range of topics.[1] A check of its published *Official Reports* down to the mid-1920s shows that very few industrialists bothered to contribute, earning the rebuke of the Archbishop of York in 1912 (see Chapter 4, s. 2 above). Because it was not in the least representative of the laity, it has been largely set aside in this book.

The Ecclesiastical Commissioners, managers of the largest bloc of assets in the Church of England, would have been a proper subject for study but for two considerations. First, there is already a definitive

---

[1] O. Chadwick, *The Victorian Church* (London, 1972), ii. 362–4.

treatment of their activities.[2] Second, it has been extraordinarily difficult to identify for the benchmark years of 1907 and 1935 the '12 eminent
laymen' who sat on the Commission. No official handbooks record their
names. No registers in the Commissioners' Archives seem to have
kept an annual tally of which 12 laymen at any given date were
Commissioners.[3] Consequently the much-needed study of the Church
Commissioners, complementing Best's work on the Ecclesiastical Commissioners, has been left to someone else.

I EDWARDIAN LAYMEN AND THEIR CHURCH OPPORTUNITIES

At the opening of the century opportunities for laymen to contribute
to the national life of the Church of England existed, but were limited.
They existed in the two Houses of Laymen (for the provinces of Canterbury and York) which met separately and (from 1898) jointly, and in
the Central Council of Diocesan Conferences. They were limited because
none of these assemblies had either legal status or power to legislate.[4]
Some progress was made in 1903 with the setting up of the Representative
Church Council, comprising the four Houses of Convocation (the
bishops and clergy of Canterbury and York) and the two Houses of
Laymen. An analysis of the membership and work of these lay bodies
will indicate the extent to which business interests participated in the
national counsels of the church.

The three bodies (the two Houses of Laymen and the Council of
Diocesan Conferences) together totalled 381 laymen: an exclusively male
preserve, in contrast to the Wesleyans' national committee memberships
(see next chapter). While numbers of laymen in the two Houses accurately reflected the population of the two provinces of Canterbury and
York (229 laymen in the Canterbury House, 112 in the York House),
the laymen's social backgrounds betrayed a massive upper-class bias,
reflected in the social origins of the bench of bishops.[5] Whereas well
under 1 per cent of the population in 1901 belonged to the peerage,

[2] G. F. A. Best, *Temporal Pillars* (Cambridge, 1963).
[3] My thanks to Mr D. A. Armstrong, Records Officer to the Church Commissioners,
for searching for these names. The list he was able to find (letter to the author, 28 Feb.
1989) indicates that very few big businessmen were involved: only one in 1907, Aretas
Akers-Douglas (later Viscount Chilston) who sat on the board of the South East &
Chatham Railway Co. in 1907.
[4] K. A. Thompson, *Bureaucracy and Church Reform* (Oxford, 1970), 125.
[5] E. R. Norman, *Church and Society in England, 1779-1970* (Oxford. 1976), 231-2.

TABLE 7.1. *Church of England company directors among lay leaders, 1907, 1935, 1955*

Industry	1907[a]		1935[b]		1955[b]	
	No.	%	No.	%	No.	%
1. Agriculture, fishing, plantations	11	4.5	5	2.5	7	6.0
2. Mining	20	8.1	10	4.9	2	1.7
3. Oil	1	0.4	3	1.5	0	0.0
4. Manufacturing	34	13.8	37	18.1	33	28.4
5. Construction	0	0.0	0	0.0	1	0.9
6. Utilities	18	7.3	23	11.3	2	1.7
7. Transport	56	22.8	22	10.8	6	5.2
8. Communications	5	2.0	1	0.5	0	0.0
9. Distribution	2	0.8	3	1.5	1	0.9
10. Insurance	32	13.0	21	10.3	11	9.5
11. Banking	23	9.3	15	7.4	7	6.0
12. Investment trusts, property	21	8.5	23	11.3	15	12.9
13. Professional services	2	0.8	1	0.5	3	2.6
14. Miscellaneous services	1	0.4	4	2.0	2	1.7
15. Unidentified	20	8.1	36	17.6	26	22.4
Total directorships	246	100.0	204	100.0	116	100.0
Total number of holders	107		64		47	
Av. per person	2.299		3.187		2.468	
Seats on Boards of 100 top cos.	16		10		6	
Men on national church committees	381		318		280	
Total persons on national church committees	381		393		368	
% of men who were co. directors	28.08		20.13		16.79	
Av. directorships per person	0.645		0.519		0.315	

[a] Houses of Laymen (Canterbury and York); Central Council of Diocesan Conferences (Laity).
[b] House of Laity, Church Assembly.

Sources: C. of E., Province of Canterbury, House of Laity, *Proceedings of Session, April, 1907* (London, 1907); C. of E., Province of York, House of Laity, *Proceedings of Session, February, 1907* (York, 1907); C. of E., Representative Church Council, *Report of the Proceedings of the Representative Church Council, July 1907* (London, 1907); C. of E., *Official Year-Book, 1907, 1935, 1955; WWW; WW 1935, 1955; WWMP, DD 1907, 1935, 1955.*

TABLE 7.2. *Church of England: sex and age composition of national lay leaderships, 1907, 1935, 1955*

	1907[a]	1935[b]	1955[b]
Sex distribution			
No. of men[c]	381	318 (80.9%)	280 (76.1%)
No. of women[c]	0	75 (19.1%)	88 (23.9%)
Total	381	393	368
Age distribution			
Men			
No. for which ages are known		291	269
Average age		63.7	62.2
Standard deviation		11.2	11.9
Women			
No. for which ages are known		47	71
Average age		57.4	59.5
Standard deviation		9.5	10.2
TOTAL NO. IN NATIONAL BODIES	381	393	368

[a] Houses of Laymen (provinces of Canterbury and York); Central Council of Diocesan Conferences (Laity).
[b] House of Laity, Church Assembly.
[c] Percentage of total in brackets.

Sources: As for Table 7.1, except for *DD*.

9 per cent (36) of the 381 laymen heading the Church of England were peers. Another 10 per cent (38) were baronets or knights (see Table 7.3). Although the occupations of all 381 have not been identified, 36 per cent (140) of them appeared in contemporary and subsequent editions of *Who's Who*—itself another indicator of social distinction. Of the 49 current and former MPs among the 381 laymen 80 per cent were Conservatives.

The educational backgrounds of those 140 identified from *Who Was Who* were distinctly upper class (see Table 7.4). Nearly 39 per cent (54) of them had attended Eton, 8 per cent Harrow, and 22 per cent other public schools.[6] Less than 3 per cent had attended the non-public school grammar schools. A correspondingly high number had passed from public school to the older universities. Of the 140 57 per cent (80) went either to Oxford or Cambridge University. Remarkably, 46 of these 'Oxbridge' men had been to one of two colleges in 1907, either Christ Church, Oxford (21), or Trinity College, Cambridge (25). Both colleges were among the larger ones in their universities but both had patrician associations. The Prince of Wales graduated at Trinity in 1861 and 'most

[6] As defined by the HMC listing of public schools in Truman & Knightley Ltd., *Schools* (12th edn., London, 1935), 164–71. The list includes a number which continued to describe themselves as grammar schools.

TABLE 7.3. *Church of England: social and political connections of national lay leaders, 1907, 1935, 1955*

	1907[a]		1935[b]		1955[b]	
	No.	%	No.	%	No.	%
Peers and peeresses (excluding offspring)	36	9.4	18	4.6	11	3.0
Knights and baronets	38	10.0	30	7.6	30	8.2
MPs (former, current)	49	12.9	20	5.1	10	2.7
Conservative, Unionist, National Unionist MPs	40		16		7	
Cons. MPs as % of all MPs in national C. of E. bodies		81.6		80		70
Total no. in national bodies	381	100.0	393	100.0	368	100.0

Note: Titles for laity of 1907 traced beyond that date in *WWW*.

[a] Houses of Laymen (Canterbury and York); Central Council of Diocesan Conferences (Laity).
[b] House of Laity, Church Assembly.

Sources: As for Table 7.2.

wealthy or aristocratic students tended to congregate in Trinity'.[7] At Oxford in the early nineteenth century Christ Church 'had established a reputation for sound education and fashionable society'.[8] Quite exceptional in appearing in the Canterbury House of Laymen was Frederick Rogers, an East End bookbinder and trade unionist who had left dame school at the age of 8, helped found Toynbee Hall, and later campaigned for old age pensions.[9]

The aristocratic element in the lay leadership of the Church of England before the First World War arguably distanced it from society's middle and lower classes. What was the extent and nature of these lay leaders' connections with the worlds of business and industry? A careful search of the *Directory of Directors* for 1907 yields some interesting findings, as may be seen in Table 7.1. It shows first that the church's lay leaders were not primarily men of business, if directorships are taken as a measure of this association. Altogether 107, or 28 per cent, of the laymen were company directors in 1907. Between them they held 246 directorships. However, only 14 per cent (34) were of companies in manufacturing industry, where the bulk of the industrial population worked and lived. A much higher proportion related to transportation companies (chiefly railways) which accounted for nearly 23 per cent of the 246 board memberships. Another 30 per cent were in financial activities, primarily

[7] S. Rothblatt, *The Revolution of the Dons* (London, 1968), 235.
[8] W. R. Ward, *Victorian Oxford* (London, 1965), 54.
[9] *WWW*.

TABLE 7.4. *Church of England: educational backgrounds of national lay leaders, 1907, 1935, 1955*

	1907[a]		1935[b]		1955[b]	
	No.	%	No.	%	No.	%
School (men only)						
Eton	54	38.6	35	11.0	24	8.6
Harrow	11	7.9	8	2.5	6	2.1
Other public schools	31	22.1	105	33.0	112	40.0
Grammar school	4	2.9	21	6.6	12	4.3
Total identified[c]	140	100.0	318	100.0	280	100.0
University						
Men						
Oxford	47	33.6	57	17.9	46	16.4
Cambridge	33	23.6	49	15.4	39	13.9
London	0	0.0	10	3.1	9	3.2
Other British universities	1	0.7	11	3.5	17	6.1
Military institution	4	2.9	8	2.5	7	2.5
Total men identified	140	100.0	318	100.0	280	100.0
Women						
Oxford	0		2	2.7	5	5.7
Cambridge	0		1	1.3	4	4.5
London	0		3	4.0	5	5.7
Other British universities	0				4	4.5
Total women identified	0		75	100.0	88	100.0
TOTAL ON NATIONAL BODY	381		393		368	

[a] Houses of Laymen (Canterbury and York); Central Council of Diocesan Conferences (Laity).
[b] House of Laity, Church Assembly.
[c] Identifications from *Who Was Who* (for 1907 individuals) and *Official YB of the C. of E.*, 1935, 1955.
Sources: As for Table 7.2.

insurance, banking, and investment trusts. By the turn of the century the activities of railway and finance companies were largely planned, co-ordinated, and evaluated in the boardrooms and clubs of London. These Anglican directors, therefore, moved in a very specific segment of the business world. In essence it was metropolitan rather than provincial, imperial rather than domestic, capital-concerned rather than labour-concerned.

The strength and nature of these church–business linkages can be probed further. How densely concentrated were directorships among these Church lay leaders with business connections and where did their commercial interests lie? How many of the directorships belonged to the big businesses of 1907? What industrial sectors were most heavily represented, in particular, how strong were links with manufacturing industry? Of the 107 Anglicans with seats on company boards only nine held five or more directorships. They were the 1st Baron Armstrong of Bamburgh and Cragside (great nephew of 1st Baron Armstrong of Cragside, founder of the armaments and shipbuilding firm that bore his name) with sixteen directorships; Sir Henry Mather Jackson 3rd Baronet with eight; Sir William B. Forwood with seven; Captain J. G. Le Marchant and Lord Wenlock, each with six; and, with five each, Alfred Baldwin, Sir Henry Howe Bemrose, the 11th Baron Kinnaird, and A. L. Stride. Despite his awesome industrial inheritance Lord Armstrong listed only one manufacturing firm among his directorships, naturally Sir W. G. Armstrong, Whitworth & Co. Ltd.; the rest were mostly of mining and plantation, utilities, railway, and financial companies. Alfred Baldwin, Unionist MP for Bewdley (West Worcestershire), Protectionist, and High Anglican, had founded the iron and steel firm that bore his name across the Midlands and South Wales. Yet he sat (as chairman) on the board of only one manufacturing firm, his own.[10] Sir Henry Bemrose, former MP for Derby, local Tory leader, Evangelical churchman, and prominent Freemason, headed the family printing business at Derby and was on the boards of two printing machinery companies. One, Linotype & Machinery Ltd., a technologically revolutionary and highly profitable firm, was then transforming the British printing trade.[11]

The other multiple directors had little or nothing to do with manufacturing. Sir William B. Forwood, Merseyside merchant-shipowner and tempered rather than extremist churchman in Liverpool's torrid sectarian climate, sat on the boards of the Cunard Steam Ship Co. (for over thirty years), the Bank of Liverpool, one insurance, one mining, and two utilities companies. His prime business interest in 1907, of which he was co-founder and first chairman, was the Liverpool Overhead Railway Co.—the first full-gauge electric railway in the world, designed to improve communications along Liverpool's congested dockland in response to Mancunian competition opened up by the Manchester Ship Canal.[12] Sir Henry Mather Jackson, of Llantilio Court, Abergavenny, split his business interests between South Wales and the Americas. He was chairman of the Corrwy Rhondda Colliery Co., Glyncorrwy Colliery Co., South Wales Mineral Railway Co., and director of the Alexandra (Newport & South Wales) Docks & Railway Co.; and he was on the boards of the Grand Trunk Pacific Railway (London committee), the Grand Trunk Railway Co. of Canada, the Marianao & Havana Railway Co., and the United Railways of the Havana & Regla Warehouses Ltd.

[10] Colin Baber and Trevor Boyns, 'Alfred Baldwin', DBB.

[11] Derby Daily Telegraph, 5 May 1911; J. O. Stubbs, 'Sir Joseph Lawrence', DBB.

[12] J. Gordon Read, 'Sir William Bower Forwood', DBB; P. J. Waller, Democracy and Sectarianism (Liverpool, 1981).

Arthur, 11th Baron Kinnaird, a staunch Evangelical leader in Edinburgh and London who generously sponsored the Student Volunteer Missionary Union in the 1890s, and its successor the Student Christian Movement through the rest of his life,[13] had predominantly financial business links. Besides Barclay & Co., the recently formed merger of Quaker banks, he was on the boards of two insurance companies (County Fire Office and Railway Passengers' Assurance), two trusts (Merchants and Trust & Agency Co. of Australasia), and a utility company (Westminster Electric Supply Corporation). Captain J. G. Le Marchant was director of three utilities companies operating in South America and the Philippines and of three investment trusts. Arthur L. Stride, chairman and managing director of the London, Tilbury & Southend Railway Co. and of Fenchurch Street Terminus, was director only of railway companies, four domestic, one Brazilian. The 3rd Baron Wenlock likewise split his business interests between domestic and foreign, mining, railway, and finance companies, including the North Eastern Railway Co. and Barclays Bank on one hand, East Gwanda Mines and the Schibaieff Petroleum Co. on the other: safe versus speculative investments. In short, of the nine multi-directors among church leaders only two, Baldwin and Bemrose, one High Church, one Evangelical, came from the manufacturing sector of the economy.

How large was the presence of these directors in the boardrooms of big business in 1907? How closely, in other words, was the established church related to big business as it moved into monopoly capitalism? One objective test, using the set of largest employers of 1907 identified in Appendix I (and admittedly weighted towards labour-intensive firms), provides an exact enough measure. Of the 246 directorships held by the 107 church lay leaders 16 belonged to companies on the list of 100 largest employers in the UK. Those 100 largest firms had between them 1,008 seats (based on a count of the seats on 91 of the 100 boards), so that 16 suggests that only 1.59 per cent of big business leaders were leading laity in the Church of England. For the national religious body with a religious density of just under 9 per cent (see Table 1.5) it seems like massive underrepresentation. Arguably the most powerful figures on the boards of large businesses were the chairmen. Here again Anglicans were poorly represented. Only three of the chairmanships of the 100 largest employer companies in the UK in 1907 were filled by church lay leaders.

[13] T. Tatlow, *The Story of the SCM of Great Britain and Ireland* (London, 1933), 24, 31, 180.

Clearly Anglican laymen at the top of big business preferred non-manufacturing associations and investments. Of the sixteen seats on the boards of the 100 largest firms two were of a mining and metal company (Wigan Coal & Iron: Lord Balcarres, chairman, and Sir Charles L. Ryan); one was of a shipping company (Cunard: of which Forwood was deputy chairman); and ten were of six railway boards. Anglicans chaired two of the railway companies: the Right Honourable J. Lloyd Wharton the North Eastern Railway and Sir George Armytage the Lancashire & Yorkshire Railway. The other eight seats were held by Lord Armstrong (the NER), Alfred Baldwin (the Great Western), Charles Bill (the North Staffs.), Sir John Talbot Llewelyn (the GWR), Miles MacInnes, a devout Evangelical (the London & North Western), Sir Walter R. Plummer (the NER), Colonel Sir Clement M. Royds (the Great Central), and Lord Wenlock (the NER). Only three of the sixteen seats belonged to men in manufacturing companies: Lord Armstrong in his family firm; W. S. Kinch of Worthington, Wigan, in the Bradford Dyers' Association; and G. Peel of Swinton, Manchester, in the Fine Cotton Spinners & Doublers' Association.

There were, of course, other businessmen among the church's lay leaders of 1907 who wielded considerable influence although their companies were not among the largest 100 employer firms. Among them were the 1st Earl Egerton, former chairman of the Manchester Ship Canal and one of the most highly placed Freemasons in the land;[14] Sir William Portal, deputy chairman of the London & South Western Railway; and William Sheepshanks, chairman of the Aire & Calder Navigation. And among the holders of the 246 directorships were clusters of individuals in a few companies: four on the board of the North Eastern Railway (see above); four on Barclays Bank board (Francis A. Bevan the chairman[15], Lord Kinnaird, Lord Wenlock, and Arthur C. P. Willyams, the first two certainly being Evangelicals); and four on the board of the Royal Insurance Co. (C. J. Bushell, George Marsham, Colonel Henry Savile, and George Winch). Such groups had the potential to exercise solid Christian influence on their fellow directors; whether they did so is unknown. Thus all the evidence suggests that the Church of England's national lay leadership had slender links with business, big business, or manufacturing. Where they were involved in business as company directors they chose transport and financial boardrooms and investments, reflecting perhaps their predominantly landed and

---

[14] E. Gaskell, *Lancashire Leaders* (London, c. 1900).
[15] Eynon Smart, 'Francis Augustus Bevan', *DBB*.

professional backgrounds. That experience, bound up with their roles as landlords, *rentiers*, or professionals and consultants, more often than not placed them outside the ruling circles of commerce and industry.

Another question remains. Who were the leaders among these 381 church laymen? Analysis of the two Houses of Laymen and the Central Council of Diocesan Committees and their subcommittees (in so far as these are known from published sources) shows that the 381 held between them 555 posts. Most (306) held only one position but 36 held three or more, and eight held five or more posts. It is these eight individuals (on the basis of criteria developed for the Methodists)[16] who may be regarded as the most active of the Church of England's laymen. Together they held 46 positions. Who were they? What interests did they represent?

The most pluralistic office holder was the 4th Marquess of Salisbury who held eight offices: chairman of the Canterbury House of Laymen, member of four committees (Standing, Parochial Lay Representatives, Ecclesiastical Dilapidations, and Workmen's Compensation Act), of the province of Canterbury's Secondary Education Council, and of the Standing Committee of the Representative Church Council. Three of the House of Laymen committee posts were ex officio because Salisbury held the highest office open to laymen in the Church of England, the chairmanship of the Canterbury House of Laymen. The other multiple office holders in the Canterbury House were Francis Charles Holiday, Wilfred Seymour de Winton (each with five posts), Sir Lewis Dibdin, and Phillip Vernon Smith LL D (each with six). In the York House of Laymen the multiple office holders were Sir Francis S. Powell MP of Bradford (six positions) and the 2nd Viscount Halifax and E. P. Charlewood (each with five). Powell and Halifax were vice-chairmen, Charlewood honorary secretary. (Viscount Cross, chairman of the York House of Laity, held four posts, just below the criterion adopted.)

Between them these eight men had little familiarity with business or manufacturing industry. Salisbury, educated at Eton and Oxford, was then in his early forties. Distinguishing himself in the South African War, he sat in the House of Commons as Conservative MP until he succeeded his famous father, the great Victorian Prime Minister, in 1903. From the family seat, Hatfield House, his political career developed through the House of Lords (where he was Lord Privy Seal 1903–5 and, briefly, President of the Board of Trade before being driven into the wilderness by the Liberal landslide of 1906), and the Court (where he

[16] See ch. 8.

was ADC to King Edward VII). The 2nd Viscount Halifax, a devout and inflexible Anglo-Catholic, for many years chaired his church party's society, the English Church Union. The quest to gain recognition for Anglican orders drove him to a futile visit to Rome in 1894 and then intermittent conversations with the Abbé Portal, all of which inflamed the ire of Protestant zealots, sparked a ritual controversy, and indirectly led to the setting up of the Royal Commission on Church Discipline in 1904.[17] Sir Francis S. Powell, octogenarian, formerly fellow of St John's College, Cambridge and a barrister by training, was a pillar of the Lancashire Tory Party and one of the small band of Unionist Free Traders to keep their parliamentary seats in the 1906 election, after which he retired. MP for Wigan for more than two decades, he championed the working classes of Lancashire against their mill-owning Liberal bosses.[18]

Several of the other leading laymen brought the judgement of the professional administrator to the highest counsels of the Church of England. Sir Lewis Dibdin, First Estates Commissioner (1905–30) and the foremost ecclesiastical lawyer of his day, was a lifelong church bureaucrat. Yet, besides an 'unparalleled knowledge of church business' on which the archbishops leaned, he harboured a deep suspicion of democratic forms, which threatened to undermine the oligarchic rule of the higher clergy and their bureaucratic advisers.[19] P. V. Smith, a Fellow of King's College, Cambridge, in the late 1860s and 1870s, trained as a barrister and practised as an Equity draftsman and conveyancer. In 1891 he became Chancellor of the Diocese of Manchester, and of three other dioceses much later in his career. In effect he too was in the mould of a church bureaucrat.[20] Another was E. P. Charlewood, Registrar of the Manchester Diocese.[21] F. C. Holiday was at the height of his career in the India Office where he was Auditor of the Home Accounts of the Government of India, 1903–8, for which he was knighted in 1909. He sat on both the Central Council of Diocesan Conferences and the Canterbury House of Laymen. In the latter he was on the committee on Parochial Lay Representation and represented the House on two

---

[17] R. Lloyd, *The Church of England in the Twentieth Century* (London, 1946–50), i. 57–8, 126–31, 134, 144–7.

[18] *Burke's Peerage and Baronetage, 1906*, 1332; P. F. Clarke, *Lancashire and the New Liberalism* (Cambridge, 1971), 29–32, 225, 245, 280, 374.

[19] Thompson, *Bureaucracy*, 168–9; *DNB*.

[20] *WWW*; *Crockford's Clerical Directory, 1929*; J. and J. A. Venn, *Alumni Cantabrigienses* (Cambridge, 1946–54).

[21] *Slater's Manchester and Salford and Suburban Directory* (Manchester, 1907), 511.

educational bodies, the Consultative Body of the National Society and the Secondary Education Council of the Province.

Only one of the eight church workhorses hailed from the business world, and a protected corner of it at that. De Winton, from the Welsh borders, was a banker with a distinctly less superior background than the others: Bradfield, Trinity College Dublin, and then a junior partnership in Wilkins & Co., Brecon Old Bank, until it was taken over by Lloyds in 1890. De Winton became a director of Lloyds in 1909. He proved to be a particularly devoted 'ecclesiastical layman',[22] sitting in the Canterbury House of Laymen for the whole of its lifetime, 1886–1920.[23] In 1907 he sat on the Standing and Parochial Lay Representation committees and on the province's Board of Missions; additionally he audited the accounts of the House of Laymen.

However they are defined, the characteristics of the Church of England's lay leaders are clear. Educationally their backgrounds were narrow and élitist. Their dominant figures were aristocratic and landed, or else bureaucratic. Invariably they were Conservatives. Their associations with business were not especially strong, their links with manufacturing industry decidedly weak. None of these findings is particularly surprising but they require demonstration for the purposes of comparison with subsequent generations and other denominations. So much for the composition of the church's lay leadership, what of their activities before the deluge of the First World War?

The Houses of Laymen, in their separate and joint meetings, faced two directions. On one side they sought to defend the church against outside threats; on the other side, to reform the church from within. Thus in 1906 the two Houses were preoccupied with debates on the current Education Bill (which offended both Anglicans and Nonconformists); in 1907 they discussed the massive Report of the Royal Commission on Ecclesiastical Discipline (and at Canterbury voted in favour of amending the Ornaments Rubric, to satisfy middle and High Church clerical consciences).[24] The paucity of evidence on these debates denies any systematic analysis of how lay leaderships or business interests lined up. However, several generalizations are possible about the role of lay leaders in general in the higher counsels of the church. First a proportion of lay leaders faced an inordinate amount of time-wasting. The Representative Church Council debated the same issues as the Houses of Lay-

---

[22] A phrase which appeared in the late 1880s: Chadwick, *Victorian Church*, ii. 364.
[23] *WWW*.
[24] C. of E., *YB 1907*, 430–5; C. of E., Province of Canterbury, House of Laymen, *Proceedings of Session* (1907), 23–4.

men.[25] So did the Central Council of Diocesan Conferences.[26] For the 38 members of both a House of Laymen and the Central Council of Diocesan Conferences this tripling of debate must have seemed unnecessarily burdensome, especially because all the assemblies were deliberative, rather than legislative. There lay a second rub: the impotence of the national lay bodies in the Church of England. The obituarist of Sir Henry Bemrose in 1911 used his opportunity to make a sharp dig in this direction: 'Sir Henry was for many years one of the two representatives of the Diocese of Southwell in the House of Laymen, but as this modern Ecclesiastical parliament is little better than a talking machine, utterly devoid of all powers of initiation and legal standing, it was not likely that a practical man of affairs of the acumen of Sir Henry could take any keen interest in its deliberations.'[27] Thirdly there was the relatively inferior position of the lay person in the Church of England, compared to the laity among the Nonconformists. Bemrose's eulogist made this point too:

In former years Sir Henry took a leading part at Church Congresses, and at the Southwell Diocesan conferences it may safely be said that no one was listened to with greater respect. Of late years he has been conspicuous by his absence from these gatherings, and his absence has been remarked upon as a significant fact. Had the accidents of birth placed Sir Henry within the Presbyterian, or Congregational, or Wesleyan Churches it is certain he would have exercised a commanding influence in any one of these respective communions, where laymen are accorded their rightful position in the management of affairs. But in the Established Church, as at present constituted, the layman, however talented and devoted, is practically powerless.[28]

Inefficiency, impotency, inferiority figured among the responses greeting laymen at the highest levels in the Church of England, in return for the financial support, the parliamentary votes, the leadership qualities they were regularly asked to render to the church. For 'men of affairs', men in business, these temporal irritations were best avoided. The situation simmered for several decades. Slowly clerical leaders, spurred by Bishop Gore and the Christian Socialists, awoke to the truth that an unreformed church was increasingly alienated from the industrial working classes. All kinds of reform were needed, from removal of the scandals of patronage to the overhaul of the church's administrative machinery

---

[25] C. of E., *YB 1907*, 433.   [26] Ibid. 435.
[27] *Derby Daily Telegraph*, 5 May 1911.   [28] Ibid.

and the engagement of the laity in the service of the church. To its credit the Representative Church Council 'recommended the appointment of the Commission on Church and State in 1913, which in turn produced the basic proposals for the subsequent constitution of the Church Assembly'.[29] In the melting pot of the First World War the dross of procrastination disappeared. Stirred by the wartime exposures of clergy to conscripts, strengthened by Lord Wolmer and a parliamentary pressure group, energized above all by William Temple and the wartime Life and Liberty Movement, the Church of England's leadership secured the Enabling Act of 1919.[30] At last the church had much of the constitutional autonomy and independence from Parliament it had sought so long. Changes in the laity's role at this national level after 1919 can now be examined.

2 LAY LEADERS BETWEEN THE WARS AND THE ROLES OF BUSINESSMEN

Amid high expectations the National Assembly of the Church of England (known more familiarily as the Church Assembly) first met in Church House, Dean's Yard, Westminster, on 30 June 1920. At long last the church would have self-government and reform. At long last 'the laity in every parish throughout the land are offered vote and voice in the management of their Church' (as the Archbishop of York promised).[31] The reality was rather different. While statutory councils at every level of church life—from the Parochial Church Council (already introduced in some dioceses[32]) to the Ruridecanal and Diocesan Conferences up to the Church Assembly—obliged the clergy to co-operate much more closely with the laity, at both local and national levels expectant lay people found their cherished hopes unfulfilled. In the parish they could not appoint the parson, nor even recommend a candidate to the patron of the living. Nor could they decide the prevailing form of service (tending towards Low or High churchmanship): that remained the responsibility of the incumbent.[33] At the national level lay influence was less clearly defined, clerical weight much less unified. So great were the post-war

---

[29] Thompson, *Bureaucracy*, 125–6.

[30] For accounts of the background to the Enabling Act see Thompson, *Bureaucracy*, ch. 6; Lloyd, *Church of England*, i. 223–53; ii. 5–9, 152.

[31] F. A. Iremonger, *William Temple* (London, 1948), 274–5.

[32] Lloyd, *Church of England*, i. 248.

[33] Iremonger, *Temple*, 277.

temporal needs of the church that the views and skills of distinguished lay people simply had to be harnessed. However, they certainly were not given free rein, and all the time they ran between the shafts of multiple interests and structures.

As Kenneth A. Thompson has shown, the Church Assembly fell victim to sectional squabbles for control of the Assembly's legislative, deliberative, and executive functions.[34] The balancing of interests between the English Church Union (the Anglo-Catholics), the Church Association (the Evangelicals), the Churchman's Union for the Advancement of Liberal Religious Thought (the Modernists), and those who wanted to identify with elements in all parties (the Broad Churchmen) meant that party interests rather than personal qualifications determined the composition of committees and the effectiveness of the Assembly in dealing with particular issues. Structural pluralism likewise hampered the efficiency of the Assembly. Although the Church Assembly met in three houses, comprising in 1920 38 bishops, 251 clergy, and 357 laity, the bishops and clergy still continued to meet in their old Convocations. This parallel, exclusively clerical structure the Anglo-Catholics saw as the repository of ultimate authority in the church: for them it was not enough that clause 14 of the Enabling Act effectively gave the bishops charge of doctrine and ritual. Many lower clergy, irritated by the cuts in their parish incomes due to the pensions and dilapidations (fabric maintenance) premiums levied by the reforming Church Assembly, likewise supported the Convocation structure as a check on the Assembly. As if these spiritual sectionalisms were not enough, the Church Assembly also faced rival structures in one of its prime temporal roles, that of managing church finance. Here the Ecclesiastical Commissioners eclipsed the Church Assembly's Central Board of Finance (CBF). The CBF had an estimated income of just under £145,000 in 1925, much more than the £29,000 received by the (quite separate) Governors of Queen Anne's Bounty but dwarfed by the £2.8 million rendered to the (again quite separate) Ecclesiastical Commissioners in 1924.[35] Given these impediments it is surprising that so many of the laity, including a number with business backgrounds, served the Church Assembly so faithfully.

Several general points of some interest emerge from a simple analysis of the Church Assembly in the mid-1930s. It was the first national body

---

[34] Thompson, *Bureaucracy*, 179–87.   [35] C. of E., *YB 1926*, 179, 218, 219.

in the Church to admit women.[36] As Table 7.2 reveals, by the mid-1930s 19 per cent of the laity were women. They included a number of widows, wives of clergy, a retired missionary, a retired training college lecturer. On average they were a younger group than the men who were mostly around retirement age. The social composition of the Church Assembly was also changing and becoming less upper class. Its proportion of peers and peeresses was half that of the Edwardian councils and its share of knights, baronets, and MPs significantly less (see Table 7.3). All this was reflected in the educational backgrounds of the Assembly's lay members. The proportion of Eton and Harrow backgrounds of leading church laymen fell from 46 to only 13 per cent between 1907 and the mid-1930s, as Table 7.4 shows. The proportionate drop in all public school backgrounds was nearly as impressive: from 68 to 46 per cent. The share of 'Oxbridge' men likewise registered a substantial fall over these three decades, from 57 to 33 per cent.

Nevertheless the Church Assembly of the mid-1930s was still not representative of society as a whole. Not one of the sixty-nine laymen listing his occupation in the 'Who's Who in the Church Assembly' could be classified as lower class.[37] The largest group (twenty-seven) were from the legal profession. Then there were eleven teachers and academics; seven Civil Servants and local government officials; and two or three medical men. Many were retired. A small group of thirteen men announced their business links: three accountants; two company secretaries; a branch inspector of Martin's Bank; a brewing company director (John Eustace Secker of Greenall, Whitley); a stockbroker (Ralph Assheton of Shaw, Loebel & Co.); and five company chairmen. The latter were Sir Clement A. Barlow, former chairman of Sotheby's, the antique dealers and auctioneers; Arthur Harrison, chairman of Harrison & Harrison, organ builders; Sir Charles Marston, chairman of Villiers Engineering Co., the renowned motorcycle manufacturers; George E. Wolstenholme, a Sheffield cutlery manufacturer; and the octogenarian Francis Priestman who had built up the family collieries into one of the largest coal businesses in the North-East before he retired.[38] The professions dominated the laity in the Church Assembly. Men in business, unless they were retired, simply did not have the time, even if they wished, to participate in the Church Assembly's spring, summer, and autumn meetings, each running from a Friday to a Monday. However, the *Official Year-Book*

[36] B. Heeney, 'The Beginnings of Church Feminism', in G. Malmgreen (ed.), *Religion in the Lives of English Women, 1760–1930* (London, 1986).

[37] C. of E., *YB 1935*, 67–108.

[38] A. A. Hall, 'Francis Priestman', *DBB*.

of the Church of England provides only a very partial, and not necessarily typical, sample of occupational structure. A fuller view comes by supplementing the Church *Year-Book* with the *Directory of Directors*.

As Table 7.1 discloses, 64 of the 318 laymen in the Church Assembly in 1935 were company directors.[39] They represented a lower proportion of leading churchmen (not including women, none of whom were company directors) than in Edwardian church councils: 20 per cent in 1935 compared to 28 per cent in 1907. Ostensibly the links between the church and the business world were weakening. On the other hand the average number of directorships held by those who were directors actually rose from 2.29 to 3.19. Where there was business commitment it was intensifying. But where were these directorships most heavily concentrated?

Using the same criterion as with the 1907 set, 12 of the 64 held 5 or more directorships: nearly 19 per cent of the church directors of 1935 compared to just over 8 per cent of the 1907 group. Seven of these 12 had evidently built up strongly local business interests. In the North-East the ageing Francis Priestman's interests (7 directorships) were mostly in collieries; while John Edward Cowen's (11) were in steel (including Consett Iron Co.), utility, and investment companies; and Henry Cecil Ferens's (5) in utilities. In Yorkshire Robert Armitage (22 directorships) had invested in collieries, steel, and utility companies. In the North-West Sir Joseph Law (6), Conservative MP for the High Peak division of Derbyshire, sat on the boards of local utility, transport, and insurance firms and in the Midlands Sir Joseph Nall (16), a longserving Conservative MP for the Hulme division of Manchester, sat on a similar range of companies, especially omnibus and motorbus firms. Across East Anglia and the South-East the interests of Sir George Courthope (15), Conservative MP for Rye 1906–45, lay in brewing, beet sugar, and railway (mostly light) companies. Apart from Viscount Wolmer (7 directorships), who sat on the boards of the Cement Makers Federation, the Hops Marketing Board, the NAAFI, Boots Pure Drug Co., and Eagle Star Insurance, the remaining four multiple directors had strong London and foreign business links. Frederick Janson Hanbury (5) sat on the main board of the family pharmaceutical firm and on those of four of its overseas subsidiaries. The 2nd Earl of Selborne (6), father of Wolmer, sat on domestic and colonial banking and insurance firms. Similarly placed were Sir Robert Kindersley (6), merchant banker and Henry Alexander Trotter (9), heavily engaged in foreign investment

---

[39] That is all those who recorded their directorships in the C. of E., *YB* or, being members of the Institute of Directors, in the *DD* for 1935.

trusts. As can be seen, the overall picture of the multi-directors suggests much stronger interests in mining, transport, utilities, and finance than in manufacturing. Links with beet sugar, pharmaceuticals, omnibuses, and motorbuses and Kindersley's directorship of the Cierva Autogiro Co. indicate some concern for the development of new technologies and industries.

More significant than densities of directorships, however, are the industrial sectors represented, the size of companies concerned, and the positions held. Compared to the set of Church of England company directors of 1907, the 1935 group exhibited increased proportions in oil, manufacturing, utilities, investment trusts and pension funds, and miscellaneous services. The shares of agriculture, insurance, banking, and, above all, transport suffered proportionate falls. The last reflected the merger of the country's 120 separate railway companies into four groups after 1921. Of all the 204 directorships only ten were attached to companies listed among the UK's largest employers in 1935. That is, big business directorships as a share of all directorships held by leading churchmen fell from 6.5 per cent to 4.9 per cent between 1907 and 1935. This suggests that churchmen were falling out of the business élite. Another measure, of church leaders' directorships as a proportion of all directorships on the boards of the 100 largest employer companies, shows that the churchmen had 0.86 per cent of the 1,157 seats on the boards of these companies (based on a count of board seats for 96 of the companies), almost a halving from 1907.

Whereas church leaders on the boards of the 100 largest companies in 1907 were predominantly on railway company boards, those in the 1935 business élite were on the boards of the big clearing banks. Three were Lloyds Bank directors: the 2nd Earl of Selborne, the 1st Baron Mamhead, a former MP for Exeter, and Major Sir Frederick Cripps, a former professional soldier and chairman of Gloucestershire County Council.[40] Two were Barclays Bank directors: Robert Armitage of Farnley Hall, Leeds, a former Lord Mayor of Leeds,[41] and Edward Mellish Clark of Cambridge (on the Bank's local board). Alfred Fowell Buxton, descendant of the Quaker and slave emancipator, was director (extraordinary) of the National Provincial Bank. In addition there were two railway company directors, Sir George Courthope (Southern Railway) and Edward Brocklehurst Fielden, Conservative MP for the Exchange

[40] *WWW.*   [41] Ibid.

Division of Manchester (deputy-chairman of the London, Midland & Scottish Railway); a director of Boots (Wolmer); and a director of Thomas Firth & John Brown (Wolstenholme). None of them, however, was chairman of any of the largest 100 companies.

First-rank figures on Britain's business landscape between the wars were few in number among leading Anglican laymen. One was Sir Robert Kindersley, partner in Lazards the merchant bankers. Henry Alexander Trotter, vice-president of the Corporation of Foreign Bond-Holders and a former Deputy-Governor of the Bank of England, 'an undistinguished figure, with no taste for power';[42] Edward Fielden, a Manchester MP and LMS deputy chairman; and Sir Charles Marston, chairman of Villiers (and formerly chairman of Sunbeam Bicycles),[43] were lesser figures. The age structure of the Church Assembly laity of 1935 suggests that the businessmen's energies, if not their influence, were valetudinarian. That may have been the case with most. Over the previous fifteen years, however, a small knot of businessmen had played a key part in the affairs of the church's Central Board of Finance.

The crucial area where church leaders perceived the need for lay involvement at a national level was finance. Here Anglican businessmen clearly believed they had much to offer in reforming church structures. Before the Church Assembly was set up, they sat on the 140-strong Central Board of Finance, established in 1914 to co-ordinate the financial functions of the dioceses. Initially it was ineffectual, meeting infrequently and starved of funds by the dioceses. During the formative years of the Church Assembly, as Thompson found, laymen who wanted greater efficiency in the central financial structures of the church encountered the opposition of archbishops who worried about loss of episcopal authority, administrators at the Ecclesiastical Commission who feared diminution of the Commission's power, diocesan interests who resented the growth of a central bureaucracy, Anglo-Catholics who smelt Erastianism, Evangelicals who caught the whiff of Romanism, and clergy who suspected their salaries would suffer.[44] Consequently when the Church Assembly took over the CBF a delicate balancing act was required of its clerical administrator, Canon Frank Partridge, secretary of the CBF 1918–34. Partridge, whose churchmanship was formed at Cuddesdon, was also financial secretary of the Church Assembly 1921–34, secretary

[42] R. S. Sayers, *Bank of England, 1891–1944* (Cambridge, 1976), 646.
[43] *Red Book of Commerce, 1911* (London, 1911), 622.
[44] Thompson, *Bureaucracy*, 188–200.

of its Legal Board 1924–33, and secretary of its Press and Publications Board 1923–33.[45]

As he saw it, he had to follow 'a practicable and sensible path between the precipice of autocratic centralization on the one hand, and the abyss of unco-ordinated differentiation on the other'.[46] With considerable skill he succeeded in mobilizing the talents of many leading laymen, including a number prominent in business, in the work of the CBF. A closer examination of the CBF's activities reveals the parts these businessmen played or were allowed to play.

One financial function of the CBF was fund-raising. This assumed critical importance under the impact of the First World War. Following the archbishops' pledge to provide bursaries for ex-servicemen to train for holy orders when the war was over, a Central Church Fund was set up under CBF auspices in 1917. At first the Finance Section of the CBF's Organization Committee handled the appeal. Advised by financial experts, the Ecclesiastical Commissioners, Central Societies, and others, they settled on a target of £5 million which 'would, with the contributions received on Church of England Sunday from year to year, enable the work of the Church to be developed on a sound financial basis'.[47] They started with a private appeal and with advertisements in the Press. The appeal was later handed over to a sub-committee (the Private Appeal Section) of the CBF's Executive Council,[48] which first met in January 1918, chaired by the 2nd Earl Brassey. Brassey's reckless energy had made his name at Eton, Balliol, and in the cavalry. In middle age his dynamism enabled him to carry leadership of the church's central fund-raising operation whilst engaging in the cause of a federal imperialism, fund-raising for his old Oxford college and for the university, and much else. In business he was managing director of a mining and lead smelting company in Sardinia and Italy, all that remained of the great Victorian contracting firm founded by his grandfather. Since 1890 he had been editor of the *Naval Annual* founded by his father. He 'transacted business at headlong speed, and rarely made mistakes, often revolutionising difficult situations in business in the very nick of time. This trait was conspicuous alike in his business, and in his administrative work.'[49]

[45] *WWW*; *Church Times*, 10 Oct. 1941.

[46] *Church Assembly News*, June 1924, quoted in Thompson, *Bureaucracy*, 199.

[47] C. of E., *YB 1919*, 380.

[48] CHA, CBF/ORG/SC/3, 'Memo on steps to be taken to press the appeal for the Central Church Fund', n.d.

[49] CHA, CBF papers, SEC/MEM/2/2, 'In memoriam Thomas Allnutt, Earl Brassey' (probably by Partridge). *WWW*.

The other pivotal layman in the CBF, particularly after the sudden death of Brassey, was Sir Robert Molesworth Kindersley (1871–1954). Through some of the most difficult years faced by the Church Assembly and the British economy Canon Partridge came to rely on Kindersley, at first in raising funds, later in stewarding them. Kindersley's background was very much that of the new generation of churchmen in business, a product of the late Victorian middle classes. The son of a manufacturing chemist, his education at Repton was curtailed by his father's straitened circumstances and he started work at the age of 15, eventually becoming private secretary to the chairman of Thames Ironworks, the last constructor of warships on the Thames. He married the daughter of a major-general in the Royal Engineers and from London's Dockland he moved into the City. In his early thirties he was partner in the stockbroking firm of David A. Bevan & Co., which had strong church connections.[50] Then in 1906 he joined the merchant bankers, Lazards & Co., as partner. When the firm became a limited company in 1919, Kindersley became chairman. From 1914 he was a Director of the Bank of England (moving from junior to senior status after the war), and from 1916 a governor of the Hudson's Bay Company. During the war he served as chairman of the War Savings Committee and was afterwards president of its successor the National Savings Committee.[51] As a City figure he was of the first rank. His contacts in the City—particularly in networks relating to shipbuilding and marine underwriting, the Stock Exchange, joint stock banking, and merchant banking—were therefore widespread, influential, and of great value to a voluntary institution with charitable functions like the CBF.

Kindersley was drawn into the circle of Partridge's lay allies in autumn 1918. The contact was Fred White (the brewery and insurance company director?), 'a great friend of mine', Partridge told Kindersley.[52] Before launching a public appeal for the Central Church Fund the CBF fundraisers wanted to secure 'promises of substantial support' from 'influential people'; Partridge wrote to Kindersley asking for 'your kind introduction to some people in the City of London'.[53] Kindersley agreed to meet Partridge and was evidently persuaded to lend his name to the

[50] From 1921, if not earlier, D. A. Bevan & Co. acted as stockbrokers for the CBF. See CHA, CBF/FIN/INV/1–7, D. A. Bevan & Co. file.

[51] D. E. Moggridge, 'Robert Molesworth Kindersley', DBB; Sayers, Bank of England, 618.

[52] CHA, CBF/FIN/INV/Kindersley files, Partridge to Kindersley, 17 Oct. 1918. This series of letters to and from Kindersley is hereafter cited as CHA, K.

[53] Ibid., Partridge to Kindersley, 17 Oct. 1918.

appeal. He recommended Lord Cunliffe, former Governor of the Bank of England, and Lord Revelstoke, head of Baring Brothers & Co., one of the most powerful merchant banks in the City: Cunliffe sent £250, Revelstoke £300.[54] Kindersley himself sent a cheque for £500 'from my firm' and mentioned the cause to Lord Cowdray, the international engineering contractor, '& hope he may be sympathetic'.[55] Cowdray was more than sympathetic: he gave the fund £10,000.[56]

Laid up by a bout of lumbago at the end of November 1918 Kindersley had time to consider the appeal and took the opportunity to pass his comments to Partridge. Recalling his War Savings experience he criticized the layout and contents of the advertisement in the *Sunday Times*, chiding that no mention was made of the administration of the appeal by laymen (a contentious principle over which Brassey and Partridge had great difficulty in persuading the archbishops to agree[57]) and adding,

I find the objects of the Fund which appeal to people most are

    Pensions for old incumbents
    Increased pay for clergy
    Education of candidates for Holy Orders drawn from fighting forces
    Strengthening of influence of Church as an antidote to Bolshevism.

I would suggest that the whole organisation of the Church through its pulpits should be utilised for propaganda for this Fund *while your advertising is going on*. Advertising without being followed up by individual effort by the organisation loses half its effect. The secret of the war savings success is this combination. How are subscriptions coming in?[58]

Over the early months of 1919 Partridge called increasingly on Kindersley's counsel. Would he comment on a scheme drafted by Lloyds Bank for church savings banks, recommend a good poster organizer (Kindersley suggested Holford Bottomley), advise allowing the Press agent to publish the names of benefactors, prescribe an autumn campaign?[59] With Lord Brassey, Kindersley gave a luncheon at Claridge's on 4 April 1919 to launch the appeal in the business world of the City.[60] Brassey invited Lord Avebury (a director of Coutts and National Provincial

[54] Ibid., Partridge to Kindersley, 28 Oct., 6 Nov. 1918, 26 Nov. 1920.
[55] Ibid., Kindersley to Partridge, 21 Nov. 1918.
[56] Ibid., same to same, 17 Apr. 1919; Partridge to Kindersley, 22 Apr. 1919.
[57] Thompson, *Bureaucracy*, 191–2.
[58] CHA, K, Kindersley to Partridge, 24 Nov. 1918.
[59] Ibid., Partridge to Kindersley, 7, 10 Jan., 16 Apr. 1919; Kindersley to Partridge, 6 May 1919.
[60] Ibid., Partridge to Kindersley, 24, 28 Mar., 1 Apr. 1919.

Banks), Viscount Goschen (director of London County Westminster & Parr's Bank and of Eagle, Star & British Dominions Insurance, and council president of the Corporation of Foreign Bondholders), Gibby Johnston, the Honourable Charles H. S. Stanhope (director of the Salinas of Mexico),[61] and Frederick Huth-Jackson (a senior Director of the Bank of England and senior partner of Frederick Huth & Co., a middling merchant bank specializing in South American trade and, unbeknown to all but a few, then running into serious difficulties with its pre-war debtors).[62] No doubt Kindersley's guests were equally influential.

Kindersley's name, with those of Brassey, Sir Trustram Eve (of J. R. Eve & Son, rating surveyors of Westminster), Sir Edward Thesiger (chairman of the Ecclesiastical Insurance Office), F. A. White (insurance and brewery director), the Honourable H. B. Portman and Lord Selborne (director of Lloyds Bank and of several African companies),[63] was appended to an appeal letter addressed to the Lord Lieutenants asking for their help in establishing county committees for raising contributions.[64] At the end of June Kindersley received an invitation from the chairman of the CBF Executive Council (Brassey) to serve on the Private Appeal Sub-committee of the Executive and also on the Finance Sub-committee, which he accepted.[65] For the autumn appeal for the Central Church Fund, three key laymen on the fund-raising committee signed personal letters to newspaper editors: Lord Selbourne to 35 provincial editors, Lord Brassey to some London dailies and Kindersley to *The Times*, the *Daily Mail*, and others. Partridge feared that unless the appeal committee moved quickly 'we shall have the Bishop of London butting in with a special appeal for the London clergy, who will get, as they got at the beginning of the year, a good lump sum each and the rest of the country will go begging'.[66] Kindersley agreed to his autograph signature being appended to the letter of appeal.[67] Almost the next letter Kindersley received from Partridge was one telling him of Brassey's accident. Dashing across a busy London street on the way from his Victoria Street offices to the House of Lords, Brassey was knocked down

---

[61] Directorships identified from *DD 1921*.

[62] Sayers, *Bank of England*, 268, 618. At the turn of the century Huth & Co's capital of £0.6m. was one-tenth that of Rothschild & Sons: S. D. Chapman, *The Rise of Merchant Banking* (London, 1984), 200.

[63] *DD 1921*.

[64] CHA, K, Partridge to Kindersley, 22 Apr. 1919 enclosure.

[65] Ibid., Partridge to Kindersley, 30 June 1919.

[66] Ibid., Partridge to Kindersley, 22 Sept., 7 Oct. 1919.

[67] Ibid., J. R. Stopford (for Kindersley) to Partridge, 11 Oct. 1919.

by a taxicab and died in hospital a few days later.[68] His death was a great blow to Partridge and the work of the CBF. It did, however, open the way for an even more appropriate figure, Kindersley himself, to act as Partridge's key financial adviser.

What had been achieved by the CBF fund-raisers under Brassey? Disappointingly little in view of all the effort made. A list of donors headed by the King and Queen and the Archbishop of Canterbury revealed that the organizers had canvassed the heights of society downwards.[69] Yet by October 1919 only £336,200 of the fund's target of £5 million had been subscribed.[70] Especially disappointing had been the response of the City. A statement of needs and their costs had been sent to peers, MPs, members of Lloyd's and of the Stock Exchange, and, in the province of York, to 'principal residents' (via the Lord Lieutenants). After the lunch at Claridges an appeal was organized to the major business sectors of the City. The response was dismal. 'The Stock Exchange produced only £475. The Chairman of Lloyds reported that it would be unwise to proceed further at Lloyds at the present time, and little resulted from the Appeal on the Coal Exchange and the Metal Exchange.'[71]

Diagnosing the situation after Brassey's death, the Organization Committee identified various reasons for the failure of the fund appeal. They blamed themselves for having set too low a standard of giving in the first place. More significantly they perceived several changes in the relationship between business and its social environment as especially obstructive. General post-war unrest and the unsettled financial situation dissuaded many people from contributing to charitable purposes. It was now impossible to appeal to firms and corporations, for however willing their directors might be they were restrained by their shareholders who 'were not Church people themselves'. Large benefactors' incomes had diminished by about a quarter from wartime inflation and heavy taxation. Lastly, 'a large proportion of those who have become wealthy during the war are men who have had no opportunity yet of grasping the responsibilities of men of substance in the matter of maintaining the public

---

[68] Ibid., Partridge to Kindersley, 11 Oct. 1919; and SEC/MEM/2/2, 'In memoriam Thomas Allnutt, Earl Brassey'.

[69] CHA, CBF/ORG/SAC/2, 'List of subscriptions of £100 and over'.

[70] CHA, K, Stopford to Partridge, 11 Oct. 1919. *The Times* on 13 Nov. 1919 reported that the Central Church Fund then stood at £303,000.

[71] CHA, CBF/ORG/SC/3, 'Memorandum on steps to be taken to press the appeal for the Central Church Fund', n.d.

services in Church and State'. No doubt these *nouveaux riches* would respond 'when an appeal is made directly to them'.[72]

Conditions relating to the supply of benefactors were certainly one side of the problem in garnering funds for the rationalized use of the church. The other side, as noted previously, comprised rivalries between those church bodies needing and demanding the attentions of public philanthropy. Partridge, more aware of the latter, confided his concerns to Kindersley. They reached one crisis point just before the Church Assembly first met in June 1920, as Partridge vividly wrote to tell Kindersley who was then in Winnipeg on Hudson's Bay Company affairs:

I think that you would have been amused had you been able to come with us to a meeting at Lambeth, when Lord Selborne, Sir Lewis Dibdin and I, like the gallant three who defended the bridge, faced the compact mass of English diocesan Bishops without a weapon in our hands. Lord Selborne told the Bishops, for the good of their souls, how poor a lead they had been giving themselves in this urgent matter, explained to them exactly what the Church ought to be doing, most of which it was not doing, and left them agape. Sir Lewis Dibdin followed and filled the mouths which were so open with the best kind of lay abuse which the ordinary parish parson is accustomed to receive. He devoted his attention in particular to the Archbishop of York [Lang] and the Bishop of London [Winnington-Ingram], and these two gentlemen looked a little bit more like whipped school boys than they can have done any time in the last fifty years. All this was leading up to the emphatic statement that the Bishops must take a lead in widening the diocesan outlook and breaking down the foolish and cut-throat policy of diocesan and central competition.[73]

The appeals for the Central Church Fund run by the CBF in 1918 and 1919 were repeated again in 1920 and 1921. While Brassey's successor as chairman of the CBF was the Earl of Selborne, his successor as chairman of the CBF's Special Appeal Committee was Kindersley. In character this Committee was heavily upper class and political. By 1921, besides Kindersley, its members were the Marquess of Bath, Countess Brassey, Sir Edward Brooksbank, the Honourable Edward Cadogan (a barrister and director of the Law Union & Rock Insurance Co.), the Marquess Camden, Lord Crawshaw (director of the American Association Inc.), C. I. de Rougemont, Viscount Goschen, Earl Grey (director of banking, insurance, and shipbuilding companies), Viscount Hambleden (senior partner of W. H. Smith & Son), Lord Hastings, the Honourable Gilbert Johnstone, Herbert Pike Pease MP (Anglican scion of the Quaker Pease dynasty of the North-East and then Assistant Postmaster-

[72] Ibid., 'Memo on steps . . .'.
[73] CHA, K, Partridge to Kindersley, 27 May 1920.

General),[74] the Marquess of Salisbury, the Earl of Selborne, and F. A. White.[75] Kindersley, at whose London house in Charles Street the Committee occasionally met,[76] was therefore an especially important link with the world of high finance. As before, he supplied the names of likely donors to the appeal. An undated list of 17 names 'suggested by Sir Robert Kindersley' ran from H. J. Mappin and Trotter (Deputy-Governor of the Bank of England) to Gordon Selfridge, F. S. Oliver, Lord Inchcape, Vivian Hugh Smith, and other figures in the high commercial circles of the City and the West End.[77] Through him Partridge sought approaches to potential benefactors. For example, 'It has been represented to me that J. Bruce Ismay [son of the founder of the White Star shipping line] ... would give a good thumping sum to the Central Church Fund if he were asked by the proper person in the proper way.'[78] Lord Selborne's attention had been drawn to the fact 'that Sir William Vestey,[79] the head of the Blue Star Line, ... is a man of immense wealth and disposed to help in philanthropic causes. He [Selborne] thinks, perhaps, that you [Kindersley] might know him or that I might approach him from some other quarter. Do you think that Anderson [Sir Alan Anderson] knows him?'[80] Again, what were the chances of Lord Cowdray increasing his £10,000 to £50,000?[81] When the substantial wealth (a will proved at £1.9 million) of another benefactor, Henry Greenwood Tetley (the fearsome and relentless force behind Courtaulds' successful exploitation of viscose rayon manufacture[82]), was announced by *The Times* in October 1921 Partridge promptly wrote to his business confidant. Tetley had earlier given £5,000 to the Central Church Fund and another £2,000 for the Service Candidates Ordination Fund, as well

[74] *WWMP.*

[75] CHA, CBF/ORG/SC/3, printed circular letter from CBF, 18 Nov, 1920; printed circular 'Central Church Fund. Special Appeal Committee. First List of Contributions received and promised towards £100,000 required in 1921.' See also CHA, K, Partridge to Kindersley, 22 Dec. 1919.

[76] CHA, K, Kindersley to Partridge, 3 Nov. 1920; Partridge to Kindersley, 15 Nov. 1920.

[77] CHA, CBF/ORG/SAC/2.

[78] CHA, K, Partridge to Kindersley, 10 Nov. 1919.

[79] Richard Perren, 'William Vestey and Edmund Hoyle Vestey', *DBB.*

[80] CHA, K, Partridge to Kindersley, 1 Dec. 1920.

[81] Ibid., Partridge to Kindersley, 1 Nov. 1920.

[82] D. C. Coleman, 'Henry Greenwood Tetley', *DBB.* Tetley's church links were developed unobtrusively and escaped the notice of his biographer and company historian, Coleman.

as more frequent sums of £100 to the CBF. His will specified £250,000 for distribution by his executors (the National Provincial & Union Bank of England and his widow) among causes in which he was interested in the British Empire. 'I think it would be well to put the case of the Central Church Fund without any delay', Partridge told Kindersley.[83]

More systematically, Kindersley signed appeal letters sent out by Partridge to the big donors who had responded to the earlier rounds of the appeal in 1918–19. These included Sir John Ellerman, the wealthy shipowner,[84] Lord Revelstoke, and Messrs R. E. Johnston, F. Bibby, C. S. Arbuthnot, and Hambleden (the last four giving £1,000 each).[85] The following year, in an attempt to find a thousand churchmen who would give £100 each, Kindersley signed most of the letters that went out.[86] Among the businessmen approached were the cigarette manufacturers H. H. Wills of Bristol and J. F. Player of Nottingham.[87] Among the 65 who appeared on the first published list of contributors were Sir Alan G. Anderson (shipowner and director of the P. & O. group), Lord Hambleden (of W. H. Smith & Sons), the Earl of Iveagh (of Guinness the brewers), Sir William Plender the accountant, Sir Thomas Royden (of Cunard), and William Sheepshanks (of the Aire & Calder Navigation and former chairman of the Yorkshire Penny Bank). Only one institutional donor, the Associated Telegraph Co., was listed.[88]

Kindersley continued to advise and help Partridge on methods of public fund-raising. He composed a public appeal letter,[89] unsuccessfully solicited an advertising arrangement with the *Daily Mail*,[90] reviewed Press advertisement,[91] and did not hesitate to relay to Partridge his continued misgivings about the inefficiencies of the church's financial structures. Attending a St Albans diocesan meeting in December 1920 he found 'as I anticipated, considerable confusion in the public mind

[83] CHA, K, Partridge to Kindersley, 14 Oct. 1921.

[84] The richest man in Britain by the time of his death in 1933: William D. Rubinstein, 'Sir John Reeves Ellerman', *DBB*.

[85] CHA, K, Partridge to Kindersley, 26 Nov. 1920.

[86] Ibid., Partridge to Kindersley, 25 Nov. 1920, 21 Sept. 1921.

[87] Ibid., Partridge to Kindersley, 7 Nov. 1921. The mention of J. F. Player must be a reference to John Dane Player, the tobacco manufacturer. See S. D. Chapman and G. Oldfield, 'John Player *et al.*', *DBB*.

[88] CHA, CBF/ORG/SC/4, printed circular, 'Central Church Fund. Special Appeal Committee. First List of Contributions . . .'

[89] CHA, K, Partridge to Kindersley, 17 Jan., 3 Mar. 1920.

[90] Ibid., Partridge to Kindersley, 25 Mar. 1920.

[91] Ibid., Kindersley to Partridge, 4 Oct. 1920.

with regard to these various appeals. I feel certain that at the present time the whole financial side of the cause is being prejudiced by this feeling that there is overlapping.'[92]

Was CBF fund-raising under Kindersley's leadership any more successful than under his predecessor Brassey? The evidence suggests not. To attain its former effectiveness the church had to replace the losses inflicted by the First World War. In spring 1921 it was estimated that during the seven years 1914–20 the church ought to have ordained 4,900 clergy. In fact only 2,400 were ordained. A rate of 700 ordinations a year required a budget of £338,504 in 1921—to cover training for the ministry (£115,104), maintenance of poorer clergy (£120,000), pensions (£58,000), religious education (£25,000), and administration (£20,000). While £226,000 of this budget would be met by diocesan levies, and £13,000 from sundry receipts, the CBF's Central Church Fund appeal was expected to raise £100,000.[93] In other words the big benefactors and the business community in London especially were faced with the challenge of giving £100,000. In producing only £19,526 6s. 11d. by February 1922, the CBF's 1921 appeal was clearly a flop. By 1926 all but £9,000 of the CBF's modest budget of £145,000 came from diocesan contributions.[94] Both Earl Brassey's and Sir Robert Kindersley's experience of fund-raising for the Church of England in the financially and economically stressed post-war world shows that big business interests, despite their perception of the church as a bulwark against Bolshevism, came nowhere near meeting their estimated shares of its financial requirements.

While Kindersley's success as a consultant fund-raiser was scarcely overwhelming, his role as an investment adviser was much more important. The four annual appeals of 1918–21, aiming at £5 million, realised something over £350,000.[95] Much of this was distributed for the church's current operating expenses. A much smaller proportion was diverted into capital accounts. To this was added trust funds received by the CBF between 1914 and 1918; totalling just over £11,000, they were placed in four separate trust accounts at the Bank of England. After the CBF assumed the added function of serving as the 'Financial Executive and

[92] Ibid., Kindersley to Partridge, 13 Dec. 1920.
[93] Ibid., enclosure with Kindersley (private secretary) to Partridge, 6 May 1921.
[94] C. of E., *YB 1926*, 179.
[95] CHA, CBF, J. R. Stopford (for Kindersley) to Partridge, 11 Oct. 1919, mentions £336,200 subscribed: more than the £250,000 mentioned by Thompson, *Bureaucracy*, 187.

Advisory Committee of the Church Assembly'[96] in 1920 it proved legally impossible to merge all the funds and so the Central Church Fund had to be administered by the CBF quite separately from the new Church Assembly Fund (mostly diocesan quotas). Much of the Central Church Fund by the mid-1920s had to be treated as capital. Between 15 June 1914 and the end of 1928 the CBF had made 57 investments costing £101,648 14s. 6d.[97]

Partridge first approached Kindersley with an investment query in March 1919, within six months of drawing him into the Central Church Fund appeal.[98] Would he recommend 5 per cent War Stock 1929–47 or 5 per cent National War Bonds 1928 for the re-investment of the interest (about £3,460) on Lord Llangattock's bequest to the Church in Wales? By the mid-1920s Kindersley, and sometimes one of his colleagues at Lazards (such as the Honourable Robert Brand[99]), was being regularly consulted by Canon Partridge for investment advice.[100] At times Kindersley's advice was unequivocal: 'I consider that the Australian Commonwealth has borrowed far more than she should have done, and her credit can in no way be compared with that of the British Government. *I* would not, therefore, recommend an exchange from War Loan to Australia 5%.'[101]

To Kindersley Partridge turned for solutions to the fresh financial problems of the CBF in the late 1920s and 1930s. In 1927 monies from the dioceses fell by nearly £3,700 while the Church Assembly Fund spent £15,000 more than its income. The Central Church Fund could relieve it by over £6,000 but this still left a deficit of £9,000. On the other hand, 'all our other finances are in a sound and indeed a flourishing condition'.[102] One way out of financial difficulties was to go to the market for capital loans. This step was taken to assist church training colleges. In 1928 the CBF raised £251,900 by issuing debentures for the Church Training Colleges Capital Fund.[103] Partridge, ever watchful for the chance to utilize his temporal connections and their expertise, sounded out Kindersley: it has been suggested that 'one or two stockbrokers interested in Church affairs like Bevan and Greenwell might be very glad

---

[96] Partridge, *Memorandum*, 6, in CHA, CBF/FIN/AC/A/1929.
[97] Partridge, *Memorandum*.
[98] CHA, K, Partridge to Kindersley, 18 Mar. 1919.
[99] Kathleen Burk, 'Robert Henry Brand', *DBB*.
[100] CHA, K, files for 1924, 1926–9.
[101] CHA, K, Kindersley to Partridge, 1 Aug. 1928.
[102] Ibid., Partridge to Kindersley, 16 Mar. 1928.
[103] CHA, CBF/FIN/AC/A/1929, CBF annual accounts, 1929, 49.

to recommend the Issue to some of our clients. I should like to have a word with you as to the possibility of this.'[104]

The Wall Street Crash in 1929, the market's response to a glut of goods and labour, triggered a world-wide collapse of prices and employment. In Britain soaring jobless figures faced the Labour Government with rising unemployment expenditures and a consequent flight from sterling. Hence came the financial crisis of 1931. The decision to impose severe economies, including a savage 10 per cent cut in unemployment benefit (in response to the misguided May Report), at the end of August split the Labour Government but failed to satisfy the international bankers. Nor did the formation of a National (part Labour, part Conservative) Government on 24 August. Snowden's traumatic budget of 10 September increased taxes and cut public sector wages. The ultimate answer, unshackling the economy from an artificially high exchange rate, came on 21 September when, in strained hopes of salvaging export markets, the National Government abandoned the gold standard. Returned to power by the electorate on 27 October, the National Government continued to pursue orthodox fiscal policies aimed at balancing the budget. Low interest rates (Bank Rate at 2 per cent), the Government's chief monetary instrument, were intended to reduce investment costs, thus stimulating industrial expansion, and to lighten the burden of the National Debt on the budget. 'A major conversion operation in March 1932 replaced 5 per cent War Loan 1929-47 (which made up over a quarter of the National Debt) with 3.5 per cent War Loan 1952 or after.'[105] Given these drastic deflationary adjustments at home and the instability of international capital markets abroad, it was not surprising that Canon Partridge appealed more urgently than ever for sound advice from CBF friends in high financial places.

The CBF's first step, the suspension of *Church Assembly Notes* for three months, was marginal compared to the measures needed to safeguard CBF investments.[106] On 21 October 1931 Partridge wrote to Kindersley for his view on the suggestion that the CBF 'would be wise to dispose of its long-dated, gilt-edged investments at present prices, and reinvest the proceeds in 4.5% Treasury Bonds, redeemable 15th April 1932.'[107] The following day Partridge urgently requested a meeting with Kindersley about CBF investments and proposed bringing with him Ralph Assheton, partner in Shaw, Loebl & Co., the CBF's stock-

[104] CHA, K, Partridge to Kindersley, 26 June 1928.
[105] G. C. Peden, *British Economic and Social Policy* (Deddington, Oxford, 1985), 99.
[106] CHA, K, Partridge to Kindersley, 1 Sept. 1931.
[107] Ibid., Partridge to Kindersley, 21 Oct. 1931.

brokers.[108] Clearly a full-scale review of the CBF's investments was under consideration. There had been two others, apparently, made in January 1925 and April 1931 by Lord Plender, the eminent accountant.[109] Incomplete documentation denies a full picture of the sequence of events which followed. What is certain is that numerous financial experts were called upon either on a formal commercial basis or on an informal perhaps more disinterested basis. For example the CBF's old stockbroker, David A. Bevan & Co., in July 1932 was advising about the conversion of 5 per cent War Loan: the interest rate might fall to 3.5 per cent but it would be tax-free and would probably succeed.[110] Plender's opinion of the accounts was taken again.[111] Others gave their less definitive services freely. By October 1932 Partridge was consulting an Investments Committee, which then consisted of Lord Grey, Bunnell Henry Burton, Ralph Assheton, and Edward Mellish Clark, all diocesan representatives in the Church Assembly.[112] This evidently got out of its depth and was expanded with the addition of City members: Sir Robert Kindersley, the Honourable Robert Brand (both still of Lazards), Henry Alexander Trotter (now a director of Alliance Assurance Co.),[113] and Sir Montague Barlow (a former MP, barrister, and chairman of Sotheby & Co. who was chairman of the London Diocesan Fund).[114] In December 1932 Partridge was telling Kindersley of the establishment of an Investments Committee.[115] The reorganized Investments Committee, under the chairmanship of Kindersley, first met on 5 April 1933 at Lazards premises in Old Broad Street.[116]

Any assessment of the performance of the CBF's investment advisers, particularly through the rough passage of the early 1930s, requires a run of data to compare with overall stock market trends. Unfortunately the CBF data is patchy and only an incomplete view of what was happening is possible. At the end of 1929, as Table 7.5 shows, the CBF's various funds had an income of £458,832 and assets of £650,975. The bulk of the income and the assets belonged to the Church Training Colleges Capital Fund, the assets of which were largely represented by three train-

[108] Ibid., Partridge to Kindersley, 22, 26 Oct. 1931.

[109] CHA, CBF/FIN/INV/3/1, Partridge to the CBF Investments Committee, 11 Oct. 1932.

[110] CHA, CBF/FIN/INV/3/1, Bevan & Co. to Partridge, 4 July 1932.

[111] Ibid., Partridge to the Investments Committee, 11 Oct. 1932.

[112] Ibid.

[113] *WW 1935*.

[114] Ibid.

[115] CHA, K, Partridge to Kindersley, 2 Dec. 1932.

[116] The printed minutes of this meeting are in CHA, CBF/FIN/INV/3/3.

TABLE 7.5. *CBF investments for the year ending 31 December 1929 (£)*

Fund	Income	Interest and dividends	Interest as % of income	Assets	Investments	Investments as % of assets
Central Church Fund	19,768	5,329	27.0	127,771	117,599	92.0
Church Assembly Fund	112,725	309	0.3	63,915	2,390	3.7
Trust Funds	2,200	1,451	66.0	35,304	30,554	86.5
Sponsors Scheme	29,317	1,554	5.3	52,593	35,087	66.7
Archbishops' Western Canada Fund	1,691	69	4.1	849		
Church Training Colleges Capital Fund	287,172	720	0.3	359,156	66,285	18.5
Church Assembly Overseas Fund	1,601	30	1.9	224		
Church Assembly Missionary Council Development Fund	1,225	61	5.0	1,633	832	50.9
Church Assembly Missionary Council Special Funds	3,133	379	12.1	9,530	7,140	74.9
TOTAL	458,832	9,902	2.2	650,975	259,887	39.9

Source: CHA, CBF/FIN/AC/A/1929, CBF annual accounts 1929.

ing colleges while the income was mostly the £251,900 raised by the issue of debentures. Nevertheless nearly 40 per cent, or nearly £260,000, of the CBF's assets were in the form of investments. Four funds accounted for the bulk of these investments: the Central Church Fund, the Trust Funds, the Sponsors' Scheme, and the Training Colleges Capital Fund. The investment record of one of these funds, the Central Church Fund (Table 7.6), apparently the only one made, shows that between 1914 and 1928 the CBF's investment advisers heavily preferred British government stocks (51 per cent of the £101,647 invested) and a narrow range of British non-government stocks, mostly local authorities and the Church Training Colleges debentures (together another 34 per cent): unexceptionably patriotic and safe choices.

The next glimpses of the CBF portfolio come in 1933 when the new Investments Committee reviewed all the investments made on behalf of the various CBF funds. The first step of the committee was a change in format so that the investments appeared not according to CBF fund but in the order of the *Stock Exchange List*. The portfolio now became familiar to the City men and facilitated their rapid appraisal of the problems it presented. Their first step was to dispose of £41,708 of 5 per cent Conversion Loan and nearly £19,000 of colonial and foreign stocks, replacing them with £10,000 Bank of England stock, £10,000 3 per cent Conversion Loan, £10,000 in local authority stocks (Manchester and the West Riding), £5,000 of India 3 per cent stock, and £5,000 of electricity company stocks.[117] In May the Committee decided to sell over 30 small holdings (under £1,000) of stocks, colonial and investment trusts being the largest groups of these. In their place they bought some of the better foreign, colonial, and industrial stocks.[118] By December 1933 the CBF's portfolio had been consolidated and restructured so that more was concentrated in local authorities and new technologies as well as gilts (see Table 7.7).

The Church Assembly Committee on Central Funds in the mid-1950s recorded in an unpublished section of its draft report that in the 1920s and 1930s the CBF 'largely under the inspiration of Canon Partridge, appears to have exercised an unquestioned dominance among the organs of the Church Assembly and to have displayed much creative activity and a frequently decisive influence upon the Assembly's policy. . . . after the departure of Canon Partridge there appears to have been a reaction against what was felt by some to have been a form of financial dictator-

---

[117] Ibid., Minutes of the Investments Committee, 5 Apr. 1933.
[118] Ibid., Minutes of the Investments Committee, 10 May 1933.

TABLE 7.6. *CBF investments made on behalf of the Central Church Fund, 1914–1928* (to nearest £)

Year	British Funds	British non-government	Imperial government	Imperial non-government	Foreign government	Foreign non-government	Total	%
1914	6,100	2,498				2,502	11,100	10.92
1915	100						100	0.10
1918	600						600	0.59
1919	14,139	2,050					16,189	15.93
1920	1,781	1,000					2,781	2.74
1921	263	10,056	2,984	1,216			14,519	14.28
1922	2,025				387		2,412	2.37
1924	8,681	2,999			154		11,834	11.64
1925	11,800				4,416		16,216	15.95
1926	200			373		243	816	0.80
1927	4,023						4,023	3.96
1928	2,644	15,800	2,613				21,057	20.72
TOTAL	52,356	34,403	5,597	1,589	4,957	2,745	101,647	100.00
%	51.5	33.8	5.5	1.6	4.9	2.7	100.00	

Source: (Frank Partridge), *Memorandum on the Funds . . . of the CBF* (London, 22 May 1929), 14–19.

ship.'[119] Partridge left the secretariat of the Church Assembly in 1934 to become Archdeacon of Oakham and two years later was appointed Bishop of Portsmouth— not the most prestigious of episcopal seats. Any suggestion of dominance that he gave to his fellow clerics in the financial affairs of the Church Assembly arose from the discreet relationships he had built up with some of the most skilled financial figures in the City. In the difficult days of his time with the CBF he must have thanked God on numerous occasions for such connections, above all for that with Kindersley: especially for Kindersley's access to the latest market information and his steady judgement in taking decisions upon it.

3 BUSINESS PEOPLE IN THE CHURCH IN THE 1940s AND 1950s

World war, atomic war, Cold War, Welfare State, loss of empire, the supremacy of science and technology, economic crises succeeded by economic growth: the vast and bewildering changes which engulfed the world and Britain in the 1940s and 1950s presented a perplexing array of moral and religious issues to the churches and the Church of England in particular. It was the established church and commanded the widest support among the British churchgoing public. Now the old certainties looked less secure than ever before. The doubt and despair engendered by the 1940s vision of a world in flames were followed by the indifference and materialism accompanying rising living standards. These external pressures threatened the church organically and structurally. Its relative membership fell drastically. The religious density of the Church of England, which stood at 8.095 in 1931 and 6.448 in 1941, slipped to 5.814 in 1951 and 3.746 in 1961.[120] At the same time the process by which the State displaced the Church as provider of welfare accelerated. For example its share of secondary education between 1950 and 1960 fell from 5.6 to 4.3 per cent of all secondary schools in England and Wales.[121] On the other hand, some gaps in the social services of the Welfare State continued to be met by the church rather than by local authorities.[122]

For lay persons within the Church of England internal changes were also unsettling. At the end of September 1944 the Archbishop of Canter-

---

[119] CHA, CBF Box 726, Committee on Central Funds file B/16/1, Part 6, paras. 31–2.

[120] R. Currie and A. Gilbert, 'Religion', in A. H. Halsey (ed.), *Trends in British Society since 1900* (London, 1972), 444.

[121] A. H. Halsey *et al.*, 'Schools', in Halsey (ed.), *Trends*.

[122] M. P. Hall and I. V. Howes, *The Church in Social Work* (London, 1965).

TABLE 7.7. *CBF investments over £1,000 in 1933*

	3 April	8 May	2 June	1 December
British Funds				
India 3.5	1,661	1,661	1,661	1,661
Conv. Loan 1940–4, 4.5%	3,824	3,824	3,824	3,824
Funding Loan 1960–90 4%	2,957	2,957	2,957	2,957
India 1948–53 4%			5,000	5,000
War Loan 3.5%	7,524	7,524	10,000	10,000
Cons. Stock 4%	5,196	5,196	5,196	5,196
Local Loans 3%	56,419	56,419	56,419	56,419
Conv. Loan 1948–53 3%		10,000	10,000	10,000
Bank of England Stock		10,000	3,000	3,000
Conv. Loan 1944–64 5%	41,708			
Cons. 2.50%	18,201	18,201	18,201	18,201
Conv. Loan 3.5%	30,722	30,722	30,722	30,822
Subtotal	168,212	146,504	146,980	147,080
Subtotal as percentage	48.77	45.93	44.30	39.56
Secs. guaranteed under Trade Facilities Acts				
London Electric Rly. 4.5% red. 2nd Deb. 1942–72	3,050	3,050	3,050	
London Passenger Transport Bd. TFA 1942–72 4.5%				3,050
Subtotal	3,050	3,050	3,050	3,050
Subtotal as percentage	0.88	0.95	0.91	0.82
Corporation and county stocks: GB and NI				
West Riding Yorks stk. 1960–79 3.5%		5,000	5,000	5,000
Manchester Corpn. 1891 red. stk. 3%		5,000	5,700	5,700
Hertfordshire Co. 1948–53 3%			5,000	5,000
Corpn. London Deb. 1940–85 4.55	2,000	2,000	2,000	2,000
Subtotal	2,000	12,000	17,700	17,700
Subtotal as percentage	0.57	3.76	5.33	4.76

TABLE 7.7. cont.

	3 April	8 May	2 June	1 December
Public boards				
Port London Inscribed 1940–60 4%	2,653	2,653	2,653	2,653
Central Electricity stk. 1963–93 3.5%				10,000
Dover Harbour Bd. deb. stk. reg. 1974 3·75%				5,000
Subtotal	2,653	2,653	2,653	17,653
Subtotal as percentage	0.76	0.83	0.79	4.474
Dominion, provincial and colonial govt. secs.				
U. of S. Africa Insc. 1945–75 5%	7,547	4,134	4,134	4,134
S. Nigeria Insc. 1930–50 3.5%	4,134	2,200	2,200	2,200
Canada 1940–60 4%	2,2200	1,046	1,046	
W. Australia Insc. 1935–55 3.5%	1,046	1,000	1,000	1,000
Victoria Cons. Insc. 1929–49 3%	1,000			
NSW Insc. 1945–65 5%	2,324		10,000	10,000
U. of S. Africa Insc. 1953–73 3.5%	2,300	2,300	2,300	2,300
NZ Insc. 1935–45 5%	2,100	2,100	2,100	
Straits Stnts Insc. 1937–67 3.5%	4,586			
Australia Reg. 1945–75 5%				
Subtotal	27,237	12,780	22,780	19,634
Subtotal as percentage	7.89	4.0	6.86	5.28
Foreign stocks, bonds, etc.				
Dutch E. Indies Loan 1933–62 5%	4,800			
China Reorg. Gold Loan 1913–60 5%				5,000
Egyptian Unified Debt Bnds. 4%	200	200		4,000
Japan Sterling Loan 1907 5%			2,000	5,000
Subtotal	5,000	200	2,000	14,000
Subtotal as percentage	1.44	0.06	0.6	3.76

TABLE 7.7. *cont.*

	3 April	8 May	2 June	1 December
Railways—British, Indian, foreign				
LNER deb. 3%	4,165	4,165	4,165	4,165
LMS deb. 4%	12,525	12,525	12,525	12,525
Fishguard & Rosslare gd. pref. 3.5%	1,400	1,400	1,400	1,400
LMS gd. 4%	273	273	1,000	1,000
GWR cons. pref. 5%	2,305	2,305	2,305	2,305
LNER 1st pref. 4%	6,000	6,000	6,000	6,000
Southern Rly. red. pref. 1964 5%	8,560	8,560	8,560	8,560
LMS pref. 4%	4,872	4,872	4,872	4,872
Assam–Bengal Rly. debs. 1934 5%	35,000	35,000	35,000	35,000
Bengal–Nagpur Rly. debs. 1937 3%	10,000	10,000	10,000	10,000
Madras & S. Mahratta Rly. deb. 1938 4%	1,964	1,964	1,964	1,964
Bengal–Nagpur Rly. debs. 1933 6%	15,000	15,000		
Buenos Ayres WR ord. stk.	1,000	1,000	1,000	1,000
Buenos Ayres GSR deb. stk. 4%	2,750	2,750	2,750	2,750
Buenos Ayres GSR ord. stk.	1,278	1,278	1,278	1,278
Subtotal	107,092	107,092	92,819	92,819
Subtotal as percentage	31.05	33.58	27.98	24.96
Commercial, industrial, electric power and light				
Trust Houses cum. pref. 6%			2,000	2,000
Shell T. & T. cum. 1st pref. £10 shs. 5%				3,000
Lever Bros. cum. pref. stk. 7%			1,000	1,000
Edmundsons Elec. Corpn. ord.			3,000	3,000
N. Eastern Elec. Supply cons. deb. 1964 3.5%				12,000
Edmundsons E. Corpn. deb. stk. 1950–80 4%		5,000	5,000	5,000
N. Eastern Elec. Supply cons. 1st mort. deb. stk. red. 4.5%	2,000	2,000	2,000	
Gas Light & Coke cons. deb. stk. irred. 3%	375	375	2,000	2,000
Subtotal	2,375	7,375	15,000	28,000
Subtotal as percentage	0.68	2.31	4.52	7.53

TABLE 7.7. *cont.*

	3 April	8 May	2 June	1 December
Investment Trusts				
Brit. Steamship Inv. Trust def. stk.	1,800	1,800	1,800	1,800
Merchants Trust perpetual deb. stk. 4%	250	250	1,750	1,750
Subtotal	2,050	2,050	3,550	3,550
Subtotal as percentage	0.59	0.64	1.07	0.95
Shipping and telegraphs and telephones				
Cunard mort. debt. stk. red. 1941–61 5%	1,000	1,000	1,000	1,000
Eastern Telegraph Co. mort. deb. stk. 4%				3,000
Subtotal	1,000	1,000	1,000	4,000
Subtotal as percentage	0.28	0.31	0.3	1.07
Unquoted on Stock Exchange lists				
Co-Partnership Tenants loan stk. 5%	2,000	2,000	2,000	2,000
Church Training Colleges cap. fund debs. 4.5%	22,200	22,200	22,200	22,300
Subtotal	24,200	24,200	24,200	24,300
Subtotal as percentage	7.01	7.58	7.29	6.53
TOTALS	344,869	318,904	331,732	371,786
All Investments	360,981	340,026	348,387	387,582

Sources: CBF lists of investments in CHA, CBF/FIN/INV/3/3.

KEY:

bnds.	bonds	irr.	irredeemable
cap.	capital	mort.	mortgage
cons.	consolidated	ord.	ordinary
conv.	conversion	pref.	preference
cum.	cumulative	red.	redeemable
deb.	debenture	reg.	registered
def.	deferred	secs.	securities
gd.	guaranteed	shs.	shares
insc.	inscribed	stk.	stock

bury, William Temple, unexpectedly died at the age of 63. With him went the hopes of fulfilling what Correlli Barnett has scornfully called the dream of the New Jerusalem, but which Temple himself saw as the great challenge of relating Christian first principles to the tangle of particular problems.[123] In place of Temple came Geoffrey Fisher, Bishop of London, who had made his name as a 'brilliant administrator and an indefatigable worker'.[124] While Temple had been intent upon Christianizing society, Fisher determined to carry out administrative and financial reforms within the church. Most immediately he dealt with the problems of war damage and of meeting the needs posed by post-war housing estates. However, in 1947 he launched the Convocations, and with them the Church Assembly, into a massive reform of the church's legal code, such as it had not seen since the seventeenth century. The object was to update the laws and law courts governing the clergy and so restore 'essential habits of good order and good conscience within the Church'.[125] The result was very different. One set of cumbersome machinery was exchanged for another. Worse, for two decades the church was distracted from her primary task of presenting the Christian faith to a world increasingly unbelieving, materialistic, and needy. What part were laymen and women, particularly those in business, able to play in this situation?

First, though, who were the church's lay leaders in the 1950s? What and where were their business interests? An analysis of the House of Laity in the Church Assembly in 1955 pinpoints the composition of the church's leading laity. The proportion of women had marginally increased over the previous twenty years, up from 19 to 24 per cent; their age structure had not much changed, however (see Table 7.2). They tended to be in their fifties or over. Social and political connections had weakened since 1935, peers and peeresses having fallen from 4.6 to 3 per cent of the House of Laity and MPs from 5.1 to 2.7 per cent; knights and baronets showed a modest rise, from 7.6 to 8.2 per cent (see Table 7.3). On the other hand, educational backgrounds showed a marked gain for the public schools which supplied nearly 51 per cent of the laymen, up from 46 per cent in 1935, while the share of known grammar school boys declined from nearly 7 to just over 4 per cent. Shares of Oxbridge graduates marginally fell from their 1935 levels;

[123] C. Barnett, *The Audit of War* (London, 1986), 12–17; W. Temple, 'Introduction', *Malvern, 1941* (London, 1941), p. vii; W. Temple, *Christianity and Social Order* (repr. London, 1976), 42–5.
[124] P. A. Welsby, *A History of the Church of England, 1945–1980* (Oxford, 1984), 9.
[125] Ibid. 41.

among the women the proportion of Oxbridge graduates more than doubled between 1935 and 1955, doubtless reflecting the widened university opportunities for women at the turn of the century and thereafter (see Table 7.4).

Professional people still dominated among those in the House of Laity who cared to record their occupations in the *Official-Year Book of the Church of England* in 1954–5. However, the legal profession, which preponderated in 1935, had been overtaken by teachers and academics of whom there were 28 (including 6 women), as compared to 20 legal men. Behind the educators came 24 men who still used their military or naval ranks, which may have been wartime relics rather than indicators of active status. Then there were 12 Civil Servants and local government officials, 3 architects or surveyors, 2 medical men, a journalist, a farmer, and one or two others. At least 60 of the 280 men in the House of Laity belonged to the professional group which contained some very distinguished men and women indeed. Among them was Sir Richard Hopkins, Second Secretary at the Treasury in the 1930s and Permanent Secretary and head of the Civil Service 1942–5, a qualified supporter of J. M. Keynes's economic policies; on retirement from the Treasury he offered his services to Archbishop Fisher, joined the CBF, and became its chairman in 1947.[126] Other members were Sir Walter Moberly, chairman of the University Grants Committee; Sir (Arthur) Wilfred Garrett, former Chief Inspector of Factories; the Oxford historians E. F. Jacob and Cecilia Ady; and the poet John Betjeman.

The business links of the 47 members of the House of Laity who were company directors, identified primarily from the *Directory of Directors, 1955*, are summarized in Table 7.1. The proportion of men who held directorships (still no women) showed a continued decline at 17 per cent in 1955 compared to 20 per cent in 1935 and 28 per cent in 1907. Likewise the average number of directorships held by each individual director slipped from its 1935 peak. On these bases capitalism was distancing or being distanced from the state church in the twentieth century. On the other hand there is evidence that the share of manufacturing directorships was rising over the long term, moving from 14 to 18 to 28 per cent between 1907 and 1955; against this, the absolute figures rose and then fell from 34 to 37 to 33 between 1907 and 1955.

By the criterion of holding five directorships, how concentrated were business connections? Less so than in 1935 but twice as concentrated

[126] *Kelly's Handbook to the Titled, Landed and Official Classes*, 1955; *The Times*, 21 Apr., 2 May 1955; G. C. Peden, 'Sir Richard Hopkins and the "Keynesian Revolution" in Employment Policy, 1929–45', *Economic History Review*, 2nd ser. 36 (1983).

as in 1907 seems to be the answer, with eight of the 47 (17 per cent) listed in the *Directory of Directors* having five or more board seats. As in 1935 they mostly displayed strong regional interests. Now there were professional men with strong backgrounds in accounting and finance. In the North-East Sir Robert Chapman (5 directorships), a chartered accountant and former Mayor of South Shields and MP for the Houghton-le-Spring division of Durham,[127] was director of George Angus & Co., the belting manufacturers, of North Eastern Investment Trust, and the North Eastern Trading Estate among other companies. Colonel Robert Mould-Graham (7), chartered accountant of Newcastle-upon-Tyne, and Lord Mayor of the city in 1954–5,[128] recorded a spread of interests across manufacturing and finance. Moving south, Folliott Sandford Henry Ward (10), a Malton solicitor and member of the North Riding County Council, had Yorkshire interests: in Leeds hotels, an insurance company, and several companies relating to pig breeding and bacon processing factories. Another Yorkshireman, Norman Baxter (5), had business interests centred on Bradford, including Greengates Worsted Co. and Sunnybank Investments. In Lancashire Harry Makin, former Mayor of Radcliffe, Manchester (if the identification is correct) had five directorships, most in North-Western brewery and property companies. Arthur Fitzgerald Rountree (6), an accountant of Oldham, had seats on the boards of various Lancashire mill and property companies and on the Liverpool & London & Globe Insurance Co. Finally, in London, Sir Richard Hopkins (9) was director of companies mostly in the distribution and finance industries, including Continental Express, Equity & Law Life Assurance, Pickfords & Hay's Wharf Shipping & Forwarding Co., and the Proprietors of Hay's Wharf. The 3rd Earl of Selborne (Roundell Cecil Palmer), long-serving member of the Church Assembly, was the eighth with five company directorships.

These members of the House of Laity may have had clusters of business interests, but were they big business interests? A check against the companies identified as the 100 largest employers in 1955 reveals that the gap separating leading church laity from the boards of largest companies, while never close, was widening. From 16 seats on the boards of the 100 largest employers in 1907 and 10 in 1935, the figure fell to 6 in 1955. Proportionately these were tiny fractions: falling from 1.59 in 1907 to 0.86 in 1935 and 0.48 per cent in 1955.[129] Three leading church laymen

---

[127] *WW 1958*.

[128] Ibid.

[129] Calculation based on the memberships of 91 of the 96 boards of largest companies in 1955.

in 1955 were on the boards of the big clearing banks: Richard Quintin Gurney, with Barclays; Selborne, with National Provincial (as deputy chairman); and Sir Philip F. C. Williams, with Lloyds. The 2nd Viscount Caldecote was on the board of English Electric. Sir Richard Hopkins was a director of the Port of London Authority. Selborne was also deputy chairman of Boots Pure Drug Co.

Which business people, then, were dominant in the affairs of the Church Assembly in the mid-1950s? The answer to this depends on the definition of key committees in the House of Laity. Presumably the Standing Committee, as the central approximation to a policy-forming caucus, was one. From an economic point of view the Central Board of Finance was the most important. Both seem to have used the available business talent in placing people with the appropriate experience and skills on these committees. Half the six lay members on the Standing Committee were company directors; so were a quarter of the sixteen lay members of the CBF. These proportions were much higher than the 13 per cent of the House of Laity (men and women) who held company directorships.

The most experienced businessmen on the two committees were George Goyder, on the Standing Committee (Sir Kenneth Grubb and Sir Robert E. Martin, though company directors, were not primarily businessmen); and on the CBF Sir Eric Gore-Browne, Sir Richard Hopkins, and Humphrey Mynors (later Sir Humphrey); William Louis Lawton, also on the CBF, was not in their league. Goyder, Mynors, and Hopkins have been encountered already. Gore-Browne, between the wars managing partner of Glyn, Mills & Co, private bankers, served as the last chairman of the Southern Railway, 1944–7. Afterwards he returned to the City, to Glyn, Mills and to Alexander's Discount Co. of which he became chairman. A friendly and approachable man, his connections with the City's financial institutions stood as high as Sir Richard Hopkins's with Whitehall. They also stood high socially: in the 1940s he was ADC to King George VI. Not surprisingly, when Hopkins died in 1955 Gore-Browne succeeded him as chairman of the CBF.[130]

What parts did these men play in the 1950s in the affairs of the Church Assembly? On the Standing Committee and in the Church Assembly George Goyder spent a great deal of time and effort, too much he recalls, discussing canon law measures. 'A pronounced Evangelical, but not a party man', who spent much of his spare time reading the sixteenth-century Reformers (as well as William Blake), 'his long and constant

---

[130] *Southern Railway Magazine*, 22 (Mar.–Apr. 1944), 25; *The Times*, 4 June 1964.

work in recent years on canon law revision has been marked by thoroughness of study, breadth of approach, and keenness of discernment'.[131] Though an economist (LSE) by training and a business manager by profession, he was one of the few laymen in the Assembly sufficiently informed to be able to argue with the clergy on theological issues, like the role of law in religion.[132] Of the nineteen major speeches he made in the Church Assembly between 1949 and 1960, nine related to church government and canon law, only three to industrial matters.[133] Sir Kenneth Grubb massively understated the irrelevance of the years of debate on canon law when he recalled it as a 'somewhat tedious subject' which 'occupied many separate sessions of the House of Laity'.[134] Indeed topics under this head were just the subjects to deter busy men of affairs from spending their spare hours in the debating chamber at Church House, as Gordon Bridge, director of Reckitt & Colman and a member of the House of Laity in the 1950s, recalled.[135]

Not all the men of business in the Church Assembly were sidetracked by Archbishop Fisher's canon law revision. Sir Richard Hopkins's abilities in analysing the national income and expenditure of the UK economy were harnessed to the church's 'national income' analysis, to its revenues and their growth. His first problem arose in 1946. Apportionment, the system by which diocesan contributions to the Church Assembly Fund were levied, established in 1921 by Canon Partridge (presumably Kindersley had something to do with it), had become seriously outdated by population movements and war damage. Since over 98 per cent of the work of the Church Assembly was financed through the dioceses the need to find a fair system was pressing.[136] Hopkins and his small subcommittee (who started in April 1946 and reported in December 1947) came up with a solution which abandoned the old criterion of diocesan population size but preserved the criteria of numbers of Easter communicants and of per caput sums actually raised by the dioceses. To lower, but not remove, the objections of dioceses penalized by the new proposals (like London), Hopkins suggested a phased introduction starting in 1950 and reaching complete implementation in 1954. Among

---

[131] *Church Times*, 9 May 1958.

[132] Author's interview with George Goyder at the Reform Club, 9 Oct. 1986.

[133] 'Major Speeches in the National Assembly of the Church of England 1949–1970 and in the National Synod of the Church of England 1970–1975 by George Goyder' (typescript list kindly provided by Mr Goyder).

[134] Sir K. Grubb, *Crypts of Power* (London, 1971), 213.

[135] Author's interview with Gordon Bridge at LSE, 20 Nov. 1986.

[136] C. of E., *YB 1954–5*, 251.

diocesan boards of finance 26 approved Hopkins's scheme, ten had reservations, only one (London) objected. In the event the scheme was carried.[137]

All that related to the revenues of the CBF. Much larger questions pertained to the total finances of the Church of England. First, while the revenues of the church were accurately known in the early 1950s, there was no reliable estimate of demands made on those resources. In 1951, at the invitation of Archbishop Fisher, Sir Richard Hopkins began to prepare a budget statement for the church as a whole. He circulated secretaries of diocesan boards of finance.[138] By May the task still demanded more time.[139] Two months later he had a draft statement ready to send out to knowledgeable critics.[140] In it he observed that 'The Church, sometimes thought to be rich, is poor. It does not need to be other. But it is not immune from the need common to all organisations, secular or otherwise, to have the minimum resources required for the fulfilment of its function.' The revenues of the church had been identified in a Church Information Board pamphlet, *The Work and Revenues of the Church of England* (1951). This showed that half the income of the Church in 1948 came from endowments, half from voluntary contributions. While well-managed endowments might increase their yield, Hopkins foresaw severe limitations to income growth from this source. New money must largely come from voluntary contributions. He judged that the church with its restricted manpower and its reorganization schemes would be able to manage with its 1939 income of £16 million plus £8 or £9 million to account for inflation, a total of £24–5 million in 1952.[141] Of the inflationary increase £1 million was covered by growth in endowment income and £3 million by a rise in voluntary parochial contributions. The conclusions sounded painfully familiar: 'parochial contributions ought with the least possible delay to be increased by fully £5 million'; the 40 per cent increase might be staged but quotas should be reached as quickly as possible and prospering parishes should hand their surpluses over to a diocesan fund for redistribution to parishes with 'a proved uncovered need'.[142] On the mechanics

[137] C. of E., Church Assembly, *Report of the Central Board of Finance on Apportionment*, CAF 210 (1948); C. of E., Church Assembly, *Report of Proceedings*, 28 (1948), 92–108.

[138] CHA, CBF Box 596, draft of Sir Richard Hopkins's proposed statement, circular letter to DBF secretaries, 29 Jan. 1952.

[139] Ibid., copy of Hopkins to the Archbishop of Canterbury, 8 May 1952.

[140] Ibid., circular letter, 31 July 1952.

[141] Ibid., draft statement in circular letter form, 31 July 1952, 2.

[142] Ibid. 3.

of fund-raising, Hopkins recommended that a single individual should ensure the parish reached its target; that churchgoers be constantly educated about the needs of the whole Church; that the personal approach be maximized; and that the effort be channelled through the ruridecanal chapters and conferences throughout the land, 'for this is a labour of love to be assumed around the whole periphery.'[143]

Businessmen's financial talent and experience was also used, as in the 1920s and 1930s, on the CBF's investment subcommittee. Not that the CBF had huge sums to invest. In 1951 its General Purposes Fund had investments with a book value of £557,376. To evaluate their portfolio the subcommittee turned to Newson-Smith & Co., the stockbroking firm of one of its members, Charles A. Chase. They advised the CBF, as a hedge against inflation, to increase its relatively low holdings of equities 'without delay' from the existing 10 per cent of total holdings to around 25 per cent.[144] The report went to Sir Richard Hopkins, Sir Philip Williams, and Humphrey Mynors. Mynors cautiously approved the report, observing that equities were also 'quite an effective method of seeing that a deflation (if and when it comes) is also reflected in our figures'. He warned against distributing equity income up to the hilt and urged the building up of an income equalization account of a few thousand pounds. On Newson-Smith's specific recommendations for equity purchases, he commented on the high cost of insurance shares, questioned whether retailers like Boots and Woolworths might not feel the pressure of the the cost of living 'during the next few years', and confessed to 'an irrational prejudice in favour of Babcock and BET and against tobacco'.[145] Mynors had no way of knowing that Britain and other advanced capitalist economies stood at the beginning of two decades of unparalleled growth, though in 1959 on the British Stock Market yields on gilts began to exceed yields on equities (reverse yield). Mynors's investment advice under the letterhead of the Bank of England exemplified the role of leading businessmen in the highest counsels of the Church of England. So did the attempt by Hopkins to develop a system for managing church finances mildly reminiscent of national income accounting. These were not the only areas in which Sir Richard Hopkins served the central financial organs of the church. He was, for example, also responsible for providing pensions advice, since the CBF

---

[143] Ibid. 4.

[144] Ibid. Box 565, Investments Subcommittee file, Newson-Smith & Co. to CBF, 8 June 1951, enclosed with C. Sawden to Sir Richard Hopkins, 14 June 1951.

[145] Ibid., Investments Subcommittee file, H. C. B. Mynors to C. Sawden, 15 June 1951.

was responsible for lay pensions which entailed matters ranging from investment to income tax.

Beyond the central organs of the Church of England, like the Church Assembly or the Church Commissioners, there was a host of voluntary bodies attached by varying degrees of formality to the church. They ranged from missionary societies, schools, and colleges to prayer cells and religious orders.[146] Most if not all depended on outside support, some of it from the business community. Space permits only the brief consideration of one example of these voluntary bodies and the nature of the relationship between them and business.

The case of *The Guardian* newspaper is doubly interesting.[147] Its proprietor, Owen Hugh Smith (1869–1958), a substantial City figure descended from Smiths the bankers (his brother Vivian Hugh Smith went into Morgan Grenfell the merchant bankers and was raised to the peerage as Lord Bicester[148]), was a close friend of Sir Richard Hopkins (who joined Smith on the board of Hay's Wharf on retiring from the Civil Service). Smith's experience with *The Guardian* illustrates how a church interest had to bow to the pressures of markets and, indirectly, of government.

Founded in 1846 as the mouthpiece of the High Church Tractarians, the weekly *Guardian* was ailing by the 1920s when Owen Hugh Smith took it over on behalf of the Life and Liberty Movement, the middle church reformers headed by William Temple. It was not a success. By the late 1930s Smith's editors (his first was Frederick Iremonger later Dean of Lichfield) had lost 14,000 readers and Smith was having to make good its losses to the tune of £3,000 to £4,000 a year. A transfer of ownership from the newspaper company to Smith personally in 1940 cut his losses and wartime pressures persuaded him to maintain his ownership. However, the readership, mainly laity and clergy with intellectual and theological tastes, continued to dwindle. Two post-war changes forced his hand. First, he was in his seventies with a young family and therefore had to make financial provision for his children which must not be threatened by loss-making investments. Second, the election of a Labour Government in 1945 led to large tax increases, both on personal income and on company profits over the next few

---

[146] See listings in the C. of E., *YB*.

[147] This section is based on the author's unpublished paper 'Laymen in the Interstices of the Church: The Case of *The Guardian*' which, by kind permission of Mrs Faith Raven, daughter of Owen Hugh Smith, is largely drawn from Smith's correspondence files relating to *The Guardian*.

[148] Kathleen Burk, 'Vivian Hugh Smith', *DBB*.

years.[149] Eventually Smith heeded his accountant rather than his editor and in 1950 decided to sell *The Guardian*.

No takers were forthcoming. Despite the best efforts of Smith, Sir Richard Hopkins, the newspaper's trustees who included Sir Walter Moberley, a string of bishops (including Hunter at Sheffield), and both archbishops (Fisher and Garbett), despite testing the market from the wealthy Colonel John J. Astor, a firm churchman and owner of *The Times*, to Sir William Goodenough, chairman of Barclays Bank, to Hunter's steel magnates like Sir Walter Benton Jones, another 'very good Churchman', no one could be found who would preserve *The Guardian* as an independent middle church newspaper. Smith eventually closed it in 1951. Its title lapsed thereby allowing the northern daily to contract its name from the *Manchester Guardian*.

Owen Hugh Smith's experience may not have been unique for a capitalist entering the uncertain waters of church-orientated markets. It boiled down to divergent religious and commercial goals and to a stealthy change in the balance between them. Smith bought the paper when it was holding its own. As it ran into chronic losses its church status and clerical customers delayed its closure. The investment became an act of charity. Eventually family circumstances and rising taxation meant that the proprietor could no longer afford to be charitable. Not surprisingly, a good number of capitalists, despite their Christian commitment, perceived the situation exactly as Owen Hugh Smith did.

The large subject of twentieth-century church finances deserves a study of its own. The examples traced in this chapter sufficiently demonstrate that in the CBF the church, both in Canon Partridge's day and in the 1940s and 1950s, brought to bear on its national economic problems the knowledge and judgement of some of the most able financial minds in the City. Just because they were powerful men in the City was, however, no guarantee that they would always be able to persuade the City to support the church, or that they themselves would have the personal resources to fund indefinitely every church-related cause.

[149] J. C. R. Dow, *The Management of the British Economy, 1945–1960* (Cambridge, 1970), 200.

8

Businessmen and Women in Methodism,
1900–1960

I THE HEYDAY OF WESLEYAN
BUSINESSMEN BEFORE 1914

In contrast to other Nonconformist denominations, the Methodist connections were highly centralized. The Wesleyans, largest of the Methodist
sects, typified Methodist structures. Their national ruling body was an
annual Conference of clerical and lay representatives, elected upwards
from chapel to circuit to district synod to Conference. Its committees
submitted proposals to Conference and, with the ministerial departmental secretaries (servicing Home Missions, Foreign Missions, and other
denominational departments), monitored the implementation of Conference decisions by synods, circuits, and local chapels. Clerical presidents and vice-presidents (occasionally laymen) of Conference, annually
elected, acted as the figureheads and spokesmen of the connections.
As the largest of the Nonconformist bodies the Wesleyans deserve close
attention. Who were the laymen who dominated their national Conference committees? What roles did the businessmen among them assume?

(a) Leading lay people in Wesleyan Methodism

Altogether the 1,671 national committee positions open to Wesleyan
laymen in 1907 were held by 875 individuals. Of these, 569 people held
one post each while, at the other extreme, one man occupied 15 positions,
as Table 8.1 shows. Which of these 875 laymen were at the core of
denominational lay leadership in 1907? Clearly the 569 holding one committee post each were not. On the other hand a large group of individuals

TABLE 8.1. *Numbers of people holding national lay committee posts in Wesleyan Methodism, 1907*

No. of posts	No. of people holding posts	Total no. of posts held by each category
1	569	569
2	140	280
3	61	183
4	29	116
5	30	150
6	9	54
7	19	133
8	5	40
9	5	45
10	1	10
11		
12	3	36
13	2	26
14	1	14
15	1	15
TOTAL	875	1,671

Notes: 76 people held 5 or more offices; 523 offices were held by such people altogether.

was needed to manage the affairs of over 70 national church committees. Crucial lay offices were the connectional treasurer and the treasurers of a dozen denominational funds, regularly re-elected by Conference. Since the least burdened of these treasurers sat on five committees, this level of committee involvement was selected as the criterion for identifying the core of Wesleyan lay leadership. Anyone with as many committee posts as a denominational treasurer would presumably have as many meetings, and almost as many opportunities for contributing to the decision-making process in the denomination.

In 1907 76 Wesleyan laymen (no women at this date) held five or more denominational committee posts. Between them they sat on all but five of the 72 denominational committees. Although they comprised only 8.7 per cent of the 875 leading Wesleyan lay people (a number were women) in the land, these 76 men held 31 per cent of available committee posts. These laymen shouldered the secular burdens of the denomination and held the centre of lay power in the connection. Who were they? How many were in business? What contributions did they make to Wesleyan Methodism at the beginning of the century?

The age structure of the group suggests that most were well seasoned yet still vigorous, being in the middle or at the height of their careers. They ranged between the ages of 34 and 79, averaging in the mid-fifties.

Only 4 per cent of these Wesleyans were 70 or over. At the other end of the range, 22 per cent were 50 and under. A handful appear to have been retired.

Evidence on social origins is too scanty for any firm conclusions to be drawn about their backgrounds. For 34 of them their father's occupation is known—24 being sons of men in business, 3 sons of professionals, and 7 sons of Wesleyan ministers. Two of the 76, Robert Perks and Sir Clarence Smith, were proud to be sons of previous presidents of the Wesleyan Conference. The 76 seem to have been a relatively well-educated group, though again the data are imperfect with information on only 53 of them. At least 15 of the 53 went to one or other of four Methodist schools (Kingswood, Bath; Wesley College, Sheffield; Woodhouse Grove, Bradford; The Leys School, Cambridge); six attended Wesleyan elementary schools; the rest attended a mixture of grammar schools, private schools, and forms of private education.

Interest centres on the occupations of these Wesleyan 'workhorses'. Several striking features emerge from a comparison between their occupational patterns and those of the occupied male workforce in the whole country, in Table 8.2. Four sectors preponderated among the Wesleyans: several manufacturing industries, distribution, finance, and the professions. At an industry level Wesleyan lay leaders heavily over-represented chemicals-petroleum, textiles, and shipping. They under-represented clothing, utilities, and road transport. Those in business owned their own enterprises. Few indeed were the managers. Twelve of the 17 professional men had, by virtue of their profession a high chance of engaging with the business world: legal men, consulting engineers and architects, a surveyor and a national journal editor. The biographical and autobiographical impressions they gave to denominational publications bring their features into focus.

The single farmer was Walter Wheeler Berry, a breezy Faversham fruit and hop grower (evidently not a strict teetotaller). He owned sufficient acres in one of the choicest parts of Kent to cultivate 10,000 cherry trees and enough hops to occupy 2,000 to 3,000 pickers for a month every season.[1] In mining Ezra Tompkins Wilks was a representative and director of Wingfield Manor Colliery Co. Ltd.;[2] John Wilcox Edge, a retired North Staffordshire potter (Edge, Malkin & Co.), sat on the boards of several North Staffordshire companies including the Sneyd Collieries Co. of which he was chairman.[3]

[1] *Wes. Mag.* (1914), 587–8.   [2] *WWM 1910.*
[3] Ibid. *1910*; *M. Rec.* 2 Aug 1900; *Wes. Mag.* (1907) 31–5.

TABLE 8.2. *Sector shares in the occupational backgrounds of 76 Wesleyan lay leaders, 1907*

Sector and industry	No.	%	Distribution of male workforce, 1911 (000)	%
Agriculture	1	1.32	1,489	11.52
Mining	2	2.63	1,202	9.30
Manufacturing				
Food	1	1.32	806	6.23
Petroleum	1	1.32		
Chemicals	4	5.26	155	1.20
Metals	4	5.26		
Engineering	1	1.32	1,795	13.88
Textiles	11	14.47	639	4.94
Leather	3	3.95	90	0.70
Glass	1	1.32	145	1.12
Timber	1	1.32	287	2.22
Paper	1	1.32	253	1.96
Other	1	1.32		
Construction	2	2.63	1,140	8.82
Transport				
Shipping	3	3.95	202	1.56
Railways	2	2.63	370	2.86
Distribution				
Wholesale	4	5.26		
Retail	4	5.26		
Finance	6	7.89	739	5.72
Professions				
Group 1[a]	12	15.79		
Group 2[b]	5	6.58	413	3.19
Public administration	2	2.63	271	2.10
Trade unions	1	1.32		
Unknown	3	3.95		
TOTAL	76	100.00	12,930	100.00

Note: The 12.93 million = occupied males in GB in 1911. In the table the following categories are omitted: armed forces, domestic offices, roads, clothing, utilities.

[a] Group 1 = solicitors, barristers, engineers, surveyors, architects, editors.
[b] Group 2 = educators, medical people.

Sources: author's data; B. R. Mitchell and P. Deane, *Abstract of British Historical Statistics* (Cambridge, 1962), 60.

In manufacturing Joseph Rank the flour miller was enjoying rapid business expansion following his early adoption of roller milling in the 1880s; in 1904 he had made the critical move to the metropolis, from Hull.[4] Thomas Barclay ran the manufacturing chemists Southall Bros.

---

[4] R. G. Burnett, *Through the Mill* (London, 1945); Jonathan Brown, 'Joseph Rank', *DBB*.

& Barclay of Birmingham;[5] James Calvert Coats was a London varnish manufacturer;[6] Thomas Robinson Ferens MP was managing director of Reckitt & Sons Ltd., starch manufacturers of Hull;[7] and Sir George Smith headed Bickford, Smith & Co, patent fuse manufacturers of Truro.[8] Moving ahead in the new petroleum industry was Charles Cheers Wakefield, lubricating oil manufacturer. His high arcing career took him from Liverpool to London and thence on a swift upward trajectory through the livery companies, Masonic lodges, and a multitude of philanthropies in the City. Eventually he would sit alongside a fellow Methodist, Walter Runciman (President of the Board of Trade in the 1930s), in the ermine and scarlet robes of a viscount of the realm.[9]

The Bissekers (cousins ?) were in metals and engineering: Henry who had spent sixteen years in South Africa before returning to Birmingham and purchasing a business manufacturing gas fittings;[10] and Tilden John Bisseker, who managed the Hall Street Metal Rolling Co. for over thirty years.[11] John Israel Parkes was a third Birmingham ferrous metal manufacturer.[12] William Henry Smith was an ironfounder at Whitchurch, Shropshire.[13] Sir George Chubb, safe and lock manufacturer, ran the nationally famous family business which pivoted between Wolverhampton and London.[14]

The relatively large group from the textile industry included self-made Alfred Brookes, director and secretary of Tootal, Broadhurst & Co. He was one of the two leading Wesleyans to sit on the boards of the 100 largest manufacturers in the UK in 1907.[15] Edward Aston was partner in Marshall & Aston, a major textile merchant house in Manchester.[16] John Robert Barlow BA headed Barlow & Jones Ltd., expanding cotton spinners of Bolton and Manchester.[17] At Rochdale Charles Heap was manging director of Samuel Heap & Sons Ltd., dyers and finishers. He had left the Wesleyan ministry and returned to the family firm on

[5] *M. Rec.* 26 July 1894; *Wes. Mag.* (1907), 535–7.
[6] *M. Rec.* 18 July 1907; *Kelly's Post Office Directory of London* (1902), ii. 2513.
[7] Mona S. Black, 'Thomas Robinson Ferens', *DBB*.
[8] *WWM 1910*; *Wes. Mag.* (1906), 725–8.
[9] *Wes. Mag.* (1916) 93–8; *WWW*.
[10] *M. Rec.* 26 July 1894.
[11] Ibid. 21 July 1892.
[12] Ibid. 26 July 1894.
[13] *WWM 1910*.
[14] *M. Rec.* 5 Aug. 1897; *Wes. Mag.* (1906), 250–2.
[15] *M. Rec.* 24 July 1902. The other was Thomas H. Bainbridge.
[16] Ibid.
[17] *WWM 1910*.

the early death of his father.[18] The other cotton manufacturers were George Crossfield of Prestwich near Manchester[19] and William Horrocks Rawson, of Wigan.[20] John Broxap was a Manchester yarn agent.[21] From the other side of the Pennines and the woollen industry came William Butterworth, woollen manufacturer (retired by 1910),[22] and Harry Dawson, wool broker,[23] both from Huddersfield. Moses Atkinson, in retirement at Harrogate, had been a Leeds linen manufacturer.[24] Charles William Early, from the much declined West of England woollen industry, was senior partner in a thriving family firm of Witney blanket makers.[25]

Three of these Wesleyan workhorses had tannery businesses: William Howell Davies MP of Bristol;[26] William Edward Walker of Bolton;[27] and Robert Harold Posnett of Runcorn and Warrington.[28] George William Kilner, partner in a glass bottle making firm, headed the London side of another family business.[29] In the timber trade Wesley North had worked up to become principal partner in a Leeds firm.[30] George Munt ran his own cardboard box making firm in London.[31] Norval Watson Helme, MP and prominent Freemason, headed a sizeable oil cloth (linoleum) manufacturing firm at Lancaster.[32]

Outside manufacturing there were two large-scale builders and contractors. Thomas Barnsley ran John Barnsley & Son of Birmingham, contractors for the Corporation Buildings, the Council House, and the Union Club in the city.[33] Henry Holloway's firm was another thriving

---

[18] Ibid.; W. T. Pike and W. B. Tracy, *Lancashire at the Opening of the Twentieth Century* (Brighton, 1903), 359; *M. Rec.* 9 Aug. 1923.

[19] *M. Rec.* 7 Aug. 1902.

[20] *WWM 1933.*

[21] *WWM 1910.*

[22] Ibid.

[23] *WWM 1933.*

[24] *M. Rec.* 22 July 1897.

[25] A. Plummer and R. E. Early, *The Blanket Makers 1669-1969* (London, 1969), 111–20; *WWM 1910.*

[26] *WWMP.*

[27] *M. Rec.* 2 May 1907.

[28] *WWM 1910.*

[29] *M. Rec.* 21 July 1892.

[30] Ibid. 22 July 1897, 28 Feb. 1907.

[31] *Kelly's PODL* (1902) i. 1426.

[32] E. Gaskell, *Lancashire Leaders* (London, c. 1900); Pike and Tracy, *Lancashire*, 126; *Wes. Mag.* (1907), 892–4; *Representative British Freemasons* (London, 1915), 289; *M. Rec.* 10 Mar. 1932.

[33] *M. Rec.* 26 July 1894.

business. Starting in 1882 he and his brother Thomas had expanded their small house-building firm into a leading London contractor. Their first big job, the Chatham Naval Barracks (worth £340,000), was completed in 1903; in 1907 they won the contract for the new General Post Office in St Martin's-le-Grand, the first large reinforced concrete building in London.[34] By 1911 they were employing 2,000 to 3,000 people.[35]

Three men were shipowners: Williamson Lamplough, with his brother Edmund S. Lamplough, had a lucrative business in London as steamship owners and underwriters,[36] Isaac A. Mack was a Liverpool shipowner;[37] and Walter Runciman MP had been in shipping in the North-East. After ten years as managing director of his father's firm, Moor Line (the second largest line in the region with 36 steamers in 1911), Runciman had just retired in order to devote himself to politics.[38] Only two of the 76 were associated with railways. Charles Sherwood Dennis trained in the office of his father Henry Dennis, goods manager of the North Eastern Railway at Hull; he then joined the Great Western Railway but rejoined the NER in 1894 as district superintendent at Darlington; a year later he was appointed general manager of the Cambrian Railway Co., one of the smaller railway companies, a post he still held in 1907.[39] Robert Perks had reached board level by specializing as a railway solicitor. He shrewdly married the daughter of a railway director, William Mewburn sen. Perks sat on the boards of the Lancashire, Derbyshire & East Coast Railway Co. 1894–1907 and of the Metropolitan District Railway Co. 1901–7 (as chairman in 1901 and deputy chairman in 1905). The latter built or electrified much of the deep-level tube railway system under London.[40] Holder of 15 offices and committee posts in 1907, Perks was the most active of all Wesleyan laymen.

Eight of these 76 Wesleyan laymen were in distribution, though only four were the proverbial English shopkeepers and none was of the corner shop variety. Thomas Hudson Bainbridge, with his brother, had inherited his father's large department store, and its branches, in Newcastle-upon-Tyne. At his death in 1912 he had 'heavy and responsible interests

[34] Ibid. 22 July 1897, 9, 16 Aug. 1923, and obituaries in the family volume kindly lent to me by Michael K. Holloway, grandson of Sir Henry; L. T. C. Rolt, *Holloways of Millbank* (London, 1958).

[35] *Red Book of Commerce, 1911* (London, 1911), 472.

[36] *M. Rec.* 24 July 1902; *Kelly's PODL* (1902) i. 1324.

[37] *M. Rec.* 30 July 1896; *Kelly's POD Liverpool* (1896).

[38] *Wes. Mag.* (1911), 573–8; *WWW*; *DNB*.

[39] *M. Rec.* 21 July 1898; *WWM 1910*.

[40] Charles E. Lee, 'Robert William Perks', *DBB*

in several other undertakings, shipbuilding, the Consett ironworks etc which have provided much remunerative employment, and contributed greatly to the prosperity of Tyneside and Durham.' Understandably he was hailed after his death as 'a Methodist merchant prince'.[41] John Rayner Batty, with two brothers, expanded his father's Manchester jewellery business (established in the 1840s) to Liverpool.[42] Thomas Cole jun. was a Sheffield draper.[43] Alfred Jermyn in 1872 had purchased a drapery business in King's Lynn where he had finally settled after training with a Cambridge draper (the Wesleyan Robert Sayle) and a firm in London's West End; he employed 120 people in 1911.[44] Those Wesleyans on the wholesale side of distribution operated in London's commodity markets. Alfred Booth, a son of the manse, was in the South African trade.[45] George Wigram McArthur and his brothers inherited a well-known Australian merchant house from their father Alexander McArthur MP and their uncle William.[46] Norman Thomas Carr Sargant, metal and colonial broker, inherited his father's business in Mincing Lane in the City.[47] Digby Frederick Shillington, who hailed from Northern Ireland, was a tea merchant.[48]

The 76 Wesleyan businessmen included four stockbrokers. William Mewburn jun.[49] and John Lees Barker[50] belonged to the Manchester firm of Mewburn & Barker. John Gibbs[51] and Sir Clarence Smith[52] each had their own London stockbroking businesses. Insurance broker Albert Wellesley Bain had a growing business in Leeds.[53] John Wesley Walker of Maidenhead chaired a building society.[54]

Among the professionals, legal men and engineers depended in part on business skills. Sir John Bamford-Slack had moved from Derby to London to develop his solicitor's practice; briefly he sat in Parliament

[41] *M. Rec.* 5 Aug. 1897, 14 Nov 1912; *Wes. Mag.* (1913), 155–6; A. and J. Airey, *The Bainbridges of Newcastle* (Newcastle-upon-Tyne, 1979), 103–30.

[42] *M. Rec.* 21 July 1898.

[43] Ibid. 21 July 1904.

[44] Ibid. 5 Aug. 1897; *Red Book of Commerce 1911*, 517.

[45] *M. Rec.* 23 July 1903.

[46] Ibid. 23 July 1903, 14 June 1923; *WWW.*

[47] *M. Rec.* 27 July 1905; *WWM 1910.*

[48] *WWM 1910.*

[49] Ibid. *1911.*

[50] Ibid. *1910.*

[51] *Wes. Mag.* (1913), 874–5.

[52] *M. Rec.* 20 July 1899, 30 July 1903; *WWMP.*

[53] Oliver M. Westall, 'Albert Wellesley Bain', *DBB.*

[54] *M. Rec.* 18 July 1907; *WWM 1910.*

and for his services to the Liberal Party was knighted in 1906.[55] The other solicitors in the cohort were the aged John Cooper of Manchester[56]; William Middlebrook of Leeds;[57] Charles W. Slater of Swansea;[58] and John Henry Turner of York (then retired to Scarborough).[59] Henry Arthur Smith, younger brother of Sir George Smith, was a London barrister who practised as an Equity draftsman and conveyancer.[60] Among the professional engineers James Botteley specialized in mining work,[61] William John Davey was partner in T. & C. Hawkesley the civil engineers,[62] and George Corderoy was senior partner in the firm of Corderoy & Corderoy, consulting surveyors who had served the Admiralty on extensive harbour and dock contracts around the world.[63] The two professional architects, Josiah Gunton of London and Ewen Harper of Birmingham, found some of their clients among their co-religionists. Gunton had designed 'close upon one hundred churches and halls for the use of our Connexion'[64] while Harper was responsible for the Central Hall in Birmingham, among other designs.[65]

The rest of the laymen comprised a surgeon (Robert Nightingale Hartley of Leeds), two Civil Servants (William J. Back and George H. Heath BA), four schoolmasters (including the heads of three Wesleyan boarding schools, Kingswood, Woodhouse Grove, and Rydal), and one trade unionist. The last would become in time the most distinguished layman of them all, with the exception of Runciman. Starting as ironfounder's apprentice, Arthur Henderson eventually sat in the first two Labour Cabinets and distinguished himself in Labour Party annals for leading the revolt against Ramsay MacDonald in 1931.[66]

Of the 76, 29 were members of the Institute of Directors and between them held 82 directorships, accounting for almost the whole of the key Methodists' presence in British boardrooms (assuming these to be representative samples) (compare Table 9.3). Of the 82 directorships only 21 can be associated with manufacturing. Preponderantly Wesleyan

---

[55] *M. Rec.* 18 Feb. 1909; *WWW*.

[56] *WWM 1910*.

[57] *M. Rec.* 22 July 1897, 30 July 1903, 2 July 1936; *WWW*; *WWM 1910, 1933*.

[58] *M. Rec.* 21 Feb. 1907.

[59] Ibid. 23 July 1896.

[60] Ibid. 18 July 1907; *WWM 1910*.

[61] *Wes. Mag.* (1913), 93–8.

[62] *M. Rec.* 25 July 1895.

[63] Ibid. 18 July 1907.

[64] Ibid. 14 Nov. 1907.

[65] *Wes. Mag.* (1916), 683.

[66] *WWMP*; *WWW*; *DNB*.

TABLE 8.3. *Social classes of 76 Wesleyan lay leaders, 1907*

Class	No.	%
Class 1		
Nobility		
Partner, owner, director of business	43	56.58
Merchant or banker	5	6.58
Landowner or farmer	1	1.32
Professional men	19	25.00
Senior manager or agent incl. TU official	5	6.58
Unknown	3	3.95
TOTAL	76	100.00

Note: None of the leaders came from Classes 2 (retailer; clerk, foreman, salesman; independent craftsman), 3 (skilled employee), or 4 (semi-skilled or unskilled employee).

businessmen sat on the boards of distribution and financial services companies. One or two cases suggest the strength of Wesleyan connections. For example, four of the 29 sat on the Star Life Assurance Co. board (Chubb, chairman; Ferens, Mewburn, and Sir Clarence Smith). Henry Holloway was a director of Albert E. Reed & Co., the paper manufacturers founded by fellow Wesleyan Albert E. Reed.[67] Two of the 76 (Bainbridge and Mewburn) had seats (only 2) on the boards of the 100 largest employers of 1907.

All the Wesleyan workhorses currently belonged to Social Class 1, on a scale of four social classes[68] (Table 8.3). None was in the nobility. Four were knights: Sir John Bamford Slack; Sir George Hayter Chubb, philanthropic manufacturer; Sir Clarence Smith, former Sheriff of London; and Sir George Smith, County Council leader in Cornwall. Noticeably a high proportion of these Wesleyan laymen lived in London or within easy commuting distance of London (see Table 8.4). Out of the 76 20 gave private addresses in London, 10 (Peter F. Wood and Sir George Chubb at Chislehurst, Walter Berry at Faversham, Ezra Wilkes at Watford, John Gibbs and George Heath at Bromley, William Mewburn at Tunbridge Wells, Charles C. Wakefield at Westcliff-on-Sea, and John Wesley Walker at Maidenhead) lived within a 40-mile radius of London, and three more (Ferens, Helme, and Howell Davies) would have been brought there regularly by parliamentary duties. Since 15.7 per cent of the population of England and Wales lived in London in

[67] *DD 1907*; Philip Sykes, 'Albert Edwin Reed', *DBB*.
[68] Charlotte Erickson's modification of the David Glass social scale. See C. Erickson, *British Industrialists* (Cambridge, 1959), 231.

TABLE 8.4. *Geographical distribution of 76 Wesleyan lay leaders, 1907*

Region	No.	%	Census population, 1911	%
London and Middlesex	21	27.63	5,667,000	15.70
South-East	10	13.16	6,055,000	16.78
East Anglia	1	1.32	1,147,000	3.18
South-West	3	3.95	2,728,000	7.56
West Midlands	10	13.16	3,276,000	9.08
East Midlands	0	0.00	2,693,000	7.46
North-West	16	21.05	5,724,000	15.86
Yorkshire	11	14.47	3,983,000	11.04
North-East	1	1.32	2,397,000	6.64
Wales	3	3.95	2,422,000	6.71
TOTAL	76	100.00	36,092,000	100.00

Sources: Author's analysis of lay leaders listed in Wesleyan Methodist Church, *Minutes of Conference* (London, 1907). B. R. Mitchell and P. Deane, *Abstract of British Historical Statistics* (Cambridge, 1962), 22. There is a discrepancy between the England and Wales and the regional population totals.

1911,[69] the presence of 28 per cent of the Wesleyan workhorses in the capital suggests an over-representation of a London mentality, if not London interests, in the counsels of Wesleyan Methodism at the beginning of the century. The argument against this was that the London Wesleyans provided most of the denomination's financial resources. The other areas well represented were the West Midlands, the North-West, and Yorkshire, reflecting the geographical strengths of the denomination. The East Midlands were unrepresented among the Wesleyan activists.

Among the 76, education and kin networks reinforced bonds of religion. For example William Butterworth (b. 1851), John Bamford-Slack (b. 1857), Charles Heap (b. 1845), Thomas Osborn (b. 1843), and Henry A. Smith (b. 1848) all attended Wesley College, Sheffield, and together must have overlapped between the mid-1850s and late-1860s. Alfred Booth (b. 1851), Robert Hartley (b. 1854), Sir Clarence Smith (b. 1849) were contemporaries at Woodhouse Grove School. Smith moved on to Kingswood where he might have met Robert Perks, who was his own age but who left in 1865.[70] Marriage drew others together. Both Perks and John Lees Barker married sisters of William Mewburn. Sir George Chubb's wife was the sister of Charles William Early the Witney blanket maker. The latter's brother, Charles Vanner Early, married a sister of Thomas Cole, the Sheffield draper.[71]

The activities of these 76 Wesleyan lay leaders were not exclusively

[69] B. R. Mitchell and P. Deane, *Abstract of British Historical Statistics* (Cambridge, 1962), 10, 22.

[70] D. Crane, *The Life-Story of Sir Robert W. Perks, Baronet, M.P.* (London, 1909), 42.

[71] *WWM 1910.*

devoted either to business or to Wesleyan Methodism. Many were civic and political leaders in their local communities. Some sat in the Commons. At least 20 were JPs. Five were serving or recent mayors (Charles Heap of Rochdale, Isaac Mack of Bootle, William Middlebrook of Morley, William Horrocks Rawson of Accrington, and John Wesley Walker of Maidenhead). Four were county councillors (Josiah Gunton, Norval Helme, Sir George Smith, and William Henry Smith). Three were aldermen (Edge of Burslem, Sir George Smith of Cornwall, William Henry Smith of Shropshire). Eight were or had been MPs: Bamford-Slack, William Howell Davies, Thomas R. Ferens, Norval Helme, Robert Perks, Walter Runciman, and Sir Clarence Smith, all Liberals, and Arthur Henderson, Labour. The dominance of Liberal interests in the highest counsels of Wesleyan Methodism is of course well known.[72] Politically Sir George Chubb played an important role. He was one of the few Nonconformist laymen with links to the Court—not with the Queen, who had little to do with Dissenters, but with the Duchess of Albany and later the Duchess's daughter Princess Alexander of Teck. As Perks jocularly remarked in an after-dinner speech, 'his friend, Sir George Hayter Chubb, never seemed happy unless he had titled friends around him'.[73]

A collective profile of the leading Wesleyan Methodist laymen of 1907 therefore reveals a narrowly selected group: generally of mid- or late middle-age; ascendant in business and capital; dominated by London perspectives; bonded by a Wesleyan education or, less frequently, marriage; and enjoying solid civic and political (usually Liberal) status. These were men rising within and between classes, despite any social handicap associated with their minority religious faith.

(b) The roles of business leaders in Wesleyan Methodism

In Wesleyan Methodism these men proved themselves first in the local chapel, as leaders and generous supporters. Usually they held office as Sunday School teachers, local preachers, or class leaders (each congregation being organized in cells or classes under the pastoral direction of an experienced layman). For example Thomas Bainbridge was an active local preacher in the Newcastle circuits and a class leader in Bruns-

[72] S. Koss, *Nonconformity in Modern British Politics* (London, 1975); D. W. Bebbington, *The Nonconformist Conscience* (London, 1982).

[73] Racal-Chubb Ltd., Chubb papers; Bebbington, *Nonconformist Conscience*, 94–6; *Methodist Times*, 12 Mar. 1903; W. L. Arnstein, 'Queen Victoria and Religion', in G. Malmgreen (ed.), *Religion in the Lives of English Women, 1760–1930* (London, 1986).

wick Chapel for forty years.[74] Sir John Bamford-Slack was another devoted local preacher. Thomas Barclay was strongly committed to the principle of class leaders.[75] Henry Bisseker superintended an adult Bible class of 1,300 members.[76] Less typically Sir George Smith revelled in the musical expression of his faith: for twenty-seven years he was organist and choirmaster of Camborne Wesleyan Chapel.[77]

With a sound record of lay leadership in the local chapel, individuals could move to positions in the circuit, as circuit steward or circuit treasurer. Advancement to the district synod was more difficult. Here powers of public speaking and debate ranked high; so did weight of social status, like that conferred by civic office or professional attainment or the acquisition of wealth. Generous benefactors to Wesleyan causes gained rapid recognition. Sir Henry Lunn critically recalled how the Wesleyan pulpit of the 1870s glorified merchant princes.[78] Even after such complacencies were disturbed by Hugh Price Hughes and his message of social Christianity, men of talent and wealth were essential in launching and leading the voluntary missions and large mission halls projected by the radicals for the needs of the poor and the inner cities. Perks and Ferens were among the businessmen who donated £1,000 or more each to the building of Kingsway Hall (designed by Josiah Gunton) for the West London Mission which had been founded by Hugh Price Hughes.[79]

From the district synod, Wesleyan laymen (with five years' continuous church membership)[80] could be elected to the annual Conference. Altogether 240 laymen represented the 35 districts into which the country, excluding Wales and Ireland, was divided (numbers being roughly proportional to the population of the districts). Another 12 attended Conference ex officio as treasurers of connectional funds (see Table 8.5) and a further 48 were elected for a term of three years by Conference itself.[81] These 300 laymen were equalled in the Representative Session by 300 ministerial representatives, but the laity were well outnumbered by a further 100 senior ministers who made up the Legal Conference (instituted after the death of John Wesley to exercise the ultimate church authority he had wielded). In the Pastoral (ministerial) session of Confer-

---

[74] Airey, *Bainbridges*, 108.
[75] *Wes. Mag.* (1907), 535.
[76] *M. Rec.* 26 July 1894.
[77] *Wes. Mag.* (1906), 726.
[78] Sir H. Lunn, *Nearing Harbour* (London, 1934). 10.
[79] P. S. Bagwell, *Outcast London* (London, 1987), 67–8.
[80] MW, *Minutes* (1906), 375.
[81] Ibid. (1906), 343–4.

ence, held in the second week of sitting, over 400 ministers representing 3,500 in the denomination at the turn of the century assembled to discuss matters specifically relating to their pastoral and theological responsibilities.

The parts played by the 76 Wesleyan lay workhorses emerge from an examination of their offices and the national church activities with which they associated. The kinds of committee on which Wesleyan laymen and women, including the 76 laymen, served are summarized in Table 8.6. In only one area did key laymen occupy more than half the committee seats allocated to the laity: internal organization. A closer look at larger individual committees shows the 76 to have predominated on Chapel Affairs (building), the Twentieth Century Fund (and its Education section), the Invalid Ministers' Rest Fund, Wesleyan Secondary Education, Wesley's Chapel, Methodism in Cambridge, the Ordinary Committee of Privileges, and the financial committee of the Theological Institution. Apart from the Twentieth Century Fund (about which more follows), these were committees dealing with fabric, the financing of church activities, and the political relations of Wesleyan Methodism.

Interest in chapel building and home missions reflected the denomination's anxiety over the condition of England question, the challenges posed by proliferating industrial-urban society and resurgent Anglicanism. To these the new central halls of the 1890s formed a major response.[82] Central halls required large urban premises and here Wesleyan businessmen played a crucial role. The Central Hall in Birmingham was not untypical of the eight major central missions in existence by 1907 (the others were in Bolton, Leeds, Liverpool, Nottingham, Sheffield, Manchester, and London). When the Birmingham Mission ran into property difficulties the national Chapel Affairs Committee (CAC) produced a solution that illustrated the way in which connectional financial and business resources could be brought to bear on a local property problem. The original Mission met on premises of 900 square yards where the Hall held only 900 people. By 1906 there was severe overcrowding. The Mission trustees decided to find new premises and bought a 2,700 square yard site on Corporation Street. The old building had a rental value of £3,700. Together with an annual income of £500 from the Mission this would cover the interest, ground rent, and working expenses incurred in building a new Central Hall, expected to cost £40,000. The problem arose because of delays in letting the old premises.

---

[82] K. S. Inglis, *Churches and the Working Classes in Victorian England* (London, 1963), 92–5.

TABLE 8.5. *Lay treasurers of Wesleyan connectional funds, 1907*

Name	Address	Occupation	Fund
Atkinson, Moses	Harrogate	linen manufacturer, retired	Local Preachers' Committee
Bamford-Slack, Sir John	London	solicitor	Temperance Committee
Barker, John Lees	Altrincham	stockbroker	Auxiliary Fund
Barlow, John Robert, BA	Bolton	cotton spinner	Children's Home
Barnsley, Thomas	Birmingham	building contractor	Education Fund
Ferens, Thomas Robinson, MP	Hull	starch manufacturer	Home Mission Fund
Lamplough, Williamson	London	steamship owner and underwriter	Missionary Society
Mewburn, William	Tunbridge Wells	stockbroker, retired	Children's Fund
Middlebrook, William	Leeds	solicitor	General Chapel Fund
Perks, Robert William, MP	London	railway director and solicitor	London Mission
Smith, Sir Clarence	London	stockbroker	Metropolitan Chapel Building Fund
Smith, Sir George	Truro	fuse manufacturer	Theological Institution Fund

Source: Minutes of Conference (London, 1906), 341–2.

TABLE 8.6. *Committee posts of 76 key Wesleyan laymen, 1907*

Committee	Key laymen		All laypersons on committee		Key laymen as % of all laypersons on committee
	No.	%	No.	%	
Chapel building					
Chapel Affairs	16	3.1	31	1.9	51.6
Trustees for Chapel Purposes	3	0.6	3	0.2	100.0
Metropolitan Chapel Building Fund	5	1.0	17	1.0	29.4
N. Wales District Chapel Fund	0	0.0	16	1.0	0.0
Extension Fund for Methodism in Scotland	0	0.0	36	2.2	0.0
S. Wales District Chapel Fund	2	0.4	9	0.5	22.2
Wesleyan Methodist Twentieth Century Fund	15	2.9	19	1.1	78.9
Total	41	7.8	131	7.8	31.3
Charitable Funds					
Auxiliary Fund for Worn-out Ministers	7	1.3	25	1.5	28.0
Children's Home and Orphanage	9	1.7	34	2.0	26.5
Children's Home, Birmingham branch	1	0.2	15	0.9	6.7
Children's Home, Frodsham branch	3	0.6	11	0.7	27.3
Children's Home, Lancashire branch	1	0.2	14	0.8	7.1
Children's Home, London branch	2	0.4	16	1.0	12.5
Children's Home, Ramsey branch	0	0.0	8	0.5	0.0
Invalid Ministers' Rest Fund	2	0.4	3	0.2	66.7
Necessitous Local Preachers	3	0.6	12	0.7	25.0
Total	28	5.4	138	8.3	20.3
Education					
Allen Library	1	0.2	6	0.4	16.7
Maintenance and Education of Ministers' Children	9	1.7	30	1.8	30.0
Trinity Hall School	8	1.5	19	1.1	42.1
Wesleyan Secondary Education	9	1.7	14	0.8	64.3
Wesley Guild	6	1.1	42	2.5	14.3

TABLE 8.6. *cont.*

Committee	Key laymen		All laypersons on committee		Key laymen as % of all laypersons on committee
	No.	%	No.	%	
Kingswood School	4	0.8	14	0.8	28.6
Twentieth C. Fund, Education Section	17	3.3	30	1.8	56.7
Wesleyan Education	16	3.1	75	4.5	21.3
Total	70	13.4	230	13.8	30.4
Home missions					
Army and Navy Board of Management	7	1.3	16	1.0	43.8
Wesley's Chapel	7	1.3	13	0.8	53.8
Home Mission	28	5.4	72	4.3	38.9
Local Preachers	14	2.7	31	1.9	45.2
Birmingham Mission	7	1.3	42	2.5	16.7
Bolton Mission	3	0.6	28	1.7	10.7
Methodism in Cambridge	16	3.1	30	1.8	53.3
Leeds Mission	5	1.0	46	2.8	10.9
Liverpool Mission	6	1.1	43	2.6	14.0
London Mission	21	4.0	62	3.7	33.9
Nottingham Mission	0	0.0	22	1.3	0.0
Methodist Settlement in London	9	1.7	28	1.7	32.1
Sheffield Mission	1	0.2	35	2.1	2.9
Methodism in South Wales	11	2.1	24	1.4	45.8
Seamen's Mission	6	1.1	14	0.8	42.9
Manchester and Salford Mission	5	1.0	63	3.8	7.9
Total	146	27.9	569	34.1	25.7
Foreign missions					
Missions (foreign)	26	5.0	86	5.1	30.2
Methodist Missionary Society	1	0.2	1	0.1	100.0
Total	27	5.2	87	5.2	31.0

TABLE 8.6. *cont.*

Committee	Key laymen		All laypersons on committee		Key laymen as % of all laypersons on committee
	No.	%	No.	%	
Internal organization					
Concerted Action	7	1.3	8	0.5	87.5
Custody of Connexional Documents	2	0.4	4	0.2	50.0
Connexional Fund	13	2.5	22	1.3	59.1
Connexional Fund, Emergency Committee	4	0.8	7	0.4	57.1
Class Leaders	15	2.9	29	1.7	51.7
Compulsory Supernumaryship	4	0.8	4	0.2	100.0
Representative Session of Conference in Ireland	1	0.2	1	0.1	100.0
Methodist Assembly	7	1.3	8	0.5	87.5
Membership Bureau	3	0.6	13	0.8	23.1
Membership	21	4.0	53	3.2	39.6
Nomination Committee	9	1.7	13	0.8	69.2
Oecumenical Conference	4	0.8	5	0.3	80.0
Convenor of Scrutineers	1	0.2	1	0.1	100.0
Representative Session of Conference in Wales	1	0.2	1	0.1	100.0
Total	92	17.6	169	10.1	54.4
External relations					
Committee of Privileges, Extraordinary	6	1.1	36	2.2	16.7
Committee of Privileges, Ordinary	21	4.0	27	1.6	77.8
Crowle Bequest (temperance)	7	1.3	7	0.4	100.0
Financial Appeals by Strangers	4	0.8	5	0.3	80.0
Legal Liability of Members of Leaders' Meeting	7	1.3	14	0.8	50.0
Religious Observance of the Lord's Day	8	1.5	22	1.3	36.4
Social Purity	3	0.6	21	1.3	14.3
Temperance	9	1.7	25	1.5	36.0
Total	65	12.4	157	9.4	41.4

TABLE 8.6. cont.

Committee	Key laymen		All laypersons on committee		Key laymen as % of all laypersons on committee
	No.	%	No.	%	
Theological education					
Didsbury Theological College	6	1.1	33	2.0	18.2
Theological Institution, General Committee	22	4.2	48	2.9	45.8
Theological Institution, Finance	4	0.8	7	0.4	57.1
Handsworth Theological College	5	1.0	32	1.9	15.6
Headingley Theological College	6	1.1	33	2.0	18.2
Richmond Theological College	0	0.0	1	0.1	0.0
Theological Institution, Sub-Committee	5	1.0	6	0.4	83.3
Wesley Deaconess Institute	6	1.1	30	1.8	20.0
Total	54	10.3	190	11.4	28.4
Summary					
Chapel building	41	7.8	131	7.8	31.3
Charitable funds	28	5.4	138	8.3	20.3
Education: church and secular	70	13.4	230	13.8	30.4
Home missions	146	27.9	569	34.1	25.7
Foreign missions	27	5.2	87	5.2	31.0
Internal organization	92	17.6	169	10.1	54.4
External relations	65	12.4	157	9.4	41.4
Theological education	54	10.3	190	11.4	28.4
TOTAL	523	100.0	1,671	100.0	31.3

The Mission trustees, who wished to sell these premises, took the matter to the denomination's CAC. Another solution then emerged.

The CAC appointed a deputation to confer with the Birmingham Mission trustees in January 1907. Out of this came a shrewd piece of property investment. The CAC took over the mortgage of £20,000 on the old Hall at 3 per cent p.a., thereby saving the Mission trust £200 p.a. Half the £40,000 cost for the new Hall could be provided almost immediately: the Mission trustees would be responsible for finding £10,000 of which nearly £6,000 had been pledged by 'gentlemen' at the Birmingham meeting in January; and the Wesleyan CAC would be asked to find a £10,000 interest-free loan, to be repaid within twenty years. For its part the CAC would be left with the safe investment of the old premises, valued at £35,000 with an annual rental value of £1,500. In twenty years, it was calculated, the only debt on the two properties would be £20,000, apart from ground rent, and this could be cleared in another ten years by a similar division of the debt between the local Mission and the national connection.[83]

Other clear evidence of businessmen's involvement in home missions and chapel building was the Twentieth Century Fund. This was launched at Conference in 1898 by Robert Perks, then MP for the Louth Division of Lincolnshire. Perks, a wily intriguer (who served as matchmaker between traditionally conservative Wesleyans and the Liberal Party), persuaded Conference that £1 million could be raised from a third of the three million adherents which he then claimed for Wesleyan Methodism. Of the sum to be raised, Perks suggested, £250,000 would afford 'material assistance to the village chapel or mission room or school' in areas where there were no wealthy laymen. Another £100,000 would be placed in the Home Missionary Fund.[84] This was a clear response to resurgent Anglicanism as well as to rampant urban deprivation.

The fund was launched and within two years its target was in sight. Four-fifths (800,000 guineas) of the Twentieth Century Fund was subscribed by individual donors of a guinea each.[85] The remaining 200,000 guineas came from donors of larger sums. At the Conference at Burslem in 1900, 'the success of the Twentieth Century Fund trembled in the Balance'. Perks, dressed in black adorned by a white orchid (the Queen's son, the Duke of Edinburgh, had just died), called on English Methodism to match the generosity of their American cousins (who had promised £4 million). Promises had been made. Money was coming in. But

[83] M. Rec. 25 July 1907, 15–16.   [84] Ibid. 28 July 1898, 31–2.
[85] Ibid. 25 July 1907, 6.

another 250,000 guineas was still needed to reach the million mark. Then Hugh Price Hughes rose. He pleaded with 'the men of means in the Conference, and throughout the Connexion'. Let them give 'not out of income, but out of capital'. In an atmosphere of high emotion sober commercial men tossed thrift and caution to the winds as, one after another, they stood up to announce a new or increased donation. Joseph Rank, the miller, announced his gift of £10,000 (which took his total gifts to the Fund to £27,000). The Vanner brothers, bankers, added £5,000 to the £5,000 they had already promised.[86] Henry Holloway, the London contractor, telegraphed his brother Tom suggesting they make a sacrificial gift of £2,000. Next morning came the reply, '"But if it is to be sacrifice make it £5,000". And it was £5,000 that the Holloway brothers gave.'[87] Perks himself gave over £10,000.[88]

Schemes which happily united the businessman's modes of thought and action with the larger objectives of the kingdom of God, and the Wesleyan Methodist Church in particular, were the forte of many Wesleyan laymen. Their variations on a church bazaar illustrate the point at a local church level.[89] No Wesleyan was more ambitious and successful in developing and pushing such projects nationally than Robert Perks MP. In spring 1907 in the correspondence columns of the *Methodist Recorder* he announced another grand enterprise. This time, however, it had secular political implications and triggered a lively debate in the pages of the denominational newspaper. Perks proposed a welfare scheme for Methodists which he called the 'Methodist Brotherhood'. Like the central halls it attempted to address the social problems of contemporary industrial society. Poverty and the injustices of the poor law were currently being confronted by the Liberal Government of which Perks was a supporter but not a member. As Perks noted in his original proposal, the Twentieth Century Fund of one million guineas, together with another £3 million it 'evoked', had been applied to 'what I may, perhaps call the plant and machinery of our vast and closely federated religious community', now it was time to mobilize human resources to serve Methodism. In brief Perks proposed to exploit the ubiquity and affluence of world-wide Methodism.[90] He had in mind four areas: emigration, employment, financial loans, and old age support. An Emigration

---

[86] Ibid. 2 Aug. 1900.
[87] *Christian World*, 16 Aug. 1923.
[88] Crane, *Perks*, 157.
[89] D. J. Jeremy, 'Chapel in a Business Career', in Jeremy (ed.), *Business and Religion in Britain* (Aldershot, 1988).
[90] *M. Rec.* 9 May 1907.

Department would assist unskilled, skilled, and professional people to find work and settlement in the Colonies. The Brotherhood's Employment Agency would serve as a labour exchange. Its Loan Society, like a Church Friendly Society or savings bank, would assist its members through temporary economic difficulty. And its scheme for encouraging 'Provision for Old Age' would be necessary, Perks thought, even if the state could ever afford a pension scheme. The whole programme promised Wesleyan businessmen a labour pool of co-religionists. There would be 'a register of the leading Methodists in every important city of the world—men who will be able and ready to assist their fellow Methodists to secure work, to bridge over some temporary difficulty, to find friends, and to push ahead'. Perks even saw a combination of emigration and loan as a means of helping failed businessmen.[91] The scheme appealed. It seemed apostolic and Wesleyan. It was practical and relevant to the social needs of the day. It was rational in its conception. Its global dimensions attracted those searching for large-scale and total solutions.

Perks published his proposals a few days before embarking with his wife and daughter on the White Star Line's *Adriatic* at Liverpool, bound for New York—his first visit to America. Then at the head of C. H. Walker & Co. Ltd., contracting engineers of Westminster, Perks was visiting New York in connection with the Georgian Bay Canal in Canada and the firm's various enterprises in South America. When he returned two months later in time to attend the Wesleyan Conference in London, the reactions of British Wesleyan laymen had been well aired, also in the columns of the *Methodist Recorder*. Opinions among laymen neatly divided into three: those who supported the Brotherhood Scheme wholeheartedly; those who gave it a cautious qualified reception; and those who opposed it. Approving and largely uncritical were Sir John Bamford-Slack; Henry Dawson, who recalled past benefits he had received from Methodist fellowship in Australia and London; John Broxap; Alfred Jermyn; Edward G. Barber, a South African-born, Kingswood-educated, London-based merchant and commission agent; Charles Heap, who saw the Local Preachers' Mutual Aid Association as a model of the principle of Methodists helping Methodists; and John Crowle-Smith, the managing director of Hazell, Watson & Viney, Manchester printers.[92]

Others had doubts. William Howell Davies MP cautioned that 'The Methodist Church will have to count the cost both in faith and works

---

[91] *M. Rec.* 9 May 1907.   [92] Ibid. 16 May 1907.

before it embarks on these schemes.' Thomas R. Ferens MP wanted
to see details of the scheme and thought 'plans for the brightening of
rural life and the retention of the young people in the villages and on
the land' preferable to emigration, a point echoed faintly by Jermyn.[93]
George Corderoy generally welcomed the ideas of 'one who sees visions
and dreams dreams to such purpose'. Least satisfactory, he believed,
was the employment agency. He had some experience of various kinds
of employment registries and had little faith in them. Above all he hoped
that Perks's scheme would 'assist in conserving the virile principle of
individual effort as distinguished from the emasculated notions too often
associated with statemanaged schemes'.[94] Sir John Scurrah Randles MP,
the Cumberland iron and steel manufacturer, dismissed pious resolutions
at conferences, synods, or committees. They might be needed but 'under
Providence the way must be shown by a leader of men'.[95]

Three lay correspondents to the *Methodist Recorder* expressed themselves totally opposed to Perks's proposals: Arthur Henderson the Labour
MP; Samuel Meggitt Johnson, a Sheffield confectionery manufacturer;[96]
and Alfred Brookes, director of Tootal, Broadhurst & Co. Henderson
approved the proposals as an indication of 'a growing desire that the
Churches should accept their full responsibility in finding a solution
for our present-day social difficulties'. But the sectarian basis of the
scheme, confined as it was to Methodists, was inimical to the application
of 'the principles of Christ to the amendment of social life'. Particularly,
how would candidates for emigration assistance be selected? Encouraging
the temporarily unemployed only 'reduced the average capacity and character of those who are left'. As for an Old Age Pension Fund, Henderson
foresaw many difficulties. Above all he believed it would only divert
'the attention of the people from pressing their claims to a pension,
as a civic right for which the community is under an obligation to make
adequate and speedy provision'.[97] Meggitt Johnson viewed all the proposals as impracticable. Steamship companies already had inducements
for attracting emigrants. As for employment schemes run by businessmen: 'the moment the Churches begin to mix up philanthropy with
business pursuits they enter upon dangerous ground'. Making loans to
failures in business, he thought, would attract men to Methodism for

[93] Ibid.

[94] Ibid. 23 May 1907.

[95] Ibid.

[96] *DD 1907*; he was related to the Bassett family (information from Sheffield Public
Library, Local Studies Library).

[97] *M. Rec.* 23 May 1907.

the wrong reasons; instead 'it is more business ability that is needed than gold'.[98] Alfred Brookes dismissed the premiss on which Perks's proposals stood: their sectarian character was inadmissible in social enterprise. Rather, Methodists should attack the problems in two ways. First, through the central halls which Wesleyans had built and were continuing to build in the major cities of the land, the poor, hungry, and unemployed could be given a measure of material aid in addition to spiritual hope. Brookes was one of the major lay supporters of the Central Hall in Manchester, the first central hall to be established.[99] Second, much more substantially on the material front, the church should 'bring its united influence to bear upon our legislators to deal with the scheme, not as Methodists for Methodists, but as British statesmen for the well-being of the State'.[100] Perks, he implied, ought to concentrate his welfare efforts in the House of Commons—where, incidentally, William Lever the Congregational soap magnate had recently introduced an abortive private bill for a tax-financed pension scheme.[101] On the clerical side both the Reverend Samuel Keeble and the Reverend Henry Carter, the denomination's specialists in social questions, were among those who expressed strong reservations about Perks's ideas. Both hinted at a preference for state action. Carter viewed old age pensions as 'the urgent business of the State'.[102]

Brookes who professed great admiration for Perks's ability and 'regarding this particular matter, his cleverness', wondered whether the manner of moving the scheme was no more than a ploy to provide Perks with the soundings he needed before presenting practical proposals to Conference.[103] It seemed to turn out that way. At Conference in mid-July 1907 Perks reviewed his Brotherhood proposals, duly tailored to meet some of his critics. He still stuck by the sectarian principle of Methodists helping Methodists, but hoped the time would come when the scheme might be expanded to non-Methodists. His chief concern was the Emigration Department. This promised to be the least contentious of his proposals. He could also support it with evidence from his Canadian tour. In Toronto he had met a generous Methodist layman who had promised

---

[98] M. Rec. 23 May 1907.
[99] J. Banks, The Story . . . so Far (Manchester, 1986), 145. Another was Edward Aston, who also made a fortune in the textile industry. Ibid. 52.
[100] M. Rec. 13 June 1907.
[101] D. Fraser, The Evolution of the British Welfare State (2nd edn., Macmillan, 1984), 153.
[102] M. Rec. 16, 23 May 1907.
[103] Ibid. 13 June 1907.

£10,000 to buy land on which the Salvation Army could settle its emigrants. He learned that 6,000 Methodists had recently passed through Quebec seeking employment in agricultural communities west of Winnipeg, 'Multitudes were going out, not knowing whither they went, to places where they had no settled occupation.'[104] Who would help them? 'Methodist preachers, and the successful laymen and workers.' Where would these emigrants locate? Here Perks, treasurer of several connectional funds, deftly shifted attention from the distant prairies to the Conference representatives, comfortably seated in post-prandial ease, in front of him in Wesley's Chapel, City Road, London, particularly his fellow businessmen. 'There were businessmen before him—men whose history he knew, whose business he knew. He knew what they were doing. He knew what some of them were making. (Loud laughter.) Might he add that he knew also what they were most generously and lavishly giving— and he would add further that they had got plenty of money left. ("Agreed" and laughter.)' Perks advocated the assistance of the Methodists to procure land in the great Colonies at the price at which it was available.[105] He briefly denied that state help would be sufficient to aid the unemployed. In conclusion he urged the 'enquiry and collection of data' (following the Reverend Henry Carter).[106] The Brotherhood scheme, which was largely overtaken by the Liberals' welfare reforms and then world war, had lost its pension and loan components by 1909.[107] Labour market intelligence for emigrants was, however, organized and limited progress noted in the minutes of succeeding Conferences. The whole episode nevertheless characterized the kinds of initiative taken by Wesleyan layman and businessmen. Likewise it illustrated the possibilities open to hard-headed Wesleyans to make very critical appraisals of visionary denominational projects.

The other area where Wesleyan laymen, again led by Sir Robert Perks, shouldered special responsibility was that of church organization. Wesleyan Methodism badly needed a more efficient organizational structure to meet the demands imposed by its own absolute growth and the technological and bureaucratic changes transforming British society. Between 1839 and 1898, as Robert Perks reminded Conference in the latter year, the denomination had more than doubled in size, so that it eventually boasted 8,391 chapels (almost entirely free from debt) with 2,181,000 sittings and 1.1 million Sunday School teachers and scholars and three

---

[104] Ibid. 25 July 1907.   [105] Ibid.
[106] Ibid.   [107] Crane, *Perks*, 166.

million adherents.[108] Despite the centralized structure of the denomination the administrative departments (for Home Missions, Chapel Affairs, and so forth) lacked a single and efficient organizational hub. This goal might be advanced by centralizing denominational departments in a single headquarters building.

The location of the central organs of Wesleyan Methodism in 1907 suggested a distinct lack of co-ordination. Centenary Hall, built in Bishopsgate Street in the City in the 1840s, 'comparatively small and about to be adapted largely for commercial purposes',[109] served as the headquarters of the Wesleyan Missionary Society. The Connexional Temperance office was in Caxton House, Westminster.[110] Home Missions, Education, the Connexional Fund, and several others were headquartered next to Wesley's Chapel in the City Road. The Connexional Sunday School Union occupied 2–3 Ludgate Circus Buildings. Outside London the Congregational Chapel Fund was based in the Central Buildings, Manchester, and the Wesleyan Methodist Trust Assurance Co. Ltd. had its offices in Fountain Street, Manchester.[111] The physical concentration of most departments in one building would allow improved communications and administrative efficiency.

One objective of the Twentieth Century Fund, and also proposed by Perks, was a single new building to house the headquarters of the Wesleyan Methodists in England. Perks's arguments echo the thinking of many a big businessman at the turn of the century when a centralized headquarters located in London increasingly acquired favour—among the 100 largest manufacturing employers at the beginning of the century 26 had headquarters in London.[112] As Perks persuasively explained in 1898 they 'needed within a reasonable distance of Charing Cross in a central position a building of a monumental character which would combine for Methodism all the purposes for which Exeter Hall was used—which would accommodate some of the Connexional Funds, and in which the evangelistic work of that noble movement the London Mission could be carried on'.[113] The Church of England was putting up a building of similar character (Church House, Westminster). The Congregationalists had in their Memorial Hall in Farringdon Street 'a hive of philan-

---

[108] *M. Rec.* 28 July 1898, 31.
[109] Ibid. 32.
[110] Ibid. 18 July 1907.
[111] MW, *Minutes* (1907), 413–18, 492, 549.
[112] C. Shaw, 'The Large Manufacturing Employers of 1907', *Business History*, 25 (1983), 48.
[113] *M. Rec.* 28 July 1898, 32.

thropic, ecclesiastical and religious enterprise'. Wesleyans 'had a great responsibility in controlling and organising the great religious and social movements of the future; and if they were to take their legitimate share in the coming century they must have adequate Church premises of the character he had indicated'.[114] In short Perks was advocating the construction of a central hall-cum-headquarters for Wesleyan Methodism.

It must be located in London. Perks's justification for London was based on the 'elasticity' in which Wesleyans gloried ('the whole genius of their Church consisted in its adaptability').[115] They must continue to modify their denominational structures, institutional and physical, to meet the changing challenge posed by secular society. Methodism was not more powerful than she was because 'their forefathers forgot and neglected London'.[116] Yet London had been rapidly growing and spreading westwards; Wesleyans should move with the population. Recent research by Clive Field has shown that in the 1850s and 1860s under 2 per cent of London's population could be accommodated in Wesleyan places of worship, compared to around 17 per cent for the Church of England (all churches combined could seat only 30 per cent of London's population).[117] Other denominations had established, or were setting up, national headquarters buildings in the heart of the capital: Wesleyans should do the same.

The manner in which the site was obtained and a vast new building financed exemplified the way in which Perks and his Wesleyan confederates masterminded denominational projects. The whole business was placed in the hands of the Twentieth Century Fund (TCF) committee. By 1907 (nine years after it was established) the TCF committee comprised 19 laymen and 16 ministers. Of the 17 laymen whose occupations are known all had one or both feet in the business world; none were just academics or professionals. So vast had been the effort needed to organize the collection and dispersal of a million guineas that the fund had required five treasurers and nine honorary secretaries. By 1907 there were four treasurers (three laymen, one minister) and eight honorary secretaries (half lay, half ministerial). The acting treasurer was, of course, Robert W. Perks MP; the lay treasurers were Thomas Hudson

---

[114] Ibid.

[115] Ibid. 31.

[116] Ibid. 32.

[117] C. D. Field, 'Methodism in Metropolitan London, 1850–1920' (Oxford D.Phil., 1974), 84.

Bainbridge, the very wealthy and generous Newcastle department store owner, and Sir George Smith, Cornish mining materials manufacturer. The secretaries were John Barnsley, Birmingham builder; Percy McArthur, Australian merchant; and William Middlebrook, Leeds solicitor.[118] Others included John Parkes, Moses Atkinson, Norval Helme MP, John R. Barlow, William Howell Davies MP, Thomas Lewis (from Bangor), Alfred Jermyn, Henry Holloway, Williamson Lamplough, and William Mewburn—all men of business experience, solid personal wealth, and tested Christian conviction.

With his vast experience of the shoals of Wesleyan Methodism and the London business world, Robert Perks, promoter and organizer of the Twentieth Century Fund, skilfully and successfully piloted the scheme for a national headquarters. London Methodists had at first wanted to see the allocated £250,000 spent on more churches and halls in the spreading suburban districts.[119] However, Perks projected something different from the usual urban central hall: it would be a complex of premises combining an auditorium to hold at least 3,000[120] with smaller meeting rooms and denominational offices. More widely and consonant with Perks's imperial vision, it would serve as the headquarters of Methodism throughout the British Empire and the world.[121]

In July 1907 Perks made a statement about progress on the Connexional Buildings site to the Wesleyan Conference. The TCF Committee had bought the decayed Royal Aquarium, close to the Houses of Parliament, for £360,000, a decision in which they 'had had to run some risk'. But Wesleyan businessmen were nothing if not canny. Shrewdly they had purchased a 110,000 square foot site,[122] very much larger than their estimated needs. A good part of the site had been sold for £200,000, leaving 35,000 square feet surrounded by streets on three sides and open spaces on the fourth for the projected Connexional Buildings. Purchasing the surplus land were none other than Messrs Holloway Bros., headed by TCF Committee member Henry Holloway. Furthermore Holloways had contracted 'to buy £100,000 more land' in two years' time. The TCF Committee would therefore pay only £60,000 for a prime site in the heart of Westminster. Contracts for clearing the site and bringing foundations to ground level had been awarded amounting to £12,600, work that would take nine months. Meantime they were negotiating

---

[118] MW, *Minutes* (1907), 89–90. [119] Crane, *Perks*, 161.
[120] *M. Rec.* 28 July 1898, 31. [121] Crane, *Perks*, 161–2.
[122] Ibid. 162.

to let parts of the Connexional Buildings and expected to raise an annual rental of £4,000 from these leases. The Holloways (who did not get the contract for the Connexional Buildings) were building a property on their part of the site which was letting well.[123]

One reason for the delay between purchase of the Aquarium site in 1902–3[124] and construction in 1907–12 was friction between moderates on Westminster Corporation (who wanted to widen Princes Street) and progressives on London County Council (who wanted to confine the improvement's costs to Westminster ratepayers). In all the tortuous negotiations and discussions, with fellow Methodists or commercial and political men outside the denomination, the pilot's hand belonged to Sir Robert Perks (made a baronet in 1909). The *Methodist Recorder* summarized his role succinctly:

The Trustees would have had far greater difficulties, involving them in fabulous costs, but for the devotion and resourcefulness—the legal knowledge, the unfailing tact and patience, and the public influence—of their Treasurer, Sir Robert Perks. Not only in the transactions connected with the purchase of the property and the sale, or leasing, of superfluous lands, but also in dealing with the highly-objectionable slum and public-house property on the other side of the building, he has rendered priceless service to Methodism.[125]

Eventually the new Central Hall and Connexional Buildings at Westminster were opened in early October 1912 with a series of meetings. A neo-classical structure, it was designed by Lanchester & Rickards (who won an open competition judged by Sir Aston Webb PRIBA) and built by Messrs Dove, also non-Methodists.[126] When all the rhetoric about the hall had finished flowing, there remained questions about the use of the buildings. The Central Hall section would follow the pattern set by other urban central halls, as a base for powerful evangelistic preaching and wide-ranging social welfare work. There were, however, the appended offices, rooms, and premises in the Connexional Buildings. In the minds of many there was the hope that the Westminster buildings would be a 'rallying ground for the various branches of Methodism'.[127] Sir William P. Hartley, the Primitive Methodist lay leader, ventured

---

[123] *M. Rec.* 25 July 1907, 14.
[124] Crane, *Perks*, 163.
[125] *M. Rec.* 26 Sept. 1912.
[126] Ibid. 10 Oct. 1912.
[127] Ibid.

TABLE 8.7. *Occupations of multiple office holders in non-Wesleyan Methodist connections, 1907*

Denomination	No. of multiple office holders	Minimum no. of offices held	No. in business	No. in manufacturing	No. not identified
Primitive Methodists	13	5	9	5	2
Bible Christians	3	3	1		1
Methodist New Con-					
nexion	9	4	9	6	
United Methodist Free	8	3	7	2	
Churches					
TOTAL	33		26	13	3

the hope that it would be a means of church union.[128] That was Sir Robert Perks's unstated goal. Methodist union would in part be predicated on a national headquarters and an adequate organizational structure. The allocation of space in the Connexional Buildings could be expected to move Methodism towards organic unity as well as administrative efficiency. So much for Wesleyan Methodism in the opening decade of the century. What of the other Methodist connections? Did businessmen occupy such a central position with them also?

2 BUSINESSMEN IN OTHER METHODIST DENOMINATIONS BEFORE 1914

The dominance of businessmen among the lay leaders of the Wesleyans was a pattern exhibited in the other Methodist sects pre-1914. The point is demonstrated by the occupational evidence about multiple office holders (see Table 8.7). The businessmen who appeared among these denominational leaders reflected a mixture of the geographical strengths and the social composition of the four denominations in question. This section attempts to identify these two dozen businessmen and then to examine their roles in the leaderships of their respective denominations.

Of these Methodist sects the largest was the Primitive Methodists, 200,000-strong and less than half the size of the Wesleyans. Historically they attracted a greater share of the lower classes than did the other Methodist groups. However, the origins of the thirteen lay leaders, as identified by their office holding, are insufficiently clear. For only four

[128] *M. Rec.* 10 Oct. 1912.

of them is father's occupation known, and they were lower middle rather than working class.[129] For nearly half of the thirteen educational backgrounds were noted in the denominational Press. Two went to grammar schools, two were educated privately, and two attended local schools.[130] Perhaps the extent to which the lay leadership of Primitive Methodism had moved from its working-class roots is suggested by the fact that only one of the thirteen was on the side of labour—John Coward, treasurer of the Durham Miners' Federation.[131] However, William McNeill, a travelling draper and town father of Crewe, was long remembered as a progressive Liberal and opponent of the intimidatory tactics of the London & North Western Railway.[132]

Three characteristics of the Primitive laymen echoed the Wesleyan lay leaders in business. Most of them were successful local or regional businessmen. They were civic leaders. And they were much honoured by their denomination. The denominational Press at the turn of the century said little about their business activities or how they made their wealth. Given the classic separation of business and religion this was hardly surprising. Of Alderman Stephen Hilton of Leicester, for example, it was observed that he was 'a successful businessman, but not spoiled by business', and no mention was made of his trade.[133]

The most successful were largely self-made in the sense that they took small inheritances and like good stewards augmented them. Such were Hartley the Liverpool preserves and marmalade manufacturer and Robinson the steam trawler owner of Cleethorpes, Lincolnshire.[134] More were in manufacturing than in distribution. Besides Hartley the jam manufacturer, Joe Brearley was a boot manufacturer of Halifax;[135] Thomas Lawrence, a boot manufacturer of Leicester;[136] and Horace

[129] Two were shopkeepers (the fathers of William Pickles Hartley and Levi Lapper Morse); one was a Nonconformist minister (the father of Edmund Charles Rawlings); and one was a fisherman (the father of Thomas Robinson). See below for sources.

[130] Hartley attended Colne Grammar School; Robinson, Humberstone Grammar School. Morse and Rawlings were educated privately. Joe Brearley went to West Grove Academy, Halifax; Thomas Lawrence, to Great Meeting School, Leicester. Sources below.

[131] *PMM* (1917), 616.

[132] Ibid. (1912), 22; W. H. Chaloner, *The Social and Economic Development of Crewe* (Manchester, 1950), 152, 163–4.

[133] *PMM* (1914), 415.

[134] For Hartley see David J. Jeremy, 'William Pickles Hartley', *DBB*; for Robinson, *PMM* (1914), 632–6; (1924), 41–3.

[135] *WWM 1910*.

[136] *WWM 1910*; *Kelly's Leicester* (1908), courtesy of Local Studies Section, Leicester Reference Library.

Rendel Mansfield, a clay products manufacturer of Spalding, Lincoln-shire.[137] Morse, who started in his father's shop in Swindon, made no attempt to move into manufacturing as Hartley had done. Instead he built up a chain of shops, numbering 20 at his death in 1913, across the South of England including Hastings, Brighton, and Eastbourne. In 1910 he described himself as a merchant rather than a shopkeeper.[138] William Beckworth, a Leeds tanner, was a director of J. Hepworth & Sons Ltd., the Leeds clothing manufacturers headed by Joseph Hepworth of the Methodist New Connexion, and also of Stead & Simpson Ltd., the Leeds tanners and Leicester shoe manufacturers and retailers among whom Wesleyans were prominent.[139] Hilton was both a shoe manufac-turer and retailer, with a chain of six shoe shops in the Leicester area.[140] One 'T. Robinson JP', possibly the Primitive Methodist, was also a direc-tor of the Eagle Insurance Co. and of the National Provincial Bank of England Ltd. in 1907.[141]

Nearly all the thirteen Primitive lay leaders were civic leaders also. Eleven of them were JPs in 1907. Five (Brearley, Linfield, Morse, McNeill, and Rawlings) were aldermen. McNeill, a gritty Scot, five times served as mayor of Crewe. Two, Mansfield and Morse, were MPs, predic-tably both Liberals. While religion and business might be compartmenta-lized, religion and politics intertwined. Mansfield's candidacy for the Spalding seat in 1900 illustrates the point. The denominational paper told its readers, 'We trust that every Primitive Methodist voter in the constituency will consider it a matter of duty on Friday, October 12th, to vote for Mr Mansfield, who is in favour of Religious Equality, Temper-ance Reform, Old Age Pensions, Better Housing of the Working Classes, Reform of the House of Lords, National and Unsectarian Education, Drastic Reform of our Army System, and Electoral Reform.'[142]

Many of these thirteen energetic laymen were honoured by their denomination. Nine of them—Coward, Hartley, Hilton, Lawrence, Lin-field, McNeill, Morse, Rawlings (a London solicitor[143]), and Robinson— had received before 1907 the highest office the denomination could offer,

[137] *PM*, 4, 18 Oct., 13 Dec. 1900; *WWM 1910*.

[138] *PMM* (1897), 563; (1912), 133–7; (1914), 151–2; *Swindon Advertiser*, 12 Sept. 1913; *WWM 1910*.

[139] *DD 1907*; *Kelly's Leeds* (1899), 381, 1024, 1082. Keith Brooker, 'Henry Simpson Gee', *DBB*.

[140] *Kelly's Leicester* (1908), courtesy of Local Studies Section, Leicester Reference Library.

[141] *DD 1907*.

[142] *PM*, 4 Oct. 1900.

[143] *PMM* (1903), 507–8; (1912), 182–7; *WWM 1910*.

that of vice-president of the Primitive Methodist Conference.[144] Quite exceptionally Sir William Hartley was elected president of the Primitive Methodist Conference (an office invariably reserved for ministers), in 1909.

The other three Methodist sects (the Bible Christians, the Methodist New Connexion, and the United Methodist Free Churches), which united in 1907 to form the United Methodist Church, were together less than three-quarters of the size of the Primitive Methodists. Smallest were the Bible Christians, confined largely to the South-West. Their three multiple office holders were George P. Dymond,[145] headmaster of Plymouth Grammar School, W. B. Luke JP of London, and Simon P. Rattenbury JP, a landowner and farmer of Callington, Cornwall.[146]

Only slightly larger than the Bible Christians was the Methodist New Connexion, the strongholds of which were Yorkshire and Lancashire. All of the MNC's nine multiple office holders at a national level were in business, six of them in manufacturing. Most came from the West Riding of Yorkshire. Joseph Hepworth, now retired to Harrogate summers and Torquay winters from his Leeds-based, self-made clothing and retailing empire, had made his mark providing cheap, ready-made clothing for national mass markets.[147] Another household name was that of John Mackintosh, the Halifax toffee manufacturer, again a self-made man, who owed much to his chapel upbringing. In his prime a heart condition limited his activities.[148] Well known in their own city and trades were three edge-tool and cutlery manufacturers from Sheffield. Sir Charles Skelton had started a business making picks, spades, and shovels in the 1850s. By the late 1890s he employed 200 people at his Sheafbank Works, Heeley, Sheffield.[149] William Frederick Jackson's firm, William Jackson & Co., of Sheaf Island Works, Pond Hill, specialized in making steel files, saws, edge tools, scissors, razors, hammers, and similar hand tools.[150] Joseph Ward, another master cutler, of Thomas W. Ward Ltd., was the third denominational leader from Sheffield.[151] George Goodall, son of a Methodist minister, had worked up from apprentice to partner

[144] K. B. Garlick, *Garlick's Methodist Registry* (London, 1983), Appendix 1.
[145] *WWM 1910*.
[146] *WWM 1910*; *BCM* (1907), 562–3; *UMM* (1924), 50–1.
[147] E. J. Connell, 'Joseph Hepworth', *DBB*.
[148] Jeremy, 'Chapel'; *UMM* (1920), 150.
[149] *Sheffield and Rotherham* (London, 1897), 78–80; *Sheffield & District WW* (Sheffield, 1905), 29. These and other sources on Skelton I owe to Dr Geoffrey Tweedale.
[150] *Kelly's Sheffield* (1898), courtesy of Sheffield Public Library, Local Studies Library.
[151] *WWM 1933*.

in the large and famous hosiery business of I. & R. Morley of Nottingham.[152] The others were Alexander Oldfield Stocks, stone merchant of Huddersfield;[153] William Peter Burnley, a Salford metal merchant;[154] and John Graves Watson, valuer, auctioneer, and house agent of Newcastle-upon-Tyne.[155]

With about 80,000 members, and twice the size of the Bible Christians and the New Connexion together, the United Methodist Free Churches were thinly spread across the country. Seven of their eight most active lay leaders were in business but only two of these men had any connection with manufacturing. One was Robert Bird, oil importer, refiner, and chemical manufacturer of Cardiff[156] who was also a director of Locket's Merthyr Collieries (1894) Ltd.[157] The other was James Duckworth of Rochdale, chairman of James Duckworth Ltd., a chain of shops, and a director of Belfield Ltd. and of four subsidiaries of Boots the chemist. The last positions gave him a claim to be engaged in manufacturing.[158] The rest were in the services sector. In London Stephen Gee was a merchant tailor[159] and William Mallinson a timber merchant.[160] Edward Scotchburn Snell was also in business in London.[161] In Liverpool John Harker was a well-known general merchant[162] and Thomas Snape in insurance, as director of the Sceptre Life Association Ltd.; he was also a director of Walkers, Parker & Co. Ltd.[163]

These were the businessmen among the 20 multiple office holders among the three sects who joined in 1907 to form the United Methodist Church. As with the Primitive Methodists, the active lay leaders were also men of substantial civic standing. Nine of them (Luke, Rattenbury, Goodall, Skelton, Stocks, Bird, Duckworth, Mallinson, and Snape) were JPs. Four were aldermen (Skelton, Stocks, Duckworth, and Snape). Two were city councillors, Burnley for Salford, Skelton for Sheffield. Two

---

[152] *Kelly's Nottingham* (1907); Doubleday Index, Local Studies Department, Nottingham County Library; *UMM* (1917), 191–2.

[153] *WWM 1910.*

[154] *Kelly's Manchester* (1906); *UMM* (1911), 415–16; (1923), 375–6.

[155] *Ward's Newcastle-upon-Tyne* (1907–8), courtesy of Newcastle-upon-Tyne City Library.

[156] *UMM* (1924), 140.

[157] *DD 1907.*

[158] Ibid. *1907; UMM* (1915), 75–8.

[159] *WWM 1910.*

[160] Sir W. Mallinson, *A Sketch of My Life* (London, 1936).

[161] *UMM* (1916), 423–5.

[162] *WWM 1910; UMM* (1917), 241–2.

[163] *MM* (1901), 293; W. T. Pike and W. B. Tracy, *Manchester and Salford at the Close of the Nineteenth Century* (Brighton, 1899); *DD 1907.*

(Duckworth and Snape) were Lancashire county councillors. Two were former MPs: Duckworth for Rochdale and Snape for the Heywood Division of SE Lancashire. The kind of political influence some of these men exerted was epitomized by Sir Charles Skelton. A Liberal, Skelton had sat on Sheffield City Council since 1880, concentrating his efforts on the work of the Highway Committee and leading the group responsible for paving Sheffield with granite. He was knighted after Queen Victoria visited Sheffield to open the new Town Hall in 1897. By the 1900s he was regarded as one of the city fathers and a thorn in the side of the Tories. A Tory obituarist recalled, 'He was a modern Puritan. Despite a certain narrowness of outlook and hardness of character always attaching to the type, and emphasised in him, there is no denying that in his private and public life he displayed in eminent degree that strongly marked individuality and those qualities of industry, self-reliance, unselfishness, and serious purpose which are the best inheritance of the race. ... Compromise was not in him.' He supported causes usually associated with the Nonconformist conscience: 'antipathy to militarism and all its influences and works'; an unbending opposition to the liquor interest; and free trade. In addition he was sceptical of the socialistic tendencies of Liberalism and had an 'amusing and rigorous antipathy to smoking'.[164] Skelton was not the only man of principle among these Methodist lay leaders in business. Duckworth, who had started in a cotton mill at the age of $6\frac{1}{2}$, lost his parliamentary seat in 1900 because, it was alleged, he passionately supported a bill to raise the minimum age of the half-timer in the Lancashire cotton industry.[165]

So much for the business and civic backgrounds of the lay leaders of the non-Wesleyan Methodist denominations in 1907, what of their roles in the churches? Many of them, not surprisingly, sat on the central bodies of their denominations. Among the Primitive Methodists twelve of the thirteen sat on the denomination's General Committee. This had responsibility for church properties, external political relations, and relations with the other Methodist bodies.[166] While they did not form a majority on this committee, which had just over 100 members, they doubtless exerted an influence over its business decisions. In the Methodist New Connexion the most senior body was the Annual Committee, 8 ministers and 8 laymen with the duty of ensuring that Conference resolutions were performed and generally conducting the work of the denomination untouched by other Conference committees. In 1907 7 of these laymen were multiple office holders, all of them

[164] *Sheffield Daily Telegraph*, 8 Oct. 1913.   [165] *UMM* (1915), 78
[166] MP, *Minutes* (1906), 125–6.

TABLE 8.8. *Offices held by multiple office holders in non-Wesleyan Methodist churches, 1907*

	Primitive Methodists		United Methodist Free Churches		Methodist New Connexion	
	No.	%	No.	%	No.	%
Chapel building	7	7.86	8	26.60	3	7.89
Charitable funds	19	21.30	1	3.33	7	18.40
Education	17	19.10	5	16.60	1	2.63
Foreign missions	10	11.20	3	10.00	3	7.89
Home missions	14	15.70			2	5.26
Internal organization	12	13.40	3	10.00	20	52.60
Theological education	10	11.20	10	33.30	2	5.26
TOTAL POSITIONS	89	100.00	30	100.00	38	100.00
TOTAL OFFICE HOLDERS	13		8		9	

businessmen (Burnley, Goodall, Hepworth, Skelton, Stocks, Ward, and Watson). Another body in the New Connexion, the Guardian Representatives, 12 ministers and 12 laymen, had a legal rather than an ecclesiastical function. Permanent members of the Connexion's Conference, they ensured the Connexion's legal existence and stood ready to guarantee it in any legal dispute.[167] In 1906–7 half the lay Guardian Representatives were multiple office holders, all of them businessmen: Burnley, Goodall, Hepworth, Skelton, Stocks, and Watson. Among the United Methodist Free Churches the central body was the Connexional Committee, comprising 36 individuals, 15 of them laymen. Only 4 of these laymen were multiple office holders but all 4 were in business: Bird, Gee, Harker, and Snape. The Connexional Committee of the Bible Christians, about 30-strong, included Dymond, Luke, and Rattenbury, the denomination's lay 'workhorses' though not much of a businessmen's contingent. In short multiple office holders and businessmen were present in the highest councils of the non-Wesleyan Methodist bodies. In the New Connexion these super-energetic men of business monopolized the lay leadership.

The analysis can be pressed further into the denominations' specialist national sub-committees. The office holding of the 30 multiple office holders in the three largest of the non-Wesleyan denominations, the Primitives, the New Connexion, and the United Free Methodists (Table 8.8), shows marked variations between them. Among the Primitive Methodists the most active laymen directed their efforts primarily into charitable funds, education, and home missions: appropriate channels for a denomination that recruited mainly from the working classes. The United Methodist Free Churches likewise seem to have used their leading laymen rationally: spread

[167] MNC, *General Rules* (London, 1889), appendix.

thinly they used their best lay resources especially in the directions of chapel building and theological education, the latter consisting mostly of committees in support of the Deaconess Institute. The New Connexion picture is distorted in favour of internal organization by the Representative Guardians and an *ad hoc* committee set up to negotiate union with the Bible Christians and the United Methodist Free Churches. Without them charitable funds would have had the greatest proportionate call on the time of the most energetic laymen.

Glimpses of the roles assumed by individual businessmen and prominent laymen in the leaderships of these Methodist denominations help to fill in the quantitative picture. Some predictably assumed duties associated with the financial functioning of their denomination. Brearley and Amos Chippindale (a multiple office holder of unidentified occupation) were honorary auditors of the Primitive Methodists,[168] Bird treasurer of the United Methodists.[169] Hartley was treasurer of the Primitive Methodist Missionary Society for three decades, starting in 1890. He was no uncritical fund-raiser, however. In 1917 he sharply criticized missionaries for running persistently unprofitable farms on Fernando Po and staggered the PMMS secretary, the Reverend Samuel Horton, by withdrawing the offer of a gift of £1,250 for the Africa Fund.[170]

Others identified with property and chapel building. Again Hartley was an outstanding example. For the Primitive Methodists he organized a Chapel Aid Association in the mid-1880s to mobilize loans for chapel building. On his own initiative, in 1907–8, he purchased Holborn Town Hall, at the junction of Clerkenwell and Gray's Inn Roads, London (which had then come on to the market); he enlarged and refurbished it and then sold it back at £31,000, two-thirds of the cost price, to the Primitive Methodist Church for its national headquarters and publishing house. His own contribution to the scheme was £17,500.[171]

In the New Connexion members of the Chapel Committee (including several businessmen like Jackson, Mackintosh, and Stocks) were trustees of connectional properties (which totalled 290 estates in 1888), indemnified against personal loss (in case of loss or damage by fire to any of the estates) to the extent of £200 each.[172] Interestingly, John Coward, of the Durham Miners' Federation, was the long-serving chairman of the Primitive Meth-

---

[168] *WWM 1910.*

[169] UMFC, *Minutes* (1907), 76.

[170] SOAS, MMS, Primitive MMS collection, Home correspondence Box 1148, Sir William P. Hartley file 1913–18, Hartley to Horton, 23 Aug. 1916, 20 Apr., 6 June 1917.

[171] A. S. Peake, *The Life of Sir William Hartley* (London, 1926), 117–29.

[172] MNC, *General Rules*, 116.

odist Insurance Co. Ltd. which was responsible for insuring the Primitives' 4,413 (in 1905) chapels. In 1906 the company had a reserve fund of £33,925 and currently underwrote 5,860 policies.[173]

Edmund Rawlings, a London solicitor, served the Primitives and the rest of Nonconformity by compiling a handbook on their legal rights: *The Free Churchman's Legal Handbook: Including a Summary of Laws Particularly Relating to Social Questions* (London, 1902). His obituarist observed,

As Connexional solicitors, and also solicitors for the National Free Church Council, the firm [Rawlings & Butt, later Rawlings, Butt & Bowyer of Walbrook EC and Hammersmith] has rendered magnificent service to the cause of Nonconformity, while the works our friend wrote on education and legal questions have been widely read, and have given guidance and help to hundreds of Free Church ministers. Dr F. B. Meyer, and other leaders, have borne splendid testimony to the value of his service as a member of the National Executive [of the NFCC], and his deep interest in all questions affecting the life and work of the Free Churches.[174]

Some, sharply conscious of their own educational deprivations, took a special interest in the theological training of ministers. William P. Hartley recruited Arthur Samuel Peake, Oxford don and one of the first 'modern' biblical scholars to emerge from Primitive Methodism, to the denomination's college at Manchester in 1892. He was responsible for extensions to the college's buildings in 1897 and 1906, the first costing £12,500, the second £20,000, much of these sums coming from Hartley's own pocket. Eventually the college bore his name.[175] For the United Methodist Free Churches Alderman James Duckworth of Rochdale was the leading campaigner for the denomination's theological college, also in Manchester. For many years it had sunk in debt. When in 1894 Duckworth was elected president of the United Methodists, a rare distinction, he resolved to raise £20,000 for an endowment fund for the college. He gave £3,000 himself for a new wing to the building and threw himself into money-raising. By 1898 his objective was reached.[176]

Others were generous benefactors and fund-raisers for almost any denominational cause. Among the Primitive Methodists Sir Robert Perks's counterpart was Sir William Hartley. Hartley, deeply influenced after his conversion by the current teaching on the Christian stewardship

[173] MP, *Minutes* (1906), 124, 164; *PMM* (1917), 617.   [174] *PMM* (1918), 94.
[175] Peake, *Hartley*, 130–53; *British Monthly* (June 1902), 321.
[176] *UMM* (1915), 77.

of wealth,[177] started in 1877 by giving away a tenth of his income, increasing this to a third as he prospered. By the end of his life his recorded gifts amounted to nearly £300,000 of which £230,000 went to causes serving the whole community rather than Primitive Methodism. His denomination received 'princely gifts' in all directions: foreign missions, London churches, rural chapels, ministerial education, and national headquarters. To the missionary Jubilee Fund in 1892 he gave £5,000 and then addressed meetings all over the country to promote the fund's £50,000 target; to the Centenary Fund, 1907–10, of which he was treasurer (which raised over £300,000), he gave £15,000; and so on.[178] Others were also generous, if not quite on Hartley's scale. Robinson, later Sir Thomas Robinson, the Grimsby trawler magnate, also made donations to the various funds of the Primitive Methodists, of which there seemed to be a conjunction of five or six national one-off efforts between 1890 and 1910.[179] In the New Connexion Joseph Hepworth and John Mackintosh were well-known benefactors, though details of their gifts were less publicized than Hartley's.[180] Among the United Methodist Free Churches James Duckworth was a prominent benefactor. Many of these men—Hartley, Mackintosh, Duckworth, Joseph Ward of Sheffield, to name only those who can be documented in biographies and obituaries—practised systematic and proportionate giving. That is, they regularly set aside fixed proportions of their gross incomes and gave these away to various religious and charitable causes. Like Mackintosh they usually gave limited proportions to any one fund, hoping to stimulate the generosity of a multitude of much less wealthy individuals. Their aim was to preserve their denominations and local churches from a destructive dependence on rich men. [181] It may be noted that a number prided themselves on creating their wealth with the aid of profit-sharing schemes. Among these were Hartley, Burnley, and Ward.[182]

Some of these laymen were valued for their wisdom as much as their wealth. Of Duckworth it was recorded,

In the counsels of Free Methodism, Sir James filled an influential place. His business genius, sound judgment, administrative gifts, and Connexional loyalty commanded the confidence and respect of all his brethren. No Annual Assembly

---

[177] For which see J. Garnett, '"Gold and the Gospel"', in W. J. Sheils and D. Wood (eds.), *The Church and Wealth* (Oxford, 1987).

[178] For the fullest details see Peake, *Hartley*.

[179] *PMM* (1924), 42.

[180] *UMM* (1911), 569; Jeremy, 'Chapel'.

[181] Jeremy, 'Chapel', 112.

[182] Peake, *Hartley*, 66–74; *UMM* (1914), 415; *PMM* (1921), 93.

seemed complete without him. Important Connexional issues were often guided to a satisfactory settlement by his tactful and judicious intervention. Many of our Departments bear today the marks of his practical wisdom and constructive genius[183]

All national leaders devoted much energy to local scenes. If they could not preach, as Hartley and Robinson could not, they taught in the Sunday School, led a Class Meeting, or served as trustees or stewards. Hartley played the organ. A man like William McNeill of Crewe, with relatively meagre sources of wealth, was held up for his personal qualities: 'How he has worked! How he has stuck!! How he has given!!! Trustee, Local Preacher, Society Steward, Circuit Steward, Sunday School Teacher and Superintendent—everything he has been and everything with all his heart.'[184] Of Levi Morse it was reported, 'He would not admit more than a share, of course, in it, but the progress of our [Primitive Methodist] cause in Swindon since he came to it has been remarkable. Seven new chapels have been built, the accommodation of two has been increased, and £5,000 spent on new Sunday Schools. The Quarterly Meeting revenue has been more than trebled. It is a great thing in any town when we have a stalwart for a leader.'[185] Such men served as figureheads on local public occasions, uniting in their persons economic power, civic influence, denominational stature, and personal piety. Sir Charles Skelton, among the Free Churches of Sheffield, was a favoured bazaar opener and a natural ornament on the platform of every big temperance meeting.[186]

In using an objective criterion like multiple office holding to identify lay leaders and hence businessmen in the denominations, it is apparent that various influential individuals will have escaped notice. Without exploring their roles, it is worth noticing that the cohorts of non-Wesleyan Methodist lay leaders of 1907 included a number who were prominent in business. Among the Primitive Methodists there was Moses Bourne, secretary of the Moira Colliery Co., the Donisthorpe Colliery Co., and the Donington Sanitary Pipe & Fire Brick Co., whose passion for preaching took him all over the North of England, frequently requiring him to 'travel all Sunday night so as to be at business on Monday morning'.[187] Sir George Green (knighted in 1911 for his services as chairman of the Scottish Liberal Association) was manager for Scotland of the Prudential

---

[183] *UMM* (1915), 77.
[184] *PMM* (1912), 20.
[185] Ibid. (1912), 137.
[186] *Sheffield Daily Independent*, 8 Oct. 1913.
[187] *PMM* (1912), 552.

Assurance Co., having worked his way up from salesman.[188] In the United Methodist Free Churches the most powerful businessman, but one who was reticent about both his benefactions and his Christian experience, was Sir Christopher Furness (later Baron Furness of Grantley). A self-made entrepreneur in shipping, coal, iron, and steel based at West Hartlepool on Teesside, he left £1.8 million when he died in middle age in 1912.[189] He held only one denominational office in 1907, trustee of the Deaconess Institute, but was a lifetime member and later secretary to the trustees of what after 1907 was the United Methodist Church, Burbank Street, West Hartlepool.[190]

3 METHODIST BUSINESSMEN IN THE 1930S AND 1950S

As the number of Methodists declined in the twentieth century, so did national opportunities for Methodist lay people. Between the 1930s and the 1950s the ratio of national committee posts to church members rose from 1:531 to 1:635.[191] Whether the laity lost representation to the clergy is presently unknown. Apparently lay women increased their representation. What is certain is that individual laymen, especially those in business, still wielded appreciable power in the church. Before turning to individual cases, however, the aggregate framework in which they operated needs outlining.

The first point to be made is that although opportunities for laymen were diminishing, lay representation was becoming much more democratic. This is suggested in Table 8.9. By the measure of concentration used in these chapters (the holding of five or more national offices), concentration of office holding fell by stages from 31 per cent in 1907 to 21 per cent in the mid-1930s and 13 per cent in the mid-1950s. Likewise the spread of concentration was shrinking, with no one holding as many as ten (or more) offices in 1955, compared to four in 1935 and eight among the Wesleyans in 1907. The table shows in retrospect just how powerful Sir Robert Perks, holder of fifteen offices in 1907, had become. Whether the trend was deliberate on the part of Methodism's policy-makers, whether it was the result of structural rationalization, or whether

---

[188] Ibid. (1913), 113–18; (1916), 712–13.
[189] Gordon Boyce, 'Christopher Furness', *DBB*.
[190] *UMM* (1913), 3–4.   [191] Table 1.7.

TABLE 8.9. *Concentrations of multiple office holders (lay and national) in Methodism, 1907, 1935, 1955*

No. of posts	1907 Wesleyans			1935 Methodists			1955 Methodists		
	No. of holders	Share of total posts	%	No. of holders	Share of total posts	%	No. of holders	Share of total posts	%
Up to 4		1,148	69		1,135	79		942	88
5	30	150	9	13	65	5	13	65	6
6	9	54	3	10	60	4	3	18	2
7	19	133	8	8	56	2	3	21	2
8	5	40	2	3	24	3	3	24	2
9	5	45	3	4	36	3	1	9	1
10	1	10	1	3	30	2			
11				1	11	1			
12	3	36	2						
13	2	26	2	1	13	1			
14	1	14	1						
15	1	15	1						
Total 5–15	76	523	31	43	295	21	23	137	13
TOTAL		1,671	100		1,430	100		1,079	100

Source: Data abstracted from annual *Conference Minutes.*

it was involuntary and the result of lay and business people having less time to spare is unclear.

Between the 1930s and the 1950s the number of lay people on national Methodist Church committees fell from 1,430 to 1,079. Had representation remained at its 1930s level the laity would have filled 1,290 posts in the 1950s. Therefore the loss of 75,000 members in twenty years statistically seems to have had a modest impact on the national representation of the laity. The disappearance of over 200 national posts has to be accounted for by other factors. One would be readjustments to Methodist Union in 1932.[192] The retirements and deaths of the lay leaders of the former Wesleyan, Primitive and United Methodist Churches evidently left unfilled gaps. Presumably too the Second World War created opportunities for slimming structures. One or two departments merged between the 1930s and the 1950s, such as the Sunday School Department which went into the new Youth Department. Another explanation, suggesting that the statistical picture is slightly illusory, is that the compilers of the *Conference Minutes* had ceased by the 1950s to list committee members of the National Children's Homes or the theological colleges. This presumably signified attempts to erase the local loyalties of divided Methodism.

Among lay leaders of the denomination, businessmen continued to predominate in the 1930s when they comprised 77 per cent of the church's 'workhorses'. However, as Table 8.10 shows, by the 1950s this proportion had dropped to under 50 per cent. Likewise falling was the number in manufacturing. Who were these businessmen and what parts did they play in the leadership of the Methodist Church?

The big difference between the 1930s and the 1950s was quantitative. Many more businessmen participated in the decision-making bodies of Methodism in the 1930s than later. In both periods the multiple office holders included men who sat on the boards or managed large national companies, though none employed sufficient to be included in the business élites identified in the first section of this study. Among the manufacturers of the inter-war cohort were J. Arthur Rank, still in the shadow of his father but moving from flour milling to films; the ageing John Esdon Henderson of John Mackintosh & Sons Ltd.;[193] and Sir Charles Hayward Bird, also ageing, of Cardiff and director of several firms in petroleum refining and chemicals including National Benzole Co.[194]

[192] For a substantial introduction to the structures of modern Methodism see G. T. Brake, *Policy and Politics in British Methodism 1932–1982* (London, 1984).

[193] Jeremy, 'Chapel', 101.

[194] *WWW*; *DD 1935*.

TABLE 8.10. *Occupations of Methodist laity holding five or more committee posts at a national level, 1907, 1935, 1955*

| | 1907 | | | | 1935 | | 1955 | |
| | Wesleyans | | All[a] | | | | | |
	No.	%	No.	%	No.[b]	%	No.[b]	%
Number of multiple office holders	76	100	109	100	43	100	23	100
Number in business (active or retired)	52	68	71	65	33	77	11	48
Number in manufacturing	29	38	42	39	11	26	4	17
Occupation unknown	2	3	6	6	5	12		
Females							5	22

[a] All Methodist denominations; Wesleyan, Primitive (holders of 5 offices at least), Methodist New Connexion (holders of 4 offices at least), United Methodist Free Churches, Bible Christians (holders of at least 3 offices).
[b] Full-time in business or company director.

Another from pre-1914 Methodism was Joseph Ward whose nine direc-torships spread across quarries, cement, coal, steel and iron, and Milford Haven Dock & Railway Co.; in 1933 he was chairman and managing director of Thomas W. Ward Ltd., steelmakers of Sheffield.[195] Sir Tho-mas Rowbotham, self-made businessman, was chairman of several Stockport engineering, metal merchanting, and tobacco firms.[196] In tex-tiles there were lesser lights among the 'workhorses'. George F. Byrom was a cotton manufacturer living at Hyde while Alexander Barlow Hillis had some connection with Abraham Barlow Ltd., bleachers and finishers of Bury.[197] John G. Withinshaw of Warrington sat on the boards of ten companies, most in the tanning industry.[198] One who followed family in both business and religion was William J. Mallinson, whose father's firm was prominent in the East End timber trade.[199] In the paper and publishing industry John Crowlesmith sat on the boards of four firms including Hazell, Watson & Viney Ltd. and the University of London Press.[200] Towering above these businessmen, if directorships are a proper criterion, was Leslie William Farrow. Still in his forties and little known outside industry, he was one of the new breed of professional managers. From the LSE he had gone into accountancy becoming a partner in Sissons, Bersey, Gain, Vincent & Co., not a well-known firm. By 1935 he was director of 20 companies, most in the paper industry, chairman of four and deputy-chairman of Wiggins, Teape & Co. (1919). In addition he was a director of Great Universal Stores, then on its upward trajectory, and of Royal Exchange Assurance, one of the oldest and most prestigious firms in insurance.[201]

Methodist lay leaders in services in 1935 included the two Holloways, Herbert John and Roland, who succeeded their father, Sir Henry Holloway (and numerous uncles and cousins), in the family firm of London builders and contractors, and their father into the offices of Methodism.[202] George (later Sir George) Knight was a retired draper and silk mercer (as he described himself in the denominational direc-tory).[203] Also in distribution were Harold William Payne, a South Africa

[195] *DD 1935; WWM 1933.*

[196] *WWW; DD 1935; WWM 1933.*

[197] *WWM 1933. DD 1955; Manchester Chamber of Commerce Official Handbook, 1935* (Manchester, *1935*), 112.

[198] *DD 1935; WWM 1933.*

[199] Geoffrey Tweedale, 'William James Mallinson', *DBB.*

[200] *DD 1935; WWM 1933.*

[201] *DD 1935; WWM 1933.*

[202] Rolt, *Holloways.*

[203] *WWW; WWM 1933.*

merchant; James E. Le Huray, a Salford metal merchant;[204] Robert Parkinson Tomlinson, a Poulton-le-Fylde corn merchant;[205] and Charles Wass, a Birkenhead coal merchant.[206] Two, Edmund S. Lamplough and William Samuel Welch, were Lloyd's underwriters and insurance brokers.[207] Best known to the general public in this group of multiple office holders were Sir Harold Bellman, managing director of the Abbey Road Building Society and leading promoter of private house owner-ship,[208] and Sir Henry Lunn, formerly a medical missionary whose pro-motion of international ecumenical conferences took him into travel clubs and the tourist business.[209] How does this group, so heavily weighted towards business, compare to the 1950s Methodist lay leaders?

Fewer in number, the 1950s activists included a smaller proportion of business people, and a much diminished share of manufacturers. They were also smaller in business stature. Only two of the eleven 'workhorses' belonged to large firms. One was William J. England, Assistant Superin-tendent of Operation on the Southern Railway in 1938–9 and Superin-tendent during the war, who had retired by the mid-1950s.[210] The other was Harold W. Danbury, a director of the Carreras Ltd., tobacco manu-facturers.[211] John A. Stead was a Sheffield razor blade manufacturer.[212] Alexander B. Hillis was now a director of A. Barlow & Sons. Richard George Burnett edited the denominational newspaper, the *Methodist Recorder*.[213] The rest came from the financial services sector or professions closely related to business: G. Ronald Birkinshaw, manager of the Willes-den Junction branch of the Midland Bank;[214] C. H. Wicks, manager of the head office of the Bank of Belgium in London[215]; E. Geoffrey Deale, manager of the Methodist Insurance Co. in Manchester;[216] David A. Solomon, a Liverpool stockbroker, later knighted;[217] Claude B. Fytche

[204] *DD 1935*; *WWM 1933*.

[205] *WWM 1933*.

[206] Ibid.; *Kelly's Liverpool* (1930).

[207] *WWM 1933*.

[208] Esmond J. Cleary, 'Charles Harold Bellman', *DBB*.

[209] *WWW*; Lunn, *Nearing Harbour*.

[210] *Directory of Railway Officials & Year Book* (1938–9, 1943–4, 1953–4); *WWFC 1951*.

[211] *DD 1955*.

[212] Letter to author from Mr Albert Law of Helmsley, York, 29 Mar. 1988.

[213] *WWFC 1951*.

[214] Letter to author from Dr Cyril J. Bennett, 24 June 1988; information from Edwin Green, Midland Bank Archivist, 2 Feb. 1989.

[215] Letter to author from Laurence S. Porter of Brentwood, Essex, 4 Apr. 1988.

[216] Letter to author from the Revd Edward Rogers, 10 June 1987.

[217] *WW 1980*.

and Stephen Weaver, accountants at Central Buildings, Westminster, Fytche in the Methodist Division of Finance, Weaver in the Central Hall. Fytche, a chartered accountant, appears to have had his own firm.[218] The rest of the 23 Methodist multiple office holders of 1955 were either professionals, housewives, or employees of Methodist institutions, like Alan A. Jacka of the National Children's Homes or Miss Hilda Porter, a former missionary to China who in 1950 founded the first Methodist International House.[219] Clearly managers were succeeding owners and the dominance of entrepreneurs, large or small, among Methodism's most active lay leaders was over.

This is not the whole picture, however. The rigidity of the multiple office criterion fails to catch a number of individuals whose Methodist offices were few but whose informal influence was very substantial indeed, in both church and business counsels. The identity of most of these people is captured in the lists of treasurers of major church funds (see Table 8.11). Here the most prominent figures straddling the boundary between church and business are to be found. One evident feature is that families, most in business, have persisted across two or more generations of lay leadership in Methodism: the Barlows, Holloways, Mackintoshes, Perkses, Ranks. For them social mobility and secular success has gone hand-in-hand with service to their church. A second impression from this table is that only the mighty in business in the 1930s, in business or the professions in the 1950s, could attain the office of treasurer to a connectional fund. The feature is, perhaps, not surprising. Treasurers generally are appointed in voluntary organizations not because they are good at bookkeeping, though that may be a consideration, but because they are good at raising money. Some may come from their own pockets. More would derive from the treasurer's friends and admirers and a wider public who would have reason to trust both the cause and the management of their donations because of the treasurer's private and public reputation. If these assumptions are correct it is plain that the most influential public men of Methodism in the 1930s are gravitating towards two funds in particular: Home Missions and the National Children's Home. The former could boast of J. Arthur Rank, the latter of Sir Josiah Stamp (see Chapter 5). In the 1950s Home Missions again claimed Rank, now better known as film magnate than flour miller (though he was both), and Lord Mackintosh of Halifax whose mother had invented the toffee on which his father had built the business and fortune that

---

[218] Information from the Revd and Mrs George Thompson Brake, 18 May 1987.
[219] Her work was celebrated in the *M. Rec* 14 May 1987.

TABLE 8.11. *Lay treasurers of major Methodist national funds, 1935, 1955*

Fund	1935 Lay treasurer	Occupation	1955 Lay treasurer	Occupation
General Purposes	Leslie William Farrow	company director	Harry W. Danbury	company director
Overseas Missions	Miss Margaret E. Byrom	daughter of cotton mfr.	F. Johnston Carey	Civil Servant
	James H. Morton	chartered accountant	John Rolfe Treadgold	provision merchant
	John G. Stirk	engineer	Mrs Russell W. Shearer	minister's wife
Ministers' Children	Herbert J. Holloway	builder and contractor	Sir Arthur L. Dixon	Civil Servant
			C. H. Wicks	bank manager
General Chapel Fund	William R. Hesketh	cotton goods merchant	David A. Solomon	stockbroker
	Alexander B. Hillis	textile bleacher and finisher	C. Soutter Smith	solicitor
Home Mission	J. Arthur Rank	flour miller	J. Arthur Rank	film and flour cos. director
	William J. Mallinson	timber merchant	Lord Mackintosh	confectionery co. chairman
London Mission	Sir R. Malcolm Perks Bt.	engineer and contractor	Charles W. Hodgson	surveyor
	Charles W. Hodgson	surveyor	Herbert J. Holloway	builder and contractor
Auxiliary Fund	Harold Hartley	professional accountant	Claude B. Fytche	chartered accountant
	William H. Slack	company managing director		
General Sustentation	John Crowlesmith	director of printing and publishing cos.	H. Raymond Tebb	chartered accountant
		stockbroker		
Ministerial Training	Lawrence Crowther	confectionery mfr.	unidentified	
	Richard Solomon	brick and hollow tile mfr.		
	William Fenton Higgins	?		
	George Parker	company director		
	Sir George W. Martin	iron and steel merchant		
	Robert Shillito Dower	builder and builders' merchant		
	Thomas Lee Gerrard	solicitor?		
		?		
	Herbert Crowther	paint and varnish mfr.		
	Rowland W. Scurrah	physical chemistry professor, Cambridge		
	George Frederick Morley			
	Prof. Thomas Martin Lowry			
Education	unidentified		unidentified	
Sunday School	Alfred John Clayton	corn miller and merchant	department merged under Youth Department	
	Fred Ogden	estate agent		

TABLE 8.11. *cont.*

Fund	1935 Lay treasurer	Occupation	1955 Lay treasurer	Occupation
Young Methodism	Herbert Barraclough	jeweller	Harold Guylee Chester	Lloyd's underwriter
National Children's Home	William Patterson	factory cashier	A. Leslie Wade unidentified	estate agent
	Sir Thomas Barlow	consulting physician		
	Sir Harold Bellman	building society director		
	Sir Josiah Stamp	railway company chairman		
	Miss Barlow	daughter of cotton mfr.		
	Frederick W. Rushbrooke	director, cycle shop chain		
	Charles T. Avery	auctioneer and estate agent		
	Roy Posnett	farmer?		
	John Gibson Withinshaw	tanner		
	Thomas Brewster Hunter	?		
	George R. Woodcock	provision and grocery merchant		
	Arthur Holgate	animal foodstuffs mfr. and merchant		
	James Herbert Pyle	baker and confectioner		
	Charles William Hobbs	gas company secretary		
	J. W. Callow	builder?		
Local Preachers	George Knight	draper and silk mercer	J. H. Charles Miller	?
Wesley Deaconess Order	William Arthur Lupton	solicitor	unnamed	
	Joseph Ward	steel mfr.		
Temperance and Social Welfare/Christian Citizenship	Isaac Foot	MP and solicitor	Isaac Foot	PC, solicitor
	Herbert Hawthorne	tile mfr.	George E. Garfoot	?

Sources: Annual *Conference Minutes* and miscellaneous biographical sources.

TABLE 8.12. *Directions of interest of Methodist multiple office holders at a national level, 1907, 1935, 1955*

	1907[a]		1935		1955	
	No.	%	No.	%	No.	%
Chapel building	41	8	13	4	6	4
Charitable funds	28	5	31	10	19	14
Education, youth work	70	13	21	7	15	11
External relations	65	12	22	7	23	17
Faith, doctrine			15	5	1	1
Foreign missions	27	5	12	4	11	8
Home missions	146	28	43	14	23	17
Internal organization	92	18	83	28	27	20
Theological education	54	10	55	18	12	9
TOTAL	523	100	295	100	137	100

[a] Wesleyans.

Source: Data abstracted from annual *Conference Minutes*.

Lord Mackintosh and his brothers had inherited and enlarged.[220] It is plain too that these men were generous towards the funds they stewarded, though in few cases are their donations known. Thus Frederick Rushbrooke, who built up the Halford Cycle Co. Ltd. from a Birmingham hardware store in the early 1890s to a national retail chain with over 200 branches in the mid-1930s, took a special interest in the National Children's Home.[221]

If prominent businessmen in Methodism are sought, there are still others. In the 1930s Lords Rochester and Runciman, honoured and renowned for their political careers rather than their business success, were two examples. Each held four national committee posts in Methodism in 1935. Ernest Henry Lamb, Baron Rochester, capped his parliamentary career as Paymaster General in Ramsay MacDonald's National Government, 1931–5. In business he had added a telephone network (before the Post Office took it over in 1912) to the family firm of Lamb Sons & Co., transport contractors.[222] The Rt Hon. Walter Runciman, President of the Board of Trade 1931–7, created Viscount Runciman of Doxford in 1937, had effectively left the family shipping business for a career in politics thirty years earlier.

So much for the characteristics and identities of the lay leaders of Methodism in the 1930s and 1950s. What parts did they play in national church life? An aggregated summary of the multiple office holders'

[220] David J. Jeremy, 'Harold Vincent Mackintosh', *DBB*; Lord Mackintosh, *By Faith and Work* (London, 1966).

[221] Alan C. McKinnon, 'Frederick William Rushbrooke', *DBB*.

[222] *The Times*, 14 Jan. 1955.

activities is shown in Table 8.12. The main points can be summarized quickly. Steadily gaining over the period 1907–55 were charitable funds, losing somewhat was chapel building. In the twenty years 1935–55 the areas gaining the interest of more active lay people were education and youth work, external relations, overseas missions, and home missions; areas losing their interest were doctrine, internal organization, and theological education. As has already been explained, there may be some statistical illusion in these figures because the official church listings ceased by the mid-1950s to identify regional committees for theological colleges and the National Children's Home. While it is tempting to relate these statistics to the general picture of a church in membership decline, in theological upheaval over the question of inter-church relations, and in structural readjustment, no such connection should be made without a much closer examination of year-by-year developments in Methodism, a task beyond the remit of this book. What can be noted is that the distribution of active lay people's interests in 1955 very closely accorded with their distribution in 1907, except that there was a greater lay involvement in external relations and rather less in home missions in 1955. Since Wesleyans lived in an age of Victorian *laissez-faire* capitalism and their mid-twentieth-century successors in the early days of the Welfare State and of managerial capitalism, a superficial reading of the evidence suggests that the lay resources of Methodism were being redirected in quantities appropriate to social circumstances.

While these active lay people kept numerous key denominational committees running, and treasurers stewarded the denominational funds in their charge—many of the individuals concerned coming from the business world—there were several other areas in which lay leaders played a significant part. Laymen in business frequently ornamented the platforms of public denominational meetings. The *Methodist Recorder* for 1934 shows them cropping up time and again. Lord Marshall (J. Arthur Rank's father-in-law), the Duke of Gloucester, and Lord Rochester took part in the opening of the Reverend J. Butterworth's Clubland Church on the Camberwell Road.[223] Lord Wakefield (from the 1907 generation of multiple office holders) was present at the annual meeting of the National Children's Home.[224] At the church's departmental meetings in May J. Arthur Rank spoke at the Home Mission meeting, Sir Josiah Stamp at the Bible Society meeting. Lord Marshall chaired the Seamen's Mission annual meeting.[225] Sir Thomas Rowbotham presided over a

[223] *M. Rec* 29 Mar. 1934.   [224] Ibid. 26 Apr. 1934.   [225] Ibid. 3, 10 May 1934.

Local Preachers' Mutual Aid Association meeting at Stockport in June.[226]
At the anniversary meetings of Tooting Central Hall J. Arthur Rank
took the chair and his father Joseph Rank, still vigorous despite his age,
addressed the meeting.[227] At the opening of Archway Hall, Highgate,
Joseph Rank (a leading promoter of central halls) was present at every
meeting, spoke of his conversion and subsequent Christian experience,
and then confessed that as treasurer of a mission hall he had been 'too
parsimonious', but warned his hearers, 'In this Mission you must study
economy. It is easy to spend money, and not so easy to get hold of
it.'[228] Another present was Charles W. Early the Witney blanket maker.
The *Methodist Recorder* began the year with an interview with Sir Josiah
Stamp, 'A Great Economist on New Year Prospects';[229] it ended it with
an interview with the Rt. Hon. Walter Runciman, 'A Cabinet Minister's
Message of Good Cheer'.[230] In contrast, by the 1950s the laity claimed
much less attention in the pages of the *Methodist Recorder*. This was
evidently an effect of their reduced role. Even in the 1930s laymen in
the Representative Session of Conference played a much less prominent
role than their forebears in the Conferences of the various Methodist
connections of 1907. It was not simply a matter of editorial reporting
as a close reading of denominational newspapers shows. In part it was
certainly due to the relative ascendancy of the clergy in Methodism.
In part it reflected the passing of the heroic individualists of the early
twentieth century. Giants had left the earth.

These prominent business figures of the 1930s were not just platform
ornaments. Sir Josiah Stamp chaired the Finance Board which oversaw
the fusion of a variety of national and local funds following the union
of Wesleyan, Primitive, and United Methodists in 1932. A summary
of Methodist property and finance is in Table 8.13. The main points
are the relative strength of the Wesleyans (both in total property values
and in relative size of debt burdens) and the complexity of the task
of merging or disposing of so many different properties, funds, and trusts.
Stamp, Leslie Farrow, and William Arthur Sturdy, a Civil Servant and
auditor of the Indian Home Accounts,[231] had five years from union to
effect a complete merger of financial systems. As part of that process
Stamp devised a survey of circuit finances whose returns were coming

---

[226] Ibid. 28 June 1934. [227] Ibid. 15 Nov. 1934.
[228] Ibid. 22 Nov. 1934. [229] Ibid. 4 Jan. 1934.
[230] Ibid. 27 Dec. 1934.
[231] *WWM 1933*; W. A. Sturdy, *Methodist Finance* (London, 1932).

TABLE 8.13. *Methodist property, 1932*

	Wesleyan Methodists		United Methodists		Primitive Methodists		Totals	
	£	No.	£	No.	£	No.	£	No.
Property								
Pre-1914 values	25,000,000		4,350,000		7,400,263		36,750,263	
1932 values	50,000,000		8,700,000		14,800,526		73,500,526	
Trusts								
Chapel trusts		8,620		2,231		4,334		15,185
Manse trusts		871				643		
Total trusts		9,491		2,231		4,977		16,699
Total trust income	1,279,795		297,169		584,845		2,161,809	
Debt	1,043,028		419,083		742,251			
Property value/debt	47.94		20.76		19.94			

Source: Minutes of the Uniting Conference of the Methodist Church, 1932, 202–3.

back in 1935.[232] For one who had organized the pioneering legal and financial integration of dozens of subsidiaries in Nobel Industries, the Methodist task must have come as a challenge of the same order.

Businessmen were of course great benefactors. This has been seen time and again in the previous sections of this chapter. For example, Charles Wass, the Birkenhead coal merchant and vice-president of the Primitive Methodist Conference in 1930, was reported as 'not only generous, but stupidly generous, and the community at large see to it that he has a full opportunity to exercise his gifts'.[233] Probably the greatest benefactors of twentieth-century Methodism were members of the Rank family. J. Arthur Rank's gifts have not been publicized but his father's major donations to Methodism have been recorded. Since the days of his early success as a flour miller, in the 1890s, Joseph Rank had given a 'high percentage of his personal profits to religious and philanthropic works'.[234] By 1933 his firm had net assets of £5,029,364 and pre-tax profits of £824,128.[235] It might be argued that he was in a position to give large sums away. So were many more who did not. Between 1921 and his death in 1943 his recorded gifts to various Methodist organizations amounted to over £3.5 million. The largest sums went to the Chapel Office (£633,575), the Wesleyan/Methodist Missionary Society (£1,135,687 in cash, £1,275,688 in Ranks Ltd. and gilt edged shares) and the Joseph Rank Benevolent Fund he set up in the 1930s (£300,000). He might be criticized for neglecting secular humanitarian causes (his largest gift in this direction appears to have been £60,000 to the Hull Royal Infirmary). However, the full extent of his benefactions is unknown, and were they known any assessment would depend on how one regards and estimates the social benefits of Methodism.[236]

The collective strength of laymen and businessmen may have diminished between the 1900s and the 1950s but in certain directions a few individual businessmen continued to exercise considerable influence. Their views, from their positions of conservatism or realism, sometimes set them against clerical minds. Sir Robert Perks's hostility to the radicalism of the Reverend Henry Carter and the Wesleyan Methodist Temperance and Social Welfare Department has been seen in Chapter 5. While he was an advocate of Methodist union, indeed it was he who pushed

---

[232] *M. Rec* 25 July 1935.   [233] *Methodist Leader,* 19 June 1930.
[234] Burnett, *Through the Mill,* 73.   [235] The Times, *Prospectuses,* 86 (1933), 210–11.
[236] Burnett, *Through the Mill,* 201–12.

it through the Wesleyan Conference,[237] Perks had little time for extra-Methodist ecumenical tendencies. He disliked ritual and pomp and it may be supposed that his objections to Carter's 'pilgrimages to Lambeth'[238] sprang as much from his churchmanship as from his politics.

Joseph Rank and his son J. Arthur Rank were also spurs where some Methodist ministers were concerned. Like other benefactors they did not give their gifts blindly, nor did they abdicate their stewardship once the gifts were promised.[239] Joseph Rank took a very close interest in the Benevolent Fund he set up in the 1930s. He answered applications, made decisions about whether and how much his Trust would give, and did not hesitate to comment on the schemes put to him either directly or, more often, through the Methodist Chapel Committee Secretary. On one proposal in 1939 he commented, 'Now I do not know why they should want Vestries for the Minister and an Office. I consider that one Vestry is quite sufficient, and there is no need to keep a room as an office, neither is there any necessity for a Quiet Room, and in my opinion these additional vestries etc are an extravagance.'[240] Later he observed, 'I am sorry to differ with some people, but I have seen too much money wasted in Methodism. I have had to work hard all my life and to deny myself of many things so that I might be in a position to do good, and I do not agree with wasting money to carry out the views of some people who do not mind how much they spend so long as they do not have to provide the money.'[241] But Rank was by no means ungenerous with his Benevolent Fund. The Reverend W. C. Jackson, secretary of the Methodist Chapel Committee, wrote to him in 1939 about Methodism in areas of highest unemployment: 'I remember, however, that you have taken a special interest in aiding the distressed areas in South Wales and that first the West Monmouth Mission, then the Ely Valley area, and now the Rhondda area are being tremendously helped by schemes that have been made possible through your great kindness.' Jackson went on to plead for Methodist churchgoers in County Durham where chapel debts had reached about £60,000.[242] Jackson was

[237] *M. Rec* 6 Dec. 1934.

[238] JRL, Keeble papers, file 5, xerox of letter from Sir R. W. Perks to Revd G. E. H. Johnson, 14 May 1926.

[239] For an interesting example of a benefactor's attempt to influence missionary policy see B. Stanley, '"The Miser of Headingley"', in Sheils and Wood (eds.), *Church and Wealth*.

[240] JRL, Joseph Rank Benevolent Fund correspondence vol. 4 (1939–50), Joseph Rank to the Revd W. C. Jackson, 8 Mar. 1939.

[241] Ibid., Rank to Jackson, 13 Mar. 1939.

[242] Ibid., Jackson to Rank, 16 Dec. 1939.

overwhelmed in January 1940 to receive a cheque for £109,000 for a Special Extension Fund from which, it was soon agreed, £25,000 should be allocated to the Durham district.[243] Debts on property might often be removed by the merger of local congregations. Where local Methodists clung to their old Wesleyan or Primitive, or whatever, allegiances, the possibilities of merger and debt removal naturally evaporated. With this Joseph Rank had no sympathy, even when it occurred in the Durham district. Of one such case he commented, 'This is most unfortunate, but as long as they persist in their present attitude they must be prepared to carry the responsibility of the debts.'[244] Neither had he any patience with congregations who accepted his loans but failed to repay them—like the West Monmouth Mission which borrowed £5,000 in 1932 over a ten-year period but in 1942 had repaid only £517. In his opinion they should still try to meet the balance.[245] He was likewise careful never to provide the full cost of a project, rarely offering more than a third, in the expectation that any more would dull local incentive.

J. Arthur Rank was equally capable of putting a flea in the ear of the Methodist Chapel Committee secretary. Having just moved from Reigate to Sutton Scotney near Winchester in 1954, Rank was interested in the state of Methodism locally. He reported to the Reverend Albert Hearn, the Chapel Committee secretary:

To my amazement I received a letter from him [the local circuit Superintendent] this week in which he says 'Unfortunately the financial resources of this Circuit have always been inadequate to maintain the work, and even the Chapel Committee were a bit dubious when I put forward a scheme to build a school-chapel for £8,000. This was eventually whittled down to four thousand, on the assumption that we might expect fifty per cent from the Rank Trust. Then on Christmas Eve (of all days) the Chapel Committee sent me an urgent letter to the effect that the Rank Trust had overspent, and no further commitments could be looked for for some time.' I have never heard such nonsense in all my life ... if in your view this is work that Methodism should be doing here, and that a school-chapel should be built, I shall be glad if you will put in the necessary application to the Secretary of the Joseph Rank Trust.[246]

The story of J. Arthur Rank's role in Methodism is one that has yet to be told. Besides his work as a multiple office holder in the 1930s and as Home Mission treasurer he made other important contributions.

[243] Ibid., Rank to Jackson, 11, 27 Jan. 1940; Jackson to Rank, 13 Jan. 1940.
[244] Ibid.. Rank to Jackson, 16 Dec. 1941.
[245] Ibid., Rank to the Revd Oliver Hornabrook, 17 June 1942.
[246] Ibid., vol. 6 (1954–5), Rank to Hearn, 21 Oct. 1954.

One related to his film interests. In the late 1920s or early 1930s,[247] while he was running an afternoon Sunday School class and an after-evening service meeting at the Reigate Methodist Church, he became interested in using the new medium of film, despite the Hollywood cheapies that were tarnishing the cinema's image. If not earlier, he would have learned about the film world's challenge to the churches as depicted by Richard G. Burnett (the Methodist journalist and eventually his father's biographer) and E. D. Martell in their book *The Devil's Camera: Menace of a Film-Ridden World*, published by the (Methodist) Epworth Press in 1932. This pulled no punches and spared no Victorian inhibitions. Theirs was a discriminating attack, however: 'We object not to the film camera but to the prostitution of it by sex-mad and cynical financiers. ... When all the possible bouquets have been handed out to those who deserve them the cinema is still revealed as at present a dread menace to civilisation.' Burnett and Martell blamed the churches for not influencing the development of the film industry and observed that 'There is a clamant opportunity for Church leaders who realise the danger of present-day tendencies and wish to make full use of the cinematograph's wonderful propaganda potentialities.'[248] It is difficult to believe that J. Arthur Rank was not influenced by this book. In 1932–3 he presented a projector to his church, used it on Sunday evenings, and later dispatched projectors to other Methodist churches around the country. In 1933 he joined the Religious Film Society and took the first steps that eventually made him the principal architect of the British film industry.[249] Few would deny that his influence put the quality of British films well above the vulgarities of the Hollywood cheapies. Within the Methodist Church his projectors and films brought the Christian message into the new medium.

In the 1950s J. Arthur Rank gave his support to one of the more exciting initiatives launched by the Methodist Church. This was the Luton Industrial Mission pioneered by the Reverend William Gowland (already noted in Chapter 6). When searching for financial support Gowland in 1955 shrewdly applied to Rank before going to the Chapel Committee. Not only might he obtain support from the Joseph Rank Benevolent Fund but also he knew or suspected that J. Arthur Rank had a lot of leverage with the Chapel Committee. Likewise the Chapel Committee made their

---

[247] My attempts to trace the exact date from either the local church or the Surrey Record Office (with whom local Methodist archives are supposed to be deposited) have failed.

[248] R. G. Burnett and E. D. Martell, *Devil's Camera* (London, 1932), 11, 123.

[249] A. Wood, *Mr Rank* (London, 1952), skates over the beginnings of his film interests at Reigate Methodist Church.

grant levels dependent on the sum likely to come from the Rank Fund.
J. Arthur Rank strongly approved the Luton project and eventually the
initial costs of £16,000 were supplied as noted earlier.

Businessmen in Methodism thus played numerous and various roles.
Despite the centralized structure of the Methodist connections and the
successor Methodist Church they found room for their skills and
resources to be used in the service of the church. Whether the decrease
in the numbers of businessmen in lay church leadership by the 1950s
arose from clericalization or secularization is a subject for another study.

9

Nonconformists and Celts, 1900–1960

Structurally the Nonconformist denominations divide between those which are centralized, like the Methodists, Presbyterians, and Quakers, and those having minimal centralized organizations, like the Baptists, Brethren, Congregationalists, and Unitarians. Centralized structures offered larger national stages for energetic and ambitious businessmen. On the other hand decentralized denominations presented many more local and regional opportunities for smaller business figures to come to the fore. Whether businessmen found opportunities to exercise their talents and ambitions within these church structures might also depend on how much space the clergy allowed them. The Methodist experience suggests that in the twentieth century the power of the clergy may have increased at the expense of lay leadership. Part of this process was the declining presence of entrepreneurs in church leaderships, though which way causation ran (whether business figures were pushed out or whether secular pursuits drew them away) is not always clear. Since this study is confined to national-level organizations it cannot pretend to find more than a partial view of the differing denominational experiences. Other work remains to be done in linking local to national activities in centralized and decentralized churches.

What is certain, as demonstrated in Table 1.7, is that shrinking church memberships left relatively more national places for lay persons to occupy. By the 1930s three denominations had over 1,000 national council and committee places to be filled annually by the laity. Besides the Methodists, already examined, the Quakers and the Church of Scotland relied substantially on the laity. This chapter looks first at the Quakers and, more briefly, at the Baptists and Congregationalists; then it turns to the roles of business people in the churches in Scotland, Wales, and Ireland.

TABLE 9.1. *Key lay people in the Society of Friends, 1907, 1935, 1955*

Total No. of posts held	1907				1935				1955			
	No. of holders	Share of total posts	%	No. of female holders	No. of holders	Share of total posts	%	No. of female holders	No. of holders	Share of total posts	%	No. of female holders
Up to 4												
5	10	50	6.45	4	9	45	4.45	2	10	50	4.10	2
6	10	60	7.74	3	8	48	4.74	2	7	42	3.44	4
7	8	56	7.23	4	5	35	3.46	1	4	28	2.30	
8	1	8	1.03		2	16	1.58		1	8	0.66	
9	1	9	1.16									
10	1	10	1.29	1					2	18	1.48	1
11												
12									1	12	0.98	
Total 5–12	31	193	24.90	12	24	144	14.23	5	25	158	12.95	6
TOTAL		775	100.00			1,012	100.00			1,220	100.00	

Sources: Minutes and Proceedings of the Yearly Meeting of Friends, for 1906; MS Committee Minutes, 1906–7, Friends' House Library; Membership List of the Meeting for Sufferings and of the Committees of the Meeting for Sufferings and Yearly Meeting, 1934–5; same for 1954–5.

I BUSINESSMEN AND WOMEN IN ENGLISH NONCONFORMITY OTHER THAN METHODISM

Several features about Quaker lay leadership appear in the aggregated data in Table 9.1. Absolutely the number of their national offices increased greatly, by well over 50 per cent, between 1907 and 1955; in comparison total membership grew at a much slower rate, by about 13 per cent. Secondly, lay leadership became less concentrated, with holders of five or more national posts halving their share of available positions (though the number of positions held by these active lay people averaged six or a little more throughout the period). Thirdly, between 1907 and 1935 the proportion of women among these key lay people fell sharply from nearly one in three to one in five.

Given the widely attested strength of links between Quakerism and business, it is surprising perhaps to find that only a very small percentage of multi-office holders were company directors (see Table 9.3). In the late nineteenth century numbers of Quaker business families were moving away from their inherited faith, becoming 'worldly', or resigning as T. A. B. Corley has shown.[1] Nevertheless between 100 and 200 Quakers in medium and large-scale business were sufficiently committed to their faith to want to debate its implications for industry, at intervals between 1918 and 1948 as seen in Chapter 5. No more than four of these seem to have had the time to become multi-office holders in their national meetings. This is not to suggest that businessmen carried little weight in Quaker circles in the twentieth century. Far from it. Rather, it underlines the fact that Quaker directors (who were also members of the Institute of Directors), men from the larger Quaker firms, seem to have had much less confidence in their denominational structures than their Methodist counterparts. Certainly this was true of George Cadbury who 'was always as it were an outrider of Quakerism, faithful to its spirit but distrustful of forms which were outworn'.[2]

In fact 12 of the 31 key lay people of 1907 had current business connections. Only one, William Harvey, director of the Friends Provident Institution, a life insurance office, was a member of the Institute of

---

[1] T. A. B. Corley, 'How Quakers Coped with Business Success', in D. J. Jeremy (ed.), *Business and Religion in Britain* (Aldershot, 1988).

[2] A. G. Gardiner, *The Life of George Cadbury* (London, 1925), 181.

Directors.[3] Alfred Lynn of Colwyn Bay was a company director of an unspecified firm. Most of the rest had some form of ownership in small firms. William Henry Wilson ran his father's collieries and brick-works at Broughton, Cumberland. Henry Lloyd Wilson was linked to the family firm of Albright & Wilson, chemical manufacturers. John Morland managed the sheepskin rug factory of C. & J. Clark at Glaston-bury. Thomas Prichard Newman of Haslemere, Surrey, was a printer. Four were in retailing: Henry Dell of Holloway, London, and Henry Stanley Newman of Leominster, both grocers; George Baynes Wetherall a tea dealer of Worcester; Thomas Sydney Marriage at Reigate, an iron-monger. One was a consulting engineer: Arthur Guy Enock, who devoted himself to solving the problems of building clean and safe milk machinery. Only one appears to have been an employee: Henry Harris who worked for the Friends' Provident Institution.

Besides this group there were two other sets among the Quaker key lay leaders of 1907 who had tenuous connections with business. One group had had business experience earlier in their lives. Thomas Barrow was a retired Lancaster woollen manufacturer. Jonathan Backhouse Hodgkin worked for four years in the family bank at Darlington before leaving in 1874 to devote himself to religious and philanthropic work. Howard Nicholson had been a coal-mine engineer in Canada before taking up full-time evangelistic work and then returning to England in 1888. The other group with business contacts were some of the ladies. Nearly half the 12 women among the 31 lay leaders came from families in business or else had married businessmen. Elizabeth Barclay Back-house was the widow of the Darlington banker James Edward Backhouse. Ethel Mary Mounsey's family were Durham coal merchants. Jane Eliza-beth Newman was the wife of printer T. P. Newman. Caroline West-combe Pumphrey was the daughter of a Worcester tallow chandler. Sarah Elizabeth Rowntree was the niece of Joseph Rowntree the cocoa manufac-turer.

By 1935 a few more company directors were appearing among the holders of multiple offices in the Society of Friends. Barrow Cadbury, nephew of George Cadbury, was a director of the British Cocoa & Choco-late Co. Ltd., the holding company of Cadburys and Frys. Roger Clark,

---

[3] William Harvey (1848–1928), educated at Ackworth, Bootham, and University Col-lege, London, had worked in linen and then silk manufacturing firms and later, in the 1880s, in his father-in-law's warehousing firm in Manchester, retiring in 1888. This and all other biographical information relating to Quakers, unless otherwise noted, comes from the DQB.

son of William Stephens Clark,[4] was a director of C. & J. Clark, the shoe manufacturing firm built up by his father at Street, Somerset, of Clark, Son & Morland, the sheepskin rug firm, and of Montserrat & Co., the Birmingham merchant and lime juice manufacturing firm. Joseph Stephenson Rowntree, third son of Joseph Rowntree by his second wife, was on the board of Rowntree & Co. J. Edward Hodgkin of Darlington was the director of twelve firms and chairman of seven of them, most related to the manufacture of engineering equipment.[5]

In addition to these four members of the Institute of Directors, the twenty-four key lay leaders of Quakerism in 1935 included four more men in business, but not necessarily at boardroom level. Robert Wilfrid Dale was a Rochester grocer; Robert Alfred Penney owned and operated a tugboat service in Poole Harbour; Edward Pease Sturge was a Lloyd's underwriter;[6] and Wilfrid Ernest Littleboy a chartered accountant. One or two had retired from business, like Alexander Cowan Wilson, a consulting civil engineer, or John Herbert Robson, a master cotton dyer who formerly worked in the family firm at Dalton near Huddersfield. Two of the five women among the twenty-four multiple office holders had slight business connections. Lucy Fryer Morland was the daughter of an umbrella maker and the sister of Harold Morland the Price Waterhouse accountant who stood trial with Lord Kylsant in the celebrated Royal Mail case in 1931.[7] (Emily) Margaret Sefton-Jones was the widow of a patent agent. Overall, though, the share of business-involved or connected people among key lay leaders in the Society of Friends declined from 22 out of 31 (71 per cent) in 1907 to 13 out of 24 (54 per cent) in 1935.

By 1955 a smaller proportion of Quaker multiple office holders had business connections. Furthermore, due to ageing, those connections mostly belonged to the past. Out of 25 key lay people none was currently a member of the Institute of Directors. Out of the 23 whose occupations have been identified, only one, Harold Reed, a bank manager, currently worked in business. Seven others had retired from business. Edmund Russell Brayshaw had retired in 1950 from the engineering firm his

---

[4] G. Barry Sutton, 'William Stephens Clark', *DBB*.

[5] There is some slight doubt about this identification. While the *DD* for 1935 lists 12 directorships for J. E. Hodgkin of Hodgkin & Young, including Darlington Merchant Credits Ltd. and Friends Trusts Ltd., none of these firms is listed against Hodgkin's name in Quaker Employers' Conference, *Quakerism and Industry* (London, 1928) or Quaker Employers' Conference, *Quakerism and Industry* (London, 1938).

[6] *Friend* (1951), 228.

[7] E. Green and M. Moss, *A Business of National Importance* (London, 1982), *passim*.

TABLE 9.2. *Directions of activity of key lay people in the Society of Friends, 1907, 1935, 1955*

Activity	1907		1935		1955	
	No. of offices	%	No. of offices	%	No. of offices	%
Property			8	5.56	6	3.80
Charitable funds			12	8.33	9	5.70
Education	3	1.55	25	17.36	12	7.59
External relations	10	5.18	26	18.06	33	20.89
Faith, doctrine			5	3.47		
Foreign missions	146	75.65	5	3.47		
Home missions	8	4.15				
Internal organization	26	13.47	45	31.25	50	31.65
Social issues			18	12.50	48	30.38
TOTAL	193	100.00	144	100.00	158	100.00

Sources: As for Table 9.1.

brother Shipley had set up in Stockport, producing gas furnaces and small tools. The associations of Barrow Cadbury, now in his nineties, Wilfrid Littleboy, and John Herbert Robson have already been noted. Robson's sister Alice had also retired from the family firm, having served it for over twenty years as its analytical chemist. William Stewart had retired in 1946 from his firm, a supplier of chemists' sundries. Crawford H. Thomson, a Post Office employee, had also retired.[8] Doris Edington was the wife of a Norwich grocer. Otherwise the key lay people of 1955 were mostly professionals and full-time employees of the Society of Friends.

What roles did these business figures play in the leadership of the Society of Friends? Clues are contained in Table 9.2. This is meaningful for the business group only for 1907 and 1935 when they constituted a majority or at least a reasonable minority of the multiple office holders. Missionary committee work clearly preoccupied Quaker lay leaders in 1907, reflecting the evangelical character of the Society in the second half of the nineteenth century. The Friends' Foreign Mission Association had a multitude of standing committees, defined by region (India, Madagascar, Syria, China, Ceylon) or by function (General Arrangements, Candidates, Literature, Finance, etc.), and on these most of the women's posts were concentrated. By 1935 Quakerism had succumbed to new currents emphasizing social issues rather than foreign missions. By this time internal organization (the affairs of the Meeting for Sufferings, its Allotments, Finance, and Office Arrangements Committees, together

[8] *Friend* (1972), 220.

with the Yearly Meeting Agenda Committee) occupied nearly a third of the committee places to which the most active lay people in the denomination gave their time.

Obtaining a more focused picture is hard because minutes tended to report the results rather than the currents of debate. The contributions of individuals among these leading lay people have been recorded, however, in the excellent files in Friends' House Library. Thomas Prichard Newman (1846–1915) the printer, for example, was recalled as 'one of the prime movers for the modernising of Yearly Meeting procedure and for a scheme whereby Friends meeting houses might be insured against fire. He was also concerned in the proposal that the old offices at Devonshire House should find a new site. On the board of the FFMA, he was one of a few Friends who developed the finance committee and was also chairman or member of the India Committee of the Association for nearly thirty years.'[9] Henry Lloyd Wilson (1862–1941) was released from duties in the family firm of Albright & Wilson by his brother Alfred and so was enabled to give much of his spare time to FFMA committees and membership of the Meeting for Sufferings.[10] The impression, and it is no more than that, gained from aggregating committee memberships is that as they became less concerned with evangelism and more with bureaucratic and social issues so entrepreneurs gave way to professionals, teachers, and social workers particularly. What is indisputable is that the denomination's formal structures never became the forum for Quaker businessmen to discuss implications of faith for business: that, as seen in Chapter 5, was organized at Woodbrooke by the associates and successors of George Cadbury. Ironically, whereas George Cadbury found Quaker thinking too traditional at the beginning of the century, by the 1950s his successors among Quaker entrepreneurs felt growing unease at its radicalism.

The same pattern of a declining involvement on the part of people in business is seen in the lay leaderships of the other main Nonconformist denominations. Using membership of the Institute of Directors as a criterion, albeit an imperfect one, it is evident from Table 9.3 that Congregationalists, Presbyterians, and Baptists fared no better than Methodists. Here there is space to do no more than identify the business people among the multiple office bearers in these denominations and indicate the extent to which the criterion is useful.

All members of the Councils of the Congregational Union of England

[9] DQB.   [10] DQB.

TABLE 9.3. *Company directors and directorships among key lay leaders in English Nonconformity, 1907, 1935, 1955*

	1907	1935	1955
Congregationalists[a]			
No. of national lay posts	178	325	401
No. of key lay leaders	171	169	217
No. of co. dirs. among key leaders	27	19	3
Co. directors as % of key leaders	15.79%	11.24%	1.38%
No. of directorships	41	56	16
No. of directorships in mfg.	9	11	2
Presbyterians			
No. of national lay posts	259	409	
No. of key lay leaders	6	23	
No. of co. dirs. among key leaders	3	0	
Co. directors as % of key leaders	50.00%		
No. of directorships	14		
No. of directorships in mfg.	2		
Baptists[a]			
No. of national lay posts	47	66	58
No. of key lay leaders	47	66	58
No. of co. dirs. among key leaders	10	12	5
Co. directors as % of key leaders	21.28%	18.18%	8.62%
No. of directorships	24	40	21
No. of directorships in mfg.	5	13	1
Methodists			
No. of national lay posts	2,428	1,430	1,079
No. of key lay leaders	92	43	23
No. of co. dirs. among key leaders	32	16	4
Co. directors as % of key leaders	34.78%	37.21%	17.39%
No. of directorships	87	60	7
No. of directorships in mfg.	21	22	1
Quakers			
No. of national lay posts	775	1,012	1,220
No. of key lay leaders	31	24	25
No. of co. dirs. among key leaders	1	4	0
Co. directors as % of key leaders	3.23%	16.67%	
No. of directorships	1	17	
No. of directorships in mfg.	0	5	

[a] These two denominations were decentralized in their structure. Key leaders have therefore been defined as all members of their respective national councils. In the other denominations key lay leaders have been defined as all those holding five or more national committee posts.

Sources: Denominational year books and the *Directory of Directors* for the appropriate dates; Tables 8.1 and 8.7 and the Methodist holders of five or more offices these tables summarize and analyse.

and Wales and the Baptist Union of Great Britain and Ireland have been regarded as key lay leaders because these two denominations, being decentralized, had relatively few lay national representatives. They can therefore be closely compared. The surprising finding of Table 9.3 is that, proportionately, the Baptists had a consistently higher number of laymen who were company directors at a time when Congregationalists (with Wesleyans) were reckoned to command the allegiance of the moneyed classes.[11]

Individually and collectively Congregational leaders in business were an imposing group. In 1907 their industrial associations were strong in the North-West, Yorkshire, and London. In the North-West they were led by textile and glass manufacturers. Arthur Adlington Haworth, Rugby-educated partner in James Dilworth & Son, yarn agents, sat on the board of the prestigious Manchester Royal Exchange, Lancashire's cotton yarn and goods market where 9,000 members sealed transactions with a verbal honour which matched that of London's Stock Exchange. Liberal MP for South Manchester 1906–12, Haworth listed his recreations in *Who's Who* as 'hunting, shooting, fishing'. He belonged to Bowdon Downs Congregational Church, 'Manchester cotton at prayer', the spiritualized suburban ideal, in the words of Clyde Binfield. On the Council of the Congregational Union of England and Wales of 1907, he was vice-chairman, lay leader of the denomination for that year.[12] Colonel William Windle Pilkington, chairman of Pilkington Bros. the St Helens glassmakers who employed 9,000 in 1907, was the only key Congregational leader in the UK business élite that year. Belonging to the Congregational church in Ormskirk Street, St Helens, he chaired the Lancashire Congregational Union.[13] William Crosfield, chairman of the Liverpool Mortgage Insurance Co., member of Liverpool's Gladstonian plutocracy, and former MP for Lincoln, was treasurer of the Congregational Union of England and Wales.[14] Behind them came lesser figures like Edward B. Dawson, director of the Lancaster Banking Co., Lancaster Catering Co., and Kiveton Park Colliery Co.; or G. Stanley Wood, chairman of the Liverpool Steam Tug Co.

In Yorkshire textile men again dominated. Mark Oldroyd, blanket and broadcloth manufacturer of Dewsbury, emerged as a remarkable entrepreneur when he successfully rebuilt the family firm following his brother's bankruptcy in 1877; he then sat as Liberal MP for Dewsbury, welding his business and political interests on a lifelong commitment as a Congregationalist.[15] At nearby Batley another woollen manufac-

---

[11] K. S. Inglis, *Churches and the Working Class in Victorian England* (London, 1963), 100–5.

[12] D. A. Farnie, 'An Index of Commercial Activity', *Business History*, 21 (1979), 97–106; *WWW*; *WWMP*; C. Binfield, *So Down to Prayers* (London, 1977), 170, 175, 239–44.

[13] T. C. Barker, *The Glassmakers Pilkington* (London, 1981), 477.

[14] P. J. Waller, *Democracy and Sectarianism* (Liverpool, 1981), 113, 182, 398, 486; *WWMP*.

[15] D. T. Jenkins, 'Mark Oldroyd', *DBB*.

turer, Theodore Cooke Taylor, also sat on the Congregational Union Council. Liberal MP for Radcliffe-cum-Farnworth near Manchester, he was best known as an exponent of profit-sharing (his own scheme has been the subject of some historical controversy) and as a severe, non-drinking, non-smoking Congregationalist. He lived to the age of 102 and was still travelling abroad seeking cloth orders in his nineties.[16]

London men clustered around Edward Spicer, chairman of Spicer Bros. Ltd.,[17] and his cousin Sir Albert Spicer, of the rival paper manufacturers and merchants James Spicer & Sons. Sir Albert Spicer was Congregationalism's answer to Wesleyan Methodism's Sir Robert Perks. He became chairman of the Congregational Union for a second time in 1907, a high honour in recognition of his thirty-plus years on the Essex Congregational Union and the London Missionary Society (of which he was also treasurer), and his role in founding Mansfield College, Oxford, the denomination's theological college (of which he was treasurer 1888–1921).[18] Alongside the Spicers ranked Halley Stewart, chairman of B. J. Forder & Son, brick manufacturers. In 1907 he was Liberal MP for Greenock. Early in his business career he took on the pastorate of a chapel in Hastings and was rare in combining business and religion so intimately.[19] Behind came men like Montagu Holmes, a London property and insurance company director, Robert Murray Hyslop, whose commercial interests were in steel,[20] and Arthur Pye-Smith director of the St Pancras Iron Work Co.

By 1935 many of the prominent businessmen on the Congregational Union Council were past their prime. The chairman of the Congregational Union was Angus Watson, the Tynesider who pioneered fish canning in Britain, capturing large markets with his 'Skipper' brand. His firm Angus Watson & Co., where he ran a profit-sharing scheme, was taken over by William Lever after the First World War and a decade or so later Watson retired from business, but not from writing and speaking about his faith.[21] The chairman of the Congregational Union Council, Harry Barber, a solicitor and company director (of Hankow Light & Power Co. and Barber Young & Co.), was in his seventies. Little is known of the Union's treasurer, W. F. Wrigley of Derby, except that he was a director of four companies.

[16] D. Boothroyd, 'Theodore Cooke Taylor', *DBB*.

[17] C. Welch, *London at the Opening of the Twentieth Century* (Brighton, 1905), 729.

[18] David J. Jeremy, 'Albert Spicer', *DBB*.

[19] Kenneth E. Jackson, 'Halley Stewart', *DBB*.

[20] *WWC*.

[21] Richard Perren, 'James Angus Watson', *DBB*.

Sir Arthur Haworth, created a baronet in 1911, now stood at the summit of Cottonopolis. Since 1909 he had been chairman of the Manchester Royal Exchange. Under his chairmanship, the longest in its 240-year history, the Exchange in 1920 reached its highest membership of 11,000 before unreversed decline began. Though he seems to have played little part in the affairs of the Manchester Chamber of Commerce (of which he was a director), and its attempts to co-ordinate efforts in the 1930s to retrieve Lancashire's lost markets, he was widely recognized as the epitome of the Lancashire businessman. Claimed an adulatory newspaper profile, Sir Arthur is '"the man" in Manchester, and the "Manchester man" in London. ... A supreme type of the Lancashire businessmen. ... The sturdy compact figure, the ruddy countenance, the keen eyes, the ever-alert mien betoken the man. "Sharp as they make 'em" is the proverbial expression heard from his admirers as they gather about the Royal Exchange, of which he is the acknowledged head.' Despite his age (in his seventies) in 1935 he was also director of English Sewing Cotton Co. and the Midland Bank as well as several smaller companies.[22] Another cotton manufacturer Harold Lee, former chairman of Tootal Broadhurst Lee & Co., was in his eighties. Halley Stewart, a baronet now, was in his nineties. The Council member with the most directorships, Frank Newton Tribe, a chartered accountant, was almost 80. He sat on the boards of ten companies chairing six of them, including the Bristol & West Building Society where, in comparison to Methodist Harold Bellman of the Abbey Road Society, he pursued cautious policies.[23] Younger businessmen, like Stanley Unwin of the publishing firm George Allen & Unwin,[24] or Bernard Hennell, a chartered accountant and company director of Putney, London, were also on the Council of the Union. However these younger businessmen, if the impression gained from the *Directory of Directors* is correct, came from smaller and more obscure companies.

By the mid-1950s scarcely any members of the Congregational Union Council were company directors. Of the three that have been identified, Bernard Hennell sat on ten boards, H. C. Leonard, a Bristol business-

[22] *WWW*; *WWMP*; *Manchester Chamber of Commerce Official Handbook, 1935* (Manchester, 1935), 73; *Manchester City News*, 11 Jan. 1930. He is barely noticed by Raymond Streat, secretary of the Manchester Chamber of Commerce in the 1930s: M. Dupree (ed.), *Lancashire and Whitehall* (Manchester, 1987), i. 72.

[23] Charles Harvey, 'Old Traditions, New Departures', in C. Harvey and J. Press (eds.), *Studies in the Business History of Bristol* (Bristol, 1988), 248.

[24] Philip Unwin, 'Stanley Unwin', *DBB*.

man,[25] on five. Symptomatic of the changes occurring in Congregationalism, as in other church leaderships, were the elections of a magistrate's clerk (B. J. Hartwell LL M) to the chair of the Union's Council and of an elocutionist and a chartered accountant to the joint honorary treasurerships of the Union.[26]

But is membership of the Institute of Directors a fair test of the presence of business people in the counsels of the Congregational Union? Businessmen outside the Institute certainly sat on the Council, like Sir Albert Spicer in 1907 and Angus Watson in 1935 and 1955: Spicer did not belong, Watson had retired. An attempt has been made to trace the occupations of all lay Council members for the three benchmark dates. Too few from the 1907 Council have been identified to be useful. In any case the evidence set out in Table 9.3 suggests that the precipitous drop in business backgrounds came between 1935 and 1955. For these dates better data are available.[27] Counting all those with known business links (i.e. trades, directorships, accounting jobs with industrial firms, but *not* professional accountants), then businessmen on the Union Council formed 40 per cent of all 169 lay people and 65 per cent of all men with known occupations in 1935. By 1955 these proportions had fallen to 22 and 49 per cent respectively. The *Directory of Directors* data exaggerated the trend but not its direction. By the 1950s these commercial men either ran small businesses, like Stanley Griffin, a jovial Plymouth builder, sanitary engineer, undertaker, and church secretary;[28] or else they were managers in large businesses like Wilfrid F. Crick, the Midland Bank's economic adviser and bank historian.[29]

Entrepreneurs and ascendant businessmen distanced themselves from the Baptists, though less sharply than they disengaged from Congregationalism. As with the latter, Table 9.3 understates the extent of businessmen's involvement in the lay leadership of the denomination. The *Directory of Directors* for 1907 does not, for example, list Alfred Caulkin, a Birmingham manufacturer,[30] or George Watson Macalpine, an Accrington colliery and brick manufacturer who represented the

---

[25] Identified, like many other lay people on the Congregational Union Council of 1955, by the Revd Dr John Huxtable: discussions with author, 7 Jan. 1986.

[26] Alec E. Glassey, former Liberal MP, was the elocutionist, A. Victor Sully the accountant: information from the Revd Dr John Huxtable.

[27] For 1935 I have used *WWC 1933* and for 1955 *WWFC*. On the 1955 Council members I have also been much helped by the Revd Dr John Huxtable, Revd Dr Geoffrey Nuttall, and Miss Margaret A. Canning, former secretary of New College, London.

[28] Information from the Revd Dr John Huxtable.

[29] A. R. Holmes and E. Green, *Midland* (London, 1986), 187, 205.

[30] C. J. L. Colvin, *The Baptist Insurance Company Limited* (London, 1980), 7.

Lancashire Association on the Baptist Union Council and chaired the Baptist Missionary Society.[31] On the other hand, of the ten Council members it does list, two qualified only because they were on the board of the Baptist Fire Insurance Co.

The other eight split between the North-East, Yorkshire, East Anglia, and London. W. Goode Davies from Newcastle-upon-Tyne was on the board of the Union Assurance Society. In Yorkshire there were John Cousin Horsfall, a Keighley worsted spinner honoured with a baronetcy in 1909,[32] and W. Dale Shaw of Longwood, Huddersfield, chairman of Woolcombers Ltd. and of Northern Counties Investment Trust Ltd. From East Anglia came John Chivers, jam manufacturer of Histon, Cambridge, and George White, shoe manufacturer of Norwich, city father and Liberal MP for North West Norfolk.[33] London businessmen, close to the Baptist Union's new headquarters building in Southampton Row, more easily served the denomination's growing administrative structures than provincial Baptists. Herbert Marnham, a young stockbroker and director of the family firm of Marnham & Co., was elected treasurer of the Baptist Union in 1900; he served until his death in 1934.[34] Henry Ernest Wood, a London surveyor and chairman of the Shenfield & Ganham Brick Co., was vice-chairman of the Baptist Fire Insurance Co. (George White of Norwich was chairman) and chairman of the London Baptist Property Board Ltd. Alfred Henry Baynes, a contractor who trained in the office of Sir Samuel Morton Peto, was secretary of the Baptist Missionary Society for many years until he retired in 1905. He was director of seven companies in 1907, all in London and most gas and water suppliers.[35] Baptist lay leaders in business, with ten of their number being aldermen, carried civic weight but, without an MP in their midst, not as much as their Congregational counterparts.

Proportionately more numerous than among the Congregationalists in 1935, businessmen in Baptist lay leadership operated on a smaller scale. Of the twelve listed in the *Directory of Directors* two were confined to the board of the Baptist Insurance Co. Of the rest four appear substantial. Robert Wilson Black, director of nine companies including Eagle,

[31] E. Gaskell, *Lancashire Leaders* (London, *c.* 1900); C. E. Wilson, *Sir George Watson Macalpine* (London, n.d.); *WWW*.

[32] *WWW*; W. H. Scott and W. T. Pike, *The West Riding of Yorkshire at the Opening of the Twentieth Century* (Brighton, 1902), 301.

[33] Zuzana Burianova, 'John Chivers', *DBB*; Keith Brooker, 'George White', ibid.

[34] F. Buffard, *Herbert Marnham* (London, n.d.); E. A. Payne, *The Baptist Union* (London, 1959), 157, *passim*.

[35] Payne, *Baptist Union*, 115, 128, 149, 167.

Star & British Dominions Insurance Co., was an estate agent and property developer in south-west London. In the 1930s he spearheaded the denomination's Forward Movement which raised £1 million in the decade for church extension. To this Black freely gave his professional knowledge on the financial, legal, and technical aspects of sites and buildings. On occasion his plans backfired. One of his schemes was to unite on a single leasehold premises in Russell Square, London, the headquarters of both the Baptist Union and the Baptist Missionary Society. However, the developer's daring offended faith in freehold property and the Baptist Assembly of 1938 rejected the plan.[36] Other directors of some weight besides Black were Harry Miller Ennals, on the boards of three companies, including two Fison ones manufacturing chemical fertilizers; Richard Bowness Hodgson, on three North East metal and engineering firms including Whessoe Foundry & Engineering Co.; and H. L. Taylor of Bristol, director of eight companies most in the paper and paper bag industry including E. S. & A. Robinson. Taylor was treasurer of the Baptist Missionary Society.

Apart from these twelve members of the Institute of Directors the Baptist Council of 1935 had another nine members with identifiable business connections. They included Arnold Clark, a glass merchant, who with Herbert Marnham was joint treasurer of the Baptist Union (Marnham did not live out the year); William Henry Mayne, a Cardiff steamship owner-manager;[37] Arthur Richardson Timson, founder of the Kettering printing machinery manufacturing firm which produced all sorts of ingenious printing machines including one to make continuous envelopes for church offerings;[38] and Seymour J. Price, later director and historian of the Temperance Permanent Building Society.[39] Taken together, the 21 men with business links on the Baptist Union Council of 1935 represented 32 per cent of the whole Council or 62 per cent of all the male Council members whose occupations have been traced.

These percentages slipped a little by 1955. Of 58 Baptist Union Council members that year 18 have been identified as connected with business, as owner, director, or manager. They comprised 31 per cent of the whole Council or 53 per cent of male members whose occupations are known.

[36] Henry Townsend, *Robert Wilson Black* (London, 1954), 74–94.
[37] *BWW.*
[38] *Timsons Limited* (Kettering, 1976).
[39] S. J. Price, *From Queen to Queen* (London, 1954).

Of the five listed in the *Directory of Directors* three, including Seymour Price, were on the boards of specifically Baptist companies. Cyril Wilson Black, son of Robert Wilson Black, chartered surveyor and Conservative MP for Wimbledon, was director of 13 companies, chiefly spanning property, hotels, and investment trusts. Still in his fifties, he was on his way to becoming one of the most influential Baptist laymen of the mid-twentieth century.[40] Charles Boardman Jewson was a director of the family timber firm his great great grandfather had founded in Norwich in 1836.[41] Unlisted in the *Directory of Directors* were, among others, Arnold S. Clark, now treasurer of the Baptist Union; F. W. Dawson, a Leeds brush manufacturer; Alfred Dickens, a Northampton leather manufacturer; Horace F. Gale, a Bedford builders merchant and founder of the Beds. & Hunts. Provident & Benevolent Society; Sir Herbert Janes, a Luton builder; A. L. Simpkin, a Sheffield confectionery manufacturer; and Ernest A. Timson, now chairman of his father's printing machinery making firm.[42] Important in local markets, most of these businessmen could not be described as national figures. Small was beautiful among Baptists.

A final comment is due about the Presbyterian Church of England, frequently the spiritual home of fugitive Scots in England. Comparisons have been confined to 1907 and 1935 because by 1955 the denomination's yearbook was listing only convenors and secretaries of committees of the ruling body, the General Assembly. Evidence from earlier years shows, as with all the other denominations, a much stronger presence of businessmen among multi-office holders before the First World War than in the 1930s. There were, however, only six lay holders of five or more national offices in 1907. Half of them were members of the Institute of Directors. By 1935 none appear to have been. There is no reason to suppose that the Presbyterian experience was any different from that of Methodists, Congregationalists, and Baptists and it may therefore be assumed that there were rather more lay leaders associated with business than Table 9.3 indicates. This is yet another area for further research.

---

[40] *WW 1958*.

[41] The Times, *Prospectuses*, 112 (1953), 238.

[42] I am grateful to my friend John Barfield, manager of the Baptist Union Corporation Ltd., for his help in making some identifications; others have been traced in *WWFC*. For Janes see *WWW* and Sir H. Janes, *The Janes Trust* (Luton, 1968). See *Baptist Times*, 6 Aug. 1987, for an obituary of Ernest Timson.

2 SCOTTISH, WELSH, AND IRISH EXPERIENCES

(a) Scotland

Divided by polity but not theology, the two largest denominations in 1907, the Church of Scotland and the United Free Church of Scotland, shared a widespread acceptance of the economics of Adam Smith. Dissenting voices were first heard among the clergy from the 1880s (see Chapter 2). By and large, however, until the 1900s free market and *laissez-faire* doctrines had almost the weight of the Westminster Confession.[43] The two churches nevertheless found support among rather different constituencies of businessmen. As the established body, the Church of Scotland historically had the allegiance of many great landed families. From the Disruption of 1843 the Free Church, with its evangelical commitment to Calvin, Knox, and the Covenanters, attracted commercial men, merchants, and manufacturers.[44] Though this social distinction can easily be exaggerated, it was clearly expressed in Free Church objections to patronage (abolished in 1874), endowments, and the principle of establishment, weak though that was.[45] Evidence of these social alliances appears among the lay leaders of the two churches in 1907.

Some of the data presented in Table 9.4 suggest that in 1907 there was little difference in business linkages between the Church of Scotland and the United Free Church. Among their activist laymen both had a greater share of industrial and commercial men than did the Methodists, the English denomination commanding the largest number of members of the Institute of Directors. Closer inspection reveals important differences, however. The seventeen company directors among the Church of Scotland multiple office holders included a majority with landed interests: Sir Ralph Anstruther had estates at Balcaskie, Fife; Lord Balfour of Burleigh had 3,000 acres; James Alexander Campbell PC, son of Sir James Campbell (who had made a fortune in wholesale drapery in Glasgow) and brother of the Prime Minister, Sir Henry Campbell Bannerman, had 4,000 acres around Brechin, in Angus;[46] the Right

---

[43] A. L. Drummond and J. Bulloch, *The Church in Late Victorian Scotland* (Edinburgh, 1978), 128; A. C. Cheyne, *The Transforming of the Kirk* (Edinburgh, 1983), 148–51.

[44] A. A. MacLaren, *Religion and Social Class* (London, 1974); C. Brown, *Social History of Religion in Scotland since 1730* (London, 1987), 150–2.

[45] A. L. Drummond and J. Bulloch, *The Church in Victorian Scotland* (Edinburgh, 1975), 329–41; idem, *Church in Late Victorian Scotland*, 79–125.

[46] G. Eyre-Todd, *WW Glasgow* (Glasgow, 1909), 35.

TABLE 9.4. *Company directors and directorships among key lay leaders in the churches in Scotland, 1907, 1935, 1955*

	1907	1935	1955
Church of Scotland			
No. of national lay posts	684	1,229	979
No. of key lay leaders	38	33	16
No. of co. dirs. among key leaders	17	15	6
Co. directors as % of key leaders	44.74%	45.45%	37.50%
No. of directorships	56	34	15
No. of directorships in mfg.	5	0	0
United Free Church of Scotland[a]			
No. of national lay posts	824	73	69
No. of key lay leaders	36	9	0
No. of co. dirs. among key leaders	17	1	
Co. directors as % of key leaders	47.22%	11.11%	
No. of directorships	36	1	
No. of directorships in mfg.	5		
Episcopal Church in Scotland[b]			
No. of national lay posts[c]	137		
No. of key lay leaders	13		
No. of co. dirs. among key leaders	4		
Co. directors as % of key leaders	30.77%		
No. of directorships	7		
No. of directorships in mfg.	0		
Scottish Baptists			
No. of national lay posts	179	311	283
No. of key lay leaders	7	27	26
No. of co. dirs. among key leaders	1	5	3
Co. directors as % of key leaders	14.29%	18.52%	11.54%
No. of directorships	4	11	5
No. of directorships in mfg.	1	1	2

Notes: Key lay people are defined as those holding five or more national committee posts, except where indicated.

Line one of Church of Scotland and UFCS figures include up to 14 'Drs' who may be 'Revd Drs'. The vast majority of these have been eliminated by cross-checking with J. A. Lamb *et al.*, *Fasti Ecclesiae Scoticanae* (Edinburgh, 1961) and Lamb, *The Fasti of the UFC* (Edinburgh, 1956), and with Prof. R. H. Campbell.

[a] Key = three or more posts in 1935, 1955.
[b] Key = three or more posts.
[c] Data unpublished 1935, 1955.

Sources: Denominational yearbooks and the *Directory of Directors* for the appropriate dates.

Honourable Walter Hugh Hepburne-Scott, Master of Polwarth, was heir to 6,000 acres. Allied to them was a crowd of legal men, most university-educated in Scotland: James Webster Barty, Perthshire land agent, solicitor, and notary public; Lewis Bilton of Edinburgh and Bellwood, Perthshire, solicitor;[47] Alexander D. M. Black, Edinburgh solicitor[48]; William

[47] A. Eddington and W. T. Pike, *Edinburgh and the Lothians at the Opening of the Twentieth Century* (Brighton, 1904), 189.
[48] Ibid.

George Black, Glasgow solicitor and author of numerous works on property and ecclesiastical law;[49] Christopher Nicholson Johnston KC, advocate, Sheriff of Perth and author of handbooks on crofter legislation and church property;[50] Sir Colin George Macrae, solicitor and JP for the counties of Edinburgh, Forfar, and Dumbarton; Alan L. Menzies, Edinburgh solicitor; and John Alexander Stevenson Millar, another solicitor and author of legal papers. In addition, there were Sir Charles Dalrymple Bt., PC, barrister, former Conservative MP for Ipswich and former Grand Master Mason of Scotland;[51] and Charles Macintosh King, JP, prominent in the public life of Stirling.[52] Although Campbell succeeded to the family business on his father's death and though he married the daughter of Sir Samuel Morton Peto, the group could scarcely be identified with anything other than Scotland's landed establishment. That much was reflected in their political allegiances. Campbell, for example, sat opposite his younger brother Henry in the House of Commons, being Conservative MP for the Universities of Glasgow and Aberdeen for twenty-five years.[53]

In contrast stood the United Free Church lay leaders. Their seventeen multiple office holders who were also company directors included no great territorial magnates. Thomas Binnie was a Glasgow property valuer of high reputation.[54] John Cowan WS (not to be confused with John Cowan DL, the industrialist) was a solicitor, as were Robert Russell Simpson,[55] David Shaw, and Robert Walker Wallace.[56] John William Gulland, Liberal MP for Dumfries Burghs, was an Edinburgh corn merchant.[57] John R. Miller was a Glasgow ironfounder.[58] Thomas Ogilvie was an Aberdeen merchant.[59] Two other multiple office holders and company directors were managers of financial institutions in Edinburgh: John Nicholson managed the Clydesdale Bank in George Street, Edin-

[49] Eyre-Todd, *WW Glasgow*, 19.

[50] Eddington and Pike, *Edinburgh*, 177.

[51] Ibid. 121.

[52] All these identifications have been made from *WWW*.

[53] Eyre-Todd, *WW Glasgow*, 35; *DNB* q.v. Sir Henry Campbell-Bannerman.

[54] UFCS, *The Principal Acts of the General Assembly* (Edinburgh, 1907), 413; Eyre-Todd, *WW Glasgow*, 16–17; J. R. Kellett, *Railways and Victorian Cities* (London, 1969), 210, 236, 302 n.

[55] *WWW*; Eddington and Pike, *Edinburgh*, 210.

[56] *DD*.

[57] *WWW*; Eddington and Pike, *Edinburgh*, 295.

[58] UFCS, *Principal Acts*, 413.

[59] Ibid.

burgh,[60] and David Paulin the Scottish Life Assurance Co.[61] James Pringle, a Scottish chartered accountant by training, had been a stockbroker before retiring in 1896.[62] For the most part these were middling men in Scotland's Edwardian commercial universe.

Of course the inclusion of individuals holding less than five offices on the committees of the General Assembly of either the Church of Scotland or the United Free Church of Scotland brought in other, sometimes bigger, figures. To the foregoing Church of Scotland lay leaders could be added the Marquess of Linlithgow, the Earl of Aberdeen, the Earl of Stair, and Lord Polwarth. In United Free Church ranks the most weighty men still had industrial and legal occupations. The denomination's thirty-six General Trustees included at least seventeen manufacturers, merchants, and financial figures (of whom six were multiple office holders). They were headed by Lord Overtoun whose chrome chemical works attained such notoriety.[63] Behind him were John M'Ausland Denny, Dumbarton shipbuilder, Robert Smith Allan and John Archibald Roxburgh, Glasgow shipowners. On the side of the law the most eminent was Thomas Shaw PC, KC, LL D, MP, the Lord Advocate of Scotland (ennobled as Lord Craigmyle).[64] Other commercial and industrial figures sat on a very limited number of United Free Church committees. Among these were John Cowan DL, son of a missionary, who through an uncle had gone into the management of Redpath, Brown & Co. and built it into a leading engineering construction business.[65] Others were Sir Michael Barker Nairn, linoleum manufacturer of Kirkcaldy who died a millionaire in 1915;[66] Sir Samuel Chisolm Bt., a wealthy grocer and former Lord Provost of Glasgow;[67] and Lord Provost Gibson of Edinburgh, another grocer.[68]

A further set of divergencies between the business-linked activists in the two denominations emerges from an analysis of their directorships. Scotland's business network, as Scott and Hughes have shown, pivoted in the 1900s on banks, investment companies and railways, and between

---

[60] Eddington and Pike, *Edinburgh*, 305.
[61] *DD*; *WWW*.
[62] J. C. Stewart, *Pioneers of a Profession* (Edinburgh, 1977), 140–1.
[63] Sydney Checkland, 'John Campbell White', *DSBB*.
[64] UFCS, *Principal Acts*, 413; *WWW*.
[65] Charles W. Munn, 'John Cowan', *DSBB*.
[66] Nicholas J. Morgan, 'Michael Barker Nairn', *DSBB*.
[67] Eyre-Todd, *WW Glasgow*, 37–8.
[68] *WWW*. I am grateful to Professor R. H. Campbell for making some of these identifications.

Edinburgh and Glasgow.[69] Of the 56 directorships held by Church of Scotland multiple office holders, 10 were in banking, 11 in investment, 12 in insurance, and 5 in railways. In comparison the United Free Church of Scotland activists had only 1 banking, 5 investment, 8 insurance, and 1 railway directorship between them. Clearly the Church of Scotland was more closely allied to capital-intensive business than the United Free Church.

The difference heightens when the companies and their positions in the business networks are identified. Half the Church of Scotland's bank directorships concentrated in the Bank of Scotland where Balfour of Burleigh was Governor. With him on the board were Anstruther, Campbell, Dalrymple, and J. Turnbull Smith LLD a chartered accountant and manager of the Life Association of Scotland.[70] Apart from this no other company-level concentrations of Church of Scotland activists are apparent among directorships. Most of the sixteen Church of Scotland company directors neatly spread their directorships (and presumably investments) across the financial sector. Typically, A. D. M. Black was on the boards of two investment companies, an insurance company and the National Bank of Scotland. The prominence of solicitors, most based in Edinburgh, is explained by their role in managing or acting as secretaries to the multitude of investment companies, many directed to foreign investment, as Scott and Hughes noticed.[71]

The most powerful businessman among the Church of Scotland activists was Sir Ralph William Anstruther. Not only was he a 'central' director, in terms of the number of directors he met on interlocking boards, but also he chaired the Nobel-Dynamite Trust Co. until 1915. This secretive and skilfully run multinational, and its Glasgow-based operating subsidiary, Nobel Explosives Co. (which he also chaired), was then buttressing its position in the international explosives market through cartel arrangements.[72] Ranking with Anstruther in the higher reaches of the Scottish business community was Balfour of Burleigh. Whereas Anstruther's background was Eton, Woolwich, and then a dozen years in the Royal Engineers before taking up the family estate and title, Balfour had followed the political route, via Eton, Oxford, and the Conservative Party into government, becoming Secretary of State

[69] J. Scott and M. Hughes, *The Anatomy of Scottish Capital* (London, 1980), ch. 1.
[70] *DD*.
[71] Scott and Hughes, *Anatomy*, 25–30.
[72] Ibid. 48; W. J. Reader, *ICI* (London, 1970–5), i. 179–98, 214, 309; neither his *WW* entry nor his obituary in *The Times*, 1, 4 Oct. 1934, mentions Anstruther's connection with the manufacture of high explosives.

for Scotland 1895–1903. His wife, the grand-daughter of the 4th Earl of Aberdeen, the Prime Minister, was Church of England. Balfour's eight directorships, were, untypically, almost all in railways and communications. At the Bank of Scotland his role was presumably that of figurehead. The company history does not suggest otherwise.[73]

No similar concentrations appeared among the United Free Church activists. Two were directors of Scottish Life Assurance (James Macdonald and John Nicholson); two of Scottish Queensland Mortgage Co. (Pringle and Simpson). Otherwise they were scattered across the boards of investment and insurance companies. There was one exception, however. Like many of their Nonconformist brethren south of the Border, the United Free Church had organized a fire insurance company, the United Free Church of Scotland Fire Insurance Trust Ltd., and on this sat five of the seventeen activists: Binnie, Macdonald, Ogilvie, Paulin, and Simpson.[74] In both denominations a much larger sample of directors might disclose additional networks.

How far did industrial interests predominate in the counsels of the Church of Scotland and the United Free Church of Scotland? No more than hints can be offered from the evidence examined here. On the basis of office holding in the respective General Assemblies, it is clear that industrialists were not the most ubiquitous laymen. In the Church of Scotland nine individuals held ten or more committee posts (see Table 9.5). Of these six were company directors but three of these were heritors, owning landed estates (Balfour of Burleigh, the Master of Polwarth, and James A. Campbell); two were solicitors (Colin Macrae and J. T. Smith). If business considerations entered their minds, they would bear upon endowment, teinds (tithes), and patronage and their implications for inter-church relations. It was as leader of the Scottish Conservatives that Balfour of Burleigh resisted disestablishment in the 1880s. But the politicization of that issue worried him. Devout churchman that he was, church unity had a higher priority.[75] But did the arithmetic of rationalization as well as spiritual unity motivate Anstruther when he and many others in 1894 entered into lengthy conversations with the Free Church and the United Presbyterians about church union?[76]

In the United Free Church of Scotland five individuals held ten or

[73] Lady F. Balfour, *A Memoir of Lord Balfour of Burleigh* (London, 1924); C. A. Malcolm, *The Bank of Scotland* (Edinburgh, 1948), 234.

[74] All information from *DD 1907*.

[75] I. G. C. Hutchison, *A Political History of Scotland* (Edinburgh, 1986), 157–62; Balfour, *Balfour of Burleigh*, 43–54, 143–58.

[76] Drummond and Bulloch, *Church in Late Victorian Scotland*, 114, 306–7.

TABLE 9.5. *Key lay people in the Church of Scotland, 1907, 1935, 1955, and the United Free Church of Scotland, 1907*

Total no. of posts held	1907			1935			1955		
	No. of holders	Share of total posts	%	No. of holders	Share of total posts	%	No. of holders	Share of total posts	%
Church of Scotland									
5	7	35	5.12	7	35	2.65	7	35	3.36
6	2	12	1.75	6	36	2.72			
7	8	56	8.19	9	63	4.77	5	35	3.36
8	5	40	5.85	4	32	2.42	3	24	2.31
9	7	63	9.21	2	18	1.36			
10	4	40	5.85	2	20	1.51			
11	2	22	3.22	1	11	0.83			
12	1	12	1.75						
13				1	13	0.98			
14				1	14	1.06	1	14	1.34
15									
16									
17									
18									
19	1	19	2.78						
20	1	20	2.92						
Total 5–12	38	319	46.64	33	242	18.31	16	108	10.37
TOTAL		684	100.00		1,229	100.00		979	100.00

TABLE 9.5. *cont.*

Total no. of posts held	1907			1935			1955		
	No. of holders	Share of total posts	%	No. of holders	Share of total posts	%	No. of holders	Share of total posts	%
United Free Church of Scotland									
5	15	75	9.01						
6	8	48	5.77						
7	5	35	4.21						
8	2	16	1.92						
9	1	9	1.08						
10									
11	1	11	1.32						
12									
13	1	13	1.56						
14	1	14	1.68						
15									
16	1	16	1.92						
17									
18									
19									
20	1	20	2.40						
Total 5–12	36	257	30.89						
TOTAL		824	100.00						

Sources: Analysis of committees listed in Church of Scotland, *Principal Acts of the General Assembly of the Church of Scotland* (Edinburgh, 1907, 1935, 1955); and United Free Church of Scotland, *Principal Acts of the General Assembly of the United Free Church of Scotland* (Glasgow, 1907).

more places on General Assembly committees in 1907. Of these four were solicitors (Wallace, Cowan, William Robson, and Simpson), only one (Ogilvie) came from the manufacturing-commercial sector. As secretaries and managers of investment and other companies in the financial sector the solicitors may have tendered advice tinged by commercial rather than purely professional calculations. It is much more likely that professional perspectives predominated in their thinking. Cowan was the United Free Church's Law Agent, responsible in the General Assembly for settling legal points. Simpson for half a century before 1924 was Deputy Clerk of the General Assembly, a role dealing with the conduct of General Assembly business.[77] Apart from directing one denomination's fire insurance company what did these active laymen with business backgrounds or linkages contribute to the life of their respective churches at the beginning of the century? Table 9.6 contains some clues. In the Church of Scotland internal organization and external relations preoccupied activist laymen. The company directors in their midst appear to have been less interested in foreign missions and more interested in theological education than the totality of key laymen. In the United Free Church of Scotland active laymen devoted their efforts towards internal organization and charitable funds. Their company directors were even more concerned with these matters than their fellows. That may be the aggregate picture but it depends on the definition of activity (which is unclear when a committee was involved in two functions, e.g. in home missions and fund-raising). And of course there are always exceptional individuals.

At least four functions performed by businessmen among the key laymen in the two Scottish churches can be identified. The role of the solicitors, crucial in a society where state and church were so closely intertwined, has been noticed above. Secondly, like their English counterparts, many of these men were benefactors to church causes. A good example in the Church of Scotland was James Campbell of Stracathro. When his duties as MP took him to London he worshipped at the Crown Court Church near Covent Garden. As London's population shifted westwards so communicants at Crown Court dwindled. Campbell decided that an additional site should be secured in the West End. As a result St Columba's Church of Scotland, Pont Street, Belgravia, was opened in 1884. It cost £20,000 and of this £12,000 came from five members of Crown Court including James Campbell of Stracathro.

[77] G. M. Reith, *Reminiscences of the UFC General Assembly* (Edinburgh, 1933), 17, 275, 302.

TABLE 9.6. *Directions of activity of key lay people in the Church of Scotland, 1907, 1935, 1955, and the United Free Church of Scotland, 1907*

Activity	1907				1935				1955			
	All key laity		DD only		All key laity		DD only		All key laity		DD only	
	No. of offices	%	No. of offices	%	No. of offices	%	No. of offices	%	No. of offices	%	No. of offices	%
Church of Scotland												
Property	0	0.00	0	0.00	7	2.45	0	0.00	4	3.13	1	2.38
Charitable funds	28	8.67	14	8.70	25	8.74	10	10.64	5	3.91	2	4.76
Education	24	7.43	10	6.21	7	2.45	2	2.13	1	0.78	1	2.38
External relations	74	22.91	37	22.98	18	6.29	9	9.57	15	11.72	5	11.90
Faith	26	8.05	14	8.70	13	4.55	3	3.19	5	3.91	0	0.00
Foreign missions	22	6.81	7	4.35	22	7.69	9	9.57	4	3.13	1	2.38
Home missions	32	9.91	15	9.32	17	5.94	6	6.38	13	10.16	5	11.90
Internal organization	81	25.08	41	25.47	106	37.06	47	50.00	51	39.84	20	47.62
Social issues	8	2.48	3	1.86	1	0.35	1	1.06	2	1.56	5	11.90
Theological education	24	7.43	20	12.42	26	9.09	7	7.45	8	6.25	5	11.90
Total	319	100.00	161	100.00	242	100.00	94	100.00	108	100.00	42	100.00
United Free Church of Scotland												
Property	9	3.30	5	3.47								
Charitable funds	37	13.55	26	18.06								
Education	22	8.06	9	6.25								
External relations	9	3.30	4	2.78								
Faith	5	1.83	4	2.78								
Foreign missions	28	10.26	11	7.64								
Home missions	19	6.96	10	6.94								
Internal organization	104	38.10	63	43.75								
Social issues	0	0.00	0	0.00								
Theological education	24	8.79	12	8.33								
Total	257	100.00	144	100.00								

Note: DD = no. of posts on committees in the various areas of activity held by key lay people who were company directors and listed as such in the *Directory of Directors*.

Sources: As for Table 9.5.

He also instigated, though never saw, the rebuilding of the Crown Court Church in 1909; to its cost of £11,000 he subscribed £1,000. In addition he was a great friend and patron of the Church of Scotland church in Dulwich.[78] In the United Free Church of Scotland the crisis of 1904 and afterwards brought a new reliance on wealthy and influential laymen. That year the rump of the Free Church (mostly Highlanders) who declined to join the United Presbyterians in the union of 1900 won an appeal to the House of Lords for ownership of all United Free Church property. The decision caused havoc. United Free Church congregations, some 500,000 church members, were obliged to abandon their churches, halls, manses, and schools to the 20,000 members of the Free Church who stayed outside the merger of 1900. Where they were able, leading laymen lent their aid. John Nicholson, manager of the Clydesdale Bank in Edinburgh and convenor of the United Free Church Finance Committee, organized and promoted an Emergency Fund for the renting of properties until the situation was settled (as it was under the Scottish Churches Act of 1905, though the allocation of properties between rival claimants took much longer).[79] Lord Overtoun gave £10,000 to the fund and was active in meetings to promote the cause of the United Free Church.[80] Thomas Ogilvie the Aberdeen merchant and Thomas Binnie the Glasgow valuer, who both died in the year preceding the General Assembly of 1913, were remembered as 'men of high Christian character, and conspicuous in the ranks of those loyal, energetic and influential laymen who came to the Church's aid in the day of her calamity, besides being all their days eager participants in all her actvities'.[81] In these troubled years Nicholson was also instrumental in locating a site for a new UFCS headquarters. Under his supervision the new headquarters building, in George Street, Edinburgh, was erected. Tragically he died just before it was opened in 1911.[82]

In two other, sometimes contradictory, directions these laymen made their presence felt in the years before 1914. One was in the defence of sectional interests. For example, in the United Free Church Thomas Ogilvie was among those defending the preservation of the denomination's theological college at Aberdeen, which he did on the floor of the General Assembly in 1907.[83] Leading laymen also lent their weight in

[78] G. C. Cameron, *Scots Kirk in London* (Oxford, 1979), 148–56, 169–73, 199–200.
[79] Reith, *Reminiscences*, 71, 77, 120, 127.
[80] Information from Professor R. H. Campbell.
[81] Reith, *Reminiscences*, 147.
[82] Ibid. 120.
[83] Ibid. 83.

the opposite direction, in favour of the uniting of the two major Protestant denominations in Scotland. In the Church of Scotland Balfour of Burleigh and Sir Ralph Anstruther strongly and actively supported such a merger. When the Free Church adjudication of 1904 burst upon the United Free Church of Scotland, Balfour offered his services as a mediator between the two denominations. Anstruther was one of the three members of the Royal Commission chaired by the Earl of Elgin and appointed by A. J. Balfour to report on the dispute. In this period John Cowan, the structural steel manufacturer and a leading Edinburgh elder in the United Free Church, similarly favoured union.[84]

All this is of course impressionistic and awaits assessment in a thorough monograph. One point is certain if the United Free Church experience was replicated in the Church of Scotland: their General Assemblies were dominated by the clergy to a far greater extent than among, say, the Wesleyans or other English Methodists in their annual Conferences. Infrequently, in George Reith's recollections of the United Free Church General Assemblies, did leading laymen engage in the cut and thrust of debate on the floor of the General Assembly. John Nicholson's intervention in 1906, when his resolution 'of deep sympathy with the evicted brethren and congregations, undertaking to stand by them to the uttermost' was adopted, was typical: rare, undisputed, and dealing with a temporal rather than a theological matter.[85]

By the 1930s the Scottish church scene had drastically changed following the union of the Church of Scotland and the United Free Church in 1929. Some 5 per cent of the old UFCS remained in a much weakened United Free Church of Scotland. Among their number was Alexander Forrester-Paton, The Leys-educated vice-chairman and director of Patons & Baldwins, the woollen yarn manufacturers who employed 7,000 people at Alloa and Halifax (thereby ranking among the 100 largest in the UK in the 1930s). Forrester-Paton took a leading part in the reconstruction of the 'Continuing Church' and between 1929 and 1948 (except for a break of two years) served as convenor of the United Free Church Finance Committee. Much of his church-directed interest centred on Alloa where his integrity, public service, and fair business dealing made him a deeply respected figure.[86]

In the nearly doubled Church of Scotland of 1935 places on General Assembly committees became much less concentrated in the hands of

[84] Ibid. 57, 70.
[85] Ibid. 77.
[86] *Alloa Circular and Hillfoots Record*, 14 Apr. 1954; information from Alastair Forrester-Paton in letters to the author, 19 Feb., 6 Apr. 1987.

activists: holders of five or more posts accounted for 47 per cent of all committee places in 1907 but for only 18 per cent in 1935, a trend which continued into the 1950s when the proportion had fallen to 10 per cent (see Table 9.5). The proportion of company directors among these activists might be expected to fall at a similar rate. It did not, as Table 9.4 shows. Well over a third of the activists were company directors until the mid-1950s. Active Scottish churchmen kept their feet firmly in commerce. Again, we can attempt to establish the identity of these lay people and the aggregate nature of their contributions to the national life of their church.

Of the 34 directorships held by the 15 company directors (Table 9.4) 12 were on the boards of insurance companies and 9 on investment and property companies. Only 2 were on bank boards. None apart from William Whitelaw operated at the centre of the Scottish business network of the 1930s.[87] Whitelaw sat on the board of the Bank of Scotland and chaired both the Forth Bridge Railway Co. and its English parent, the giant London & North Eastern Railway. The other bank director was Lord Polwarth who sat on the board of the British Linen Bank, now a subsidiary of Barclays. Four of the activists were directors of the Church of Scotland Fire Insurance Trust, which biased the group's business interests towards the insurance industry. Two of them, Archibald Campbell Black KC, Sheriff of Stirling, Dumbarton, and Clackmannan, and William Huntley Buist, head of a firm of cabinetmakers and then Lord Provost of Dundee,[88] had no other directorships. W. G. C. Hanna was chairman of the Scottish Cities Investment Trust and a director of Scottish Life Assurance. The fourth, Sir John Archibald Roxburgh, chaired Roxburgh, Colin Scott & Co., a shipping firm.[89] Only one of the 15 did not have a board seat on a financial company of some kind, and he sat only on the board of his family firm. This was Sir James Macfarlane, chairman of Macfarlane, Lang & Co. the Glasgow biscuit and bread manufacturers he had headed since 1908.[90]

The aggregate contributions of these men to the work of the General Assembly of the Church of Scotland is indicated in Table 9.6. Matters of property, foreign missions, internal organization (above all), and theological education became more important than in 1907 to all the activists; external relations, faith and doctrine, home missions, and social issues,

[87] See Scott and Hughes, *Anatomy*, 100, 117–25 for the identities of the multiple directors forming these networks.

[88] *Scottish Biographies, 1938* (Glasgow, 1938)

[89] Eyre-Todd, *WW Glasgow*, 183.

[90] *Scottish Biographies, 1938*. Other identifications from *DD* and *WWW*.

less important. The changes no doubt reflected the results of merging with the United Free Church. The company directors among the multiple office holders of 1935 evinced appreciably more interest than the whole group of activists in all areas bar property, faith (and doctrine), and theological education. Perhaps William Whitelaw was typical of these devout Scottish businessmen:

He took a leading part in the affairs of the Church and attended the General Assembly, at which he often spoke. For many years he devoted himself to the work of the committee which took charge of the smaller livings and sought to improve the stipends of those who ministered in poor and scattered districts. When the movement for union of the national Church with the United Free Church began to make headway Whitelaw was one of its most ardent supporters. His long service to the Church of Scotland was acknowledged in 1937 by the presentation to him of his portrait.[91]

Outside the group of multiple office holders on the committees of the General Assembly, sometimes outside the General Assembly itself, were other men of business no less committed to the work of the church. Two, identified as leading Scottish industrialists in the late 1930s, will serve as examples.[92] Sir James Lithgow, shipbuilder, central figure in the rationalization of the Scottish shipbuilding industry, and, as chairman of William Beardmore, a member of the UK business élite, launched several consequential initiatives in the Church of Scotland by his discreet and large generosity—guided and shared often by his reclusive brother Henry. In the cause of church renewal he made gifts of £35,000 to the National Church Extension Fund, set up after the 1929 union. Locally, at Port Glasgow where the early Lithgow yards were located, he matched funds raised by the minister and congregation for restoring the local parish church; and he admitted the minister, the Reverend Harry C. Whitley, into his shipyards as an industrial chaplain. Far more daring was his support of the Reverend Dr George MacLeod (later Lord Mac-Leod), minister of Govan in downtown Glasgow where the Fairfield yards (acquired by Lithgow in 1935) stood. MacLeod, holder of the MC and bar as a result of actions on the Western Front, emerged from the First World War as an active pacifist. Lithgow's first encounter with him proved an embarrassment. MacLeod declined his invitation to attend and ask a blessing on the launch of a Fairfield-built cruiser: there had been no such benediction at the recent launch of the *Queen Mary* and it seemed wrong to MacLeod to bless a warship. Lithgow neverthe-

[91] *The Times*, 21 Jan. 1946.   [92] Scott and Hughes, *Anatomy*, 86.

less persisted. MacLeod attended subsequent launches of merchant vessels and revealed to Lithgow his plans for an unusual approach to church renewal in inner-city Glasgow. The essence of this was that a team, partly of craftsmen, partly of divinity students, would spend their summers on the Isle of Iona, studying, rebuilding the monastery, and developing a community life which they would carry back into Scotland's cities. Lithgow caught something of this vision and started his association with MacLeod's Iona project with a gift of £5,000. In 1943 Sir James Lithgow and his wife instigated the Iona Youth Trust under the auspices of the Church of Scotland's Youth Committee, anonymously endowing it with a covenanted annuity of £20,000 for ten years. At no time did Lithgow concede ground to MacLeod's pacifist, radical, anti-capitalist views. But he was large-minded enough to see that MacLeod could make novel contributions towards the goals of the faith they both shared. His largest gift to the Church of Scotland also arose from a personal contact. Enquiring of the Reverend Harry Whitley why an increasingly infirm minister would not retire, he learned that his pension would be too small for him to live on. Lithgow went to Church of Scotland headquarters to ascertain the facts. Soon after, in July 1946, he ordered the Commercial Bank of Scotland to send all his securities to the Church of Scotland. They were valued at almost £235,000 and were used to assist retiring ministers, missionaries, and sisters of the Women's Home Mission.[93]

The other example is Sir John Craig, chairman of Colvilles the leading Scottish steelmakers. Whereas Lithgow and his brother inherited their father's shipbuilding business, Craig was the fourth son of an iron puddler who started in the steelworks as an office boy. His sheer diligence marked him out. Promotion followed, first by the Colville brothers and then, after they died in 1916, by the senior officials who, with Craig, had earlier become shareholders. Craig steered the firm through the depressed inter-war period, the rationalization of the industry, and into post-1945 investment in the Ravenscraig Works at Motherwell. As the chairman of a firm employing 17,000 in 1955, Sir John Craig (as he became) reached the UK business élite. He did so without losing his Christian faith. In his early manhood he worshipped at Motherwell Dalziel Free Church (which joined the Church of Scotland in 1929), serving as an elder for over fifty years.[94]

By the mid-1950s there were many fewer multiple office holders on

[93] Anthony Slaven, 'James Lithgow', *DSBB*; M. Reid, *James Lithgow* (London, 1964), 175–83, 217–19, 229–32; H. C. Whitley, *Laughter in Heaven* (London, 1962), 40–5, 85–95, 127–34.
[94] Peter L. Payne, 'John Craig', *DSBB*.

General Assembly committees (Table 9.5). Of the six who were members of the Institute of Directors, two (D. B. Bogle and George Waddell Harvey) were solicitors and one (Francis H. N. Walker) was an investment fund manager. The latter's firm, Scottish American Investment Co., ranked fourth by assets among Scottish investment firms.[95] Only one of these activists was titled and he was in semi-retirement. Sir James Fletcher Simpson, formerly managing director of the East India merchants Gordon Woodroffe & Co. London (and before that of Gordon Woodroffe & Co. (Madras) Ltd.), had been chairman of the powerful Madras Chamber of Commerce in the early 1920s.[96] Ownership of a considerable segment of Scotland's primary and secondary industrial sectors had changed hands between the 1930s and 1950s. In the case of the various nationalizations this meant take-over by English interests. Possibly this helps to explain the much diminished presence of businessmen in the leadership of the churches of Scotland, a part of the country where churchgoing was least dented before the 1950s.

Of the non-presbyterian churches in Scotland the Episcopal Church attracted aristocratic and landed interests, the Baptists industrial and commercial men. Absence of data precludes in-depth investigation of the former. The Baptists, however, had in their ranks some of the period's most powerful industrialists in Scotland. The data in Table 9.4 certainly give a very false impression in their case. The single multiple office holder and member of the Institute of Directors in 1907 was Adam Nimmo, coalmaster. His father, also a Baptist, founded the family firm centred on Slamannan, Stirlingshire.[97] By the time of his father's death in 1912 Adam Nimmo was chairman of James Nimmo & Co. and a director of the Fife Coal Co., one of the largest colliery combines in the UK. During the First World War he was a leading figure in the Coal Control by which the Board of Trade administered the industry during the latter part of the war. In the series of bitter confrontations between coalmasters and unions which culminated in the General Strike he was 'the most forceful and intransigent member of the Mining Association central council at a time when the affairs of the coalmining industry dominated industrial politics'.[98] By 1935, still a Baptist multiple office holder, he was chairman of the Fife Coal Co. and on the boards of Shotts Iron, Ailsa Investment Trust, and Scottish Boiler & General Insurance. Living in central Glasgow, he attended one of the key churches in the denomina-

[95] Scott and Hughes, *Anatomy*, 134.
[96] *WWW*; *Red Book of Commerce, 1911* (London, 1911), 395.
[97] Maurice W. Kirby and Sheila Hamilton, 'James Nimmo', *DSBB*.
[98] Maurice W. Kirby and Sheila Hamilton, 'Adam Nimmo', *DSBB*.

tion, Adelaide Place Baptist Church. Here the Baptist Union of Scotland had been formed in 1869 (when the congregation met in Hope Street). Here William Quarrier, the multiple shop retailer and 'paladin of Scottish evangelical philanthropists', was a deacon.[99] Here the denomination's theological college met in an upper room until the First World War at least.[100] Nimmo in 1907 held nine denominational places, in 1935 five. For 1907 it is easier to list the denominational committees on which he did not sit (primarily the Foreign Mission Committee). In 1935 (and now Sir Adam Nimmo KBE) his preferences were confined to property and administration. He was convenor and member of the Loan and Building Committee and member of the committees for Church House, Ministerial Recognition and the Year Book.[101] Interestingly, although he served as denominational treasurer 1913–22, he was not elected as president, the highest office in the church. For some considerable time he also served the Baptist Theological College as its treasurer.[102]

Outside the multiple office holders the most influential business people among the Baptists in Scotland were members of the Coats family, sewing thread manufacturers of Paisley. Their experience illustrates some of the complications that can arise when business wealth is injected into a local church. By the early twentieth century the Coats had spread out into a many-branched clan. The firm founder, James Coats (1774–1857), had ten sons and one daughter. James and Peter Coats, inheritors in 1830 of the thread side of their father's business, had, along with their fraternal partners Thomas and Andrew Coats, all died by 1907. Under the direction of Archibald Coats, second son of Peter, the firm had been converted into a private limited company (1883), had developed into a multinational with plants in the USA and across Europe to Russia, and in 1896 had finally taken over its main British rivals.[103]

Though the second generation were brought up as Baptists only Thomas seems to have made a mark on the denomination. 'Very busy

[99] O. Checkland, *Philanthropy in Victorian Scotland* (Edinburgh, 1980), 258–65; D. W. Bebbington (ed.), *The Baptists in Scotland* (Glasgow, 1988), 150.

[100] Bebbington (ed.), *Baptists*, 82.

[101] BU of S., *YB 1907, 1935*.

[102] D. B. Murray, *The First Hundred Years* (Glasgow, 1969), 75, which observes that there were two cousins named Adam Nimmo both active in the Baptist Church. There is the possibility therefore that in 1907 two different people held the nine offices I have ascribed to Adam Nimmo the coalmaster. In the BU of S., *YB 1907*, the multiple office holder is Adam Nimmo MA.

[103] A. Coats, *From the Cottage to the Castle* (Paisley, 1896), 40; M. Blair, *The Paisley Thread Industry* (Paisley, 1907), 44–53; J. B. K. Hunter, 'Archibald Coats', *DSBB*; idem, 'Thomas Coats', ibid; idem, 'Otto Ernest Philippi', ibid.

and very prosperous as he was, Thomas Coats never bowed the knee to Mammon'—which would have been very easy for him since he left £1.3 million at his death. He became well known for his charitable gifts to the town of Paisley (a park and an observatory), his donations to all sorts of emergency relief funds and to various Baptist churches, not least Storie Street Baptist Church, Paisley, where he was a member.[104] After his death in 1883 his widow, his five sons, and five daughters determined to build a new Baptist church in Paisley worthy of his memory. In his life neither he nor his brother Sir Peter Coats 'ever allowed the question of cost to stand in the way of the realisation of their ideal'.[105] The memorial would be raised on the same principle.

The result was the Thomas Coats Memorial Church, Paisley, a Nonconformist cathedral unsurpassed in Britain.[106] Designed by Hippolyte J. Blanc, the French architect then in Edinburgh, its Gothic lines in massive red sandstone rise up from a vast flight of steps, ascend to a triple-arched main doorway, and culminate in a 220-foot high crown tower. Inside the finest craftsmanship adorned vestibule, parquet-floored nave (seating 1,000), and marble-floored chancel. The permanently visible baptistry was also in Italian marble. Both the marble-and-alabaster pulpit and the bronze lectern were designed by Blanc. The richly carved organ with four manuals and 3,040 pipes was by William Hill & Son of London (whence it was taken to Paisley on a special train of twelve wagons). A hall below the sanctuary seated 500. Separate vestries for the minister (with its own handsome, self-contained toilet), deacons, organist/choirmaster, and choir (men and women separately accommodated) adjoined. This 'Baptist cathedral' took nine years to build and cost £150,000. Opened in 1894 it was indeed a fitting memorial.[107]

Less fitting were the restrictions imposed by the family on the use of the new church. The buildings and property were to belong to the Coats family. The sanctuary would be used only for religious and musical services. Social meetings would be confined to the Hall. Bible classes might meet in the Hall but not Sunday School classes. The Coats family

[104] *Paisley and Renfrewshire Gazette*, 12 May 1894; *Paisley Daily Express*, 18 Feb. 1918; Bebbington (ed.), *Baptists*, 52, 155–6.
[105] *Paisley and Renfrewshire Gazette*, 12 May 1894.
[106] C. Binfield, 'Business Paternalism and the Congregational Ideal', in D. J. Jeremy (ed.), *Business and Religion in Britain* (Aldershot, 1988), 133.
[107] D. D. Hair *et al.*, *The Thomas Coats Memorial Church* (Paisley, 1945); author's impressions when shown around by the caretaker Mr Sam Caldwell, 8 Oct. 1986; D. Norval, *The Organ* (Paisley, 1985); information from Local History Department, Paisley Central Library, letter to author, 3 July 1987.

would be responsible for the upkeep of the buildings, appointing and paying the caretakers; they would also pay the expenses of an organist and choir and 'reserve the right to use the church on week days for organ recitals and other musical services of a religious character.' No seat rents would be charged, however. Nor would conditions of membership be changed.[108] Some of these conditions were insensitive. Presumably Sunday School work was excluded from the premises because of the hazard of hooliganism.[109] Whatever the reason, it forced the congregation to find another site and build another set of halls (in Walker Street) at a cost of £8,152: a high opportunity cost and an unhealthy physical division between religious education and religious worship which rarely occurred elsewhere.[110] Removal of the responsibility for the building from the congregation created a debilitating dependence on the rich man in the midst, a risk which pious but prudent businessmen avoided.[111]

The Coats family's control over the choir also opened the possibility of their control over liturgy, as had happened at Christ Church, Port Sunlight, with William Lever. Indeed the impending opening of the Thomas Coats Memorial Church in May 1894 stirred George H. Coats, curer and retailer of hams and director of psalmody with the Storie Street congregation for twenty-five years, to deliver and publish a lecture on *An Ideal Baptist Church*. In calling for a new reverence in worship, going as far as kneeling, a uniformed choir, and its own collection of hymns and psalms pointed for chanting, he was surely anticipating the higher liturgical mode invited by the new church's architectural forms.[112] Other Baptists reading G. H. Coats's pamphlet found in the Thomas Coats Memorial Church what might be called a sacramental model for Baptist worship, more suited to upper- and middle-class tastes than to the more uninhibited traditions of the lower classes. George Holms Coats was the son of Bailie William Holms Coats of Paisley and brother of the Reverend Dr Jervis Coats, minister of Govan Baptist Church and President of the Baptist Theological College in Glasgow. Though not in the same family line as the thread manufacturers he was distantly related to them and clearly welcomed the upward liturgical shift that the other side of the family envisaged in their memorial to their father. Later though, G. H. Coats lost his faith and thought more critically

---

[108] Hair *et al.*, *Thomas Coats Memorial Church*, 69.

[109] D. J. Jeremy *et al.*, *A Century of Grace* (Southend-on-Sea, 1982), 49.

[110] Hair *et al.*, *Thomas Coats Memorial Church*, 85–9.

[111] D. J. Jeremy, 'Chapel in a Business Career', in Jeremy (ed.), *Business and Religion*.

[112] Murray, *First Hundred Years*, 57; Hair *et al.*, *Thomas Coats Memorial Church*, 68–9.

about the changes that followed the move into the Memorial Church.[113] In essence they risked turning the church into the fief of a single family, by destroying its theocratic-egalitarian character, imposing a new formality in worship, and perhaps converting the church into an extension of the Coats' thread mills.

Did this in fact happen? It is doubtful. First, the people of Paisley, on account of Scotland's religious divisions, had several other denominational brands from which to choose. Second, the Coats family were not confined to the Baptist denomination. Sir Peter Coats had switched to the United Presbyterians, for example. Thirdly, there was another Baptist church (in George Street, Paisley), to which those uncomfortable in the 'cathedral' might go. Finally, it may be observed that the Coats were not the only rich clan to attend the Thomas Coats Memorial Church. Another wealthy business family was the McCallums, headed by Sir John M. McCallum MP, soap manufacturer and deacon in the church.[114]

There is evidence on the other side, however. Some of the former practices which bound the congregation together were abandoned when they removed from Storie Street to the Thomas Coats Memorial Church. The effects were questionable. Backslidden in old age, George H. Coats, who resigned in 1916 after fifty years with the church, recalled,

It is interesting perhaps to know that the question of plurality of elders, though it has fallen into disuse, has never been re-considered by the Church; neither has the continuance of the Love Feast. They have simply been dropped, and the fine brotherly feeling and human interest which they fostered have perhaps suffered by their disuse. There is little hope of these practices being revived however under the conditions as they at present exist in the magnificent buildings called The Thomas Coats Memorial Church.[115]

Returning to the samples of key Baptist lay leaders in 1907, 1935, and 1955, it is noticeable that no member of the Coats family appears in these samples in 1907. That year Sir Thomas Glen Coats, 1st Baronet and son of Thomas Coats, held just one post on the committees of the Baptist Union of Scotland, membership of the Loan and Building Fund, of which he was treasurer. In Paisley he was the 'vital link between the congregation and the Coats family. He had many times acted as chairman at important meetings of the church; and so deep and active

---

[113] G. H. Coats, *Rambling Recollections* (printed privately), *passim*; Eyre-Todd, *WW Glasgow*, 44.

[114] Hair *et al.*, *Thomas Coats Memorial Church*, 93, 96, 99; Bebbington (ed.), *Baptists*, 52.

[115] Coats, *Rambling Recollections*, 139.

was his interest in it that he might have been called its President.'[116] At his death in 1922 Sir Thomas Glen Coats left over £1.651 million, £300,000 more than his father (though comparison is distorted by war-time inflation).[117] By 1935 there were two Coats among the Baptist activists, Miss O. M. Coats and Thomas Coats. The latter was a director of J. & P. Coats and of Cardiff Collieries. Both appear among the key lay leaders of 1955 together with Mrs Thomas Coats. Thomas Coats still retained his two directorships. The other multiple office holder among the Scottish Baptists of 1955 was Charles S. Muir, chairman and managing director of Charles Muir (Castle Bakery) Ltd. of Glasgow and director of Kyles of Bute Hydropathic Ltd. In short, what the lay leaderships of the Baptists of Scotland lacked in numbers they made up in weight. Nor were they so clerically dominated as the presbyterian denominations.

(b) Wales

If Table 9.7 reveals anything about the identity of businessmen in the life of the churches in Wales, it is that they were not members of the Institute of Directors. Whether this meant they were small business people or middle managers, or that they had little sense of solidarity with their English counterparts, will only come from more detailed study than is possible here.

The three Nonconformist bodies, the Independents, Calvinistic Methodists, and Baptists, were led, in so far as laymen played a part in denominational affairs, by men of local standing.[118] With the Independents, for example, there were seven JPs among the two dozen or so (the number is not precise because so many Joneses shared the same initials) who held the 36 national positions in 1907. The Calvinistic Methodists, a somewhat larger body (see Table 1.7), mustered a dozen JPs, at least one alderman, and two MPs (David Davies and J. Herbert Lewis) among the laymen who held the 112 national places on the committees of their General Assembly.[119]

---

[116] Hair et al., *Thomas Coats Memorial Church*, 102. For his career see *Bailie*, No. 711 (2 June 1886); *Paisley and Renfrewshire Gazette*, 15 July 1922.

[117] W. D. Rubinstein, 'British Millionaires', *Bulletin of the Institute of Historical Research*, 47 (1974), 209, 216.

[118] For the Nonconformist background see E. T. Davies, *Religion in the Industrial Revolution in South Wales* (Cardiff, 1965), 44–96.

[119] The annual handbooks of these two denominations are in Welsh. I am most grateful to my colleague John Hacche for translating the Methodists' handbooks and to the Revd Dr R. Tudur Jones of Bala-Bangor College, Bangor, for supplying relevant pages of the Independents' handbooks complete with English translation.

TABLE 9.7. *Company directorships among key lay leaders in the churches in Wales and Ireland, 1907, 1935, 1955*

	1907	1935	1955
Wales			
Church in Wales[a]			
No. of national lay posts	n/a	457	486
No. of key lay leaders		6	10
No. of co. dirs. among lay leaders		2	2
Co. directors as % of key leaders		33.33%	20.00%
No. of directorships		5	4
No. of directorships in mfg.		2	0
Independents (Congregationalists)			
No. of national lay posts	36	50	39
No. of key lay leaders	1		
No. of co. dirs. among lay leaders	0		
Co. directors as % of key leaders			
No. of directorships			
No. of directorships in mfg.			
Calvinistic Methodists (Presbyterians)[b]			
No. of national lay posts	112	137	137
No. of key lay leaders	3	3	6
No. of co. dirs. among lay leaders	1		0
Co. directors as % of key leaders	33.33%		
No. of directorships	1		
No. of directorships in mfg.			
Baptists			
No. of national lay posts	11	n/a	18
No. of key lay leaders			
No. of co. dirs. among lay leaders			
Co. directors as % of key leaders			
No. of directorships			
No. of directorships in mfg.			
Ireland			
Church of Ireland			
No. of national lay posts	603	644	596
No. of key lay leaders	16	19	13
No. of co. dirs. among lay leaders	6	0	1
Co. directors as % of key leaders	37.5%		7.69%
No. of directorships	13		3
No. of directorships in mfg.			1
Presbyterian Church in Ireland			
No. of national lay posts	431	438	416
No. of key lay leaders	20	24	18
No. of co. dirs. among lay leaders	7	3	3
Co. directors as % of key leaders	35.00%	12.50%	16.67%
No. of directorships	10	3	7
No. of directorships in mfg.	2		4

Note: Unless stated otherwise, key lay people are those holding five or more national posts.

[a] Key years: 1936, 1959.
[b] Key = four or more posts in 1907, 1933, 1954.

Sources: As for Table 9.4.

On the basis of multiple office holding, the only man to hold as many as five posts in any of the three benchmark years among the Independents was Josiah Thomas JP, a marine surveyor of Liverpool in 1907. 'He had a great interest in periodical literature. He was the proprietor of *Y Tyst* (the weekly organ of the Welsh Independents); he bought the children's magazine, *Tywysydd y Plant* and the weekly newspaper, *Y Celt*; he edited the Independents' monthly journal, *Y Dysgedydd*; he was the Chairman of the Union of Welsh Independents in 1905 and delivered his address at the meetings at Tredegar in that year on "The Cry from the Pew."'[120]

Only one of the laymen in these two denominations has been identified as a member of the Institute of Directors. J. E. Powell JP (a Presbyterian) of Wrexham was on the local board of the Alliance Assurance Co. in 1907. Nothing useful can presently be said about the Welsh Baptists: for one of the sample years their records are missing; for the other years the records provide no clues to identity (essential given so many shared names).[121]

There is clearly much more to be learned about the lay leadership in Welsh Nonconformity during the twentieth century, both in Wales and in the Welsh communities in cities like London, Manchester, and Liverpool. The *Dictionary of Business Biography* includes two entries on Welsh Nonconformist businessmen: William Evans, the Rhondda grocer and mineral water manufacturer (of Corona 'pop' fame) who in 1930–1 served as president of the Baptist Union of Wales; and Sir William Price, who engineered the merger of most London dairies with United Dairies, his own firm, during the First World War, and was elder and treasurer of the Presbyterian Church of Wales in Shirland Road, Paddington.[122]

Episcopalians in Wales relied for their leadership much more on the landed and ruling classes than the Nonconformists. In the Welsh Church the clergy were more radical than the laity, indeed more radical than the contemporary councils of Welsh Nonconformity at the end of the nineteenth century.[123] Perhaps it was easier to criticize industrialization from rural vantage points than from industrial ones.

Episcopalians had no higher a proportion of company directors among

---

[120] Revd Dr R. Tudur Jones to author, 20 Feb. 1989, information derived from *Y Dysgedydd* (1913), 530–1, 533–2.

[121] I am grateful to the Revd P. D. Richards, assistant secretary of the Baptist Union of Wales, for sending me lists of Council members for 1907 and 1955.

[122] Colin Baber and Trevor Boyns, 'William Evans', *DBB*; P. J. Atkins, 'William Price', *ibid.*

[123] Davies, *Religion*, 130–2.

their lay leaders, if Table 9.7 tells the whole story, than the Nonconformists. Disestablished by the Liberal Government in 1914 the Church in Wales had come into being in 1920. Its supreme legislative body was the Governing Body, parallel to the Church of England's Church Assembly, presided over by the Archbishop of Wales and meeting once a year. Its 502 members included 320 lay persons. The crucial financial and administrative body, however, was the Representative Body of the Church in Wales. 'It bears somewhat the same relation to the Governing Body as the Board of Finance in various dioceses bears to the Diocesan Conference.'[124] For this reason the identification of key lay people has been based on the Representative Body and its committees (offering 137 positions in 1936, 166 in 1959).

The results are in Table 9.7. In absolute terms only two activists were members of the Institute of Directors in 1936 and only two in 1959. Sir Watkin Randle Kynaston Mainwaring Kt., of St Asaph, educated at Eton and Christ Church, Oxford, a minor political figure with First World War experience in Egypt, was director of Gillett Bros. Discount Co.[125] William Edward Cecil Tregoning, educated at Harrow and Trinity, Cambridge, had succeeded to the multi-generational family business of steel and tinplate manufacture John S. Tregoning & Co. and was director of three related companies.[126] In 1959 (the church's *Official Handbook* was not published in 1955) the same representation of heavy industry and finance recurred. Robert Wynne Bankes, son of Lord Justice Sir John Eldon Bankes, educated at Eton and University College, Oxford, and Inner Temple, was secretary of the Institute of Chartered Accountants, 1935–49; in 1955 he was director of Halkyn District United Mines. David Wyamar Vaughan, Rugby-educated, had worked up through Barclays Bank becoming a director of the Cardiff and Swansea boards and then of the main board.[127] In Wales the social distinctions, if not the social concerns, of Nonconformity and erstwhile Establishment were clearly extrapolated into business.

(c) Ireland: South and North

At the beginning of the century the socio-economic dimension of the Irish church scene reflected that of the rest of the United Kingdom: episcopalians drew their strength from the landed, ruling classes, other

[124] C. of E., *YB 1926*, 463.

[125] *WW 1935*.

[126] *WW Wales 1937*; *DD 1935*; W. E. Minchinton, 'The Tinplate Maker and Technical Change', *Explorations in Entrepreneurial History*, 7 (1970).

[127] *DD 1955*; *WW 1958*.

Protestants (here Presbyterians) from the industrial urban middle classes. Table 9.7 summarizes the situation. In the Presbyterian Church in Ireland the proportion of lay leaders who were also members of the Institute of Directors was from the 1930s consistently higher than in the episcopalian Church of Ireland.

In the Church of Ireland laymen sat in the House of Representatives of the General Synod and on Synod's 17 or so committees. Here representatives of the Irish ruling classes—landlords and gentry, most with military or legal experience, judges and barristers—met regularly to discuss church education, clerical training, missions, Sunday observance, and the administrative affairs of the church. Few lacked titles, estates, or a seat on the magistrates' bench. Typical of the six company directors among the activists of 1907 were Sir James Creed Meredith and Hugh de Fellenberg Montgomery. Meredith was the product of Trinity College Dublin and the Irish Bar; a minor Civil Servant, he became secretary of the Royal University of Ireland. Besides being one of the honorary secretaries of the General Synod, he was Deputy Grand Master of the Freemasons in Ireland. In the business world he sat on the Irish board of the Yorkshire Insurance Co. and on that of the Irish Civil Services Permanent Building Society.[128] Montgomery, who had a Swiss mother, was educated at Christ Church, Oxford, held land in the Clogher valley, and was a member of the Board of Agriculture for Ireland; he was a JP of Co. Fermanagh and had served as Sheriff of both Co. Fermanagh and Co. Tyrone. His clubs were the Travellers', Alpine, and University, Dublin. His solitary directorship was of the Clogher Valley Railway Co.[129] Clearly neither was primarily entrepreneur or manager: their business connections were simply expressions of other interests. None of these men seems to have taken a prominent part in the Dublin Chamber of Commerce which was dominated by old merchant families.[130] Any alliance between Church and business decayed after Irish independence in 1922. By the 1940s the Church of Ireland's minority status in the Republic was being sharply underlined in many directions.[131] By the 1950s the single company director among the Church of Ireland's lay activists was Captain John C. Herdman OBE DL, of Sion Mills, Co.

[128] E. M. Cosgrave and W. T. Pike (eds.), *Dublin and County Dublin in the Twentieth Century* (Brighton, 1908), 106.

[129] R. M. Young and W. T. Pike (eds.), *Belfast and the Province of Ulster in the Twentieth Century* (Brighton, 1909), 429.

[130] L. M. Cullen, *Princes and Pirates* (Dublin, 1983), 69–91.

[131] J. H. Whyte, 'Political Life in the South', in M. Hurley (ed.), *Irish Anglicanism* (Dublin, 1970).

Tyrone, chairman of Strabane & Letterkenny Railway Co. and director of Hugh Stevenson & Co. and Spamount Woollen Co.

Somewhat different were the business connections of the Presbyterian Church in Ireland lay leaders. These men depended on business and industry for their livelihood. With that they carried civic weight. At the beginning of the century Sir Robert Anderson, for instance, had a finger in many pies: textiles, firewood, property, and Vulcanite. He had been High Sheriff of Belfast in 1902 and was Lord Mayor of the city in 1908–9. Sir William James Baxter was head of W. J. Baxter, chemist and wholesale merchant of Coleraine. Robert Smyth was a Strabane grain merchant and miller; William Moffat Clow, a Glasgow-born corn miller at Portadown; James Harper, a Londonderry leather manufacturer; and Joseph Cuthbert, a Belfast-based South African merchant apparently trading in leather.[132] Above them stood Sir William Crawford. The son of a Presbyterian clergyman, he had worked his way up to become senior managing director and vice-chairman of the York Street Flax Spinning Co. which, employing 4,500 in 1907, placed him in the British business élite of that year. He was as powerful in Presbyterian affairs as a layman could be, sitting on fourteen committees of the church's Assembly.[133] None of their successors in 1935 and 1955 reached the commercial and industrial stature of these men.

The great omission in this analysis, as with the other regions (as explained in the Introduction), is any treatment of business figures in the Catholic Church, the dominant church in the South of Ireland and in the Republic after 1922. A thorough historical investigation is badly needed to do justice to the topic of entrepreneurship in Ireland, both north and south of the Border.

---

[132] Young and Pike (eds.), *Belfast*, 326, 327, 359, 369, 390, 453.
[133] Emily Boyle, 'William Crawford', *DBB*; Young and Pike, (eds.), *Belfast*, 329.

10

Interdenominational Scenes, 1900–1960

I BUSINESS PEOPLE IN INTERDENOMINATIONAL SOCIETIES, 1900–1960

The identity and functions of business people in the work of inter-denominational Christian enterprises can be discovered in at least three ways. The careers of members of the business élites will yield some cases, the lists of presidents, vice-presidents etc. of the societies them-selves will produce others. Case studies of the interdenominational orga-nizations themselves will be most illuminating. Here there is limited space for case-studies. One is presented in the second section of this chapter.

If interest is confined to specifically Christian interdenominational societies—the British and Foreign Bible Society (BFBS) or the YMCA for example, as opposed to more vaguely religious groups like Free-masonry or Moral Re-armament—three impressions remain. First, there is a welter of such societies. A separate study would be necessary to quantify and analyse the dozens recorded in the advertisement pages of the churches' national year books or *The Annual Charities Register and Digest*. Second, the most numerous interdenominational societies emerged from the evangelical wings of the churches. Evangelicals had little difficulty in recognizing one another's orders in the various denomi-nations, which made co-operation between them much easier than for High Churchmen. Bible religion united; apostolic succession religion divided. Third, among the various societies there was a distinct division between the older, more respectable organizations whose activities had upper-class support and even royal patronage, and the newer, more aggressive societies not yet wholly socially acceptable.

The biographies assembled for the business élites of 1907, 1935, and 1955 reveal very few individuals linked to any of these religious interdenominational societies: less than two dozen individuals out of the 476 whose obituaries have been assembled. With these men associations with the BFBS and the YMCA, two of the older societies, cropped up most often. Among chairmen, George Cadbury, Joseph Storrs Fry, Sir Josiah Stamp, and Sir John Laing were vice-presidents of the BFBS. Sir Frank Gill of Standard Telephones & Cables and vicar's warden at Christ Church, Beckenham, was on the BFBS Committee, its governing body, from 1945 until his death.[1] W. H. Wills (Lord Winterstoke) of Imperial Tobacco was a strong supporter of the Society. None of the managing directors was a BFBS vice-president.

The YMCA, founded by businessmen, recruited more strongly among the heads of big businesses.[2] YMCA vice-presidents in the three benchmark years of this study included George Cadbury, Joseph Storrs Fry, Sir William Henry Houldsworth (Fine Cotton Spinners & Doublers), Richard Pilkington, William Windle Pilkington, Lord Bennett of Edgbaston (Lucas), Sir John Craig, E. L. Hann and A. G. B. Owen. Sir John Dewrance (Babcock & Wilcox) was a YMCA supporter. At Blackburn the YMCA branch president was Brigadier-General Arthur Birtwistle (Birtwistle & Fielding), and in Manchester Sir William Clare Lees (Bleachers' Association) was on the board of management.[3] Both these men were managing directors.

Among the newer interdenominational bodies the roles of Lord Hambleden, Samuel Courtauld, Basil Smallpeice, and Sir Gordon Radley in connection with the British Council of Churches, Christian Frontier, and Christian Teamwork have been examined in Chapter 6. Not all active Christian business leaders gave priority to the more reasoned, apologetic, infiltrational approach to pagan society which those organizations represented. Sir John Laing and Sir Alfred Owen, one Brethren the other Anglican but both strong evangelicals, promoted a direct, evangelistic approach in presenting their faith to the world. For John Laing this took him into such organizations as the Crusader Union (on its national Committee in 1935 and 1955) and Inter-Varsity Fellow-

---

[1] My thanks to Mrs Ingrid Roderick, Records Administrator of the Bible Society, and Peter Young, the S.T.C. company historian, for this information.

[2] C. Binfield, *George Williams and the YMCA* (London, 1973).

[3] *Northern Daily Telegraph*, 13 May 1937; Roger Lloyd-Jones, 'William Clare Lees', *DBB*.

ship (on whose Business Advisory Committee he sat in 1935[4]). With a number of other business and professional people, like P. S. Henman, in the mid-1940s Laing was instrumental in the founding and funding of the London Bible College, an interdenominational institution of higher education committed to evangelical scholarship.[5] A. G. B. Owen's intitiatives in evangelism are examined in the case study below.

A glance at the vice-presidents of these various 'penumbra' societies reveals that the YMCA and the BFBS collected the longest lists.[6] In 1907 the YMCA had 150 vice-presidents, the BFBS 64 (clergy and laity). By 1935 the YMCA's list had shrunk to 95 and the BFBS's grown to 81. In 1955 the YMCA list stood at 85 while the BFBS's had contracted to 61. No similar religious societies could match these in length or eminence; not even the Boys' Brigade which originated in and drew much of its strength from Scotland, the most religious part of the UK.[7] By 1955 the BFBS had the patronage of the Queen and the Queen Mother; the YWCA had the Queen as patron also. In the peerage they could call on a stream of powerful figures and families: Aberdeen, Brassey, Dartmouth, Halifax, Kinnaird, Salisbury, and the rest. Among them and beyond them were numerous businessmen: Astor, Kinnaird (banking and insurance), Leverhulme, Luke, Rochester, Wolseley, and (outside the peerage) Sir Henry Bemrose, Sir George Chubb, Sir Algernon Coote, John Cory (South Wales coal firms), Williamson Lamplough, Joseph Rank, Robert Leatham Barclay, Robert Noton Barclay, Sir Harold Mackintosh, Sir William Mallinson, Sir Albert Spicer, Joseph Herbert Tritton (banking), Alderman Sir George White. Names familiar in the lay leaderships of the denominations, these men, their wives and widows, lent the voluntary Christian societies the weight and reputation needed for their work. Between the 1930s and the 1950s, as in the churches themselves, businessmen proportionately diminished: though whether this was a push or pull effect is impossible presently to tell. Much more

[4] Information from Miss Heather Keep, Assistant Director, Crusaders; *Inter-Varsity Magazine* (Lent Term 1935).

[5] R. Coad, *Laing: The Biography of Sir John W. Laing CBE* (London, 1979), 191–2; David J. Jeremy, 'Philip Sydney Henman', *DBB*.

[6] Lists of vice-presidents for 1907, 1935, and 1955 of the BFBS and the YMCA have been kindly supplied me by Mrs Roderick of the Bible Society and C. John Naylor, secretary of the National Council of YMCAs. I am grateful also to the officials and archivists of the Boys' Brigade, the Girls' Brigade, Barnardos, Crusaders, the Oxford Group (MRA), UCCF (formerly IVF), Young Life, and the YWCA who all supplied similar information; space unfortunately prevented the inclusion of details in my analysis.

[7] In terms of numbers of BB members per thousand of the population. See J. Springhall *et al.*, *Sure and Stedfast* (London, 1983), *passim*, 258.

work needs to be done on this aspect of the subject. What can emerge is illustrated by the following case-study.

2 BUSINESSMEN AND THE BILLY GRAHAM GREATER LONDON CRUSADE, 1954

Unknown in 1946–7, Billy Graham, Cliff Barrows, and their thirty-strong evangelistic team seven years later captured national media attention in Britain. Over twelve weeks (1 March–22 May 1954) the meetings, most nights in Harringay Arena, attracted over two million attendances and brought 38,000 'decisions for Christ'. Whatever the detractors said, the Billy Graham team made a remarkable impression on the people of London and the provinces (reached by television relay services).[8] Recalling the accusation against earlier generations of industrialists, that they used religion as a means of workforce control, the question arises about the Billy Graham Crusade. How far was it promoted and paid for by big business interests? Who were the businessmen backing Billy Graham? What were their motives? What was their precise role? How successful were they in mobilizing finance? The papers of A. G. B. Owen (encountered in earlier chapters), chairman of the Crusade Finance Sub-committee, offer answers to these and related questions.

Of the sixteen members of the Crusade's Executive Committee seven were clergymen (the most senior being the Right Reverend Hugh R. Gough, Bishop of Barking); another member, Eric Hutchings, was a British Youth for Christ evangelist[9]; and three, including the chairman (Major-General D. J. Wilson-Haffenden[10]), had military titles.[11] Of the remaining five three were company chairmen. One was A. G. B. Owen. He had come into contact with Billy Graham in 1946–7 when

[8] F. Colquhoun, *Harringay Story* (London, 1955); C. T. Cook, *London Hears Billy Graham* (London, 1954).

[9] A. Eric Hutchings (1910–82) was a former insurance company inspector from Manchester who became a powerful evangelist in the inter-war years. He was appointed Field Director for British Youth for Christ, offshoot of YFC International, in 1947. J. E. Tuck, *Your Master Proclaim* (London, 1968). I am grateful to Mrs Audrey Jones of Spurgeon's College for information on Eric Hutchings.

[10] *The Times*, 2 June 1986: Wilson-Haffenden (1901–86) was the son of a Baptist minister; a career officer in the Indian Army between the wars, he was responsible for provisioning the retreating troops at Dunkirk; after the war he served the Church Missionary Society as financial and administrative secretary.

[11] For lists of members of the Executive Committee and the Council of Reference of the Crusade see *London Crusade News*, No. 5 (Feb. 1954).

Graham and Cliff Barrows as evangelists for Youth for Christ International Inc. (founded in Chicago in 1944 by a businessman, George M. Wilson, and the pastor and broadcaster Torrey M. Johnson) had made an unremarked preaching tour of Britain. Graham and Barrows visited Birmingham and out of that encounter came Birmingham Youth for Christ. Owen effectively led Birmingham YFC, which focused on Saturday night youth rallies in Birmingham Town Hall. In 1951 he had helped organize and fund the BYFC's two weeks of meetings led by the English Baptist evangelist the Reverend Stephen F. Olford. Experience of that local campaign, which cost £1,300 to promote, equipped Owen for the mission to London in 1954.[12] Besides Owen there was (Alexander) Lindsay Glegg (1882–1975), son of Sir Alexander Glegg of Aberdeen, educated at Dulwich College and chairman of linoleum manufacturing companies in west London, with pullulating interests in a host of evangelical societies from Christian Endeavour and Crusaders to the Advent Testimony and Preparation Movement.[13] The third was John Henderson (b. 1888), Conservative MP for Cathcart, Glasgow since 1946, chairman of J. Henderson Ltd., produce importers of Glasgow, and contributor to various religious periodicals as well as chairman of the Houses of Parliament Christian Fellowship.[14] Of the other two members, Oliver Stott was assistant managing director of William Dibben & Sons Ltd., builders' merchants of Southampton.[15] Douglas S. Young was an engineer.[16]

Behind the Executive Committee stood a Council of Reference. Of these 50 men 25 were ministers and clergymen, two were evangelists (Stephen Olford and Tom Rees). Only three of the 23 laymen have been identified as active in business: Alderman Cyril Black, Conservative MP, Wimbledon property developer, and Baptist;[17] George Goyder, managing director of British International Paper Ltd.;[18] and John W. Laing CBE, chairman of one of the two largest building and construction companies in the UK.[19] One other businessman sometimes attended meetings of the Executive Committee and its associated sub-committees

[12] These remarks are based on the author's unpublished paper 'Businessmen in Interdenominational Activity: Birmingham Youth for Christ, 1940s–1950s' to appear in the *Baptist Quarterly* in 1990.

[13] *WWW*; *DD 1954*.

[14] *WW 1958*; *DD 1955*.

[15] *DD 1954*.

[16] Judging by his qualifications.

[17] *DD 1954*; Henry Townsend, *Robert Wilson Black* (London, 1954), 42.

[18] *WW 1986*; above ch. 6.

[19] Coad, *Laing*, 200.

by virtue of his position as honorary treasurer of the (World's) Evangelical Alliance, an umbrella organization which with the Billy Graham Evangelistic Association sponsored the Crusade: namely John H. Cordle, managing director of the family textile firm E. W. Cordle & Son Ltd. and member of the Church Assembly 1946–53. He was already known to A. G. B. Owen: their families had met at Sheringham CSSM and the Owens later took summer holidays in the roomy Cordle home at Eaton Mascot, Shropshire. John Cordle's later career veered away from evangelical norms: he was twice divorced and, Tory MP for Bournemouth since 1959, he was forced in 1977 to resign his seat as a result of his links with the corrupt architect John Poulson.[20] Cordle's name appeared as an Executive Committee member on Crusade letterhead during 1953 but by early 1954 had been dropped.

The key committee from a business point of view was the Finance Committee, though this was not seen as such at first. It was chaired by A. G. B. Owen the Crusade treasurer.[21] On 25 March 1953 F. Roy Cattell, secretary of the Evangelical Alliance and executive secretary of the Crusade, wrote to AGB introducing the Executive Committee's plans and AGB to his new responsibilities as honorary treasurer. Cattell added, 'this all means that the initial campaign of preparation over here is laying stress upon prayer rather than finance. A little later I think it will be advisable to form a Finance Committee and probably appoint an Assistant Treasurer who is in London and to whom I can refer over matters of detail.'[22] Part of Cattell's confident neglect of finance arose from the Billy Graham Team's assurance that they would meet all their own personal expenses (including salaries) and transatlantic travel costs from US sources. Moreover the Americans had sent over $5,000 to fund the necessary administrative system prior to a general appeal (the Evangelical Alliance having very limited resources for this purpose).[23]

Negotiations to bring Billy Graham to London for the crusade had commenced much earlier: in August 1951 Graham's wish to stage such a visit was communicated to the (World's) Evangelical Alliance; in March 1952 he visited England and met about 800 church leaders at a reception at Church House, Westminster; an official invitation from

[20] *WWMP*; A. Doig, *Corruption and Misconduct in Contemporary British Politics* (Harmondsworth, 1984), 150–4.
[21] AGBO was invited to become treasurer in Feb. 1953: ROA, 1953 GR.2, F. Roy Cattell to AGBO, 27 Feb. 1953.
[22] Ibid., Cattell to AGBO, 25 Mar. 1953.
[23] Ibid., Cattell to AGBO, 25 Mar. 1953 enclosure (Minute 9 of Crusade Executive Committee, held 29 Jan. 1953).

the Evangelical Alliance followed; and in November 1952 Jerry Beavan, Graham's executive secretary, met the (EA) Council to co-ordinate plans, deciding that a separate organization, the Executive Committee and its Council of Reference, would be needed. By mid-May 1953 a Finance Committee was formed, comprising AGB (chairman), Lindsay Glegg, Oliver Stott and the Revd Arthur Goodwin Hudson (Vicar of St Mary Magdalene, Holloway, North London). Stott was assistant treasurer.[24]

Clearly A. G. B. Owen was the key figure in developing the Crusade's finances. His Finance Committee did not meet until 2 October 1953 (assembling in the Kent House offices of the Owen Organization in Great Titchfield Street in London's West End). Three major items were considered: the terms of an agreement for the hire of Harringay Arena; the financial arrangement between the Billy Graham organization and the London Crusade Committee; and the method and timing of fund-raising in England.[25] After the meeting AGB expressed his anxiety that excessive power was deputed to the general manager of Harringay Arena: 'I do hope that this power can be limited if he has any complaint against ourselves.'[26] (The agreement allowed the general manager or his deputy 'to visit at any time all parts of the Arena and Market Building and . . . be at liberty to suspend or control in any way he may deem necessary any matter or proceeding which in his judgement is not in accordance with the conditions or objects of the agreement' but without rendering the company or its manager liable in damages.[27]) Cattell con-tacted Group Captain Wilson of Harringay Arena and obtained assur-ances that the clause was there to comply with the terms of the hall's licence and to meet police regulations regarding the control of public disturbances; managerial disagreement with anything said from the Crusade platform would not lead to suspension of the meeting and Wilson was prepared to confirm this in writing.[28]

The second item, the financial arrangements between the Americans and the British, would recur throughout the Crusade. At this time it was agreed that a budget with a schedule of dates when various payments

[24] Colquhoun, *Harringay Story*, 17–28; ROA, 1953 GR.2, Cattell to AGBO, 14 May 1953; *WW 1963*.

[25] ROA, 1953 GR.2, Minutes of Finance Committee, 2 Oct. 1953.

[26] Ibid., AGBO to Cattell, 6 Oct. 1953.

[27] Ibid., copy of memo of agreement between Harringay Arena Ltd. and the hirers (Billy Graham Organization and the Evangelical Alliance) clause 10, attached to Finance Committee Minutes of 2 Oct. 1953.

[28] Ibid., Cattell to AGBO, 9 Oct. 1953.

fell due be drawn up, and that provision be made for sufficient money to be available in the Crusade account to meet commitments. The Finance Committee also decided to take out an indemnity insurance policy against the possibility that Billy Graham could not fulfil his engagement. Coverage of £60,000 (£28,000 for the Harringay rent) cost just over £2,000.[29] That Finance Committee meeting also heard that 2,000 square feet of office space 'of the building at Holborn Tube Station' was to be rented at £2,299 per annum, the Evangelical Alliance having an option to lease for seven years.

The third item, when and how financial support should be raised, brought decisions about principles. Most money, it was agreed, would not be received until the Crusade was under way. Before the Crusade, money would come from regular giving by prayer partners (8,000 of whom were then enlisted) who would be urged to take up shares of £1, and also from collections taken at the showing of *Oil Town USA*, a Billy Graham film being circulated in the churches.

Jerry Beavan, representing the Billy Graham Evangelistic Association, was present at the Finance Committe meeting on 4 November 1953 and reported that the American side had set a target of $311,000 for their share of the Crusade (a figure reached from experience of holding similar crusades in the USA). To date $30,000 (approximately £10,700) had already been raised in the USA and sent to Britain.[30] The Kresge Foundation, endowed and run by the Methodist head of a large American chain store,[31] had voted to help the Greater London Crusade financially and the Ford Foundation were considering an application for support. Following this American example the British Finance Committee discussed whether they too should approach 'the various trusts and funds in this country'. No doubt the view was expressed—as it was vigorously expressed to Roy Cattell a few months later by the secretary of the London Banks' Christian Union—that appealing to industrial sources was 'going down into Egypt' and that instead 'the whole cost of the Campaign, at least as far as this country is concerned, should be borne by Christian people *only* and that no appeal should be made to the world in general'.[32] Although arguments were unrecorded there was 'considerable discussion' before it was agreed that AGB would lead a deputation to the

[29] Ibid., Finance Committee Minutes, 2 Oct. 1953.

[30] Ibid., Finance Committee Minutes, 4 Nov. 1953.

[31] J. Ingham, *Biographical Dictionary of American Business Leaders* (Westport, Conn., 1983), s.v. 'Sebastian Spering Kresge'.

[32] ROA, 1954 GR.2, London Banks' Christian Union to Cattell, 24 Feb. 1954.

Federation of British Industries sometime in January, with the object of raising financial support.[33]

By the Finance Committee's meeting on 8 December 1953 the dimensions of the Crusade budget were becoming clearer. The British could expect £50,000 from America, leaving an estimated £50,000 to be raised in Britain. Half of this would come from Crusade collections, half from appeals. As for expenditures, the services of Messrs Frederick Aldridge Ltd. the advertising agents (who were arranging publicity largely under the direction of Jerry Beavan) would cost £20,000 and the hire of the Harringay Arena £28,000.[34] Three cars had been purchased. However, a broad breakdown was still not available for general release. AGB noted with displeasure that decisions taken at the November meeting were not being implemented—no English publicity brochure had been prepared for example—and wrote a stiff letter to Cattell. Cattell replied on 21 December to assure AGB that after 5 January the respective responsibilities of himself and Beavan would be more carefully defined and that 'however much pressure there is from other quarters this matter of finance will have top priority in all our work in the office, and of myself particularly'.[35] The matter was rectified by the Committee at its meeting on 16 December. An appeal brochure, entirely different from that deployed by the Billy Graham team in America, was to be drafted and 10,000 copies printed, with a copy and a covering letter signed by A. G. B. Owen going to every member of the Federation of British Industries. Other recipients of the appeal brochure would be 'Trusts, the City Guilds and every other possible source'.[36]

Thus the businessmen, particularly A. G. B. Owen, ensured that the internal accounting system of the Greater London Crusade was run efficiently and equitably in relation to American commitments and to the Evangelical Alliance (which was recompensed £3,000 for its estimated costs at the early stages of the Crusade, between 1951 and November 1953).[37] The businessmen also appear to have been decisive in taking the view that, like the Billy Graham Evangelistic Association Inc., they should appeal for funds to all likely sympathizers, not just to committed Christians. How did A. G. B. Owen set about the task of raising a sum first estimated at around £25,000? What success did he and the Finance Committee meet with?

[33] ROA, 1953 GR.2, Finance Committee Minutes, 4 Nov. 1953.
[34] Ibid., Finance Committee Minutes, 8 Dec. 1953; Colquhoun, *Harringay Story*, 42.
[35] ROA, 1953 GR.2, AGBO to Cattell, 14 Dec. 1953; Cattell to AGBO, 21 Dec. 1953.
[36] Ibid., Finance Committee Minutes, 16 Dec. 1953.
[37] Ibid., Cattell to AGBO, 21 Dec. 1953.

Their main effort to attract donations comprised the dispatch of 7,500 copies (the Publicity Committee cut the number by 2,500[38]) of the appeal brochure *Whither ...?* Of these 5,000 were sent to FBI members with a letter from AGB on Rubery Owen letterhead. AGB also solicited statements of support from Lord Brabazon of Tara and J. Arthur Rank. Brabazon was suggested by Cattell because he had 'recently opened the Bible Society Exhibition and made a very fine speech there, and incidentally he happens to be one of the directors of the Harringay Arena concern'. He was moreover a director of Leyland Motors and the David Brown Corporation so would have known of AGB through trade connections.[39] Both sent warm statements for AGB to include in the appeal brochure sent to FBI members.[40] The Finance Committee agreed that 'other Trusts, the City Companies, Lloyd's, Stockbrokers and large city companies should also be asked to help' and that the chairman of the Evangelical Alliance, Lieutenant-General Sir Arthur Smith, a distinguished Guards officer who retired in 1947 as Chief of General Staff, India, be asked to sign the letter. Additionally 150 Trusts were to be approached and 'men of substance' were to be asked to contribute £100 (Lindsay Glegg's suggestion).[41]

Given that the interests of most industrialists would not obviously coincide with the purpose of converting individuals to Christ, the objective of the Crusade, on what did A. G. B. Owen base his appeal to fellow members of the FBI? In the climate of Cold War and exhausted imperial power he turned to ideological and nationalistic pleas, baldly expressed in a brief letter. The key parts read, 'We, in this country, are facing tremendous difficulties, not the least of these being the growth of Communism which is seeking to infiltrate the whole of our national life. The only answer to this is a militant Christianity. Dr Billy Graham brings such a message to the British people, and the coming Crusade is the result of his desire to present to our people the message which has had such a marked effect upon the American way of life.' He went on to explain that 'our American friends' were meeting from American resources their own travelling and living expenses 'together with 50% of the total cost of the actual Crusade'. On the British side 'we are most anxious to match their generosity with our own gifts, and to bear

[38] Ibid., Publicity Committee Minutes, 31 Dec. 1953.
[39] Ibid., Cattell to AGBO, 21 Dec. 1953; *DD 1953*.
[40] ROA, 1954 GR.2, Lord Brabazon to AGBO, 11 Jan. 1954; J. Arthur Rank to AGBO, 13 Jan. 1954, relayed to AGBO in London by telegram from Darlaston 15 January 1954.
[41] Ibid., Finance Committee Minutes, 15 Jan. 1954.

TABLE 10.1. *Business and other sources of income of the Billy Graham Crusade to London,*
1954 (£)

Source	On 15 March 1954	On 30 June 1954
Collections	4,000	50,626
(excluding 12, 13 March)		
Chairman's appeal	14,000	48,435
A. G. B. Owen's appeal to business	1,367	
Other gifts	13,618	
TOTAL	32,985	99,061

Sources: ROA, 1954 GR.2, Executive Committee Minutes, 15 Mar. 1954; published financial statement
of the Greater London Crusade audited by Turquand Youngs & Co., 27 Sept. 1954.

our full share of this burden. I would, therefore, ask you to give the
Crusade all the financial support you can'.[42]

What sort of response did the circularization of the 5,000 FBI members
firms elicit? In the final accounting Crusade income totalled £171,357
of which £50,626 came from collections, £48,435 from donations,
£40,729 from the Billy Graham Evangelistic Association, £19,722 from
the sale of books and royalties, and £11,845 from film broadcast, relay,
and radio appeal receipts.[43] If A. G. B. Owen's files give anything like
a complete picture of industry's share then he must have been very disappointed with the reponse of his fellow industrialists. A list of donors
to whom he sent personal acknowledgements included 72 with company
addresses. Their gifts totalled £1,236. Most gave £25 or less; only ten
gave more than £25 and of these just three firms each gave the largest
sum of £100: Rubery, Owen & Co. Ltd.; A. E. Clarke Ltd. of Southwark
Street, London; and James Mackie & Sons Ltd., the Belfast engineering
firm.[44] The Executive Committee heard on 15 March 1954, six weeks
after the letter to FBI members had been sent and two weeks after the
Crusade had begun, how receipts from collections and donations stood.
These figures may be compared to the final totals (see Table 10.1).

The published accounts do not provide any breakdown of gifts and
an itemized listing is unavailable. However, since A. G. B. Owen's appeal
was directed at industry it is clear that industry and industrialists were

[42] Ibid., circular letter from AGBO on Rubery, Owen & Co. Ltd. chairman's office
letterhead, 21 Jan. 1954.

[43] Ibid., Published Financial Statement of the Greater London Crusade audited by
Turquand, Youngs & Co., 27 Sept. 1954.

[44] Ibid., undated list under Sept. 1954 date.

not much interested in supporting the Crusade as a buttress against Communism. FBI members' scepticism of evangelical Christianity evidently far outweighed their fears of Communism. The responses to AGB's letter are instructive. Most who sent donations were small manufacturing firms in the Midlands or in the engineering industry, presumably familiar with the reputations of AGB and Rubery Owen. Managing directors would hardly deny AGB support for one of his favoured charities. The only really large firms which sent any support—and that in relatively small sums of money—were Rolls–Royce (£10), Associated Portland Cement Manufacturers (£10), Guinness Exports (10 guineas), and Reckitt & Colman (£50).[45] Heads of the smaller firms most frequently gave right-wing political reasons for supporting the Crusade. They voiced political concerns that had preoccupied them since the 1920s and earlier.[46] Thus the chairman of Chaseside Engineering Co. of Hertford declared, 'the need of this country today is for a military Christianity, and that is why I am supporting financially the force of Moral Re-Armament'. He sent 10 guineas.[47] A director of Chamberlain Industries Ltd. of Leyton sent 5 guineas explaining, 'We feel that this is a useful and, in fact, necessary work, as so many organisations, including communism, show much lively activity, whereas the Christian organisations of the country do not give so much indication to the masses of the work which they are doing quietly. This Crusade should help to show people that Christianity as a force can be as militant as the undesirable activities which receive so much prominence.'[48] The argument was a dangerous one, but that was the risk in making an ideologically slanted appeal. AGB sensed the difficulties in his clouded reply to another donor who was worried about the anti-Communist posture of the Crusade: 'I am in full agreement with the comments you make with regard to the offering of the Christan Gospel as an alternative to either Communism or any other "... ism" but I am afraid in these days whilst there are still some to whom it means everything, to very many an appeal such as this can only have a practical application if it is linked up with some evil which we are fighting, such as Communism.'[49]

---

[45] Ibid., sundry replies to AGBO's circular to FBI members.
[46] R. P. T. Davenport-Hines, *Dudley Docker* (Cambridge, 1984), 105–19.
[47] ROA, 1954 GR.2, G. H. Jackson to AGBO, 17 Feb. 1954.
[48] Ibid., L. R. H. Bell to AGBO, 16 Feb. 1954.
[49] Ibid., AGBO to N. Denison of Messrs Samuel Denison & Son Ltd., Hunslet Foundry, Leeds, 2 Mar. 1954.

Those who wrote declining to support the Greater London Crusade included the Austin Motor Co., T. Avery, Beechams, BICC, Cadburys, Charterhouse Finance Corporation, Crosfields, Courtaulds, EMI, Renold Chain, and Ruston & Hornsby, among others. Where given, the reason most frequently cited was existing commitment to many other causes, appeals, charities. Sometimes a critical reply came back. The chairman of Redferns Rubber Works Ltd. wanted a new message: not personal salvation but 'the spiritual values of the Christian heritage'.[50] From Wolaston Hall, Northampshire, the volatile chemical manufacturer and radical Baptist-turned-Quaker Ernest Bader shuddered at the prospect of 'an atomic fury' and passionately urged AGB 'to turn this Crusade at Harringay into an august occasion for honest Christian peace making'. Though claiming to be 'a supporter of the planned Billy Graham Crusade' he sent no donation to AGB.[51] From the other end of the religious spectrum Price Waterhouse & Co., the accountancy firm, explained, 'because of our other commitments we cannot support them [some charities] ourselves through association as auditors or otherwise. [AGB had reminded them of earlier services for Rubery Owen & Co.] I am afraid that your Crusade must fall into this catagory. There is in your case, perhaps, the additional reason that at the present time the name of our senior partner Sir Nicholas Waterhouse is associated with the Westminster Abbey Appeal.' Price Waterhouse also declined to act as auditors for the Crusade, on the grounds that the firm's name might be 'exhibited indiscriminately' in violation of the Institute of Chartered Accountants' rules about advertising by members.[52] The matter did not discourage Turquand, Youngs, another leading firm of professional accountants, from taking the appointment.

If the national business community made a relatively tiny contribution to the Billy Graham Crusade to London of 1954, the businessmen on the Executive Council and on the Council of Reference played a significant part. A. G. B. Owen's hand ensured an efficient accounting system, especially in keeping the accounts of the Evangelical Alliance, the Billy Graham Evangelistic Association and the Greater London Crusade separate. John Laing's services were available when, early on, it was planned to import a prefabricated 'tabernacle' from the USA and to

---

[50] Ibid., T. H. Redfern to AGBO, 1 Feb. 1954.
[51] Ibid., Ernest Bader to AGBO, 17 Feb. 1954.
[52] Ibid., T. Howorth of Price Waterhouse & Co. to AGBO, 14 Jan., 8 Feb. 1954.

set it up on a London site.[53] Oliver Stott restrained Roy Cattell's opti-
mism with a healthy dose of realism.[54]

The businessmen with political positions played an important public
relations role. On 26 February they held a Dinner of Welcome at the
House of Commons for Billy Graham and his team. Organized by 5
MPs (John Henderson, Cyril Black, Richard Reader Harris (all Conservatives), Horace Holmes and George Thomas (Labour)), and chaired
by the Honourable Lancelot W. Joynson-Hicks MP, the 241 guests
included 9 peers, 20 MPs, numerous church leaders headed by the Bishop
of Barking and the Dean of Westminster, and various other guests ranging from Field Marshal Earl Alexander of Tunis to the architect Basil
Spence. A Dinner of Farewell, held at the Dorchester Hotel, Park Lane,
London, on 24 May 1954, was hosted by Lord and Lady Luke—Lord
Luke was inheritor of the Bovril business and a leading Anglican layman.[55]

Success for the Crusade at a business level hinged on revenues meeting
expenditures. The size of attendances and of numbers of enquiries so
exceeded the organizers' expectations that additional meetings, broadcast relays, and a much larger budget for the follow up of enquirers
became necessary. Levels of expenditure rose and the only way of
humanly meeting them was through the publicity of the advertising
agents (by dint of American influence, the Crusade profile was already
high), the persuasiveness of the Crusade meetings and messages, and
the safety-net of American support. Once the Crusade was in motion
Owen and his associates could not apply customary business principles
to closing the gap between revenue and expenditure because the equivalent of the production line, the Crusade meetings, grew in size and at
a rate beyond their control. So therefore did the Crusade budget. As
the published figures showed, this went beyond projections derived from
American experience, (see Table 10.2).

Running a high speed, large-scale charity, for that was essentially the

[53] ROA, 1953 GR.2, Cattell to AGBO 27 Feb. 1953; Minutes of a Special Meeting
of the Executive Committee, 15 May 1953. The plans of a circular aluminium tabernacle
300 feet in diameter, being built by the firm of R. G. LeTourneau (a well-known evangelical
in the USA) manufacturer of earth-moving equipment, were passed to Messrs John
Laing & Son (John W. Laing being the chairman of the Buildings Sub-committee of
the Crusade). In the event they were not needed.

[54] ROA, 1954 GR.2, Stott to AGBO, 2 Mar. 1954; AGBO to Stott, 17 Mar. 1954.
In mid-March money was reaching AGBO at the rate of £100 a week while collections
averaged £600 a night.

[55] Ibid., Menu and guest list for Dinner of Welcome, 26 Feb. 1954; AGBO and Mrs
AGBO to Lord and Lady Luke, 11 May 1954.

TABLE 10.2. *Projected and actual costs of the Billy Graham Crusade to London, 1954* (£)

Category of expense	Budget estimate	Actual cost
Rental and insurance of Harringay, White City, and Wembley arenas	33,000	46,670
Publicity	50,280	52,595
Administration	11,750	37,187
Books, including those given away		16,602
Miscellaneous (mostly cost of following up enquirers with literature by post)		14,324
Contingencies	5,000	
TOTAL	100,030	167,378
Final statement figure of income		171,357
Excess of income over expenditure		3,979

Source: ROA, 1954 GR.2, draft (6) of Auditors' Statement of Income and Expenditure for the Billy Graham Greater London Crusade for the period 1 Jan. 1952 to 31 August 1954; auditors' statement, 27 Sept. 1954.

business nature of the Greater London Crusade, was a new experience for the businessmen in charge. Inevitably they and their clerical associates made some mistakes. They apparently overestimated the potential support from British industrialists, who contrasted with American ones. They exaggerated the attractiveness of an anti-Communist slant to their appeal for financial support. One tactical error embarrassed the Finance Committee during the Crusade. An over-enthusiastic member of the Council of Reference persuaded A. G. B. Owen to approach Lord Brabazon, director of Daimler Hire Ltd., for the loan of car and chauffeur for the use of Billy Graham in London. After one of Brabazon's co-directors had agreed to put a Daimler at Billy Graham's disposal for two weeks, Roy Cattell, the Crusade secretary, learned about the arrangement and had to inform AGB ,'the matter was all arranged some time ago from America through the Ford Motor Company, who have put two cars and two drivers at the disposal of the team for the whole time they are here'.[56]

More serious was the decision taken by the Executive Committee on 29 March to announce, once £50,000 had been received from all British sources, that collections would continue but that they would be directed to additional Crusade expenses, to reduce the need for further help from the USA and to build up a fund for future evangelism.[57]

[56] Ibid., W. J. R. Horsburgh to AGBO, 7 Mar. 1954; telegram from Rivers Fletcher to AGBO, 11 Mar. 1954; AGBO to Horsburgh, 19 Mar. 1954; E. L. Marshall to AGBO, 19 Mar. 1954; Cattell to AGBO, 29 Mar. 1954.

[57] Ibid., Executive Committee Minutes, 29 Mar. 1954; Finance Committee Minutes, 14 Apr. 1954.

The announcement was made at the Harringay Arena on 14 April. The impression was left that Crusade expenses had been met and that further revenues would be set aside for future evangelistic work. In fact the £50,000 covered only the original estimated British share of the £100,000 budget. In the event the British share of the budget came to £120,000. Consequently all further income was consumed by Crusade costs, leaving only £1,000 for a permanent evangelistic fund. The point left some ill feeling. Kenneth de Courcy, a minor diplomat between the wars and a religious publisher after 1945, wrote to members of the Executive Committee remonstrating at the apparent dissimulation and righteously concluding, 'It is somewhat disillusioning to some of us to find that the appeals made in the case of the Greater London Crusade were not quite as strictly accurate as is required by the most worldly business man in putting forward a Prospectus, and that the City can indeed show a higher standard of ethics in this respect than Evangelism.'[58] This was rather harsh and de Courcy fully understood how the mistake had been made. It did illustrate the unwisdom of announcing budget intentions halfway through a high-speed charity project of the dimensions of an urban crusade.

The questions posed at the beginning of this section have received some rather unexpected answers. Industrialists' money provided about 1 per cent of the £120,000 that had to be raised from British sources for the Greater London Crusade of 1954. The Billy Graham team provided their own costs and nearly £41,000 for Crusade funds; what proportion of the American contribution of £50,000 came from American industrialists is unknown. Of course individuals in business might have, and probably did, make anonymous donations which could have been channelled variously into Crusade funds. Certainly the lure of anti-Communism, which might be expected to have attracted a lot of funds, failed miserably. An exploration of the identity of the British businessmen behind the Billy Graham Crusade shows them to have been few in number. Only two, Alfred Owen and John Laing, were large employers. The other half-dozen were probably personally wealthy but were definitely not in the same league as, say, J. Arthur Rank. Their motives in sponsoring the Crusade were superficially political—as outlined in A. G. B. Owen's circular to FBI members. But that objective counted for little with Owen, Laing, Glegg, and their associates in comparison to the goal of seeing people come to the personal experience of conversion to Christ. They were evangelicals and the spiritual experience of the

[58] Ibid., Kenneth de Courcy to AGBO, 18 Nov. 1954; *WW 1963*.

individual still mattered far more to them than the collective experience of society. Owen admitted as much in his letter to N. Denison. The businessmen's role in the Crusade was to raise money and to keep the finances in order. They do not appear to have been particularly good at raising money[59] but were thoroughly competent in administering it on behalf of a snowballing voluntary enterprise.

[59] Indeed one of Sir Alfred Owen's sons recalls that four of the businessmen involved in the Crusade organization (A. G. B. Owen, Cyril Black, John Laing, and one other) had to find £5,000 each in order to make up a shortfall between Crusade expenditure and income. (Telephone conversation with Mr A. David Owen, 14 July 1989.)

CONCLUSION

What answers to the questions posed at the outset of this study emerge from the evidence marshalled here? First, what of the role of religion in business? The initial target was to discover the extent and nature of Christian inputs into the lives of the leaders of big business. An objective sampling of three business élites, the heads of the largest employers in 1907, 1935, and 1955, found that the vast majority were brought up in Victorian or Edwardian Britain; that over 75 per cent were sons of middle-class parents; that about a fifth came from London and a fifth from Scotland; that at least 41 per cent of all the chairmen and 30 per cent of all managing directors attended public schools; and that 30 cent of all chairmen and 24 per cent of all managing directors went to university. These figures take no account of the unknown cases. It could be that at least 56 per cent of chairmen and 48 per cent of managing directors went to a public school of some description. All these circumstances strongly suggest that the majority of business leaders encountered the teaching and spirit of Protestant Christianity in their early years. An almost universal experience before 1914, churchgoing in the early lives of most of the business leaders can be safely assumed.

Minimally received religious influences among the business élites took the form of public school religion. Among Nonconformists or, in Scotland and Ireland, presbyterians, the local chapel or church was a more potent experience. Neither can family and kin networks be discounted. Overall, the nature of the religious influences to which business leaders were exposed is predictably clear. Anglicanism, the religion of the state, was paramount. Between 31 and 40 per cent of all chairmen and 16 to 30 per cent of all managing directors (again including cases for whom there are no data) received significant Church of England influences in their upbringing. Slightly more received episcopalian influences of all kinds. Presbyterian influences were present in around 6 per cent of all chairmen in 1907 and 1935, tailing to 2 per cent in 1955. Nonconformist backgrounds accounted for 11–13 per cent of all the élite throughout the period, again including unknown cases; for managing directors the proportion was 6–8 per cent. If unknowns are removed all these percentages might be as much as doubled.

The nature of Christian influence in the backgrounds of the business leaders was defined in other respects. Against a background of rising secularization the churches in 1900 were not only failing to keep pace with population growth and industrial-urban culture, they still had not reached adequate theological and ethical responses to the issues of industrialization. For two centuries theology had been cut off from economic questions by the triumph of Puritan individualism latterly reinforced by Adam Smith's economics. Between the 1880s and the early 1920s this position was reversed in the major denominations. Clerics and laity in the churches now pronounced not only on the morality of individual businessmen but upon the structures and foundation of capitalism itself. The injustices and pain of industrial society led to cries by the most radical clergy, at times echoing Marx, for the abolition of private property, the elimination of competition, the participation of workers in management, and much else. Some policies, like Major Douglas's Social Credit, were economic nonsense. Although such extreme policies issued only from the High Church segment of the Anglican Church, they disturbed, confused, and estranged men of capital across the denominations. In the formation of business values, the second area proposed for consideration at the beginning of this study, the churches offered no clear and adequate guidelines to business leaders until, against the threats and agonies of the Second World War, world crisis provided the catalyst for new thinking and new action.

What impact did Christian beliefs have on business in the first half of the twentieth century? How extensive was Christian influence on business? These are the most difficult questions to answer. They shift attention from received religious influences to adult affiliations and commitments. They demand evidence from a society which was, in reaction to Victorian norms, increasingly reticent towards religion. They require exploration of the scarcely detectable gradation from reticence to indifference to hostility. Despite the problems, some pointers emerge from the evidence of the foregoing chapters.

First a distinction needs to be made between the business leaders and the firms they ran. As individual people, 56 per cent of all the chairmen and 35 per cent of all the managing directors of 1907 had detectable Christian religious preferences (these could be 20 per cent higher if unknowns are excluded). By 1955 these proportions had fallen to 29 and 24 per cent respectively (inflatable by 10–15 per cent if excluding unknowns). What these preferences amounted to was another matter, of course. An educated guess suggests that in only a very small minority of cases, perhaps 5 to 10 per cent, did they imply the kind of Christian commitment displayed by J. Arthur Rank, John Craig, John Laing, or Alfred Owen. So much for individuals.

When these individuals are set in their companies two questions arise. How many of them injected their religious beliefs into their businesses? In what forms were these beliefs manifested? A one-in-ten sampling of largest employers in the decade before 1914, the period of highest religious observance in the twentieth century, found that six were family firms or were firms run by strong paternalistic figures. In these six most chairmen and managing directors had some kind of church adherence in their private lives, commonly Anglican. However, there is little evidence to show that they extended their religious convictions into their firms either as an instrument to control employees or in order to achieve religious proselytizing. The closest to these stances occurred in one firm where the proprietor endowed a church near the firm's works and in another firm where the proprietor was a pillar of the nearby parish church. Only 10 per cent of firms, on this evidence, even set up the kind of physical religious plant which at Port Sunlight William Lever transmuted into an adjunct of the company structure. On the other hand all these family firms offered welfare benefits of various kinds and probably regarded these as expressions of their Christian convictions and caring. Hence before 1914 maybe between 10 and 60 per cent of firms had policies which could be regarded as outcomes of the Christian faith of their chairmen or managing directors. How far this was the product of a general level of social expectations, how far it was driven by strongly held Christian principles, as in the case of the Quakers, it is almost impossible to tell: apart from the Quakers, employers did not formally assemble in denominational groups to discuss their common problems of business ethics.

Given the climate of apathy towards religion, by the late 1950s very few if any among the minority of firms that were still in family ownership resorted to Lever's religious devices. The nearest was Rubery Owen and those firms which were admitting industrial chaplains. It has not been possible to quantify their number. As for extent of Christian influence within the firm, by the 1950s in both family-run and managerial corporations among the largest employers religious initiatives were either confined to private individual observance (which was squeezed into lunch hours, as in the case of Sir Gordon Radley, or out-of-work meetings) or to clergy entering the firm as industrial chaplains (and then catering more for workers than managers). Very exceptional was Sir Alfred Owen's personal involvement in sponsoring first an Anglican chaplain and then a group of consultants headed by a clergyman, Bruce Reed of Christian Teamwork, to engage his workforce in Christian dialogue. Welfare had now become systematized and operated not from the chairman's desk but from the personnel manager's office, divorcing it from managerial caprice and religious preference. The major exceptions to this would survive in areas, such as Northern Ireland, Liverpool, and Glasgow, where Protestant and Catholic divisions in the community were extrapolated into business. These have not been investigated.

It could be argued from the evidence assembled that Christianity in business made its greatest impact in two specific areas during the period in question. First, within the older mode of paternalism the model developed by George Cadbury and his family at Bournville reached the peak of sensitive community-based entrepreneurship. For its fine balance between employer provision and respect for the freedom of individual employees, Bournville has rarely been matched in Britain. Working conditions were of the highest order. Housing arrangements and community facilities were similar to those at Port Sunlight with the crucial difference that a man losing his job at Bournville did not lose his house and full church membership at the same time. Yet fundamental business policies were submitted to religious principle. As in the case of indentured labour in cocoa plantations, no expense was spared to determine the true facts. When it was ascertained that their suppliers' labour policies contravened Quaker moral principles the Cadburys and Rowntrees did not hesitate to sacrifice commercial interest to moral principle. While the facts of the case were in doubt they prudently but slowly reduced their dependence on such suppliers. Analyses of modern Quaker industrialists are badly needed to discover the typicality of George Cadbury's position on business ethics.

Secondly, the deep concerns of Christian business leaders to relate faith and business led to the emergence of important forums of debate. True, they were no more than debating arenas. Yet only those who deny the value of self-criticism would regard them as inconsequential. While effects cannot be measured, it is more than likely that such forums played an important part in shaping the attitudes of individual business leaders. Again, there is room for more research. Two forums of debate

have been considered in this study. First there were the decennial conferences of Quaker employers, held in 1918, 1928, 1938, and 1948 at
Bournville. These recorded not only differences of opinion but also
achievements. In considering wartime governmental proposals for industrial councils at all levels of employers and employees (the Whitley Councils) they put clear limits on the extent to which they were willing to
admit workers into management, particularly financial management.
However, some firms, including Cadburys, were experimenting with
works councils in the 1920s. The condition of their workers was a strong
and abiding concern of Quaker employers, deriving originally from their
Christian views of the dignity of the individual. Both Cadburys and
Rowntrees had set up personnel departments before the First World
War; Seebohm Rowntree had precisely defined the living wage, which
all enlightened employers should aim to provide, as early as 1918; and
in the 1930s they were studying the 'human relations' work of American
social scientists. Out of the Quaker employers' conferences came also
Seebohm Rowntree's Oxford conferences for employers. Quaker thinking received international attention: Rowntree's ideas (Quakers in 1928
thought) possibly had guided those framing the labour clauses in the
Treaty of Versailles; the American churches were certainly influenced
by the thinking of Quaker employers.

The other highly influential forum of debate centred on the work
of Dr J. H. Oldham, an associate of Archbishop William Temple in
the movement to relate the faith to the modern world. Oldham's idea
was to help Christian lay people in all spheres of activity to apply Christian
principles to their particular areas of competence. With the support of
clerical church leaders and the aid of a few people in business, like the
3rd Viscount Hambleden, head of W. H. Smith & Son, or Harold Judd,
a professional accountant in the City, he promoted two vehicles for
debate: the *Christian News-Letter* and the Christian Frontier Council.
Under Oldham's leadership these two instruments, the weekly magazine
and the CFC with its regular meetings, exchanges of discussion papers,
and annual conferences, brought together a mixture of extremely able
people, never more so than in the war years. Fast-rising politicians,
Whitehall manadarins, academics, men from the City, people in industry,
all were linked by the quest to translate Christian principles into practical
policies. The business people included Samuel Courtauld IV, then at
the end of his career, and Basil Smallpeice (later managing director
of BOAC), in the early stages of his. Another was George Goyder whose
book on the future of private enterprise inspired one of the most radical
experiments, albeit in a small-scale firm, in company organization, the

Scott Bader Commonwealth. That in turn became a model for the new thinking about small-scale business and intermediate technology which E. F. Schumacher brought to public attention in the 1970s.

So much for an assessment of the role of religion in business. What of business people in church leaderships? This study produces quantitative findings on which to base some evaluation. Three trends are evident. First, over time, the business presence among activists in the churches' national lay leaderships diminished between 1900 and 1960. The most drastic decrease came after the 1930s. Second, at the beginning of the century all denominations could boast men of business among their leading supporters. The Church of England had the highest proportion of the business élite; they also had City men, merchant bankers for example, in their ranks. The Wesleyans, a shade lower, had some prominent company chairmen like Perks or emerging big business entrepreneurs like Joseph Rank. The Congregationalists too had men at or near the top of their respective industries, like Arthur Haworth or Albert Spicer. In Scotland, where the various forms of presbyterianism cramped the role of the laity, landed magnates appeared in the General Assembly committees of the Church of Scotland, industrialists more frequently in the General Assembly committees of the United Free Church of Scotland. Third, these businessmen took on a wide range of tasks in the service of their denominations.

In trying to evaluate the influence of businessmen in the churches, one question must be 'What were the churches' needs, how did they change and were the attitudes, skills, and resources of business people appropriate to those needs?' Down to the 1930s the denominations were concerned with three problems: their declining growth rates; the organization of national structures; and the forging of mergers. Meeting them in part depended on fund-raising. The evidence suggests that the presence of entrepreneurs and managers at the beginning of the century was amply appropriate. The denominations needed funds, fund-raisers, and then investment advice to support the work of mission at home and abroad. In Conference, Wesleyan ministers called on their laity to spoil the Egyptians. In fact it was the Israelites who were spoiled if the enormous gifts of Joseph Rank are recalled. Of fund-raisers in the churches Robert Perks had no peer. Among fund managers at the service of the churches Kindersley and Brand, who advised Canon Partridge at the Church of England's Central Board of Finance between the wars, probably had no equal.

Funds were used to meet the primary need at the turn of the century: to organize and where possible build national denominational headquarters. In providing these headquarters, in London, Edinburgh or another provincial centre, businessmen played a big part. Among Wesleyans Sir Robert Perks was the pivotal figure; among Primitive Methodists, Sir William Pickles Hartley; in the United Free Church of Scotland it was John Nicholson, a bank manager. The formation and direction of companies to insure church property presented another demand on business skills deriving from nineteenth-century church growth and consolidation.

Then there were schemes for church unity. In Scotland Lord Balfour of Burleigh played a prominent part in urging the union of the United Free Church of Scotland with the Church of Scotland. In English Methodism businessmen were at the forefront of movements which led to mergers in 1907 and 1932. A number, most prominently Sir Josiah Stamp, planned, co-ordinated, and monitored the financial and property aspects of church union. A wider ecumenical movement was served in England between the 1890s and the 1940s by Sir Henry Lunn and Viscount Hambleden of W. H. Smith & Son. In Lunn's case the religious interest took him into organizing tours and foreign holidays.

The third need presented by the churches throughout the twentieth century was to steady and reverse their declining growth rates. While much less spectacular than in fund-raising, here too businessmen took part. In Wesleyan Methodism they were behind the central halls by which the denomination planned to reached the unchurched urban industrial populace at the turn of the century. Population movements and the rise of suburbia cast doubts between the wars on the effectiveness of concentrated investments like central halls. A more widely spread support of local church building schemes seemed more appropriate. Here Joseph Rank and his son J Arthur Rank served Methodism by setting up a generous Benevolent Fund. In the Church of England business people administered funds to finance the training and maintenance of clergy, through the work of the Central Board of Finance and the diocesan DBFs. On a limited scale businessmen seized new technology to serve the cause of evangelism: J. Arthur Rank's use of film was the outstanding example. When they felt that the mainline denominations were failing, some Christian businessmen supported new initiatives in evangelism like the Billy Graham organization's Crusade to London in 1954. Prominent among these were Alfred Owen and John Laing. Interestingly, neither in the 1920s, when Kindersley appealed to the City on behalf of the Church of England's needs, nor in the 1950s, when A. G. B. Owen circulated members of the FBI to support Billy Graham, did many businessmen or corporations respond financially to the argument that Christianity was a proper ideological bulwark for capitalism against Bolshevism and Communism. British industrialists and City men evidently did not see Christianity as the indispensable political ally of capitalism: a point which would have heartened radicals in the churches.

Much of this sounds very positive. Were there debits to the involvement of businessmen and business interests in the churches? There is some evidence that rich men could stifle local initiative. Besides William Lever's undemocratic and un-Congregational interventions in the life of Christ Church, Port Sunlight, there was the case of the Thomas Coats Memorial Church, Paisley. Stamp, through his writings at least, gave comfort to those who wished to preserve the notion of a distinct separation between the pulpit and the managing director's office; had he lived to see the Christian Frontier Council he might have altered his views. It might be argued that criticisms made by Arthur Henderson of Perks's schemes—that they served the sectional interests of Methodism rather than the whole community—might be levelled at some of the other philanthropies of business benefactors: but this could be much debated. Oldham's failure to set up a network of local support groups, to turn the principles and insights hammered out in the national-level *Christian News-Letter* and the Christian Frontier Council into precisely worked policies, might be interpreted as an opportunity lost by leading lay people in the denominations. The role of rich men and businessmen in the life of the churches deserves many more local studies.

By the 1950s professional people outnumbered business people among the lay activists in the denominations. What they, by definition, supposedly lacked was the drive of their predecessors. Judging by the experience of the Church of England's National Assembly, committed to canon law revision for a decade by Archbishop Fisher, it was no wonder that entrepreneurs, men of action rather than ceaseless debate, departed. Was it a great loss? If the central structures of the denominations were in danger of becoming excessively bureaucratic—and there is some evidence that they were—then a dose of entrepreneurial appraisal would have been beneficial.

In standing back and looking at the question of 'business and the churches' one general impression remains. From the evidence available about behaviour at leaderships levels, the impact of business on the churches has on balance been more substantial than the impact of the churches on business. This may be a reflection of the rising tide of secularism in twentieth-century British society. Alternatively, Christian values may have contributed to the attitudes and values of business leaders in ways which defy historical evidence or with effects that are too easily misread as arising from simple decency. Whatever the case, this study has attempted to open up to further enquiry and public interest the important but neglected topic of interactions between business and religion in a world in which ideology and economics regularly intersect.

Largest Employers in the UK in 1907, 1935, 1955, by Industry

1907			1935			1955		
No. of employees	Firm	SIC	No. of employees	Firm	SIC	No. of employees	Firm	SIC
16,000	United Collieries Ltd.	2	14,193	Manchester Collieries Ltd.	2	704,000	National Coal Board	2
12,947	Fife Coal Co.	2	13,636	Lambton, Hetton & Joicey Collieries	2	35,000	Lyons (J.) & Co. Ltd.	3
12,000	Sir James Joicey & Co.	2	13,512	Powell Duffryn Steam Coal Co.	2	25,000	Imperial Tobacco Co.	3
10,000	Wigan Coal & Iron Co.	2	12,697	Wigan Coal Corporation Ltd.	2	20,000	Cadbury Brothers Ltd.	3
6,000	Powell Duffryn Steam Coal Co.	2	12,558	Amalgamated Anthracite Collieries Ltd.	2	20,000	Ranks Ltd.	3
5,300	Pease & Partners Ltd.	2	8,090	Welsh Associated Collieries Ltd.	3	20,000	Allied Bakeries	3
4,604	Wemyss Coal Co.	2	7,490	Ocean Coal Co.	3	19,000	Rowntree & Co. Ltd.	3
4,146	Summerlee Iron Co. Ltd.	2	7,322	Butterley Co. Ltd.	3	11,000	United Dairies	3
6,500	Huntley & Palmers	3	6,921	Consett Iron Co. Ltd.	5	26,239	British Petroleum/Anglo-Iranian	4
6,000	Imperial Tobacco Co.	3	6,568	Fife Coal Co. Ltd.	5	25,362	Shell Transport & Trading	4
4,683	Cadbury Brothers	3	30,000	Lyons (J.) & Co. Ltd.	5	15,000	Esso Petroleum Co. Ltd.	4
4,600	Fry (J. S.) & Sons Ltd.	3	30,000	Imperial Tobacco Co.	6	115,306	Imperial Chemical Industries Ltd.	5
12,000	United Alkali Co.	5	11,685	Cadbury Brothers Ltd.	6	50,287	Unilever Ltd.	5
8,000	Kynoch Ltd.	5	7,245	Associated Biscuit Manufacturers Ltd.	3	35,938	Boots Pure Drug Co. Ltd.	5
4,700	Lever Brothers	5	7,000	Tate & Lyle Ltd.	3	20,000	Distillers Co. Ltd.	5
21,710	Guest, Keen & Nettlefolds	5				13,000	British Oxygen Co. Ltd.	5
20,000	Brown (John) & Co.	6				62,000	Guest, Keen & Nettlefolds Ltd.	6
18,000	Bolckow, Vaughan & Co.	6				42,000	Stewarts & Lloyds Ltd.	6
10,602	Stewarts & Lloyds Ltd.	6						
9,500	Dorman, Long & Co.	6						

No.	Firm	Ch.
7,000	Thomas (Richard)	6
6,500	Staveley Coal & Iron Co. Ltd.	6
6,000	Stanton Ironworks Ltd.	6
5,694	Steel Co. of Scotland	6
25,000	Armstrong (Sir W. G.), Whitworth & Co.	7
22,500	Vickers Sons & Maxim	7
15,651	Royal Ordnance Factories	7
12,000	Platt Brothers	7
7,000	Singer Manufacturing Co. Ltd.	7
5,050	Fairbairn Lawson Combe Barbour Ltd.	7
5,000	Dobson & Barlow	7
5,000	Howard & Bullough Ltd.	7
4,200	Hetherington (John) & Sons	7
4,150	Birmingham Small Arms Co. Ltd.	7
6,000	General Electric Co.	9
5,000	British Westinghouse Electric & Mfg Co.	9
4,150	Siemens Brothers & Co.	9
25,580	Royal Dockyards	10
8,500	Harland & Wolff	10
8,000	Workman, Clark & Co.	10
7,500	Palmers Shipbuilding & Iron Co.	10
6,000	Fairfield Shipbuilding & Engineering Co.	10
5,000	Scott's Shipbuilding & Engineering Co.	10
4,600	Swan, Hunter, & Wigham Richardson Ltd.	10
9,396	Shell Transport & Trading Co.	4
7,274	Anglo-Persian Oil Co.	4
60,000	Unilever Ltd.	5
56,119	Imperial Chemical Industries Ltd.	5
18,697	Boot's Pure Drug Co.	5
8,100	Reckitt & Sons Ltd.	5
30,000	Guest, Keen & Nettlefolds Ltd.	6
27,452	Dorman, Long & Co. Ltd.	6
25,000	United Steel Cos. Ltd.	6
19,450	Lancashire Steel Corporation	6
14,000	Stewarts & Lloyds Ltd.	6
11,513	Brown (John) & Co. Ltd.	6
10,000	Thomas (Richard) & Co. Ltd.	6
9,100	British Iron & Steel Co. Ltd.	6
24,600	Textile Machinery Makers Ltd.	7
15,000	Tube Investments Ltd.	7
14,231	Ordnance Factories	7
8,700	Babcock & Wilcox Ltd.	7
8,103	Singer Manufacturing Co.	7
8,000	National Cash Register Co.	7
6,837	Naval Ordnance Depots	7
30,000	Associated Electrical Industries Ltd.	9
24,000	General Electric Co.	9
20,000	Lucas (Joseph) Ltd.	9
14,000	Electric & Musical Industries Ltd.	9
34,785	United Steel Cos. Ltd.	6
31,000	Dorman, Long & Co. Ltd.	6
25,500	Richard Thomas & Baldwins	6
20,750	Steel Co. of Wales	6
17,000	Colvilles Ltd.	6
16,500	English Steel Corporation	6
12,500	Summers (John) & Sons Ltd.	6
32,000	Tube Investments Ltd.	7
15,845	Babcock & Wilcox Ltd.	7
12,950	Singer Manufacturing Co. Ltd.	7
87,000	Associated Electrical Industries	9
60,000	General Electric Co. Ltd.	9
45,000	Lucas (Joseph) Industries Ltd.	9
39,000	British Insulated Callender's Cables Ltd.	9
39,000	English Electric Co.	9
22,900	Standard Telephones & Cables Ltd.	9
16,800	Smith (S.) & Sons	9
16,000	Mullard Co.	9
15,894	Plessey Co. Ltd.	9
11,378	Ferranti Ltd.	9
70,000	Vickers Ltd.	10
32,000	Harland & Wolff Ltd.	10
75,000	Hawker Siddeley Group Ltd.	11
37,500	Rolls-Royce Ltd.	11
25,990	De Havilland Aircraft Co.	11
24,773	Ford Motor Co.	11

1907			1935			1955		
No. of employees	Firm	SIC	No. of employees	Firm	SIC	No. of employees	Firm	SIC
4,500	Beardmore (William) & Co. Ltd.	10	14,000	Callender's Cable & Construction Co. Ltd.	9	23,000	British Motor Corporation Ltd.	11
4,127	Hawthorn (R. & W.), Leslie & Co.	10	8,200	British Insulated Cables Ltd.	9	21,000	Bristol Aeroplane Co.	11
14,000	Metropolitan Amalgamated Rly. Carriage & Wagon Co.	11	7,911	Standard Telephones & Cables Ltd.	9	18,000	Birmingham Small Arms Co. Ltd.	11
			7,000	Ferranti Ltd.	9	17,300	Rootes Motors Ltd.	11
7,854	North British Locomotive Co.	11	44,162	Vickers Ltd.	9	16,151	Vauxhall Motors	11
			31,680	Naval Dockyards	10	14,000	Leyland Motors Ltd.	11
30,000	Fine Cotton Spinners & Doublers Association	13	22,570	Harland & Wolff Ltd.	10	13,000	Standard Motor Co.	11
20,500	Calico Printers Association	13	8,000	Beardmore (William) & Co. Ltd.	10	24,818	Metal Box Co.	12
12,700	Coats, J. & P.	13	19,000	Austin Motor Co.	10	12,000	Rubery, Owen & Co.	12
11,280	Bleachers Association Ltd.	13	13,800	Hawker Siddeley Aircraft Co. Ltd.	11	25,381	Courtaulds Ltd.	13
8,000	Rylands & Sons Ltd.	13	10,200	Morris Motors Ltd.	11	13,212	British Celanese Ltd.	13
8,000	Morley, I. & R.	13	8,605	Ford Motor Co.	11	20,000	Sears Holdings Ltd.	15
7,500	Bradford Dyers Association	13	8,000	Singer & Co.	11	20,302	Pilkington Brothers Ltd.	16
6,000	Horrockses, Crewdson & Co.	13	7,000	Vauxhall Motors Ltd.	11	20,000	Turner & Newall Ltd.	16
			6,900	Rolls-Royce Ltd.	11	11,000	Associated Portland Cement Mfrs.	16
5,000	Birtwistle & Fielding	13	12,813	Metal Box Co.	12	11,400	Reed (Albert E.) & Co. Ltd.	16
5,000	Hibernian Lace Co.	13	30,000	Fine Cotton Spinners & Doublers Association	13	10,500	Amalgamated Press	18
5,000	Irish Lace Depot	13	22,889	Courtaulds Ltd.	13	100,000	Dunlop Rubber Co. Ltd.	18
5,000	United Turkey Red Co. Ltd.	13	15,000	Lancashire Cotton Corporation	13	22,000	Wimpey (George) & Co.	19
5,000	Lister & Co. Ltd.	13	10,500	Combined Egyptian Mills Ltd.	13	15,000	Laing (John) & Son (Holdings) Ltd.	20
4,500	Cox Brothers	13	10,000	Coats (J. & P.) Ltd.	13	190,022	British Electricity Authority	20
4,500	York Street Flax Spinning Co.	13				143,378	Gas Council	21
5,000	Bayer (Charles) & Co.	15				801,199	British Transport	21

9,000	Pilkington Brothers	16
6,147	Associated Portland Cement Mfrs.	16
4,500	Doulton & Co.	16
5,000	Waterlow & Sons Ltd.	18
7,500	McAlpine (Robert) & Sons	20
15,000	Gas Light & Coke Co.	21
7,000	South Metropolitan Gas Co.	21
212,310	General Post Office	22
77,662	London & North Western Rly.	22
70,014	Great Western Rly.	22
66,839	Midland Rly.	22
47,980	North Eastern Rly.	22
34,900	Lancashire & Yorkshire Rly.	22
32,422	Great Northern Rly.	22
29,289	Great Eastern Rly.	22
25,469	Great Central Rly.	22
24,063	North British Rly.	22
21,545	Caledonian Rly.	22
18,837	South Eastern & Chatham Rly.	22
15,095	London, Brighton & South Coast Rly.	22
8,775	Glasgow & South Western Rly.	22
8,500	Pickfords Ltd.	22
8,111	Great Southern & Western Rly.	22
5,555	Great Northern Rly. (Ireland)	22
5,000	Glasgow Corporation Tramways	22
4,823	North Staffordshire Rly.	22
8,500	Bleachers Association Ltd.	13
8,150	Bradford Dyers Association Ltd.	13
8,000	Rylands & Sons Ltd.	13
8,000	Amalgamated Cotton Mills Trust Ltd.	13
8,000	British Ropes Ltd.	13
7,500	Hoyle (Joshua) & Sons Ltd.	13
7,000	Patons & Baldwins Ltd.	13
6,500	Horrockses, Crewdson & Co. Ltd.	13
10,000	Pilkington Brothers Ltd.	16
7,000	London Brick Co. & Forders Ltd.	16
6,720	Associated Portland Cement Mfrs.	16
28,000	Dunlop Rubber	19
22,000	Gas Light & Coke Co.	21
231,877	General Post Office	22
222,220	London Midland & Scottish Rly. Co.	22
171,339	London & North Eastern Rly. Co.	22
95,729	Great Western Railway Co.	22
77,500	London Passenger Transport Board	22
65,005	Southern Railway Co.	22
13,000	Cunard Steamship Co. Ltd.	22
9,785	Port of London Authority	22
8,033	Glasgow Corporation Transport	22
49,182	Co-operative Wholesale Society	23
	Commission	22
337,465	General Post Office	22
70,000	British Electric Traction Co.	22
17,989	British Overseas Airways Corporation	22
16,000	British Broadcasting Corporation	22
15,000	Cunard Steamship Co. Ltd.	22
12,000	Port of London Authority	22
11,580	Glasgow Corporation Transport	22
60,000	Great Universal Stores Ltd.	23
60,000	Woolworth (F. W.) & Co. Ltd.	23
52,087	Co-operative Wholesale Society	23
32,000	Home & Colonial Stores	23
28,403	Marks & Spencer	23
20,000	Burton (Montague) Ltd.	23
18,104	Smith (W. H.) & Son	23
17,000	United Drapery Stores Ltd.	23
15,000	International Tea Co.'s Stores	23
14,000	Lewis's Investment Trust Ltd.	23
14,000	Fraser (House of) Ltd.	23
13,828	Scottish Co-operative Wholesale Society	23
12,254	Lewis (John) Partnership	23
11,000	Debenhams Ltd.	23
20,205	Barclays Bank Ltd.	24

1907

No. of employees	Firm	SIC
4,791	Cheshire Lines Committee	22
4,600	London & India Docks Co.	22
4,346	London General Omnibus Co.	22
4,340	Cunard Steamship Co.	22
4,162	Taff Vale Rly.	22
16,982	Co-operative Wholesale Societies Ltd.	23
8,285	Smith (W. H.), & Son	23
7,109	Scottish Co-operative Wholesalers	23
6,275	Army & Navy Co-operative Societies	23
6,000	Whiteley (William) Ltd.	23
1,420,054	Total	
14,201	Average	
23,888	Standard deviation	

1935

No. of employees	Firm	SIC
25,000	Woolworth (F. W.) & Co.	23
15,000	Home & Colonial Stores	23
14,273	Smith (W. H.), & Son	23
12,314	Scottish Co-operative Wholesalers	23
12,000	Lewis's Investment Trust Ltd.	23
11,555	Marks & Spencer Ltd.	23
11,000	Burton (Montague) Ltd.	23
6,930	Debenhams Ltd.	23
6,700	Barker (John) & Co. Ltd.	23
6,292	Harrod's Ltd.	23
17,318	Prudential Assurance Co.	24
13,070	Midland Bank Ltd.	24
12,993	Lloyds Bank Ltd.	24
12,977	Barclays Bank Ltd.	24
9,000	Westminster Bank Ltd.	24
8,000	National Provincial Bank Ltd.	24
2,260,181	Total	
22,602	Average	
36,337	Standard deviation	

1955

No. of employees	Firm	SIC
19,922	Prudential Assurance Co. Ltd.	24
18,351	Lloyds Bank Ltd.	24
17,000	Midland Bank Ltd.	24
12,000	Westminster Bank Ltd.	24
11,000	National Provincial Bank Ltd.	24
26,000	Rank (J. Arthur) Organization/Odeon Theatres Ltd.	26
12,500	Associated British Picture Corporation	26
4,643,512	Total	
48,370	Average	
111,225	Standard deviation	

Notes: Total number of firms 1907, 1935: 100; 1955: 96.

SIC: Industry groups:

1 agriculture, forestry, fishing (excluded)
2 mining and quarrying
3 food, drink, tobacco
4 coal and petroleum products
5 chemicals and allied industries
6 metal manufacture
7 mechanical engineering
8 instrument engineering
9 electrical engineering

10 shipbuilding and marine engineering
11 vehicle construction
12 metal goods not specified elsewhere
13 textiles
14 leather, leather goods, and fur
15 clothing and footwear
16 bricks, pottery, glass, cement
17 timber, furniture
18 paper, printing, publishing

19 other manufacturing industries
20 construction
21 gas, electricity, water
22 transport and communication
23 distributive trades
24 insurance, banking, finance, and business services
25 professional and scientific services
26 miscellaneous services
27 public administration and defence (excluded)

(Standard Industrial Classifications, 1968: two digits orders)

Sources: C. Shaw, 'The Large Manufacturing Employers of 1907', *Business History*, 25 (1983); L. Johnman, 'The Largest Manufacturing Companies of 1935', *Business History*, 28 (1986): author's data for non-manufacturing companies 1907, 1935, and for all companies 1955.

NB.: In the case of diversified firms there is some arbitrariness in assigning the company to a single industry, e.g. the coal and iron firms.

Business Leaders, 1907, 1935, 1955: Alphabetical List

Name	Year	Company	SIC[a] position
Abell, George Foster	1935	Lloyds Bank Ltd.	24 m[b]
Akers-Douglas, Aretas, PC, MP	1907	South Eastern & Chatham Rly.	22 m
Allen, Henry	1907	Bleachers Association Ltd.	13 m
Amos, James	1955	BTC Road Passenger Service, Scottish Omnibuses	22 m
Anderson, John, 1st Visc. Waverley	1955	Port of London Authority	22 c
Anson, Sir George Wilfrid	1955	Imperial Tobacco Co.	3 m
Armstrong, Col. Oliver Carlton (Indian Army)	1907	Beardmore (William) & Co. Ltd.	10 m
Armytage, Sir George John	1907	Lancashire & Yorkshire Rly.	22 c
Askew, Sidney Bruce	1955	Ranks Ltd.	3 m
Aspinall, John Audley Frederick	1907	Lancashire & Yorkshire Rly.	22 m
Austin, Sir Herbert	1935	Austin Motor Co.	11 c
Awdry, Charles	1907	Smith, W. H.	23 m
Baillieu, Clive Latham, 1st Baron Baillieu	1955	Dunlop Rubber Co. Ltd.	19 c
Banks, Sir Donald	1935	General Post Office	22 c
Barlow, Robert	1935	Metal Box Co.	12 m
Barlow, Sir Robert	1955	Metal Box Co.	12 c
Barnett, Sir Ben Lewis	1955	General Post Office	22 m
Barrie, Robert	1907	Lever Brothers	5 m
Bartlett, Charles John	1935	Vauxhall Motors Ltd.	11 m
Bass, John	1907	Waterlow & Sons Ltd.	18 m
Bates, Denis H.	1955	Cunard Steamship Co. Ltd.	22 c
Bates, Sir Percy Elly	1935	Cunard Steamship Co. Ltd.	22 c
Baxendale, Joseph William	1907	Pickfords Ltd.	22 c
Baxendale, Lloyd Henry	1907	Pickfords Ltd.	22 m
Baxter, James	1955	Singer Manufacturing Co. Ltd.	7 c
Baxter, James	1955	Singer Manufacturing Co. Ltd.	7 m
Bayer, Charles	1907	Bayer (Charles) & Co.	15 c
Bayer, Charles	1907	Bayer (Charles) & Co.	15 m
Beale, Sir John Field	1935	British Iron & Steel Co. Ltd.	6 c
Beale, Sir John Field	1935	Guest, Keen & Nettlefolds Ltd.	6 c
Beardmore, William	1907	Beardmore (William) & Co. Ltd.	10 c
Beasley, Ammon	1907	Taff Vale Rly.	22 m

Name	Year	Company	SIC[a] position
Beaton, Neil Scobie	1935	Scottish Co-operative Wholesale Society	23 c
Beckett, Hon. Rupert Evelyn	1935	Westminster Bank Ltd.	24 c
Bedford, John	1955	Debenhams Ltd.	23 m
Beharrell, George Edward	1955	Dunlop Rubber Co. Ltd.	19 m
Beharrell, Sir John George	1935	Dunlop Rubber	19 m
Bennett, Peter Frederick Blaker	1935	Lucas (Joseph) Ltd.	9 m
Bennett, Peter Frederick Blaker, 1st Baron Bennett	1955	Lucas (Joseph) Industries Ltd.	9 m
Benson, Air Cdre. Constantine Edward	1955	Burton (Montague) Ltd.	23 c
Bernard, Sir Dallas Gerald Mercer	1955	Courtaulds Ltd.	13 m
Berry, John Seymour, 2nd Visc. Camrose	1955	Amalgamated Press	18 m
Berry, Hon. William Michael,	1955	Amalgamated Press	18 c
Birtwistle, Albert	1907	Birtwistle & Fielding	13 c
Birtwistle, Arthur	1907	Birtwistle & Fielding	13 m
Bonsor, Henry Cosmo Orme	1907	South Eastern & Chatham Rly.	22 c
Boot, John Campbell, 2nd Baron Trent	1935	Boot's Pure Drug Co.	5 c
Boothman, W. T.	1935	Amalgamated Cotton Mills Trust	13 m
Bowman, James	1955	National Coal Board	2 a
Brock, John	1907	United Alkali Co.	5 c
Brocklehurst, Robert Walter Douglas Phillips	1935	Fine Cotton Spinners & Doublers Association	13 m
Brodrick, Thomas	1907	Co-operative Wholesale Societies Ltd.	23 m
Brown, James	1907	Scott's Shipbuilding & Engineering Co.	10 m
Browne, Sir Benjamin Chapman	1907	Hawthorn (R. & W.), Leslie & Co.	10 c
Browne, Edward Humphrey	1955	NCB West Midlands Division	2 m
Bryant, Frederick	1935	Naval Dockyards	10 m
Buckley, Harold	1955	Co-operative Wholesale Society	23 m
Bullock, William Edward	1935	Singer & Co.	11 c
Bullock, William Edward	1935	Singer & Co.	11 m
Bullough, Sir George	1907	Howard & Bullough Ltd.	7 c
Burbidge, Sir Richard Woodman	1935	Harrods Ltd.	23 c
Burbidge, Sir Richard Woodman	1935	Harrods Ltd.	23 m
Burn, Sir Joseph	1935	Prudential Assurance Co.	24 m
Burrows, Robert Abraham	1935	Manchester Collieries Ltd.	2 m
Burton, Sir Montague Maurice	1935	Burton (Montague) Ltd.	23 c
Burton, Sir Montague Maurice	1935	Burton (Montague) Ltd.	23 m
Bury, Oliver Robert Hawke	1907	Great Northern Rly.	22 m

Name	Year	Company	SIC[a] position
Butterworth, Alexander Kaye	1907	North Eastern Rly.	22 m
Byng, Gustav	1907	General Electric Co.	9 c
Cadbury, Edward	1935	Cadbury Brothers Ltd.	3 m
Cadbury, George	1907	Cadbury Brothers	3 c
Cadbury, George	1907	Cadbury Brothers	3 m
Cadbury, Laurence John	1955	Cadbury Brothers Ltd.	3 c
Cadbury, Paul Strangman	1955	Cadbury Brothers Ltd.	3 m
Cadbury, William Adlington	1935	Cadbury Brothers Ltd.	3 c
Cadman, Sir John	1935	Anglo-Persian Oil Co.	4 c
Cadogan, Sir Alexander George Montagu, PC OM	1955	British Broadcasting Corporation	22 c
Caird, Patrick Tennant	1907	Glasgow & South Western Rly.	22 c
Callender, Sir Thomas Octavius	1935	Callender's Cable & Construction Co. Ltd.	9 m
Campbell, Colin Frederick,	1935	National Provincial Bank Ltd.	24 c
Carlisle, Alexander Montgomery, PC	1907	Harland & Wolff	10 m
Carlow, Charles	1907	Fife Coal Co.	2 c
Carlow, Charles	1907	Fife Coal Co.	2 m
Carlow, Charles Augustus	1935	Fife Coal Co. Ltd.	2 m
Carlton, Newcomb	1907	British Westinghouse Electric & Mfg. Co.	9 m
Carnegie, Francis	1935	Ordnance Factories	7 c
Carnelley, William	1907	Rylands & Sons Ltd.	13 c
Chamberlain, Arthur	1907	Kynoch Ltd.	5 c
Chamberlain, Arthur	1935	Tube Investments Ltd.	7 c
Chambers, Stanley Paul	1955	Imperial Chemical Industries Ltd.	5 m
Chauvin, G. Von	1907	Siemens Brothers & Co.	9 m
Chesterfield, Arthur Desborough	1955	Westminster Bank Ltd.	24 m
Christie, Henry	1907	United Turkey Red Co. Ltd.	13 m
Christie, John Hyde	1907	United Turkey Red Co. Ltd.	13 c
Church, W. C.	1935	Boot's Pure Drug Co.	5 m
Citrine, Walter McLennan, 1st Baron Citrine	1955	British Electricity Authority	21 c
Clark, Alfred Corning	1935	Electric & Musical Industries Ltd.	9 c
Clark, Allen George	1955	Plessey Co. Ltd.	9 c
Clark, Allen George	1955	Plessey Co. Ltd.	9 m
Clark, George Smith	1907	Workman, Clark & Co.	10 m
Clark, James Oscar Max	1935	Coats (J. & P.) Ltd.	13 c
Clark, William	1907	Steel Co. of Scotland	6 m
Clore, Charles	1955	Sears Holdings Ltd.	15 c
Coats, Archibald	1907	Coats (J. & P.)	13 c
Coats, Ernest Symington	1935	Coats (J. & P.) Ltd.	13 m
Cohen, H. L.	1935	Lewis's Investment Trust Ltd.	23 c
Cohen, Rex Arthur Louis	1955	Lewis's Investment Trust Ltd.	23 m
Cohen, Sir Robert Waley	1935	Shell Transport & Trading Co.	4 m
Collier, Joseph	1955	United Drapery Stores Ltd.	23 m

Name	Year	Company	SIC[a] position
Cooke, James H., JP	1907	Hibernian Lace Co.	13 c
Cooper, David	1907	Glasgow & South Western Rly.	22 m
Cooper, Francis d'Arcy	1935	Unilever Ltd.	5 c
Cope, Sir Alfred	1935	Amalgamated Anthracite Colleries Ltd.	2 m
Cornwall, Ernest	1935	National Provincial Bank Ltd.	24 m
Cornwallis, Wykeham Stanley, 2nd Baron Cornwallis	1955	Reed (Albert E.) & Co. Ltd.	18 c
Courtauld, Samuel IV	1935	Courtaulds Ltd.	13 c
Cozens-Hardy, Edward Herbert, 3rd Baron Cozens-Hardy	1935	Pilkington Brothers Ltd.	16 m
Craig, Sir John	1955	Colvilles Ltd.	6 c
Crawford, Sir William	1907	York Street Flax Spinning Co.	13 m
Crompton, John Gilbert	1907	Stanton Ironworks Co.	6 c
Cross, Herbert Shepherd	1907	Bleachers Association Ltd.	13 c
Cruddas, William Donaldson	1907	Armstrong (Sir W. G.), Whitworth & Co.	7 m
Cunliffe-Lister, Samuel, 2nd Baron Masham	1907	Lister & Co. Ltd.	13 c
Dalrymple, James	1907	Glasgow Corporation Tramways	22 m
Dannatt, Cecil	1955	Associated Electrical Industries Ltd.	9 m
Davidson, J. E.	1907	United Alkali Co.	5 m
Davidson, John M.	1955	Scottish Co-operative Wholesale Society	23 c
Davies, David 1st Baron Davies	1935	Ocean Coal Co.	2 c
Davis, Sir Herbert	1955	Unilever Ltd.	5 m
Davis, John Henry Harris	1955	Rank Organization/Odeon Theatres Ltd.	26 m
Dawson, Frank Harold	1955	Cunard Steamship Co. Ltd.	22 m
de Ferranti, Gerard Vincent Sebastian Ziani	1935	Ferranti Ltd.	9 c
de Ferranti, Gerard Vincent Sebastian Ziani	1935	Ferranti Ltd.	9 m
de Ferranti, Sir Gerard Vincent Sebastian Ziani	1955	Ferranti Ltd.	9 c
de Ferranti, Sir Gerard Vincent Sebastian Ziani	1955	Ferranti Ltd.	9 m
Deeds, Edward Andrew	1935	National Cash Register Co.	7 c
Dent, Charles Hastings	1907	Great Southern & Western Rly.	22 m
Dewrance, Sir John	1935	Babcock & Wilcox Ltd.	7 c
Dick, Alick Sydney	1955	Standard Motor Co.	11 m
Dillon, Malcolm	1907	Palmers Shipbuilding & Iron Co. Ltd.	10 m
Dixon, Alfred Herbert	1907	Fine Cotton Spinners & Doublers Association	13 m
Dobson, Benjamin A. Palin	1935	Textile Machinery Makers Ltd.	7 m

Name	Year	Company	SIC[a] position
Dobson, Benjamin Palin	1907	Dobson & Barlow	7 m
Docker, Bernard Dudley Frank	1955	Birmingham Small Arms Co. Ltd.	11 c
Docker, Bernard Dudley Frank	1955	Birmingham Small Arms Co. Ltd.	11 m
Docker, Frank Dudley	1907	Metropolitan Amalgamated Rly. Carriage & Wagon Co. Ltd.	11 c
Dodd, John, JP	1907	Platt Brothers	7 c
Donaldson, Hay Frederick	1907	Royal Ordnance Factories	7 c
Dorman, Arthur John	1907	Dorman, Long & Co.	6 c
Dorman, Arthur John	1907	Dorman, Long & Co.	6 m
Douglas, George	1907	Bradford Dyers Association Ltd.	13 m
Douglas, George	1935	Bradford Dyers Association Ltd.	13 c
Doulton, Henry Lewis	1907	Doulton & Co.	16 c
Doulton, Henry Lewis	1907	Doulton & Co.	16 m
Drayton, Harold Charles Gilbert	1955	British Electric Traction Co.	22 c
Ducat, David	1955	Metal Box Co.	12 m
Dudley, Sir William Edward	1935	Co-operative Wholesale Society	23 c
Dumble, Capt. Wilfrid Chatterton	1907	London General Omnibus Co.	22 m
Earle, Sir George Foster	1955	Associated Portland Cement Manufacturers	16 c
Eccles, Josiah	1955	British Electricity Authority	21 m
Edington, William Gerald	1955	Midland Bank Ltd.	24 m
Edmond, Francis	1935	Wigan Coal Corporation Ltd.	2 m
Elliot, Sir John Blumenfeld	1955	BTC London Transport Executive	22 m
Elliott, Albert George	1955	Rolls-Royce Ltd.	11 m
Ellis, Charles Edward	1907	Brown (John) & Co.	6 m
Engelbach, Charles Richard Fox	1935	Austin Motor Co.	11 m
Ennis, Lawrence	1935	Dorman, Long & Co. Ltd.	6 m
Eriks, Sierd Sint	1955	Mullard Co.	9 c
Eriks, Sierd Sint	1955	Mullard Co.	9 m
Evans, Thomas, CBE, JP	1935	Ocean Coal Co.	2 m
Fairfax, Albert Kirby, 12th Baron	1935	Amalgamated Cotton Mills Trust Ltd.	13 c
Fay, Samuel	1907	Great Central Rly.	22 m
Firth, Sir William John	1935	Thomas (Richard) & Co. Ltd.	6 c
Firth, Sir William John	1935	Thomas (Richard) & Co. Ltd.	6 m
Fitzpayne, E. R. L.	1955	Glasgow Corporation Transport Department	22 m
Fleck, Sir Alexander	1955	Imperial Chemical Industries Ltd.	5 c
Fletcher, Eric George Molyneaux, MP	1955	Associated British Picture Corporation Ltd.	26 m

Name	Year	Company	SIC[a] position
Forbes, William de Guise	1907	London, Brighton & South Coast Rly.	22 m
Ford, Leslie Ewart	1955	Port of London Authority	22 m
Forman, Henry Buxton	1907	General Post Office	22 m
Forrester-Paton, Alexander	1935	Patons & Baldwins Ltd.	13 m
Fortescue-Flannery, Sir James	1935	Callender's Cable & Construction Co. Ltd.	9 c
Franks, Sir Oliver Shewell, PC	1955	Lloyds Bank Ltd.	24 c
Fraser, Capt. Bruce Austin	1935	Naval Ordnance Depots	7 c
Fraser, Hugh	1955	Fraser (House of) Ltd.	23 c
Fraser, Hugh	1955	Fraser (House of) Ltd.	23 m
Fraser, William Lionel	1955	Babcock & Wilcox Ltd.	7 c
Fraser, William Milligan	1935	Anglo-Persian Oil Co.	4 m
Fraser, William Milligan, 1st Baron Strathalmond	1955	British Petroleum Co./Anglo-Iranian Oil Co.	4 c
Fraser, William Milligan, 1st Baron Strathalmond	1955	British Petroleum Co./Anglo-Iranian Oil Co.	4 m
Fry, Francis James	1907	Fry (J. S.) & Sons Ltd.	3 m
Fry, Joseph Storrs	1907	Fry (J. S.) & Sons Ltd.	3 c
Galloway, W. W.	1935	Horrockses, Crewdson & Co. Ltd.	13 c
Gamage, Leslie	1955	General Electric Co. Ltd.	9 m
Gardiner, Thomas Robert	1935	General Post Office	22 m
Gardner, Walter Frank	1955	Prudential Assurance Co. Ltd.	24 m
Gavey, John	1907	General Post Office	22 m
Geddes, Sir Eric Campbell, PC	1935	Dunlop Rubber	19 c
Gemmell, David	1907	United Collieries Ltd.	2 m
George, Edward James	1935	Consett Iron Co. Ltd.	2 m
Gibbs, Walter Durant, 4th Baron Aldenham	1955	Westminster Bank Ltd.	24 c
Gill, Frank	1935	Standard Telephones & Cables Ltd.	9 c
Gillespie, Col. James John	1935	British Ropes Ltd.	13 c
Gluckstein, Isidore Montague	1955	Lyons (J.) & Co. Ltd.	3 c
Gluckstein, Isidore Montague	1955	Lyons (J.) & Co. Ltd.	3 m
Godber, Sir Frederick	1955	Shell Transport & Trading Co.	4 c
Godber, Sir Frederick	1955	Shell Transport & Trading Co.	4 m
Gooday, John Francis Sykes	1907	Great Eastern Rly.	22 m
Gordon-Smith, Ralph	1955	Smith (S.) & Sons	9 c
Gordon-Smith, Ralph	1955	Smith (S.) & Sons	9 m
Goulding, Edward Alfred, 1st Baron Wargrave	1935	Rolls-Royce Ltd.	11 c
Goulding, Sir William Joshua	1907	Great Southern & Western Rly.	22 c
Gracie, Alexander	1907	Fairfield Shipbuilding & Engineering Co.	10 m
Grand, Keith Walter Chamberlain	1955	BTC British Rlys., Western Region	22 m
Granet, William Guy	1907	Midland Rly.	22 m
Greenwood, Hamar, 1st Baron Greenwood	1935	Dorman, Long & Co. Ltd.	6 c

Name	Year	Company	SIC[a] position
Greig, Alexander	1935	Home & Colonial Stores Ltd.	23 m
Gresley, Herbert Nigel	1935	London & North Eastern Rly. Co.	22 m
Grosvenor, Richard de Aquila, Baron Stalbridge	1907	London & North Western Rly.	22 c
Grosvenor, Robert Wellesley, 2nd Baron Ebury	1907	Army & Navy Co-operative Society	23 c
Gwinner, A.	1907	Siemens Brothers & Co.	9 c
Hague, Sir Charles Kenneth Felix	1955	Babcock & Wilcox Ltd.	7 m
Hamilton, Claud John, Lord	1907	Great Eastern Rly.	22 c
Hanbury-Williams, Sir John Coldbrook	1955	Courtaulds Ltd.	13 c
Hann, Douglas Alfred	1935	Powell Duffryn Steam Coal Co.	2 m
Hann, Edmund Lawrence	1935	Powell Duffryn Steam Coal	2 c
Hann, Edmund Mills	1907	Powell Duffryn Steam Coal Co.	2 m
Hanson, Harry	1955	Turner & Newall Ltd.	16 m
Hardy, Thomas	1907	London & India Docks Co.	22 m
Harris, Col. Lionel Herbert	1955	General Post Office	22 m
Harrison, Sir Frederick	1907	London & North Western Rly.	22 m
Hartley, Sir Harold Brewer	1935	London Midland & Scottish Rly. Co.	22 m
Harvey, Robert James Paterson	1955	General Post Office	22 m
Hayman, Sir Cecil George Graham	1955	Distillers Co. Ltd.	5 m
Henderson, Sir Alexander	1907	Great Central Rly.	22 c
Hennessy, Sir Patrick	1955	Ford Motor Co.	11 m
Hepworth, F.	1935	Metal Box Co.	12 c
Hewit, R. P.	1907	Calico Printers Association	13 c
Hewlett, Alfred	1907	Wigan Coal & Iron Co.	2 m
Heyworth, Sir Geoffrey	1955	Unilever Ltd.	5 c
Hill, Edward John	1955	Lloyds Bank Ltd.	24 m
Hill, W. E.	1955	Vauxhall Motors Ltd.	11 m
Hilton, Robert Stuart	1935	United Steel Cos. Ltd.	6 m
Hilton, William, JP	1907	Platt Brothers	7 m
Hirst, Hugo	1907	General Electric Co.	9 m
Hirst, Hugo, Baron Hirst	1935	General Electric Co.	9 c
Hitchon, Alfred	1907	Howard & Bullough Ltd.	7 m
Hives, Ernest Walter, 1st Baron Hives	1955	Rolls-Royce Ltd.	11 c
Hogg, Oliver Frederick Gillilan	1935	Ordnance Factories	7 m
Holden, Sir George	1935	Combined Egyptian Mills Ltd.	13 m
Hole, Francis George	1955	BTC Hotels & Catering Services Division	26 m
Holland-Martin, Robert M.	1935	Southern Rly. Co.	22 c
Hollins, Sir Frank	1907	Horrockses, Crewdson & Co.	13 c
Hollins, Sir Frank	1907	Horrockses, Crewdson & Co.	13 m
Holmes, Maj.-Gen. Noel Galway	1955	NCB North Eastern Division	2 m

Name	Year	Company	SIC[a] position
Hopkins, C. P.	1955	BTC British Rlys., Southern Region	22 m
Hornby, Charles Harry St John	1935	Smith (W.H.), & Son	23 m
Hornby, Michael Charles St John	1955	Smith (W. H.) & Son	23 m
Horne, Sir Robert Stevenson, PC	1935	Great Western Railway Co.	22 c
Horne, Sir William Edgar	1935	Prudential Assurance Co.	24 c
Houldsworth, Sir Hubert Stanley	1955	National Coal Board	26 c
Houldsworth, Sir William Henry	1907	Fine Cotton Spinners & Doublers Association	13 c
Howard, Henry	1907	Stewarts & Lloyds Ltd.	6 m
Hoyle, Lt.-Col. Joshua Craven	1935	Hoyle (Joshua) & Sons Ltd.	13 c
Hubbard, Charles H.	1935	Woolworth (F. W.) & Co.	23 m
Hunter, Sir Ellis	1955	Dorman, Long & Co. Ltd.	6 c
Hunter, Sir Ellis	1955	Dorman, Long & Co. Ltd.	6 m
Hunter, George Burton	1907	Swan, Hunter, & Wigham Richardson Ltd.	10 c
Hutchison, James Seller	1955	British Oxygen Co. Ltd.	5 c
Hutton, Lucius Octavius	1907	Great Northern Rly. (Ireland)	22 c
Huxham, Frank, ACA	1907	Kynoch Ltd.	5 m
Hyde, Frederick	1935	Midland Bank Ltd.	24 m
Inglis, James Charles	1907	Great Western Rly.	22 m
Jackson, William Fulton	1907	North British Rly.	22 m
Jackson, William Lawies, 1st Baron Allerton	1907	Cheshire Lines Committee	22 c
Jackson, William Lawies, 1st Baron Allerton	1907	Great Northern Rly.	22 c
Jacob, Lt.-Col. Sir Edward Ian Claud	1955	British Broadcasting Corporation	22 m
Jacobson, Lionel	1955	Burton (Montague) Ltd.	23 m
James, John Ernest	1935	Lancashire Steel Corporation	6 c
James, John Ernest	1935	Lancashire Steel Corporation	6 m
Johns, Sir Arthur William	1935	Naval Dockyards	10 c
Johnson, Henry	1935	Courtaulds Ltd.	13 m
Johnson-Ferguson, Sir Jabez Edward	1907	Bolckow, Vaughan & Co.	6 c
Joicey, James, 1st Baron Joicey	1935	Lambton, Hetton & Joicey Collieries Ltd.	2 c
Joicey, James, 1st Baron Joicey	1907	Sir James Joicey & Co.	2 c
Joicey, James Arthur, 2nd Baron Joicey	1935	Lambton, Hetton & Joicey Collieries Ltd.	2 m
Joicey, Maj. William James	1907	Sir James Joicey & Co.	2 m
Jones, Henry Frank Harding	1955	Gas Council	21 m
Jones, Walter Benton	1935	United Steel Cos. Ltd.	6 c
Jones, Sir Walter Benton	1955	United Steel Cos. Ltd.	6 c
Keen, Arthur	1907	Guest, Keen & Nettlefolds	12 c
Keen, Arthur Thomas	1907	Guest, Keen & Nettlefolds	12 m
Kennedy, Stanley	1955	BTC Road Passenger Services, Tilling Group	22 m

Name	Year	Company	SIC[a] position
King, Sir James	1907	Caledonian Rly.	22 c
Kirkham, G. W. C.	1907	Rylands & Sons Ltd.	13 m
Laing, John Maurice	1955	Laing (John) & Son (Holdings) Ltd.	20 m
Laing, John William	1955	Laing (John) & Son (Holdings) Ltd.	20 c
Lancaster, Robert Fisher	1935	Co-operative Wholesale Society	23 m
Law, R. U.	1955	Wimpey (George) & Co.	20 m
Lawrence, Gen. the Hon. Sir Herbert Alexander	1935	Vickers Ltd.	10 c
Lawrie, John	1907	Whiteley (William) Ltd.	23 m
Lawson, Sir Arthur Tredgold	1907	Fairbairn Lawson Combe Barbour Ltd.	7 c
Lawson, H.	1907	Army & Navy Co-operative Society	23 m
Leake, Sidney Henry	1955	Lewis's Investment Trust Ltd.	23 c
Leckie, Robert W.	1935	Scottish Co-operative Wholesale Society	23 m
Lee, Albert George	1935	General Post Office	22 m
Lee, Herbert William	1935	Fine Cotton Spinners & Doublers Association	13 c
Lee, Lennox Bartram	1907	Calico Printers Association	13 m
Lees, Sir William Clare	1935	Bleachers Association Ltd.	13 m
Lemon, Ernest John Hutchings	1935	London Midland & Scottish Rly. Co.	22 m
Letch, Sir Robert	1955	BTC Docks Division	22 m
Lever, Sir Ernest Harry	1955	Richard Thomas & Baldwins	6c
Lever, Sir Ernest Harry	1955	Steel Co. of Wales	6 c
Lever, William Hesketh	1907	Lever Brothers	5 c
Lewis, John Spedan	1955	Lewis (John) Partnership	23 c
Lewis, John Spedan	1955	Lewis (John) Partnership	23 m
Lidbury, Charles	1935	Westminster Bank Ltd.	24 m
Lindsay, David Alexander Edward, 27th Earl Crawford	1935	Wigan Coal Corporation Ltd.	2 c
Lindsay, James Ludovic, 26th Earl Crawford	1907	Wigan Coal & Iron Co.	2 c
Lister, S. J.	1935	Cunard Steamship Co. Ltd.	22 m
Lithgow, Sir James	1935	Beardmore (William) & Co. Ltd.	10 c
Livesey, Sir George Thomas	1907	South Metropolitan Gas Co.	21 c
Livesey, Sir George Thomas	1907	South Metropolitan Gas Co.	21 m
Llewellyn, Sir David Richard	1935	Welsh Associated Collieries Ltd.	2 c
Llewellyn, William Morgan	1935	Welsh Associated Collieries Ltd.	2 m
Lloyd, A. W.	1935	Stewarts & Lloyds Ltd.	6 m
Longden, J. A. MICE	1907	Stanton Ironworks Co.	6 m
Lord, Leonard Percy	1935	Morris Motors Ltd.	11 m
Lord, Sir Leonard Percy	1955	British Motor Corporation Ltd.	11 c

Name	Year	Company	SIC[a] position
Lord, Sir Leonard Percy	1955	British Motor Corporation Ltd.	11 m
Lorimer, William	1907	North British Locomotive Co.	11 c
Lorimer, William	1907	Steel Co. of Scotland	6 c
Lusk, William C.	1935	Associated Electrical Industries Ltd.	9 m
Lyle, Charles Ernest Leonard	1935	Tate & Lyle Ltd.	3 c
Lyttelton, Oliver, 1st Visc. Chandos	1955	Associated Electrical Industries Ltd.	9 c
M'Allister, Robert	1955	Glasgow Corporation Transport Department	22 c
McAlpine, Robert	1907	McAlpine (Robert) & Sons	20 c
McAlpine, William Hepburn	1907	McAlpine (Robert) & Sons	20 m
McCance, Sir Andrew	1955	Colvilles Ltd.	6 m
Macdiarmid, Allan Campbell	1935	Stewarts & Lloyds Ltd.	6 c
McFadzean, William Hunter	1955	British Insulated Callender's Cables Ltd.	9 c
McFadzean, William Hunter	1955	British Insulated Callender's Cables Ltd.	9 m
M'Farlane, James	1907	Glasgow Corporation Tramways	22 c
McGowan, Sir Harry Duncan	1935	Imperial Chemical Industries Ltd.	5 c
McGowan, Sir Harry Duncan	1935	Imperial Chemical Industries Ltd.	5 m
McKenna, Reginald, PC	1935	Midland Bank Ltd.	24 m
Mackinnon, Lachland	1935	Glasgow Corporation Transport Department	22 m
McKinstry, Archibald	1935	Babcock & Wilcox Ltd.	7 m
McLaren, Sir Charles Benjamin Bright	1907	Palmers Shipbuilding & Iron Co. Ltd.	10 c
McLaren, Sir Charles Benjamin Bright	1907	Brown (John) & Co.	6 c
McLaren, Henry Duncan, 2nd Baron Aberconway	1935	Brown (John) & Co. Ltd.	6 c
M'Lean, Bailie Alexander	1935	Glasgow Corporation Transport Department	22 c
MacPherson, W. W.	1907	Fairbairn Lawson Combe Barbour Ltd.	7 m
Maggs, Leonard	1955	United Dairies	3 c
Maggs, Leonard	1955	United Dairies	3 m
Markham, Charles Paxton	1907	Staveley Coal & Iron Co. Ltd.	6 c
Markland, Stanley	1955	Leyland Motors Ltd.	11 m
Marks, Simon	1935	Marks & Spencer Ltd.	23 c
Marks, Sir Simon	1955	Marks & Spencer Ltd.	23 c
Marquis, Frederick James	1935	Lewis's Investment Trust Ltd.	23 m
Marshall, James Brown	1907	Royal Dockyards	10 m
Martel, Charles Philip	1907	Royal Ordnance Factories	7 m
Martin, Sir James	1935	Home & Colonial Stores Ltd.	23 c
Martin, Robert M.	1907	Irish Lace Depot	13 m

Name	Year	Company	SIC[a] position
Maxwell, William	1907	Scottish Co-operative Wholesale Soc. Ltd.	23 c
Millar, Robert	1907	Caledonian Rly.	22 m
Milne, Sir James	1935	Great Western Rly. Co.	22 m
Milne-Watson, David	1907	Gas Light & Coke Co.	21 m
Milne-Watson, Sir David	1935	Gas Light & Coke Co.	21 c
Milne-Watson, Sir David	1935	Gas Light & Coke Co.	21 m
Milne-Watson, Michael	1955	Gas Council	21 m
Mitchell, Sir Godfrey Way	1955	Wimpey (George) & Co.	20 c
Montague-Douglas-Scott, John Chas., Earl of Dalkeith	1907	North British Rly.	22 c
Moorhouse, A. P.	1907	Cunard Steamship Co.	22 m
Morgan, Sir Frank William	1955	Prudential Assurance Co. Ltd.	24 c
Morley, Howard	1907	Morley, I. & R.	13 m
Morley, Samuel Hope	1907	Morley, I. & R.	13 c
Morris, William Richard, Baron Nuffield	1935	Morris Motors Ltd.	11 c
Mosley, Tonman	1907	North Staffordshire Rly.	22 c
Mountain, Sir Brian Edward Stanley	1955	United Drapery Stores Ltd.	23 c
Mungall, Henry, JP	1907	United Collieries Ltd.	2 c
Neilson, John	1907	Summerlee Iron Co. Ltd.	2 c
Neilson, Col. John Beaumont	1935	Vickers Ltd.	10 m
Neilson, William	1907	Summerlee Iron Co. Ltd.	2 m
Nelson, Sir George Horatio	1955	English Electric Co.	9 c
Nelson, Sir George Horatio	1955	English Electric Co.	9 m
Nimmo, Sir Adam	1935	Fife Coal Co. Ltd.	2 c
Nisbett, G. H.	1935	British Insulated Cables Ltd.	9 m
Nixon, Wilfrid Ernest	1955	De Havilland Aircraft Co. Ltd.	11 c
Nixon, Wilfrid Ernest	1955	De Havilland Aircraft Co. Ltd.	11 m
Noble, Sir Andrew	1907	Armstrong (Sir W.G.), Whitworth & Co.	7 c
Ormsby-Gore, William George Arthur, 4th Baron Harlech	1955	Midland Bank Ltd.	24 c
Orr, William James	1935	Lancashire Cotton Corporation	13 c
Owen, Alfred George Beech	1955	Rubery, Owen & Co.	12 c
Owen, David John	1935	Port of London Authority	22 m
Owen, Ernest	1955	Rubery, Owen & Co.	12 m
Owtram, W. W.	1935	Horrockses, Crewdson & Co. Ltd.	13 m
O'Hagan, Henry Osborne	1907	Associated Portland Cement Mfrs. (1900)	16 m
Paget, Sir George Ernest	1907	Midland Rly.	22 c
Palmer, Charles Eric	1935	Associated Biscuit Manufacturers Ltd.	3 c
Palmer, W. Howard	1907	Huntley & Palmers	3 c
Park, Franklin Atwood	1907	Singer Manufacturing Co. Ltd.	7 c
Park, Franklin Atwood	1907	Singer Manufacturing Co. Ltd.	7 m
Parker, Ronald William	1955	NCB Scottish Division	2 m

Name	Year	Company	SIC[a] position
Peacock, Kenneth Swift	1955	Guest, Keen & Nettlefolds Ltd.	6 c
Peacock, Kenneth Swift	1955	Guest, Keen & Nettlefolds Ltd.	6 m
Peacock, Thomas Swift	1935	Guest, Keen & Nettlefolds Ltd.	6 m
Pearce, Sir George William	1907	Fairfield Shipbuilding & Engineering Co.	10 c
Pearson, John	1907	Scottish Co-operative Wholesale Soc. Ltd.	23 m
Pease, Arthur Francis	1907	Pease & Partners Ltd.	2 c
Pease, John William Beaumont	1935	Lloyds Bank Ltd.	24 c
Perry, Sir Percival Lea Dewhurst	1935	Ford Motor Co.	11 c
Perry, Sir Percival Lea Dewhurst	1935	Ford Motor Co.	11 m
Phelps, Douglas Vandeleur	1955	Pilkington Brothers Ltd.	16 m
Philippi, Otto Ernst	1907	Coats (J. & P.)	13 m
Phillipps, William Douglas	1907	North Staffordshire Rly.	22 m
Pick, Frank	1935	London Passenger Transport Board	22 m
Pickworth, Frederick	1955	English Steel Corporation	6 m
Pilkington, Geoffrey Langton	1935	Pilkington Brothers Ltd.	16 c
Pilkington, Richard	1907	Pilkington Brothers	16 m
Pilkington, Sir William Henry	1955	Pilkington Brothers Ltd.	16 c
Pilkington, William Windle	1907	Pilkington Brothers	16 c
Pilling, Walter, JP	1935	Hoyle (Joshua) & Sons Ltd.	13 m
Pinion, James	1907	Cheshire Lines Committee	22 m
Pirrie, William James, Baron	1907	Harland & Wolff	10 c
Platt, Frank	1935	Lancashire Cotton Corporation	13 m
Player, John Dane	1935	Imperial Tobacco Co.	3 m
Plews, Henry	1907	Great Northern Rly. (Ireland)	22 m
Pode, Edward Julian	1955	Steel Co. of Wales	6 m
Pole, Felix John Clewett	1935	Associated Electrical Industries Ltd.	9 c
Pollitt, Arthur	1935	Rylands & Sons Ltd.	13 m
Ponsonby, Edward, 8th Earl Bessborough	1907	London, Brighton & South Coast Rly.	22 c
Pound, John	1907	London General Omnibus Co.	22 c
Preston, Sir Walter Reuben, MP	1935	Textile Machinery Makers Ltd.	7 c
Procter, William Thomson	1935	Patons & Baldwins Ltd.	13 c
Quig, Alexander Johnstone	1955	Imperial Chemical Industries Ltd.	5 m
Radley, Sir William Gordon	1955	General Post Office	22 c
Railing, Sir Harry	1955	General Electric Co. Ltd.	9 c
Railing, Max John	1935	General Electric Co.	9 m
Ramsden, Joseph	1935	Manchester Collieries Ltd.	2 c
Rank, Joseph Arthur	1955	Rank Organization/Odeon Theatres Ltd.	26 c

Name	Year	Company	SIC[a] position
Rank, Joseph Arthur	1955	Ranks Ltd.	3 c
Reade, Robert Henry Sturrock	1907	York Street Flax Spinning Co.	13 c
Rebbeck, Frederick Ernest	1935	Harland & Wolff Ltd.	10 c
Rebbeck, Frederick Ernest	1935	Harland & Wolff Ltd.	10 m
Rebbeck, Sir Frederick Ernest	1955	Harland & Wolff Ltd.	10 c
Rebbeck, Sir Frederick Ernest	1955	Harland & Wolff Ltd.	10 m
Reckitt, Sir Philip Bealby	1935	Reckitt & Sons Ltd.	5 c
Rees, David Morgan	1955	NCB South Western Division	2 m
Reid, Hugh	1907	North British Locomotive Co.	11 m
Reincke, H. A.	1935	Beardmore (William) & Co. Ltd.	10 m
Reiss, John Anthony Ewart	1955	Associated Portland Cement Manufacturers	16 m
Reixach, Jose	1907	Lister & Co. Ltd.	13 m
Rhodes, Sir Edward	1935	Rylands & Sons Ltd.	13 c
Richardson, John Wigham	1907	Swan, Hunter, & Wigham Richardson Ltd.	10 m
Richmond, Sir Frederick Henry	1935	Debenhams Ltd.	23 c
Rickey, Walter J.	1935	Singer Manufacturing Co.	7 c
Rickey, Walter J.	1935	Singer Manufacturing Co.	7 m
Ringham, Reginald	1955	NCB East Midlands Division	2 m
Ritchie, Charles, 2nd Baron Ritchie of Dundee	1935	Port of London Authority	22 c
Robarts, David John	1955	National Provincial Bank Ltd.	24 c
Robertson, Gen. Sir Brian Hubert	1955	British Transport Commission	22 c
Robertson, Capt. Gerard Walter Trevelyan	1935	Naval Ordnance Depots	7 m
Robinson, Sir Thomas	1935	Bradford Dyers Association	13 m
Roger, Sir Alexander Forbes Proctor	1935	British Insulated Cables Ltd.	9 c
Rogers, Sir Hallewell	1907	Birmingham Small Arms Co. Ltd.	7 c
Rollason, James	1935	Tube Investments Ltd.	7 m
Rollason, Neville Howard	1955	Summers (John) & Sons Ltd.	6 m
Rootes, Sir Reginald Claud	1955	Rootes Motors Ltd.	11 m
Rootes, Sir William Edward	1955	Rootes Motors Ltd.	11 c
Ross, Sir Henry James	1955	Distillers Co. Ltd.	5 c
Rowell, Herbert Babington	1907	Hawthorn (R. & W.), Leslie & Co.	10 m
Royle, Sir Lancelot Carrington	1955	Home & Colonial Stores	23 c
Royle, Sir Lancelot Carrington	1955	Home & Colonial Stores	23 m
Rushton, James Lever	1907	Dobson & Barlow	7 c
Russell, Maj.-Gen. George Neville	1955	BTC British Road Services Division	22 m
Sainer, Leonard	1955	Sears Holdings Ltd.	15 m
Salmon, Henry	1935	Lyons (J.) & Co. Ltd.	3 m
Salmon, Sir Isidore	1935	Lyons (J.) & Co. Ltd.	3 c
Samuel, Walter Horace, 2nd Viscount Bearsted	1935	Shell Transport & Trading Co.	4 c

Name	Year	Company	SIC[a] position
Savage, John Percival	1955	Boots Pure Drug Co. Ltd.	5 c
Savage, John Percival	1955	Boots Pure Drug Co. Ltd.	5 m
Sayer, H. J., JP	1935	Lucas (Joseph) Ltd.	9 c
Schicht, George	1935	Unilever Ltd.	5 m
Scott, Charles Cuningham	1907	Scott's Shipbuilding & Engineering Co.	10 c
Scott, Charles James Cater	1907	London & India Docks Co.	22 c
Self, Sir Albert Henry	1955	British Electricity Authority	21 m
Shackleford, William C.	1907	Metropolitan Amalgamated Rly. Carriage & Wagon Co. Ltd.	11 m
Shaw, Joseph	1907	Powell Duffryn Steam Coal Co.	2 c
Shepherd, William Walker Frederick	1955	Turner & Newall Ltd.	16 c
Shillito, John	1907	Co-operative Wholesale Societies Ltd.	23 c
Short, Herbert Arthur	1955	BTC British Rlys., North Eastern Region	22 m
Shute, Col. Sir John Joseph	1935	Combined Egyptian Mills Ltd.	13 c
Sidgreaves, Arthur Frederick	1935	Rolls-Royce Ltd.	11 m
Sieff, Israel Moses	1935	Marks & Spencer Ltd.	23 m
Sieff, Israel Moses	1955	Marks & Spencer Ltd.	23 m
Sigrist, Frederick	1935	Hawker Siddeley Aircraft Co. Ltd.	11 m
Sinclair, Sir Leonard	1955	Esso Petroleum Co. Ltd.	4 c
Sinclair, Sir Robert John	1955	Imperial Tobacco Co.	3 c
Skinner, Ernest Harry Dudley	1955	NCB Durham Division	2 m
Skinner, Sir Sydney Martyn	1935	Barker (John) & Co. Ltd.	23 c
Skinner, Sir Sydney Martyn	1935	Barker (John) & Co. Ltd.	23 m
Smallpeice, Basil	1955	British Overseas Airways Corporation	22 m
Smith, Sir Alexander Rowland	1955	Ford Motor Co.	11 c
Smith, Andrew	1907	Hibernian Lace Co.	13 m
Smith, Clarence Dalrymple	1935	Consett Iron Co. Ltd.	2 c
Smith, Hon. David John	1955	Smith (W. H.) & Son	23 c
Smith, Henry Babington	1907	General Post Office	22 c
Smith, Herbert	1935	British Ropes Ltd.	13 m
Smith, William Frederick Danvers	1907	Smith, W. H.	23 c
Smith, Sir William George Verdon	1955	Bristol Aeroplane Co.	11 c
Smith, William Henry, 3rd Visc. Hambleden	1935	Smith (W. H.), & Son	23 c
Smith (Templar-Smith), Sir Harold Charles	1955	Gas Council	21 c
Snape, Thomas Henry	1907	Hetherington (John) & Sons	7 m
Sopwith, Thomas Octave Murdoch	1935	Hawker Siddeley Aircraft Co. Ltd.	11 c
Sopwith, Sir Thomas Octave Murdoch	1955	Hawker Siddeley Group Ltd.	11 c

Name	Year	Company	SIC[a] position
Spencer, Henry Francis	1955	Richard Thomas & Baldwins	6 m
Spencer, Thomas George	1935	Standard Telephones & Cables Ltd.	9 m
Spencer, Sir Thomas George	1955	Standard Telephones & Cables Ltd.	9 c
Spencer, Sir Thomas George	1955	Standard Telephones & Cables Ltd.	9 m
Spencer, Victor A. F. C., Visc. Churchill	1907	Great Western Rly.	22 c
Spilman, G. H.	1955	British Celanese Ltd.	13 m
Spink, Frederick	1955	Rowntree & Co. Ltd.	3 m
Spriggs, Sir Frank Spencer	1955	Hawker Siddeley Group Ltd.	11 m
Spurrier, Sir Henry	1955	Leyland Motors Ltd.	11 c
Stamp, Sir Josiah Charles	1935	London Midland & Scottish Rly. Co.	22 c
Stanley, Albert Henry, 1st Baron Ashfield	1935	London Passenger Transport Board	22 c
Stedeford, Sir Ivan Arthur Rice	1955	Tube Investments Ltd.	7 c
Stedeford, Sir Ivan Arthur Rice	1955	Tube Investments Ltd.	7 m
Steel, Gerald	1955	United Steel Cos. Ltd.	6 m
Stephenson, William Lawrence	1935	Woolworth (F. W.) & Co.	23 c
Sterling, Louis Saul	1935	Electric & Musical Industries Ltd.	9 m
Stewart, Andrew Graham	1955	Stewarts & Lloyds Ltd.	6 c
Stewart, Andrew Graham	1955	Stewarts & Lloyds Ltd.	6 m
Stewart, John Graham	1907	Stewarts & Lloyds Ltd.	6 c
Stewart, Percy Malcolm	1935	Associated Portland Cement Manufacturers	16 c
Stewart, Percy Malcolm	1935	Associated Portland Cement Manufacturers	16 m
Stewart, Percy Malcolm	1935	London Brick Co. & Forders Ltd.	16 c
Stewart, Percy Malcolm	1935	London Brick Co. & Forders Ltd.	16 m
Stirling, John A.	1955	Scottish Co-operative Wholesale Society	23 m
Stobart, Frank	1907	Pease & Partners Ltd.	2 m
Storr, Walter William	1907	Bolckow, Vaughan & Co.	6 m
Summers, Richard Felix	1955	Summers (John) & Sons Ltd.	6 c
Sutcliffe, Henry	1907	Bradford Dyers Association	13 c
Swash, Stanley Victor	1955	Woolworth (F. W.) & Co. Ltd.	23 c
Sykes, Sir Alan John	1935	Bleachers Association Ltd.	13 c
Szarvasy, Frederick Alexander	1935	Amalgamated Anthracite Collieries Ltd.	2 c
Tate, George Vernon	1935	Tate & Lyle Ltd.	3 m
Tedder, Arthur William, 1st Baron Tedder	1955	Standard Motor Co.	11 c
Tett, Hugh Charles	1955	Esso Petroleum Co. Ltd.	4 m
Thomas, Richard	1907	Thomas (Richard)	6 c
Thomas, Richard	1907	Thomas (Richard)	6 m

Name	Year	Company	SIC[a] position
Thomas, Sir William Miles Webster	1955	British Overseas Airways Corporation	22 c
Thornton, Ronald	1955	Barclays Bank Ltd.	24 m
Tuke, Anthony William	1935	Barclays Bank Ltd.	24 m
Tuke, Anthony William	1955	Barclays Bank Ltd.	24 c
Tuke, William Favill	1935	Barclays Bank Ltd.	24 c
Turner, W. Joseph	1955	Woolworth (F. W.) & Co.Ltd.	23 m
Vansittart, Guy Nicholas	1955	Vauxhall Motors Ltd.	11 c
Vassal, Robert Lowe Grant	1907	Taff Vale Rly.	22 c
Vickers, Albert	1907	Vickers Sons & Maxim	7 m
Vickers, Thomas Edward	1907	Vickers Sons & Maxim	7 c
Walker, Sir Herbert Ashcombe	1935	Southern Railway Co.	22 m
Walker, Philip Gordon	1955	Reed (Albert E.) & Co. Ltd.	18 m
Wallace, William	1955	Rowntree & Co. Ltd.	3 c
Wallis, Hubert	1907	Birmingham Small Arms Co. Ltd.	7 m
Walton, Leslie	1935	Vauxhall Motors Ltd.	11 c
Waring, Arthur Bertram	1955	Lucas (Joseph) Industries Ltd.	9 c
Warter, Sir Philip Allan	1955	Associated British Picture Corporation Ltd.	26 c
Waterlow, Sir Philip Hickson	1907	Waterlow & Sons Ltd.	18 c
Watkins, James William	1955	BTC British Rlys., London Midland Region	22 m
Watson, William	1907	Cunard Steamship Co.	22 c
Watt, William Warnock	1955	British Oxygen Co. Ltd.	5 m
Watts, Sir Philip	1907	Royal Dockyards	10 c
Wedgwood, Sir Ralph Lewis	1935	London & North Eastern Rly. Co.	22 m
Weeks, Lt.-Gen. Sir Ronald Morce	1955	English Steel Corporation	6 c
Weeks, Lt.-Gen. Sir Ronald Morce	1955	Vickers Ltd.	10 c
Wemyss, Randolph Gordon Erskine	1907	Wemyss Coal Co.	2 c
Wemyss, Randolph Gordon Erskine	1907	Wemyss Coal Co.	2 m
Westinghouse, George	1907	British Westinghouse Electric & Mfg. Co.	9 c
Westlake, Henry	1907	Staveley Coal & Iron Co. Ltd.	6 m
Weston, Willard Garfield	1955	Allied Bakeries	3 c
Weston, Willard Garfield	1955	Allied Bakeries	3 m
Wharton, John Lloyd, PC	1907	North Eastern Rly. Co.	22 c
Whigham, G. H.	1955	British Celanese Ltd.	13 c
Whitby, W. H.	1907	Hetherington (John) & Sons	7 c
White, F. A.	1907	Associated Portland Cement Mfrs. (1900)	16 c
White, George Stanley Midleton	1955	Bristol Aeroplane Co.	11 m
Whitelaw, William	1935	London & North Eastern Rly. Co.	22 c

Name	Year	Company	SIC[a] position
Whiteley, William	1907	Whiteley (William) Ltd.	23 c
Williams, Clement Hilton	1935	Associated Biscuit Manufacturers Ltd.	3 m
Williams, Leonard John	1955	National Provincial Bank Ltd.	24 m
Williams, Thomas Edward, 1st Baron Williams	1955	Co-operative Wholesale Society	23 c
Williams, William Bullivant	1907	Huntley & Palmers	3 m
Wills, George Alfred	1907	Imperial Tobacco Co.	3 m
Wills, Gilbert Alan Hamilton, 1st Baron Dulverton	1935	Imperial Tobacco Co.	3 c
Wills, John Spencer	1955	British Electric Traction Co.	22 m
Wills, William Henry, 1st Baron Winterstoke	1907	Imperial Tobacco Co.	3 c
Wilson, Frank	1955	International Tea Co.'s Stores	23 c
Wilson, Frank	1955	International Tea Co.'s Stores	23 m
Wolfson, Isaac	1955	Great Universal Stores Ltd.	23 c
Wolfson, Isaac	1955	Great Universal Stores Ltd.	23 m
Woodall, Corbet	1907	Gas Light & Coke Co.	21 c
Workman, Francis	1907	Workman, Clark & Co.	10 c
Wrench, Frederick Stringer, PC	1907	Irish Lace Depot	13 c
Wright, A. L.	1935	Butterley Co. Ltd.	2 m
Wright, Arthur Fitzherbert	1935	Butterley Co. Ltd.	2 c
Wright, George Maurice	1935	Debenhams Ltd.	23 m
Wright, George Maurice	1955	Debenhams Ltd.	23 c
Wright, Sir William Charles	1935	British Iron & Steel Co. Ltd.	6 m
Young, Sir James Reid	1955	Vickers Ltd.	10 m
?	1935	Brown (John) & Co. Ltd.	6 m
?	1907	Cox Brothers	13 m
?	1907	Cox Brothers	13 c
?	1935	National Cash Register Co.	7 m
?	1935	Reckitt & Sons Ltd.	5 m

[a] As defined by the 1968 Standard Industrial Classification and the firm's primary activity (see Appendix 1).

[b] c: chairman; m: managing director.

NB.: Titles, etc., shown are the highest held at the benchmark dates.

Bibliography

Manuscript sources

Birmingham University Library: Cadbury papers.

British Council of Churches, London: Christian Frontier Council papers. Council on the Christian Faith and the Common Life papers. Misc. papers, incl. Conference on Chaplaincies among Munitions Workers, 1942.

Christ Church, Port Sunlight: Divine Services Minute Book and Ruling Committee Minute Book.

Church Commissioners, Archives, London: Reports of Committees, 1907.

Church of England, General Synod, Archives: Central Board of Finance papers. Social and Industrial Council papers.

Erickson Workcards: biographical data cards prepared by Professor Charlotte Erickson for her book *British Industrialists* and kindly lent by her to the author.

Friends' House Library, London: Files of the Dictionary of Quaker Biography. MS minutes of committees of Yearly Meeting and Meeting for Sufferings. MS minutes of the Friends' Foreign Mission Association.

Glasgow University Archives: Robert Stevenson Horne papers.

Grubb Institute, London: Revd Bruce Reed's personal papers.

John Rylands Library, Manchester: Methodist Archives: Joseph Rank Benevolent Trust correspondence. Methodist Archives: Samuel Keeble papers.

Manchester University Library: Sheffield Industrial Mission papers, William Temple College papers.

Mrs Faith Raven, Ardtornish House, Oban: Owen Hugh Smith papers.

Quarry Bank, Styal, Cheshire: Bleachers' Association papers.

Racal Chubb, Feltham, Middlesex: Chubb papers.

Rubery Owen Holdings Ltd., Darlaston: Sir Alfred Owen papers.

School of Oriental & African Studies, London: Methodist Missionary Society, Primitive Methodist Missionary Society papers.

Scott Bader Co. Ltd., Wellingborough: Scott Bader Commonwealth papers.

Scottish Record Office: Quarter Sessions records.

Sion College, Library, London: Industrial Christian Fellowship, executive committee minutes.

Interviews

Atkinson, Reverend Michael, 12 February 1987.
Bader, Mr. Godric, various dates 1984–86.

Bliss, Dr Kathleen, 27 November 1986.
Brett, Canon Paul, 2 December 1986.
Bridge, Mr Gordon, 20 November 1986.
Cadbury, Sir Adrian, 26 June 1986.
Clark, Mr Oswald W. H., 25 November 1986
Goyder, Mr George, 9 October 1986.
Huxtable, Reverend Dr John, 7 January 1986.
Jenkins, Mrs Grace (née Owen), 27 February 1985.
Owen, Mr. A. David, 27 February 1985.
Owen, Lady Eileen, 27 February 1985.
Preston, Professor Ronald, also Mr Jack Keiser, 10 March 1987.
Radley, Lady Dorothy, 27 October 1986.
Raven, Mrs Faith (née Smith), 18 December 1986.
Reed, Reverend Bruce, also Miss Jean Hutton, 3 December 1986.
Self, Professor Peter, 12 December 1986.
Smallpeice, Sir Basil, 25 November 1986.
Stansfield, Mr Ronald G., 4 November 1986.
Taylor, Mrs Hannah (née Cadbury), 13 August 1986.

Theses and unpublished papers

BELDEN, D. C., 'The Origins and Development of the Oxford Group (Moral Rearmament)' (Oxford D.Phil., 1976).

BROWN, C. G., 'Religion and the Development of an Urban Society: Glasgow 1780–1914' (Glasgow Ph.D., 1981).

DORMAN, A., 'A History of the Singer Company (UK) Ltd. (Clydebank Factory)' (typescript, 1972; copy in Clydebank Public Library).

FIELD, C. D., 'Methodism in Metropolitan London, 1850–1920' (Oxford D.Phil., 1974).

JEREMY, D. J., 'The devices of a Paternalist: William Hesketh Lever and Port Sunlight, 1889–1914' (Unpublished paper given at a conference on entrepreneurship at the École des Hautes Études Commerciales, University of Montreal, 1–4 May 1986). Forthcoming (1991) publication in *Business History*.

—— 'Businessmen in Interdenominational Activity: Birmingham Youth for Christ, 1940s–1950s' to appear in the *Baptist Quarterly* in 1990,

—— 'Laymen in the Interstices of the Church: The Case of *The Guardian*'.

LURKINGS, E. H., 'The Origins, Context and Ideology of Industrial Mission, 1875–1975' (London, Ph.D., 1981).

McDERMOTT, M. C., 'Singers Clydebank: The Anatomy of Closure' (Glasgow University, honours thesis in economic history, 1982).

MELLING, J. L., 'British Employers and the Development of Industrial Welfare, c 1880–1920: An Industrial and Regional Comparison' (Glasgow Ph.D., 1980).

STUBLEY, P., 'The Churches and the Iron and Steel Industry in Middlesbrough, 1890–1914' (Durham MA, 1979).

Journals and newspapers

Alloa Circular and Hillfoots Records.
Bailie.
Bible Christian Magazine.
Birmingham Daily Post.
Bolton Evening News.
Bolton Journal.
Bournville Works Magazine.
British Monthly.
British Youth for Christ Newsletter.
Christian World.
Church Times.
Daily Mirror.
Derby Daily Telegraph.
Evangelism Today.
Friend.
Goodwill.
Guardian.
Industrial Christian Fellowship, *Annual Reports.*
London Crusade News.
Manchester City News.
Methodist Monthly.
Methodist Recorder.
Midland Chronicle.
Northern Daily Telegraph.
Paisley and Renfrewshire Gazette.
Paisley Daily Express.
Port Sunlight Monthly Journal.
Primitive Methodist Magazine.
Progress (Lever Brothers Ltd.).
Railway Gazette.
Reading Standard.
Red S. Review (Singer).
Rubery Owen News.
Sheffield Daily Independent.
Shipbuilder.
Swindon Advertiser.
Tablet.
Times, The.
United Methodist Magazine.
Wesleyan Magazine.

Books and booklets

AIREY, A. and J., *The Bainbridges of Newcastle: A Family History, 1679-1976* (Newcastle-upon-Tyne, 1979).

ALDERMAN, G., *The Railway Interest* (Leicester, 1973).

BAGWELL, P. S., *Outcast London: A Christian Response: The West London Mission of the Methodist Church, 1887-1987* (London, 1987).

BAKER, D., *Partnership in Excellence: A Late-Victorian Educational Venture: The Leys School Cambridge, 1875-1975* (Cambridge, 1975).

BALFOUR, Lady F., *A Memoir of Lord Balfour of Burleigh* (London, 1924).

BANKS, J., *The Story ... so Far: The First 100 Years of the Manchester and Salford Methodist Mission* (Manchester, 1986).

Baptist Union of England and Wales, *Baptist Handbook* (London, 1907, 1935, 1955).

—— *The Baptist Who's Who* (London, 1933).

Baptist Union of Scotland, *Scottish Baptist Yearbook* (Glasgow, 1907, 1935, 1955).

BARKER, T. C., *The Glassmakers Pilkington: The Rise of an International Company, 1826-1939* (London, 1981).

BARNES, J., *Ahead of His Time: Bishop Barnes of Birmingham* (London, 1979).

BARNETT, C., *The Audit of War: The Illusion and Reality of Britain as a Great Nation* (London, 1986).

BEBBINGTON, D. W., *The Nonconformist Conscience: Chapel and Politics, 1870-1914* (London, 1982).

—— (ed.), *The Baptists in Scotland: A History* (Glasgow, 1988).

BELLMAN, H., *Cornish Cockney: Reminiscences and Reflections* (London, 1947).

BEST, G. F. A., *Temporal Pillars* (Cambridge, 1963).

BINFIELD, C., *So Down to Prayers: Studies in English Nonconformity, 1790-1920* (London, 1977).

—— *George Williams and the YMCA: A Study in Victorian Social Attitudes* (London, 1973).

BISHOP, T. J. H., and WILKINSON, R., *Winchester and the Public School Élite* (London, 1967).

BLAIR, M., *The Paisley Thread Industry* (Paisley, 1907).

Bournville Village Trust, *The Bournville Village Trust, 1900-1955* (Bournville, 1955).

BRADLEY, I. C., *Enlightened Entrepreneurs* (London, 1987).

BRAKE, G. T., *Policy and Politics in British Methodism 1932-1982* (London, 1984).

BRETT-JAMES, N. G., *Mill Hill* (London, 1938).

BRIERLEY, P, (ed.), *UK Christian Handbook 1983 Edition* (London, 1982).

BRIGGS, A., and MACCARTNEY, A., *Toynbee Hall: The First Hundred Years* (London, 1954).

BRIGGS, J. H. Y., and SELLERS, I. (eds.), *Victorian Nonconformity* (London, 1962).

BROWN, C., *The Social History of Religion in Scotland since 1730* (London, 1987).

BROWN, F. K., *Fathers of the Victorians: The Age of Wilberforce* (Cambridge, 1961).

BROWN, K. D., *A Social History of the Nonconformist Ministry in England and Wales 1800–1930* (Oxford, 1988).

BUFFARD, F., *Herbert Marnham* (London, nd).

BUNYAN, J., *The Pilgrim's Progress* (repr. London, 1947).

Burke's Landed Gentry, 1937

Burke's Peerage and Baronetage, 1906

BURNETT, R. G., *Through the Mill: The Life of Joseph Rank* (London, 1945).

—— and MARTELL, E. D., *Devil's Camera: Menace of a Film-Ridden World* (London, 1932).

BUTLIN, Sir B., *The Billy Butlin Story* (London, 1982).

CADBURY, Sir, A., *Laurence John Cadbury, 1889–1982* (printed privately, 1982).

CADBURY, E., *Experiments in Industrial Organization* (London, 1912).

CADBURY, W. A., *Labour in Portugese West Africa* (London, 1910).

CAMERON, G. C., *Scots Kirk in London* (Oxford, 1979).

Catholic Church, *The Catholic Directory, Ecclesiastical Register and Almanack* (London, 1907, 1935, 1955).

—— *The Catholic Who's Who and Year-Book* (London, 1931, 1938, 1952).

CHADWICK, O., *The Victorian Church*, i: *1829–1859* (London, 1971)

—— *The Victorian Church, Part* ii *1860–1901* (London, 1972).

CHALONER, W. H., *The Social and Economic Development of Crewe, 1780–1923* (Manchester, 1950).

CHANDLER, A. D. jun, *Strategy and Structure: Chapters in the History of Industrial Enterprise* (Cambridge, Mass, 1962).

—— *The Visible Hand: The Managerial Revolution in American Business* (Cambridge, Mass, 1977).

CHANNON, D., *The Strategy and Structure of British Enterprise* (London, 1973).

CHAPMAN, S. D., *The Rise of Merchant Banking* (London, 1984).

CHECKLAND, O., *Philanthropy in Victorian Scotland: Social Welfare and the Voluntary Principle* (Edinburgh, 1980).

CHEYNE, A. C., *The Transforming of the Kirk: Victorian Scotland's Religious Revolution* (Edinburgh, 1983).

Christian Teamwork, *Introduction to Christian Teamwork* (London, 1957).

—— *Industrial Life Report No. 6* (London, 1962).

—— *Christians Entering Industry* (London, 1963).

—— *Christian Consultants: A Constructive Approach to the Problems of Industry, the Local Church, Young People and the Community* (London, 1963).

Church in Wales, *Official Handbook of the Church in Wales* (London, 1936, 1959).

Church of England, *The Official Year-Book of the Church of England* (London, 1900 onwards).

—— Anglican bishops, *Conference at Lambeth Palace, 1920: Encyclical Letter from the Bishops with the Resolutions and Reports* (London, 1920).

Church of England, Archbishops' Committee, *Christianity and Industrial Problems. Being the Report of the Archbishops' Fifth Committee of Inquiry* (London, 1918).

—— Church (National) Assembly, *Report of Proceedings* (London, 1920–60).

—— Church Congress, *Official Reports of the Church Congress* (various places, 1890–1930).

—— Province of Canterbury, House of Laity, *Proceedings of Session, April, 1907* (London, 1907).

—— Province of York, House of Laity, *Proceedings of Session, February, 1907* (York, 1907).

—— Representative Church Council, *Report of the Proceedings of the Representative Church Council, July 1907* (London, 1907).

Church of Ireland, *Journal of the Session of the General Synod* (Dublin 1907, 1935, 1955).

Church of Scotland, *Principal Acts of the General Assembly of the Church of Scotland* (Edinburgh, 1907, 1935, 1955).

—— *Reports to the General Assembly* (1940–60).

—— *The Church of Scotland Year Book* (1902–5).

—— *see also* Lamb, J. A. *and* Scott, H.

CLARKE, P. F., *Lancashire and the New Liberalism* (Cambridge, 1971).

COAD, R., *Laing. The Biography of Sir John W. Laing CBE (1879-1978)* (London, 1979).

—— *A History of the Brethren Movement* (2nd edn., London, 1976).

COATS, A., *From the Cottage to the Castle* (Paisley, 1896).

COATS, G. H., *Rambling Recollections* (1920 printed privately).

COLEMAN, D. C., *Courtaulds: An Economic and Social History* (2 vols., Oxford, 1969).

COLQUHOUN, F., *Harringay Story: The Official Record of the Billy Graham Greater London Crusade 1954* (London, 1955).

COLVIN, C. J. L., *The Baptist Insurance Company Limited: A Short History of Seventy-Five Years, 1905-1980* (London, 1980).

Complete Peerage.

[COPEC] Conference on Christian Politics, Economics and Citizenship, Reports, vol. ix: Industry and Property (London, 1924)

Congregational Union of England and Wales, *Congregational Year Book* (London, 1908, 1936, 1937, 1956).

—— *Who's Who in Congregationalism* (London, 1933).

COOK, C. T., *London Hears Billy Graham: The Greater London Crusade* (London, 1954).

CORLEY, T. A. B., *Quaker Enterprise in Biscuits: Huntley & Palmers of Reading, 1822-1972* (London, 1972).

COSGRAVE, E. M., and PIKE, W. T. (eds.), *Dublin and County Dublin in the Twentieth Century* (Brighton, 1908).

COTTRELL, P. L., *Industrial Finance, 1830–1914: The Finance and Organization of English Manufacturing Industry* (London, 1980).

COURTAULD, S., *Ideals and Industry* (Cambridge, 1949).

COX, J., *The English Churches in a Secular Society: Lambeth, 1870–1930* (London, 1982).

CRANE, D., *The Life-Story of Sir Robert W. Perks, Baronet, M.P.* (London, 1909)

CREESE, W. L., *The Search for Environment: The Garden City: Before and After* (New Haven, Conn., 1966).

Crockford's Clerical Directory (various years).

CROSFIELD, J. F., *A History of the Cadbury Family* (2 vols., printed privately, 1985).

CULLEN, L. M., *Princes and Pirates: The Dublin Chamber of Commerce 1783–1983* (Dublin, 1983).

CURRIE, R., *Methodism Divided: A Study in the Sociology of Ecumenicalism* (London, 1968).

—— GILBERT, A., and HORSLEY, L., *Churches and Church-Goers: Patterns of Church Growth in the British Isles since 1700* (Oxford, 1977).

CURTIS, S. J., *History of Education in Great Britain* (4th edn, London, 1957).

DANCY, J. C., *The Public Schools and the Future* (London, 1963).

DANGERFIELD, G., *The Strange Death of Liberal England* (London, 1936).

DAVENPORT-HINES, R. P. T., *Dudley Docker: The Life and Times of a Trade Warrior* (Cambridge, 1984).

DAVIES, E. T., *Religion in the Industrial Revolution in South Wales* (Cardiff, 1965).

Dictionary of National Biography.

Directory of Railway Officials & Year Book (various years).

Dobson & Barlow, *Samuel Crompton: The Inventor of the Spinning Mule* (Bolton, 1927).

DOIG, A., *Corruption and Misconduct in Contemporary British Politics* (Harmondsworth, 1984).

DOUGAN, D., *The Great Gun-Maker: The Story of Lord Armstrong* (Newcastle-upon-Tyne, 1970).

DOUGLAS, C. H., *The Douglas Manual: A Rescension of Passages from the Works of C. H. Douglas Outlining Social Credit* (London, 1934).

DOW, J. C. R., *The Management of the British Economy, 1945–1960* (Cambridge, 1970).

DRUMMOND, A. L., and BULLOCH, J., *The Church in Victorian Scotland, 1843–1874* (Edinburgh, 1975).

—— *The Church in Late Victorian Scotland, 1874–1900* (Edinburgh, 1978).

DUDLEY, J., *The Life of Edward Grubb, 1854–1939* (London, 1946).

DUFFY, J., *A Question of Slavery* (Oxford, 1967).

DUNKLEY, C. (ed.), *The Official Report of the Church Congress Held at Middlesbrough on September 30–October 4, 1912* (London, 1912).

DUPREE, M. (ed.), *Lancashire and Whitehall: The Diary of Sir Raymond Streat* (2 vols., Manchester, 1987).

DURBIN, E., *New Jerusalems: The Labour Party and the Economics of Democratic Socialism* (London, 1985).

DYOS, H. J., *Victorian Suburb: A Study of the Growth of Camberwell* (Leicester, 1961).

EDDINGTON, A., and PIKE, W. T., *Edinburgh and the Lothians at the Opening of the Twentieth Century* (Brighton, 1904).

EDWARDS, M. L., *S. E. Keeble: Pioneer and Prophet* (London, 1949).

Episcopal Church in Scotland, *Year Book for the Episcopal Church in Scotland* (Edinburgh, 1906–7, 1935–6, 1955–6).

ERICKSON, C., *British Industrialists: Steel and Hosiery, 1850–1950* (Cambridge, 1959).

EYLES, D., *Royal Doulton, 1815–1965: The Rise and Expansion of the Royal Doulton Potteries* (London, 1965).

EYRE-TODD, G., *Who's Who in Glasgow in 1909* (Glasgow, 1909).

FITZGERALD, R., *British Labour Management and Industrial Welfare, 1846–1939* (Beckenham, 1988).

FORSYTH, P. T., *A Holy Church the Moral Guide of Society* (London, c. 1905).

FRASER, B., and HOARE, M., *Sure and Stedfast: A History of the Boys' Brigade, 1883–1983* (Glasgow, 1983).

FRASER, D., *The Evolution of the British Welfare State* (2nd edn., Macmillan, 1984).

FRASER, W. L., *All to the Good* (London, 1965).

(Free Church Federal Council), *Who's Who in the Free Churches* (London, 1951).

GARDINER, A. G., *The Life of George Cadbury* (London, 1925).

GARLICK, K. B., *Garlick's Methodist Registry* (London, 1983).

GARVIE, A., *The Christian Ideal for Human Society* (London, 1930).

GASKELL, E., *Lancashire Leaders* (London, c. 1900).

GAULDIE, E., *Cruel Habitations: A History of Working-Class Housing, 1780–1918* (London, 1974).

GAY, J. D., *The Geography of Religion in England* (London, 1971).

GEORGE, W. L., *Labour and Housing at Port Sunlight* (London, 1909).

GILBERT, A. D., *Religion and Society in Industrial England: Church, Chapel and Social Change, 1740–1914* (London, 1976).

GORE, C. (intro.), *Property: Its Rights and Duties* (London, 1913).

GOSPEL, H., and LITTLER, C. (eds.), *Managerial Strategies and Industrial Relations* (London, 1983).

GOURVISH, T. R., *Mark Huish and the London & North Western Railway: A Study of Management* (Leicester, 1972).

GOWLAND, D. A., *Methodist Secessions: The Origins of Free Methodism in Three Lancashire Towns* (Manchester, 1979).

GOWLAND, W., *Militant and Triumphant* (London, 1954).

GOYDER, G., *The Future of Private Enterprise* (Oxford, 1951).

GREEN B., *The Practice of Evangelism* (London, 1951).

GREEN, E., and MOSS, M., *A Business of National Importance: The Royal Mail Shipping Group. 1903–1937* (London, 1982).

GREEN, R. W. (ed.), *Protestantism and Capitalism: The Weber Thesis and Its Critics* (Boston, 1959).

GRUBB, E., *Social Aspects of the Quaker Faith* (London, 1899).

—— *Christianity and Business* (London, 1912).

GRUBB, Sir K., *Crypts of Power: An Autobiography* (London, 1971).

HAILSHAM, Lord (Quintin Hogg), *The Door Wherein I Went* (London, 1975).

HAIR, D. D., et al., *The Thomas Coats Memorial Church, Paisley, Jubilee Book, 1944* (Paisley, 1945).

HALL, M. P., and HOWES, I. V., *The Church in Social Work: A Study of Moral Welfare Work Undertaken by the Church of England* (London, 1965).

HALSEY, A. H. (ed.), *Trends in British Society since 1900: A Guide to the Changing Social Structure of Britain* (London, 1972).

HANNAH, L., *The Rise of the Corporate Economy* (2nd edn. London, 1983).

—— *Inventing Retirement: The Development of Occupational Pensions in Britain* (Cambridge, 1986).

HARVEY, C., and PRESS, J. (eds.), *Studies in the Business History of Bristol* (Bristol, 1988).

HARVEY, J., et al., *Competition: A Study in Human Motive* (London, 1917).

HEASEMAN, K., *Evangelicals in Action: An Appraisal of their Social Work* (London, 1962).

HENNOCK, E. P., *Fit and Proper Persons: Ideal and Reality in Nineteenth Century Urban Government* (London, 1973).

HEWITT, G. (ed.), *Strategist for the Spirit: Leslie Hunter, Bishop of Sheffield, 1939–1962* (Oxford, 1985).

HICHENS, W. L., *The New Spirit in Industrial Relations* (London, 1919).

HODGKIN, J. E., *Quakerism and Industry: Being the Full Record of a Conference of Employers, 1918* (Darlington, 1918).

HOE, S., *The Man Who Gave His Company Away: A Biography of Ernest Bader, Founder of the Scott Bader Commonwealth* (London, 1978).

HOLLAND, H., *The Road to Farnham Castle: The Story behind the Centre for International Briefing* (Farnham, 1986).

HOLMES, A. R., and GREEN, E., *Midland: 150 Years of Banking Business* (London, 1986).

HOOLEY, E. T., *Hooley's Confessions* (London, 1924).

HOUNSHELL, D. A., *From the American System to Mass Production, 1800–1932: The Development of Manufacturing Technology in the United States* (Baltimore, 1984).

HUBBARD, E. and SHIPPOBOTTOM, M., *A Guide to Port Sunlight Village* (Liverpool, 1988).

HUNTER, L. S., *John Hunter, DD: A Life* (London, 1921).

HURLEY, M. (ed.), *Irish Anglicanism, 1869–1969: Essays on the Role of Anglicanism in Irish Life* (Dublin, 1970).

HUTCHISON, I. G. C., *A Political History of Scotland, 1832–1924: Parties, Elections and Issues* (Edinburgh, 1986).

INGHAM, J., *Biographical Dictionary of American Business Leaders* (4 vols., Westport, Conn., 1983).

INGLEBY, A. G., *Pioneer Days in Darkest Africa: A Record of the Life and Work of Charles A. Swan* (London, 1946).

INGLIS, K. S., *Churches and the Working Classes in Victorian England* (London, 1963).

INMAN, P. A., *No Going Back: An Autobiography* (London, 1952).

INMAN, Peggy, *Labour in the Munitions Industries* (London, 1957).

Institute of Directors, *Directory of Directors* (1907, 1935, 1951, 1955).

IREMONGER, F. A., *William Temple, Archbishop of Canterbury: His Life and Letters* (London, 1948).

ISICHEI, E., *Victorian Quakers* (Oxford, 1970).

JAMES, W., *The Varieties of Religious Experience: A Study in Human Nature* (1902, repr. London, 1947).

JANES, Sir H., *The Janes Trust: The History of the Trust Described by the Founder* (Luton, 1968).

JEREMY, D. J. (ed.), *Business and Religion in Britain* (Aldershot, 1988).

—— BARFIELD, J., and NEWMAN, K. S., *A Century of Grace: The History of Avenue Baptist Church, Southend-on-Sea 1876–1976* (Southend-on-Sea, 1982).

—— and SHAW, C. (eds.), *Dictionary of Business Biography* (5 vols., London, 1984–6).

JOHNSON, D., *Contending for the Faith: A History of the Evangelical Movement in the Universities and Colleges* (Leicester, 1979).

JONES, J. H., *Josiah Stamp, Public Servant: The Life of the First Baron Stamp of Shortlands* (London, 1964).

JONES, R. T., *Congregationalism in England, 1662–1962* (London, 1962).

JOYCE, P., *Work, Society and Politics: The Culture of the Factory in Later Victorian England* (Brighton, 1980).

KEEBLE, S. E., *Industrial Day Dreams: Studies in Industrial Ethics and Economics* (London, 1907).

KEISER, J., *College to Foundation: An Outline History of William Temple College, 1947–1976* (Manchester, 1986).

KELLETT, J. R., *Railways and Victorian Cities* (London, 1969).

Kelly's Directories of Leeds, Leicester, Liverpool, London (*PODL*), Manchester, Nottingham, Sheffield (various dates).

Kelly's Handbook to the Titled, Landed and Official Classes, 1955 (London, 1955).

KETTLER, D., MEJA, V., and STEHR, N., *Karl Mannheim* (London, 1984).

KIRBY, M. C., *Men of Business and Politics: The Rise and Fall of the Quaker Pease Dynasty of North-East England, 1700–1943* (London, 1984).

KITSON-CLARK, G., *The English Inheritance: An Historical Essay* (London, 1950).

KNAPP, A. W., *The Cocoa and Chocolate Industry: The Tree, the Bean, the Beverage* (London, 1930).

KNIGHT, S., *The Brotherhood: The Secret World of the Freemasons* (London, 1983).

KOSS, S., *Nonconformity in Modern British Politics* (London, 1975).

Kynoch Ltd., *Under Five Flags. The Story of Kynoch Works, Witton, Birmingham, 1862-1962* (Birmingham, 1962).

Laing, J. & Son Ltd.., *Teamwork: The Story of John Laing and Son Limited* (London, 1950).

LAMB, J. A. (ed.), *The Fasti of the United Free Church of Scotland, 1900-1929* (Edinburgh, 1956).

—— *Fasti Ecclesiae Scoticanae: The Succession of Ministers in the Church of Scotland from the Reformation*, vol. ix (Edinburgh, 1961).

LEAN, G., *Frank Buchman: A Life* (London, 1985).

Lever Bros., *The Co-Partnership Trust in Lever Brothers Ltd.* (Port Sunlight, 1909).

Leys School, *Old Leysian Directory and Handbook of The Leys School, Cambridge* (7th edn., Cambridge, 1908).

—— *Handbook and Directory of Leys School* (12th edn., Cambridge, 1934; 15th edn., Cambridge, 1956).

LLOYD, R., *The Church of England in the Twentieth Century* (2 vols., London, 1946-50).

LUNN, Sir H., *Nearing Harbour: The Log of Sir Henry S. Lunn* (London, 1934).

LYON, D., *The Steeple's Shadow on the Myths and Realities of Secularisation* (London, 1985).

MACK, E. C., *Public Schools and British Opinion, 1780-1860* (New York, 1938).

—— *Public Schools and British Opinion since 1860* (New York, 1941).

MACKINTOSH, Lord (of Halifax), *By Faith and Work: The Autobiography of the Rt. Hon. the First Viscount Mackintosh of Halifax* (London, 1966).

MACLAREN, A. A., *Religion and Social Class: The Disruption Years in Aberdeen* (London, 1974).

McLEAN, I., *The Legend of Red Clydeside* (Edinburgh, 1983).

McLEOD, H., *Class and Religion in the Late Victorian City* (London, 1974).

MACROSTY, H. W., *The Trust Movement in British Industry: A Study of Business Organisation* (London, 1907).

MALCOLM, C. A., *The Bank of Scotland* (Edinburgh, 1948).

MALLINSON, Sir W., *A Sketch of My Life* (London, 1936).

MALMGREEN, G. (ed.), *Religion in the Lives of English Women, 1760-1930* (London, 1986).

Manchester Chamber of Commerce Official Handbook, 1935 (Manchester, 1935).

MANWARING, R., *From Controversy to Co-existence: Evangelicals in the Church of England, 1914-1980* (Cambridge, 1985).

MARX, K., and ENGELS, F., *Manifesto of the Communist Party* (repr. of 1888 English ed., Moscow, 1955).

MEAKIN, B., *Model Factories and Villages: Ideal Conditions of Labour and Housing* (London, 1905).

MELLONE, S. H., *Liberty and Religion: The First Century of the British and Foreign Unitarian Association* (London, 1925).

(Methodist) Bible Christians, *Minutes of Annual Conference of the People Denominated Bible Christians, 1907* (London, 1907).

Methodist Church, *Declarations of Conference on Social Questions* (London, 1959).

—— *The Methodist Book-Almanack, 1934* (London, 1934).

—— *The Methodist Local Preachers' Who's Who 1934* (London, 1934).

Methodist Church, *Minutes of the Uniting Conference of the Methodist Church, 1932* (London, 1932).

—— *Who's Who in Methodism, 1933* (London, 1933).

Methodist New Connexion, *The General Rules of the Methodist New Connexion Revised and Approved at Their Ninety-Third Annual Conference . . . 1889* (London, 1889).

—— *Minutes of Annual Conference of Methodist New Connexion* (London, 1906, 1907).

(Methodist) Primitive Methodists, *Minutes of the Primitive Methodist Conference* (London, 1906, 1907).

(Methodist) United Methodist Free Churches, *Minutes of the Assembly of United Methodist Free Churches* (London, 1907).

(Methodist) Wesleyan Methodist Church, *Minutes of Conference* (London 1906, 1907).

MIDDLEMAS, K., *Politics in Industrial Society: The Experience of the British System since 1911* (London, 1979).

MITCHELL, B. R., and DEANE, P., *Abstract of British Historical Statistics* (Cambridge, 1962).

MORISHIMA, M., *Ideology and Economic Activity* (London: LSE Suntory Toyota International Centre for Economics and Related Disciplines, 1986).

MOWAT, C. L., *Britain between the Wars, 1918–1940* (London, 1956).

MURRAY, D. B., *The First Hundred Years: The Baptist Union of Scotland* (Glasgow, 1969).

MURRAY, K. M. E., *Caught in the Web of Words: James A. H. Murray and the Oxford English Dictionary* (New Haven Conn., 1977).

NEWCOMER, M., *The Big Business Executive and the Factors that Made Him* (New York, 1955).

NEWSOME, D., *Godliness and Good Learning: Four Studies on a Victorian Ideal* (London, 1961).

NORMAN, E. R., *Church and Society in England, 1779–1970: A Historical Study* (Oxford, 1976).

—— *The Victorian Christian Socialists* (Cambridge, 1987).

NORVAL, D., *The Organ, Thomas Coats Memorial Baptist Church* (Paisley, 1985).

OLIVER, J., *The Church and Social Order: Social Thought in the Church of England, 1918–1939* (London, 1968).

OLSEN, D. J., *The Growth of Victorian London* (London, 1976).

OSBORNE, G. S., *Scottish and English Schools: A Comparative Survey of the Last Fifty Years* (London, 1966).

OWEN, R., *Tedder* (London, 1952).

Parliamentary Papers.

PARTRIDGE, F., *The Soul of Wealth* (London, 1918).

—— *Memorandum on the Funds, Investments and Capital of the Central Board of Finance of the Church of England* (London, 22 May 1929).

PATTERSON, D., and THOMSON. D. P. (eds.), *The Scottish Churches Handbook* (Edinburgh, 1933).

PAYNE, E. A., *The Baptist Union: A Short History* (London, 1959).

PAYNE, P. L., *British Entrepreneurship in the Nineteenth Century* (2nd edn., London, 1988).

PEAKE, A. S., *The Life of Sir William Hartley* (London, 1926).

PEART-BINNS, J. S., *Maurice B. Reckitt: A Life* (Basingstoke, 1988).

PEDEN, G. C., *British Economic and Social Policy, Lloyd George to Margaret Thatcher* (Deddington, Oxford, 1985).

PERKS, Sir R., *Sir Robert William Perks, Baronet* (London, 1936).

PIKE, W. T., and TRACY, W. B., *Manchester and Salford at the Close of the Nineteenth Century: Contemporary Biographies* (Brighton, 1899).

—— *Lancashire at the Opening of the Twentieth Century* (Brighton, 1903).

Pilgrim Trust, *Men Without Work* (1938).

PLUMMER, A., and EARLY, R. E., *The Blanket Makers, 1669-1969: A History of Charles Early & Marriott (Witney) Ltd.* (London, 1969).

POLLARD, S., *The Development of the British Economy 1918-1980* (London, 1983).

POLLOCK, J. C., *Billy Graham: Highlights of the Story* (Basingstoke, 1984).

Presbyterian Church in Ireland, *Minutes of the Proceedings of the General Assembly* (Belfast, 1907, 1935, 1955).

Presbyterian Church of England, *Official Hand-Books of the Presbyterian Church of England* (London, 1907-8, 1935-6, 1955-56).

Presbyterian Church of Wales, *Year Books* (1906, 1933, 1954).

PRESTON, R. H., *Church and Society in the Late Twentieth Century: The Economic and Political Task* (London, 1983).

PRICE, S. J., *From Queen to Queen* (London, 1954).

PRITCHARD, F. C., *Methodist Secondary Education: A History of the Contribution of Methodism to Secondary Education in the United Kingdom* (London, 1949).

PROCHASKA, F. K., *Women and Philanthropy in Nineteenth Century England* (Oxford, 1980).

PURCELL, W., *Woodbine Willie: A Study of Geoffrey Studdert Kennedy* (London, 1962).

Quaker Employers' Conference, *Quakerism and Industry, Being the Full Record of a Conference of Employers 1928* (London, 1928).

—— *Quakerism and Industry: Being the Papers Read at a Conference of Quaker Employers 1938* (London, 1938).

—— *Quakerism and Industry: Conference of Quaker Employers* (London, 1948).

Quakers (Society of Friends), *Church Government, Being the Third Part of Christian Discipline in the Religious Society of Friends in Great Britain* (London, 1931).

Quakers (Society of Friends), *Extracts from the Minutes and Proceedings of the Yearly Meeting of Friends* (London, 1906).

—— *Membership List of the Meeting for Sufferings and of the Committees of the Meeting for Sufferings and Yearly Meeting* (London, 1934–5, 1954–5).

RAWLINGS, E. C., *The Free Churchman's Legal Handbook* (London, 1902).

READER, W. J., *Imperial Chemical Industries: A History* (2 vols. London, 1970–5).

—— *At Duty's Call: A Study in Obsolete Patriotism* (Manchester, 1988).

—— *Professional Men: The Rise of the Professional Classes in Nineteenth Century England* (London, 1966).

Red Book of Commerce, 1911 (London, 1911).

REID, M., *James Lithgow, Master of Work* (London, 1964).

REITH, G. M. *Reminiscences of the United Free Church General Assembly (1900–1929)* (Edinburgh, 1933).

Representative British Freemasons (London, 1915).

ROBERTS, D., *Paternalism in Early Victorian England* (New Brunswick, NJ, 1979).

RODERICK, G. W., and STEPHENS, M. D., *Education and Industry in the Nineteenth Century: The English Disease?* (London, 1978).

ROGERS, E., *A Christian Commentary on Communism* (London, 1959).

ROLT, L. T. C., *Holloways of Millbank: The First Seventy-Five Years* (London, 1958).

ROTHBLATT, S., *The Revolution of the Dons: Cambridge and Society in Victorian England* (London, 1968).

ROWDON, H. H., *The Origins of the Brethren* (London, 1967).

ROWNTREE, B. S., *Poverty: A Study of Town Life* (London, 1901; 4th edn., 1902).

Rubery Owen & Co. Ltd., *Rubery, Owen & Co. Ltd. 1884–1944* (printed privately, n.d.).

RUBINSTEIN, W. D., *Men of Property: The Very Wealthy in Britain since the Industrial Revolution* (London, 1981).

Salvation Army, *Year Book, 1955* (London, 1955).

SAMUELSSON, K., *Religion and Economic Action* (London, 1959).

SANDERSON, M., *The Universities and British Industry, 1850–1970* (London, 1972).

—— *Education, Economic Change and Society in England, 1780–1870* (London, 1983).

SAYERS, R. S., *The Bank of England, 1891–1944* (3 vols., Cambridge, 1976).

SCHUMACHER, E. F., *Small is Beautiful: A Study of Economics as if People Mattered* (London, 1973).

SCOTT, H. (ed.), *Fasti Ecclesiae Scoticanae: The Succession of Ministers in the Church of Scotland from the Reformation* (8 vols., Edinburgh, 1915–50).

SCOTT, J., and HUGHES, M., *The Anatomy of Scottish Capital: Scottish Companies and Scottish Capital, 1900–1979* (London, 1980).

SCOTT, W. H., and PIKE, W. T., *The West Riding of Yorkshire at the Opening of the Twentieth Century* (Brighton, 1902).

Scottish Biographies, 1938 (Glasgow, 1938).

SEKON, G. A., *The Railway Year Book for 1908* (London, 1908).

Sheffield & District Who's Who (Sheffield, 1905).

Sheffield and Rotherham (Illustrated, Up-to-date) (London, 1897).

SHEILS, W. J., and WOOD, D. (eds.), *The Church and Wealth* (Oxford, 1987).

SHELDON, C. M., *In His Steps, or What Would Jesus Do?* (New York, 1897).

SKINNER, W. B., *The Mining Manual* (London, 1907).

Slater's Manchester and Salford and Suburban Directory (Manchester, 1907).

SLAVEN, A., and CHECKLAND, S. (eds.), *Dictionary of Scottish Business Biography, 1860-1960*, i *The Staple Industries* (Aberdeen, 1986).

SMALLPEICE, Sir B., *Of Comets and Queens* (Shrewsbury, 1981).

Society of Friends *see* Quakers

SPRINGHALL, J., FRASER, B., and HOARE, M., *Sure and Stedfast: A History of the Boy's Brigade, 1883 to 1983* (London, 1983).

STAMP, A. M., *Josiah Stamp and the Limitations of Economics* (London, 1970).

STAMP, J. C., *The Christian Ethic as an Economic Factor* (London, 1926).

—— *Some Economic Factors in Modern Life* (London, 1929).

—— *Criticism and Other Addresses* (London, 1931).

—— *Motive and Method in a Christian Order* (London, 1936).

—— *Christianity and Economics* (London, 1939).

STANWORTH, P., and GIDDENS, A. (eds.), *Élites and Power in British Society* (Cambridge, 1974).

STENTON, M., and LEES, S., *Who's Who of British Members of Parliament* (4 vols., Hassocks, Sussex, 1976-81).

STEWART, J. C., *Pioneers of a Profession: Chartered Accountants to 1879* (Edinburgh, 1977).

STEWART, W. A. C., *Quakers and Education as Seen in Their Schools in England* (London, 1953).

Stock Exchange Official Intelligence for 1907 (London, 1907).

Stock Exchange Official Year-Book (London, 1935, 1955).

STUDDERT-KENNEDY, G., *Dog-Collar Democracy: The Industrial Christian Fellowship, 1919-1929* (London, 1982).

STURDY, W. A., *Methodist Finance: Past, Present and Future* (London, 1932).

SWAN, C. A., *The Slavery of To-Day or the Present Position of the Open Sore of Africa* (Glasgow, 1909).

TATLOW, T., *The Story of the Student Christian Movement of Great Britain and Ireland* (London, 1933).

TAWNEY, R. H., *Religion and the Rise of Capitalism* (London, 1936).

TEMPLE, W., *Christianity and Social Order* (repr London, 1976).

—— (ed.), *Malvern, 1941: The Life of the Church and the Order of Society: Being the Proceedings of the Archbishop of York's Conference* (London, 1941).

The Times, *Prospectuses of Public Companies* (London, various dates).

THOMPSON, E. P, *The Making of the English Working Class* (London, 1965).

THOMPSON, F. M. L., *English Landed Society in the Nineteenth Century* (London, 1963).

THOMPSON, K. A., *Bureaucracy and Church Reform: The Organizational Response of the Church of England to Social Change, 1800–1965* (Oxford, 1970).

THOMSON, D. P., and PATTERSON, D. (eds.), *The Scottish Churches Handbook* (Edinburgh, 1933).

TIMPSON, G. F. (ed.), *Sir James A. H. Murray: A Self Portrait* (printed privately, 1957).

Timsons Limited: Eighty Years and Beyond (Kettering, 1976).

TOWNSEND, Henry, *Robert Wilson Black* (London, 1954).

Truman & Knightley Ltd., *Schools* (12th ed, London, 1935).

TUCK, J. E., *Your Master Proclaim: The Story of Eric Hutchings and His Team* (London, 1968).

TURNBULL, G., *A History of the Calico Printing Industry of Great Britain* (Altrincham, 1951).

Two Centuries of Shipbuilding by the Scotts at Greenock (3rd edn., Manchester, 1950).

United Free Church of Scotland, *The Principal Acts of the General Assembly of the United Free Church of Scotland* (Edinburgh, 1907).

Union of Welsh Independents, *Report of the Annual Meetings* (1907, 1935, 1956).

Unitarian and Free Christian Churches, *Year Book of the General Assembly* (London, 1935, 1955).

(Unitarians) British and Foreign Unitarian Association, *Essex Hall Year Book* (London, 1907).

United Free Church of Scotland, *The Principal Acts of the General Assembly of the United Free Church of Scotland* (Glasgow, 1907).

—— *Handbook of the United Free Church of Scotland* (Glasgow, 1935, 1955).

—— *Minutes of the Proceedings of the General Assembly* (Glasgow, 1935).

VENN, J. and J. A., *Alumni Cantabriqienses*, Part II (6 vols., Cambridge, 1946–54).

VIDLER, A. R., *Scenes from a Clerical Life: An Autobiography* (London, 1977).

WAGNER, G., *The Chocolate Conscience* (London, 1987).

WAINWRIGHT, D., *Henderson: A History of the Life of Alexander Henderson, First Lord Faringdon, and of Henderson Administration* (London, 1985).

WALLACE, W., *'I Was Concerned': The Autobiography of William Wallace* (privately printed, 1985).

WALLER, P. J., *Democracy and Sectarianism: A Political and Social History of Liverpool, 1868–1939* (Liverpool, 1981).

WALLER, R. J., *The Dukeries Transformed: The Social and Political Development of a Twentieth-Century Coalfield* (Oxford, 1983).

WARD, W. R., *Victorian Oxford* (London, 1965).

—— (ed.), *The Correspondence of Jabez Bunting* (London, 1976).

Ward's Directory of Newcastle-upon-Tyne.

WATSON, A., *The Faith of a Business Man and Other Addresses* (London, 1936).

WEBER, T. P., *Living in the Shadow of the Second Coming: American Premillenialism, 1875–1925* (Oxford, 1979).

WEDGWOOD, J., *The Economics of Inheritance* (London, 1929).

WELCH, C., *London at the Opening of the Twentieth Century: Contemporary Biographies* (Brighton, 1905).

WELSBY, P. A., *A History of the Church of England, 1945–1980* (Oxford, 1984).

WEST, W. M. S., *To Be a Pilgrim: A Memoir of Ernest A. Payne* (Guildford, 1983).

WHITLEY, H. C., *Laughter in Heaven* (London, 1962).

Who's Who

Who Was Who, 1897–1980 (8 vols., London, 1920–81).

Who's Who in Wales (Cardiff, 1921 and 1937).

WICKHAM, E. R., *Church and People in an Industrial City* (London, 1957).

WILSON, C., *First with the News: The History of W. H. Smith, 1792–1972* (London, 1985).

—— *The History of Unilever: A Study in Economic Growth and Social Change* (3 vols., London, 1954–68).

WILSON, C. E., *Sir George Watson Macalpine* (London, n.d.).

WOLFE, K. M., *The Churches and the British Broadcasting Corporation, 1922–1956: The Politics of Broadcast Religion* (London, 1984).

WOOD, A., *Mr Rank: A Study of J. Arthur Rank and British Films* (London, 1952).

WOOD, F. P. and M. S., *Youth Advancing: The Story of What God Has Done through the National Young Life Campaign* (London, 1961).

YEO, S., *Religion and Voluntary Organizations in Crisis* (London, 1976).

YOUNG, G. M. (ed.), *Early Victorian England, 1830–1865* (2 vols., Oxford, 1934).

YOUNG, R. M., and PIKE, W. T. (eds.), *Belfast and the Province of Ulster in the Twentieth Century* (Brighton, 1909).

Articles and pamphlets

ALLEN, E. A., 'Public School Élites in Early-Victorian England: The Boys at Harrow and Merchant Taylors' School from 1825 to 1850' *Journal of British Studies*, 21 (1982).

ARNSTEIN, W. L., 'Queen Victoria and Religion', in Malmgreen (ed.), *Religion*.

ATKINSON, M., 'A Sort of Episcopal Fly on the Walls of British Industry', in Hewitt (ed.), *Strategist for the Spirit*.

BAHLMAN, D. W. R., 'Politics and Church Patronage in the Victorian Age', *Victorian Studies*, 22 (1979).

BINFIELD, C., 'Business Paternalism and the Congregational Ideal: A Preliminary Reconnoitre', in Jeremy (ed.), *Business and Religion*.

BLISS, K., 'The Legacy of J. H. Oldham', *International Bulletin of Missionary Research* (Jan. 1984).

BOWERS, F. and B., 'Bloomsbury Chapel and Mercantile Morality: The Case of Sir Morton Peto', *Baptist Quarterly* (1984).

BRAYSHAW, S. N., 'Planning Industry for the Utilisation of All Available Abilities', in Quaker Employers, *Quakerism and Industry* (1938).

CADBURY, E., 'Welcome', in Quaker Employers, *Quakerism and Industry* (1928).

CADBURY, G. jun., 'Training for Business Management', ibid.

CADBURY, L. J., 'Public Control of Industry', in Quaker Employers, *Quakerism and Industry (1938)*.

CAMPBELL, R. H., 'A Critique of the Christian Businessman and His Paternalism', in Jeremy (ed.), *Business and Religion*.

CHECKLAND, S. G., 'Cultural Factors and British Business Men, 1815–1914', in K. Nakagawa (ed.), *Social Order and Entrepreneurship* (Tokyo, 1977).

CHILD, J., 'Quaker Employers and Industrial Relations', *Sociological Review* NS 12 (1964).

CHURCH, R. A., 'Profit-Sharing and Labour Relations in England in the Nineteenth Century', *International Review of Social History*, 16 (1972).

COLLIER, H. E., 'The Needs of Everyman', in Quaker Employers, *Quakerism and Industry* (1938).

CORLEY, T. A. B., 'How Quakers Coped with Business Success: Quaker Industrialists 1860–1914', in Jeremy (ed.), *Business and Religion*.

COURTAULD, S., 'An Industrialist's Reflections on the Future Relations of Government and Industry', *Economic Journal* 52 (1942).

CURRIE, R. and GILBERT, A., 'Religion', in Halsey (ed.), *Trends*.

DELLHEIM, C. 'The Creation of a Company Culture: *Cadburys*, 1861–1931', *American Historical Review* 92 (1985).

DIAPER, S., 'J. S. Fry & Sons: Growth and Decline in the Chocolate Industry since 1800', in Harvey and Press (eds.), *Studies*.

FARNIE, D. A., 'An Index of Commercial Activity: The Membership of the Manchester Royal Exchange, 1809–1948', *Business History*, 21 (1979).

FORRESTER-PATON, A., 'The Romance of Paton's Yarn' (typescript, the firm and family).

GARNETT, J., '"Gold and the Gospel": Systematic Beneficence in Mid-Nineteenth Century England', in Sheils and Wood (eds.), *Church and Wealth*.

GOSPEL, H., 'Managerial Structure and Strategies: An Introduction', in Gospel and Littler (eds.), *Managerial Strategies*.

GUY, J. H., 'Quandary of a Financial Executive in Competitive Business', in Quaker Employers, *Quakerism and Industry* (1938).

HALSEY, A. H., SHEEHAN, J., and VAIZEY, J., 'Schools', in Halsey (ed.), *Trends*.

HARVEY, C., 'Old Traditions, New Departures: The Later History of the Bristol & West Building Society', in Harvey and Press (eds.), *Studies*.

HEENEY, B., 'The Beginnings of Church Feminism: Women and the Councils of the Church of England, 1897–1919', in Malmgreen (ed.), *Religion*.

HOLLAND, H. S., 'Property and Personality', in Gore (intro.), *Property*.

JEREMY, D. J., 'Important Questions about Business and Religion in Modern Britain', in Jeremy (ed.), *Business and Religion*.

—— 'Chapel in a Business Career: The Case of John Mackintosh (1868–1920)', ibid.

JEREMY, D. J., 'Religious Links of Individuals Listed in the *Dictionary of Business Biography*', in ibid.

JOHNMAN, L., 'The Largest Manufacturing Companies of 1935', *Business History*, 28 (1986).

KIRBY, M. W., 'The Failure of a Quaker Business Dynasty: The Peases of Darlington, 1830–1902', in Jeremy (ed.), *Business and Religion*.

MATTHEWS, D., 'Profit-Sharing in the Gas Industry, 1889–1949', *Business History*, 30 (1988).

MINCHINTON, W. E., 'The Tinplate Maker and Technical Change', *Explorations in Entrepreneurial History*, 7 (1970).

MORE, C., 'Armaments and Profits: The Case of Fairfield', *Business History*, 24 (1982).

MORISHIMA, M., 'Ideology and Economic Activity' (London: Suntory Toyota International Centre for Economics and Related Disciplines, 1986).

MUNSON, J. E. B., 'The Oxford Movement by the End of the Nineteenth Century: The Anglo-Catholic Clergy', *Church History*, 44 (1975).

OLDHAM, J. H., 'The Frontier Idea', *Frontier* (1960).

OWEN, A. G. B., 'Lessons from the Experience of a Business Man: An Address Given at the Evening Public Meeting of the British Bible Union' (June 1946).

PAYNE, H. H., 'An Experiment in Giving the Workers a Greater Share of Control and Product', in Quaker Employers, *Quakerism and Industry* (1938).

PAYNE, P. L., 'The Emergence of the Large Scale Company in Great Britain, 1870–1914', *Economic History Review*, 2nd ser. 20 (1967).

PEDEN, G. C., 'Sir Richard Hopkins and the "Keynesian Revolution" in Employment Policy, 1929–45', *Economic History Review*, 2nd ser. 36 (1983).

PERKS, R. B., 'Real Profit Sharing: William Thomson & Sons of Huddersfield, 1886–1925', *Business History*, 24 (1982).

PRIESTMAN, W. D., 'Priestman's Profit-Sharing Scheme', in Hodgkin (ed.), *Quakerism and Industry*.

RADLEY, W. G., 'The Romance of Communications', *Crusaders' Magazine* (Feb. 1935).

—— 'Through Electrical Eyes: How Television Works', *Crusaders' Magazine* (July 1935).

—— '"TIM": The Post Office Talking Clock', *Crusaders' Magazine* (Feb. 1936).

ROWLINSON, M., 'The Early Application of Scientific Management by Cadbury', *Business History*, 30 (1988).

ROWNTREE, A. S., 'The Industrial Outlook', in Hodgkin (ed.), *Quakerism and Industry*.

—— 'Review of Industrial Changes during the Last Ten Years', in Quaker Employers, *Quakerism and Industry* (1928).

ROWNTREE, B. S., 'Wages', in Hodgkin (ed.), *Quakerism and Industry*.

RUBINSTEIN, W. D., 'British Millionaires', *Bulletin of the Institute of Historical Research* 47 (1974).

SHAW, C., 'The Large Manufacturing Employers of 1907', *Business History*, 25 (1983).

SHEWELL, J. B., 'The Status of the Worker', in Hodgkin (ed.), *Quakerism and Industry*.

SMALLPEICE, B., 'My Faith and My Job', *Accountant*, 15 Sept. 1945.

—— 'The Profit Motive in Industry', *Christian News-Letter*, Supp. to No. 152 (23 Sept. 1942), repr. in *Accountant*, 3 Oct. 1942.

—— 'The Managers of Industry', *Christian News-Letter*, Supp. to No. 180 (21 Apr. 1943).

STANLEY, B., ' "The Miser of Headingley": Robert Arthington and the Baptist Missionary Society, 1877–1900', in Sheils and Wood (eds.), *Church and Wealth*.

STANSFIELD, R. G., 'Social Responsibilities of Industry: Two Approaches', *Frontier*, 2 (1951).

STANWORTH, P., and Giddens, A., 'An Economic Élite: A Demographic Profile of Company Chairmen', in Stanworth and Giddens (eds.), *Élites and Power*.

STOKES, H. F. S., 'Security of the Worker', in Quaker Employers, *Quakerism and Industry* (1928).

TANNER, H. G., 'Review of Industrial Changes in the Last Ten Years', in Quaker Employers, *Quakerism and Industry* (1938).

TYSON, R. E., 'The Failure of the City of Glasgow Bank and the Rise of Independent Auditing', *Accountant's Magazine* (Apr. 1974).

WALLACE, W., 'The Workers' Share of the Product', in Quaker Employers, *Quakerism and Industry* (1928).

—— 'Quaker Ideals in Industry: The Practical Conditions and the Practical Steps', in Quaker Employers, *Quakerism and Industry* (1938).

WHITING, G. E., 'The Friends' Appointment Board', in Quaker Employers, *Quakerism and Industry* (1938).

WHYTE, J. H., 'Political Life in the South', in Hurley (ed.), *Irish Anglicanism*.

WILKS, M., '*Thesaurus Ecclesiae*', in Sheils and Wood (eds.), *Church and Wealth*.

INDEX

Individuals are usually identified by full name and highest lifetime title.